SAN JUAN ISLANDS

DON PITCHER

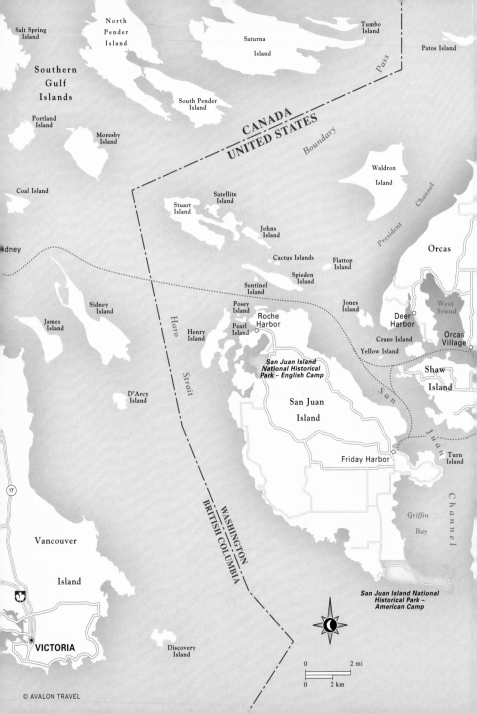

Contents

DISCOVER
the San Juan Islands

Nestled between the Washington mainland and Vancouver Island, the San Juan Islands offer a perfect getaway. The islands are equidistant from two major Northwest cities, Seattle to the south and Vancouver to the north. Despite this proximity, they remain largely rural. You'll find a host of bed-and-breakfasts, distinctive art galleries, specialty farms selling everything from alpaca garments to oysters, and fine restaurants where your waiter might also be the owner.

From the air, it's easy to imagine the San Juan archipelago as broken pieces from a shattered plate. They encompass 176 named islands, and a total of 743 islands, islets, and reefs at low tide (or 428 at high tide). Thirty of these are inhabited. Some 16,000 people live on the islands year-round, half of them on San Juan Island, home to Friday Harbor, the islands' only incorporated town. The three largest islands—Orcas, San Juan, and Lopez—form a cluster of oddly shaped puzzle pieces around Shaw Island, with many of the smaller islands strewn outward to the north and east from this hub.

Clockwise from top left: sea kayaking; Judd Cove Preserve on Orcas Island; hummingbird; Doe Bay Café on Orcas Island; sheep and goats on Lopez Island; Pelindaba Lavender Farm on San Juan Island.

As soon as the island-bound ferry leaves the dock, a sense of timelessness descends on all on board. Visiting the San Juans means escaping to rocky shorelines and dark evergreen forests, a place where the natural world dominates. Birders gather to watch for eagles or murres, clusters of cyclists huddle around maps and plot their next adventure, and spotting a passing whale is a big event. Locals read books and sip coffee at window tables, and children wave excitedly to passing sailboats. The pace of life here is slow—and all the better for it.

Clockwise from top left: sunset at Beach Haven Resort on Orcas Island; Admiralty Head Lighthouse on Whidbey Island; poppies at Cattle Point on San Juan Island; Orcas Hotel on Orcas Island.

Planning Your Trip

Where to Go

Gateways to the Islands

Most visitors to the San Juan Islands arrive on board Washington State Ferries that depart from the town of **Anacortes.** Nearby is popular Deception Pass State Park, and farther south is bucolic **Whidbey Island,** with the artsy towns of Coupeville and Langley. The island provides a scenic access route for people driving up from **Seattle.** Another entry point is **Bellingham,** with its museums, historic Fairhaven neighborhood, and shore-hugging Chuckanut Drive. **Victoria,** the elegant capital of British Columbia, Canada, lies nearby on the southern tip of Vancouver Island.

San Juan Island

San Juan Island is the most visited island. It comprises 55 square miles. The main town, **Friday Harbor,** is a picturesque spot, and it boasts the Whale Museum, fine dining and lodging, and abundant opportunities for whale-watching and sea kayaking. **Roche Harbor** has a busy marina, gorgeous grounds, historic buildings, and a sculpture garden. **San Juan Island National Historical Park** reveals the island's vivid history, with protected English Camp on the western shore and great beaches at American Camp. Other island attractions include a much-photographed lighthouse, the only whale-watching park in the nation at **Lime Kiln Point State Park,** wineries, a lavender farm, and an alpaca farm.

Orcas Island

The "Gem of the San Juans," Orcas Island is the most diverse island in the archipelago. It's also the largest: 57 square miles, stretching 12 miles

Downtown Friday Harbor

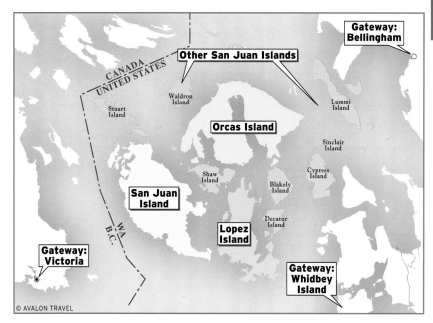

Other San Juan Islands

Gateway: Bellingham

CANADA
UNITED STATES

Waldron Island

Stuart Island

Lummi Island

Orcas Island

Sinclair Island

Shaw Island

Cypress Island

Blakely Island

San Juan Island

W.A.
B.C.

Decatur Island

Lopez Island

Gateway: Victoria

Gateway: Whidbey Island

© AVALON TRAVEL

across by 8 miles north to south. The main settlement is **Eastsound,** with its picture-perfect inns, cozy cafés, earthy farmers market, and even a skateboard park. Elsewhere on Orcas are marinas, resorts, and pottery studios. The east side of the island is dominated by woodsy **Moran State Park,** with mountaintop vistas, miles of trails, camping, and lakes for swimming. Nearby is the century-old mansion at **Rosario Resort.**

Lopez Island

Quiet and slow paced, Lopez Island covers 30 square miles. It's a destination for bicyclists who pedal a 30-mile paved loop that traverses gently rolling farm country. "The Wave" isn't a surfer's term here, but one applied to the ubiquitous hands that lift off steering wheels to acknowledge every passing car or bike. B&Bs and vacation rentals are scattered around the island, and **Lopez Village** has shops, restaurants, a little museum, and a nearby organic vineyard. **Spencer Spit State Park** is popular for camping and for its long beach and its kayaking opportunities.

Other Islands

Once you get beyond the three largest islands, the number of visitors decreases markedly. State ferries visit Shaw Island, but not the other islands, where access is by water taxi, boat, kayak, or plane. **Shaw Island** offers hiking and camping options. **Lummi Island** provides snug lodging and four-star dining. Many of the smaller islands in the San Juans are maintained as marine state parks, most notably **Sucia Island, Jones Island,** and **Stuart Island,** all of which have protected coves and hiking trails.

Know Before You Go

When to Go

The San Juans are primarily a **summer** destination. Heading to the islands between mid-June and early September will put you among throngs of fellow travelers. Many of the best **accommodations** fill up far in advance, especially on weekends, when **some resorts are booked a year or more ahead.** Summers are primarily warm and dry, with lush floral displays and plenty of chances to view killer whales just offshore. July and August each average only an inch of rain per month, and May, June, and September are also reasonably dry. If you don't mind the wait for a table at the restaurants and lengthy ferry lines—and if you can get lodging reservations—this is a great time to visit. On weekends, leave your vehicle in Anacortes to avoid lengthy waits at the ferry terminal. Both Orcas and San Juan Islands have car rentals, and a shuttle bus service is available on San Juan Island.

Spring and **fall** provide ideal times to visit. By May, many plants are already flowering—don't miss the wildflower displays on Yellow Island—but school is still in session, so most folks haven't yet headed out on vacation. **Lodging prices** aren't at peak summer rates. Fall brings a bit of color to the trees, cooler temperatures, and relative peace and quiet. By mid-November, long ferry lines are gone, prices drop, B&Bs have rooms on short notice, and it's easy to take a romantic walk down an unpopulated beach. Holiday weekends can be busy, but for much of the **winter,** you'll have the place to yourself. This is also the chilliest and rainiest part of the year, with an occasional dusting of snow.

Transportation

Whether you're aboard a state ferry threading its way through the islands or in a small floatplane dipping down to a watery landing, getting to the islands is half the fun. Access is primarily by **Washington State Ferries** from the town of

cyclist on Lopez Island

kayaks on Whidbey Island

riding the ferry

Anacortes (an 81-mile drive north from Seattle along I-5), but quite a few visitors fly in, while others ride private passenger ferries, motorboats, or sailboats to the islands. The state ferry system links the four main islands—San Juan, Orcas, Lopez, and Shaw—with Anacortes, with some ferries continuing westward to the Canadian port of Sidney (20 miles north of Victoria) on Vancouver Island. **Bikes** and **kayaks** are welcome on board these ferries, making the islands an ideal destination for adventurous travelers. **Private ferries** and **tour boats** run from Seattle, Bellingham, and Port Townsend. Scheduled **floatplane** and **wheeled-plane flights** are available from Seattle, Anacortes, and Bellingham.

Many island visitors bring their own vehicles on board the state ferries, but you can also **rent a car** or take a **local taxi** once you arrive. If you're flying into Seattle, the Sea-Tac Rental Car Facility has all the major car rental companies in one location. Getting around Seattle is easy and cheap, with the Link Light Rail System connecting the airport with downtown, and all sorts of bus and streetcar options serving other parts of the city.

If you don't have a vehicle, San Juan Transit **shuttle buses** provide reasonably priced transportation on San Juan, Orcas, and Lopez Islands during the summer. All three islands also have **bike rentals,** including electric-assist bikes for the hills.

What to Pack

Everyone and everything (from oranges to cement) must get to the islands by boats, ferries, or planes. So, bring anything essential with you. **Shorts** and **T-shirts** are ubiquitous throughout the summer, though you will want long-sleeve shirts and pants for cooler evenings and cloudy or rainy days. Carry a **light jacket** for rainy days or on-the-water trips. Keep it casual when it comes to clothing: Even the most upscale island restaurants don't require a sports jacket or tie. In winter, dress in **layers.** Bring a sweater or two, gloves, a hat, and a Gore-Tex or other breathable rain jacket. Don't forget **binoculars, camera, cell phone** (of course), **sunscreen,** and **sunglasses.** Bring **passports** if you plan any cross-border travel into Canada.

Best of the San Juans

The San Juan Islands are an easy half-day drive and ferry ride from Seattle or Vancouver. Expect crowds on summer weekends; avoid them by visiting in the off-season or in the middle of the week. Even at their most crowded, the San Juans offer a peaceful respite from city living.

Each of the islands makes a perfect weekend trip. If you have more time, combine the itineraries below for a full 10-day getaway. Leave your vehicle in **Anacortes** to avoid the lengthy ferry lines. Both Orcas and San Juan Islands have taxis and car rentals, and an excellent shuttle service is available on San Juan Island. Some lodgings also provide limited transportation. It's easy to get from one island to the next via the ferry system.

San Juan Island Getaway

Always a favorite of visitors, San Juan Island is great for an extra-long weekend escape, with plenty to do and a range of lodging and food choices. The ferry docks right at Friday Harbor, making this a good base for your trip.

DAY 1

Drive to Anacortes, stopping to see Washington Park and other sights, before boarding the Washington State Ferries for the town of **Friday Harbor** on **San Juan Island.** There are many lodging choices in Friday Harbor, including well-maintained rooms at family-friendly **Discovery Inn,** swanky rooms at **Island Inn at 123 West,** or a unique lakeside setting at **Lakedale Resort.**

DAY 2

In Friday Harbor visit the **Whale Museum,** and then take a half-day whale-watching trip or head to **Lime Kiln Point State Park** to watch from the shore (recommended to reduce impact). Drive south along the coast, stopping at tiny **Westside Scenic Preserve** to soak up the view before visiting fragrant **Pelindaba Lavender Farm,** the cuddly alpacas at **Krystal Acres Ranch,** and the tasting rooms at **San Juan Vineyards** and **Westcott Bay Cider.**

Lakedale Resort

kayaks on Lopez Island

English Camp within San Juan Island National Historical Park

DAY 3

Time for a history lesson. This is a full day, so get an early start or choose a couple of sights instead of trying to see them all. Drive over to **English Camp** for a hike up Mount Young in this portion of **San Juan Island National Historical Park,** and then head to beautiful **Roche Harbor** for lunch and a saunter through the **San Juan Islands Sculpture Park.** Take a short detour to **Westcott Bay Shellfish Co.** to sample the fresh oysters, and then continue south to **American Camp** for a hike through the flower-filled meadows or a stroll along **South Beach**—one of the finest beaches in the islands. End the day with dinner in downtown Friday Harbor (reservations advised) at **Coho Restaurant** or **Backdoor Kitchen.**

DAY 4

Max out your time in Friday Harbor before ferrying back to Anacortes. Do a little browsing at **Griffin Bay Bookstore,** buy an ice cream cone from **The Sweet Retreat & Espresso,** browse the galleries, or rent a bike and pedal the loop road around Pear Point, stopping for a picnic lunch at **Jacksons Beach.**

Orcas Island Getaway

Orcas Island is too big to really take in over a long weekend, but this short trip provides a sampler that will make you wish for more time there.

DAY 1

Catch an early ferry for a timely start on this diverse island. With a central base in the **Eastsound** area, you can easily get to most of the sights on the island. **Outlook Inn** features a great in-town setting and a variety of room choices, including inexpensive ones in the historic main building. Families will enjoy the staterooms at **Inn at Ship Bay** or earthy **Doe Bay Resort & Retreat,** while **Golden Tree Hostel** appeals to young travelers.

You may want to spend time exploring the sights around Eastsound, such as the **Orcas Island Historical Museum,** or rent a sit-on-top kayak from **Crescent Beach Kayaks** to paddle the protected bay.

DAY 2

Explore **Moran State Park**, including the paved road to the stone tower atop **Mount Constitution.** Hike the trails, try some mountain biking, or play in the waters of **Cascade Lake.** Be sure to take the detour to **Rosario Resort** for a visit to this historical getaway. **Orcas Island Artworks** is nearby, with works by 40 or so local artists and a fine café.

DAY 3

Take it easy on your last day on Orcas Island. Grab brunch at **Roses Bakery Café** and tour the local galleries and gift shops in Eastsound before heading back to the ferry.

Lopez Island Getaway

Lopez is all about relaxing, so this weekend adventure is short on activities and long on letting go.

DAY 1

Arrive at the Anacortes ferry terminal and get on board for a truly relaxing weekend. In Lopez Village you can wander through the handful of shops and restaurants and the town's museum, and then stroll over to **Weeks Wetland Preserve** to watch migrating birds.

Once you've settled into your lodging place (**Edenwild Boutique Inn** and **Lopez Farm Cottages** are especially nice), enjoy a waterside dinner at **Galley Restaurant and Lounge** and then take a sunset walk along the beach at **Otis Perkins County Park.**

DAY 2

Get a gourmet picnic lunch from **Vita's Wildly Delicious,** and if you're in town on a summer Saturday, walk across the road to check out the **Lopez Island Farmers Market.** Rent a bike from **Lopez Bicycle Works** or **Village Cycles** to see the island at an appropriately slow pace, stopping for a leisurely break at one of the beaches; **Watmough Bay** and **Agate Beach** are great choices. If you'd rather explore Lopez from "see" level, rent a kayak from **Orcas Outdoor Center** in **Spencer Spit State Park** for a paddle to nearby James Island.

DAY 3

Drop by **Isabel's Espresso** in Lopez Village for a cappuccino, and then head across the street to **Holly B's Bakery** for a giant cinnamon roll before catching the ferry back to Anacortes. If you have time, drive the scenic route south to Seattle via **Deception Pass State Park** and **Whidbey Island.**

Family Camping

Family trips don't have to resemble the 1983 comedy *National Lampoon's Vacation.* On the San Juan Islands, it's easy to bring the family, rent a cottage or house (around $900-1,300/week), and launch out on day trips from this base. The following itinerary is a budget trip to Lopez and Orcas Islands; similar trips are also very popular on San Juan Island.

Day 1

Load up the minivan and drive to Anacortes, where you have time to stock up on snacks and diapers at the Market. Because you made reservations, you won't need to wait long to roll on board

a ferry heading toward **Lopez Island,** where you set up camp at **Spencer Spit State Park.**

Day 2

If you brought bikes along, everyone can hop on for a ride around the island; if not, they're available for rent at Spencer Spit from **Outdoor Adventures Center** or in Lopez Village at **Village Cycles.** Afterward, return to Spencer Spit, where the kids can roast marshmallows over a campfire.

Day 3

Enjoy another day of biking around the island; break up the ride with a hike through the forest at

Romancing the Islands

With beautiful scenery, cozy cottages, candlelit restaurants, and upscale day spas, the San Juans are perfect for romance. They're a favorite spot for both weddings and honeymoons. Start your romantic getaway here:

SAN JUAN ISLAND

Romantic Lodging
- Roche Harbor Resort (page 149)
- Friday Harbor Grand B&B (page 152)
- Snug Harbor Resort (page 151)

Dining
- Backdoor Kitchen (page 140)
- Coho Restaurant (page 140)
- Duck Soup Inn (page 141)

Outdoor Escapes
- South Beach (page 117)
- Lime Kiln Point Lighthouse (page 122)
- San Juan Vineyards (page 125)
- Pelindaba Lavender Farm (page 127)
- San Juan Island Sculpture Park (page 121)

ORCAS ISLAND

Romantic Lodging
- Beach Haven Resort (page 198)
- Cabins-on-the-Point (page 203)
- The Inn on Orcas Island (page 206)

Dining
- Inn at Ship Bay (page 189)
- New Leaf Café (page 189)
- West Sound Café (page 194)
- Hogstone's Wood Oven (page 190)

Outdoor Escapes
- Mount Constitution (page 168)
- Turtleback Mountain (page 173)
- Doe Bay Resort & Retreat (page 198)
- Judd Cove Preserve (page 176)

relaxing on Orcas Island

LOPEZ ISLAND

Romantic Lodging
- Bay Houses and Garden Cottages (page 232)
- Lopez Farm Cottages (page 233)
- Edenwild Boutique Inn (page 231)
- MacKaye Harbor Inn (page 233)

Dining
- Holly B's Bakery (page 229)
- Haven Kitchen & Bar (page 228)
- The Bay (page 228)
- Vita's Wildly Delicious (page 229)

Outdoor Escapes
- Spencer Spit State Park (page 221)
- Iceberg Point (page 222)
- Watmough Head (page 224)
- Shark Reef Sanctuary (page 223)

Farm Fresh

With a revitalized back-to-the-land movement focusing on regionally produced foods, the San Juans have become home to a growing number of small farms, farmers markets, and organic products. Many local restaurants make a point of buying fresh island products. Find **summer farmers markets** on Saturdays in Friday Harbor, Eastsound, and Lopez Village, plus Anacortes, Bellingham, and Whidbey Island. Here are a few additional farm-fresh options:

SAN JUAN ISLAND

- Westcott Bay Shellfish Co. (page 142)
- Krystal Acres Ranch (page 125)
- San Juan Vineyards (page 125)
- Westcott Bay Cider (page 126)
- Pelindaba Lavender Farm (page 127)

ORCAS ISLAND

- Orcas Moon Alpacas (page 184)
- Once in a Blue Moon Farm (page 204)

LOPEZ ISLAND

- Lopez Island Vineyards & Winery (page 220)
- Horse Drawn Farm (page 221)
- Lopez Island Farm (page 221)

Orcas Island Farmers Market

OTHER ISLANDS

- Whidbey Island Greenbank Farm, Whidbey Island (page 50)
- Taylor Shellfish Farm near Bellingham (page 66)
- Our Lady of the Rock Monastery, Shaw Island (page 245)

Shark Reef Park and the chance to look for colorful stones at **Agate Beach County Park.** Get a panino at **Vita's Wildly Delicious,** and wander the handful of shops and galleries in nearby **Lopez Village.**

Day 4

Pack everyone up and take the ferry to **Orcas Island.** Drive up to **Eastsound** for lunch at **Island Skillet,** then continue to the island's eastern end to **Moran State Park** and its abundant campsites among the trees (the best ones are at South End Campground).

Day 5

Drive the twisting road up **Mount Constitution** to take in the island vistas, and then head back down to **Cascade Lake** for swimming and paddleboarding with other families, plus a balanced lunch of hot dogs, lemonade, and popcorn. Everyone knows sugar works wonders in helping kids relax, so throw in an ice cream cone or three.

Day 6

Lots of options today. Take a hike up **Turtleback Mountain,** or hop on a whale-watching trip offered by **Deer Harbor Charters.** Browse **Orcas**

Orcas Island Pottery

Turtleback Mountain Preserve

Island Pottery (fun treehouse and swings for kids) on the west side of Orcas before a side trip to watch the daredevils at **Orcas Island Skateboard Park**.

Day 7

Put the kids in day care at **Orcas Island Children's House** or **Kaleidoscope Preschool** and take the time to explore the shops of Eastsound, brunching at **Roses Bakery Café**. If you're feeling ambitious, join a day trip to Sucia Island from **Shearwater Kayaks,** or rent a

mountain bike from **Wildlife Cycles.** On your way to get the kids, stop by **Orcas Food Co-Op** to pick up fresh seafood to cook back at the campsite.

Day 8

It's time to exit the islands, but if you take an afternoon ferry, you'll have time for a short hike in **Obstruction Pass State Park** or **Judd Cove Preserve** before heading out. Waiting in your car as the ferry approaches the terminal, with the kids sleeping peacefully in the backseat, you may think that family trips aren't so bad after all.

Exploring the Outer Islands

The vast majority of visitors to the San Juans focus all their attention on the most accessible islands: San Juan, Orcas, and Lopez. With a little effort (and some cash), you can discover an entirely different world. The following tour mixes time on the main islands with trips to lesser-known islands and state marine parks. All sorts of other options exist, and if you want to create your own itinerary, you should consider hiking

and camping on **Cypress Island** (access by water taxi from Anacortes), **Stuart Island** (water taxi from San Juan Island), or **Matia Island** (water taxi from Anacortes). The trip below begins in Bellingham and assumes that you have a car.

Bellingham to Lummi Island
DAY 1

Drive northwest from Bellingham on I-5 and

take Exit 260 to the ferry for **Lummi Island.** Once on Lummi, stop at **Beach Store Café** for lunch, check out the art at **Sisters Bountiful Mercantile,** and then tour the island roads before settling in for a gourmet dinner and plush accommodations at the **Willows Inn** (reserve months ahead for the Willows).

Anacortes to Guemes Island
DAYS 2-4

Return to the mainland in the morning, stopping in Bellingham's **Fairhaven** district for a foamy espresso at **Tony's Coffee & Teas.** Then you're off down winding **Chuckanut Drive** with its arching trees, bay vistas, and seafood restaurants, but be sure to turn off on the narrow side road to **Taylor Shellfish Farms** for some fresh Manila clams. Chuckanut Drive eventually connects to U.S. Highway 20 and Anacortes—an interesting town with several fine restaurants. Stop for lunch or early dinner at friendly **Adrift Restaurant.** Then catch the little ferry from Anacortes to **Guemes Island.** You've booked three tranquil nights at **Guemes Island Resort,** with a choice of attractive cabins on the water or rustic yurts beneath tall trees. The low-key resort is a delightful place to chill out, so bring a book or two, set up a massage, relax in the sauna, play table tennis with the kids, or borrow a rowboat to drop a crab pot for dinner. Groceries and meals are available on Guemes from the tasty **Dig's Kitchen** food truck.

Anacortes to Orcas Island
DAY 5

Leave Guemes Island behind and drive onto the ferry to Anacortes again. Get a hearty breakfast at **Calico Cupboard Café & Bakery** before catching a state ferry to **Orcas Island,** where you've booked two nights at **Spring Bay on Orcas Island.** Stop at Eastsound along the way to check out the shops and galleries, and have dinner at **Hogstone's Wood Oven.** Orcas is a fine base from which to explore surrounding islands and has its own array of attractions.

Day 6

This easy day begins with a short kayak tour from Spring Bay and a big breakfast (both included in your stay). Do a bit of hiking within nearby **Obstruction Pass State Park,** or drive the roads of Orcas Island to see local sights. Dinner is a vegetarian affair at earthy **Doe Bay Resort & Retreat.**

Day 7

If you're traveling in May or June—when flowers are at their peak—a day trip to **Yellow Island** is a vividly verdant option. **Shearwater Adventures** has kayak day trips to the island from Deer Harbor on Orcas. As an alternative, rent a skiff from **Orcas Boat Rentals** and head over to nearby **Jones Island** for an easy forest hike with deer, raccoons, and other creatures for company. Return to Orcas Island and catch the ferry back to Anacortes the next morning.

With More Time

With more time, plan on a multi-night kayak tour that includes time on **Patos Island** with its picturesque lighthouse and **Sucia Island** with its maze of trails leading to hidden coves. This is a good introduction to kayaking; several companies on Orcas, San Juan, and Lopez Islands offer extended sea kayak trips. San Juan Island-based **Discovery Sea Kayaks** leads multi-night tours. For the one-day version, **Outer Island Excursions** has daily ferry service to Sucia from Orcas.

Gateways to the Islands

Look for ★ to find recommended
sights, activities, dining, and lodging.

Highlights

★ **W. T. Preston:** This historic stern-wheeler operated around Puget Sound from 1940 through the 1970s. It's now open for self-guided tours (page 27).

★ **Washington Park:** This Anacortes waterfront park has camping, hiking trails, and a scenic two-mile loop road (page 28).

★ **Deception Pass State Park:** Known for the arching bridge that links Whidbey and Fidalgo Islands, this park has hundreds of campsites, miles of hiking trails, freshwater lakes, and sandy beaches (page 30).

★ **Fort Casey State Park:** This park has it all—a dramatic location, picturesque lighthouse, enormous old cannons, and plenty of space for camping, picnicking, and kite-flying (page 51).

★ **Ebey's Landing National Historical Reserve:** These preserved farmlands are bordered by an impressive shoreline of cliffs and beaches (page 52).

★ **Fairhaven:** Bellingham's historic district is a great place to search for that perfect gift or enjoy a fine meal (page 61).

★ **Whatcom Museum:** Transformed by the addition of the striking Lightcatcher building, this museum houses regional art (page 62).

★ **Chuckanut Drive:** This scenic road stretches south from Fairhaven, passing tall trees and the waters of Samish Bay before emerging into the Skagit Valley (page 63).

★ **Pike Place Market:** Immerse yourself in the sights, sounds, and smells (both flowery and fishy) of Seattle's marketplace (page 78).

★ **Royal British Columbia Museum:** If you visit only one museum in Victoria, make it this one, where you can come face-to-face with an Ice Age woolly mammoth (page 86).

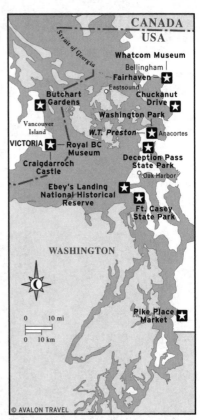

★ **Craigdarroch Castle:** To get a feel for the wealth of the Victorian Era, take a tour of this extravagant castle (page 93).

★ **Butchart Gardens:** Make time to visit one of the world's most delightful gardens (page 94).

The San Juan Islands can be approached from several directions and have numerous gateways. Getting there can be half the fun.

Located 80 miles north of Seattle, the town of Anacortes is Washington's primary gateway to the San Juan Islands, with state ferries departing several times a day year-round. It offers a good mix of restaurants, reasonably priced lodging, and sights to see, including Washington Park and the historic sternwheeler *W. T. Preston*. A few miles south of town is Deception Pass State Park, famous for the high arched bridge that links Fidalgo Island with Whidbey Island to the south.

Whidbey Island is a scenic access route for people driving up from Seattle. One of the longest islands in America, Whidbey has one large town, Oak Harbor, and two smaller—and far more interesting—ones: Langley and Coupeville. Colorful Whidbey Island Greenbank Farm is a fun stop, with loganberry wines and other treats for sale, and just up the road is Meerkerk Rhododendron Gardens. Visit Fort Casey State Park to check out the disappearing guns and Admiralty Head Lighthouse, or take in the verdant fields and a gorgeous coastline of Ebey's Landing National Historical Reserve.

The city of Bellingham is a destination in its own right, but it also provides a jumping-off point for whale-watching tours to the San Juan Islands. The historic Fairhaven district boasts a collection of nicely restored buildings from the 1880s, many fine shops, and the multimodal transportation center for trains, buses, boats, and the Alaska State Ferry. Downtown Bellingham is home to the Whatcom Museum and a couple of offbeat collections. South of Bellingham, scenic Chuckanut Drive hugs the coast through lush forests before entering farm country.

Seattle is a travel hub and the primary access point for people flying into Washington State, with private passenger ferries and air taxis connecting to the San Juans—and enough attractions to keep visitors busy en route, including bustling Pike Place Market, the landmark Space Needle, and the mesmerizing EMP Museum.

Previous: Anacortes from Cap Sante Park; Seattle's famous Pike Place Market. **Above:** the Space Needle at Seattle Center.

Gateways to the Islands

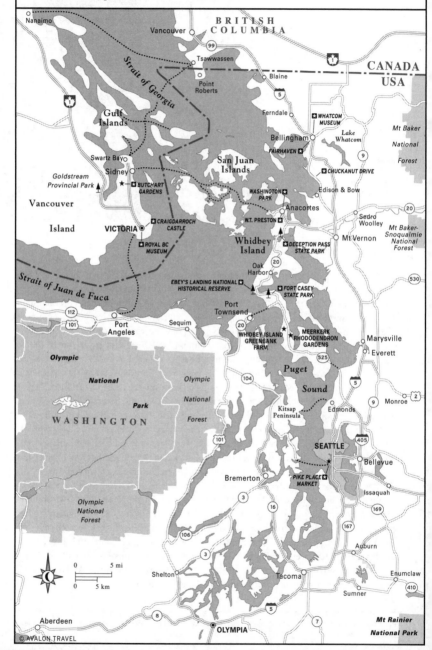

© AVALON TRAVEL

Beautiful Victoria, capital of British Columbia, is just a ferry ride from the San Juans, making it easy to see in the same trip. Situated on the southern tip of Canada's Vancouver Island, picture-perfect Victoria is as close as you'll come to London on this side of the Atlantic, with traditional high tea, double-decker bus tours, and formal gardens. Washington State Ferries depart for the San Juan Islands from the town of Sidney, 20 miles north of Victoria.

Anacortes

Many visitors know Anacortes (anna-KOR-tez) only as the launching point for the San Juan Islands, but this city of 15,000 is far more than a ferry dock. With a casual end-of-the-road atmosphere, it's also one of the more pleasant cities of its size in Puget Sound. The city is 80 miles north of Seattle and 90 miles south of Vancouver.

Although it looks like part of the mainland, Anacortes is officially on **Fidalgo Island;** Swinomish Slough cuts a sluggish, narrow swath from the La Conner area around the hills known as Fidalgo Head. The slough is kept open for boaters and is spanned by a beautiful curving arc of a bridge.

HISTORY

Anglos first resided on the island in the 1850s, but William Munks, who called himself "The King of Fidalgo Island," claimed to be the first permanent settler and opened a store in 1869. A geologist named Amos Bowman tried to persuade the company he worked for, the Canadian Pacific Railroad, to establish its western terminus at Fidalgo—despite the fact that Bowman had never seen the island. When the railroad refused, Bowman came down to check out the land himself, bought 168 acres of it, and opened a store, a wharf, and the Anna Curtis Post Office, named after his wife, in 1879. Bowman was so determined to get a railroad—any railroad—into Anacortes that he published a newspaper, *The Northwest Enterprise,* to draw people and businesses to his town.

He was so convincing that the population boomed to more than 3,000 people, even though, by 1890, the town's five railroad depots had yet to see a train pull up. The Burlington Northern Railroad eventually came, and residents found financial success in salmon canneries, shingle factories, and lumber mills. Anacortes grew to prominence as a shipping and fishing port; by its heyday in 1911, it was home to seven canneries and proclaimed itself the "salmon canning capital of the world." Workers were needed for all these plants, and Anacortes became a major entry point of illegal laborers from China and Japan; several outlaws made a prosperous living smuggling in both workers and opium. Anacortes's title for salmon canning has long since been lost as salmon stocks dwindled in Puget Sound due to overfishing, but the city still maintains a strong seaward orientation.

ANACORTES TODAY

Anacortes relies on the Tesoro and Shell oil refineries, Dakota Creek shipyard, two seafood processing plants (including the Trident Seafoods plant, which turns Alaskan pollock into fish burgers for Burger King and Long John Silver's), and tourists en route to the San Juan Islands. A fleet of gillnetters and seiners supplies salmon for local markets, and many of the boats here head north to Alaska each summer. In recent years, the city has grown with the increase in tourism as well as retirees who enjoy the mild, relatively dry weather. A gateway arch at the corner of Commercial Avenue and 11th Street welcomes visitors to downtown Anacortes—now a National Historic District—and many of the historic Victorian buildings have been restored. What do locals call Anacortes? A-Town, of course.

Anacortes and Vicinity

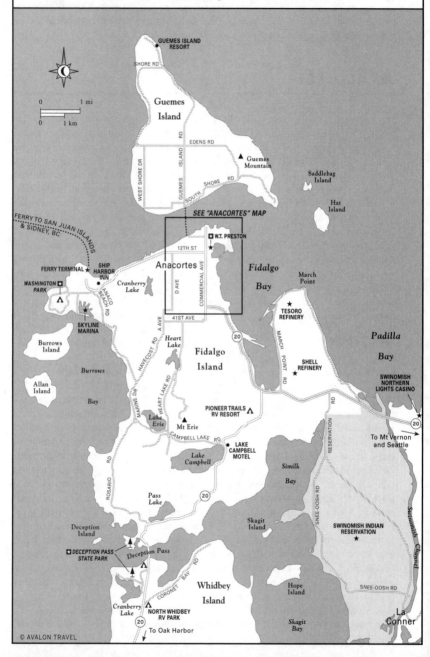

GUEMES ISLAND RESORT

SHORE RD

Guemes
Island

EDENS RD

Guemes
Mountain

Saddlebag
Island

WEST SHORE DR

GUEMES ISLAND RD

SOUTH SHORE RD

Hat
Island

SEE "ANACORTES" MAP

FERRY TO SAN JUAN ISLANDS
& SIDNEY, BC

W.T. PRESTON

12TH ST

FERRY TERMINAL

SHIP HARBOR INN

Anacortes

*Fidalgo
Bay*

March
Point

WASHINGTON PARK

Cranberry
Lake

D AVE

COMMERCIAL AVE

TESORO
REFINERY

SKYLINE MARINA

41ST AVE

20

*Padilla

Bay*

A AVE

ANACO BEACH RD

Burrows
Island

Burrows

Heart
Lake

*Fidalgo
Island*

SHELL
REFINERY

MARCH POINT RD

SWINOMISH NORTHERN LIGHTS CASINO

Allan
Island

MARINE DR

HEART LAKE RD

Bay

Lake
Erie

PIONEER TRAILS
RV RESORT

20

To Mt Vernon
and Seattle

Mt Erie

LAKE
CAMPBELL
MOTEL

RESERVATION RD

CAMPBELL LAKE RD

ROSARIO RD

*Lake
Campbell*

*Similk

Bay*

SWINOMISH INDIAN
RESERVATION

20

Pass
Lake

Skagit
Island

SNEE-OOSH RD

Deception
Island

DECEPTION PASS
STATE PARK

Deception Pass

CORONET BAY RD

*Whidbey
Island*

Hope
Island

SNEE-OOSH RD

La
Conner

Cranberry
Lake

NORTH WHIDBEY
RV PARK

20

To Oak Harbor

*Skagit
Bay*

Swinomish Channel

0   1 mi
0   1 km

© AVALON TRAVEL

SIGHTS
Museums and Historic Sites

The **Anacortes Museum** (1305 8th St., 360/293-1915, http://museum.cityofana-cortes.org, 10am-4pm Tues.-Sat., 1pm-4pm Sun., donation) has changing exhibits on local history. Drop by the visitors center for a *Walking Tour of Historic Downtown Anacortes* brochure detailing 30 historic buildings. Dozens of small **historical murals** adorn local buildings, including the mural of Anna Curtis across the street from the visitors center.

Don't miss **Causland Park,** which covers a city block at 8th Street and N Avenue (right across from the museum). The park's playfully ornate mosaic walls, gazebo, and amphitheater were built in 1920 with colorful stones from area islands. Nearby are a number of 1890s homes and buildings, many restored to their original splendor. The home owned and built by Amos and Anna Curtis Bowman in 1891 stands at 1815 8th Street. At 807 4th Street, an architect's office is now housed in what was probably the finest bordello in the county in the 1890s. The little church at 5th and R was built by its Presbyterian congregation in 1889; still in use is the Episcopal Church at 7th and M, built in 1896.

Founded in 1913, **Marine Supply & Hardware Co.** (2nd St. and Commercial Ave., 360/293-3014, www.marinesupplyan-dhardware.com) is the oldest continuously operating marine supply store west of the Mississippi. The original oiled wood floors and oak cabinets are still here, along with a potpourri of supplies. It's a fascinating place to visit, with three generations of the Demopoulos family running things.

★ *W. T. Preston*

Remnants of Anacortes's earlier days are scattered throughout town, including the fascinating historic stern-wheeler *W. T. Preston* (next to the marina at 7th St. and R Ave., 360/293-1916, http://museum.cityofanacortes.org, 10am-4pm Tues.-Sat. June-Aug., 10am-4pm Sat. and 11am-4pm Sun. Apr.-May and Sept.-Oct., closed Nov.-Mar., $5 adults, $4 seniors, $3 ages 5-16, free for children under 5). Now a National Historic Landmark, the *Preston* operated as a snag boat for the U.S. Army Corps of Engineers from 1940 to 1981, when she was given to the city of Anacortes. The last stern-wheeler operating on Puget Sound, it kept waterways clear of debris by towing off snags, logs, and stumps that piled up against bridge supports. Step into the **Maritime Heritage**

historic snagboat *W.T. Preston*

Center (360/299-1984) to learn about the importance of fishing and boat building to the region, and then walk up the ramp for a self-guided tour of the vessel.

Adjacent to the *Preston* is the 1911 Burlington Northern Railroad Depot at 7th and R, now home to the Depot Arts Center, plus the Anacortes Farmers Market on summer Saturdays.

Not far from the Preston is **Dakota Creek Industries** (820 4th St., 306/293-9575, www.dakotacreek.com), a large shipbuilding and repair shipyard. No tours are offered, but you can watch the action from the street. The company can accommodate vessels up to 400 feet long, and there's always something interesting going on. Dakota Creek recently completed two 238-foot oceanographic research vessels named for astronauts, the R/V Sally Ride and the R/V Neil Armstrong.

Viewpoints

Five miles south of downtown Anacortes, 1,270-foot **Mount Erie** is the tallest hill on Fidalgo Island. A steep and winding road rises 1.5 miles to a partially wooded summit, where four short trails lead to dizzying views of the Olympics, Mount Baker, Mount Rainier, and Puget Sound. Don't miss the two lower overlooks, located 0.25 mile downhill from the summit. Get to Mount Erie by following Heart Lake Road south from town past Heart Lake to the signed turnoff at Mount Erie Road. Trails lead from various points along Mount Erie Road into other parts of Anacortes Community Forest Lands.

For a low-elevation viewpoint of Anacortes, the Cascades, and the Skagit Valley, visit **Cap Sante Park** on the city's east side, following 4th Street to West Avenue. Scramble up the boulders for a better look at Mount Baker, the San Juans, and the Anacortes refineries that turn Alaskan oil into gasoline. Not far away, a short paved trail leads to **Rotary Park** next to Cap Sante Boat Haven, where you'll find a covered picnic table overlooking the busy harbor.

★ Washington Park

Three miles west of downtown Anacortes, **Washington Park** is a strikingly beautiful preserve with 220 waterfront acres on Rosario Strait affording views of the San Juans and Olympics. Visitors can walk, bike, or drive the skinny two-mile paved scenic loop. Stop off at one of many waterfront picnic areas, including the oft-photographed leaning tree, where a now-dead Douglas fir hangs precariously over the water.

Other facilities include a busy boat launch, several miles of hiking trails offering views of the San Juans and the Olympics, a playground, and crowded campsites with showers and laundry facilities. The original park acreage was donated by one of Fidalgo Island's earliest pioneers, Tonjes Havekost, who said, "Make my cemetery a park for everybody." His grave stands on the southern edge of the park, overlooking Burrows Channel. The Anacortes Women's Club bought additional acreage in 1922 from the sale of lemon pies—they paid just $2,500 for 75 beachfront acres.

Guemes Island

Skagit County operates a **ferry** (www.skagitcounty.net, $12 round-trip for a car and driver) to residential Guemes (GWEE-mes) Island from 6th Street and I Avenue. Take your bicycle along for a scenic tour of this rural, almost level island that is home to 500 year-round residents, and twice that many in the summer. The black-tailed deer population is almost certainly much higher. You'll find a mile-long public shoreline on the southwest end, with a pleasant agate-strewn beach; the best access is reached by turning left off the ferry and following South Shore Drive to its junction with West Shore Drive. Kids will enjoy the playground near the center of Guemes. **Guemes Island Resort** on the north end of the island provides lodging and a few food items. If you aren't staying here, stop at the adjacent **Young's Park** for a delightful beach picnic. Find good meals at **Dig's Kitchen** (360/826-2233, www.dogisland-goods.com), a brightly painted food truck on

Anacortes

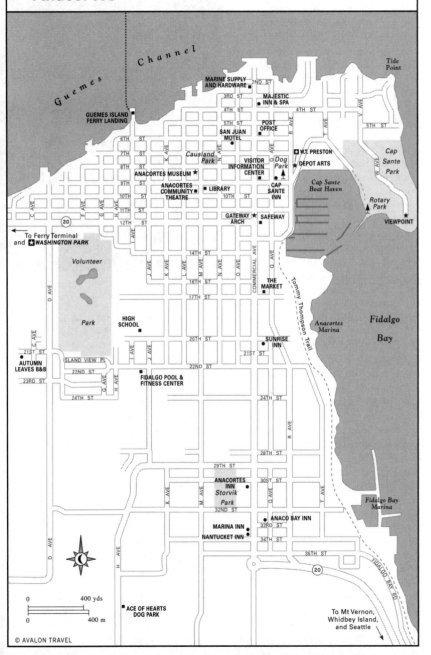

© AVALON TRAVEL

the grounds of Guemes Island Resort. Learn more about the island at www.linetime.org.

A 1.2-mile hiking trail climbs to the 700-foot summit of **Guemes Mountain**—the highest point on the island—providing vistas in all directions. Access the trailhead by driving straight from the ferry landing for 1.5 miles and turning right on Edens Road. Continue another 1.5 miles to a small parking area; the trailhead is on the left side. Find details at www.skagitlandtrust.org.

Next to the ferry landing on Guemes, the welcoming **Guemes Island General Store** (7885 Guemes Island Rd., 360/293-4548, www.guemesislandstore.com, 8:30am-8pm Sun. and Wed.-Fri., 8:30am-11pm Fri.-Sat.) has groceries and supplies. Its motto: "If we don't have it, we'll explain how you can get along without it." Stop by for breakfasts, baked goods, lunchtime sandwiches and salads, and light dinners, with beer on draft at the small bar and a covered deck to take in the ferry action. Live music is offered most Friday nights, and Wi-Fi is free. The store is owned by Guemes Island Resort.

★ Deception Pass State Park

Washington's most popular state park, **Deception Pass State Park** (360/675-2417, www.parks.wa.gov) has facilities that rival those of national parks: swimming at two lakes, 4 miles of shoreline, 28 miles of hiking trails, freshwater and saltwater fishing, boating, picnicking, rowboat rentals, boat launches, viewpoints, an environmental learning center, and several hundred campsites. The park, nine miles south of Anacortes on Highway 20, covers almost 3,600 forested acres on both sides of spectacular Deception Pass Bridge. (The north side is on Fidalgo Island, while the south end is on Whidbey Island.)

When Captain George Vancouver first sighted this waterway in 1792, he called it Port Gardner. But when he realized the inlet was actually a tidal passage between two islands, he renamed it Deception Pass. Because of the strong tidal currents that can reach nine

Deception Pass Bridge

knots, the passage was avoided by sailing ships until 1852, when Captain Thomas Coupe (for whom nearby Coupeville is named) sailed a fully rigged three-masted vessel through the narrow entrance.

For a unique perspective, take a speedy catamaran tour through the passage from **Deception Pass Tours** (888/909-8687, www.deceptionpasstours.com). These hour-long trips start in Oak Harbor and cost $33 per person. The company also has orca whale-watching trips ($89 adults, $79 kids and seniors) in the summer, plus gray whale-watching trips in March and April.

DECEPTION PASS BRIDGE

Completed in 1935, **Deception Pass Bridge,** a steel cantilever-truss structure, links Fidalgo, Pass, and Whidbey Islands. Much of the work was done by the Civilian Conservation Corps (CCC), which also built many other park structures. The bridge towers 182 feet above the water. It's estimated that each year more than three million people stop

The Maiden of Deception Pass

The Samish Indians told the story of the beautiful maiden of Deception Pass, Ko-Kwal-Alwoot. She was gathering shellfish along the beach when the sea spirit saw her and became enamored; when he took her hand, Ko-Kwal-Alwoot became terrified, but the sea spirit reassured her, saying he only wished to gaze upon her loveliness. She returned often, listening to the sea spirit's declarations of love.

One day a young man came from the sea to ask Ko-Kwal-Alwoot's father for permission to marry her. Her father, suspecting that living underwater would be hazardous to his daughter's health, refused, despite the sea spirit's claim that Ko-Kwal-Alwoot would have eternal life. Miffed, the sea spirit brought drought and famine to the old man's people until he agreed to give his daughter away. There was one condition: that she return once every year so the old man could be sure she was properly cared for. The agreement was made, and the people watched as Ko-Kwal-Alwoot walked into the water until only her hair, floating in the current, was visible. The famine and drought ended at once.

Ko-Kwal-Alwoot kept her promise for the next four years, returning to visit her people, but every time she came she was covered with more and more barnacles and seemed anxious to return to the sea. On her last visit, her people told her she need not return unless she wanted to; ever since that time, she has provided abundant shellfish and clean springwater to that area. Legend has it that her hair can be seen floating to and fro with the tide in Deception Pass.

Today, this Samish legend is inscribed on a story pole on Fidalgo Island within Deception Pass State Park. To get there, follow Highway 20 to Fidalgo Island; go west at Pass Lake, following the signs for Bowman Bay and Rosario Beach, and hike the trail toward Rosario Head.

---

at the bridge to peer over the edge at the turbulent water and whirlpools far below, or to enjoy the sunset vistas. A delightful scenic trail leads down from the southwest side of the bridge to a beautiful beach. The beach is also accessible by taking the road to the North Beach picnic area.

OTHER SIGHTS

Bowman Bay is just north of the bridge on the west side of the highway and has campsites, a boat launch, a picnic area, and a fishing pier, plus a **CCC Interpretive Center** (Thurs.-Mon., hours vary, summers only) inside one of the attractive structures the corps built. Three rooms contain displays on the CCC and the men who worked for it in the 1930s. You may find one of the original CCC workers on duty, ready to talk about the old times. **Anacortes Kayak Tours** (360/588-1117 or 800/992-1801, www.anacorteskayaktours.com) guides family friendly 1.5-hour paddles ($39 adults, $35 kids) from its kiosk here.

Rosario Beach, just north of Bowman Bay, features a delightful picnic ground with CCC-built stone shelters. A 0.5-mile hiking trail circles Rosario Head, the wooded point of land that juts into Rosario Bay (technically, this is part of the 75-acre Sharpe County Park). The shoreline is a fine place to explore tidepools. The **Maiden of Deception Pass** totem pole commemorates the tale of a Samish girl who became the bride of the water spirit. **Rosario Beach Marine Laboratory** (www.wallawalla.edu) is adjacent, and an underwater park offshore is popular with scuba divers.

A mile south of the Deception Pass Bridge is the turnoff to Coronet Bay Road. This road ends three miles out at **Hoypus Point,** a good place to fish for salmon or to ride bikes, with striking views of Mount Baker.

LAKES AND HIKES

Only electric motors, canoes, and rowboats are allowed on the park's lakes. You can observe beaver dams, muskrats, and mink in the marshes on the south side of shallow

Cranberry Lake, which also hosts a seasonal concession stand. Trout fishing is good here, and the warm water makes it a favorite swimming hole. North of the bridge is **Pass Lake,** another place to fish or paddle.

A 15-minute hike to the highest point on the island, 400-foot **Goose Rock,** provides views of the San Juan Islands, Mount Baker, Victoria, and Fidalgo Island. You may possibly see a bald eagle soaring overhead. The trail starts at the south end of the bridge, heading east from either side of the highway; take the wide trail as it follows the pass, and then take one of the unmarked spur trails uphill to the top. Other hiking trails lead throughout the park, ranging from short nature paths to unimproved trails for experienced hikers only.

SPORTS AND RECREATION
Whale-Watching

Two local companies offer four- to five-hour whale-watching trips from Anacortes, both using large 100-foot vessels. **Island Adventures** (1801 Commercial Ave., 360/293-2428 or 800/465-4604, www.orcawhales.com, $109 adults, $99 seniors, $49 kids) boasts a fast 150-passenger boat that can find orcas even when they've moved into Canadian waters around the Southern Gulf Islands. The company operates most of the year, shifting to humpback and gray whales in the winter and spring months. (They operate from Everett in the off-season.)

Mystic Sea Charters (819 Commercial Ave., 360/588-8000 or 800/308-9387, www.mysticseacharters.com, $95 adults, $85 seniors, $49 kids under 18) offers five-hour whale-watching trips on a comfortable 100-foot boat with room for 75 folks. They look for orcas in the summer, and in spring they add trips in search of migrating gray whales.

Outer Island Excursions (360/376-3711, www.outerislandx.com) offers whale-watching trips from Skyline Marina (2201 Skyline Way). The cost is $109 adults, $99 seniors, $89 teens, and $69 kids.

Sea Kayaking

Anacortes Kayak Tours (2009 Skyline Way, 360/588-1117 or 800/992-1801, www.anacorteskayaktours.com) operates from the Island Adventures Center, which also leads whale-watching trips. Nearby Burrows Bay is a popular destination for three-hour ($79) or five-hour paddles ($99) departing from Skyline Marina. The company's most popular trips are inexpensive 1.5-hour paddles ($39) from Bowman Bay at Deception Pass State Park.

Boating and Fishing

Anacortes is home to the second-largest bareboat charter fleet in the world. You'll find dozens of power yachts and sailboats heading out from two impressive marinas: **Anacortes Marina** (2415 T Ave., 360/293-4543, www.anacortesmarina.com) and **Cap Sante Boat Haven** (1019 Q Ave., 360/293-0694, www.portofanacortes.com). Cap Sante has guest moorage. The largest charter companies are **ABC Yacht Charters** (360/293-9533 or 800/426-2313, www.abcyachtcharters.com), **Anacortes Yacht Charters** (360/293-4555 or 800/233-3004, www.anacortesyachtcharters.com), **Crown Yacht Charters** (800/426-2313, www.crownyachtcharters.com), and **Ship Harbor Yacht Charters** (360/299-9193 or 877/772-6582, www.shipharboryachts.com).

For fishing trips, contact **Highliner Charters** (360/770-0341, www.highlinercharters.com), **Jolly Mon Charters** (360/202-2664, www.jollymonanacortes.com), **Outer Island Excursions** (360/376-3711, www.outerislandx.com), **R&R Charters** (360/941-6515, www.randrfishingcharters.com), or **Catchmore Charters** (360/293-7093, www.catchmorecharters.com).

Hiking and Biking

The **Tommy Thompson Trail** is a paved 3.5-mile bike/pedestrian path that starts at the downtown marina, extends south to Fidalgo Bay RV Park, and then crosses to March Point atop an old railway trestle over Fidalgo Bay.

Rent bikes at **Skagit Cycle Center** (1620 Commercial Ave., 360/588-8776, www.skagit-cyclecenter.com).

Some of the finest local hiking is at Deception Pass State Park. For more options, stop by the Anacortes visitors center for a guide to trails within the 2,800-acre **Anacortes Community Forest Lands** (360/293-1918, www.cityofanacortes.org) around Mount Erie and Cranberry, Whistle, and Heart Lakes. More than 50 miles of trails are here, and many of them can be linked into loop hikes; get a map for $10.

The 3.5-mile **Whistle Lake Shore Loop** circles small Whistle Lake, offering water views, lots of bird life, and old-growth stands of Douglas fir and western red cedar. An easy and almost level path, the **Erie View Trail** departs from Heart Lake Road and follows a seasonal creek to a fine view of Mount Erie a mile out. Return the same way.

From the trailhead at the intersection of Mount Erie and Heart Lake Roads, hike the 0.5-mile **Pine Ridge Loop Trail** for more views of Mount Erie and Sugarloaf. This moderately difficult hike takes from one to two hours. Another short hike is the 1.6-mile **Sugarloaf Trail,** starting on Ray Auld Drive, six miles from its intersection with Heart Lake

Road. Follow the trail from the marshy trailhead straight up, ignoring side trails. To the west, enjoy views of Port Townsend, the San Juan Islands, and the Strait of Juan de Fuca; to the north, Bellingham.

The Cranberry Lake area also has hiking paths, including a mile-long **Loop Trail** that starts at the end of 29th Street. This easy loop hike provides bluff-top views of Cranberry Lake and old-growth Douglas fir forests, where some trees are seven feet in diameter.

Other Recreation

Swinomish Golf Links (12518 Christianson Rd., 855/794-6563, www.swinomishcasino-andlodge.com) is an 18-hole course with Puget Sound vistas. Swim at the public **Fidalgo Pool & Fitness Center** (1603 22nd St., 360/293-0673, www.fidalgopool.com, $8); a complete exercise center is also available here. **Bayside Fitness** (8212 S. March Point Rd., 360/293-0123, www.baysidefitness.com) has day passes for $15; child care and massage are available.

Anacortes Diving & Supply (2502 Commercial Ave., 360/293-2070, www.ana-cortesdiving.com) is a full-service shop that runs dive trips to the San Juans and surrounding areas. **Diver's Dream Charters**

Cap Sante Boat Haven

(360/202-0076, www.lujacsquest.com) provides dive transportation on board the 42-foot *Lu-Jac's Quest*.

SHOPPING

Anacortes is becoming a popular destination for antiquing, with a number of downtown shops specializing in historical Northwest items. Meet regional authors during book and poetry readings at **Watermark Book Company** (612 Commercial Ave., 360/293-4277, www.watermarkbookcompany). Housed in a lovingly restored historic building, Perfect for bibliophiles, **Pelican Bay Books** (520 Commercial St., 360/293-1852) is a great little used book store with thousands of titles.

Local galleries present changing exhibits during monthly **First Friday Art Walks** (www.anacortesart.com). The **Scott Milo Gallery** (420 Commercial Ave., 360/293-6938, www.scottmilo.com) has a variety of artists and changing exhibits.

The **Anacortes Oil and Vinegar Bar** (704 Commercial Ave., 360/293-6410, www.anacortesoilandvinegarbar.com) carries many types of olive oil, infused olive oils, and vinegars from around the world. This is a good place to taste the difference between standard Costco olive oil and its gourmet cousins.

ENTERTAINMENT AND EVENTS

The **Anacortes Community Theatre** (918 M Ave., 360/293-6829, www.acttheatre.com) stages plays, musicals, and annual Christmas performances. The **Vela Luka Croatian Dancers** (www.velaluka.org) is a local group that performs all over the world. This is the most obvious example of Anacortes's Croatian community; at one time, nearly a quarter of the local population were of Croatian descent.

The small **Anacortes Cinemas** (415 O St., 360/293-7000) shows first-run films. Find live music on weekends at three downtown bars, which sometimes share a cover charge: **Rockfish Grill & Anacortes Brewery** (320 Commercial Ave., 360/293-3666, www.rockfishgrill.com), **H2O** (314 Commercial Ave., 360/755-3956, www.anacortesh2o.com), and **Brown Lantern Ale House** (412 Commercial Ave., 360/293-2544, www.brownlantern.com).

High Society (8630 S. March Point Rd., 360/661-0168, www.420highsociety.com) is the only pot dispensary in Anacortes.

Drop some cash at **Swinomish Casino & Lodge** (just across the Highway 20 bridge on Fidalgo Island, 360/293-2691 or 888/288-8883, www.swinomishcasinoandlodge.com), which offers bingo, slots, table games, keno, and off-track betting. The gift shop sells Native arts, and the lounge has live music (no cover) on Saturday nights and comedy every Friday. A free shuttle is available from town, and a 98-room hotel and a convention center are also here.

Festivals and Events

Throughout the month of April, the ever-popular **Skagit Valley Tulip Festival** (360/428-5959, www.tulipfestival.org) brings activities to Anacortes, La Conner, and Mount Vernon, with everything from garden tours to a quilt show. Another popular April event is the **Spring Wine Festival,** with tastings from 30 regional wineries and food sampling from six local restaurants.

The Heart of Anacortes (www.the-heartofanacortes.com) is an outdoor venue for music and performance on 4th Street behind Rockfish Grill, with lots of action all summer and fall.

The **Anacortes Waterfront Festival,** held at Cap Sante Boat Haven on Q Avenue in early June, celebrates the city's maritime heritage with a food court and beer garden, live music, free boat rides, craft booths, marine swap meet, and kids' activities.

Anacortes hosts a parade and fireworks on the **4th of July.** During **Shipwreck Days Flea Market** (www.shipwreckfest.com) on the third Saturday in July, more than 300 vendors turn downtown Anacortes into a giant garage sale.

The **Anacortes Arts Festival** (360/293-6211, www.anacortesartsfestival.com), held the first weekend of August, attracts more than 70,000 people with a juried fine art show, 250 arts and crafts booths, kids' events, ethnic foods, classic cars, and plenty of live music and entertainment. Especially fun is the quick-and-dirty boat building contest, which gives participants five hours to construct a wooden boat.

Oyster Run (360/435-9103 www.oyster-run.org), which takes place the last weekend of September, brings thousands of motorcyclists to Anacortes; it's a great time for leather lovers. You'll also find stunt cyclists, a beer garden, vendors, and oysters on the half shell. More drinking takes place at the annual **Oktoberfest Bier on the Pier,** where 30 breweries roll out the tasting barrels.

FOOD
Fine Dining
If you eat just one meal in Anacortes, make sure it's at the nautically themed ★ **Adrift Restaurant** (510 Commercial Ave., 360/588-0653, 8am-9pm Mon.-Thurs., 8am-10pm Fri.-Sat., 8am-2pm Sun., $15-31). Unpretentious and quirky, Adrift has a raucous atmosphere and serves from-scratch meals from its open kitchen. Owner Nichole Holbert cranks out unusual breakfasts (served till 4pm) and creative lunches. Try the fried egg sandwich with bacon and cheese, the cottage cheese pancakes, or the Skagit burger ($13 for a quarter-pounder) topped with garlic aioli. Many items are locally grown and organic. Dinner entrées start around $14 for a roasted pork, black bean, and sweet potato taco. The menu changes often, but always has several staples, including an amazing cioppino ($29) with a rich tomato wine sauce and big chunks of clams, mussels, halibut, salmon, and crab, all seasoned with saffron and fennel. Nightly seafood and steak specials are worth considering, along with the delicious Dungeness crab cake appetizers and Thursday night sushi. This is slow food worth the wait. If you get bored, peruse the nautical décor and the eclectic collection of old books (including some first editions); I found *The Muzzleloading Hunter*

and *Offset Lithographic Printmaking* next to each other. If you find one you like, buy it for $5. Reservations are advised.

★ **A'Town Bistro** (418 Commercial Ave., 360/899-4001, www.atownbistro. com, 11:30am-9pm Mon-Thurs., 11:30am-10pm Fri.-Sat., closed Sun., $14-35) has excellent local food in a casual setting. The menu changes with the seasons, but typically includes wild boar burger, an amazing made-to-order clam chowder with focaccia, Mediterranean chicken, polenta fries, and a simple but tasty Tuscan angel hair pasta. Amazing desserts too, including crème brûlée and berry crisp. A few tables out front provide al fresco dining.

Housed within the Majestic Inn, the **5th Street Bistro** (419 Commercial Ave., 360/299-1400 or 877/370-0100, www.majesticinnandspa.com, 6:30am-9:30pm Mon.-Sat., 7:30am-9:30pm Sun., $17-27) is open three meals a day. The setting is elegant, with black linen tablecloths, big windows, and an upscale menu of king salmon, butternut squash gnocchi, and Dungeness crab strudel. A special three-course early-evening meal (served 4pm-6pm) is just $25 per person. Eggs Benedicts and crepes are popular for breakfast, along with a grilled turkey and brie sandwich for lunch. The dramatic rooftop lounge is available in the summer for drinks, light meals, and views of town and the busy shipyard.

Seafood
Anthony's (1207 Q Ave., 360/588-0333, www.anthonys.com, 11am-9:30pm Sun.-Thurs., 11am-10:30pm Fri.-Sat., $18-38) is the local incarnation of the upmarket Northwest chain. Enormous windows provide a Cap Sante Marina view, while two large decks and a covered patio with an outdoor fireplace add to the lively appeal. The menu encompasses regional seafood and steaks, along with a $22 four-course sunset dinner on weeknights 4pm-6pm. Adjacent to Anthony's is its playful cousin, **The Cabana,** a covered patio where the back half of the restaurant opens to bocce ball courts and harborside tables. This

is a casual seat-yourself place with a simple menu ($8-19) of fish tacos, burgers, fish-and-chips, pan-fried oysters, and salads. It's open for breakfast too. Happy hour is daily 3pm-6pm, with good drink specials. Hang out in the Adirondack chairs or join in a fun bocce ball game.

Bob's Chowder Bar (3320 Commercial Ave., 360/299-8000, www.bobschowderbar. com, 11am-9:30pm Mon.-Sat., closed Sun., $5-11) is the spot for quick seafood meals such as oyster burgers, clam chowder, fish tacos, chicken strip baskets, and grilled wild salmon. The priciest item is $12, making Bob's popular with families.

International

Greek Islands Restaurant (2001 Commercial Ave., 360/293-6911, 11am-2pm and 4pm-8pm Tues.-Sat., $10-17) serves lamb souvlaki, moussaka, chicken shish kebab, spanakopita, and other Mediterranean specialties. Everything is made from scratch at this authentic slice of the Old World, where chef Manolis Chondroyannos cooks the food and his friendly wife, Anna, greets diners. This is the real deal.

Find traditional Mexican plates, seafood, burritos, and vegetarian dishes at **Agave Taqueria** (2520 Commercial Ave., 360/588-1288, 11am-9pm daily, $5-11). This simple, clean, and unpretentious hometown spot is popular for south-of-the-border meals. Pull up to the drive-through if you're in a hurry. Big burritos are $10, while traditional Mexican plates cost $12-15.

★ **Frida's Gourmet Mexican Cuisine** (416 Commercial Ave., 360/299-2120, www. fridascourmet.com, 11am-9pm Sun.-Thurs., 11am-10pm Fri.-Sat., $17-23) is an enormous step above most Mexican restaurants. The setting is upscale, with Mexican art on the wall—the restaurant is named for painter Frida Kahlo—and the food is beautifully presented. This isn't a place where the enchiladas, rice, and beans all flow into one big gloppy pile. The chile rellenos, chicken mole poblano, burrito fajita, chicken tamales, and crepas Guadalupe posada are all recommended. Frida's bar has more than 400 types of tequila, and there's even a 42-ounce margarita for those with a thirst for life. But don't drive after this!

Don't come to **Naung Mai Thai Kitchen** (3015 Commercial Ave., 360588-1183, 11am-9pm Tues.-Sun., $11-14) for a fine-dining experience; the building is run-down and the interior is tiny and plain at best. Fortunately,

bocce ball court at The Cabana

the flavorful Thai food makes up for any lack of ambience, with three dozen or so spicy options, including Panang curry, tom kha, larb salad, pad see-ew, and pineapple fried rice. Avoid the nothing-special setting and get your meal to go.

Lucky Chopsticks (1407 Commercial Ave., 360/588-8899, www.luckychopsticks. net, 11am-9pm Tues.-Sun., $9-14) is a friendly spot for Chinese food, including Mongolian chicken and egg flower soup. It's in a strip mall next to Compass Wines.

For Japanese food, try **Teriyaki Time** (910 11th St., 360/588-8025, 11am-9pm Mon.-Fri., 11am-8pm Sat., $6-8) or **Tokyo Japanese Restaurant** (818 Commercial Ave., 360/293-9898, noon-8pm Mon.-Fri., 3:30pm-8pm Sat., $11-25), which has a sushi bar and bento box lunches.

Pubs and Pizza

Yes, it is a bowling alley, but **San Juan Lanes** (2821 Commercial Ave., 360/293-7500, www. sanjuanlanes.com, 7am-10pm Mon.-Thurs., 7am-11pm Fri.-Sat., 7am-9pm Sun., $8-17) is also a good spot for all-American diner fare at a reasonable price. Breakfast is served all day, and the menu includes burgers, pizzas, pasta, salads, sandwiches, soups, and some of the best fish-and-chips in town. In addition to bowling, San Juan Lanes has an arcade with plenty of family games, plus a sports bar and lounge.

You certainly won't go wrong with a lunch or dinner at **Rockfish Grill & Anacortes Brewery** (320 Commercial Ave., 360/588-1720, www.rockfishgrill.com, 11am-10pm Sat.-Thurs., 11am-11pm Fri., $11-16), where the menu includes burgers, seafood, and sandwiches, along with nachos, sweet potato waffle fries, wings, and fresh ales from the on-site brewery. It's a bar, but families are welcome. **H2O** (314 Commercial Ave., 360/755-3956, www.anacortesh2o.com, 3pm-11pm Sun.-Thurs., 3pm-1am Fri.-Sat., $7-15) is next door, with the same owners but a totally different menu. Entrées include smoked pork tacos, oysters, a candied-bacon beer burger, and

truffle fries. Note that kids are not allowed, and the bands get very loud.

A few doors away is ★ **Brown Lantern Ale House** (412 Commercial Ave., 360/293-2544, www.brownlantern.com, $8-15), where the burgers, street tacos, and the halibut and chips are all noteworthy. The pool table and shuffleboard see plenty of action, and the bar is packed with sports memorabilia. Daily happy hour drink specials pull folks in.

Village Pizza (807 Commercial Ave., 360/293-7847, 11am-9pm daily, $10-24) has so-so pizzas, subs, grinders, and more; a medium cheese pizza is $13. The same owners run the connected Wheelhouse Bar, where you can order a pizza with your beer.

Breakfast and Lunch

Start your day at **Calico Cupboard Café & Bakery** (901 Commercial Ave., 360/293-7315, www.calicocupboardcafe.com, 7am-3pm daily, $9-13) for homemade country breakfasts—served all day—and healthy lunches. The extensive menu includes plenty of vegetarian and gluten-free options; a favorite is the roasted butternut squash hash. Be sure to save room for dessert; the cinnamon rolls and apple dumplings are legendary. Get there early on weekends to avoid a lengthy wait.

Penguin Coffee (2110 Commercial Ave., 360/588-8321, 5:30am-6pm Mon.-Fri., 6am-6pm Sat.-Sun.) serves Tully's Coffee and amazing cookies, scones, biscotti, and other treats from Jalillah's Cookies (located behind the coffee shop).

Johnny Picasso's (501 Commercial Ave., 360/299-2755, www.johnnypicasso.com, 8am-5pm Mon.-Sat., 10am-5pm Sun.) combines the best espresso in town with a studio where you can paint ceramic pottery or craft fused-glass pieces. There's free Wi-Fi as well.

Just looking to maximize your calorie, fat, and sugar consumption? Get a dozen to go at **Donut House** (2719 Commercial Ave., 360/293-4053, 24 hours daily); the drive-up window obviates the need to expend needless energy walking inside. Free Wi-Fi too.

Wine and Spirits

For an impressive selection of wines—including the most extensive selection of Washington wines anywhere—stop by **Compass Wines** (1405 Commercial Ave., 360/293-6500, www.compasswines.com, 10am-6pm Mon.-Sat., 11am-5pm Sun.).

Deception Distilling (9946 Padilla Heights Rd., 360/588-1000, www.deception-distilling.com, 8:30am-4:30pm Mon.-Fri., 8:30am-2pm Sat.), just south of Anacortes, is a craft distillery of various spirits, including vodka, gin, and a distinctive apple pie moonshine. You can see the tall brass stills from the tasting room.

Markets

Stock up on groceries for the San Juans at two big stores along Commercial Avenue: **Safeway** (911 11th St., 360/293-5393, www.safeway.com, daily 24 hours) and **The Market** (1519 Commercial Ave., 360/588-8181, www.themarketsllc.com, 6am-11pm daily).

Seabear Wild Salmon (605 30th St., 800/645-3474, www.seabear.com, 8:30am-5pm Mon.-Fri., 10am-4pm Sat., noon-4pm Sun) sells smoked Alaska salmon, Washington-made items, and other treats. Drop by to sample the fish or watch a video on the processing operation.

The **Anacortes Farmers Market** (611 R Ave., 360/293-7922, www.anacortesfarmersmarket.org, 9am-2pm Sat. early May-Oct.) takes place at the Depot Arts Center. It's a good place to buy fresh produce, baked goods, flowers, artisan cheeses, handmade crafts, clothing, and jams.

ACCOMMODATIONS

Anacortes is blessed with an abundance of comfortable hotels, motels, and B&Bs. Make reservations far ahead for the summer months; some places fill up by March for the peak season in July and August. The Anacortes Chamber of Commerce website (www.anacortes.org) has links to many local lodging options, including guesthouses and cottages. Find additional listings through **VRBO** (www.vrbo.com) and **Airbnb** (www.airbnb.com).

Hotels and Inns

Downtown across from the marina, **Cap Sante Inn** (906 9th St., 360/293-0602 or 800/852-0846, www.capsanteinn.com, $95-99 d) is a good mid-priced motel offering clean rooms, comfy beds, and Wi-Fi, plus microwaves and fridges. A two-bedroom suite sleeps six for $160. Pets ($10 extra) are allowed. Guests are likely to be greeted by the owner's dogs, and there's a dog park less than a block away.

Similar rates are offered at **Anacortes Inn** (3006 Commercial Ave., 360/293-3153 or 800/327-7976, www.anacortesinn.com, $100 d), where rooms include fridges and microwaves (some have full kitchens with dishes) and guests enjoy a seasonal outdoor pool, Wi-Fi, and continental breakfast. Special rates are often available, so call ahead.

Another reasonably priced choice is **Fidalgo Country Inn** (7645 State Rte. 20, 360/293-3494 or 855/823-5544, www.fidalgocountryinn.com, $110-120 d), with an outdoor pool, hot tub, continental breakfast, and Wi-Fi. It's on the south end of Anacortes, a five-minute drive from downtown.

Islands Inn (3401 Commercial Ave., 360/293-4644 or 866/331-3328, www.islandsinn.com, $109-124 d) offers comfortable motel rooms—most with fireplaces and some with separate bedrooms—plus a large suite ($149 d) containing a fireplace and jetted tub. An outdoor pool and hot tub are on the premises, and continental breakfast and Wi-Fi are included.

On the south end of town, **Anaco Bay Inn** (916 33rd St., 360/299-3320 or 877/299-3320, www.anacobayinn.com, $134 d) is Anacortes's newest lodging place. The immaculate rooms have gas fireplaces, microwaves, and fridges; larger ones include kitchenettes and jetted tubs. Two-bedroom apartment suites with full kitchens ($159 d) are also available. A continental breakfast and Wi-Fi are included.

Just up the street is **Marina Inn** (3300

Commercial Ave., 360/293-1100 or 800/231-5198, www.marinainnwa.com, $114-134 d), with big and immaculate rooms, in-room fridges and microwaves, a light breakfast, and Wi-Fi. Some rooms have Jacuzzi tubs and king beds.

Formerly known as Anaco Inn, **Sunrise Inn Villas and Suites** (905 20th St., 360/293-8833 or 888/293-8833, www.sunriseinnanacortes.com, $129-349 d) underwent a major renovation in 2015, with the addition of a dozen suites. Rooms are immaculate and large; all include gas fireplaces, jetted tubs, microwaves, fridges, continental breakfast, and Wi-Fi. Some also include kitchenettes or jetted tubs, and apartment-style villas are available. Rates vary widely depending on the season and whether you arrive on a weekday or weekend.

In the heart of town, ★ **Majestic Inn** (419 Commercial Ave., 360/299-1400 or 877/370-0100, www.majesticinnandspa.com, $187-320 d) exudes historical elegance. It was built in 1889, but the building has been completely updated with such amenities as a fine-dining restaurant (5th Street Bistro) and lounge, full-service spa, and Wi-Fi. The 52 guest rooms are spread over two buildings, and many are luxurious two-room suites. All include plush robes, soaking tubs, waterfall showers, and Wi-Fi. Rooftop dining is available in the summer.

Anyone heading out to the San Juans should consider homey ★ **Anacortes Ship Harbor Inn** (5316 Ferry Terminal Rd., 360/293-5177 or 800/852-8568, www.shipharborinn.com), located close to the ferry west of town. It's quiet and peaceful, with water vistas, Wi-Fi, a barbecue area, clean small rooms ($199 d), cottages with kitchenettes and fireplaces ($219-229 d), and family apartments ($419-449 d). A hot breakfast is included, and you're likely to encounter deer and rabbits on the lawn.

Built in 1925, **Nantucket Inn** (3402 Commercial Ave., 360/333-5282, www.nantucketinnanacortes.com) is a classic three-story colonial-style home with eight guest rooms, all with private baths, continental breakfasts, and Wi-Fi. The two queen-bed rooms are $169 d, while king rooms and suites run $199-239 d. The grounds are popular for weddings and family reunions.

Bed-and-Breakfasts

Autumn Leaves B&B (2301 21st St., 360/293-4920, www.autumn-leaves.com, $195 d) is a large contemporary home with three guest rooms furnished with French antiques, gas fireplaces, jetted tubs, and Wi-Fi. Rates include a gourmet breakfast. No kids under 14 are allowed.

Built in 1996, ★ **Gateway B&B** (407 2nd St., 360/293-9870, www.gatewaybbanacortes.com, $175-250 d) blends the charm of a classic Victorian home with the features guests expect today. A wraparound porch faces Guemes Channel, and the four upstairs guest rooms and suites all have private baths, queen or king beds, private baths, and Wi-Fi. Owners Mike and Nancy serve a delicious breakfast in the dining room each morning, and their friendly Boston terrier greets visitors. No kids under age 12.

Sail over to **The Ship House Inn B&B** (12876 Marine Dr., 360/293-1093, www.shiphouseinn.com, $98-159 d), where the nautical theme carries through three cute cottages, one of which has a boat-shaped space from which to watch the sunset. The smallest units have twin bunk beds. A filling breakfast is served in the galley room facing the water. The cliff-top location makes it best for older kids only.

Resorts

Located on the north end of Guemes Island and accessible via a five-minute ferry ride ($12 round-trip) from Anacortes, **Guemes Island Resort** (325 Guemes Island Rd., 360/293-6643 or 800/965-6643, www.guemesislandresort.com) is a delightful family escape. Six waterfront cabins—each with a kitchen and woodstove—face a grassy lawn with views of Mount Baker; these cost $196-225/night. The larger units sleep up to six. Other options include three private beach houses ($285-570/

night), three deluxe cabins ($260-285/night) with private hot tubs, and five comfortable yurts ($97-115 d) for upscale camping in the trees. There are no TVs, radios, or in-room phones in any of these, but guests are welcome to use the rowboats, sea kayaks, wood-fired sauna, Ping-Pong table, yard games, hiking trail, boat launch, Wi-Fi, and crab pots. Massage and a Dutchtub (wood-fired hot tub filled with saltwater) are available. The resort books far ahead for the peak Dungeness crabbing season during July and August. There's a minimum stay of three nights (four nights for the houses) during the summer and holidays, and many families book lodging for a full week (lower rates).

Located just uphill from the resort, Dig's Kitchen (360/826-2233, www.dogislandgoods. com, $7-18) is a food truck with picnic tables out front and a good menu of burgers, fish-and-chips, salads, sandwiches, thin-crust pizzas, and seasonal specials.

Camping

Three miles west of Anacortes and close to the ferry terminal, city-run **Washington Park** (360/293-1918, www.cityofanacortes.org, $20 tents, $26 RVs) has 75 crowded campsites in a peaceful wooded setting, as well as showers, picnic tables, boat launches, and a delightful beach and playground. No reservations, but the campground is open all year.

Nine miles south of Anacortes, **Deception Pass State Park** (360/675-2417, www.parks.wa.gov, $35 tents, $45 RVs, $12 bikes) has some of the finest camping in this part of Washington, with tall Douglas firs and a gorgeous lakeside location. Unfortunately, the park's popularity means that you'll be accompanied by a multitude of fellow visitors. There are 310 tent and RV sites at Deception Pass, and the facility includes hot showers and dump stations. The primary campground along Cranberry Lake has year-round sites, and a second seasonal campground is just north of the bridge at Bowman Bay, with additional sites at the former Sunrise Resort. The park also rents

several cabins at $79-91 per night. The nicest of these, the Ben Ure Cabin, is a modern two-person unit with a large deck overlooking Cornet Bay. It's accessible by kayak. If possible, make reservations ($10 fee) well in advance of a midsummer visit by calling 888/226-7688 or booking online at www.washingtongooingtocamp.com. Head to the park's outdoor amphitheater on weekend evenings in the summer for natural history lectures and presentations.

Exceptionally popular with RVers—and with good reason—**Pioneer Trails RV Resort** (527 Miller Rd., 360/293-5355, www.pioneertrails.com) sits on 28 acres of forested land south of town off Highway 20. Immaculate sites cost $36 ($49 for those with a private cabana), and cabins are $49-59. No tent camping is permitted.

A sprawling RV park just south of town, **Fidalgo Bay Resort** (4701 Fidalgo Bay Rd., 360/293-5353, www.fidalgobay.com, $36-49) has beach access, seafood cookouts, a fitness center, and Wi-Fi. Other RV options include **Swinomish Casino & Lodge** (12885 Casino Dr., 360/293-2691 or 888/288-8883, www.swinomishcasinoandlodge.com, $32-35) and **Lighthouse RV Park** (6060 Sands Way, 360/770-4334, www.lighthouseministorageandrvpark.com, $35); the latter isn't much more than a gravel lot with crammed-together sites near Skyline Marina. You can also park RVs at **Cap Sante Marina** in Anacortes; guests check in at the harbormaster's office (360/293-0694).

North Whidbey RV Park (565 W. Cornet Bay Rd., 360/675-9597 or 888/462-2674, www.northwhidbeyrvpark.com, $33) is nine miles south of Anacortes and across the road from Deception Pass State Park.

INFORMATION AND SERVICES

For maps, brochures, and up-to-date information, drop by the **Anacortes Visitor Information Center** (819 Commercial Ave., 360/293-3832, www.anacortes.org, 9am-5pm daily Mar.-Nov., 10am-4pm Sat.-Sun.

Dec.-Feb.). Across the street is a mural of Anna Curtis, for whom the town was named. Also check out the *Anacortes American* newspaper's website (www.goanacortes.com) for local information and news.

Island Hospital (1211 24th St., 360/299-1300, www.islandhospital.org) has a 24-hour emergency room and 43 beds. The only hospital on the San Juan Islands is a limited facility in Friday Harbor, so this is the primary regional facility for the islands. The hospital also has a **Walk-In Clinic** (360/299-4311, 8am-8pm Mon.-Sat., 9am-5pm Sun.) for non-emergency visits. **Anacortes Family Medicine** (2511 M Ave., 360/299-4211) is the local medical clinic.

If your pet gets sick or hurt, head to **Anacortes Animal Hospital** (2504 Commercial Ave., 360/293-3431) or **Fidalgo Animal Medical Center** (3303 Commercial Ave., 360/293-2186, www.fidalgovets.com). Leave your dogs or cats at **Sunnyhill Kennels & Catterey** (8033 Summit Rd., 360/293-3434, www.sunnyhillkennels.com) if you don't want to have them on the San Juans. Dog lovers will appreciate the big fenced-in **Ace of Hearts Rotary Dog Park** at H Avenue and 38th Street.

Spacious **Anacortes Library** (1220 10th St., 360/293-1910, http://library.cityofanacortes.org, 10am-7pm Mon., 11am-7pm Tues.-Fri., noon-5pm Sat.-Sun.) has a kids' room and a dozen computers with free Internet access and Wi-Fi.

GETTING THERE AND AROUND
Washington State Ferries

To reach the San Juan Islands or Sidney, British Columbia, via state ferry, you have no choice but to leave from Anacortes—and ferry traffic keeps a good portion of local businesses in business. The **Washington State Ferries** website (www.wsdot.wa.gov/ferries) has details on the ferry system, including current wait times in Anacortes. Call 206/464-6400 or 888/808-7977 for information and reservations.

RESERVATIONS

If you are traveling on the ferry during a busy time of year, be sure to make **Save A Spot** vehicle reservations online at www.wsdot.wa.gov/ferries/reservations. Use your credit card to hold space for standard vehicles on ferries up to two months prior to your sailing to the islands. You'll receive a confirmation email, but won't be billed for travel until you board. You can change or cancel reservations until 5pm the day prior to travel. Be sure to bring the bar code printout or your reservation confirmation number.

ANACORTES TERMINAL

Located on 12th Street, the Anacortes ferry terminal has a small gift shop and a café. Warning: Anacortes police often stop folks speeding to catch the ferry. Keep your speed down or you might get delayed considerably longer, with a fine to boot!

If you're bringing your car and have a reservation, arrive an hour ahead of your scheduled sailing. If you don't have a reservation and are driving, get there at least two hours ahead (or more) to wait as a standby. A small beach nearby is fun for a stroll or to keep the kids from bugging you too much, but keep an eye on the ferry traffic so you don't find yourself at the other end of the beach when cars start loading. Avoid delays by leaving your car in the parking lot next to the terminal (800/828-4197, $25 for three days or $40 for a week); there's always space for walk-on passengers.

TO THE SAN JUANS

For travel to the San Juan Islands, the state ferries charge higher rates in summer (May-Sept.) than in the off-season. Peak-season summertime fares from Anacortes to Friday Harbor—the last stop in the United States—are $14 for adult passengers in a vehicle and walk-ons, or $64 for a standard car and driver. Bikes are $4 extra, and kayaks cost $21 more. Summertime fares from Anacortes to the other islands are $14 for passengers or $45 for a car and driver to Lopez Island, and $14 for passengers or $54 for a car and driver to Orcas or Shaw Islands. Credit cards are accepted at all ferry terminals, but checks are not.

Westbound travel between the islands (such as from Lopez to Orcas) costs $28 for a car and driver, and is free for passengers or walk-ons. Eastbound interisland travel is free within the San Juans (e.g., Orcas to Lopez) or from the islands eastward to Anacortes. If you're planning to visit all the islands, save money by heading straight to Friday Harbor on San Juan Island, and then work your way back through the others at no additional charge.

TO VANCOUVER ISLAND

Twice a day (once daily in winter; no service Jan.-Mar.), a ferry heads from Anacortes to **Sidney, British Columbia,** 20 miles north of Victoria on Vancouver Island. One-way peak-season fares to Sidney are $20 for adult passengers in a vehicle and walk-ons or $67 for a car and driver. Bikes are $6 extra, and kayaks cost $23 more. The charge is the same in the opposite direction (Sidney to Anacortes) or from Sidney to Friday Harbor, but if you stop in Friday Harbor, there are no additional costs to continue east all the way to Anacortes. Save A Spot vehicle reservations are highly recommended for this route. You will be crossing an international border, so passports are required (for kids a passport or birth certificate will do).

Other Transportation
GUEMES FERRY

Skagit County operates the small **Guemes Island Ferry** (6th St. and I Ave., 360/419-7618, www.skagitcounty.net) to this nearby residential island. The five-minute crossing from Anacortes costs $12 round-trip for a car and driver, and $4 adults, $2.50 kids and seniors round-trip for passengers or walk-ons. The ferry departs hourly (more often during commute hours) from 6:30am till at least 8pm daily (till 11pm on weekends). It doesn't run between 11:30am and 1pm.

WATER TAXIS

Based at Skyline Marina in Anacortes, **Island Express Charters** (360/299-2875 or 877/473-9777, www.islandexpresscharters. com) has two high-speed landing crafts with plenty of space for kayaks, bikes, and gear. They'll head most anywhere in the San Juans for $90 per person round-trip to the closer islands. Add $20 round-trip for bikes or $30-40 for kayaks. Parking is free while you're on the islands.

In business since 1992, **Paraclete Charters** (Skyline Marina, 360/420-5187, www.paracletecharters.com) runs three boats (the largest can carry 64 folks) from Anacortes. Prices depend on your destination and number of people, but you don't need to charter an entire boat, and there's space for kayaks, bikes, and pets.

AIR

Departing from **Anacortes Airport** (360/299-1828, www.portofanacortes.com/airport), **San Juan Airlines** (360/293-4691 or 800/874-4434, www.sanjuanairlines.com) offers commuter flights year-round to Lopez, San Juan, Orcas, and Blakely Islands in the San Juans, plus flightseeing and air charters.

BUS AND SHUTTLE VAN

Skagit Transit (360/757-4433, www.skagittransit.org, $1) has daily bus connections from Anacortes (including the ferry terminal, Guemes Island ferry, and Washington Park) to Mount Vernon, La Conner, and other parts of Skagit County. All SKAT buses have bike racks. **Airporter Shuttle** (360/380-8800 or 800/235-5247, www.airporter.com) runs vans between Anacortes and Sea-Tac Airport at least 10 times daily year-round; the fare is $76 one-way ($65 kids) to the Anacortes ferry terminal.

TAXI AND CAR

Call **Mert's Taxi** (360/708-6358, www.mertstaxi.com) for rides around town or out to the ferry terminal. Car rentals are available from **U-Save Auto Rental** (360/293-8686 or 877/451-6985, www.usave.net) and **Enterprise Rent a Car** (360/293-4325 or 800/261-7331, www.enterprise.com).

Whidbey Island

One of the longest islands in the Lower 48, Whidbey Island encompasses 208 square miles in its 45-mile length. No spot on it is more than 5 miles from the water.

Whidbey is a favorite place for a Sunday-afternoon drive, with Deception Pass State Park the primary "stop and gawk" spot along the way. Also popular are the quaint towns of Coupeville and Langley, the quiet shoreline and picturesque agricultural land of Ebey's Landing National Historical Reserve, and wild places such as South Whidbey State Park and Fort Casey State Park. The largest metropolitan center, Oak Harbor, is home to Whidbey Naval Air Station.

EXPLORING THE ISLAND

Whidbey is a perfect destination for a day trip or a weekend outing, with lots to explore and a wide variety of places to stay. The island is also great for cyclists, with many miles of quiet back roads and well-maintained bike paths. The charm of the picturesque towns of Langley and Coupeville is natural—a result of their history, not a theme created to attract tourism.

For a fast day tour, ride the Mukilteo-Clinton ferry to the south end of the island and take a leisurely drive up-island, with stops in each town and park. To really do Whidbey right, you'll need more than a day. Take the time to explore the many natural areas and historical sites, camp out in one of the excellent state parks, or stay in a local bed-and-breakfast. Reservations are highly recommended for summer weekends.

Contact **Whidbey-Camano Tourism** (888/747-7777, www.whidbeycamanoislands. com) for information on Whidbey.

GETTING THERE

To drive onto Whidbey Island, you have only one option: the Deception Pass Bridge at the island's north end. To get there, go west on Highway 20 from I-5. Access to the south

end of Whidbey is a relaxing **Washington State Ferries** (206/464-6400 for general info or 888/808-7977 in Washington and British Columbia only) ride from Mukilteo or Port Townsend. Find all the details—including current ferry wait times—at www.wsdot. wa.gov/ferries.

The **Mukilteo-Clinton** ferry departs every half hour 5am-1am, and the 20-minute crossing costs $5 round-trip for passengers or walk-ons, $1 extra for bikes, and $11 one-way for a car and driver. (No charge for eastbound passengers and bikes.) The busiest times are the weekday commute (westbound in the morning and eastbound in the evening), Saturday mornings (after 9am en route to the island), and late in the afternoon on Sundays. Sunday evenings after 7pm are quieter, so just enjoy the island and let folks in a hurry wait in the ferry line while you sit on a beach or in a café.

From the Olympic Peninsula, board the ferry in **Port Townsend** to arrive at the **Keystone-Coupeville** landing next to Fort Casey State Park a half hour later. These perpetually full ferries operate every 90 minutes between 6:30am and 8:30pm in the summer, and one-way fares are $4 for passengers ($0.50 extra one-way for bikes), or $14 for a car and driver. Unlike most other Washington State Ferries, reservations are highly recommended for this one. Be sure to make a **ferry reservation** within 24 hours of your departure at www.wsdot.wa.gov/ferries, or by calling 206/464-6400 or 888/808-7977. You can also make a reservation at the tollbooth a few hours prior to your sailing, or take your chances without one (not advised). Twenty spaces are kept for vehicles without reservations, but you may be waiting for hours if you miss the boat.

Heading to Whidbey from Sea-Tac Airport? Take the **Whidbey-Sea-Tac Shuttle** (360/679-4003 or 877/679-4003,

Whidbey Island

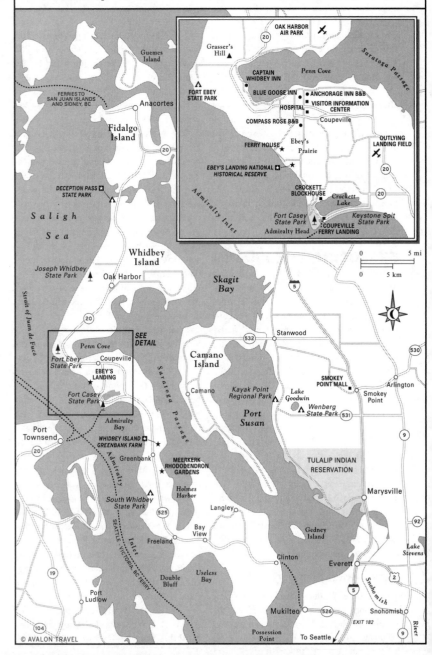

OAK HARBOR AIR PARK
(20)
Grasser's Hill ▲
Saratoga Passage
Penn Cove
CAPTAIN WHIDBEY INN
BLUE GOOSE INN ● ■ ANCHORAGE INN B&B
FORT EBEY STATE PARK
HOSPITAL ■ ■ VISITOR INFORMATION CENTER
COMPASS ROSE B&B ●
Coupeville
OUTLYING LANDING FIELD
FERRY HOUSE ★ Ebey's Prairie
(20)
EBEY'S LANDING NATIONAL HISTORICAL RESERVE ●
CROCKETT BLOCKHOUSE
Crockett Lake
Fort Casey State Park
Keystone Spit State Park
Admiralty Inlet
Admiralty Head
COUPEVILLE FERRY LANDING

0   5 mi
0   5 km

Guemes Island
FERRIES TO SAN JUAN ISLANDS AND SIDNEY, BC
Anacortes
Fidalgo Island
(20)
DECEPTION PASS STATE PARK
Saligh Sea
Whidbey Island
Oak Harbor
Skagit Bay
Joseph Whidbey State Park
(20)
SEE DETAIL
Strait of Juan de Fuca
Fort Ebey State Park
Penn Cove
Coupeville
EBEY'S LANDING
Fort Casey State Park
Admiralty Bay
Saratoga Passage
(5)
Stanwood
(532)
Camano Island
Camano
Kayak Point Regional Park
Lake Goodwin
Port Susan
Wenberg State Park
(531)
SMOKEY POINT MALL
Arlington
Smokey Point
(9)
Port Townsend
(20)
WHIDBEY ISLAND GREENBANK FARM
Greenbank
MEERKERK RHODODENDRON GARDENS
Holmes Harbor
South Whidbey State Park
(525)
Langley
Bay View
Freeland
Gedney Island
TULALIP INDIAN RESERVATION
Marysville
(92)
Lake Stevens
Admiralty Inlet
SEATTLE VICTORIA BC FERRY
(19)
Port Ludlow
(104)
Double Bluff
Useless Bay
Clinton
Everett
Snohomish River
(5)
(2)
Snohomish
(9)
Mukilteo
(526)
EXIT 182
To Seattle
Possession Point

© AVALON TRAVEL

www.seatacshuttle.com), with frequent daily runs up the island. The cost is $40 one-way between Sea-Tac and Whidbey Island.

GETTING AROUND

Whidbey Island seems like it was designed for biking. The rolling hills, clean air, and beautiful weather are inspiring enough; occasional whale and eagle sightings add to the pleasure. **Island Transit** (360/678-7771 or 800/240-8747, www.islandtransit.org) is a *free* bus system that operates Monday-Friday all across Whidbey Island, from Clinton on the south to Deception Pass on the north. All buses have bike racks, and you can flag buses down.

LANGLEY

This tiny waterfront artists' community (pop. 1,100) is a great browsing stop, and several of its lodging establishments have views across Saratoga Passage to Camano Island and beyond. You'll find gourmet restaurants, boutiques, bed-and-breakfasts, bookstores, and art galleries.

Langley may be the only Washington town founded by a teenager. In 1880, an ambitious 15-year-old German immigrant named Jacob Anthes settled here. Because he was too young to file for a homestead, Anthes spent $100 to buy 120 acres of land, adding to his holdings with a 160-acre homestead claim when he reached 21. He later built a store and post office and teamed up with Judge J. W. Langley to plat the new town.

Sights

Langley's main attraction is simply the town itself, situated right along Saratoga Passage. A favorite downtown spot for photos is the life-size bronze **Boy and Dog,** by local sculptor Georgia Gerber. The 160-foot fishing pier offers water views and a chance to pull out your fishing pole, and the beach is popular for picnicking and swimming. It's hard to miss the rabbits that hop all over Langley, especially at dawn and dusk.

Tiny **South Whidbey Historical Museum** (312 2nd St., 360/730-3367, www.

southwhidbeyhistory.org, 1pm-4pm Fri.-Sun. June-Aug., 1pm-4pm Sat.-Sun. Sept.-May) has local memorabilia in a century-old building. Across the street at the corner is a small park with a colorful shelter and tables.

Seawall Park off 1st Street is the spot for a beach fix. Watch for eagles, herons, and gray whales—especially in spring. Ring the whale bell if you see one.

Near the town of Clinton, **Whidbey Institute at Chinook** (6449 Old Pietila Rd., 360/341-1884, www.whidbeyinstitute.org) offers a variety of educational and environmental programs. The 100-acre site has lovely wooded trails and a spacious retreat center.

Langley Whale Center (117 Anthes St., 360/331-3543, www.orcanetwork.org, 11am-5pm Thurs.-Sat., free) is a project of the nonprofit Orca Network. The center provides information and exhibits on orcas, gray whales, and other whales and marine mammals.

Recreation

At Bayview Corner, **Bayview Bicycles** (360/331-7980) rents mountain and hybrid bikes and has bike maps. **Whidbey Island Kayaking Company** (360/221-0229 or 800/233-4319, www.whidbeyislandkayaking.com) leads trips of varying length, starting with a two-hour kayak trip ($59) from the south end of the island.

Kids love the **Castle Park Playground** at 5495 Maxwelton Road, with all sorts of towers, ramparts, swings, and slides.

Shopping

Tiny Langley is home to several fine art galleries, most notably **Museo Gallery** (215 1st St., 360/221-7737, www.museo.cc) and **Brackenwood Gallery** (302 1st St., 360/221-2978, www.brackenwoodgallery.com), both of which feature unusual and highly creative pieces. Brackenwood has works by internationally known sculptor Georgia Gerber, whose ever-popular metal pig is a landmark at Seattle's Pike Place Market. Cooperatively run **Whidbey Art Gallery** (220 2nd St.,

360/221-7675, www.whidbeyartists.com) is another excellent spot with pieces by Whidbey artists. The **Langley First Saturday Art Walk** takes place monthly at local galleries.

The **Whidbey Island Center for the Arts** (565 Camano Ave., 360/221-8262, www.wicaonline.com) has concerts and plays throughout the year. Housed within the old fire station, **Callahan's FireHouse Studio & Gallery** (179 2nd St., 360/221-1242, www.callahansfirehouse.com) is a fun place to watch glassblowers at work or to produce your own pieces. In a half-hour session you get to create a colorful sea float, tumbler, or paperweight.

Gregor Rare Books (197 2nd St., 360/221-8331, www.gregorbooks.com) specializes in 20th-century masterpieces. **Moonraker Books** (209 1st St., 360/221-6962) carries a fine selection of regional titles.

Whidbey Island Winery (5237 S. Langley Rd., 360/221-2040, www.whidbeyislandwinery.com, tastings 11am-5pm Wed.-Mon.) is a family operation that produces white wines from estate-grown Madeleine Angevine and Madeleine Sylvaner grapes, along with surprisingly good rhubarb wines and a number of reds crafted from eastern Washington grapes. Stop for a picnic overlooking the adjacent vineyard and apple orchard.

For a different kind of buzz, **Whidbey Island Cannabis Company** (5826 S. Kramer Rd., 360/321-6151, www.whidbeyislandcannabisco.com) has marijuana products. This was the first cannabis store to be issued a retail license in Washington State.

Entertainment and Events

The Clyde Theatre (217 1st St., 360/221-5525, www.theclyde.net) is the only place to watch first-run movies on the south end of Whidbey.

In late February, **Langley Mystery Weekend** attracts sleuths in search of a make-believe murderer. Clues are planted all over town, and actors serve up information to help (or confuse) the hundreds of amateur detectives. The main summertime event—it's been around for over 40 years—is

Choochokam Festival of the Arts (www.choochokamarts.org) on the second weekend in July. The festival attracts thousands of visitors to 1st Street with live music, art exhibits, a street dance, beer garden, and half-marathon race. A free shuttle bus runs from the Clinton ferry terminal, so you won't need to bring a car.

The **Whidbey Island Fair** (360/221-4677, www.fair.whidbeyislandfair.com) is a four-day event held the third week of August that includes a carnival, parade, music, and 4-H exhibits. For something a bit less countrified, return to Langley for **DjangoFest Northwest** (www.djangofest.com) in mid-September, celebrating the life and music of acclaimed Gypsy jazz guitarist Django Reinhardt.

A local acting company puts on the **Island Shakespeare Festival** (5476 Maxwelton Rd., www.islandshakespearefest.org), with outdoor performances of classic plays Thursday-Sunday evenings July-mid-September.

Food

Langley is blessed with fine and surprisingly reasonable restaurants. Start your morning at the ever-busy ★ **Useless Bay Coffee** (121 2nd St., 360/221-4515, www.uselessbaycoffee.com, 7:30am-4:30pm daily, $6-11), where owner Des Rock is a coffee connoisseur, roasting his own beans in a small on-the-premises roaster. Get a morning latte, grilled panini on homemade bread, breakfast tacos, or granola parfait. Take your coffee outside to enjoy it amid the flowers. Check the blackboard for the day's specials. There's occasional live music in an adjacent band shell. (Useless Bay received its name because of its uselessness to large ships. It's shallow, leading to enormous tidal flats at low tide.)

A bit hard to find—but worth the search—is **Mukilteo Coffee Roasters Café in the Woods** (5331 Crawford Rd., 360/321-5270, 8am-4pm Mon.-Sat., closed Sun., $7-12). The café has a peaceful wooded setting, with a brunch menu of huevos rancheros, salads, wraps, and burgers. It's located south of Bayview Corner between Langley and the main highway.

For comfort food, **Braeburn Restaurant** (197 2nd St., 360/221-3211, www.braeburnlangley.com, 8am-4pm Mon.-Fri., 7am-4pm Sat.-Sun., $9-13) serves stuffed French toast or corned beef hash for breakfast along with curry chicken salad or meatloaf sandwich (and lots more) for lunch. Enjoy patio dining in the summer.

A French-inspired Northwest bistro, ★ **Prima Bistro** (upstairs at 201 1st St., 360/221-4060, www.primabistro.com, 11:30am-9pm daily, $16-28 dinner entrées), serves steak frites, seafood specials, great burgers, Penn Cove mussels, and salads. Save room for a slice of molten chocolate s'mores cake. Lunch favorites include confit of Muscovy duck, truffled prawns, and salade Niçoise. Get beer on tap and mixed drinks at the cozy bar, or step out on the deck for alfresco dining with a water view. There is live music every Thursday. Call ahead for reservations on busy summer weekends. Downstairs, the **Star Store** (360/221-5222, www.starstorewhidbey.com) is a fun place to explore, with gourmet groceries, clothing, housewares, and imported items.

Up the street a bit, the Garibyan brothers have gained an enormous local following for their artfully presented Greek and Middle Eastern dishes at **Café Langley** (113 1st St., 360/221-3090, www.cafelangley.com, 11:30am-2:30pm and 5pm-9pm daily, $16-21). Try the chicken marsala gnocchi or crab cakes with mango salsa.

Right on the water, **Village Pizzeria** (106 1st St., 360/221-3363, 11:30am-10pm daily June-Sept., 11:30am-9pm daily Oct.-May, cash only) crafts New York-style thin-crust pizzas. House specialties are a vegetarian pesto and garlic pizza, and the Village Special: homemade meatball and sausage, pepperoni, onions, peppers, mushrooms, olives, and anchovies. The European-style grilled chicken is also popular. The restaurant gets crowded and very loud on weekends, so don't come here for quiet conversations. Get a $3-4 slice or a pie

to go if you're in a hurry. Credit cards aren't accepted, but there's an ATM if you're short on cash.

The **South Whidbey Tilth Farmers Market** (Hwy. 525 at Thompson Rd., 360/579-2892, www.southwhidbeytilth.org, 11am-2pm Sun. May-mid-Oct.) has all-organic fruits and vegetables, plus flowers, baked goods, and seafood. The **Bayview Farmers Market** (360/321-4302, www.bayviewfarmersmarket.com, 10am-2pm Sat. May-Oct.) is located behind the Star Store at the intersection of Bayview Road and Highway 525.

Hidden behind All Washed Up Laundromat, **Sundance Bakery** (630 2nd St., 360/222-2392, 6am-5pm daily May-Sept., reduced winter hours) is a locals' place where the European-style breads and pastries are made using rye and wheat grown on Whidbey Island. Fresh breads, cinnamon rolls, cookies, beignets, and other treats are baked in a wood-fired brick oven. A fun old-school pinball parlor is adjacent.

Bringing a taste of South America to Langley, **Portico Latin Bistro** (220 1st Ave., 360/221-8141, www.porticolatinbistro.com, $14-15) has a menu of chicken enchiladas, Jamaica jerk chicken, roasted pineapple salads, fish tacos, fresh-squeezed guava juice, and a memorable plantain tart topped with caramel and whipped cream. The setting is casual, with bright yellow walls, a back waterside deck, and occasional live music.

★ **Orchard Kitchen** (5574 Bayview Rd., 360/321-1517, www.orchardkitchen.com) is located on a five-acre organic farm near Bayview Corner. Owner/chef Vincent Nattress offers farmhouse dinners Thursday-Saturday evenings, with a single seating at 6:30pm for $63 per person. Meals are served family-style, and the emphasis is on freshness, fun, and flavor. Each week's menu reflects seasonal ingredients from the farm. Because of its popularity and limited seating, it's wise to book well in advance for a meal at Orchard Kitchen.

The ★ **Inn at Langley** (400 1st St., 360/221-3033, www.innatlangley.com, Thurs.-Sun. summer, Fri.-Sun. rest of the year) is

Whidbey's four-star restaurant, serving memorable six-course Northwest cuisine dinners that emphasize local ingredients. Celebrity chef Matt Costello puts on quite a performance in the open kitchen, explaining each step as he prepares the meal. Dinner here is highly recommended, but you'll need to reserve a week or two ahead, or a month in advance for Saturday nights. The cost for these memorable culinary extravaganzas is $155 per person; wines are additional. Meals start at 7pm most nights (6pm on Sundays) and last three hours.

Wine and Spirits

Whidbey Island is home to eight wineries and distillers, with several in the Langley/Freeland area. Pick up a Wine & Spirits Trail map from the visitors center, or find it online at www. whidbeyislandvintners.org. Three of the most interesting are **Whidbey Island Winery** (5237 Langley Rd., 360/221-2040, www.whidbeyislandwinery.com), **Spoiled Dog Winery** (5881 Maxwelton Rd., Clinton, 360/661-6226, www.spoileddogwinery.com), and **Whidbey Island Distillery** (3466 Craw Rd., 360/221-4715, www.whidbeydistillery.com).

2nd St. Wine Shop (221 2nd St., 360/221-3121, www.2ndstreetwineshop.com) focuses exclusively on wines from Washington State.

Accommodations

The Langley Visitors Center has details on a multitude of local bed-and-breakfasts and inns and keeps track of vacancies. Stop by the visitors center to see photos of each place. Add a 10.4 percent lodging tax to all rates. Additional weekly or nightly rentals can be found on **Airbnb** (www.airbnb.com) or **VRBO** (www.vrbo.com).

HOTELS AND INNS

The 16-room **Saratoga Inn** (201 Cascade Ave., 360/221-5801 or 836/749-5565, www. saratogainnwhidbeyisland.com, $195-235 d) combines the privacy of a hotel with the amenities of a B&B, including a buffet breakfast and afternoon wine and hors d'oeuvres.

The spacious rooms are attractively appointed, and all include gas fireplaces, guest robes, Wi-Fi, and bikes to roll around town. Honeymooners will love the private carriage house suite ($325 d), which has a two-person tub and a full kitchen.

Designed by its architect-owner, **Langley Motel** (526 Camano Ave., 360/221-6070 or 866/276-8292, www.langleymotel.com, $115-155 d) has five units with 1950s retro-style simple rooms and full kitchens. There's a two-night minimum on weekends.

Located right along the beach and just up from the marina, **Boatyard Inn** (200 Wharf St., 360/221-5120, www.boatyardinn.com, $220-325 d) has spacious and modern studio units, loft suites, and a town house. Most of these feature waterfront decks, and all include mini-kitchens and Wi-Fi. A two-night minimum is required on summer weekends.

The luxurious 26-unit ★ **Inn at Langley** (400 1st St., 360/221-3033, www.innatlangley. com) has rooms ($325-345 d), suites ($400 d), and cottages ($500-600 d), each with its own private patio overlooking Saratoga Passage, a jetted tub, wood-burning fireplace, fridge, continental breakfast, and Wi-Fi. A two-night minimum is required on weekends, and no kids under age 12 are permitted, but pets are accepted for an extra fee. Also on the premises is a renowned restaurant, along with The Spa, providing massage, aromatherapy, body masks, and more.

BED-AND-BREAKFASTS

You can find links to local bed-and-breakfasts at **Whidbey Island B&B Association** (www. whidbeyislandbandb.com). Most of these require a two-night minimum stay on summer weekends.

★ **Country Cottage of Langley B&B** (215 6th St., 360/221-8709 or 800/713-3860, www.acountrycottage.com, $149-209 d) comprises a 1920s Craftsman-style farmhouse and six cottages, all with water views, private entrances, and decks. A gourmet breakfast is served in the main house or brought to your cottage. Three cottages also feature in-room

Jacuzzis and fireplaces. Kids are welcome, and pets are accepted (fee).

Eagles Nest Inn (4680 Saratoga Rd., 360/221-5331, www.eaglesnestinn.com, $169-189 d) is a delightful bed-and-breakfast getaway in a lush forested setting. The octagonal house is capped with an "eagle's nest" room with windows on all sides and outstanding views. Three other guest rooms are a bit larger, and the Saratoga Room has a private balcony, fireplace, and soaking tub. Amenities include a full breakfast, outdoor hot tub, private baths, Wi-Fi, and hiking trails within adjacent Saratoga Woods Preserve. The feeders outside attract birds and chipmunks, and deer are frequent visitors to the grounds. A two-night minimum is required.

★ **Guest House Log Cottages** (24371 State Rte. 525, 360/678-3115 or 800/997-3115, www.guesthouselogcottages.com, $165-375 d) consists of six cottages on 25 acres of woods and fields. All are nicely maintained, with private baths, fireplaces, and jetted tubs, and they are stocked with breakfast ingredients. The cottages are for couples in search of a quiet escape, so no kids are allowed. Other amenities include an outdoor pool and hot tub, and a pretty wildlife pond. Deer are commonly seen in the morning. The luxurious lodge ($375 d) is easily the finest unit and a perfect honeymoon spot, with a big deck hanging over the edge of the pond. There is no Wi-Fi in the rooms, but it is available in the commons area around the pool and hot tub.

In Clinton, five miles west of Langley, **Farmhouse B&B** (2740 Sunshine Ln., 360/321-6288 or 888/888-7022, www.farmhousebb.com, $139-189 d) gets kudos from guests for its peaceful setting on Useless Bay, dramatic vistas, four immaculate suites, flower gardens, and playful donkeys. A sandy beach is nearby, and rooms include private baths, private entrances, fireplaces, kitchens, jetted tubs (in some rooms), Wi-Fi, in-suite breakfasts, and access to an outdoor hot tub. Older children only.

A charming 1930s farmhouse in Clinton, **Maxwelton Aerie Alpacas** (7224 S. Maxwelton Rd., 206/819-3710, www.maxweltonaerie.com) has a magnificent location overlooking Useless Bay, with stairs to a long and secluded beach. Guests love to visit with and feed the 24 alpacas in the adjacent pasture. The house sleeps up to eight people for $365; add $30 per person for additional guests (max of 12). There's a three-night minimum in the summer, or two nights in the off-season. This is a magical spot that is perfect for families.

CAMPING

Unfortunately, the campground at **South Whidbey State Park** closed in 2015 because of the danger from falling trees; many of the park's older trees are weakened from decay. **Island County Fairgrounds** (819 Camano Ave., 360/221-7950, www.portofsouthwhidbey.com, $20 tents, $25 RVs) has year-round RV hookups and a few tent spaces. Showers are available, with additional coin-operated showers at the marina on Wharf Street.

Information

Drop by the **Langley Visitors Center** (208 Anthes Ave., 360/221-6765, www.visitlangley.com, 11am-4pm daily year-round) for the full scoop on Langley. You can also get brochures from a kiosk at Langley Road and Highway 525; it's staffed on summer weekends.

The **Langley Library** (104 2nd St., 360/221-4383, www.sno-isle.com, 11am-7pm Mon. and Wed., 10am-6pm Tues. and Thurs.-Sat.) has computers and free Wi-Fi access.

FREELAND AND GREENBANK

Home to 2,000 people, the town of **Freeland** has an unusual history. The area was settled in the early 1900s by socialists who believed in the communal ownership of land, hence the name. The commune only lasted a few years before infighting led to the breakup of the group. Freeland is not a tourist attraction and the downtown is forgettable, but the town does have lodging, restaurants, and several places worth a visit, including South Whidbey

State Park, Greenbank Farm, and Meerkerk Rhododendron Gardens. Tiny **Greenbank** is an unincorporated area seven miles north of Freeland on Highway 525.

One unique local attraction is **Earth Sanctuary** (360/331-6667, www.earthsanctuary.org, $7), a 72-acre preserve where art and ecology mix in a druid-friendly, sacred-aura, in-touch-with-the-earth locale that includes two miles of trails, a stone circle, Tibetan prayer wheel, labyrinth, retreat center, and more. It's open daily during daylight hours. Get local info from the **Greater Freeland Chamber of Commerce** (5575 Harbor Ave., 360/331-1980, www.freeland-wa.org, 10am-3pm daily).

Food

Looking for a reasonably priced all-American breakfast? **Freeland Café** (1642 E. Main St., 360/331-9945, www.freelandcafe.com, 6am-9pm daily, $6-10 breakfasts) serves good diner fare in a frumpy setting. Breakfast is available all day, with blueberry pancakes, omelets, and a popular Hawaiian-style breakfast of sausage, eggs, and rice. The café also serves burgers, steaks, and other fare for lunch and dinner, but breakfast is the main attraction. The café has been in business for over 40 years.

In Freeland, **China City** (1804 Scott Rd., 360/331-8899, www.chinacityrestaurant.com, 11am-9pm daily for food, bar open till midnight, $9-14) is a good option for vegetarians and anyone looking for Asian cooking on Whidbey. The setting is stylish, with a koi pond near the entrance and a wide selection of traditional favorites and combination dinners. Try the famous walnut shrimp or vegetable hofun. China City has a second restaurant in Oak Harbor.

Located along scenic Holmes Harbor, ★ **Gordon's on Blueberry Hill** (5438 Woodard Ave., 360/331-7515, www.gordonsonblueberryhill.com, Tues.-Fri. 11:30am-2pm and 5pm-8pm, 4pm-8pm Sat.-Sun., $22-34) is Freeland's white-linen dining choice. Chef and co-owner Gordon Stewart brings a bit of New Orleans to the menu with spicy seafood jambalaya, bouillabaisse, and sambuca prawns, but the restaurant also features London broil, spinach ravioli, linguini with mussels and clams, and more. Reservations are advised.

Accommodations

Harbor Inn (1606 Main St., 360/331-6900, www.harborinn.us, $133-145 d) has reasonably priced motel units with microwaves, fridges, seasonal continental breakfast, and Wi-Fi. Rooms are not fancy, but are clean and well maintained. The inn is right in Freeland and just a short walk to shopping and restaurants. Add $15 for dogs.

SOUTH WHIDBEY STATE PARK

Easily the island's most underrated park, **South Whidbey State Park** (360/331-4559, www.parks.wa.gov) has outstanding hiking and picnicking, plus clamming and crabbing on a narrow sandy beach and striking Olympic Mountains views. The 85 acres of old-growth Douglas fir and western red cedar protect resident black-tailed deer, foxes, raccoons, rabbits, bald eagles, ospreys, and pileated woodpeckers. Be sure to hike the **Wilbert Trail,** a mile-long path that circles through these ancient forests; it starts directly across from the park entrance. Get to the park by heading northeast from Freeland on Bush Point Road; it becomes Smugglers Cove Road and continues past the park, a distance of seven miles.

★ WHIDBEY ISLAND GREENBANK FARM

The large red barn at **Whidbey Island Greenbank Farm** (14 miles north of the ferry dock at Clinton, 360/222-3151) is a well-known sight to anyone driving across Whidbey Island. Built in 1904, the barn was once the centerpiece for the world's largest loganberry farm. The berries aren't grown here anymore, and the land is now owned by the Port of Coupeville and covered with solar panels. The farm's wine shop (www.gbfwine.

com) sells loganberry wine—produced elsewhere—along with grape and fruit wines from local wineries. Besides wines, the shop has preserves, jellies, and loganberry wine-filled chocolates. The buildings also houses **Whidbey Pies Café** (360/678-1288, www.whidbeypies.com), serving 10 or so types of pies daily at $6 per slice or $20 for a whole pie. Three fine art galleries are also worth a look at Greenbank Farm, and there's a popular off-leash **dog park** out front. Look for great blue herons in the farm's pond; their nests can be seen in the trees on the other side of Highway 525.

Greenbank Farm is open daily 10am-5pm in the summer, and Monday-Friday 11am-5pm, Saturday-Sunday 10am-5pm the rest of the year.

MEERKERK RHODODENDRON GARDENS

The delightful **Meerkerk Rhododendron Gardens** (360/678-1912, www.meerkerkgardens.org, 9am-4pm daily, $5, free for children) boast more than 1,500 varieties of rhododendron species and hybrids on a 53-acre site just south of Greenbank off Resort Road. Begun by Max and Anne Meerkerk in the 1960s, the gardens are now maintained by the not-for-profit Seattle Rhododendron Society. A quaint stone structure serves as a visitors center. Peak season for "rhodies" is in late April and early May. By the way, the coast rhododendron is Washington's state flower.

★ FORT CASEY STATE PARK

Fort Casey State Park (360/678-4519, www.parks.wa.gov, $10 parking fee) is a historic U.S. Army post three miles south of Coupeville next to the Keystone ferry dock. It has two miles of beach, an underwater park, a boat ramp, hiking trails, picnic areas, spectacular Olympics views, and campsites, plus good fishing in remarkably clear water. The parade field is popular for kite flying and Frisbee.

Fort Casey was one of the "Iron Triangle" of forts that guarded the entrance to Puget Sound and the Bremerton Naval Shipyard at the turn of the 20th century. This deadly crossfire consisted of Fort Casey, Fort Worden at Port Townsend, and Fort Flagler on Marrowstone Island; fortunately, the guns were never fired at an enemy vessel. Fort Casey's big weapons were the ingenious 10-inch disappearing carriage guns; the recoil sent them swinging back down out of sight for reloading, giving the sighter a terrific ride. By 1920, advances in naval warfare made them obsolete, so they were melted down. During World War II, Fort Casey was primarily a training site, although antiaircraft guns were mounted on the fortifications. The fort was closed after the war and purchased by the State of Washington in 1956 for a state park.

Sights

If you're arriving on Whidbey Island by ferry from Port Townsend, get to Fort Casey by taking an immediate left onto Engle Road as soon as you exit the ferry terminal. Much of the fort is open for public viewing, including ammunition bunkers, observation towers, underground storage facilities (bring your flashlight), gun catwalks, and the main attraction: two disappearing 10-inch guns, each weighing 33 tons. Because the originals are long gone, these were brought here in 1968 from an old American fort in the Philippines. Park volunteers lead informative 45-minute tours of Fort Casey on Fridays at 1pm and Saturday-Sunday at 1pm and 2:30pm late May-August.

Be sure to visit the **Admiralty Head Lighthouse Interpretive Center** (360/678-1186, 11am-5pm daily June-Aug., reduced hours Sept.-May, free), where you can learn about coast artillery and the fort's 1890 defense post. The lighthouse itself has not been used since 1927, but you can climb to the top for a wonderful view of Puget Sound and the Olympic Mountains. The hilltop location is a great place to watch ferries crossing from Port Townsend, and kids will have fun on the beach.

The fort's historic buildings are now used as a conference center and the Fort Casey Inn, both run by Seattle Pacific University (www.fortcaseyinn.com). Also nearby is shallow **Crockett Lake,** a good place to look for migratory and resident birds, including great blue herons, belted kingfishers, and northern harriers. You might also see Savannah sparrows and pigeon guillemots on the adjacent **Keystone Spit**.

The **Crockett Blockhouse,** one of four remaining fortifications built in the 1850s to defend against Indian attacks, stands on the north shore of the lake. An offshore underwater park is popular with divers. Northeast of Crockett Lake is **Outlying Landing Field**, used by U.S. Navy pilots to simulate aircraft-carrier landings. Navy jets often do touch-and-go landings at the field, providing for a bit of aerial excitement.

Camping

The small and crowded campground ($30 tents or $40 RVs) at Fort Casey has 21 sites and is open year-round. Shower facilities are available. The exposed campsites are right on the water next to the busy ferry terminal. Pleasant hiking trails lead through the wooded grounds and uphill to the fort's cannons. Make **reservations** ($10 extra) online at http://washington.goingtocamp.com, or by calling 888/226-7688.

★ EBEY'S LANDING NATIONAL HISTORICAL RESERVE

Ebey's Landing National Historical Reserve (360/678-6084, www.nps.gov/ebla), two miles southwest of Coupeville center, has easily the most striking coastal view on the island; no wonder portions of the 1999 movie *Snow Falling on Cedars* were filmed here. As the roads of the reserve wind through acres of rich farmland, the glimpses of water and cliffs might remind you of the Northern California or Oregon coastline; views of the majestic Olympics add to the drama.

The native Skagit people who originally occupied this land were generally friendly toward the white settlers, but their northern neighbors were considerably less forgiving of the invaders. Alaska's Kake tribe of the Tlingit people had a fierce reputation, as exemplified by the following incident recorded by Richard Meade (1871):

> In 1855 a party of Kakes, on a visit south to Puget Sound, became involved in some

road near Ebey's Landing National Historical Reserve

trouble there, which caused a United States vessel to open fire on them, and during the affair one of the Kake chiefs was killed. This took place over 800 miles from the Kake settlements on Kupreanof Island. The next year the tribe sent a canoe-load of fighting men all the way from Clarence Straits in Russian America to Whidby's Island in Washington Territory, and attacked and beheaded an ex-collector—not of internal revenue, for that might have been pardonable—but of customs, and returned safely with his skull and scalp to their villages. Such people are, therefore, not to be despised, and are quite capable of giving much trouble in the future unless wisely and firmly governed.

The beheaded man was Colonel Isaac Ebey, the first settler on Whidbey Island; his head was eventually recovered and reunited with his body before being buried at Sunnyside Cemetery. To fend off further attacks (which never came), the pioneers built seven blockhouses in the 1850s, four of which still stand.

The Anglo settlers were attracted to this part of Whidbey Island by the expansive prairies and fertile black soil. These prairies occupy the sites of shallow ice age lakes; when the water dried up, the rich, deep soil remained. The indigenous practice of burning helped keep them open over the centuries that followed, and the white settlers simply took up residence on this prime land.

Managed by the National Park Service and covering 17,400 acres, Ebey's Landing National Historical Reserve helps keep this land rural and agricultural through scenic easements, land donations, tax incentives, and zoning. Approximately 90 percent of the land remains in private hands. Created in 1978, this was America's first national historical reserve.

Sights

The main attraction at Ebey's Landing National Historical Reserve is simply the country itself: bucolic farmland, densely wooded ridges, and steep coastal bluffs. An informative driving and bicycling brochure, available at the Coupeville museum, provides a detailed tour of Ebey's Landing.

For a scenic bike ride or drive, turn onto Hill Road (two miles south of Coupeville) and follow it through the second-growth stand of Douglas fir trees. It emerges on a high bluff overlooking Admiralty Inlet before dropping to the shoreline at tiny **Ebey's Landing State Park.** From the small parking area at the water's edge, hike the 1.5-mile trail along the bluff above **Parego Lagoon** for a view of the coastline, the Olympics, and the Strait of Juan de Fuca that shouldn't be missed. The lagoon is a fine place to look for migratory birds. Return along the beach, or continue northward to Fort Ebey State Park (three miles from Ebey's Landing). Along the way, keep your eyes open for gem-quality stones, such as agate, jasper, and black and green jade, plus quartz and petrified wood.

Several historical sights are out on Cemetery Road, accessible from Cook Road. Colonel Isaac Ebey is buried at **Sunnyside Cemetery.** The **Davis Blockhouse,** another of the blockhouses used to defend against Tlingit and Haida attacks, stands at the edge of the cemetery; it was moved here in 1915. Park your car at the aptly named **Prairie Overlook.** Farms spread out below, and the horizon is marked by snowcapped Mount Baker to the north and Mount Rainier to the south. Walk up the dirt road past the little park headquarters building (9am-5pm Mon.-Fri.) to the restored **Jacob Ebey House** (staffed 10am-4pm Thurs.-Sun. June-Sept.), which has historical exhibits in the two front rooms. A blockhouse is right out front. The home was built in 1855 by the father of Isaac Ebey.

Occupying a bluff above Ebey's Landing, **Ferry House** is one of the oldest buildings in Washington. It was built in 1860 by Winfield Ebey, the brother of Isaac Ebey. Ferry House originally served as an inn and tavern for people arriving by ferry. Now owned by the National Park Service, the house itself is not safe to enter, but you can walk around the outside.

COUPEVILLE

The second-oldest town in Washington, the "Port of Sea Captains" was founded and laid out in 1852 by Captain Thomas Coupe, the first man to sail through Deception Pass. The protected harbor at Penn Cove was a perfect site for the village that became Coupeville (pop. 1,800). In the town's early years, timber from Whidbey was shipped to San Francisco to feed the building boom created by the gold rush. Today, modern businesses operate from Victorian-era buildings amid the nation's largest historical preservation district. Coupeville is the county seat for Island County and has the only public hospital on Whidbey. Downtown has an immaculate cluster of false-fronted shops and restaurants right on the harbor and a long wharf once used to ship local produce and logs to the mainland. This is a cat-friendly town; perhaps half the downtown businesses have one inside. Summer weekends are busy times, but in the winter months, life in Coupeville slows to a crawl and downtown is quiet.

Jacob Ebey House

Sights

The town's most obvious attraction is picturesque **Coupeville Wharf,** which extends into Penn Cove. You'll find several marine exhibits (including a gray whale skeleton suspended from the ceiling) in the building at the end of the wharf.

The **Island County Museum** (908 NW Alexander St., 360/678-3310, www.islandhistory.org, 10am-4pm Mon.- Sat., 1pm-4pm Sun., $4 adults, $3 seniors and kids, $8 families) has pioneer relics, including a shadow box with flowers made from human hair, interesting newsreels from the 1930s, a 1902 Holsman car (the first car on Whidbey), woolly mammoth bones, and changing exhibits. Out front is a lovely garden with drought-tolerant native plants and herbs.

Another of the original Whidbey Island fortifications, the **Alexander Blockhouse,** built in 1855, stands outside the museum; it was moved here in the 1930s. An adjacent shelter houses two turn-of-the-20th-century Native American racing canoes.

Penn Cove

For a scenic drive, head northwest from Coupeville along Madrona Way, named for the Pacific madrone (also called madrona) trees whose distinctive red bark and leathery green leaves line the roadway. Quite a few summer cottages and cozy homes can be found here, along with the one-of-a-kind Captain Whidbey Inn. Offshore are dozens of floating pens where mussels grow on lines hanging in Penn Cove. On the northwest corner of Penn Cove, Highway 20 passes scenic **Grasser's Hill,** where hedgerows alternate with open farmland. Development restrictions prevent this open country from becoming a mass of condos. Just north of here are the historic **San de Fuca schoolhouse** (now a vacation rental) and **Captain Whidbey Inn.**

Fort Ebey State Park

Located southwest of Coupeville on

Admiralty Inlet, **Fort Ebey State Park** (360/678-4636, www.parks.wa.gov) has campsites, a large picnic area, three miles of beach, and several miles of hiking trails within its 644 acres. The fort was constructed during World War II, though its gun batteries were never needed. The concrete platforms remain, along with cavernous bunkers, but the big guns have long since been removed. Thanks to its location in the Olympics' rain shadow, the park is one of the few places in western Washington where cactus grows, but it also has stands of second-growth forest and great views across the Strait of Juan de Fuca.

Although not as well-known as other parks on Whidbey, Fort Ebey is still a favorite summertime spot. Much of its popularity stems from tiny **Lake Pondilla,** a glacial sinkhole—and a bass fisher's and swimmer's delight. Follow the signs from the north parking lot for a two-block hike to the lake; half a dozen picnic tables and a camping area are reserved for hikers and bicyclists. A maze of hiking and biking trails lead along the bluffs south from here and down to the beach. Adventurous folks (after consulting a tide chart and with a bit of care) can walk all the way to Fort Casey State Park, eight miles away.

Recreation

Coupeville Cycle and Sport (186 Fort Casey Rd., 360/672-0510, www.coupevillecycleandsport.com) rents hybrid bikes for $35/day, including free delivery of bikes in the Coupeville area.

Coupeville is a great place for a taste of the sailing past. Built in 1925, and now owned by the Coupeville Maritime Heritage Foundation, the *Suva* (360/320-4337, www.shcoonersuva.org) is a beautiful 68-foot racing schooner. The boat heads out Wednesday-Sunday afternoons all summer, and costs $75 per person for a 2.5-hour sail. Another beautiful sailboat, the *Cutty Sark* (360/678-5567, www.svcuttysark.com) is a classic 52-foot ketch built from teak in 1960. Join captain John Colby Stone for a day sail from

Coupeville: $300 for up to six people on a two-hour trip.

Entertainment and Events

In existence for over 30 years, **Pacific Northwest Art School** (15 NW Birch St., 360/678-3396 or 866/678-3396, www.pacificnorthwestartschool.org) teaches dozens of workshops throughout the year, from photography and watercolor painting to lost-wax jewelry and Japanese stencil making.

In early March, the **Penn Cove MusselFest** (www.thepenncovemusselsfestival.com) features chowder tasting, farm tours, music, and other activities. The **Penn Cove Water Festival** (www.penncovewaterfestival.com) in mid-May brings tribal canoe races, dance performances, Native American arts and crafts, traditional foods, and games for kids. The event attracts tribes and visitors from all over Puget Sound. In existence for over 50 years, the mid-August **Coupeville Arts and Crafts Festival** (www.coupevillefestival.com) is another big event, with musical entertainment, arts and crafts, gallery openings, kids' activities, and food.

Concerts on the Cove (360/678-6821, www.concertsonthecove.org) includes all sorts of productions, from acrobats to musical performances. Their Sundays in the Park series provides a fine way to spend a lazy afternoon during July and August.

Shopping

In business since 1994, the cooperatively run **Penn Cove Gallery** (360/678-1176, www.penncovegallery.com) has artwork in a variety of media by Whidbey artists.

At **Lavender Wind Farm** (2530 Darst Rd., 360/544-4132 or 877/242-7716, www.lavenderwind.com), owner Sarah Richards grows nine varieties of organic lavender for bouquets and various products, including distilled essential oils and homemade lavender ice cream bars. The eight-acre farm north of Fort Ebey State Park off West Beach Road has a lavender labyrinth, picnic tables, and beautiful views of the Olympic Mountains. Lavender Wind also has a Coupeville shop at 15 NW Coveland Street selling lavender gifts of all types, from shampoo and candles to lavender granola.

Food

Pastry aficionados shouldn't miss **Knead & Feed** (4 Front St., 360/678-5431, www. kneadandfeed.com, 9am-3pm Mon.-Fri., 8am-3pm Sat.-Sun., $6-12), where tempting marionberry bear claws, slices of rhubarb pie, and enormous walnut caramel rolls await. The bakery is upstairs, with a separate downstairs restaurant where waterside tables face Penn Cove. Breakfast scrambles, French toast, and lunchtime sandwiches and homemade soups provide more substantial fare.

With a waterside location and diverse menu, **Front Street Grill** (20 Front St., 360/682-2551, www.fsgcoupeville.com, 11am-9pm Mon.-Thurs., 11am-10pm Fri., 8am-10pm Sat., 8am-9pm Sun.) is loud, fun, and a family favorite. Start with coconut green curry mussels or Kobe-style beef sliders, and then order a mushroom Swiss burger or Dan's spicy seafood fettuccine, topping the evening off with a raspberry pomegranate margarita and orange crème brûlée.

Find dependably good pub grub—including fish-and-chips, Reuben sandwiches, and steamed mussels—inside **Toby's Tavern** (8 NW Front St., 360/678-4222, www.tobysuds. com, $9-19). The 1884 red building contains a pool table and is open to all ages, with food service till 9pm. Built in 1875 as a mercantile, this is one of the oldest buildings on Whidbey. It's been a tavern since 1938, a few years after the end of Prohibition.

Mosquito Fleet Chili (12 NW Front St., 360/678-2900, 10am-8pm Mon.-Sat., $6-14) serves traditional American breakfasts in a waterside setting. It dishes up great homemade chili and corn bread, or try the salmon asparagus quiche, tomato basil bisque soup, clam chowder, or just a big slice of pecan pie.

Austrian-born owner/chef Andreas Wurzrainer has transformed ★ **Christopher's** (103 NW Coveland St., 360/678-5480, www.christophersonwhidbey. com, 11:30am-2pm and 5pm-8pm Wed.-Sun., $16-30 entrées) into one of the finest dining choices on Whidbey. The restaurant has an upscale setting and such specialties as bacon-wrapped pork tenderloin, raspberry barbecued salmon, and notable Caesar salads, plus classic clam chowder from the soup pot. Save space for the decadent chocolate mousse served in a dark chocolate tulip shell. Reservations are advised. There's live piano music on Friday and Saturday nights.

★ **The Oystercatcher** (901 Grace St., 360/678-0683, www.oystercatcherwhidbey. com, noon-3pm and 5pm-9pm Wed.-Sun.; closed first two weeks of January, $30-34) is a wonderful little place where the limited menu changes frequently. Owner/chefs Tyler and Sara Hansen serve gourmet seafood (including Penn Cove oysters), beef, duck, and pork dishes, with a nice selection of wines as accompaniment. It's casually elegant, but kids are welcome. Call ahead for reservations. Dine in the beer garden if the weather cooperates.

Historic **Captain Whidbey Inn** (2072 W. Captain Whidbey Inn Rd., 360/678-4097 or 800/366-4097, www.captainwhidbey.com, noon-9pm Wed.-Sun., $26-41) is surrounded by colorful madrone trees and faces pretty Penn Cove. Even if you aren't staying here, be sure to stop and take in the scenery, or order a martini in the bar and enjoy a meal in the restaurant. Dinners feature veal osso buco, duck confit, cedar plank salmon, and ahi poke. Happy hour specials are 4pm-6pm Wednesday-Friday at the tavern, which serves a menu of burgers, sandwiches, steamer clams, seafood chowder, and smoked salmon fettuccine.

The **Coupeville Farmers Market** (www. coupevillemarket.com, 10am-2pm Sat. Apr.-Oct.) takes place at the Community Green at 8th and Alexander Streets.

Accommodations

Coupeville is blessed with many historic buildings, several of which have been turned into bed-and-breakfasts and inns, but be sure to make reservations for summer weekends. Find links to local lodgings at www.coupevillelodging.com.

HOTELS AND INNS

Conveniently located in the heart of town, **Coupeville Inn** (200 NW Coveland St., 360/678-6668 or 800/247-6162, www.thecoupevilleinn.com) is in a French mansard-style building. The 24 hotel rooms ($105-170 d) provide waterside views of Penn Cove. Other options include a two-bedroom apartment unit ($225 d), a beach suite ($175 d), and a lovely two-bedroom house ($275 for up to four people). All rooms have fridges, private baths, Wi-Fi, and a continental breakfast.

Captain Whidbey Inn (2072 W. Captain Whidbey Inn Rd., 360/678-4097 or 800/366-4097, www.captainwhidbey.com) is a classic two-story inn built in 1907 from madrone logs. Small rooms in the main lodge are $103-115 d, but note these have "European-style" shared baths down the hall; request a waterside room. Newer guest rooms and suites with private baths are $175-192 d, and four modern cabins containing wood-burning fireplaces, decks, private baths, and hot tub access cost $210-240 d. Continental breakfast is available in the dining room each morning. The expansive grounds, studded with Pacific madrone trees, face Penn Cove.

Adjacent to Fort Casey State Park, **Fort Casey Inn** (1124 S. Engle Rd., 360/678-5050 or 866/661-6604, www.fortcaseyinn.com) consists of 10 restored Georgian Revival homes that served as officers' quarters during World War I. Most of these large two-story homes are divided into two units each, with complete kitchens, private baths, and access to a heated outdoor pool, but there are no phones, TVs, or Wi-Fi. These are authentically historic places, not luxury condos. The homes' basements were to be used as bomb shelters in case of attack, and some still have the original steel-shuttered windows. The duplexes sleep four or five guests for $170 per night. The old doctor's house ($360) is separate from the others, providing more privacy.

You're likely to encounter deer on the lawn most evenings, and both Fort Casey and Crockett Lake (good bird-watching) are a short walk away. Fort Casey Inn is owned by Seattle Pacific University, which also manages the adjacent Camp Casey Conference Center.

BED-AND-BREAKFASTS

Anchorage Inn B&B (807 N. Main St., 360/678-5581 or 877/230-1313, www.anchorage-inn.com, $109-179 d) has seven guest rooms with private baths in a large and luxurious Victorian-style home with a wraparound porch, cozy parlor, and in-town location. The largest room fills the 3rd floor, providing views of Penn Cove and Mount Baker. A big sit-down breakfast is included, as is Wi-Fi.

One of the most striking local places is **Compass Rose B&B** (508 S. Main St., 360/678-5318 or 800/237-3881, www.compassrosebandb.com, $140 d), a Queen Anne Victorian built in 1890 and packed with antiques and Persian rugs. It's almost like stepping into a museum. The two guest rooms have queen-size or king-size beds, and an elegant candlelight breakfast is served on fine china and crystal. "Extremely well-behaved" kids (antiques, after all) are welcome. Gregarious owners Jan and Marshall Bronson—he's a retired naval captain—also own a vintage 1933 Packard.

Occupying two adjacent Victorian-era homes—both in the National Register of Historic Places—★ **The Blue Goose Inn** (702 N. Main St., 360/678-4284 or 877/678-4284, www.bluegoosecoupeville.com, $159-219 d) provides tasteful B&B accommodations. The inn consists of Kineth House and Coup-Gillespie House—built in 1887 and 1891, respectively—with a total of seven guest rooms with private baths, along with superb breakfasts and Wi-Fi. The location is perfect, right in the heart of Coupeville. No children under 12 are permitted.

Halfway between Coupeville and Oak Harbor, **Spinnaker Tea Garden B&B** (1872 Arnold Rd., 360/678-4481, www.spinnakerteabb.com, $125 d or $195 for four guests) has a country location with five acres of fields and gardens overlooking Penn Cove. The two rooms have private baths, and one can be combined with an adjacent room as a family suite. A delicious breakfast is included.

Garden Isle Guest Cottages (207 NW Coveland St., 360/678-5641, www.garden-islecottages.com) consists of two immaculate cottages ($150-160 d) with mini-kitchens, a hot tub, private baths, continental breakfast, and Wi-Fi. A separate vacation house ($265 d, add $15 each for extra guests) has three bedrooms, three baths, a full kitchen, and more; a two-night minimum is required.

CAMPING

Find year-round camping ($30 tents, $40 RVs) at **Fort Casey State Park** (three miles south of Coupeville, 360/678-4519) or **Fort Ebey State Park** (five miles west of Coupeville, 360/678-4636, www.parks.wa.gov). Make reservations ($10 extra) online at http://washington.goingtocamp.com, or by calling 888/226-7688.

Rhododendron Park, a Washington Department of Natural Resources property, is 1.5 miles south of Coupeville on State Highway 20. It's easy to miss; look for the small blue camping sign on the highway. Here you'll find eight free in-the-woods seasonal campsites with water and vault toilets. The park contains second-growth Douglas fir trees, along with rhododendrons that bloom in April and May.

Information and Services

For local information and brochures, stop by the **Coupeville Chamber & Visitor Information Center** (905 NW Alexander St., 360/678-5434, www.coupevillechamber.com, 10am-4pm daily May-Oct., 11am-3pm daily Nov.-Apr.), housed within the old firehouse. Another helpful website is www.cometocoupeville.com.

The **Coupeville Library** (788 NW Alexander St., 360/678-4911, www.sno-isle.com, 10am-8pm Mon. and Wed., 10am-6pm Tues. and Thurs.-Sat., 1pm-5pm Sun.) has computers and free Wi-Fi access.

Whidbey General Hospital (101 N. Main St., 360/678-5151, www.whidbeygen.org) is the only public hospital on the island.

OAK HARBOR

Settled first by sea captains, then the Irish, and at the turn of the 20th century by immigrants from Holland, Oak Harbor (pop. 22,000) takes its name from the many ancient Garry oak trees that grew here; those remaining are protected by law. The oldest of these are almost 300 years old. **Smith Park**, downtown at SE Midway and SE 9th Avenue, is one of only two parks in Washington made up entirely of Garry oak trees. The town's visitors center has a pamphlet detailing locations of other large oaks around town.

Oak Harbor was founded by three men in the early 1850s: a Swiss named Ulrich Freund, a Norwegian named Martin Tafton, and a New Englander named C. W. Sumner. The military arrived during World War II and remains the primary economic force. The city's historic waterside downtown retains a bit of character, but the main drag—Highway 20—is yet another sad example of the malling of America. This is the only place on the island where you'll find burger joints, shopping malls, traffic jams, and noise. It's on a far smaller scale than many Puget Sound cities, but comes as a shock if you've just driven in from genteel Coupeville and Langley.

Whidbey Island Naval Air Station

Oak Harbor's main employer is the largest naval air base in the Northwest, **Whidbey Island Naval Air Station** (360/257-2211, www.cnic.navy.mil/whidbey). The Naval Air Station is home to electronic warfare squadrons, including reconnaissance aircraft (EA-18G Growlers), along with surveillance planes (P-3 Orion and EP-3E Aries). The base employs more than 10,000 military and civilian personnel and is a favorite of Navy personnel. The area is filled with military retirees who appreciate the scenic setting and mild weather.

The **PBY Museum** (270 SE Pioneer Way, 360/240-9500, www.pbymf.org, 11am-5pm Wed.-Sat., $7 adults, $6 seniors and military, free for kids under 6) is at the Navy's Seaplane Base in Oak Harbor. Out front is the main attraction, a lovingly restored PBY Catalina, an amphibious "flying boat" used to patrol the Pacific during World War II. Inside the museum, you can climb inside the nose turret to see how it felt to be a gunner on these vintage planes. The PBY flight simulator is a big hit with kids of all ages, and a 30-minute film provides a fascinating historical overview.

Recreation

Windjammer Park (360/279-4500, www.oakharbor.org), on Beeksma Drive, has a sandy beach with piles of driftwood, sheltered picnic tables, saltwater swimming in the lagoon, a gazebo, tennis courts, baseball diamonds, RV camping, and a monumental **Dutch-style windmill.** There's a nice view of the peaceful and protected harbor from here, and a great kiddie playground. Look for ducks along the shore. **Smith Park** at Midway Boulevard has old Garry oak trees and a large boulder left behind by the last ice age.

Joseph Whidbey State Park (360/902-8844, www.parks.wa.gov), just south of Whidbey Island Naval Air Station on Swantown Road, is largely undeveloped, with picnic tables and a few trails. The real attraction here is a long and scenic beach, one of the finest on the island. No camping is permitted.

The hip-roofed **Neil Barn** (100 E. Whidbey Ave.) was once the largest barn on the West Coast. The distinctive **water tower** out front houses a small historical museum that's open occasionally.

Swim outdoors at the seasonal **Windjammer Park** (360/579-5551, free), where a man-made lagoon sits next to a Dutch-style windmill. **Harborsup** (360/632-1601, www.harborsup.com) has stand-up paddleboarding tours and rentals at the park.

John Vanderzicht Memorial Pool (85 SE Jerome St., 360/675-7665, www.oakharborpool.com, $5) contains an indoor pool, sauna, two hot tubs, a ball swing, an inflatable octopus, and a wading pool.

Shopping

Named for the majestic trees of Oak Harbor, **Garry Oak Gallery** (830 SE Pioneer Way, 360/240-0222, www.garryoakgallery.com) is a nice downtown co-op with works by local artists.

Kaleafa Cannabis Company (33858 State Rte. 20, 360/682-2420, www.kaleafa.com) sells marijuana products.

Entertainment and Events

Whidbey Playhouse Community Theatre (630 SE Midway Blvd., 360/679-2237, www.whidbeyplayhouse.com) puts on plays throughout the year in a 93-year-old former church.

Here since 1959, **Blue Fox Drive-In Theatre** (two miles south of town at 1403 Monroe Landing Rd., 360/675-5667, www.bluefoxdrivein.com) is one of only five surviving outdoor movie theaters in Washington. Locals say they serve the best pizzas in Oak Harbor. Your ten-year-old will love the go-kart track, open during the day.

The **Whidbey Island Marathon** (www.whidbeyislandmarathon.com) in mid-April attracts more than 2,000 runners to its hilly course. A bit less grueling, **Holland Happening** (www.hollandhappening.org) on the last weekend of April includes a street fair, carnival, and parade. The **4th of July** festivities include a big parade and fireworks, followed the third week of July by **Whidbey Island Race Week** (www.whidbeyislandraceweek.com), one of the world's top 20 yachting regattas.

The **Oak Harbor Music Festival** (www.oakharborfestival.com) brings bands, art, food, and family fun to downtown Oak

Harbor. It takes place over Labor Day Weekend in early September.

Food

For a quick start to your day, **Whidbey Coffee** (980 SE Pioneer Way, 360/331-8121, www.whidbeycoffee.com) has more than a dozen locations in the region, but the best may be their one in downtown Oak Harbor. It's classy and cozy, with a drive-through if you're in a hurry.

For iced drinks, be sure to check out **Honeymoon Bay Coffee Roasters** (1100 SW Bowmer St., 800/781-7261, www.honeymoonbaycoffee.com, 7am-6pm Mon.-Fri., 8am-6pm Sat., 9am-3pm Sun.), where the ice cubes are made from yesterday's drip coffee. The shop is in a strip mall behind Wal-Mart.

As might be expected given the strong military presence in Oak Harbor, most restaurants serve up the traditional American food groups: McDonald's, pizza, and steak. But one place provides a notable exception: ★ **Frasers Gourmet Hideaway** (1191 SE Dock St., 360/279-1231, www.frasersgh.com, 4:30pm-9:30pm Tues.-Sat., closed Sun. and Mon., $24-39). Trained in France, chef Scott Fraser blends European and Northwest cooking traditions at the town's fine-dining establishment. Frasers serves beef tenderloin, rack of lamb, seared scallops, and more in a classy downtown setting. Be sure to try the spicy shrimp and grits appetizer. The restaurant has several tables on the wraparound porch.

Seabolt's Smokehouse & Deli (31640 State Route 20, 360/675-6485 or 800/574-1120, www.seabolts.com, 9am-9pm Mon.-Sat., 10am-8pm Sun., $11-18) attracts locals with halibut and chips, seafood gumbo, fish tacos, and more.

Jada's Thai Kitchen (270 SE Cabot Dr., 360/679-8907, 11am-8:30pm daily, $9-18) is the best Thai place in Oak Harbor, with dozens of choices from crab Rangoon and Shui Mei dumplings to salmon teriyaki and sizzling duck. Patrons rave about Jada's unique avocado curry. Save room for a dessert of coconut ice cream with fried bananas.

Flyers Restaurant and Brewery (32295 State Route 20, 360/675-5858, www.eatatflyers.com, 11am-9pm Mon.-Thurs., 11am-11pm Fri., 9am-11pm Sat., 9am-9pm Sun., $9-25) has a family-friendly atmosphere. The pub fare includes skillet nachos, 15 variations on the burger theme, waffle fries, sandwiches, salads, pizzas, and 10 brewed-on-the-premises beers. Fittingly enough, you can get a flight of eight beers from Flyers. A side deck opens on sunny days, and the restaurant opens for breakfast on weekends.

Downtown's **Rustica** (670 SE Pioneer Way, 360/675-4053, www.rusticacafe.com, 11am-8pm Mon.-Tues., 11am-9pm Thurs.-Sat., 10am-8pm Sun., $15-29 dinner entrées) is bright, cheery, and upscale, with patio dining and farm-to-table Italian-inspired food. Dinner favorites include short ribs, smoked pork chop, and seafood risotto, or choose a lighter menu 2pm-6pm when small-plate tapas are served. The Sunday brunch menu features shrimp and grits, smoked salmon frittata, focaccia French toast, and more. Rustica has live music many weekends and a nice wine selection.

The **Oak Harbor Farmers Market** (360/678-4288, 4pm-7pm Thurs. mid-May-Sept.) takes place next to the visitors center along Highway 20.

Accommodations

Oak Harbor has the least expensive lodging on Whidbey, but as always, location matters, and you won't find the charm of Coupeville or Langley here.

Best Western Plus Harbor Plaza (33175 State Rte. 20, 360/679-4567 or 800/927-5478, www.bestwestern.com/harborplaza, $140 d) is a good family-owned hotel with amenities that include an outdoor heated pool, hot tub, fitness center, microwaves, fridges, Wi-Fi, and continental breakfast.

Adjacent to the Best Western, **Candlewood Suites** (33221 State Rte. 20, 360/279-2222 or 877/226-3539, www.ihg.com, $165-185 d) is the newest hotel in Oak Harbor. Its spacious suites all have full kitchens and recliners. The hotel also features a fitness center, library of DVDs, outdoor grill, and Wi-Fi.

In the center of town, **Acorn Motor Inn** (31530 State Route 20, 360/675-6646 or 800/280-6646) has large, recently remodeled rooms with fridges, microwaves, and a light breakfast. The price varies dramatically in the summer, starting around $89-99 d on weeknights, sometimes rising to $199 d for the same room on a weekend.

Rooms at **Coachman Inn** (35959 State Rte. 20, 360/675-0727 or 800/635-0043, www.thecoachmaninn.com, $120-200 d) range from standard units and Jacuzzi suites to a two-bedroom town house apartment and a penthouse suite. The hotel includes a small outdoor pool, hot tub, exercise room, fridges, microwaves, Wi-Fi, and a hot breakfast. It's also pet friendly ($10 extra).

CAMPING
City-run **Staysail RV Park** (at the end of Beeksma Dr., 360/279-4756, www.oakharbor. org, $25 RVs with full hookups, no tents) has limited RV sites along the lagoon within Windjammer Park. No reservations, but the park does have hot showers.

Beautiful **Deception Pass State Park** (360/675-2417, www.parks.wa.gov, $35 tents, $45 RVs, $12 bikes) is nine miles north; it's described in the *Anacortes* section. In addition, the local Wal-Mart parking lot (1250 SW Erie St., 360/279-0665) becomes an unofficial RV park each summer.

Information
The **Oak Harbor Visitor Center** (32630 Hwy. 20, 360/675-3735, www.oakharborchamber.com, 8am-7pm Mon.-Sat. and noon-5pm Sun. May-Oct., 8am-7pm Mon.-Sat. Nov.-Apr.) is a good source for local information. The **Oak Harbor Library** (1000 SE Regatta Dr., 360/675-5115, www.sno-isle.com, 9am-8pm Mon.-Thurs., 10am-6pm Fri.-Sat., 1pm-5pm Sun.) has computers and free Wi-Fi access.

Bellingham

With a population topping 82,000, Bellingham is no longer a town, though it still maintains a friendly small-town feel. The city is an almost perfect blend of the old and the new, with stately homes, extraordinary museums, and an abundance of cultural events, plus many fine shops and restaurants. Bellingham's big paper mill closed in 2007, but the town continues to flourish with Western Washington University—the third-largest university in the state—and increasing numbers of tourists. The town pegs the livability meter, consistently getting stellar reviews in those "best places to live" magazine rankings.

Bellingham is a jumping-off point for private ferries and whale-watching trips to the San Juan Islands; it is also where northbound travelers catch Alaska Marine Highway ferries. The terminal for all these boats is in Bellingham's historic Fairhaven district. In addition, the city is only 43 miles from the ferry terminal at Anacortes, and the route takes you along beautiful Chuckanut Drive. Because of this, Bellingham is a popular stopping point for people driving down from Vancouver en route to the San Juans, and a regional shopping destination.

Downtown Bellingham has some of the most confusing streets anywhere on the West Coast, with streets heading at odd angles in all directions.

SIGHTS
★ Fairhaven
This historic section of Bellingham has quite a few buildings constructed in the late 1880s. At the time, rumors were circulating that Fairhaven would be the western terminus for the Great Northern Railroad. (The railroad chose Tacoma instead.) The buildings are

now part of the Fairhaven Historic District; pick up a walking-tour map from the visitors center. A wonderful two-mile walkway connects Fairhaven with downtown Bellingham, including a portion that extends over the bay.

Several interesting shops and galleries can be found in the district. **Good Earth Pottery** (1000 Harris Ave., 360/671-3998, www.goodearthpots.com) has fine ceramics. In the same building, the cooperatively owned **Artwood** (360/647-1628, www.artwoodgallery.com) sells handcrafted woodworking. **Chuckanut Bay Gallery** (700 Chuckanut Dr., 360/734-4885, www.chuckanutbaygallery.com) is a lovely stop a mile or so south of Fairhaven at the start of Chuckanut Drive, with quality pieces by regional artisans.

One of the most popular places in Fairhaven—or in all of Bellingham for that matter—**Village Books** (1200 11th St., 360/671-2626 or 800/392-2665, www.villagebooks.com) has frequent book readings, workshops, and signings. Look for used titles just up the street at **Eclipse Bookstore** (1104 11th Ave., 360/647-8165).

historic Fairhaven

★ Whatcom Museum

In the last few years, Bellingham's stodgy old downtown museum has been transformed into a modern cultural center—the Art District—surrounded by burgeoning cafés, galleries, and other businesses. **Whatcom Museum** (360/778-8930, www.whatcommuseum.org) consists of Old City Hall and the new Lightcatcher building. Commanding a high bluff at 121 Prospect Street, **Old City Hall** (noon-5pm Thurs.-Sun.) is an ornate redbrick building capped by a four-corner cupola and a central clock tower. Constructed in 1892, it remained in use until 1939. The building now houses historical displays from Bellingham's early days.

The Lightcatcher (250 Flora St., noon-5pm Wed.-Sun.) provides a vastly different experience. Designed by architect Jim Olson, this 42,000-square-foot museum debuted in 2009. A curving translucent wall of glass—37 feet high and 180 feet long—dominates the building, separating the exterior courtyard from interior galleries. The building integrates natural materials and even has a green roof covered with plants and solar arrays. Exhibition spaces contain changing exhibits of art, and a family gallery has activities for kids. Admission to both The Lightcatcher and Old City Hall is $10 adults, $8 seniors, military, and students, and $5 for children under age five. Admission on Thursdays is just $5.

Other Museums

Make it a point to visit **Mindport** (210 W. Holly St., 360/647-5614, www.mindport.org, noon-6pm Wed.-Fri., 10am-5pm Sat., noon-4pm Sun., $2), a creative science center that will amuse, fascinate, and educate both kids and adults. The exhibits are mostly made from reused junk, with a touch of whimsy thrown in. It's great fun, particularly a backwards speech device that's bound to make you laugh.

Don't miss the fascinating **Spark Museum of Electrical Invention** (1312 Bay St., 360/738-3886, www.sparkmuseum.

org, 11am-5pm Wed.-Sun., $8 adults, $5 kids under age 11), with more than a thousand radios, some dating from the early 1900s. But this place isn't just about radios; it's also about the dawn of the electrical age and all the bizarre creations of that era, including a theremin you can play. In this age of computers, this throwback to the past still entertains kids of all ages. Don't miss the weekend MegaZapper demonstrations ($12 adults, $9 kids); they're literally shocking.

The **Bellingham Railway Museum** (1320 Commercial St., 360/393-7540, www.bellinghamrailwaymuseum.org, noon-5pm Tues.-Sat., $5 adults, $3 kids) features model-railroad displays and exhibits on historical railroads.

The **Marine Life Center** (1801 Roeder Ave., 360/671-2431, www.marinelifecenter.org, 10am-6pm daily June-Aug., 11am-5pm daily Sept.-May, free) showcases marinelife and habitats in Puget Sound. The touch pool provides an up-close-and-personal experience with sea urchins, sea stars, hermit crabs, and other creatures.

Western Washington University

The 215-acre campus of **Western Washington University** (I-5 Exit 252, 360/650-3861, www.wwu.edu) is home to 15,000 students. Visitors appreciate the **Outdoor Sculpture Garden,** with two dozen works scattered across the campus. Overlooking Bellingham Bay and accessible via a footpath from the university, **Sehome Hill Arboretum** provides 3.5 miles of trails and splendid views of the San Juans and Mount Baker, plus 180 acres of tall Douglas firs, wildflowers, and big-leaf maples.

★ CHUCKANUT DRIVE

One of the most scenic stretches of highway in the state, **Chuckanut Drive** (Hwy. 11) stretches south from Fairhaven and then across the Skagit Valley. ("Chuckanut" is a Salish word that means "beach on a bay with a small entrance.") The Bellingham Visitors Center has a helpful brochure detailing attractions along the way, or you can visit www.chuckanutdrive.com. The road doesn't have a straight stretch for seven miles as it swoops and swerves along the face of a cliff. Grand views span across to Anacortes, Guemes Island, and, farther north, the San Juan Islands. With no shoulder, a narrow strip of pavement, and tight corners, it's a bit dicey for bikes (especially on weekends when traffic is heaviest), but the views are stunning.

tree-lined Chuckanut Drive

Bellingham

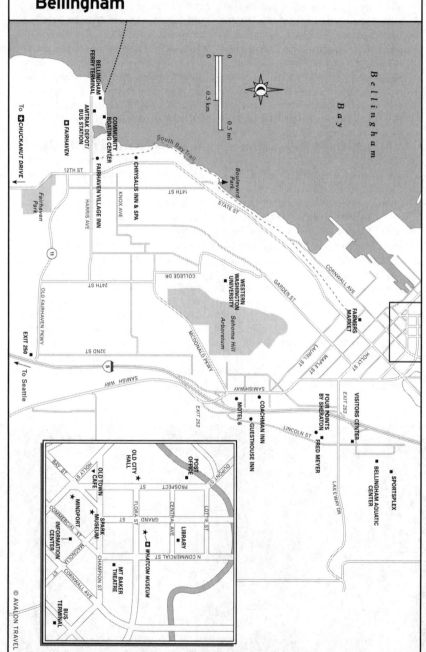

To ★ CHUCKANUT DRIVE

★ FAIRHAVEN

BELLINGHAM FERRY TERMINAL

AMTRAK DEPOT/ BUS STATION

COMMUNITY BOATING CENTER

South Bay Trail

Boulevard Park

Bellingham Bay

FAIRHAVEN VILLAGE INN

CHRYSALIS INN & SPA

Fairhaven Park

12TH ST

HARRIS AVE

KNOX AVE

14TH ST

STATE ST

11

OLD FAIRHAVEN PKWY

24TH ST

COLLEGE DR

WESTERN WASHINGTON UNIVERSITY

Sehome Hill Arboretum

GARDEN ST

CORNWALL AVE

FARMERS MARKET

LAUREL ST

MAPLE ST

HOLLY ST

EXIT 250

32ND ST

5

MCDONALD PKWY

To Seattle

SAMISH WAY

EXIT 252

SAMISH WAY

MOTEL 6

COACHMAN INN

GUESTHOUSE INN

FOUR POINTS BY SHERATON

FRED MEYER

LINCOLN ST

EXIT 253

VISITORS CENTER

LAKEWAY DR

BELLINGHAM AQUATIC CENTER

SPORTSPLEX

BAY ST

HOLLY ST

STATION ST

OLD CITY HALL

OLDTOWN CAFE

COMMERCIAL ST

MINDPORT

INFORMATION CENTER

MEMORIAL ST

SPARK MUSEUM

PROSPECT ST

FLORA ST

GRAND AVE

CENTRAL AVE

POST OFFICE

DUPONT ST

LIBRARY

LOTTIE ST

N COMMERCIAL ST

WHATCOM MUSEUM

CHAMPION ST

MT BAKER THEATRE

CORNWALL AVE

BUS TERMINAL

0   0
0.5 Km
0.5 mi

© AVALON TRAVEL

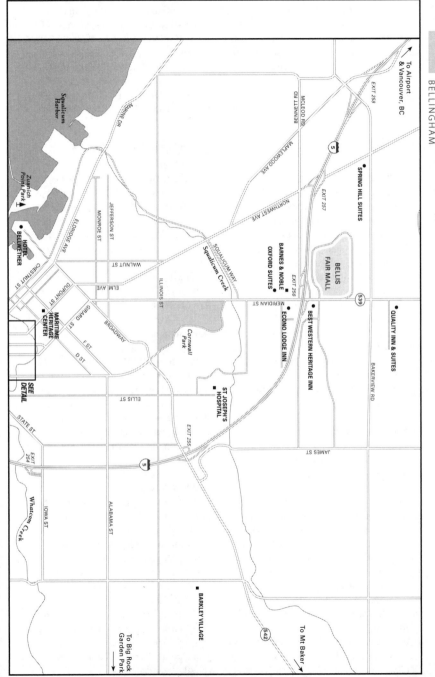

Two excellent restaurants are located along Chuckanut Drive.

While on Chuckanut Drive, you will also pass the road to **Taylor Shellfish Farms** (2182 Chuckanut Dr., 360/766-6002, www.taylorshellfishfarms.com). Take this steep one-lane road to the bay to purchase fresh oysters, Manila clams, geoduck clams, and crab. It's the largest producer of Manila clams in the United States. Signs describe the operation, with tours by appointment.

Larrabee State Park

Established in 1923 as the first state park in Washington, **Larrabee State Park** (360/676-2093, www.parks.wa.gov, $10 parking fee) occupies one of the most beautiful stretches of mountainous country along Chuckanut Drive and has a popular campground. Covering more than 2,500 acres, the park borders Samish Bay and boasts a boat launch, a sandy beach for sunning, and tidepools for marine explorations. Nine miles of hiking trails include the southern end of the **Interurban Trail,** connecting the park with Bellingham. Other trails lead to scenic Fragrance and Lost Lakes for trout fishing and to dramatic vistas from the 1,941-foot summit of **Chuckanut Mountain.**

Edison and Bow

At the south end of Chuckanut Drive—14 miles from Bellingham—the road emerges into open farmland at the tiny towns of Bow and Edison. Bow is little more than a wide spot in the road, with a gun shop on one side and a notable café and bakery on the opposite side. Turn off the highway and drive a mile past farms and fields to tiny Edison, where historic buildings are being transformed by a new generation. You'll find a bakery, café, and an art gallery.

South from Edison the road passes **Padilla Bay National Estuarine Research Reserve.** This shallow bay is home to the **Breazeale Interpretive Center** (10441 Bayview-Edison Rd., 360/428-1558, www.padillabay.gov, 10am-5pm Wed.-Sun., free). Stop by to learn more about this important estuary; there's even a hands-on room for kids. Nearby is tiny **Bay View State Park** (360/757-0227, www.parks.wa.gov), with access to the bay, a two-mile shoreline trail, and campsites for $25-40; reservations can be made for $10 extra at 888/226-7688 or through the park website. Six small cabins ($69-79) are also available at the park.

CITY AND COUNTY PARKS

Whatcom County (360/676-6985, www.co.whatcom.wa.us/parks) has one of the best collections of city- and county-owned parks in the state. In Bellingham alone, there are more than 35 places that qualify as parks, including greenbelts, fitness areas, and trails. These parks range from less than half an acre to more than a thousand acres.

Beautiful **Samish County Park** (at I-5 Exit 246 south of Bellingham, 360/733-2362) is a 39-acre county park along Lake Samish with swimming, fishing, boating, picnicking, hiking, boat rentals, and a playground.

Whatcom Falls Park (near Lake Whatcom at 1401 Electric Ave.) has hiking trails, tennis courts, a playground, a picnic area, and a state fish hatchery on 241 acres. With 12 acres on the lake itself, **Bloedel Donovan Park** (2214 Electric Ave.) includes a swimming beach, boat launch, playground, and picnic area.

Covering more than 1,000 acres, **Lake Padden Park** (4882 Samish Way; I-5 Exit 252) has hiking and horse trails, a golf course, picnic areas, and a playground, plus swimming, fishing, and nonmotorized boating.

Stimpson Family Nature Reserve has four miles of hiking trails through lush old-growth forests, with two ponds and wetland areas. It's near Lake Whatcom about five miles east of downtown.

Overlooking Squalicum Harbor, **Zuanich Point Park** is an outstanding place for picnics, kite flying, and play. A children's play area, paved bike path, and dock add to the appeal.

In Bellingham, don't miss **Boulevard Park,** where the main attraction is a 2,700-foot scenic overwater walkway. The walkway is part of the two-mile South Bay Trail connecting Fairhaven with downtown Bellingham. The best access is from Boulevard Park off South State Street.

RECREATION
Whale-Watching

San Juan Cruises (360/738-8099 or 800/443-4552, www.whales.com, Fri.-Sat. May-Sept.) departs Bellingham for all-day cruises to the San Juan Islands on the 149-passenger *Victoria Star 2*. These trips combine a two-hour stop in Friday Harbor with a three-hour whale-watching voyage and lunch; $109 adults, $55 ages 6-17, free for children under 6. Half-day trips are a bit cheaper, and the company also runs evening specialty cruises focusing on wine, beer, or crab dinners. Special birding trips to see Smith Island puffins and seabirds around Sucia and Patos Islands take place several times each summer. Sunday-only trips to Sucia Island State Park ($89 adults, $45 ages 6-17, free for children under 6) includes 2.5 hours on the island and a picnic lunch on the beach.

Outer Island Excursions (360/376-3711, www.outerislandx.com) has whale-watching trips from Gooseberry Point north of Bellingham. The cost is $109 adults, $99 seniors, $89 teens, and $69 kids.

Kayaking and SUP

Located near the Amtrak station in Fairhaven, **Community Boating Center** (555 Harris Ave., 360/714-8891, www.boatingcenter.org) is a nonprofit place where you can rent wind- and human-powered watercraft. Prices for kayaks, rowboats, and stand-up paddleboards are $45 for four hours or $75 for all day. Small sailboats start at $35 for two hours.

Moondance Sea Kayaking Adventures (360/738-7664, www.moondancekayak.com) leads sea kayak tours in the area, from half-day paddles ($70) to five-day San Juan trips ($875). The company

operates from Larrabee State Park south of Bellingham.

Sailing

The city's visitors center has a complete listing of sailing and fishing charter operators and cruises. **Gato Verde Adventure Sailing** (360/220-3215, www.gatoverde.com) has day sails on board a 42-foot catamaran; it's the first plug-in diesel-electric hybrid charter boat on the West Coast. For something truly unique, take an evening sail on the 160-foot **Schooner Zodiac** (206/719-7622, www.schoonerzodiac.com). Built in 1924 for the Johnson & Johnson heirs, the two-masted schooner was later the last working pilot schooner in the nation, and is now listed in the National Register of Historic Places. Three-hour sailing trips are $79 adults, $59 kids and include full dinners.

Bellingham is a major center for boaters heading to the San Juans, with the following companies offering powerboat or sailing charters: **Bellhaven Charters** (360/733-6636 or 877/310-9471, www.bellhaven.net), **Bellingham Yachts Sales and Charters** (360/671-0990 or 877/310-9446, www.bellinghamyachts.com), **Northwest Explorations** (360/676-1248 or 800/826-1430, www.nwexplorations.com), **San Juan Sailing** (360/671-4300 or 800/677-7245, www.sanjuansailing.com), and **San Juan Yachting** (360/671-4300 or 800/670-8089, www.sanjuanyachting.com). (San Juan Sailing and San Juan Yachting are essentially the same company, but with a different focus.)

Hiking

Stop by the visitors center for descriptions and maps of more than 20 hiking trails in and around Bellingham, including trails in Whatcom Falls Park, Sehome Hill Arboretum, and the nearby Mt. Baker-Snoqualmie National Forest.

The **Interurban Trail** is a nine-mile path that follows a former railroad bed from Old Fairhaven Parkway south to Larrabee State Park. Continue north from Fairhaven to

Bellingham via the paved two-mile **South Bay Trail,** a portion of which is on pilings over Bellingham Bay. It's a great place for a jog or bike ride.

Bikes

The city's visitors center has a handout describing local biking paths. Favorites include the seven-mile Interurban Trail from Fairhaven to Larrabee State Park, the two-mile South Bay Trail connecting downtown with Bellingham, and five miles of single-track trails around Lake Padden.

Rent bikes from **Fairhaven Bicycle** (1108 11th St., 360/733-4433, www.fairhavenbike.com) or **Jack's Bicycle Center** (1907 Iowa St., 360/733-1955, www.jacksbicyclecenter.net). Full-suspension bikes cost $40-60 per day.

Swimming and Skating

Bellingham's **Arne Hanna Aquatic Center** (1114 Potter St., 360/657-7665, www.cob.org/ahac) has an indoor pool, wading pool, diving tank, and waterslide. It costs $4 for a one-day pass. A second pool is available at **Whatcom Family YMCA** (1256 N. State St., 360/763-8630, www.whatcomymca.org). In the summer, you can also swim at **Lake Padden Park** (4882 Samish Way, 360/676-6985), **Lake Samish** (673 N. Lake Samish Dr., 360/733-2362), and **Bloedel Donovan Park** (2214 Electric Ave., 360/676-6985).

For year-round indoor ice skating, head to **Sportsplex** (1225 Civic Field Way, 360/676-1919, www.bellinghamsportsplex.com).

SHOPPING

Bellingham has a diverse arts community, with many fine galleries, including several described above in Fairhaven. The nonprofit **Allied Arts of Whatcom County** (1418 Cornwall Ave., 360/676-8548, www.alliedarts.org) has a large downtown gallery, and puts on several festivals and other events. They also produce a helpful guide to local galleries, available at the visitors center.

For outdoor gear, head to **REI** (400 36th St.,

360/647-8955, www.rei.com) or the locally owned **Yeager's Sporting Goods** (3101 Northwest Ave., 360/733-1080, www.yeagerssportinggoods.com). Yeager's also houses the best toy store in Bellingham.

The city has a near-total **ban on plastic bags,** and adds a $0.05 charge to all purchases using paper bags.

ENTERTAINMENT AND EVENTS

Opened in 1927 as a vaudeville and movie palace, historic **Mt. Baker Theatre** (106 N. Commercial St., 360/733-5793, www.mountbakertheatre.com) hosts a dynamic calendar of live music and theater events, as well as the **Whatcom Symphony Orchestra** (360/756-6752, www.whatcomsymphony.com). A **Brown Bag Music Series** (360/647-2060) features concerts on the public library lawn each Friday mid-June-August.

Housed in a state-of-the-art downtown cinema, **Pickford Film Center** (1318 Bay St., 360/647-1300, www.pickfordcinema.org) shows independent, art house, documentary, and foreign films.

At **Bellingham Beer Week** (www.bellinghambeerweek.com) in mid-August the town bursts with 10 days of beer parties, music, and other events.

Given its young and hip population, it probably isn't surprising that Bellingham has 10 different **marijuana shops**; find them on websites such as www.leafly.com or www.weedmaps.com.

Founded by comedian and Bellingham resident Ryan Stiles, **The Upfront Theatre** (1208 Bay St., 360/733-8855, www.theupfront.com) is a 100-seat cabaret-style venue with live improv comedy Thursday-Saturday nights.

For the latest on the local music scene, pick up a copy of *Cascadia Weekly* (www.cascadiaweekly.com) or *Bellingham Herald's Take 5* (www.bellinghamherald.com). The **Wild Buffalo** (208 W. Holly St., 360/746-8733, www.wildbuffalo.net) and **Boundary Bay Brewery & Bistro** (1107 Railroad Ave.,

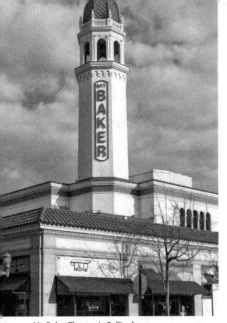

Mt. Baker Theatre in Bellingham

running, bicycling, canoeing, mountain biking, and finally kayaking across Bellingham Bay to the finish in the Fairhaven district. An annual event since 1973, the race is the highlight of a weeklong festival that includes parades, a street fair with crafts, live music and dancing, food, and a beer garden on Sunday after the race.

There's a big **Fourth of July** fireworks show over Bellingham Harbor each summer, and each July, the city hosts the two-week **Bellingham Festival of Music** (360/676-5997, www.bellinghamfestival.org), with outstanding classical and jazz performances. In October, the **Whatcom Artist Studio Tour** (www.studiotour.net) provides an open house for more than 50 local artisans.

FOOD

Bellingham has an amazing variety of creative eating establishments. Head to Fairhaven and just walk around to see what looks interesting, or visit the downtown Arts District surrounding the Whatcom Museum.

Eclectic

Fairhaven's **Dirty Dan Harris' Restaurant** (1211 11th St., 360/676-1011, www.dirtydanharris.com, 5pm-10pm daily, $25-36) serves prime rib, steaks, and fresh seafood dinners in a classy 1800s-style saloon. It's named for Daniel Jefferson Harris, a feisty eccentric best known for his bathing habits—or lack thereof—who platted the town's streets, built a dock, and sold lots to the thousands of folks who rolled into Fairhaven in 1883. He made a small fortune in the process. Save a small fortune with $4 happy hour drinks and $6 crab cake sliders.

If you aren't looking for the gourmet-variety burger, **Boomer's Drive-In** (310 N. Samish Way, 360/647-2666, www.boomersdrivein.com, 11am-10pm Sun.-Thurs., 11am-11pm Fri.-Sat.) has the finest anywhere around, served with waffle fries. They serve great milk shakes too, with carhop service under the canopy for a blast from the past.

EAT Restaurant and Bar (1200

360/647-5593, www.bbaybrewery.com) are good first stops for live bands. **The Green Frog Café** (1015 N. State St., 360/756-1213, www.acoustictavern.com) attracts singer-songwriter artists with a tiny stage and more than 20 microbrews on tap. **Temple Bar** (306 W. Champion St., 360/676-8660, www.templebarbellingham.com) is a great little wine bar with live music every Saturday and surprisingly good food. It's especially popular during happy hour, when a featured bottle of wine and a small plate of cheese, bread, olives, and fruit is just $18. **Skylark's Hidden Café** (1308 11th St., 360/715-3642, www.skylarkshiddencafe.com, 8am-midnight daily) has live jazz on weekends.

Downtown Art Walks (www.downtownbellingham.com) attract gallery enthusiasts the first Friday of each month. Bellingham's **Ski to Sea Race** (360/746-8861, www.skitosea.com), held Memorial Day weekend, tests the physical endurance and athletic skills of its participants over an 85-mile course that includes cross-country and downhill skiing,

Cornwall Ave., 360/306-3917, www.4u2eat. com, 11:30am-9pm Mon.-Thurs., 11:30am-11pm Fri., 10am-11pm Sat., 10am-2pm Sun., $13-28) is a casual bistro serving "American farm-to-table with a French twist." Even the cheeseburgers are unique, accompanied by homemade barbecue sauce and garlic fries. There's an excellent selection of wines, and the weekend brunch menu includes eggs Benedict, grilled hanger steak, and brioche French toast.

Keenan's at the Pier (804 10th St., 360/756-0005, www.thechrysalisinn.com, 7am-9pm daily, $22-38) is located within Chrysalis Inn & Spa in Fairhaven. Lunchtime sandwiches, rice bowls, and fish tacos are replaced by rack of lamb, eggplant parmesan, roasted chicken breast, and New York strip steak at dinner. The bar mixes great cocktails, and the pier is a lovely place for an after-dinner stroll.

Seafood

A pair of special-occasion seafood places hug Chuckanut Drive south of Bellingham. Famous for its sunset views from the back deck, **Chuckanut Manor Seafood & Grill** (360/766-6191, www.chuckanutmanor.com, 11:30am-9pm Tues.-Sat., 10:30am-9pm Sun., $19-50) is located at the southern end of Chuckanut Drive. The restaurant specializes in fresh seafood, including grilled Samish Bay oysters, coconut prawns, and pan-seared Alaskan halibut. Reservations are recommended. Sunday buffet brunches ($26) are also popular. The restaurant has been here since 1963. Clinging to the side of a hill at Mile 10, **The Oyster Bar** (2578 Chuckanut Dr., 360/766-6185, www.theoysterbar.net, 11:30am-10pm daily, $28-50) has two levels of windows facing the San Juan Islands and a back deck facing Samish Bay. In business since 1929, this friendly, iconic fine-dining place serves oysters on the half shell (of course), but fresh fish and other seafood are featured attractions on an always-changing menu. The wine list is equally notable. Reservations are essential, especially on weekends.

Fairhaven Fish & Chips (1020 Harris Ave., 360/733-5021, 11am-5:30pm Tues.-Sun., $10-15) is one of Bellingham's funkier eateries. It's hard to miss the aging London double-decker bus on the corner of Harris and 11th in Fairhaven. Step up the window to order traditional cod or halibut and chips, and enjoy them on the picnic tables out front. Afterwards, get a cone with soft-serve ice cream; more than 50 flavors are offered.

A popular downtown café housed in a historic building, **Rock & Rye Oyster House** (1145 N. State St., 360/746-6130, www.rock-rye.com, 3pm-11pm Tues.-Sun., $18-27) stars Puget Sound oysters, gnocchi, and duck confit. Happy hour appetizers are a good deal: pork tacos, poutine, and cioppino sauté are $5 or less. There's a covered patio out back, and a big drink menu

International

At Bellingham Marina near the Bellwether Hotel, the classy **Giuseppe's Al Porto Ristorante Italiano** (21 Bellwether Way, 360/714-8412, www.giuseppesitalian.com, 11:30am-9pm daily, $18-36) has delicious pastas and a large outside terrace for waterside dining. Dinner entrees range from simple spaghetti dishes to rack of lamb. The $18 three-course early dinners (served 3pm-6pm) are a good deal.

D'Anna's Italian Café (1317 N. State St., 360/714-0188, www.dannascafeitaliano.com, 11am-10pm Mon.-Fri., 11:30am-10am Sat., 4pm-10pm Sun., $11-33) is a bright bistro serving homemade red pepper ravioli, pancetta brandy chicken, linguini with fresh clams, pasta primavera, caprese sandwiches, Caesar salads, and more, with a couple of outside tables. Gluten-free pastas are available. The space is bright and open, with redbrick walls and an open kitchen.

In the heart of downtown, **Tadeo's Restaurant** (207 E. Holly St., 360/647-1862, 7am-10pm Mon.-Wed., 11am-9pm Sun.-Thurs., 11am-11pm Fri., 11am-2am Sat., $10-15) serves real-deal Mexican food, with made-from-scratch corn tortillas and salsas.

It's a family-run place where the food makes up for the low-key, utilitarian setting. (The owners started in a food truck before expanding to the restaurant.) Favorites include tacos al carbon, hefty burritos, carne asada, and $6 lunch specials. Tadeo's has Friday night karaoke and Saturday night dancing till 2am. There is free Wi-Fi.

At last count Bellingham had 18 different Thai restaurants. Two of the best are **Busara Thai Cuisine** (conveniently adjacent to REI at 404 36th St., 360/734-8088, www.busara-bellingham.com, 11:30am-9:30pm Mon.-Sat., 11:30am-9pm Sun., $10-17) and **Thai House Restaurant** (187 Telegraph Rd., 360/734-5111, www.bellinghamthaihouse.com, 11:30am-3pm, 5pm-9pm Mon.-Thurs., 11:30am-3pm, 5pm-9:30pm Fri., noon-9:30pm Sat., noon-9pm Sun., $10-16). **Little Tokyo** (2915 Newmarket Place in Barkley Village, 360/752-2222, www.littletokyowa.com, 11am-9pm Mon.-Fri., noon-9pm Sat., 4pm-9pm Sun., $10-20) is a casual sushi bar and Japanese restaurant open for lunch and dinner. The bento boxes and teriyaki are popular.

For those who crave authentic Vietnamese comfort food, **Pho 99** (3503 Byron St., 360/647-8471, www.pho99.us, 11am-9:30pm Mon.-Fri., 10am-9:30pm Sat.-Sun., $8-11) is a godsend. Choose from a big variety of pho noodle soups, along with rice plates, vermicelli bowls, fresh rolls, and vegetarian dishes. The setting is no-frills, and its proximity to Western Washington University makes it a student favorite.

Bellingham's best Greek eatery, **Café Akroteri** (1219 Cornwall Ave., 360/676-5554, www.cafeakroteri.com, 11am-9pm Mon.-Thurs., 11am-9:30pm Fri., noon-9:30pm Sat., 4pm-9pm Sun., $15-21) is a good lunch and dinner spot for gyros, Greek salads, souvlaki, dolmades, moussaka, and vegetarian specials.

Housed within the Bellingham Public Market at 1530 Cornwall Avenue, **Ambo Ethiopian Cuisine** (360/927-8714, www.amboethiopiancuisine.wordpress.com, 11am-8pm Mon.-Sat., $8-12) is a little café with traditional Ethiopian fare. This is finger food at

its best, with a leavened sourdough flatbread called injera at the heart of most meals. Doro wat (chicken stew) is especially popular. The café is in the back of a rather odd collection of earthy businesses, including **Terra Organic & Natural Foods** (www.terraorganicfood.com), **Mount Baker Books** (used books), and **Electric Beet Juice Co.** (360/676-7477, www.electricbeetjuiceco.com, 8am-6pm Mon.-Fri., 9am-5pm Sat., 11am-3pm Sun.) with organic juices, smoothies, and vegan treats.

A Peruvian deli near downtown, **Café Rumba Sanguchería** (1140 N. State St., 360/746-8280, www.caferumbabham.com, 11am-7pm Mon.-Fri., 11am-8pm Tues.-Fri., 11am-6pm Sat., 11am-5pm Sun., $9) crafts unusual sandwiches, all served with a side of *papas con aji escabeche*—boiled and grilled potatoes with salsa. The *pavo* (turkey) version is especially popular, and order a fruity Inca Cola for the full effect. The café comes alive with salsa dancing on the first and third Saturdays of every month.

Pizza

Bellingham has at least 60 pizza establishments, from crank-em-out national chain joints to upscale gourmet pizza restaurants. Nearly all of these now offer gluten-free crust options. One of five pizza places in Fairhaven, **Ovn** (1148 10th St., 360/393-4327, www.ovnwoodfiredpizza.com, 11:30am-9:30pm Mon.-Thurs., 11:30am-10:30pm Fri.-Sat., 11:30am-9pm Sun., $13-16) bakes wood-fired pizzas. The setting is trendy and upscale, with a three-ton oven imported from Italy and vegetarian options and dipping sauces to spice up the crust. Ovn is next to Village Inn, a block away from the busiest part of Fairhaven.

La Fiamma (200 E. Chestnut St., 360/647-0060, www.lafiamma.com, 11am-10pm Mon.-Thurs., 11am-10:30pm Fri., 9am-10:30pm Sat., noon-10pm Sun., $10-25) is a stylish but family-friendly spot with crunchy wood-fired pizzas (including a potato-gorgonzola-fennel sausage version), panini, and salads. A large cheese pizza costs $19; locals call it the best in town.

Part of a local chain of Hawaiian-themed pizza places, **Coconut Kenny's** (2220 James St., 360/647-9273, www.coconutkennys.com, 11am-9pm daily, $15-20) serves thick-crust pies, including the Big Kahuna, piled high with pepperoni, ham, sausage, bacon, red onions, mushrooms, tomatoes, green onions, and black olives. They also serve great sandwiches on Hawaiian bread baked in the shop; try the Maui cheesesteak. The décor is tiki kitsch.

Breakfast and Lunch

Enjoy great breakfasts and lunches at ★ **Old Town Café** (316 W. Holly St., 360/671-4431, www.theoldtowncafe.com, 6:30am-3pm Mon.-Sat., 8am-2pm Sun., $8-10), an earthy downtown brunch place where the line of customers stretches out the door most mornings. Try the Number Nine: two poached eggs on a biscuit with cheese sauce, tomatoes, and home fries. The atmosphere is laid-back and noisy.

A different dining experience can be found a few blocks away at **The Little Cheerful Café** (133 E. Holly St., 360/738-8824, 7am-2pm daily, $8-12), where the staff is, of course, cheerful. The setting is casual, and the breakfasts are always great—especially the house favorites, crab cakes with sliced avocado eggs Benedict—and served in ample portions. Everything on the menu is available all day, so you can start your morning with the Yuppie Scramble (artichoke hearts, tomato, red onion, asparagus, sun-dried tomatoes, and goat cheese), and end it with the aptly named Myocardial Infarction burger (2,500 calories). Sidewalk seating is available, but be prepared to wait if you show up after 10am on weekends. No credit cards.

A Victorian building in Fairhaven houses spacious **Skylark's Hidden Café** (1308 11th St., 360/715-3642, www.skylarkshiddencafe.com, 8am-midnight daily, $10-22), serving filling breakfasts, deli sandwiches, soups, fresh seafood, award-winning clam chowder, steaks, and much more. Everything is made in-house, including the fresh lemonade made from hand-squeezed lemons. No

longer hidden, the café has expanded from its backstreet location to a beautiful two-level building with a hardwood bar (14 single malt scotches) and live jazz on weekends. The late-night small-plates menu includes standards such as buffalo wings and nachos, along with scampi-style prawns, grilled coppa caprese, and a unique Thai peanut rockfish burger.

Magdalena's Creperie (1200 10th St., 360/483-8569, www.magdalenascreperie.com, 9am-4pm Mon.-Fri., 8am-4pm Sat.-Sun., $8-13) has a big choice of delicious sweet and savory crepes, authentic Polish pierogi, sandwiches, and espresso. Magdalena's is adjacent to Fairhaven Village Inn, an upscale boutique hotel along the sometimes-noisy railroad tracks.

It isn't in Bellingham, but ★ **Rhododendron Café** (5521 Chuckanut Dr., Bow, 360/766-6667, www.rhodycafe.com, 11:30am-8pm Wed.-Fri., 10am-8pm Sat.-Sun., closed Mon.-Tues., $11-20 breakfasts, $17-28 dinner entrées) is certainly worth the drive. This little country café is the centerpiece of the town of Bow, 14 miles south of Bellingham. Weekend brunch is always a draw, with steak and eggs, Greek omelets, huckleberry waffles, and eggs Benedict. Check the blackboard for lunch and dinner, including various ethnic specialties and Northwest cuisine.

Next door to Rhododendron Café is **Farm to Market Bakery** (5507 Chuckanut Dr., Bow, 360/766-6240, 9am-4pm Wed.-Sun., $3-6), serving fresh cinnamon rolls, lime-soaked polenta cake, lemon bars, triple chocolate pecan brownies, and other sweets.

Coffee and Sweets

Many Bellingham places make espresso, but one stands out: **Tony's Coffee & Teas** (1101 Harris Ave., 360/733-6319, www.tonyscoffee.com, 7am-6pm daily), where the smell of roasting coffee wafts through the air. There's another location downtown, but the Fairhaven one is the real deal. Read the newspaper, sample the carrot cake, play a game of chess, or just take in the scene. This is as close to Berkeley as you'll get this far north. The owners also run **Harris Ave. Café** (360/738-0802, 8am-2pm daily, $6-14) next door, with delicious brunches and a shady patio.

Also in Fairhaven, **Rustic Coffee and Wine Bar** (1319 11th St., 360/306-8794, www.rusticcoffeeandwinebar.com, 6:30am-7pm Mon.-Thurs., 6:30am-9pm Fri.-Sat., 7am-6pm Sun.) provides an upscale variation on the coffee theme, with quiche, breakfast wraps, sandwiches, cheeses, and wine by the glass or bottle.

A popular regional chain, **Woods Coffee** (www.woodscoffee.com) has 11 Bellingham cafés—all with Wi-Fi—open daily, generally 6:30am-8pm. In addition to all the standard coffee drinks, they serve sandwiches, salads, and baked goods. Stop by the striking café in the historic Flatiron Building (10 Prospect St., 360/392-8116). For killer views with your cappuccino, head to the Boulevard Park location (470 Bay View Rd., 360/738-4771); it's right on the water, with a deck and windows fronting Bellingham Bay, along with a fireplace, comfy leather chairs, and upstairs seating.

If you're in Fairhaven and want great sandwiches, bagels, quiche, a slice of famous peanut butter pie, or just a scoop of ice cream, drop by **Colophon Café** inside Village Books (1210 11th St., 360/647-0092, www.colophoncafe.com, 9am-9pm Mon.-Thurs., 9am-10pm Fri.-Sat., 10am-8pm Sun.).

Breweries

If you're a fan of craft beer, Bellingham will make you think you died and went to heaven. At last count 15 different breweries were in Bellingham. Pick up a **Tap Trails** (www.taptrails.com) map at the visitors center and head out to sample the beers and collect "passport" stamps from all of them. **Food trucks** park in front of many of these breweries, providing inexpensive and tasty food. Most breweries allow folks to bring in food not purchased on site.

Find award-winning brews at **Boundary Bay Brewery & Bistro** (1107 Railroad Ave., 360/647-5593, www.bbaybrewery.com, $9-13), the largest brewpub in Washington and the 10th biggest in the nation. Established in 1995, it is the oldest brewery in Bellingham, with seven house-brewed beers on tap and a pub menu of fish tacos, enchiladas, bangers and mash, burgers, pizza, salads, sandwiches, and more. The big doors open onto a flower-filled deck and beer garden, where you'll hear live music most nights. The brewery is right across the street from the farmers market.

Chuckanut Brewery & Kitchen (601

Tony's Coffee & Teas

W. Holly St., 360/752-3377, www.chuckanutbreweryandkitchen.com, 11am-9:30pm Sun.-Thurs., 11am-10pm Fri.-Sat., $9-14) specializes in European-style craft beers—including the Chuckanut Helles Lager, a gold medal winner at the 2016 Great American Beer Festival (GABF)—but crafts nearly 20 varieties. The diverse menu complements the beers, with pizzas, fish chowder, mac and cheese, meatloaf, and a sausage-and-beer combo ($9, includes a pint). The brewery was named small brewing company and brewer of the year at the 2011 GABF.

Kulshan Brewing Company (2238 James St., 360/389-5348, www.kulshanbrewing.com, 11am-11pm daily) is another favorite, with award-winning beers that include Bastard Kat IPA, Red Cap Irish Red Ale, and Transporter Porter. Kulshan lacks a kitchen, but food trucks park in the lot.

Elizabeth Station (1400 W. Holly St., 360/733-8982, www.estationbeer.com, 10am-midnight daily) is a perpetually busy establishment in the heart of downtown. The brewery has 16 beers on tap, plus coolers filled with hundreds of different bottled beers and ciders from around the world, all organized by region. Get an order of chili nachos, or return in the morning for a fix of Fruit Loops and Captain Crunch from the cereal bar.

Other places well worth a visit for food and beer are **Aslan Brewing** (1330 N. Forest St., 360/778-2088, www.aslanbrewing.com, 11am-11pm Mon.-Thurs., 11am-midnight Fri.-Sat., 11am-10pm Sun.)—the state's only organic brewery—and **Wander Brewing** (1807 Dean Ave., 360/647-6152, www.wanderbrewing.com, 3pm-9pm Mon.-Thurs., noon-10pm Fri.-Sat., noon-7pm Sun.).

Bakeries and Sweets

For a treat in Fairhaven, drop by **Sirena Gelato** (960 Harris Ave., 360/733-6700, www.sirenagelato.com, noon-9pm Mon.-Sat., noon-8pm Sun.). Choose from Thai coconut milk, Madagascar vanilla, salted caramel, and other flavors, plus dairy-free fruit sorbets.

Find European-style breads, plus sandwiches, salads, and soups, at **Avenue Bread Co.** (1313 Railroad Ave., 360/715-3354, www.avenuebread.com, 7am-5pm daily, $5-10). There are additional Avenue Bread shops in Fairhaven at 1135 11th Street and in the Sunnyland neighborhood at 2301 James Street. Try their Eggenue, an English muffin egg sandwich with bacon, gorgonzola, spinach, and tomato.

The Bagelry (1319 Railroad Ave., 360/676-5288, www.bagelrybellingham.com, 7am-4pm Mon.-Fri., 7:30am-4pm Sat., 8am-3pm) is a popular place with a baker's dozen types of New York-style bagels, along with bagel sandwiches, omelets, and espresso.

The exceptionally popular **Mount Bakery Café** (308 W. Champion St., 360/715-2195, www.mountbakery.com, 8am-3:30pm daily, $6-11) serves savory and sweet crepes, "Bellingham's best Benedicts," frittatas, waffles, BLTs, a quiche of the day, and amazing tarts, croissants, chocolate truffle cakes, and other sweet treats. The crème brûlée is to die for. Mount Bakery Café is in the heart of the Art District, with a second shop in Fairhaven at 1217 Harris Avenue.

Markets

Bellingham's **Community Food Co-Op** (1220 N. Forest St., 360/734-8158, www.communityfood.coop, 7am-10pm daily) is a spacious natural foods market. Across the street is **Co-Op Bakery Café** (405 E. Holly St., 7am-8pm daily), with an outdoor patio and assorted baked goods, smoothies, espresso, and more.

The **Bellingham Farmers Market** (1100 Railroad Ave., 360/647-2060, www.bellinghamfarmers.org, 10am-3pm Sat. Apr.-mid-Dec.) is housed within Depot Market Square. A second farmers market takes place behind Village Books in Fairhaven; it's held Wednesdays, noon-5pm from June through September.

ACCOMMODATIONS

Bellingham Whatcom County Tourism (904 Potter St., 360/671-3990 or 800/487-2032, www.bellingham.org) keeps track of local lodging availability on summer weekends. Stop by the office for brochures and discount coupons, or to check out photographs of local bed-and-breakfasts. An abundance of weekend soccer tournaments creates crowded conditions in summer, so lodging can be a challenge. Call months ahead for the peak of summer to ensure a space. Add 10.7 percent tax to the rates quoted below.

Lodging rates are relatively high in Bellingham, and the few budget options suffer from a host of problems. In addition to the hotels listed below, booking sites such as **Airbnb** (www.airbnb.com), **CouchSurfing** (www.couchsurfing.org), **FlipKey** (www.flipkey.com), **VRBO** (www.vrbo.com), and **Homeaway** (www.homeaway.com) have dozens of nightly or weekly rentals in the Bellingham area.

Under $150

Coachman Inn (120 N. Samish Way, 360/671-9000 or 800/962-6641, www.coachmaninnmotel.com, $120 d) has simple but well-maintained rooms, fridges, Wi-Fi, a sauna, continental breakfast, and a small seasonal pool.

Motel 6 (3701 Byron St., I-5 Exit 252, 360/671-4494 or 800/466-8356, www.motel6.com, $112 d) has economy rooms, an outdoor pool, and Wi-Fi.

GuestHouse Inn (805 Lakeway Dr., 360/671-9600 or 800/214-8378, www.guesthouseintl.com, $140-150 d) is a fine moderately priced option, with clean rooms, a continental breakfast, an indoor hot tub, and Wi-Fi. It's right off I-5 at Exit 253, so choose a room away from the freeway if you're a light sleeper.

Two reasonably priced places offer similar facilities, including a seasonal outdoor pool, hot tub, in-room microwaves and fridges, continental breakfast, and Wi-Fi: **EconoLodge Inn & Suites** (3750 Meridian St., 360/671-4600, www.choicehotels.com, $119-160 d), and **Quality Inn & Suites** (100 E. Kellogg Rd., 360/647-8000, www.qualityinnbellingham.com, $144-154 d).

Popular with business travelers and convenient to the airport, **Hampton Inn Bellingham Airport** (3985 Bennett Dr., 360/676-7700 or 800/426-7866, www.hamptoninn.com, $129-134 d) includes a heated seasonal outdoor pool, fitness room, buffet breakfast, and airport and ferry shuttle. Some rooms have jetted tubs.

Best Western Plus Heritage Inn (151 E. McLeod Rd., 360/647-1912 or 800/528-1234, www.bestwestern.com/heritageinnbellingham, $220-230 weekends, $130-150 weekdays) has the look of a New England colonial building and features attractive grounds, 90 fashionable rooms, a seasonal outdoor pool, indoor hot tub, fitness center, airport shuttle, Wi-Fi, and a filling hot breakfast. Reserve a room facing away from I-5.

Over $150

One of Bellingham's finer lodging places, **Four Points by Sheraton** (714 Lakeway Dr., I-5 Exit 256, 360/671-1011 or 888/671-1011, www.fourpointsbellingham.com, $265-279 d) is a four-story hotel arranged around a large central atrium with an indoor pool, restaurant, and bar. Other amenities include a fitness center, hot tub, Wi-Fi, and a free airport shuttle. The hotel is within walking distance of downtown and just a block from the visitors center.

A 22-room boutique hotel, ★ **Fairhaven Village Inn** (1200 10th St., 360/733-1311 or 877/733-1100, www.fairhavenvillageinn.com, $239-259 d) blends well with its historic Fairhaven neighbors. Rooms are spacious and include gas fireplaces, plush king-size beds, small decks, a continental breakfast, Wi-Fi, and other amenities. The Interurban Trail starts nearby, providing a good spot for a morning run.

One of Bellingham's most indulgent lodging choices, **Hotel Bellwether** (1 Bellwether Way, 360/392-3100 or 877/411-1200, www.hotelbellwether.com) offers a harborside location, large rooms (many with king-size beds), balconies, Italian furnishings, gas fireplaces, large TVs, marble baths with jetted tubs, a lavish breakfast buffet, and Wi-Fi. Peak-season weekend rates start at $319 d for the smaller rooms facing the plaza, $329 d for more spacious ones. The lavish three-level lighthouse building is a favorite bridal suite. Downstairs is the classy Harborside Restaurant and Lounge, and golfers will appreciate the small putting green.

The acclaimed **Chrysalis Inn & Spa** (804 10th St., 360/756-0005 or 888/808-0005, www.thechrysalisinn.com, $259-359 d) is another gorgeous waterside option with ultra-luxurious rooms (two-person baths, gas fireplaces, and window seats), a breakfast buffet, an impressive lobby, a wine bar, and a decadent spa. The hotel also houses Keenan's at the Pier, which is popular for lunch, dinner, and drinks. Unfortunately, the hotel's trackside location can bring train noise throughout the night.

Bellingham has several newly constructed suites hotels along I-5 on the north end of town, perfect for quick access to the freeway and airport. Among these is **SpringHill Suites Bellingham** (4040 Northwest Ave., 360/714-9600 or 888/236-2427, www.marriott.com, $156-170 d), with well-appointed rooms with microwaves, fridges, and 42-inch TVs. Amenities include hot breakfasts, a pool and fitness center, and a restaurant.

Bed-and-Breakfasts

★ **Tree Frog Night Inn** (1727 Mt. Baker Hwy., 360/676-2300, www.treefrognight. com, $165-190 d for multiple nights, add $25 each for extra guests) consists of an elegant, environmentally friendly cottage with two guest suites and a guest room. Nearby are gardens, a forest, and a pond. Suites have small porches, luxurious furnishings, private baths, robes, organic breakfasts, and a bottle of local wine. Private massage and spa packages are available.

Located along scenic Chuckanut Drive south of Bellingham, **Chuckanut Manor B&B** (3056 Chuckanut Dr., 360/766-6191, www.chuckanutmanor.com, $160 d or $230 for four) is a two-bedroom apartment suite

with a large deck facing Samish Bay, including a full kitchen and private bath with jetted tub. It's old-fashioned, but has a killer location with plenty of room. A continental breakfast is provided, and Chuckanut Manor Seafood & Grill is downstairs. Railroad tracks are just down the hill, so trains may sing to you in the night. The owners also manage the Bay House just down the road ($160 d); pets are allowed at that property.

A 20-minute drive north of downtown Bellingham, **Anderson Creek Lodge** (5602 Mission Rd., 360/966-0598, www.andersoncreek.com, $155-205 d) has three guest rooms and a suite, all with private baths, king beds, a filling hot breakfast, and Wi-Fi. The lodge is set on 35 acres of fields and forests, with llamas, deer, and other creatures.

On the woodsy shore of Lake Whatcom just east of Bellingham, ★ **MoonDance Inn** (4737 Cable St., 360/647-2997, www.bellinghambandb.com, $135-180 d, $35 each for extra guests) provides a beautiful setting, luxury accommodations, full breakfasts, a private dock, fire pit, lakeside beach, canoes, kayaks, volleyball, and Wi-Fi. Five guest rooms all have private baths, and kids are accepted.

Camping

The closest public campsites are seven miles south of Bellingham at **Larrabee State Park** (360/676-2093, www.parks.wa.gov, $25 tents, $30 RVs). Year-round sites are available, along with showers. Make reservations ($10 extra) at 888/226-7688 or online at http://washington. goingtocamp.com.

At **Bellingham RV Park** (3939 Bennett Dr., 360/752-1224 or 888/372-1224, www.bellinghamrvpark.com), RV hookups cost $40.

INFORMATION

For maps, a slew of brochures, historical walking tours, and general information, visit the **Bellingham Whatcom County Tourism Visitors Center** (904 Potter St., I-5 Exit 253, 360/671-3990 or 800/487-2032, www.bellingham.org, 9am-5pm daily). The **Downtown Information Center** (1301

Commercial St., 11am-5pm Mon.-Sat.) has brochures and a location in the center of the action. Other information kiosks are inside the Bellingham Cruise Terminal (where the Alaska ferry docks), Bellis Fair Mall, and at the airport.

GETTING THERE AND AROUND

The **Bellingham Cruise Terminal** (www.portofbellingham.com), three blocks downhill from Fairhaven, is where you can catch whale-watching boats to the San Juans, and the **Alaska Marine Highway** (360/676-8445 or 800/642-0066, www.ferryalaska.com) ferries to Alaska on Fridays and Saturdays.

Car and Taxi

Avis (360/676-8840 or 800/230-4898, www.avis.com), **Budget** (360/671-3800, www.budget.com), **Enterprise** (360/714-0243 or 855/266-9565, www.enterprise.com), and **Hertz** (360/733-8336 or 800/654-4173, www.hertz.com) all have airport car rentals. Local taxi companies include **Yellow Cab** (360/733-8294, www.yellowcabinc.com) and **Bellingham Taxi** (360/220-4990, www.taxi-bellingham.com).

Train

Amtrak (360/734-8851 or 800/872-7245, www.amtrakcascades.com) provides twice-daily train connections on its *Cascades* train north to Vancouver, British Columbia, and south to Mount Vernon, Stanwood, Everett, Edmonds, and Seattle. It stops at the Fairhaven depot, just a short walk from the Bellingham Cruise Terminal.

Air

Located just north of the city, **Bellingham International Airport** (4255 Mitchell Way, 360/671-5674, www.portofbellingham.com) is a popular departure point for many Canadians because they can get more convenient flights to some U.S. destinations and cheaper tickets; the parking—$8-12 per day—is a big savings too. Because of this, air traffic has grown rapidly in the last decade.

Alaska Airlines (800/252-7522, www.alaskaair.com) connects Bellingham with Sea-Tac, Portland, Las Vegas, Maui, and Kona. **Allegiant Air** (702/505-8888, www.allegiantair.com) connects Bellingham with Los Angeles, Las Vegas, Long Beach, Oakland, Palm Springs, San Diego, and Phoenix.

San Juan Airlines (360/293-4691 or 800/874-4434, www.sanjuanairlines.com) has daily service to San Juan, Orcas, Lopez, and Blakely in the San Juan Islands, along with charter flights and flightseeing.

Shuttle

If you're flying into Sea-Tac Airport, catch the **Airporter Shuttle** (360/380-8800 or 866/235-5247, www.airporter.com) van to Bellingham for $39 one-way ($33 kids). **Quick Shuttle Service** (604/940-4428 or 800/665-2122, www.quickcoach.com) has service rom the Bellingham airport to both the Vancouver airport and downtown Vancouver for $29 one-way ($10 kids).

SeaTac Direct (360/733-3666, www.seatacdirect.com) has bus connections between Sea-Tac and Bellingham three times a day. They are $50 one-way, with a four-person minimum.

Bus

Locally, **Whatcom Transit Authority** (360/676-7433, www.ridewta.com, $1)—better known as WTA—provides daily bus service throughout Bellingham and the rest of the county, including Ferndale, Lynden, Blaine, and the Lummi Indian Reservation. **Greyhound** (401 Harris Ave., 360/733-5251 or 800/231-2222, www.greyhound.com) has nationwide bus connections from the Amtrak depot in Fairhaven.

BoltBus (877/265-8287, www.boltbus.com) travels the I-5 corridor from Seattle north to Bellingham and Vancouver, and south to Portland. Fares are reasonable and the buses all have Wi-Fi, reserved seating, and ample legroom.

Seattle

Seattle is not only the largest city in the Pacific Northwest, but a delightful place to spend several days—or weeks—of adventurous sightseeing. Below is a skim-the-surface version of this eminently livable city with a booming economy. For a taste of city life, pick up one of the free newspapers on racks all over town. Both *The Stranger* and *Seattle Weekly* are packed with events and things to do, from art openings and rock concerts to pot shops.

SIGHTS

★ PIKE PLACE MARKET

If you only have a day in the city, be sure to take in **Pike Place Market** (85 Pike St., 206/682-7453, www.pikeplacemarket.org) for a wonderful introduction to Seattle at its best. Located downtown at the waterfront end of Stewart Street, it's open daily. The true heart and soul of Seattle, Pike Place is where visitors and locals buy the freshest fish, most colorful flowers, and most squeezable produce in town. Listen to the street musicians, enjoy the parade of humanity, pose atop Rachel the pig (sculpted by a Whidbey Island artist), and explore myriad shops and eateries (my favorite is Crepe de France), but watch out for flying fish. Head "Down Under" for additional shops, and explore vendors selling all sorts of unique arts and crafts. New in 2017 is Pike Place MarketFront, with a grand public plaza and viewing deck, shops, restaurants, and artist tables, plus parking and low-income housing. For something different, be sure to ask for directions to the market's infamous gum wall, coated with thousands of pieces of already-been-chewed gum.

WATERFRONT PARK

From Pike Place Market, you can easily walk down to **Waterfront Park** (1301 Alaskan Way, 206/684-4075, www.seattle.gov/parks), which offers beautiful views of Puget Sound along with benches and tables from which to admire them. If that's not close enough to the water, board one of the **Argosy Cruises** (Pier 55, 1101 Alaskan Way, 206/623-1445 or 800/642-7816, www.argosycruises.com) that leave from Pier 55 for a one-hour spin around Elliott Bay.

Pike Place Market

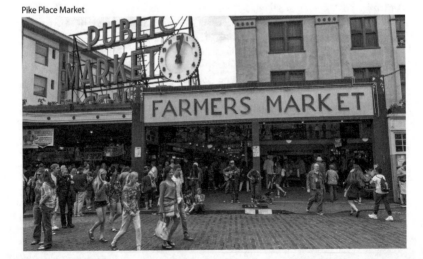

Seattle

To Anacortes, Vancouver, Whidbey Island, and the San Juan Islands

Golden Gardens Park

NW 85TH ST

NE 95TH ST

99

5

522

513

24TH AVE NW

15TH AVE NW

8TH AVE NW

32ND AVE NW

NE 75TH ST

BALLARD

NW 65TH ST

Green Lake Park

Green Lake

NE 65TH ST

NW MARKET ST

Discovery Park

WOODLAND PARK ZOO ★

N 50TH ST

FREMONT

34TH AVE W

UNIVERSITY DISTRICT

NE 45TH ST

★ **BURKE MUSEUM**

★ **HENRY ART GALLERY**

UNIVERSITY OF WASHINGTON

Union Bay

EVERGREEN POINT/ FLOATING BRIDGE

520

W DRAVUS ST

THORNDYKE AVE W

15TH AVE

MAGNOLIA

QUEEN ANNE

Lake Union

99

Portage Bay

5

Washington Park

Volunteer Park

Lake Washington

SPACE NEEDLE

PACIFIC SCIENCE CENTER

EMP MUSEUM/CHIHULY GLASS

SEATTLE CENTER

Lake Union Park

CAPITOL HILL

MADISON PARK

UNION ST

VICTORIA CLIPPER

Elliott Bay

To San Juan Island and Victoria

SEATTLE ART MUSEUM ★

PIKE PLACE MARKET ☐

SEATTLE AQUARIUM ★★

★ **SEATTLE GREAT WHEEL**

CHERRY ST

WASHINGTON BLVD

To Bainbridge Island

To Bremerton

Duwamish Head

PIONEER SQUARE

23RD AVE E

CENTURYLINK FIELD ★

★ **SAFECO FIELD**

Alki Beach Park

LAKE WASHINGTON FLOATING BRIDGE

90

ALKI AVE SW

S HOLGATE ST

RAINIER AVE

ADMIRAL WAY

Harbor Island

WEST SEATTLE

1ST AVE S

99

900

Colman Park

0   1 mi

0   1 km

DELRIDGE WAY SW

W MARGINAL WAY SW

SPOKANE ST

Duwamish Waterway

5

15TH AVE S

BEACON AV

38TH AVE S

SOUTH SEATTLE

Genesee Playfield

© AVALON TRAVEL

At Pier 57, the **Seattle Great Wheel** (1301 Alaskan Way, 206/623-8600, www.seattlegreatwheel.com, 11am-10pm Mon.-Thurs., 11am-midnight Fri., 10am-midnight Sat., 10am-10pm Sun., shorter hours in winter, $13 adults, $11 seniors, $8.50 children 4-11, free children under 4) is the best seat in the city: 175 feet up in the sky. Opened in 2012, the newest city icon offers views that extend over the waterfront and out over Puget Sound and the surrounding islands and mountains.

SEATTLE AQUARIUM

Along the waterfront, the **Seattle Aquarium** (1483 Alaskan Way, 206/386-4320, www.seattleaquarium.org, 9:30am-5pm daily, $22 adults, $15 children 4-12, free children under 4) is the best way—short of donning scuba gear—to see the colorful marinelife inhabiting Puget Sound's icy depths. Get your hands wet in tidepools and marvel at 350 species of aquatic animals on display, including harbor seals, sharks, giant Pacific octopuses, and sea otters. The 400,000-gallon Underwater Dome alone is worth the trip: Descend into a half-sphere to find scores of deep-sea creatures surrounding you.

SEATTLE ART MUSEUM

The entrance to the **Seattle Art Museum** (SAM, 1300 1st Ave., 206/654-3100, www.seattleartmuseum.org, 10am-9pm Thurs., 10am-5pm Wed. and Fri.-Sun., closed Mon.-Tues., $19.50 adults, $12.50 youth 13-19, free children under 13) is marked by a 48-foot kinetic sculpture, *Hammering Man,* that towers over the sidewalk as though he's about to smash his hammer into the concrete. The museum is renowned for its cultural displays of Native American, Asian, and African American art. The spacious, three-level building includes a café and gift shop.

PIONEER SQUARE

South of the downtown core lies the **Pioneer Square Historic District** (1st Ave. and Yesler Way). Seattle's oldest neighborhood features 19th-century buildings nestled alongside modern art galleries, cafés, and nightclubs. Today, the square is the starting point of the **Bill Speidel's Underground Tour** (608 1st Ave., 206/682-4646, www.undergroundtour.com, $16 adults, $8 children), an entertaining excursion through the original streets beneath the current city. It's also the location of the **Klondike Gold Rush National Historical Park Museum** (319 2nd Ave. S., 206/553-7220, www.nps.gov/klse, 9am-5pm daily, free), which traces Seattle's gold rush history through educational exhibits, films, historical photos, and activities. There's even a free walking tour (10am daily mid-June to Labor Day weekend).

At night, revelers come to enjoy the square's many restaurants, bars, and clubs, especially when the Mariners or Seahawks are playing. Safeco Field, the Mariners' home base, sits a few blocks south of Pioneer Square.

VOLUNTEER PARK

New York has Central Park; San Francisco has Golden Gate Park; and Seattle has **Volunteer Park** (accessible from 4th or 5th Ave. E., 206/684-4743, www.seattle.gov/parks, 6am-10pm daily). Stroll the many trails framed in greenery to the conservatory, a glass building filled with rooms of blooming flowers and seasonal displays. A short walk to the other side of the park leads to a spiral staircase that ascends the 75-foot water tower and offers sweeping city views.

KERRY PARK

A small, perfectly manicured lawn and a few benches is all you'll find in **Kerry Park** (corner of 2nd Ave. W. and W. Highland Dr., free), but people don't come here for the seating. If there is one place to see everything it's from the perch of this quiet neighborhood park. Amateur and professional photographers, locals, and tourists come here for sweeping views of downtown Seattle, the Space Needle, Mount Rainier, the waterfront, and, best of all, the sunset.

SEATTLE CENTER

Adjacent to lower Queen Anne and a short distance north of downtown is the tourist mecca known as **Seattle Center** (305 Harrison St., 206/684-7200, www.seattlecenter.com, 7am-9pm daily, free). Built for the 1962 World's Fair, it encompasses fairgrounds, the International Fountain, and a year-round arts and entertainment complex. It's the north terminus of the **Seattle Center Monorail** (www.seattlemonorail.com, $2), which transports visitors between Seattle Center and downtown approximately every 10 minutes. Seattle Center is also the location of the landmark Space Needle and the EMP Museum, and it hosts the kid-friendly **Pacific Science Center** (206/443-2001, www.pacificsciencecenter.org) and the astounding **Chihuly Garden and Glass** (305 Harrison St., 206/753-4940, www.chihulygardenandglass.com, 10am-9pm Sun.-Thurs., 10am-10pm Fri.-Sat., $18 adults, $12 children 4-12, free children under 4, add $2/ticket if purchased at the door).

SPACE NEEDLE

First sketched on a napkin by artist Edward E. Carlson in a coffee shop, the **Space Needle** (400 Broad St., 206/905-2100, www.spaceneedle.com, 8am-midnight daily, $19-24 adults, $9.50-15 youth) dominated the 1962 Seattle World's Fair and has since become a celebrated Seattle icon. Traveling at a speed of 10 mph, the elevators glide 605 feet up to the observation deck, where panoramic, 360-degree views of the entire city and Puget Sound leave visitors breathless. With 25 lightning rods on its roof and elevators that reduce speed when winds reach 35 mph, the Space Needle was built to withstand the rough winds and thunderstorms that bless the Pacific Northwest.

EMP MUSEUM

At the mesmerizing **EMP Museum** (325 5th Ave. N., 206/367-5483, www.empmuseum.org, 10am-5pm daily, $23), everyone gets to be 17 again as they explore the strange pop culture worlds of rock music and science fiction.

(EMP stands for Experience Music Project.) The building's rounded metal exterior—based on the curves in electric guitars—was designed by famed architect Frank O. Gehry.

FOOD

Organic and fresh breakfast and lunch is always perfect at ★ **Portage Bay Café** (4130 Roosevelt Way NE, 206/547-8230, www.portagebaycafe.com, 7:30am-2:30pm daily, $11 and up), which serves delicious waffles and pancakes topped with colorful berries and fresh cream. The menu has all the home-style favorites, along with some new ones like their crab cakes Benedict.

★ **The Wild Ginger** (1401 3rd Ave., 206/623-4450, www.wildginger.net, 11:30am-3pm and 5pm-11pm Mon.-Fri., 11:30am-3pm and 4:30pm-11pm Sat., 4pm-9pm Sun., $18 and up) mixes diverse Asian flavors in Thai, Indonesian, and Szechuan dishes. The *satay* is the best you'll find in the city.

Before Seattle gained fame for serving up some of the best espressos and café lattes, it was known for delivering the freshest seafood right off the boat and to your plate. **Elliott's Oyster House** (1201 Alaskan Way, 206/623-4340, www.elliottsoysterhouse.com, 11am-10pm Sun.-Thurs., 11am-11pm Fri.-Sat., $9-38) still serves the freshest wild salmon and Dungeness crab, while giving shellfish lovers 40 different varieties of oysters. There is an extensive selection of wine, cocktails, and draft beers, all served with an excellent waterfront view of Elliott Bay.

The Metropolitan Grill (820 2nd Ave., 206/624-3287, www.themetropolitangrill.com, 11am-10pm Mon.-Thurs., 11am-10:30pm Fri., 4pm-11pm Sat., 4pm-9pm Sun., $20 and up) is where the best steaks are served in an elegant atmosphere with private booths or, if you prefer, wide-open tables. The onion rings are thickly cut, making a great appetizer, and the crab cakes are perfect. Entrées include great steak choices, as well as seafood and a tasty grilled portabello mushroom.

A rooftop terrace in the summer, comfortable dining room seating, and trapeze artists swinging overhead while you eat—that's the unique atmosphere and allure of the **Pink Door** (1919 Post Alley, 206/443-3241, www. thepinkdoor.net, 11:30am-10pm Mon.-Thurs., 11:30am-11pm Fri.-Sat., 4pm-10pm Sun., $25 and up), a favorite among Seattleites and visitors alike. American-Italian-style cooking is served for lunch and dinner.

Once one of Seattle's best-kept secrets, **Volunteer Park Café** (1501 17th Ave. E, 206/328-3155, http://alwaysfreshgoodness. com, 7am-4:30pm and 5:30pm-9pm Tues.-Fri., 8am-4:30pm and 5:30pm-9pm Sat., 8am-4:30pm Sun., $12 and up) has been "discovered" and is now a favorite of many. Serving farm-fresh American cuisine for breakfast, lunch, and dinner, all made with local and seasonal ingredients from the Pacific Northwest, the café serves up meals that build community around the dinner table.

ACCOMMODATIONS

Seattle's lodging choices cover the spectrum from basic hostels all the way up to five-star hotels. The **Seattle Bed & Breakfast Association** (206/547-1020, www.lodginginseattle.com) includes 14 comfortable and friendly places to stay around Seattle, and online sites such as **Airbnb** (www.airbnb. com) or **VRBO** (www.vrbo.com) provide hundreds more lodging options, from basic apartment units to sumptuous Lake Union houseboats.

Downtown

Backpacking travelers willing to sleep in a bunk bed should check out the **Green Tortoise Hostel** (105 Pike St., 206/340-1222, www.greentortoise.net, $36/person). Each bed has a storage locker and privacy curtain, with a bathroom down the hall, kitchen access, luggage storage, and Wi-Fi. Bike rentals are available.

Just a short walk from Pike Place Market, **Mayflower Park** (405 Olive Way, 206/623-8700 or 800/426-5100, www.mayflowerpark. com, $259-289 d) is a good downtown option.

Quaint **Pensione Nichols B&B** (1923 1st Ave., 206/441-7125, www.pensionenichols. com, $180-220 d including breakfast) occupies a century-old building in a great location close to Pike Place. It's a European-style place with small rooms and shared baths.

A fine downtown place is **Best Western Plus Pioneer Square Hotel** (77 Yesler Way, 206/340-1234, www.bestwestern.com, $329 d).

Three elegant high-end places are **Inn at the Market** (86 Pine St., 206/443-3600 or 800/446-4484, www.innatthemarket.com, $325-485 d), **Four Seasons Hotel Seattle** (99 Union St., 206/749-7000, www.fourseasons.com, $700-1,400 d), and **Hotel 1000** (1000 1st Ave., 206/957-1000 or 877/315-1088, www.hotel1000seattle.com, $655-755 d).

Seattle's only waterfront hotel, **The Edgewater** (2411 Alaskan Way, 206/728-7000 or 800/624-0670, www.edgewaterhotel. com, $227-455 d), is on Pier 67, close to the departure point for Clipper Vacations ferries to Victoria and the San Juans.

North of Downtown

Two recommended hotels near the Space Needle and within walking distance of downtown are **Mediterranean Inn** (425 Queen Anne Ave., 206/428-4700, www.mediterranean-inn.com, $259 d) and **The Loyal Inn** (2301 8th Ave., 206/682-0200, www.loyalinn. com, $309-319 d). **MarQueen Hotel** (600 Queen Anne Ave. N., 206/282-7407, www. marqueen.com, $219 d) is a charming boutique hotel at a great location in the Queen Anne District north of the Space Needle.

If you have a car, good options include three University District places: **University Inn** (4140 Roosevelt Way NE, 206/632-5055 or 866/866-7977, www.universityinnseattle.com, $199-269 d), **University Motel Suites** (4731 12th Ave. NE, 206/522-4724, www.universitymotelsuites.com, $150-155 d), and the luxurious **Hotel Deca** (4507 Brooklyn Ave., NE, 206/634-2000, www.hoteldeca.com, $389 d).

Nexus Hotel (2140 N. Northgate Way, 206/365-0700 or 800/435-0754, www.hotelnexusseattle.com, $188 d) is in north Seattle off I-5.

Near the Airport

Sea-Tac International Airport is a dozen miles south from downtown Seattle in the gritty city of Tukwila, where the main drag—International Boulevard—is lined with chain hotels, fast-food joints, airporter parking lots, gas stations, and quickie marts. If you can tolerate the neighborhood, or have an early flight, this may be your best lodging option.

For airport lodging that won't break the bank, try **Sleep Inn SeaTac Airport** (20406 International Blvd., 206/878-3600, www.choicehotels.com, $179 d), **Best Western Seattle Airport Hotel** (20717 International Blvd., 206/878-3300, www.bestwestern.com, $189-199 d), **Days Inn Seatac Airport** (19015 International Blvd., 206/244-3600, www.wyndhamhotels.com, $110-118 d), or **Holiday Inn Express Seattle SeaTac Airport** (19621 International Blvd., 206/824-3200, www.ihg.com, $177-211 d).

INFORMATION

The **Seattle Convention and Visitors Bureau** (7th Ave. at Pike St., 206/461-5800 or 866/732-2695, www.visitseattle.org) stocks the *Visit Seattle*, a fat compendium of local entertainment, shopping, and sights. Also check out the CVB's useful lodging and restaurant guides. The **Market Information Center** (10am-6pm daily) in the southwest corner of Pike Place Market has additional local info. Sea-Tac Airport has a small information center with the usual blizzard of brochures and freebie papers. It's near the baggage claim area.

Located inside the REI store at 222 Yale Avenue N, the **Ranger Station** (206/470-4060 or 800/270-7504, www.discovernw.org) has details on natural areas around the state, including National Park Service, U.S. Forest Service, Washington State Parks, and Department of Natural Resources lands.

Useful websites for Seattle information include the **City of Seattle**'s official website (www.seattle.gov), Microsoft's **Citysearch** site (www.seattle.citysearch.com), and those of local newspapers: *Seattle Times* (www.seattletimes.com) and *Seattle Weekly* (www.seattleweekly.com).

GETTING THERE AND AROUND
Air

Seattle's airport is 12 miles south of the city and midway between Seattle and Tacoma, hence the name **Sea-Tac International Airport** (www.portseattle.org/seatac). It's the primary entry point for flights into Washington State, but there are no direct flights from Sea-Tac to the San Juan Islands; you'll need to go to either Lake Union or Boeing Field in Seattle. The airport has undergone a significant upgrade in the last few years and is a pleasant place to spend a couple of hours in transit. The central terminal has enormous windows facing the runways and a good selection of reasonably priced dining choices.

All major domestic, and many international, airlines operate out of Sea-Tac, and foreign travelers can change money in the main terminal. A **Visitor Information Booth** (open daily May-Sept., brochures available anytime) is close to the baggage claim area. Most major national car rental companies operate from the new **Sea-Tac Rental Car Facility,** a five-minute shuttle ride from the airport. Catch a free shuttle from outside the baggage claims area.

The fastest and least expensive way to reach downtown Seattle from the airport—just $3—is aboard a **Link Light Rail Train,** operated by Sound Transit (206/398-5000 or 800/201-4900, www.soundtransit.org). These trains run every 6 to 15 minutes daily 6am-11pm and take you directly to Pioneer Square, University Street, and Westlake (near Pike Place Market) downtown, and then continue to Capitol Hill and the University of Washington. City buses provide connections to other parts of Seattle.

The islands are served by **Kenmore Air** (425/486-1257 or 866/435-9524, www.kenmoreair.com)—the world's largest seaplane operation—with flights to San Juan, Orcas, and Lopez Islands from Seattle's Lake Union.

Pack light for your trip; a 25-pound baggage weight limit is in effect, with a charge for excess baggage. A free shuttle provides transport to Lake Union from Sea-Tac. Wheeled-plane flights to San Juan and Orcas Islands depart from Boeing Field (www.kingcounty.gov) on the south end of Seattle; the baggage weight limit on these is 70 pounds. Kenmore also offers flightseeing trips and charters to other destinations in the San Juans, including Cypress, Sucia, Stuart, and Jones Islands. A shuttle van is available between Sea-Tac and Lake Union ($15) or Boeing Field ($10).

Charter flights to the San Juans can be cheaper than scheduled flights if you have four or more passengers. **San Juan Airlines** (360/293-4691 or 800/874-4434, www.sanjua-nairlines.com) and **Island Air** (360/378-2376 or 888/378-2376, www.sanjuan-islandair.com) provide charter flights from Boeing Field.

Ferries

You will see a constant parade of Washington State Ferries departing from downtown Seattle, but none of these go to the San Juans. Instead, you'll need to get to Anacortes, where state ferries head to the islands. There is, however, a private ferry with daily service to the islands from Seattle: the passenger-only *Victoria Clipper* (2701 Alaskan Way, Pier 69, 206/448-5000 or 800/888-2535, www.clippervacations.com), a family of three large high-speed catamarans with day trips between Seattle and San Juan Island. Rates vary with a convoluted schedule, including discounts on weekdays and if you book at least a day ahead. Adults pay $81-98 round-trip and kids are $41-49. Combine transportation from Seattle with a 2.5-hour whale-watching trip for $25-30 extra. The company has a multitude of other travel options in the Northwest, including packages that add a night's lodging on San Juan Island, or a three-day/two-night visit to San Juan Island and Victoria. You can also use this as transportation to the islands from Seattle, traveling north one day and returning later. In addition, *Victoria Clipper* has year-round service between Seattle and Victoria for $154 round-trip (less if purchased in advance).

Shuttles

Airporter Shuttle (360/380-8800 or 866/235-5247, www.airporter.com, $76 one-way adults, $65 kids) makes connections between Sea-Tac and the ferry terminal at Anacortes, along with Bellingham and points north all the way to Vancouver.

Island Airporter (360/378-7438, www.is-landairporter.com) provides direct van service daily from Sea-Tac to San Juan Island. The bus departs the airport and heads straight to the Anacortes ferry, where it drives on for San Juan Island, and then continues to Friday Harbor ($50) and Roche Harbor ($57). You'll need to add the ferry fare ($13), but it's approximately half the standard rate because you're on a bus. Vans operate once a day in each direction Monday-Saturday in summer and Monday-Friday in winter.

Train and Bus

King County Metro (http://metro.kingcounty. gov)—better known as simply **Metro**—is Seattle's public transit system, with a mix of buses, light-rail, and streetcars. The Link Light Rail system is particularly traveler friendly, with fast and frequent service connecting Sea-Tac with downtown and other neighborhoods. Buses cost $2.50 adults, $1.50 ages 6-18, or $1 seniors.

Amtrak trains serve Seattle from the King Street Station (3rd Ave. S. and S. King St., 206/464-1930 or 800/872-7245, www.amtrak-cascades.com). The Amtrak *Cascades* train connects Seattle with Vancouver, stopping at Mount Vernon twice daily in each direction. Trains do not stop in Anacortes (where Washington State Ferries depart for the San Juan Islands), and the Mount Vernon station is 18 miles away.

Greyhound (206/628-5526 or 800/231-2222, www.greyhound.com) has daily bus service throughout the Lower 48 and to Vancouver, British Columbia, from its bus terminal at 9th and Stewart. It's the same story here as for Amtrak; Greyhound's closest stop is the town of Mount Vernon, 18 miles from the ferry terminal in Anacortes.

BoltBus (877/265-8287, www.boltbus. com) travels the I-5 corridor from Seattle north to Bellingham and Vancouver, and south to Portland. Fares are reasonable and the buses all have Wi-Fi, reserved seating, and ample legroom.

SeaTac Direct (360/733-3666, www.seatacdirect.com) has bus connections between SeaTac and Bellingham three times a day for $50 one-way with a four-person minimum.

Car

Sea-Tac International Airport has all the national car rental companies. If you're driving from Seattle, it's 81 miles (94 miles from Sea-Tac) to Anacortes, where you catch the Washington State Ferries to the San Juans. The ride is straightforward: follow I-5 north to Mount Vernon at Exit 230 and then turn west onto Highway 20, which goes straight into Anacortes. The ferry terminal is three miles west of downtown Anacortes via 12th Street.

Alternatively, you can take the more **scenic** route to Anacortes via Whidbey Island. For this option, drive on I-5 north to Exit 182 and follow State Highway 525 (Mukilteo Speedway) to the Mukilteo ferry terminal, where you catch the state ferry to Whidbey Island. Once on Whidbey, it's 57 miles to Anacortes. The total distance from Seattle to Anacortes via this route is almost the same (83 miles from Seattle or 97 miles from Sea-Tac), but the trip takes considerably longer and costs more because of the ferry ride. The chance to explore beautiful Whidbey Island easily makes the longer route worth your time.

Be sure to **fill your tank in Anacortes** before driving on the ferry. Because of the extra cost of shipping fuel (and because they can get away with it), gas stations on the islands charge at least 30 percent more than on the mainland.

Smart cars are a great way to get around Seattle if you don't have a rental vehicle. **Car2Go** (www.car2go.com) has cute two-seat vehicles all over the city. Find one on the street or with the Car2Go app, and use your smart phone to unlock the car and pay by the minute. There's no charge for parking; just find a place with on-street parking to end your ride.

Victoria

Most people first see the city of Victoria, British Columbia, from the Inner Harbour as they arrive by boat, the way people have done for almost 150 years. Ferries, fishing boats, and seaplanes bob in the harbor, with a backdrop of manicured lawns, flower gardens, and striking urban architecture. Despite the pressures that go with city life, easygoing Victorians still find time for a stroll along the waterfront, a round of golf, or a night out at a fine-dining restaurant. Discovering Victoria's English roots has been a longtime favorite with visitors: High tea, double-decker bus tours, and exploring formal gardens remain some of the city's true joys.

SIGHTS

The epicenter of downtown Victoria is the Inner Harbour, which is flanked by the parliament buildings, the city's main museum, and the landmark Fairmont Empress Hotel. Government Street leads uphill from the waterfront through a concentration of shops and restaurants while, parallel to the west, Douglas Street is the core of a small central business district.

Inner Harbour

Initially, the harbor extended farther inland; before the construction of the massive stone causeway that now forms the marina, the area on which the impressive Empress Hotel now stands was a deep, oozing mudflat. Walk along the lower level and then up the steps in the middle to come face-to-face with an unamused Captain James Cook; the bronze statue commemorates the first recorded British landing in 1778. Above the northeast corner of the harbor is the **Victoria Visitor Centre** (812 Wharf St., 250/953-2033, www.tourismvictoria.com), the perfect place to start your city exploration. Be sure to return to the Inner Harbour after dark, when the parliament buildings are outlined in lights and the Empress is floodlit.

FAIRMONT EMPRESS
Overlooking the Inner Harbour, the ivy-covered 1908 **Fairmont Empress** (721 Government St., 250/384-8111 or 800/257-7544, www.fairmont.com) is Victoria's most recognizable landmark. Its architect was Francis Rattenbury, who also designed the parliament buildings and Crystal Garden. It's worthwhile walking through the hotel lobby to gaze at the interior razzle-dazzle or partake in traditional afternoon tea. Browse through the conservatory and gift shops, drool over the menus of the various restaurants, see what tours are available, and exchange currency if you're desperate (banks give a better exchange rate). Get a feeling for the hotel's history by joining a tour.

★ ROYAL BRITISH COLUMBIA MUSEUM
Canada's most-visited museum and easily one of North America's best, the **Royal British Columbia Museum** (675 Belleville St., 250/356-7226, http://royalbcmuseum.bc.ca, 10am-5pm daily, CAN$24 adults, CAN$17 seniors and youth) is a must for even the most jaded museum-goer. Its fine *Natural History* galleries are extraordinarily true to life, complete with appropriate sounds and smells. Come face-to-face with an ice age woolly mammoth, stroll through a coastal forest full of deer and tweeting birds, meander along a seashore or tidal marsh, and then descend into the *Open Ocean* exhibit via submarine—a real trip not recommended for claustrophobics. The *First Peoples* galleries hold a fine collection of artifacts from the island's first human inhabitants, the Nuu-chah-nulth (Nootka). Take a tour through time via the time capsules; walk along an early-1900s street; and experience hands-on exhibits on industrialization and the gold rush. The museum's **theater** (9am-8pm daily, additional charge) shows nature-oriented IMAX films.

Victoria's Inner Harbour

PARLIAMENT BUILDINGS

Satisfy your lust for governmental, historical, and architectural knowledge all in one by taking a free tour of the harborside **Provincial Legislative Buildings,** aka the parliament buildings, designed by Francis Rattenbury and completed in 1897. The exterior is British Columbia Haddington Island stone, and if you walk around the buildings you'll no doubt spot many a stern or gruesome face staring down from the stonework.

On either side of the main entrance stand statues of Sir James Douglas, who chose the location of Victoria, and Sir Matthew Baillie Begbie, who was in charge of law and order during the gold rush period. Atop the copper-covered dome stands a gilded statue of Captain George Vancouver, the first mariner to circumnavigate Vancouver Island. Walk through the main entrance and into the memorial rotunda, look skyward for a dramatic view of the central dome, and then continue upstairs to peer into the legislative chamber. Free guided tours are offered every 20 minutes, 9am-noon and 1pm-5pm daily in summer, less frequently (Mon.-Fri. only) in winter. Tour times differ according to the goings-on inside; for current times, call the **tour office** at 250/387-3046.

ROBERT BATEMAN CENTRE

Along the waterfront on Belleville Street, across the road from the parliament buildings, is the ornate former Canadian Pacific Railway steamship terminal, now the **Robert Bateman Centre** (470 Belleville St., 250/940-3630, http://batemancentre. org, 10am-6pm Sun.-Wed. and 10am-9pm Thurs.-Fri. in summer, 10am-5pm Tues.-Sun. the rest of the year, CAN$12.50 adults, CAN$8.50 seniors and students). Renowned as one of the world's greatest wildlife artists, Bateman resides on nearby Salt Spring Island. Each themed gallery is dedicated to a different subject—British Columbia and Africa are the highlights. Another gallery is dedicated to children and includes a hand-on nature learning area.

LAUREL POINT

For an enjoyable short walk from downtown, continue along Belleville Street from the parliament buildings, passing a conglomeration of modern hotels, ferry terminals, and intriguing architecture dating back to the late 19th century. A path leads down through a shady park to Laurel Point, hugging the waterfront and providing good views. If you're feeling energetic, continue to **Fisherman's Wharf,** where an eclectic array of floating homes are tied up to floating wharves.

Old Town

The oldest section of Victoria lies immediately north of the Inner Harbour between Wharf and Government Streets. Start by walking north from the Inner Harbour along historical Wharf Street, where Hudson's Bay Company furs were loaded onto ships bound for England, gold seekers arrived in search of fortune, and shopkeepers first established businesses. Cross the road to cobblestoned **Bastion Square,** lined with old gas lamps and decorative architecture dating from the late 1800s. This was the original site chosen by James Douglas in 1843 for Fort Victoria, the Hudson's Bay Company trading post. At one time the square held a courthouse, jail, and gallows. Today, restored buildings house touristy restaurants, cafés, nightclubs, and fashionable offices.

MARITIME MUSEUM OF BRITISH COLUMBIA

At the top (east) end of Bastion Square, the **Maritime Museum of British Columbia** (28 Bastion Sq., 250/385-4222, www.mmbc. bc.ca, 10am-4pm daily, until 5pm in summer, CAN$10 adults, CAN$8 seniors, children under 13 free) traces the history of seafaring exploration, commercial ventures, and passenger travel through displays of dugout canoes, model ships, Royal Navy charts, figureheads, photographs, naval uniforms, and bells. One room is devoted to exhibits chronicling the circumnavigation of the world, and another holds a theater.

Greater Victoria

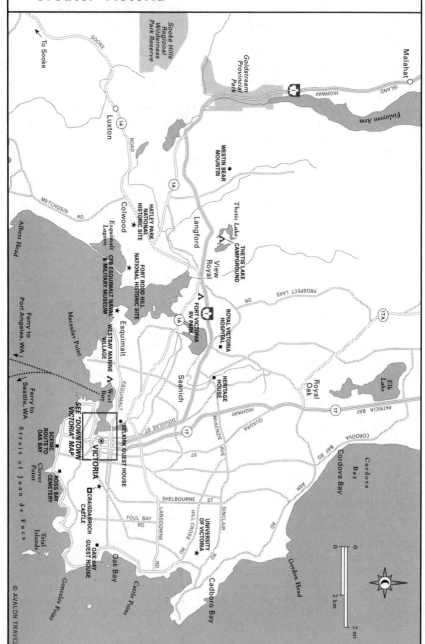

© AVALON TRAVEL

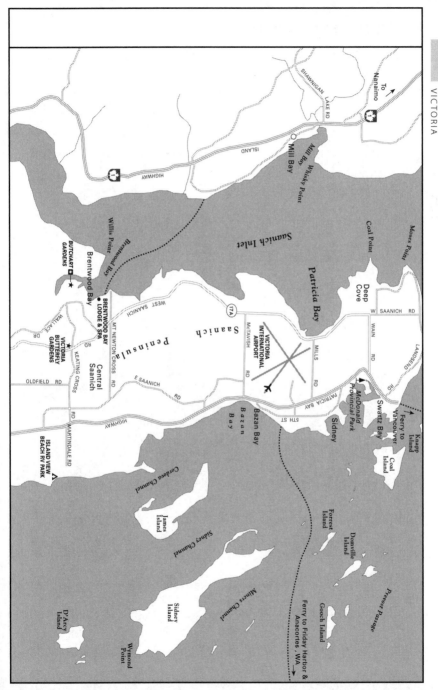

Downtown Victoria

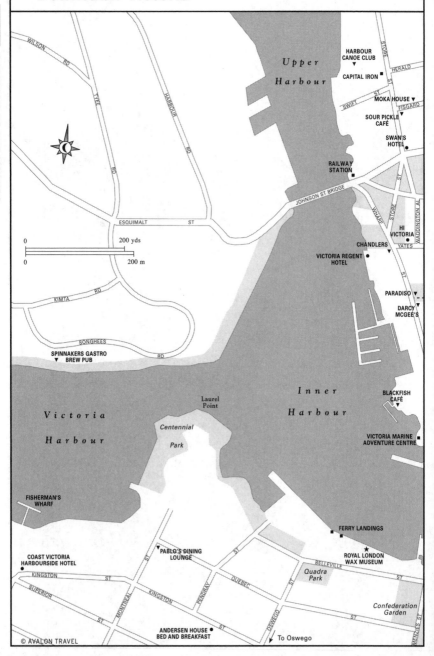

Upper Harbour

HARBOUR CANOE CLUB

CAPITAL IRON

MOKA HOUSE ▼

SOUR PICKLE CAFÉ

SWAN'S HOTEL

RAILWAY STATION

WILSON RD

TYEE RD

HARBOUR RD

ESQUIMALT ST

JOHNSON ST BRIDGE

STORE ST

HERALD

SWIFT ST

FISGARD

HI VICTORIA

CHANDLERS

VICTORIA REGENT HOTEL

PARADISO ▼

DARCY MCGEE'S

STORE ST

WHARF ST

YATES

WADDINGTON AL

KIMTA RD

SONGHEES RD

SPINNAKERS GASTRO ▼ BREW PUB

0   200 yds
0   200 m

Victoria Harbour

Laurel Point

Centennial Park

Inner Harbour

BLACKFISH CAFÉ ▼

VICTORIA MARINE ADVENTURE CENTRE

FISHERMAN'S WHARF

COAST VICTORIA HARBOURSIDE HOTEL

KINGSTON ST

SUPERIOR ST

MONTREAL ST

KINGSTON

PENDRAY ST

PABLO'S DINING LOUNGE

QUEBEC

OSWEGO ST

BELLEVILLE

Quadra Park

FERRY LANDINGS

ROYAL LONDON WAX MUSEUM ★

Confederation Garden

MENZIES ST

ANDERSEN HOUSE BED AND BREAKFAST ●

↓ To Oswego

© AVALON TRAVEL

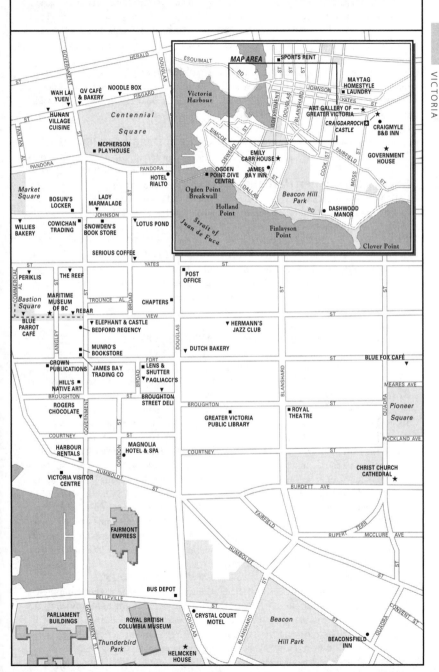

CENTENNIAL SQUARE

Centennial Square, bounded by Government Street, Douglas Street, Pandora Avenue, and Fisgard Street, is lined with many buildings dating from the 1880s and 1890s, refurbished in recent times for all to appreciate. Don't miss the 1878 **City Hall** (fronting Douglas Street) and the imposing Greek-style building of the Hudson's Bay Company. In the heart of Centennial Square is **Spirit Square,** dedicated to First Nations people, where you'll find totem poles and a garden.

South of the Inner Harbour
EMILY CARR HOUSE

In 1871 artist Emily Carr was born in this upper-class Victorian-era home, which now hosts visitors as the **Emily Carr House** (207 Government St., 250/383-5843, www.emily-carr.com, 11am-4pm Tues.-Sat. May-Sept., CAN$7 adults, CAN$6 seniors and students, CAN$4.50 children). Carr moved to the mainland at an early age, escaping the confines of the capital to draw and write about the First Nations people and the wilderness in which she lived. She is best remembered today for her painting, a medium she took up in later years.

BEACON HILL PARK

Known to Coast Salish as Meeacan (a First Nations word for "belly"), for its resemblance to a man lying on his back, this large tract of land immediately south of downtown was protected as parkland in 1882. Today the 25-hectare (62-acre) park is an oasis that extends from the back of the Royal BC Museum along Douglas Street out to cliffs that offer spectacular views of the Strait of Juan de Fuca and, on a clear day, the distant Olympic Mountains.

The park is geographically divided in two by Dallas Road. On the downtown side of the road are landscaped gardens protected by grand Garry oak trees, along with tennis courts, bowling greens, playgrounds, mini-golf, bird-filled ponds, and even a cricket pitch.

Beacon Hill Childrens Farm (Circle Dr., 250/381-2532, www.beaconhillchildrensfarm.ca, 10am-4pm April-Oct., CAN$3.50 adults, CAN$2.50 children) is home to chickens, pigs, donkeys, and goats. Peacocks run free through the surrounding greenery.

Rockland

This historical part of downtown lies behind the Inner Harbour, east of Douglas Street, and is easily accessible on foot.

CHRIST CHURCH CATHEDRAL

On the corner of Quadra and Courtney Streets, **Christ Church Cathedral** (250/383-2714) is the seat of the Bishop of the Diocese of British Columbia. Built in 1896 in 13th-century Gothic style, it's one of Canada's largest churches. Self-guided tours are possible (8:30am-5pm Mon.-Fri. and 7:30am-8:30pm Sun., free). In summer, the cathedral sponsors free choral recitals each Saturday at 4pm. The park next to the cathedral is a shady haven to rest weary feet, and the gravestones make fascinating reading.

ART GALLERY OF GREATER VICTORIA

From Christ Church Cathedral, walk up Rockland Avenue for four blocks through the Rockland district, passing stately mansions and colorful gardens. Turn left on Moss Street and you'll come to the 1889 Spencer Mansion and its modern wing, which together make up the **Art Gallery of Greater Victoria** (1040 Moss St., 250/384-4101, www.aggv.ca, 10am-5pm daily, until 9pm Thurs., CAN$13 adults, CAN$11 seniors, CAN$2.50 children). The gallery contains Canada's finest collection of Japanese art, a range of contemporary art, an Emily Carr gallery, and traveling exhibits, as well as a Japanese garden with a Shinto shrine.

GOVERNMENT HOUSE

Continue up Rockland Avenue from the art gallery to reach **Government House,** the official residence of the lieutenant governor, the queen's representative in British Columbia. Open to the public throughout the year are an English-style garden, rose garden, and rhododendron garden, along with green velvety lawns and picture-perfect flower beds. On the front side of the property, vegetation has been left in a more natural state, with gravel paths leading to inviting benches with city views.

★ CRAIGDARROCH CASTLE

A short walk up (east) from the art gallery along Rockland Avenue and left on Joan Crescent brings you to the baronial four-story mansion known as **Craigdarroch Castle** (1050 Joan Cres., 250/592-5323, http://thecastle.ca, 9am-7pm daily in summer, 10am-4:30pm daily the rest of the year, CAN$14 adults, CAN$13 seniors, CAN$5 children). From downtown take bus 11 (Uplands) or 14 (University) to Joan Crescent, then walk 100 meters (110 yards) up the hill. The architectural masterpiece was built in 1890 for Robert Dunsmuir, a wealthy industrialist and politician who died just before the building was completed. Tour the mansion with volunteer guides, admiring the polished wood, stained glass windows, Victorian-era furnishings, and city views from upstairs.

Scenic Route to Oak Bay

This driving route starts south of the Inner Harbour and follows the coastline of the Strait of Juan de Fuca all the way to the University of Victoria. Allow around one hour to reach the university, but allow at least half a day if you plan on multiple stops. If you don't have your own transportation, most city tours take in the sights along the route.

You can take Douglas Street south alongside Beacon Hill Park to access the Strait of Juan de Fuca, but it's best to continue east along the Inner Harbour to the mouth of Victoria Harbour proper along Belleville and then Kingston Street to **Ogden Point Breakwall,** the official starting point of the scenic drive (marked by small blue signs). The breakwall is only 3 meters (10 feet) wide, but it extends for 800 meters (0.5 mile) into the strait. It's a popular place for a stroll, especially in the early morning.

For the first few kilometers beyond the breakwater, the Olympic Mountains are clearly visible across the Strait of Juan de Fuca, and a string of roadside lookouts allow you to stop and take in the panorama, including **Clover Point.** East beyond Clover Point, **Ross Bay Cemetery** is the final resting place of many of early Victoria's most prominent residents. including artist Emily Carr; British Columbia's first governor, Sir James Douglas; members of the coal-baron Dunsmuir family; and Billy Barker, of gold rush fame. The gates are open weekdays during daylight hours.

Continue through the well-manicured fairways of Victoria Golf Club on Gonzales Point to Cadboro Bay, home to the **Royal Victoria Yacht Club.** The **University of Victoria** lies on a ridge above Cadboro Bay; from here head southwest along Cadboro Bay Road and then Yates Street to get back downtown, or to go north take Sinclair Road and then Mackenzie Avenue to reach Highway 17, the main route north up the Saanich Peninsula toward famous Butchart Gardens.

Goldstream Provincial Park

Lying 20 kilometers (12 miles) from the heart of Victoria, this 390-hectare (960-acre) park straddles the TransCanada Highway northwest of downtown on its loop around the south end of Saanich Inlet. The park's most distinctive natural feature is the Goldstream River, which flows north into the Finlayson Arm of Saanich Inlet. Forests of ancient Douglas fir and western red cedar flank the river; orchids flourish in forested glades; and at higher elevations forests of lodgepole pine, western hemlock, and maple thrive. From late October through December, **salmon** fight their way upriver through the park to spawn on the same shallow gravel bars where they themselves were born. **Bald eagles** arrive in December, feeding off the salmon until February.

To reach the excellent **Freeman King Visitor Centre** (250/478-9414, www.goldstreampark.com, 9am-4:30pm daily, free), look for the parking lot on the east side of the TransCanada Highway 2 kilometers (1.2 miles) north of the campground turnoff. From the main parking area, the center is an easy 400-meter (440-yard) walk along a forested trail.

Saanich Peninsula

The Saanich Peninsula is the finger of land that extends north from downtown. It holds Victoria's most famous attraction, Butchart Gardens, as well as Victoria International Airport and the main arrival point for ferries from Tsawwassen. If you've caught the ferry over to Vancouver Island from Tsawwassen, you'll have arrived at **Swartz Bay,** on the northern tip of the Saanich Peninsula; from here it's a clear run down Highway 17 to downtown Victoria and the waterfront town of Sidney. If you're coming from Goldstream Provincial Park, head north, or from Nanaimo on Highway 1, head south, to reach **Mill Bay,** where a ferry departs regularly for **Brentwood Bay** on the Saanich Peninsula. (Brentwood Bay is home to Butchart Gardens.) Ferries run in both directions nine times daily; for details, contact **BC Ferries** (250/386-3431, www.bcferries.com).

★ BUTCHART GARDENS

Carved from an abandoned quarry, the delightful **Butchart Gardens** (800 Benvenuto Dr., Brentwood Bay, 250/652-4422, www.butchartgardens.com) are Victoria's best-known attraction. They're approximately 20 kilometers (12.4 miles) north of downtown. The gardens are open every day of the year from 9am, closing in summer at 10pm and in winter at 4pm, with varying closing hours in other seasons. Admission in summer is CAN$32 for adults, CAN$16 for youth aged 13-17, and CAN$3 for children aged 5-12; admission in winter is around 60 percent of those rates.

A Canadian cement pioneer, R. P. Butchart, built a mansion near his quarries. He and his wife, Jennie, traveled extensively, collecting rare and exotic shrubs, trees, and plants from around the world. By 1904 the quarries had been abandoned, and the couple began to beautify them by transplanting their collection into formal gardens interspersed with concrete footpaths, small bridges, waterfalls, ponds, and fountains. The gardens now contain more than 5,000 varieties of flowers, and the extensive test nurseries grow some 35,000 new bulbs and more than 100 new roses every year. Go there in spring, summer, or early autumn to treat your eyes and nose to a marvelous sensual experience (many gardeners would give their right hands to be able to work in these gardens). Highlights include the Sunken Garden (the original quarry site) with its water features and annuals; the formal Rose Garden, set around a central lawn; and the Japanese Garden, from where views extend to Saanich Inlet. In winter when little is blooming, the basic design of the gardens can best be appreciated. Summer visitors are in for a special treat on Saturday nights (July and August only), when spectacular fireworks light up the garden.

As you may imagine, the attraction is busy throughout spring and summer. Try to arrive as early as possible, before the tour buses. On the grounds, pick up a flower guide and follow the suggested route (allow at least two hours). Afterward, choose from a variety of eateries and browse the gift shop, which specializes in—you guessed it—floral items.

VICTORIA BUTTERFLY GARDENS

Near Butchart Gardens, **Victoria Butterfly Gardens** (1461 Benvenuto Dr., 250/652-3822, www.butterflygardens.com, 9am-7pm daily in summer, 9:30am-4:30pm daily Mar. to mid-May and Oct., CAN$17 adults, CAN$11 seniors, CAN$6 children) offers the chance to view and photograph spectacular butterflies at close range. Thousands of butterflies, encompassing species from around the world, live here, flying freely around the enclosed gardens and feeding on the nectar provided by colorful tropical plants. You can also get up close and personal with exotic birds such as parrots and cockatoos.

TOURS

Throughout the day and into the evening, **Victoria Carriage Tours** (250/383-2207 or 877/663-2207, www.victoriacarriage.com) line up along Menzies Street at Belleville Street awaiting passengers. A 30-minute tour around the downtown waterfront precinct costs CAN$100 per carriage (seating up to six people), a 45-minute tour costs CAN$145, or take a 60-minute Royal Tour for CAN$185. Tours run 9am-midnight in summer and bookings aren't necessary, though there's often a line.

Double-decker **bus tours** are operated by **Gray Line** (250/744-3566 or 800/663-8390, www.grayline.com) from beside the Inner Harbour. To get oriented while also learning some city history, take the 90-minute Grand City Drive Tour. It departs from the harbor front every half hour 9:30am-4pm (CAN$28 adults, CAN$17 children). There's also a tour to Butchart Gardens (CAN$56, including garden admission).

Victoria Harbour Ferry (250/708-0201, www.victoriaharbourferry.com) offers tours of the harbor and Gorge Waterway. Boats seat around 20 passengers and depart regularly 9am-8:15pm from below the Empress Hotel. The 45-minute loop tour allows passengers the chance to get on and off at will;

tickets are CAN$26 per adult, CAN$24 per senior, CAN$14 per child. Or travel just pieces of the entire loop for CAN$5-10 (adult ticket) per sector.

Whale-watching tours depart from the Inner Harbour; operators include **Orca Spirit Adventures** (250/383-8411 or 888/672-6722, www.orcaspirit.com) and **Prince of Whales** (250/383-4884 or 888/383-4884, www.princeofwhales.com). Whales can be sighted mid-April to October, along with sea lions, porpoises, and seals. Trips last 2-3 hours, are generally made in sturdy inflatable boats with an onboard naturalist, and cost CAN$90-110 per person.

SHOPPING

Victoria is a shopper's delight. In the Inner Harbour, **Government and Douglas Streets** form the main strip of tourist and gift shops.

Farther up Government Street from the harbor are more stylish shops, such as **James Bay Trading Co.** (1102 Government St., 250/388-5477, 9am-7pm daily), which specializes in First Nations art and crafts from the island's coastal communities. Also recommended is **Hill's Native Art** (1008 Government St., 250/385-3911, www.hills.ca,

Victoria Harbour Ferry

9am-7pm daily), selling a wide range of authentic First Nations souvenirs including original prints, Inuit carvings, totem poles, and jewelry. **Munro's Books** (1108 Government St., 250/382-2464 or 888/243-2464, www.munrobooks.com, 9am-9pm Mon.-Sat., 9:30am-6pm Sun.), in a magnificent neoclassical building, holds a comprehensive collection of fiction and nonfiction. The largest bookstore in town is **Chapters** (1212 Douglas St., 250/380-9009, www.chapters.indigo.ca, 8am-11pm Mon.-Sat., 9am-11pm Sun.). **Cowichan Trading** (1328 Government St., 250/383-0321, www.cowichantrading.com, 9am-6pm daily) specializes in Cowichan sweaters and other products hand-knitted by the Cowichan people of Vancouver Island. Traditions also continue at **Rogers Chocolates** (913 Government St., 250/881-8771, www.rogerschocolates.com), which is set up like a candy store of the early 1900s, when Charles Rogers first began selling his homemade chocolates to the local kids.

Linking Broad and Government Streets (near View Street), the cobblestoned **Trounce Alley** is off most visitors' radars, but it's worth searching out for the spiritual gifts at Instinct Art & Gifts and the 1862 W&J Wilson men's clothing store. Cross under the arch across Fisgard Street and enter Chinatown, with vendors selling produce and Asian curios, and then wander down **Fan Tan Alley,** Canada's narrowest street, and through an eclectic array of shops and boutiques.

Fort Street between Cook and Quadra Streets has been branded **Mosaic Village** in recognition of the wide variety of local merchants in the area—antique shops, art galleries, clothing boutiques, and cooking supply stores. Most shops and all major department stores are generally open 9:30am-5:30pm Monday-Saturday and stay open for late-night shopping Thursday and Friday nights until 9pm.

In Old Town, colorful, two-story **Market Square** was once the haunt of sailors, sealers, and whalers, who came ashore looking for booze and brothels. It's been jazzed up, and today shops here specialize in everything from kayaks to condoms.

Throughout summer, local artisans sell their wares at the **Bastion Square Public Market** (11am-5:30pm Thurs.-Sat.).

NIGHTLIFE

Most of Victoria's nightclubs double as live music venues attracting a great variety of acts. **Club 9one9,** in the Strathcona Hotel (919 Douglas St., 250/383-7137), has been a city hot spot for more than 30 years. It comes alive with live rock-and-roll some nights and a DJ spinning the latest dance tunes on other nights. In the same hotel, **Big Bad John's** is the city's main country music venue. At the bottom of Bastion Square, **Darcy's Pub** (1127 Wharf St., 250/380-1322) is a great place for lunch or an afternoon drink, but after dark it dishes up live rock to a working-class crowd.

Victoria boasts several good jazz venues. The best of these is **Hermann's Jazz Club** (753 View St., 250/388-9166, www.hermannsjaxzz.com, Wed.-Sat.). Check the **Victoria Jazz Society website** (www.jazzvictoria.ca) for a schedule of local jazz performances.

FESTIVALS

Queen Victoria's birthday has been celebrated in Canada since 1834 and is especially relevant to her namesake city. The Inner Harbour is alive with weekend festivities that culminate in the **Victoria Day Parade** (downtown, Mon. preceding May 25). The parade takes two hours to pass a single spot. (Although Queen Victoria's actual birthday was May 24, the event is celebrated with a public holiday on the Monday preceding May 25.)

At **Victoria Jazzfest International** (downtown, 250/388-4423, www.jazzvictoria.ca, last week of June), more than 300 musicians from around the world descend on the city for this weeklong celebration at various venues.

At **Symphony Splash** (Inner Harbour, 250/385-9771, www.victoriasymphony.ca, first Sun. in Aug.), the local symphony orchestra performs from a barge moored in the Inner Harbour to masses crowded around the shore. This unique musical event attracts upwards of 40,000 spectators who line the shore or watch from kayaks.

The water comes alive during the **Victoria Dragon Boat Festival** (Inner Harbour, 250/704-2500, www.victoriadragonboat.com, middle weekend of Aug.), with 90 dragon boat teams competing along a short course stretching across the Inner Harbour. Onshore entertainment includes the Forbidden City Food Court, classical music performances, First Nations dancing, and lots of children's events.

The **Victoria Fringe Theatre Festival** (throughout the city, 250/383-2663, www. victoriafringe.com, last week of Aug.) is a celebration of alternative theater, with more than 350 acts performing at venues throughout the city, including outside along the harbor foreshore and inside at the Conservatory of Music on Pandora Street. All tickets are around CAN$12-18.

Tourism Victoria (www.tourismvictoria. com) has an easy-to-navigate event schedule for the entire year.

FOOD

Although Victoria has traditionally been associated with quaint tea rooms dotted around the suburbs, today's chefs favor produce organically grown and sourced from island farms. Locally sourced seafood—halibut, shrimp, mussels, crab, and salmon—also features prominently on most restaurant menus.

Although locals are often disdainful of the touristy restaurants clustered around the Inner Harbour, many have water views and all are handy to downtown accommodations. Unlike in many cities, ethnic restaurants are not confined to particular streets. On the upscale end, Fort Street east of Douglas has a proliferation of restaurants that are as trendy as it gets on the island.

Traditional English fare, including afternoon tea, is served everywhere from motherly corner cafés to the grand Fairmont Empress. For the full experience, choose kippers and poached eggs for breakfast, a ploughman's lunch (crusty bread, a chunk of cheese, pickled onions), and then roast beef with Yorkshire pudding (a crispy pastry made with drippings and doused with gravy) in the evening.

Seafood

Fish-and-chips is a British tradition and is sold as such at a number of places around town. Down on the docks below downtown, at the foot of Broughton Street, **Red Fish Blue Fish** (1006 Wharf St., 250/298-6877, www.redfish-bluefish.com, 11:30am-7pm, CAN$10-20) is a takeout place ensconced in a brightly painted shipping container. Unusual for a fish-and-chip joint, the emphasis is on wild, sustainable fisheries. Prices reflect the waterfront location (CAN$20 for two pieces of halibut with chips), but the quality of fish is excellent. Other choices include a grilled scallop burger and wild salmon fish tacos. Expect a line in summer.

For the best quality, ★ **Fairfield Fish & Chips** (1275 Fairfield Rd., 250/380-6880, 11:30am-7:30pm Tues.-Sat., CAN$7-10.50) is a winner. Fish choices include halibut, haddock, cod, and rockfish, which are served with perfectly cooked chips. Other options include a halibut burger and deep-fried oysters. The shop is located along Fairfield Road at Moss Street.

The location alone makes ★ **Barb's Place** (Fisherman's Wharf, at the foot of St. Lawrence St., 250/384-6515, www.barbsfishandchips.com, 11am-dusk daily March-Oct., CAN$9-18), a sea-level eatery on a floating dock, my other favorite. It's not a restaurant as such, but a shack surrounded by outdoor table settings, some protected from the elements by a canvas tent. The food is as fresh as it gets. Choose cod and chips, halibut and chips, or clam chowder, or splurge on a steamed crab. Adding to the charm are the surrounding floating houses and the seals that hang out waiting for handouts. An enjoyable way to reach Barb's is by ferry from the Inner Harbour. Also on Fisherman's Wharf is **The Fish Store** (250/383-6462, www.

floatingfishstore.com, 11am-6pm daily, longer hours in summer), which sells a wide variety of local seafood, as well as fish-and-chips, fish tacos, and other light meals.

Occupying a prime downtown location on a floating dock amid whale-watching boats, seaplanes, and shiny white leisure craft, the ★ **Flying Otter Grill** (950 Wharf St., 250/414-4220, www.flyingottergrill.com, 11am-10pm Mon.-Fri., 8am-10pm Sat.-Sun., CAN$16-22) is just steps from the main tourist trail, but it's far enough removed to make it a popular haunt with locals wanting a quiet, casual waterfront meal. The setting alone makes the Flying Otter a winner, but the menu is a knockout. Choose pan-fried oysters or grilled chili-lime marinated prawns to share, and then move on to mains like seafood risotto. To get there, walk north along the harbor from the information center.

Asian

Victoria's small Chinatown surrounds a short, colorful strip of Fisgard Street between Store and Government Streets. The restaurants welcome everyone, and generally the menus are filled with all of the familiar Westernized Chinese choices. Near the top (east) end of Fisgard is **QV Café and Bakery** (1701 Government St., 250/384-8831, 7am-11pm daily, CAN$7-12), offering inexpensive Western-style breakfasts in the morning and Chinese delicacies the rest of the day.

One of the least expensive places in the area is **Wah Lai Yuen** (560 Fisgard St., 250/381-5355, 10am-8pm daily, CAN$8-16), a simply decorated, well-lit restaurant with fast and efficient service. The wonton soups are particularly good, as are the Szechwan prawns, or get adventurous and order salted squid. Out front is a bakery with offerings such as peanut almond soft cake.

Mediterranean

The energetic atmosphere at ★ **Café Brio** (944 Fort St., 250/383-0009, www.cafebrio.com, from 5:30pm daily, CAN$22-32) is contagious, and the food is as good as anywhere in Victoria. The Mediterranean-inspired dining room is adorned with lively artwork and built around a U-shaped bar, while out front are a handful of tables on an alfresco terrace. A creative menu features local, seasonal produce executed with expertise and flair. The charcuterie, prepared in-house, is always a good choice to start, followed by wild salmon prepared however your server suggests. Order the sticky date toffee pudding, even if you're full.

Italian

One of the most popular restaurants in downtown Victoria is **Pagliacci's** (1011 Broad St., 250/386-1662, www.pagliaccis.ca, 11:30am-3pm and 5:30pm-10pm daily, CAN$14-29), known for hearty Italian food, homemade bread, great desserts, and loads of atmosphere. Small and always busy, the restaurant attracts a lively local crowd, many with children; you'll inevitably have to wait for a table during the busiest times (no reservations taken). Pasta options include a prawn fettuccine topped with tomato mint sauce.

Vegetarian

★ **Rebar Modern Food** (50 Bastion Sq., 250/361-9223, www.rebarmodernfood.com, 8:30am-9pm Mon.-Sat., 8:30am-3:30pm Sun., CAN$8.50-17) is a cheerful, always-busy 1970s-style vegetarian restaurant with a loyal local following. Dishes such as the almond burger at lunch and Thai tiger prawn curry at dinner are full of flavor and made with only the freshest ingredients. Still hungry? Try the nutty carrot cake. Children are catered to with fun choices such as banana and peanut butter on sunflower seed bread. It's worth stopping by just for juice: vegetable and fruit juices, power tonics, and wheatgrass infusions are made to order for CAN$6.50.

Caribbean

The Reef (533 Yates St., 250/388-5375, www.thereefrestaurant.com, lunch and dinner daily, CAN$15-20) is as un-Victoria-like as one could imagine, but it's incredibly popular for its upbeat atmosphere, tasty food, and island-friendly service. The kitchen concentrates on the Caribbean classics, with jerk seasoning and tropical fruit juices featured in most dishes. Highlights include any of the West Indian curries, *ackee* (fruit) with salted codfish, plantain chips with jerk mayo, and chicken marinated in coconut milk and then roasted. Of course, you'll need to order a fruity drink for the full effect—a traditional favorite like a piña colada or something a little more hip, like a rum-infused banana smoothie.

Cafés

Broughton Street Deli (648 Broughton St., 250/380-9988, www.broughtonstreetdeli.com, 7am-4pm Mon.-Fri., 9am-3pm Sat., breakfast CAN$10-13, lunch CAN$6-9) occupies a tiny space at street level of a redbrick building. Soups made from scratch daily are CAN$5 and sandwiches are just CAN$7.

With walls decorated with original art and an eclectic array of table arrangements, **Mo:Le Restaurant** (554 Pandora St., 250/385-6653, www.molerestaurant.ca, 8am-3pm Mon.-Fri., 8am-4pm Sat.-Sun., lunches CAN$10-15) impresses with creative yet well-priced cooking—think shrimp eggs Benedict, yam omelet, maple-balsam grilled vegetable sandwich, and more.

Well worth searching out, **Blue Fox Café** (919 Fort St., 250/380-1683, www.thebluefoxcafe.com, 7:30am-4pm Mon.-Fri., 8am-3pm Sat.-Sun., lunches CAN$7-12) nearly always has a line for tables. Breakfast includes Eggs Benedict Pacifico (with smoked salmon and avocado) and Apple Charlotte (French toast with apples and maple syrup). At lunch, try an oversized Waldorf salad or a curried chicken burger with sweet date chutney. Almost everything is under CAN$12.

Casual Dining

At the foot of Bastion Square, a cobbled pedestrian mall, **The Local Kitchen** (1205 Wharf St., 250/385-1999, www.localkitchenandbar.com, 11:30am-10pm Sun.-Thurs., 11:30am-1am Fri.-Sat., CAN$18-24) offers a menu of simple, globally inspired cooking, although the outdoor tables are reason enough to stop by. The West Coast seafood kebab, the Tofino linguine—it's all excellent.

In Old Town, the small **Sour Pickle Café** (1623 Store St., 250/384-9390, 7:30am-4:30pm Mon.-Fri., lunch CAN$7-12) comes alive with funky music and an enthusiastic staff. The menu offers bagels, full cooked breakfasts, soup of the day, healthy sandwiches, and delicious single-serve pizzas.

Pubs

Right in the heart of downtown is the **Elephant & Castle** (corner of Government St. and View St., 250/383-5858, www.elephantcastle.com, lunch and dinner daily, CAN$13-23). This English-style pub features exposed beams, oak paneling, and traditional pub decor. A few umbrella-shaded tables line the sidewalk out front. You'll find all the traditional favorites, such as steak and kidney pie and fish-and-chips.

Swan's Hotel & Brewpub (506 Pandora St., 250/361-3310, www.swanshotel.com, 7am-1am daily, CAN$12-20) is home to a stylish brewpub with matching food, such as a portobello burger and a smoked salmon wrap.

While these pubs exude the English traditions for which Victoria is famous, **Spinnakers Gastro Brewpub** (308 Catherine St., Esquimalt, 250/386-2739, www.spinnakers.com, from 11am daily, CAN$13-29) is in a class by itself. It was Canada's first in-house brewpub, and it's as popular today as when it opened in 1985. The crowds come for the beer but also for great food served up in a casual, modern atmosphere. British-style pub fare, such as a ploughman's lunch, is served in the bar, while West Coast and seafood dishes such as sea bass basted in an ale sauce are offered in the downstairs restaurant.

Coffeehouses

While Victoria is generally associated with afternoon tea, there are some serious coffee lovers in the capital. A good percentage of these

Afternoon Tea

Afternoon tea, that terribly English tradition that started in the 1840s as a between-meal snack, is one ritual you should definitely partake in while visiting Victoria. Many North Americans don't realize that there is a difference between afternoon tea and high tea, and even in Victoria the names are sometimes used in place of one another. Afternoon tea is the lighter version, featuring fine teas (no tea bags) accompanied by delicate crustless sandwiches, scones with clotted cream and preserves, and a selection of other small treats. High tea (traditionally taken later in the day, around 6pm) is more substantial — more like dinner in North America.

The best place to immerse yourself in the ritual is at one of the smaller tearooms scattered around the outskirts of downtown. **White Heather Tea Room** (1885 Oak Bay Ave., 250/595-8020, www.whiteheather-tearoom.com, 10am-5pm Tues.-Sat., CAN$18-26) has a small, homey setting, with a great deal of attention given to all aspects of afternoon tea — right down to the handmade tea cozies.

If the sun is shining, a pleasant place to enjoy afternoon tea is **Point Ellice House** (2616 Pleasant St., 250/380-6506, www.pointellicehouse.com, 11am-4pm Thurs.-Mon. May-June, 11am-5pm daily July-early Sept., CAN$25 adults, CAN$13 children), a waterfront property along the Gorge Waterway. The price includes a tour of the property. As you'd expect, it's a touristy affair at **Butchart Gardens** (800 Benvenuto Dr., Brentwood Bay, 250/652-4422, www.butchartgardens.com, from noon daily, CAN$32), with Cornish pasties, quiche, and more.

The **Fairmont Empress** (721 Government St., 250/389-2727, www.fairmont.com, CAN$75) offers the grandest of grand afternoon teas, but you pay for it. Still, it's so popular that you must book at least a week in advance through summer and reserve a table at one of seven sitting times between noon and 5pm.

Finally, **Murchies** (1110 Government St., 250/381-5451, www.murchies.com, 9am-6pm daily, CAN$6-11), in the heart of the downtown tourist precinct, sells teas from around the world as well as tea paraphernalia such as teapots, gift sets, and collector tins. The adjacent café pours teas from all over the globe in a North American-style coffeehouse.

consider **Moka House** (various locations, including 345 Cook St., 250/388-7377, 6am-midnight daily) as pouring the best coffee. As a bonus, the bagels are excellent and wireless Internet is free. The focus at minimalist **Habit Coffee** (552 Pandora St., 250/294-1127, 7am-6pm Mon.-Fri., 8am-6pm Sat.-Sun.) is most definitely the coffee, though it offers an eclectic collection of magazines to browse through.

Bakeries

In Old Town, **Willies Bakery** (537 Johnson St., 250/381-8414, www.willies.ca, 7am-4pm Mon.-Fri., 8:30am-4pm Sat., 8am-4pm Sun., lunch CAN$6.50-9.50) is an old-style café offering cakes, pastries, and sodas, with a quiet cobbled courtyard in which to enjoy them.

On the same side of downtown, **Cascadia Bakery** (1812 Government St., 250/380-6606, 7am-5pm Mon.-Fri., 8am-4pm Sat., 9am-3pm

Sun., lunch CAN$7-10) is best known for its hand-shaped, preservative-free breads, but also offers freshly made granola and tasty lunches.

Ignore the dated furnishings at the **Dutch Bakery** (718 Fort St., 250/383-9725, www.thedutchbakery.com, 7:30am-5pm Mon.-Sat.) and tuck into freshly baked goodies and handmade chocolates.

ACCOMMODATIONS

Victoria accommodations come in all shapes and sizes. A couple of downtown hostels cater to travelers on a budget, but there are also a surprising number of convenient roadside motels with rooms for under CAN$100, including one right off the Inner Harbour. Bed-and-breakfasts are where Victoria really shines, with rooms starting at CAN$100. In the same price range are boutique hotels.

In the off-season (Oct.-May), the nightly rates quoted here are discounted up to 50 percent, but occupancy rates are high as Canadians flock to the country's winter hot spot. Arriving without a reservation is unwise, especially in the summer months. As a last resort, staff at the **Victoria Visitor Centre** (Wharf St., 250/953-2022 or 800/663-3883, www.tourismvictoria.com) can offer help finding a room.

Most of these options within are within walking distance of the Inner Harbour.

Under CAN$50

In the heart of the oldest section of downtown Victoria is **HI-Victoria** (516 Yates St., 250/385-4511 or 888/883-0099, www.hi-hostels.ca, dorm CAN$40; private room CAN$88-105 s or d). The totally renovated 108-bed hostel enjoys a great location only a stone's throw from the harbor. Separate dorms and bathroom facilities for men and women are complemented by two fully equipped kitchens, a large meeting room, lounge, library, game room, travel services, public Internet terminals, and an informative bulletin board. There are a limited number of private rooms.

Housed in the upper stories of an old commercial building, **Ocean Island Backpackers Inn** (791 Pandora Ave., 250/385-1788 or 888/888-4180, www.ocean-island.com, dorm CAN$30 per person; private room CAN$38-117 d) lies just a couple of blocks from downtown. This a party place, but on the plus side, the lodging is clean, modern, and welcoming throughout. Guests have use of kitchen facilities, a laundry room, and a computer for Internet access. There's also plenty of space to relax, such as a reading room, music room (guitars supplied), television room, and street-level bar open until midnight. Private rooms range from CAN$38 for a super-small single to CAN$117 for an en suite that sleeps a family of four.

CAN$100-200

Dating to 1911 and once home to artist Emily Carr, **James Bay Inn** (270 Government St., 250/384-7151 or 800/836-2649, www.jamesbayinn.com, CAN$139-189 d) is five blocks from the harbor and within easy walking distance of all city sights and Beacon Hill Park. From the outside, the hotel has a clunky, un-inspiring look, but a bright and breezy decor and new beds in the simply furnished rooms make it a pleasant place to rest your head. All guests enjoy discounted food and drink at the downstairs restaurant and pub.

East of downtown in the suburb of Oak Bay, the Tudor-style **Oak Bay Guest House** (1052 Newport Ave., 250/598-3812 or 800/575-3812, www.oakbayguesthouse.com, CAN$149-229 d), one block from the waterfront, has been taking in guests since 1922. It offers 11 smallish antique-filled rooms, each with a private balcony and a bathroom. The Sun Lounge holds a small library and tea- and coffee-making facilities while the Foyer Lounge features plush chairs set around an open fireplace. Rates include a delicious four-course breakfast.

If you're looking for a modern feel, centrally located ★ **Swans Suite Hotel** (506 Pandora Ave., 250/361-3310 or 800/668-7926, www.swanshotel.com, CAN$125-205 s or d) is an excellent choice. Located above a restaurant/pub complex that was built in the 1880s as a grain storehouse, each of the 30 split-level suites holds a loft, full kitchen, dining area, and bedroom. The furnishings are casual yet elegantly rustic, with West Coast artwork adorning the walls and fresh flowers in every room. In the off-season, all rooms are discounted up to 40 percent.

CAN$200-300

Separated from downtown by Beacon Hill Park, **Dashwood Manor** (1 Cook St., 250/385-5517 or 800/667-5517, www.dashwoodmanor.com, CAN$189-249 d), a 1912 Tudor-style heritage house on a bluff overlooking the Strait of Juan de Fuca, enjoys a panoramic view of the entire Olympic mountain range. The 11 guest rooms are elegantly furnished, and hosts Michael Dwyer and David Marshall will happily recount the historical details of each room. The Oxford Grand room (CAN$249) holds a chandelier, stone fireplace, and antiques.

Just four blocks from the Inner Harbour, the 1905 ★ **Beaconsfield Inn** (988 Humboldt St., 250/384-4044 or 888/884-4044, www.beaconsfieldinn.com, CAN$219-279 d) is exactly what you may imagine a Victorian bed-and-breakfast should be. Original mahogany floors, high ceilings, classical moldings, imported antiques, and fresh flowers from the garden create an upscale historical charm throughout. Each of the nine guest rooms is individually decorated in a style matching the Edwardian era. The Emily Carr Suite has a rich burgundy and green color scheme, Emily Carr prints on the walls, a regal mahogany bed topped by a goose-down comforter, an oversized bathroom and double-jetted tub, and separate sitting area with a fireplace. After checking in, you'll be invited to join other guests for high tea in the library and then encouraged to return for a glass of sherry before heading out for dinner. As you may expect, breakfast—served in a formal dining room or more casual conservatory—is a grand affair, with multiple courses of hearty fare delivered to your table by your impeccably presented host.

Very different from Victoria's traditional accommodations is the contemporary **Parkside Hotel & Spa** (810 Humboldt St., 250/716-2651 or 855/616-3557, www.parksidevictoria.com, starting at CAN$299 d). Within walking distance of the Inner Harbour, the guest rooms have a contemporary ambience, and each has one or two bedrooms, a full kitchen with stainless steel appliances, and large wall-mounted TVs. Rooms on the upper floors have city views. Other highlights include a fitness room, indoor pool, theater, and underground parking.

Sitting on a point of land jutting into the Inner Harbour, the **Inn at Laurel Point** (680 Montreal St., 250/386-8721 or 800/663-7667, www.laurelpoint.com, CAN$238-264 d) offers a distinct resort atmosphere within walking distance of downtown. Two wings hold around 200 rooms; each has a water view and private balcony, but well worth the extra money are the Terrace Suites. Amenities include an indoor pool, beautifully landscaped Japanese-style gardens, a sauna, a small fitness facility, Aura Restaurant, a lounge, and a gift shop.

Over CAN$300

Enjoying a waterfront location right downtown is the **Victoria Regent** (1234 Wharf St., 250/386-2211 or 800/663-7472, www.victoriaregent.com, CAN$259-489 s or d). The exterior of this renovated building is nothing special, but inside, the rooms are spacious and comfortable. The best-value rooms at the Regent are the suites, which include a full kitchen, balcony, wireless Internet, and a daily newspaper.

The ★ **Magnolia Hotel & Spa** (623 Courtney St., 250/381-0999 or 877/624-6654, www.magnoliahotel.com, from CAN$339 d) is a European-style boutique hotel just up the hill from the harbor. It features an elegant interior with mahogany-paneled walls, Persian rugs, chandeliers, a gold-leafed ceiling, and fresh flowers throughout public areas. The rooms are each elegantly furnished and feature floor-to-ceiling windows, heritage-style furniture in a contemporary room layout, richly colored fabrics, down duvets, a work desk with cordless phone, and coffee-making facilities. Many also feature a gas fireplace. The bathrooms are huge, with each having marble trim, a soaker tub, and separate shower stall. The hotel is also home to the Magnolia Spa and a stylish Mediterranean-themed restaurant. Rates include a light breakfast, daily newspaper, passes to a nearby fitness facility, and unlike at most other downtown hotels, free parking. Off-season rates cost CAN$169-209, single or double.

The grand old **Fairmont Empress** (721 Government St., 250/384-8111 or 800/257-7544, www.fairmont.com, from CAN$649 d) is Victoria's best-loved accommodation. Covered in ivy and with only magnificent gardens separating it from the Inner Harbour, it's also in the city's best location. Designed by Francis Rattenbury in 1908, the Empress is one of the original Canadian Pacific Railway hotels. Rooms are offered in 90 different configurations, but as in other hotels of the era, most are small. Each is filled with Victorian period furnishings and antiques. The least expensive Fairmont Rooms start at CAN$389 in summer, but if you really want to stay in this Canadian landmark, consider upgrading to a Fairmont Gold room. Although not necessarily larger, these rooms have harbor views, a private check-in, nightly turndown service, and a private lounge where hors d'oeuvres are served in the evening. If you can't afford to stay at the Empress, plan on at least visiting one of the restaurants or the regal Lobby Lounge.

INFORMATION AND SERVICES
Tourist Offices

Tourism Victoria runs the bright, modern **Victoria Visitor Centre** (812 Wharf St., 250/953-2033 or 800/663-3883, www.tourismvictoria.com, 8:30am-8:30pm daily May-Sept., 9am-5pm daily the rest of the year), which overlooks the Inner Harbour.

The friendly staff can answer most of your questions. They also book accommodations, tours and charters, restaurants, entertainment, and transportation, all at no extra cost; sell local bus passes and map books with detailed area-by-area maps; and stock an enormous selection of tourist brochures. While there, pick up the free *Accommodations* publication and the free local news and entertainment papers—it's the best way to find out what's happening in Victoria while you're in town.

When coming off the ferry from Vancouver, stop in at the **Sidney Visitor Centre** (10382 Pat Bay Hwy., 250/656-0525, www.sidney.ca, 9am-5pm daily in summer), which is just off the highway along the road leading into Sooke.

Emergency Services

In a medical emergency, call 911 or contact **Victoria General Hospital** (1 Hospital Way, 250/727-4212, www.vgh.mb.ca). For cases that aren't urgent, a handy facility is **James Bay Medical Treatment Centre** (230 Menzies St., 250/388-9934). For dental care, try the **Cresta Dental Centre** (3170 Tillicum Rd., 250/384-7711, www.crestadental.ca). You can fill prescriptions at **Shopper's Drug Mart**

the Fairmont Empress hotel

(1222 Douglas St., 250/381-4321, www.shoppersdrugmart.ca, 7am-7pm daily).

GETTING THERE AND AROUND

Air

Victoria International Airport (www.victoriaairport.com), the island's main airport, is on the Saanich Peninsula, 20 kilometers (12.4 miles) north of Victoria's city center. **Air Canada** (604/688-5515 or 888/247-2262, www.aircanada.ca), **Alaska Airlines** (800/426-0333, www.alaskaair.com), **Delta** (800/221-1212, www.delta.com), **United** (800/864-8331, www.united.com), **Pacific Coastal** (604/273-8666 or 800/663-2872, www.pacificcoastal.com), and **WestJet** (604/606-5525 or 800/538-5696, www.westjet.com) all have scheduled flights.

Once you've collected your baggage from the carousels, it's impossible to miss the rental car outlets (Avis, Budget, Hertz, and National) across the room, where you'll also find a currency exchange and information booth. Outside is a taxi stand and ticket booth for the airporter. The modern terminal also houses a lounge, various eateries, and a profusion of greenery.

Several companies operate scheduled seaplane flights to Victoria's Inner Harbour, including **Harbour Air** (604/274-1277 or 800/665-0212, www.harbourair.com) to Vancouver and **Kenmore Air** (425/486-1257 or 866/435-9524, www.kenmoreair.com) to Seattle's Lake Union.

The **YYJ Airport Shuttle** (778/351-4995 or 855/351-4995, www.yyjairportshuttle.com, CAN$25 adults, CAN$15 children one-way) operates buses between the airport and major downtown hotels. A taxi costs approximately CAN$70 to downtown.

Ferry

FROM VANCOUVER

BC Ferries (250/386-3431 or 888/223-3779, www.bcferries.com) links Vancouver and Victoria with a fleet of ferries that operate year-round. Ferries depart Vancouver from **Tsawwassen,** south of Vancouver International Airport and **Horseshoe Bay,** on Vancouver's North Shore. They terminate on Vancouver Island at **Swartz Bay,** 32 kilometers (20 miles) north of Victoria. On weekends and holidays, the one-way fare on either route costs adults CAN$18, children 5-11 CAN$9, and vehicles CAN$57. Limited vehicle reservations (CAN$15-22) are accepted at 604/444-2890 or 888/724-5223, or online at www.bcferries.com. Seniors travel free Monday-Thursday, but must pay for their vehicles.

In high season (late June to mid-Sept.), the ferries run about once an hour, 7am-10pm. The rest of the year they run a little less frequently. Both crossings take around 90 minutes. Expect a wait in summer, particularly if you have an oversized vehicle (each ferry can accommodate far fewer large vehicles than standard-size cars and trucks).

Try to plan your travel outside peak times, which include summer weekends, especially Friday afternoon sailings from Tsawwassen and Sunday afternoon sailings from Swartz Bay. Most travelers don't make reservations but simply arrive and prepare themselves to wait for the next ferry if the first one fills. Both terminals have shops with food and magazines as well as summertime booths selling everything from crafts to mini donuts.

FROM WASHINGTON STATE

From downtown Seattle (Pier 69), **Clipper Vacations** (800/888-2535, www.clippervacations.com, US$92 adults one-way, US$155 round-trip) runs passenger-only ferries to Victoria's Inner Harbour. In summer, sailings are made five times daily, with the service running the rest of the year on a reduced schedule. Travel is discounted off-season and year-round for seniors and children.

North of Seattle, Anacortes is the departure point for **Washington State Ferries** (206/464-6400, 250/381-1551, or 888/808-7977, www.wsdof.wa.gov/ferries, US$20 adults, US$10 seniors or youth, US$67 vehicle and driver) to Sidney (on Vancouver Island, 32 kilometers/20 miles north of Victoria), with a stop made en route in the San Juan Islands. To ensure a space, make Save A Spot vehicle reservations online at www.wsdot.wa.gov/ferries/reservations.

The final option is to travel from Port Angeles to Victoria. The **MV Coho** (250/386-2202 or 360/457-4491, www.cohoferry.com, US$19 adults, US$9 children, US$64vehicle and driver) runs year-round, with up to four crossings daily in summer.

Bus

Most central attractions can be reached on foot. However, the **Victoria Regional Transit System** (250/385-2551, www.bc-transit.com/victoria) is excellent, and it's easy to jump on and off and get everywhere you want to go. Pick up an *Explore Victoria* brochure at the information center for details of all the major sights, parks, beaches, and shopping areas and the buses needed to reach them. Bus fare for travel within the entire city is CAN$2.50. Transfers are good for travel in one direction within 90 minutes of purchase. A day pass costs CAN$5 per person.

Bike

Victoria doesn't have the great network of bicycle paths that Vancouver boasts, but bike rental shops are nevertheless plentiful. Try **Sports Rent** (1950 Government St., 250/385-7368) or **Oak Bay Bicycles** (1990 Oak Bay Ave., 250/598-4111, www.oakbaybikes.com). Expect to pay from around CAN$10 per hour, CAN$40 per day.

Taxi

Taxis operate on a meter system, charging CAN$3.30 at the initial flag drop plus around CAN$2 per kilometer. Call **Blue Bird Cabs** (250/382-8294 or 800/665-7055, www.taxi-cab.com), **Empress Taxi** (250/381-2222), or **Victoria Taxi** (250/383-7111).

San Juan Island

Delightful, diverse San Juan is an island with something to please almost any traveler. White clapboard buildings, busy shops, art galleries, and fine restaurants are tucked into the hills surrounding its main town, Friday Harbor.

Beyond it, the country quickly opens into expansive farms and fields, forests, hills, and rocky shorelines.

On the south end of the island, the land is grassy and open, with a couple of long beaches. The western shore is relatively undeveloped and rugged, with the only whale-watching park in the nation at Lime Kiln Point State Park. Two historical and especially scenic areas—English Camp on the west side and American Camp on the southeast end of the island—compose San Juan Island National Historical Park.

San Juan Island is 20 miles long and 7 miles wide, covering a total of 55 square miles. It's the second-largest island in the archipelago (Orcas is slightly bigger). Friday Harbor is the only incorporated town in the chain, and also the county seat, the commercial center of the San Juans, and home to around a third of San Juan Island's 7,600 residents. It is a U.S. Customs port of entry, as is Roche Harbor on

the northwest end of the island. Roche Harbor is regionally famous for its superb deepwater marina and historic buildings that are now part of a popular resort.

Notable visitors to the San Juans have included U.S. presidents Theodore Roosevelt and Howard Taft, who both overnighted at Roche Harbor while in office. More recently, movie star John Wayne and 1970s rocker Steve Miller have owned homes here (Wayne owned nearby Spieden Island for a number of years).

PLANNING YOUR TIME

San Juan Island is popular both with weekend vacationers and those with more time on their hands. It's possible to fly directly to the island, but most visitors arrive by state ferry. A ferry trip requires getting to Anacortes (or Sidney if you're visiting from Vancouver Island), waiting in line for an hour or more, and then sailing to Friday Harbor. Unless you get a very early start and leave late the evening of your

Previous: Waterfront Park in Friday Harbor; beach on the south end of San Juan Island. **Above:** the Port of Friday Harbor.

Look for ★ to find recommended
sights, activities, dining, and lodging.

Highlights

★ **The Whale Museum:** Learn about killer whales and other marine mammals at this informative museum in Friday Harbor. Kids love to try on the whale costumes (page 113).

★ **San Juan Islands Museum of Art:** Enjoy both the striking glass-enclosed atrium gallery and the changing exhibits (page 115).

★ **San Juan Island National Historical Park:** This park commemorates the conflict between the United States and Britain for control of the islands. English Camp has historic buildings and a formal garden, while American Camp is a windswept, open spot with the best beaches anywhere in the San Juans (page 115).

★ **Roche Harbor:** This beautiful marina and resort has a historic hotel, flower-packed gardens, and abundant recreation options (page 120).

★ **Lime Kiln Point State Park:** Often called Whale Watch Park, this west-side natural area has a photogenic lighthouse and underwater hydrophones to listen for the whales passing offshore (page 121).

★ **San Juan Vineyards:** This boutique winery produces wines from 10 acres of Madeleine Angevine and Siegerrebe grapes (page 125).

★ **Pelindaba Lavender Farm:** The fragrance reaches you before you even see the 20 acres of organic lavender (page 127).

★ **Whale-Watching:** Each year, more than a half-million people board whale-watching boats in the San Juans; most remember spotting a whale as the highlight of their trip (page 128).

★ **Sea Kayaking:** Kayaking is an adventurous way to explore the surrounding waters. Several companies lead both day trips and multi-night paddles (page 130).

San Juan Island

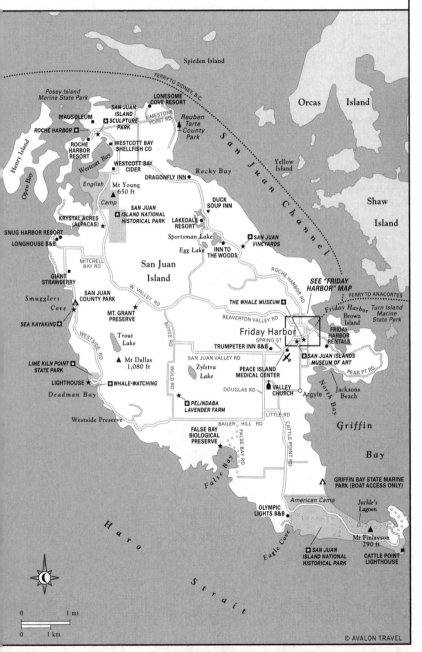

Spieden Island

FERRY TO SIDNEY, B.C.

Posey Island
Marine State Park

Orcas Island

LONESOME
COVE RESORT

MAUSOLEUM

SAN JUAN
ISLAND
SCULPTURE
PARK

Reuben
Tarte
County
Park

ROCHE HARBOR

LIMESTONE POINT RD

Yellow
Island

Shaw

ROCHE
HARBOR
RESORT

WESTCOTT BAY
SHELLFISH CO

WESTCOTT BAY
CIDER

Westcott Bay

Island

San Juan Channel

Henry Island

Open Bay

English

DRAGONFLY INN

Rocky Bay

Camp

Mt Young
650 ft

DUCK
SOUP INN

KRYSTAL ACRES
(ALPACAS)

SAN JUAN
ISLAND NATIONAL
HISTORICAL PARK

LAKEDALE
RESORT

SNUG HARBOR RESORT

Sportsman Lake

SAN JUAN
VINEYARDS

LONGHOUSE B&B

Egg Lake

INN TO
THE WOODS

MITCHELL
BAY RD

San Juan
Island

ROCHE HARBOR RD

SEE "FRIDAY
HARBOR" MAP

GIANT
STRAWBERRY

W VALLEY RD

THE WHALE MUSEUM

FERRY TO ANACORTES

Smugglers
Cove

SAN JUAN
COUNTY PARK

BEAVERTON VALLEY RD

Friday Harbor

Turn Island
Marine
State Park

MT. GRANT
PRESERVE

Brown
Island

SEA KAYAKING

Trout
Lake

BOYCE RD

Friday Harbor

FRIDAY
HARBOR
RENTALS

WESTSIDE RD

SPRING ST

TRUMPETER INN B&B

SAN JUAN ISLANDS
MUSEUM OF ART

LIME KILN POINT
STATE PARK

Mt Dallas
1,080 ft

WOLD RD

SAN JUAN VALLEY RD

PEAR PT RD

Zylstra
Lake

LIGHTHOUSE

WHALE-WATCHING

PEACE ISLAND
MEDICAL CENTER

Jacksons
Beach

Deadman Bay

DOUGLAS RD

VALLEY
CHURCH

Argyle

North Bay

PELINDABA
LAVENDER FARM

LITTLE RD

Griffin

Westside Preserve

BAILER HILL RD

CATTLE POINT RD

FALSE BAY
BIOLOGICAL
PRESERVE

FALSE BAY RD

Bay

False Bay

Haro

GRIFFIN BAY STATE MARINE
PARK (BOAT ACCESS ONLY)

American Camp

OLYMPIC
LIGHTS B&B

Jackle's
Lagoon

Eagle Cove

SAN JUAN
ISLAND NATIONAL
HISTORICAL PARK

Mt Finlayson
290 ft

CATTLE POINT
LIGHTHOUSE

Strait

0   1 mi

0   1 km

© AVALON TRAVEL

return, you can lose big chunks of your weekend to travel. Take as much time as you can afford, but even a short trip can be fun.

Friday Harbor is the center of action on San Juan Island, and a good base from which to explore surrounding areas. It's also home to the fun and educational **Whale Museum,** several fine restaurants, and a multitude of gift shops and galleries. After visiting the museum, many visitors climb on board one of the many **whale-watching** boats that converge on orcas feeding in nearby waters. There is controversy over the impacts of whale-watching boats, with the museum recommending onshore whale-watching. The best place for that is **Lime Kiln Point State Park** on the undeveloped west side of the island. Just north of Lime Kiln Point is a small county park that serves as a popular put-in point for guided and private groups of **sea kayakers.**

San Juan Island National Historical Park and **Roche Harbor** mix history with grand scenery. The park commemorates the Pig War with the restored bases once occupied by American and British soldiers, while Roche Harbor features gracious gardens, an old clapboard hotel, a busy harbor, and an intriguing mix of nature and art at **San Juan Island Sculpture Park.**

On the south end of the island, **Pelindaba Lavender Farm** grows fragrant lavender flowers for a variety of uses and has a big shop in the heart of Friday Harbor. These attractions are just a starting point, and inveterate travelers will discover all sorts of other delights on San Juan Island.

It's easy to see Friday Harbor sights on foot, but for many of the most interesting spots around San Juan, you'll need transport. **San Juan Transit** (360/378-8887, www.sanjuantransit.com, daily mid-May-early Sept.) provides an inexpensive way to see the sights in the summer, with stops at many destinations. You can also get off or on anywhere along the route; just flag it down for a ride. Buses can carry bikes and luggage, and fares are $5 each way ($3 for kids under 12), or $15 for an all-day pass ($5 kids). The San Juan Transit office is in the Cannery Landing building adjacent to the ferry dock.

HISTORY

The Pig War, a turf battle between the United States and Britain, threatened to escalate into violent conflict in 1859. Once tensions eased, both sides stationed troops on San Juan Island to protect their interests until a settlement could be reached. That settlement did not

watching whales from the south end of San Juan Island

come until 1872, when the United States was awarded the islands by an arbitrator, Kaiser Wilhelm I of Germany.

San Juan Town and Friday Harbor

Shortly after American soldiers landed on the southern end of San Juan Island in 1859, a settlement sprang up along nearby Griffin Bay. Originally called San Juan Town, it would later be known as Old Town. The turmoil over ownership of the islands made them ripe for all sorts of illicit activities, the primary one being the uncontrolled selling of alcohol. Within a year, the entire area was verging on anarchy, with robberies, attacks on women at any time of the day or night, rampant drunkenness by both Native Americans and whites, saloon brawls, prostitution, and even murder. The American military stepped in to restore order, but San Juan Town's reputation was already ruined.

The name Friday Harbor comes from an early settler called **Joe Friday.** Born in Hawaii, Friday was brought to the San Juans by the Hudson's Bay Company to tend sheep. His original name is unknown, but it's possible the British sailors who recruited him wanted something they could pronounce, naming him after Friday, the fictional character in *Robinson Crusoe*. Joe Friday settled along the protected cove others came to call Friday's Harbor, and the town grew up on land where his sheep had grazed. Friday was one of many Hawaiians who were brought to the San Juan Islands and Gulf Islands by the British. The Hawaiians were called Kanakas by others, and Kanaka Bay on the southwest side of San Juan Island is named for them. There was a mass exodus of Kanaka from the San Juans after the islands were awarded to the Americans in 1872. Many moved to Victoria, while others followed their flocks of sheep to Salt Spring Island in the Gulf Islands. Of course, it didn't help that Kanaka were given citizenship by the British, while Americans viewed them with suspicion, denying them basic rights.

One of the few reputable civilians on San Juan in the early years was **Edward Warbass,** who came to the island to run the U.S. Army's post store and stayed around to become justice of the peace, a state legislator, and the crafter of a bill that created San Juan County. Warbass is best known today as the father of Friday Harbor. Fed up with the boozing reputation of San Juan Town, he resolved to create a grand metropolis at a protected harbor on the east side of the island. He claimed that it would rival Seattle.

In 1873, Warbass staked 160 acres for the new San Juan County seat on the shores of Friday's harbor, erected a shack for the courthouse, and waited in vain for the hordes to arrive. It was three years before the first settler, other than Warbass, finally moved in to open a store, and almost a decade before the town contained more than a handful of homes and residents. In 1882, a second store opened at Friday Harbor, creating competition that led the owners to add a backroom bar. This was what folks really needed: cheap beer. Within a few months, the island's economic focus shifted to Friday Harbor, and over the next few years, San Juan Town became a ghost town. A fire in 1890 destroyed all that remained of Old Town, but nobody shed any tears. Friday Harbor was now clearly the chief—and only—town on the island, and it remains so today, with some 2,200 permanent residents.

The Lime King

Today, Roche Harbor is famous for its beautiful protected harbor, large marina, and immaculately maintained historic buildings, which operate as the largest resort on San Juan Island. By 1850 the Hudson's Bay Company had built a log trading post along the shore. In 1881, the brothers Robert and Richard Scurr bought the harbor and began mining an incredibly rich deposit of lime.

In 1884, **John S. McMillin,** a Tacoma lawyer, learned of the limestone and bought the land for $40,000. By 1886, McMillin's Tacoma and Roche Harbor Lime Company had begun operation. The old Hudson's Bay bunkhouse became the basis for his **Hotel de Haro,** a still-standing structure that has hosted presidents and paupers over the decades. Business boomed, and by the 1890s, Roche Harbor had become not only the primary employer in the San Juans, but also the largest producer of lime west of the Mississippi. The lime was mined from 13 hillside quarries. Workers drilled holes for dynamite and then used sledgehammers to crush the rock once it had been blasted loose. The rock was hauled to kilns by horse-drawn wagon. In later years, a steam locomotive carried the ore, and this in turn was replaced by trucks.

The limestone was processed in brick-lined kilns along the shore of Roche Harbor. The rock was dumped into steel receptacles lined with firebrick and then heated with wood fires. The intense heat eventually changed the rock into lime. It took 4,000 acres of forest just to keep the kilns running; each kiln burned 10 cords of wood every six hours! The company had its own small fleet of ships to transport the lime to markets as far away as San Francisco and Hawaii.

The company continued to grow, adding a modern lime factory and a barrel works, along with docks and warehouses that extended hundreds of feet into the bay. McMillin built a company town that included segregated housing for nearly 800 Asian and white employees. Single men were barracked in large bunkhouses, and families were housed in rows of trim and well-kept cottages. Payment was in scrip, useable only at the company store on the wharf; alcohol was banned, and the company even owned a school and church.

McMillin prospered immensely from all this development, buying out his partners and running his various businesses in ways that would lead to fraud charges (they were later dismissed). For half a century, John McMillin was the undisputed king of San Juan Island. When union organizers demanded a wage increase at the quarries, he summarily fired 50 men associated with the union. McMillin also used his money, power, and influence to dictate local politics for years, handpicking candidates for office. On the plus side, McMillin did continue to provide jobs when hard times came in the Depression of the 1930s. He died in 1936 and is buried in the Masonic symbol-covered family mausoleum just above Roche Harbor—built, of course, with cement from the local limeworks.

The quarries at Roche Harbor finally closed in 1956, and a Seattle businessman and physician, Dr. Reuben J. Tarte, purchased all 4,000 acres and 12 miles of coastline. Over the next three decades, he and his family restored the aging hotel and other buildings. The complex has been sold twice since and is currently owned by Rich Komen and SaltChuk Resources (the billion-dollar parent of Totem Ocean Trailer Express, Foss Maritime, and other companies), who have continued the process of transforming this old lime operation into the finest resort in the San Juans.

Sights

★ THE WHALE MUSEUM

One of the must-see places on San Juan Island, **The Whale Museum** (62 1st St. N.,360/378-4710 or 800/946-7227, www.whalemuseum.org, 9am-6pm daily late May-Sept., 10am-4pm daily the rest of the year, closed Thanksgiving, Christmas, and early January, $6 adults, $5 seniors, $3 ages 5-18 and college students, free for military members and kids under 5) opened its doors in 1979 as the first museum in America dedicated to the interpretation of living whales in the wild. Exhibits focus on whale biology and human-whale interactions, with a spotlight on the famous resident orca populations of the Salish Sea.

Downstairs are several free exhibits that introduce you to these incredible animals, including details on recent sightings. The main collection is up a narrow staircase bordered by a colorful whale mural. The exhibits begin with the legends of the Salish people who first lived here. One room in the museum shows a video about whales in the Salish Sea that provides an excellent overview. Another small room has exhibits especially for children, and they'll love the chance to dress-up with orca fins and tails for photos to send to the grandparents. The large exhibit hall upstairs contains life-size models and the full skeletons of a baby gray whale, plus adult killer and minke whales. A big wall chart shows the genealogy of local pods. Step into a phone booth to hear the songs of various whales and other marine mammals; learn about hydrophones and how the noises from vessels can be a problem for whales; examine whale fetuses; and compare the pickled brains of a spotted dolphin, a fin whale, and a human. The museum operates a network of hydrophones to monitor whale locations, vocalizations, and noise from vessel traffic.

There's also a gift shop with books on whales, educational toys, games, videos and CDs, clothing, T-shirts, and jewelry. Group tours and educational programs are available year-round. You can "adopt" one of the local whales (population of 82 in 2015) for $35. If you come upon a stranded seal, sea lion, or other marine mammal, do not handle it, but instead immediately call the museum's **Stranded Marine Mammal Hotline** at 800/562-8832.

SAN JUAN ISLAND
SIGHTS

The Whale Museum

Friday Harbor

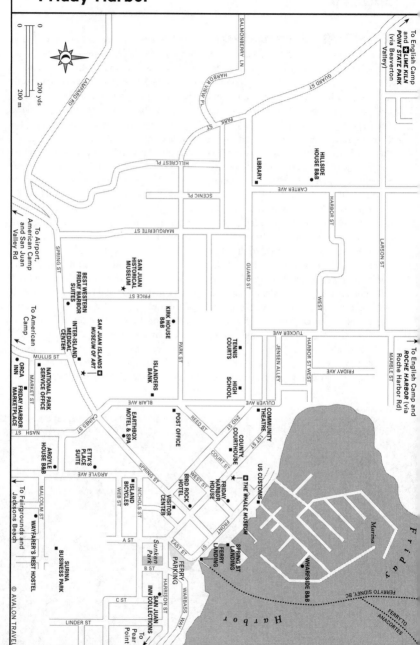

0
0

200 yds
200 m

To English Camp
and ✪ LIME KILN
POINT STATE PARK
(via Beaverton
Valley)

SALMONBERRY LN

HARBOR VIEW PL

GUARD ST

PARK ST

HILLCREST PL

LIBRARY ■

HILLSIDE
HOUSE B&B ■

CARTER AVE

HARBOR ST

LARSON ST

SCENIC PL

MARGUERITE ST

SPRING ST

SAN JUAN
HISTORICAL
MUSEUM ★

PRICE ST

BEST WESTERN
FRIDAY HARBOR
SUITES ■

To Airport,
American Camp
and San Juan
Valley Rd

KIRK HOUSE B&B ■

To American
Camp

INTER-ISLAND
MEDICAL
CENTER ■

SAN JUAN ISLANDS ✪
MUSEUM OF ART

GUARD ST

WEST

TUCKER AVE

TENNIS
COURTS ■

HIGH
SCHOOL ■

To English Camp and
ROCHE HARBOR (via
Roche Harbor Rd)

MARBLE ST

HARBOR AVE

FRIDAY AVE

MULLIS ST

PARK ST

ISLANDERS
BANK ■

JENSEN ALLEY

HARBOR ST WEST

MARKET ST

NATIONAL PARK
SERVICE OFFICE ■

● ORCA
INN

FRIDAY HARBOR
MARKETPLACE ■

CAINES ST

NASH ST

EARTHBOX
MOTEL & SPA ●

BLAIR AVE

POST OFFICE ■

REED ST

2ND ST

1ST ST

CULVER AVE

COMMUNITY ★
THEATRE

COUNTY ■
COURTHOUSE

US CUSTOMS

✪ THE WHALE MUSEUM

ETTA'S
PLACE
SUITE ●

SPRING ST

COURT S ST

FRIDAY
HARBOR
HOUSE ●

ARGYLE
HOUSE B&B ●

ARGYLE AVE

ISLAND
BICYCLES ■

WEB ST

NICHOLS ST

MALCOLM ST

VISITOR
CENTER ●

BIRD ROCK
HOTEL ●

WEST ST

FRONT ST

A ST

To Fairgrounds and
Jacksons Beach

WAYFARER'S REST HOSTEL ●

SURINA
BUSINESS PARK ■

Sunken
Park

EAST ST

1ST ST

FERRY
PARKING

SPRING ST
LANDING

FERRY
LANDING

WHARFSIDE B&B ●

Marina

F r i d a y

B ST

C ST

LINDER ST

SAN JUAN ■
INN COLLECTIONS

HARRISON ST

WARBASS WAY

To
Pear
Point

H a r b o r

FERRY TO SIDNEY, BC

FERRY TO
ANACORTES

© AVALON TRAVEL

★ SAN JUAN ISLANDS MUSEUM OF ART

Friday Harbor's most stunning building houses the **San Juan Islands Museum of Art** (540 Spring St., 360/370-5050, www.sjima.org, 11am-6pm Thurs.-Mon. May-Sept., 11am-5pm Fri.-Mon. Oct.-Apr., $10, free for kids under 18). Towering glass windows in the IMA's Atrium Gallery provide a visually enticing space for changing exhibits. The focus is primarily contemporary and includes sculpture, painting, photography, and more; there's something new almost any time you visit. The museum's two other galleries showcase its permanent collection.

SAN JUAN HISTORICAL MUSEUM

In 1894, James King built the two-story farmhouse that now houses the **San Juan Historical Museum** (405 Price St., 360/378-3949, www.sjmuseum.org, 10am-4pm Wed.-Sat. and 1pm-4pm Sun. May-Sept., 1pm-4pm Sat. Apr. and Oct., by appointment only in winter, $5 adults, $4 seniors, $3 ages 5-18, free for kids under 5). Inside are fascinating antiques, old photos, and historical artifacts, while outside you'll find a variety of old farm equipment, the first county jail, a log cabin, barn, milk house, and carriage house. A replica 19th-century barn at the museum is expected to be completed in 2018, with images, historical artifacts, and interactive displays detailing the fishing, farming, logging, and lime history of San Juan Island. Those interested in a more in-depth look at local history will want to check out the resource center, with an extensive collection of historical photos, oral histories, and genealogical information. The little gift shop sells books, cards, and toys. Various museum activities take place throughout the year, including outdoor concerts Wednesday evenings mid-July-mid-August and the Fourth of July Pig War picnic.

A number of other historic structures dot the island. One of the nicest is **Valley Church,** on Madden Lane two miles south of Friday Harbor. The church was built in 1892, and two cemeteries are nearby.

OTHER FRIDAY HARBOR SIGHTS

Head up Front Street from the ferry landing for a couple of hidden attractions. Next to the ferry is **Spring Street Landing** (www.portfridayharbor.org), which houses a collection of shops and restaurants, along with an interesting 400-gallon **saltwater aquarium** containing surf perch, sea stars, anemones, sea cucumbers, tube worms, scallops, sea urchins, and other creatures from nearby waters.

A short distance farther at Waterfront Park is *Interaction,* a large and striking wood sculpture by First Nations Canadian artist Susan Point. The piece is inspired by traditional Coast Salish house posts but uses contemporary techniques to represent the interface between people and their environment on San Juan Island.

Next to the Whale Museum, the **American Legion Veterans Museum** (1st St., 360/298-1940, www.wateringholegallery.com/museum, 10am-2pm Fri.-Sun. in summer, free) houses weapons and memorabilia from past wars, most notably a Union flag from the Battle of Shiloh during the Civil War.

★ SAN JUAN ISLAND NATIONAL HISTORICAL PARK

In one of the stranger pieces of Northwest history, the killing of a pig by an American settler nearly set off a war between the United States and Britain. Conflict was averted when saner heads prevailed, and the San Juan Islands were eventually declared American territory. The sites where the American and British forces were based during the standoff are now part of **San Juan Island National Historical Park** (650 Mullis St., 360/378-2240, www.nps.gov/sajh), with administrative offices in Friday Harbor. The park itself is in two sections on different sides of the island: American Camp on the south end and English Camp on the western shore. Both sites have small visitors centers, along with picnic areas and beach access for day use only. The grounds of both are open year-round, but they do not have campgrounds.

Summertime activities include guided daily historical and nature walks at American Camp, living history exhibitions Saturday noon-3pm at English Camp, and various talks and demonstrations on summer weekends. Check the park website for details on these and other offerings.

American Camp

On the southeast corner of San Juan Island, 1,200-acre American Camp sits on a grassy, windswept peninsula six miles from Friday Harbor. This is a magnificent place on a sunny summer afternoon, with both the Cascades and Olympics in view. It's also a deliciously lonely place to explore on a rainy winter day.

The **American Camp Visitor Center** (360/378-2240, 8:30am-5pm daily late May-early Sept., 8:30am-4:30pm Wed.-Sun. the rest of the year) houses a few historical exhibits, along with a tiny snuff spoon, a toothbrush, bottles, pipes, marbles, a comb, a chamber pot, and other small items found in archaeological excavations of the military encampments. Also on exhibit are Native Lummi items from other local excavations. Be sure to pick up the park brochure at trailheads for a self-guided mile-long walking tour. There's an active **bald eagle nest** in a tree beside the visitors center; take a look through the spotting scope out front. A brand-new interpretive center is in the works for American Camp, but don't expect to see it before 2019.

Three original buildings remain at American Camp from the occupation in the 1860s—two officers' quarters and a laundress's quarters—along with an earthen gun fortification (redoubt) that was constructed by an army engineer named Henry M. Robert. You probably know him from a still-in-print book he wrote in 1876: Robert's Rules of Order, the internationally used manual of parliamentary procedure.

One of the two **Officers' Quarters** buildings once housed George E. Pickett, who later fought for the Confederacy and who became known for his division's role in the disastrous "Pickett's Charge" during the Battle of Gettysburg. This building—oldest on the San Juan Islands—was built in 1856 at Fort Bellingham, and moved to San Juan Island three years later during the Pig War. A second Officers' Quarters building on the grounds was constructed in 1875, and later moved to Friday Harbor after the Pig War. The Park Service returned it to the original location at American Camp in 2010. Both Officers' Quarters buildings are open to the public on summer weekends.

A long white picket fence circles the grounds, and a trail leads downhill past the site of **Belle Vue Farm** near Grandma's Cove. Belle Vue was the old Hudson's Bay Company farm and the home of the British-owned pig that American Lyman Cutlar shot.

American Camp is a fun place for a hike at any time of the year, with all-encompassing vistas, a long sandy beach, three bird-filled lagoons, and a protected cove with tall trees. Bright orange poppies line the slopes in early summer, and killer whales are often visible offshore; just look for the cluster of small boats trailing them. If the weather is sunny and the wind isn't too strong, you certainly won't go wrong with a trek up the towering summit of **Mount Finlayson.** OK, it's hardly a mountain at just 290 feet, so leave your climbing ropes and carabiners at home, but you're bound to be pleased at the summit panorama. On a clear day, you can pick out Mount Baker, Mount Rainier, the Olympic Mountains, and Vancouver Island. There are several routes up the hill; a good one starts at the Jakle's Lagoon Trailhead, where parking is available. The path climbs grassy and flower-filled slopes (with scattered boulders for variety), and for the next mile you can take deep breaths of fresh air, practice a little tai chi, pull out the binoculars to check for whales, eat a peanut butter sandwich, or kiss your sweetie. Once you reach the end near Third Lagoon, you can return on a separate path above Griffin Bay. Follow an old roadbed through a canopy of Douglas fir, western red cedar, and Western hemlock along **Jakle's Lagoon** to reach your original starting point. The total loop is around 3.5 miles, but you can come up with shorter versions if you just want a quick view from the hill or a one-mile round-trip saunter to the lagoon.

A maze of short trails covers the open country around the American Camp Visitor Center, taking you to the historical locations (marked by signs) of the Hudson's Bay Company farm, the officers' quarters, laundress's quarters, and redoubt, and then downhill to the shore along pretty **Grandma's Cove.** This cove is less than a mile round-trip from the visitors center. The prairie at American Camp is home to the **island marble butterfly,** a species long thought extinct. Prior to its rediscovery in 1998, the butterfly hadn't been seen for 90 years.

If beaches are your thing, don't miss driftwood-jammed **South Beach,** a truly wonderful place for a sunset walk (or run). A parking lot is right next to South Beach, and you can hike a mile or so in either direction on this, San Juan Island's longest public beach. It's also one of the best beaches anywhere in the archipelago. It can become a log-walk at the highest tides, so check a tide chart before heading out. This is also a good place to watch for birds, including terns, gulls, plovers, ruddy turnstones, greater and lesser yellowlegs, and bald eagles. Tidepools on the western end of the beach have a multitude of marine life. Restrooms and picnic tables are available.

On the north side of the peninsula along Griffin Bay, **Fourth of July Beach** is another easy walk. It's a short hike from the parking area to the beach, and from here you can walk to Old Town Lagoon, site of the rough-around-the-edges town that was the first settlement on the island.

Near the tip of the peninsula is tiny **Cattle Point Interpretive Area,** where you'll find a picnic shelter housed in an old powerhouse. You can walk to **Cattle Point Lighthouse** via a trail that starts 150 yards down the road to the south. Two pretty pocket-size beaches are just down from the powerhouse parking area. Some private residences are located on the eastern end of the peninsula, as this area lies outside the boundaries of San Juan Island National Historical Park.

English Camp

Nine miles from Friday Harbor on the northwest side of the island, **English Camp** (360/378-4409, 9am-5pm daily June-early Sept., closed the rest of the year) covers more than 900 acres and includes four buildings from the 1860s that have been restored: a small white barracks, a hospital, a commissary, and a picturesque **blockhouse.** The latter sits right at the water's edge and has a peculiar design. The second story is rotated 45 degrees from the bottom level, allowing troops to repel attacks from any side. Fortunately, the attack never came. Befitting the civilized British modus operandi, the camp had a small **formal garden,** an impressive replica of which has been reestablished.

Park volunteers staff the barracks building during the summer and show a video that explains the Pig War. Be sure to pick up the park brochure for a self-guided walking tour of the historical sites. A spotting scope is often set up outside the barracks, providing a good view of an active **osprey nest** on a nearby dead tree. As with American Camp, it's day use only here, with no camping allowed.

English Camp is a quiet and peaceful spot with protected waters on both sides of Bell Point. It contrasts sharply with American Camp's exposed and windswept location. The grounds include several old pear trees from a homestead family who lived here after the British military departed in 1872. Enormous **bigleaf maples** are also on the grounds, one of which was once officially the world's largest (it's surrounded by a picket fence). The loss of two major limbs reduced its spread, so the beautiful tree is now ranked the world's eleventh largest. It is estimated to be over 340

The Pig War

Because of vague wording in the Oregon Treaty of 1846—which established the boundary between the United States and Canada—the San Juan Islands became the focus of an international incident, later known as the Pig War. The treaty noted that the boundary would extend "to the middle of the channel which separates the continent from Vancouver's Island and thence southerly through the middle of the said channel, and of Fuca's Straits, to the Pacific Ocean." Unfortunately, there are two such channels: Britain claimed the boundary was Rosario Strait, while the United States preferred Haro Strait. In dispute were the San Juan Islands, which lie between them.

COLLISION COURSE

Western Canada was under the control of a man with fierce loyalties to both the Hudson's Bay Company and England, governor James Douglas. In 1851, he set up a fishing operation on San Juan Island. Two years later, he sent Charles Griffin—for whom Griffin Bay is named—to establish Belle Vue Farm on the southern end of the island. Crops were planted, shepherds tended sheep, and a few pigs rounded out the farm.

HOG WILD

By 1859, around 18 American settlers had moved to San Juan Island, including Lyman A. Cutlar, who began clearing land for a home and a potato patch. Unfortunately, the place he chose was in the midst of land grazed by Hudson's Bay Company sheep. A boar from Belle Vue Farm kept wandering into Cutlar's potatoes; each time he'd chase it out. Complaints to Griffin got him nowhere; he suggested the problem was Cutlar's weak fence. On June 15, 1859, Cutlar awoke to see Griffin's herdsman laughing as the pig rooted in the potatoes once again. With a shot from his rifle, the pig was dead.

Cutlar offered to pay for the pig. Griffin's response: "You Americans are nothing but a nuisance." He claimed the boar was worth $100 and Cutlar stormed out. Later that day, the British threatened to haul Cutlar to Victoria for trial; Cutlar threatened to shoot anyone who attempted to do so.

Within days, an American steamer arrived, carrying a company of soldiers under arrogant Captain George E. Pickett. Already known for his Mexican War exploits, he would later gain infamy as a Confederate general who led "Pickett's charge" during the Battle of Gettysburg. His troops set up a camp near the Hudson's Bay Company wharf. It was an odd choice. Instead of putting his men out of range of British naval guns, Pickett chose an exposed beach. When the number of warships grew, he moved to the opposite beach. This puzzled the British officers, who didn't know he had graduated last in his class at West Point: 59th out of 59.

---

years old, making it the oldest known bigleaf maple. The park has photos from the 1860s with British officers' wives standing next to this grand old tree.

A 650-foot hill, **Mount Young,** rises directly behind Garrison Bay, with meadow openings atop its forested slopes. The 0.75-mile Mount Young Trail starts at the far end of the English Camp parking lot, crosses the road, and climbs to the little **British cemetery** where six Royal Marines are buried—though none of them died in a battle over the islands. One especially poignant gravestone reads:

William Taylor Aged 34 years Who was accidentally shot By his Brother Jan. 26th 1868. This Tablet is erected by his Sorrowing Brother.

Beyond this, the trail continues up through second-growth forests to the open summit of Mount Young, where you are treated to outstanding vistas across the archipelago. Old Garry oak trees grow up here as well. Many more trails crisscross the **Mitchell Hill** area just south of Mount Young.

An easy alternative walk departs from the blockhouse and leads along an almost-level

AN ESCALATING CRISIS

Governor Douglas didn't take kindly to the sudden American military presence. He ordered three British warships under Captain Geoffrey Hornby to occupy the island, but to avoid a military collision. Douglas's superior, Rear Admiral Robert L. Baynes, who arrived two days later, was appalled, saying he would not "involve two great nations in a war over a squabble about a pig." Still, five of Her Majesty's ships stood ready to open fire.

In the meantime, General Harney continued to build up his forces on San Juan, and by the end of August, 461 American soldiers--protected by an earthen redoubt, 14 field pieces, and eight naval guns--faced off against the British ships. All this military bluster had taken place without any instructions from Washington DC. When President James Buchanan heard the news, he sent Lieutenant General Winfield Scott to seek a peaceful settlement. After much bickering, both sides agreed to leave a token force until an agreement could be brokered.

SHARING THE ISLAND

The Americans stayed on the south end of the island at "Fort Pickett," as **American Camp** came to be called. Crushing boredom, bad food, and dreadful quarters made this a hardship post. On March 21, 1860, British Royal Marines landed on the west side of the island, building **English Camp,** with prim white buildings and a formal garden, at beautiful Garrison Bay. The British were no less bored and unhappy and than the Americans.

The crisis on San Juan died down as a much bigger event rose over the horizon: the Civil War. By 1861, nearly everyone had forgotten about the silly argument over a pig. In the years that followed, the two camps gradually developing a camaraderie that led to joint celebrations of the Fourth of July and Queen Victoria's birthday.

AMERICA TAKES OVER

Finally, a deal was struck to let an arbitrator decide the final boundary: Kaiser Wilhelm I of Germany awarded the islands to the United States in 1872. The Royal Marines withdrew and many British settlers changed their citizenship, allowing them to keep their land as American homesteaders. The Pig War is barely a footnote today, but it marked a turning point in relations between Britain and America. Their last conflict had just one casualty: a pig.

path to the tip of **Bell Point** and then back along Westcott Bay; it's about a mile round-trip. This little wooded peninsula is a great place for a picnic lunch. Keep your eyes open for Canada geese and wild turkeys below, and bald eagles and turkey vultures over-head. Additional trails connect the park with Westcott Bay and Roche Harbor.

Above the parade grounds at English Camp is the historic **Crook House,** built in 1903 by homesteaders after the Royal Marines left. When the Park Service took over in 1968, they discovered a chamber pot under a trap door in the attic. The original inhabitant, William Crook had filled the pot with the family's savings. The Crook House is currently being restored, and will eventually house park offices.

The park hosts an event called **Encampment** the last weekend of July, where you can meet British and American "soldiers" in mid-19th-century period costume. Old-fashioned canvas tents host demonstrations on blacksmithing, small arms, black pow-der demonstrations, woodworking, march-ing, and cookery. Activities include croquet, cricket, and 19th-century baseball. The finale is a candlelight ball in the barracks building.

★ ROCHE HARBOR

On the north end of San Juan Island, 10 miles from Friday Harbor, Roche Harbor (360/378-2155 or 800/451-8910, www.rocheharbor.com) is a delightful step into the past. (Most locals pronounce the word "Roche" as RO-sch, not roach or ro-SHAY.) It's named for Richard Roche, a British surveyor and midshipman during two 19th-century expeditions of the area.

Resort and Marina

Hotel de Haro was built in 1886 by John McMillin of the Hudson's Bay Company, but later grew into the distinctive three-story mansion of today. President Theodore Roosevelt visited it twice, in 1906 and 1907, and it later hosted President William Howard Taft. The property's quarries operated till 1956, when they were essentially mined out. Pick up the fascinating *Walking Tour of Historic Roche Harbor* brochure at the hotel and start your exploration of this picturesque harbor.

The white-clapboard hotel, now in the National Register of Historic Places, has been lovingly restored. If it isn't occupied, you can peek in the **presidential suite** (room 2A) upstairs where Roosevelt stayed, or see his 1907 signature in the guest book below his portrait. The sloping floors, creaking steps, crooked windows, and antique furnishings add some charm to the gracious setting. At the top of the stairs you'll see hand-cut timbers from the original bunkhouse.

Take some time to explore the area around the hotel. Out front is a wonderful **formal garden** with rose trellises and brilliant swaths of various flowers throughout the summer. The yellow brick road between the garden and the hotel was built from firebricks that once lined the limekilns. McMillin's home is now a waterside restaurant, facing the protected and busy harbor filled with sailboats, motorboats, and kayaks. Roche Harbor is still the primary U.S. Customs port of entry for boaters heading to the San Juans from Canadian waters. The old general store is still in use and well worth a visit. Behind it, warehouses once stretched hundreds of feet into the bay, holding up to 20,000 barrels of lime. Across the parking lot are the two original **stone kilns** built by the Scurr brothers in 1881. The 13 old lime quarries are uphill behind the resort, but you need to exercise caution because the slopes are unstable.

Join a free game of bocce ball on the courts nearby, or saunter down the row of **Artist Kiosks** showcasing photography, jewelry,

Hotel de Haro

hand-knit pieces, and watercolors—not to mention scoops of ice cream. The booths are next to the parking lot and are open daily late June-early September and on weekends in the spring and fall. Midsummer moped and bike rentals are available across from the San Juan Island Sculpture Park, uphill from Roche Harbor.

Just up from the hotel is the quaint little New England-style **Our Lady of Good Voyage Chapel,** built in 1892. John McMillin was a devout Methodist, but when Reuben Tarte bought Roche Harbor in 1956, he turned this building into the only privately owned Catholic church in America. Mass is held on Easter Sunday and periodically throughout the summer. Other denominations also use the chapel, and it's a favorite spot for a wedding-with-a-view. A carillon was added in 1972, followed a few years later by a stained glass window that depicts two of the late Dr. Tarte's devotions: medicine and tennis.

A short walk north of the church are nine simple cottages once used by McMillin's employees; they're now rented out to guests. Ten larger cottages were torn down, along with the old Japanese settlement on the south side of the harbor. The Japanese buildings were replaced by ugly condos in the 1970s, a glaring affront to this historic site. More recent developments have been more appropriate to the site, including tasteful additions in the last few years of upscale lodging, a spa, and other facilities behind and adjacent to Hotel de Haro.

A moving—and simultaneously comical— **Colors Ceremony** takes place each evening at sunset mid-May-late September, as the U.S., Canadian, and British flags are lowered as the national anthems play, followed by a recording of taps and a shot from the cannon. This event always attracts a big crowd. Surprise your friends by having a message read to them during the ceremony; just leave the message at the front desk of Hotel de Haro in advance.

Afterglow Vista Mausoleum

The exuberant McMillin family mausoleum, **Afterglow Vista,** is about a mile from Hotel de Haro. Located north of the cottages and a 0.25-mile hike up a dirt trail (signed), the mausoleum's centerpiece is a stone temple packed with Masonic symbols and containing the family's ashes in chair-shaped crypts around a limestone table. A broken column symbolizes the "unfinished state" of life, but the planned bronze dome with a Maltese cross was never added. Some folks claim that on full-moon nights, a ghostly McMillin family can be seen talking and laughing around the mausoleum table. Could this be the true meaning of the Afterglow Vista name?

San Juan Island Sculpture Park

Covering 20 acres near the entrance to Roche Harbor, **San Juan Island Sculpture Park** (9083 Roche Harbor Rd., 360/370-5050, www.sjisculpturepark.com, daily dawn-dusk, $5 donation, kids under 12 free) is home to more than 150 large stone, wood, bronze, glass, and metal sculptures created by renowned sculptors. It's the largest sculpture park in the Pacific Northwest. Trails wend through a diverse habitat of forest, meadow, pond, wetland, and shoreline. The sculptures change every few months, so there's always something new to see (and touch). All of these are also for sale if you have a few thousand dollars lying around; just peruse the binder inside the gatehouse for prices and artist info. Children can build their own sculptures at the Starfish Project area with found objects, and dogs are welcome. Birders should pick up the brochure on the 120 or so species that have been seen in this diverse habitat. Nearby is a **fly-in aviation community,** where planes taxi down Cessna Avenue and park in hangars next to the houses.

★ LIME KILN POINT STATE PARK

Lime Kiln Point State Park (360/378-2044, www.parks.wa.gov), locally known as Whale Watch Park, is a premier spot to look for killer whales as they pass along Haro Strait on the island's west side. It's the only park in the nation dedicated primarily to whale-watching. Sit here long enough on a summer day (it may be quite a while), and you're likely to see killer whales and possibly minke whales, Dall's porpoises, or harbor porpoises. Day use of the park costs $10 per vehicle ($30 for an annual pass).

Picturesque **Lime Kiln Point Lighthouse** was completed in 1919. Researchers from the Whale Museum use the lighthouse as a base to observe whale and vessel behavior, as well as to study whale vocalizations and underwater noise via offshore hydrophones. If there aren't any whales, you can take in the vistas that stretch from Vancouver Island to the Olympic Peninsula. If it's foggy, you'll get a fine view of the fog.

The park has plenty of parking and a wheelchair-accessible trail to the whale-viewing area. A small **interpretive center** next to the parking lot is staffed daily 10am-4pm late May-mid-September, but it closes when whales are passing by the lighthouse. No camping is available, but there are picnic tables, drinking water, and privies. Tune your radio to 88.1 FM when you approach the park to hear a broadcast of underwater sounds—including whales if they happen to be in the area. (You're more likely, however, to hear the loud drone of ship motors.) A small stand called **Red Checkered Picnics** (360/370-5810, 10am-5pm May-Sept.) sells ready-made picnic lunches, juices, salads, and ice cream treats.

In the summer, park staff, volunteers, and researchers lead not-for-the-claustrophobic lighthouse tours (7pm-sunset Thurs. and Sat. late May-early Sept.). At other times, you can watch a video on whales at the interpretive center, listen to underwater sounds from the hydrophone at the lighthouse (or online at www.seasound.org), take in the view, or pull out binoculars to scan for orcas, seals, and marine birds. Also known as FOLKS, the **Friends of Lime Kiln Society** (www.folkssji.org) is a volunteer group that works to protect the park.

A short loop hike leads past one of the restored **limekilns,** along with others in disrepair, before the trail heads south to the old quarry and on to **Deadman Bay Preserve.** A separate trail leads to Deadman Bay from West Side Road just south of the park (it's just before the 15 mph sign). Stop at the pebbly cove to explore the tidepools and look for multicolored beach glass. The name Deadman Bay originated in the 1880s when Ben Ure smuggled Chinese immigrants into Puget Sound.

Lime Kiln Point Lighthouse

He operated near Deception Pass, tying his cargo of immigrants in burlap bags. If customs officials approached, he would throw them overboard, with tides and currents sometimes carrying them north and west to this cove on San Juan Island.

The trail continues out of the park and onto adjacent land within the **Limekiln Preserve,** owned by the San Juan County Land Bank. South of Limekiln, West Side Road hugs the steep shoreline of San Juan Island. This stretch of road is part of the Land Bank's **Westside Scenic Preserve,** where three pullouts provide additional chances to watch for whales and to take in panoramic views of Vancouver Island and the Olympic Mountains.

SAN JUAN COUNTY PARK

On the west side of the island at Smallpox Bay, **San Juan County Park** (360/378-8420, www.co.san-juan.wa.us/parks) is the only public camping spot on San Juan. In addition to camping, the 12-acre park has a grassy day-use area overlooking the water, a pebble beach, pretty forests, picnic tables, restrooms, drinking water, and a boat launch. The waters here are popular with kayakers and divers, and this is a good place to watch for wild turkeys on land and killer whales offshore. Portions of the 1998 film *Practical Magic* were filmed in the park.

Smallpox Bay got its name in the 1860s when two sick sailors from an unknown boat were put ashore to prevent them from contaminating the rest of the crew with smallpox. Local Coast Salish people, who had no immunity to the disease, helped the men, and smallpox quickly spread across San Juan Island. The feverish victims jumped into the bay to cool off and died of pneumonia. The few survivors burned their possessions and fled the island.

REUBEN TARTE COUNTY PARK

The tiny day-use-only **Reuben Tarte County Park** (360/378-8420, www.co.san-juan.wa.us/ parks) is a secluded and delightful place to escape the Friday Harbor crowds. Located on the north end of the island near Limestone Point, it consists of a rocky point with two minor coves facing Haro Strait. The ferry connecting the islands with Sidney, British Columbia, goes right past the park. This is one of the few pieces of public land on the north end of San Juan Island; everything else around here is posted No Trespassing.

Get to Reuben Tarte by following Roche Harbor Road eight miles from Friday Harbor and turning right onto Rouleau Road. Follow it a mile, then turn right onto Limestone Point Road. After another mile, turn right again onto San Juan Drive and continue 0.25 mile to the park, located on the left. You should probably park at the top and hike down the steep paved road to Reuben Tarte, as only a couple of parking spaces are available at the bottom. There are no facilities (other than an outhouse) here, but bring your picnic lunch for a delightful afternoon along the shore.

FALSE BAY BIOLOGICAL PRESERVE

Owned by the University of Washington, **False Bay Biological Preserve** is a half-mile-wide undeveloped bay on the south end of San Juan Island. This large and shallow bay becomes a mudflat when the tide is out, though there are some sandy stretches along the shore. It's an easy stroll, and a good place to look for gulls, ducks, and shorebirds. Access is from a pullout off False Bay Road; follow the road around the east side of the bay.

MOUNT GRANT PRESERVE

Covering 141 acres, the extraordinary **Mount Grant Preserve** was slated for development and a paved road had been built to the top for a dozen planned homesites. Fortunately, local environmental organizations stepped in to purchase the land before it could be parceled out. The preserve is still a work in progress (not all the $3 million price has been raised), but hikers can head up the road to

Killer Whales

Killer whales are a major attraction for visitors to the San Juan Islands. Each year more than 500,000 people board commercial whale-watching trips in the waters off Washington and British Columbia, pumping $10 million into the economy. Why all this attention? These intelligent, beautiful animals share close family bonds, communicate long distances underwater, enjoy play, and share our taste for salmon (though theirs is in the raw, sashimi form).

NATURAL HISTORY

With a range from tropical seas south to the edge of Antarctica and north into the Bering Sea, killer whales are the second-most widely distributed mammals on the planet; only humans range farther. Like humans, some females may live a century or longer (males have a shorter lifespan), with sexual maturity around age 15. At birth, the calves are 8 feet long and weigh more than 400 pounds. By adulthood, females are around 23 feet long, while males can reach 30 feet. A member of the order of cetaceans—whales, dolphins, and porpoises—the killer whale might best be viewed as a large dolphin that happens to have *whale* in its name.

Killer whales, *Orcinus orca,* have long had a reputation befitting their murderous name. Historically, they were regarded as bloodthirsty predators. More recently, the "Save the Whales" crowd has promoted them as lovable creatures that should instead be called by the more lyrical name, orcas. (Ironically, the word "orca" comes from a Latin word meaning "kingdom of the dead.") The cuddly orca frenzy was fueled in part by the three *Free Willy* movies. The truth is much more complex; some killer whales known as residents hunt only fish. Others, called transient killer whales, kill marine mammals, including sea otters, sea lions, porpoises, and even other whales.

---

the 740-foot summit for astounding 360-degree views. Continue along the ridge through grassy areas and old-growth Douglas fir forests, and loop back to your starting point, a distance of 1.8 miles.

The road is open to cars 9am-7pm most Sundays July-September, but the rest of the time it is foot or bike access only. Access to Mount Grant is off West Valley Road; look for the small sign approximately five miles from Friday Harbor.

BEACHES, TRAILS, AND NATURAL AREAS

Day-use-only spots are scattered around San Juan Island. **Jacksons Beach** is a small public beach a mile south of Friday Harbor off Argyle Avenue. It has a sandy shore littered with driftwood, a boat ramp, picnic tables, sand volleyball courts, and restrooms.

Eagle Cove sits on the south end of the island just west of American Camp and is a favorite of sportfishers who enjoy the delightful pocket beach. Two north-end bodies of water,

Egg Lake and **Sportsmans Lake,** are also popular with anglers in search of trout.

Sunken Park in Friday Harbor is a little pocket park with a gazebo, basketball court, and picnic area.

The **San Juan County Land Bank** (350 Court St., 360/378-4402, www.sjclandbank. org) owns several hundred acres of protected lands on San Juan Island that are open to the public, including Westside Scenic Preserve, Deadman Bay Preserve, Mount Grant Preserve, Cady Mountain Preserve, and Limekiln Preserve.

The **San Juan Trails Committee** (www. sanjuanislandtrails.org) helps maintain and develop hiking trails on the island. Its website has descriptions and downloadable maps for trails in a dozen different locations. Some of the most interesting are in the **Roche Harbor Highlands** and at **English Camp** and **American Camp.** The six-mile **Town to American Camp Trail** follows roads to the park.

For something completely different, check

Killer whales travel in matrilineal groups called pods. These consist of extended families that follow the eldest female. Even the males may remain for life within these extended families. Surprisingly, not all mating takes place with other pods, and there is some evidence of inbreeding. Intensive research has revealed a highly complex social structure and diverse patterns of behavior, including a vocal dialect for each pod that is distinctive from one population to the next.

Killer whales can be surprisingly kind to members of their own pod. In 1973, a British Columbia ferry collided with a young killer whale, seriously injuring it with the propeller. Other members of the pod rushed to the calf's aid, physically supporting it for two weeks to help it breathe. Unfortunately, the animal later died of its wounds.

RESIDENT KILLER WHALES

Nearly 300 resident killer whales swim in the waters along Washington and British Columbia. They are divided into two groups: a large northern community of approximately 210 whales in 16 pods found mainly in British Columbia's Johnstone Strait, and a smaller southern community of whales in the Salish Sea around the San Juan Islands. These southern residents are subdivided into family groups known as J, K, and L pods.

With 35 members (as of 2017), L pod is the largest, followed by J pod with 24 members and K pod with around 19 individuals. The J pod is most often seen by whale-watchers because it spends time in local waters year-round. The matriarch of J pod was born in 1911, with four generations of descendants. Both K and L pods head to the outer coast of Washington and Vancouver Island, and even as far south as Monterey Bay, California, during the winter and spring.

out the whimsical creations of local artist Kevin Roth on West Side Road. You'll find a Beatles-esque **Yellow Submarine,** along with a **giant red strawberry** and SpongeBob-inspired **giant yellow pineapple.** All are created from recycled metal and big enough to climb inside. Guaranteed to please the kid in anyone!

FARMS AND VINEYARDS

Several dozen small farms dot the San Juan Island landscape, producing such specialty products as cider apples, wines, miniature horses, alpacas, medicinal herbs, strawberries, goat cheese, organic vegetables, and rabbits (do they really need more of these?). Fall farm tours take place in late September each year. Many local farm products are sold at the **San Juan Farmers Market** in Friday Harbor, held on summer Saturdays.

Krystal Acres Ranch

Fans of the friendly alpaca will certainly want to visit **Krystal Acres Ranch** (3501 Valley Rd., 0.5 mile south of English Camp, 360/378-6125, www.krystalacres.com, 10am-5pm daily Apr.-Dec., 11am-4pm daily Jan.-Mar.), a picturesque 80-acre farm bordered by white picket fences. The multicolored herd is a favorite of photographers who happen by, and the teddy bear-faced alpacas are bound to elicit "I want one" from any child. A walking path leads between pastures containing more than 60 grazing alpacas—some worth many thousands of dollars as breeding stock. The gift shop (open daily year-round) sells locally produced alpaca yarn and socks, along with stuffed animals and Peruvian clothing. Owners Kris and Albert Olson will be happy to tell you about alpacas and their immaculate ranch. The animals' hair is sheared in early June, so the alpacas will look closely cropped for a while after that.

★ San Juan Vineyards

The award-winning **San Juan Vineyards** (3136 Roche Harbor Rd., 360/378-9463, www.sanjuanvineyards.com) is housed inside a

Saving the Whales

When intensive research on the islands' resident killer whales began in 1976, the southern community consisted of 71 individuals. It gradually increased to a peak of 98 in 1995, but declined to 78 whales in 2001, prompting scientists to request protection under the Endangered Species Act. As of 2017, the three pods contained only 79 whales; scientists are alarmed that the population could be in serious trouble.

Several factors contribute to this decline. Because they are long-lived top-level predators, killer whales concentrate environmental contaminants in their fatty tissue, including high levels of toxins like polychlorinated biphenyls (PCBs), flame retardants (PBDEs), and dioxins. PCB levels in the southern community killer whales are among the highest ever found in whales. Another problem is that their primary food source, salmon, is on the decline; half of the local salmon runs are threatened with extinction. When the whales lack food, they consume stored blubber that contains PCBs, which can cause reproductive and other problems.

During the 1960s and 1970s, some 48 young killer whales from this population were captured in Puget Sound for aquariums around the world; only one of these is still alive, a female known as Lolita, living in the Miami Seaquarium in Florida. The loss of this 10-year age cohort of females is still being felt.

What role does whale-watching have in the whales' decline? Boat noise can mask echolocation, possibly making it harder for killer whales to find what little food is available to them. Current research suggests that the dramatic increase in boat traffic may also be causing whales to compensate for boat noise in the way they communicate.

The Whale Museum in Friday Harbor recommends that people watch whales responsibly either from shore or with a whale-watching company that belongs to the **Pacific Whale Watch Association** (www.pacificwhalewatch.org). The company should be one that hires professional naturalists and follows the Be Whale Wise guidelines. As a consumer, you can help by supporting habitat protection for salmon, limiting the use of chemicals, and voting for politicians who support environmental protection.

restored one-room schoolhouse built in 1896 and originally located along Sportsmans Lake. The little five-acre vineyard grows Madeleine Angevine and Siegerrebe grapes. The winery produces a limited bottling of these—and they sell out quickly—but most of what it crafts comes from eastern Washington grapes, including chardonnay, cabernet sauvignon, pinot gris, riesling, rose, cabernet Franc, and Mono Vino.

The Mona Vino—a red wine blend—is named for the friendly and much-photographed **dromedary camel** that lives across the road (he loves carrots, but watch your fingers). Drop by for wine-tasting (three samples for $5) daily 11am-5pm in the summer, and on weekends in the spring and fall. Call for an appointment at other times. The second Saturday in June brings barrel tasting, with food and wine. Grapes are harvested in early October by local volunteers. Join them for the picking and partying fun.

Westcott Bay Cider

Apples have a lengthy history on the San Juan Islands. Many orchards were planted by early settlers, and by 1900 this was perhaps the most important apple-producing region in the state. Eastern Washington apples have long taken over that crown, but apple and other fruit trees are again being planted on the San Juans. One sign of this resurgence is **Westcott Bay Cider** (12 Anderson Lane, 360/378-2606, www.westcottbaycider.com), located on the west side of the island near Roche Harbor. New orchards were planted here in 1996, and Westcott Bay Cider opened a few years later.

The winery produces and bottles traditional English-style ciders, from very dry to

Lavender Lemonade

- 2 cups water
- 6 sprigs fresh lavender spikes, or 2 teaspoons dried Pelindaba lavender
- juice of 3 lemons (about ½ cup)
- 1 quart water
- ½ cup sugar, or to taste, or ½ cup Pelindaba Lavender Syrup, or to taste
- additional lavender for garnish

Bring the 2 cups of water to a boil. Add lavender, cover the pan, and let it steep over very low heat for 30 minutes. Strain and reserve the liquid, which is the lavender tea you will use later.

Roll the lemons on a hard surface to help release the juices. Cut and squeeze them, straining out the seeds. To the quart of water, add ⅓ cup of the lavender tea, lemon juice, and sugar or lavender syrup (to taste). Stir well to dissolve. Chill and serve over ice. Garnish with a fresh lavender spike. Makes 1 quart of lemonade.

Recipe courtesy of Pelindaba Lavender Farm

medium sweet using 16 different kinds of cider apples, including such heritage varieties as Yarlington Mill, Dabinett, Brown Snout, Sweet Coppin, Cox's Orange Pippins, and Kingston Black. You've probably never heard of these bittersweet and bittersharp little apples, with their high tannin and acidity, because they're grown for cider production, not eating. The juice is fermented to a 6.8 percent alcohol content.

In 2010, a brass pot still was added to distill apple brandy and gin. It's part of the same business, but is called **San Juan Island Distillery** (www.sjidistillery.com). Visitors can sample hard cider, apple brandy, and a dozen kinds of gin at the winery, and the tasting room is open Saturdays 1pm-4pm year-round, and Sundays 1pm-4pm in the summer, or by appointment at other times. Closed in January and February. Cider, brandy, and gin are available for purchase or from Kings Market in Friday Harbor. Locals join in for a big apple harvest party each October.

★ Pelindaba Lavender Farm

Pelindaba Lavender Farm (off Wold Rd. at 33 Hawthorne Lane, 360/378-4248 or 866/819-1911, www.pelindabalavender.com) grows these pungent flowering plants on 20 acres on the south side of the island. Owner Stephen Robins has 25,000 plants in production on his organic farm, plus a distillery to extract the oil. Lavender flowers and essential oils are used in a wide range of products, all of which are made here: body oil, eye pillows, sachets, lavender pepper, pet shampoo, and even a lavender-based product that kills pond algae. Lavender ice cream and lemonade are available in midsummer. A lavender cookbook is available, and there's a cutting field if you're just looking for a fresh bouquet during the flowering season July-September; you'll see the most color in July. Pick up a brochure or borrow an iPod for a self-guided tour of the fields, drying racks, and distillery. Drop by on weekends in July and August for informative free 45-minute talks about lavender, how it is processed and distilled, and its many uses; these start at 2pm.

The gift shop is open daily 9:30am-5:30pm May-October, with limited hours the rest of the year. The farm also hosts the annual **Lavender Festival** the third weekend of July, with tours, distillation demonstrations, craft workshops, lavender-accented foods, music, and kid activities.

Recreation

★ WHALE-WATCHING

For thousands of visitors, seeing whales is *the* highlight of a trip to San Juan Island. Whale-watching has become a major business for the island. July and August are the peak months to see resident killer whales, and in summer a flotilla of boats and kayaks hovers around pods of whales, trailing them as they move. Boat operators insist that they are not negatively impacting the whales, and most local companies are members of the **Pacific Whale Watch Association** (www.pacificwhale-watchassociation.org), which follows the "Be Whale Wise" code of conduct to minimize disturbances to the whales.

The Whale Museum encourages folks to watch from shore, especially from such places as Lime Kiln Point State Park (aka Whale Watch Park) and American Camp. Drop by the museum to ask where whales have been reported that day and then take a bike, car, or shuttle bus over for the day. It's cheaper than a boat and you won't need to worry about impacting the whales.

Quite a few companies run scheduled whale-watching trips, and each has its advantages and disadvantages. Some companies promise "guaranteed whales" in their brochures. In reality, the entire fleet knows where the whales are, so you're probably as likely to see them on one boat as another.

Some of the bigger outfits have flashy brochures and larger boats that pack folks on, while the small operators offer more intimate trips, though their boats may be slower and bounce around a lot (not good if you get seasick easily). Operators based on the west side of San Juan Island at Snug Harbor or Roche Harbor are often closer to the whales, but fast boats can get there from Friday Harbor, and the whales aren't always in that area. Many companies have hydrophones to listen in on whale conversations.

You'll generally pay a lower price for the larger boats that hold 50 or more passengers, and more for the little "six-pack" vessels. Prices vary widely, and a three- or four-hour trip costs $99-129 for adults or $69-115 for kids. Approximately half that time will be spent around the whales, with the remainder

watching orcas off San Juan Island

Whale-Watching Tips

Dozens of commercial operators run some 85 whale-watching trips around the San Juan Islands. Some are based on San Juan and Orcas Islands; others launch from Victoria and Seattle. Operated by The Whale Museum, the **Soundwatch Boater Education Program** works to protect the whales from vessel impacts through education and "report cards" on commercial whale-watching companies. Flagrant violations are reported to the National Marine Fisheries Service and Fisheries & Oceans Canada, which may impose stiff fines for whale harassment. Boaters heading out on their own should pick up a copy of the *Be Whale Wise* guidelines from The Whale Museum in Friday Harbor or learn more at www.bewhalewise.org. Boaters and kayakers must stay at least 200 yards from whales and keep out of their path.

WHERE ARE THE WHALES?

The best time to see whales is July and August, when salmon are plentiful in Puget Sound and orcas are seen 90 percent of the time. The J pod is typically present year-round, while the K and L pods often head farther out to sea to hunt December through April, when most of the salmon are elsewhere.

The best viewing is in Haro Strait; the least intrusive way to watch whales is on shore at **Lime Kiln Point State Park** (aka Whale Watch Park). But whales move almost constantly and may be seen elsewhere around the San Juans, particularly near Stuart and Waldron Islands northwest of Orcas Island. The Whale Museum's website, www.whalemuseum.org, shows which pods have historically been seen around the San Juans, plus webcams showing the current view from the park, along with live audio from underwater hydrophones just offshore. Other good viewing spots are San Juan County Park and South Beach.

CHOOSING A TOUR

Not all tours are created equal. Some brag about personalized trips aboard boats that hold just six passengers; others talk up their speedy boats, colorful captains, stable larger vessels, or hydrophones. From an environmental standpoint, larger boats mean fewer vessels bobbing around the whales. You'll also hear complaints about the small inflatable Zodiac boats that buzz around the whales like angry bees. They have a bad reputation for "leapfrogging": intentionally positioning the boats where the whales are expected to surface. This practice gives tourists a thrill, but is frowned upon by whale researchers and more reputable operators.

Take the time to learn more about the companies and how they operate. Ask about onboard naturalists' training and affiliated organizations. Companies listed in this book are all members of the **Pacific Whale Watch Association** (www.pacificwhalewatchassociation.org), which has a code of conduct that tries to minimize disturbances to the whales. A particularly good company is also the oldest on the islands: **Deer Harbor Charters** (360/376-5989 or 800/544-5758, www.deerharborcharters.com), based on Orcas Island. **The Whale Museum** (360/378-4710 or 800/946-7227, www.whalemuseum.org) does not lead trips; in fact, it encourages shore-based viewing instead. A local environmental group, **Orca Relief** (www.orcarelief.org), opposes all boat-based whale-watching.

LEARNING MORE

Killer Whales, by John K. B. Ford, Graeme M. Ellis, and Kenneth C. Balcomb (UBC Press, www.ubc-press.ca), is the definitive volume on these whales, with a detailed natural history and a genealogy of the British Columbia and Washington whales. Balcomb heads the nonprofit **Center for Whale Research** (360/378-5835, www.whaleresearch.com). The center doesn't have facilities for visitors, but it does take volunteers for seasonal research projects. Another good organization is **Orca Network** (866/672-2638, www.orcanetwork.org).

in transit. In the peak season, be sure to make reservations for these very popular trips. Bring a warm jacket, snacks, drinks, a camera, and binoculars.

In addition to killer whales, keep your eyes open for Dall's porpoises, harbor porpoises, harbor seals, Steller sea lions, bald eagles, and many species of seabirds. You might also spot an occasional minke or gray whale.

A good small company, **Maya's Legacy Whale Watching** (360/378-7996, www. sanjuanislandwhalewatch.com) has two six-passenger boats based in Snug Harbor, and a 16-passenger vessel that heads out from Friday Harbor.

Friday Harbor-based **Western Prince Cruises** (360/378-5315 or 800/757-6722, www.orcawhalewatch.com) uses a fast bio-diesel-powered 46-foot boat that holds a maximum of 30 guests. They also operate a 27-foot high-speed boat for those who don't mind wind in their faces.

San Juan Excursions (360/378-6636 or 800/809-4253, www.watchwhales.com) operates the classic 65-foot *Odyssey,* a wooden boat with space for 97 passengers. Three tours depart from Friday Harbor and typically last 3.5 hours.

San Juan Safaris (360/378-1323 or 800/450-6858, www.sanjuansafaris.com) is based in Spring Street Landing at the Friday Harbor marina. The company has a speedy open boat (exposure suits provided) for the more adventurous, and a larger boat with a heated cabin for more comfort.

San Juan Outfitters (360/378-1962 or 866/810-1483, www.sanjuanislandoutfitters. com) has 3.5-hour trips out of Roche Harbor with a 24-passenger boat. Trips depart twice daily in midsummer.

Black Fish Whale & Wildlife Tours (360/370-5696, www.sanjuanislandwhales. com) has both a 30-foot vessel and a six-passenger boat operating from Friday Harbor. In addition to the standard three-hour whale-watching trips, Black Fish also runs day trips to state parks on Jones Island and Sucia Island.

(Black Fish also operates under the name San Juan Island Whale & Wildlife Tours.)

Spirit of Orca (360/378-0302 or 888/221-1331, www.spiritoforca.com) has a fast six-passenger 26-foot boat with water taxi service from Friday Harbor.

Maya's Legacy Whale Watching heads out year-round; the other companies typically operate April-September when whales are more plentiful. Wintertime trips focus on seals, bald eagles, and other wildlife.

A number of companies lead **sea kayak trips** along the west coast of San Juan Island—through prime orca waters. Kayaks are quiet and don't leave behind the odor from exhaust fumes, but kayakers should raft up (stick close to each other) to minimize their impacts on the whales. Look for kayak companies that depart from San Juan County Park or Snug Harbor.

★ SEA KAYAKING

Sea kayaking is exceptionally popular in the waters around San Juan Island, with local companies offering both day trips and multi-night tours. Each company has its own specialties, so ask around before deciding, particularly on a multiday kayaking trip. Some companies take large groups, while others limit sizes and have a better guide-to-client ratio. Reservations are recommended for summer weekends. Most companies operate late April-September.

Day Trips

Several companies lead short sea-kayaking paddles from San Juan Island in the summer months. No experience is needed, but you should be in decent physical condition, and most don't allow young children. You aren't likely to get too far in such a short time, but this will at least provide a guided introduction to saltwater paddling under protected conditions. If you're looking for whales, go with a company whose trips begin from San Juan County Park; Friday Harbor and Roche Harbor are fun but busy places to paddle. All companies provide free transportation from Friday Harbor.

Discovery Sea Kayaks (260 Spring St., 360/378-2559 or 866/461-2559, www.discoveryseakayak.com) has some of the most experienced local guides, and the emphasis is on small groups—generally fewer than six people. Discovery has the only kayak shop on San Juan Island and offers kayaking lessons. Day trips cover the west side of the island, departing from San Juan County Park; a six-hour trip is $107, and four-hour sunset paddles are $80. More unique are the nighttime bioluminescence trips (three hours for $125) to Griffin Bay. Marine dinoflagellates emit green light when the water is disturbed by paddles or kayaks, creating an otherworldly experience.

In business since 1986, **Outdoor Odysseys** (360/378-3533 or 800/647-4621, www.outdoorodysseys.com) has day trips ($79) departing from San Juan County Park. Kayakers spend four hours on the water (longer than other companies), and trips include a lunch, something not offered by other operators. Guides are some of the most experienced around.

The largest kayaking company in the islands, **Crystal Seas Kayaking** (40 Spring St., 360/378-4223 or 877/732-7877, www.crystalseas.com) operates from Snug Harbor Marina on San Juan's west side, offering family-friendly three-hour paddles ($99) for a quick sample, along with six-hour day trips ($125) that cover more coastline and increase your likelihood of viewing whales. Group sizes never exceed eight clients.

San Juan Kayak Expeditions (360/378-4436, www.sanjuankayak.com) has day tours from quiet Griffin Bay near Friday Harbor; $75 for three hours or $110 for all day.

Sea Quest Expeditions (360/378-5767 or 888/589-4253, www.sea-quest-kayak.com) leads day trips from San Juan County Park. Guides all have scientific backgrounds and emphasize natural history during their three-hour ($79) and six-hour ($95) trips.

San Juan Outfitters (360/378-1962 or 866/810-1483, www.sanjuanislandoutfitters.com) heads out daily from Roche Harbor and Friday Harbor in the summer. In addition to standard three-hour tours ($99) from both ports, San Juan Outfitters also has other tours, including five-hour "whale sanctuary" paddles ($115) from Roche Harbor to San Juan County Park (or vice versa); these tours provide a better chance of encountering whales. The company also rents stand-up

sea kayaking

paddleboards, sit-on-top kayaks, and pedal boats in both Friday Harbor and Roche Harbor.

Multiday Kayak Tours

It takes time to really get a taste of the islands, and multiday kayaking treks provide a fun way to explore places most visitors will never see.

At **San Juan Kayak Expeditions** (360/378-4436, www.sanjuankayak.com), owner-operator Tim Thomsen personally leads many trips—as he has for more than 35 years. He's even invented a unique sail that allows kayakers to take advantage of the winds when conditions are right. Three-day trips are $595, and four-day trips cost $695.

The highly experienced guides at **Discovery Sea Kayaks** (260 Spring St., 360/378-2559 or 866/461-2559, www.discoveryseakayaks.com) lead all-inclusive three- to five-day adventures to the more remote parts of the archipelago, including Sucia, Patos, Matia, and Jones Islands. Overnight trips have a maximum of just eight clients, and the itinerary is flexible.

A respected kayak company with highly experienced guides, **Outdoor Odysseys** (360/378-3533 or 800/647-4621, www.outdoorodysseys.com) has two-day whale adventures ($400), three-day tours ($600) that depart San Juan Island for remote Stuart Island, and more leisurely four-day paddles ($800) to Stuart, Jones, and other islands. The company also offers a range of special-interest tours, including three-day yoga and kayaking ($650) and women-only three-day trips ($650). All trips begin from beautiful San Juan County Park on the west side of the island.

Another long-established company, **Sea Quest Expeditions** (360/378-5767 or 888/589-4253, www.sea-quest-kayak.com) has multiday trips to Stuart, Jones, Posey, Turn, and other islands. Group sizes are often larger than other companies.

Crystal Seas Kayaking (40 Spring St., 360/378-4223 or 877/732-7877, www.crystalseas.com) offers a wide variety of two- to six-day trips, including kayak-and-camping trips, inn-to-inn soft adventures, and multisport trips that combine kayaking, biking, and lodging at inns. A two-day, one-night trip is $780, while a six-day, five-night adventure costs $2,180. Groups are kept small—not more than eight people. Crystal Seas Kayaking is a sister company to both Terra Trek (bike tours) and San Juan Excursions (whale-watching); all three have the same owners.

Multi-night kayak trips are also available from **San Juan Outfitters** (360/378-1962 or 866/810-1483, www.sanjuanislandoutfitters.com), with three-night "Island Hopper" trips to Jones and Stuart Islands for $639, including all meals and camping equipment.

Kayak and Paddleboard Rentals

On the waterfront, **Friday Harbor Marine** (360/378-6702, www.fridayharbormarine.com) has kayak rentals of all types, including a rather bizarre sit-on-top Mirage that uses foot pedals to turn a propeller. They also rent dinghies, runabouts, sailboats, and stand-up paddleboards.

Also based in Friday Harbor, **San Juan Kayak Expeditions** (275 A St., 360/378-4436, www.sanjuankayak.com) rents fiberglass double kayaks with gear for $150 per day. Both Friday Harbor Marine and San Juan Kayak charge lower rates for multiday rentals.

San Juan Outfitters (360/378-1962 or 866/810-1483, www.sanjuanislandoutfitters.com) rents sit-on-top kayaks, stand-up paddleboards, and pedal-powered boats for playing around in hectic Roche Harbor.

Lakedale Resort (360/378-2350 or 800/617-2267, www.lakedale.com) rents kayaks, stand-up paddleboards, canoes, paddleboats, and rowboats for use on Neva Lake, four miles from Friday Harbor on Roche Harbor Road.

Located on picturesque Griffin Bay 1.5 miles from downtown Friday Harbor, **Springtide SUP** (254 Jackson Beach Rd.,

360/298-5317, www.springtidesup.com) has stand-up paddleboard lessons, tours, and rentals. The location is quiet and relaxing, and board rentals are $30 per hour, including a 10-minute lesson.

Kayaks can be launched from the public dock just north of the Friday Harbor ferry landing ($10), but parking can be a challenge. Other options include Shipyard Cove (0.5 mile from Friday Harbor), Pinedrona Cove (near Turn Island), Jacksons Beach, San Juan County Park ($7), Roche Harbor ($10), Snug Harbor ($10), American Camp, and English Camp. People planning their own kayak trip to the islands should get a copy of Randel Washburne's *Kayaking Puget Sound, the San Juans, and Gulf Islands* (The Mountaineers, www.mountaineers.org), with information on routes, safety issues, and more.

BOATING

Sailing and powerboating are very big on San Juan Island, and the surrounding waters fill with a flotilla of watercraft on summer weekends. Two large marinas at Roche Harbor and Friday Harbor offer guest moorage, motorboat charters, sailboat rentals, sailing trips, fishing charters, and showers, with lodging, restaurants, and other amenities close by. Public boat-launch ramps are located at San Juan County Park, Friday Harbor, Roche Harbor, Shipyard Cove Marina, Snug Harbor, and Jacksons Beach. A launch fee is charged at most of these locations.

Founded in 1964, the **San Juan Island Yacht Club** (273 Front St., 360/378-3434, www.sjiyc.com) sponsors a dozen or so local cruises for powerboats and sailboats each year, along with the biggest sailing event of the year, the Shaw Island Classic in early August.

Friday Harbor Marine (360/378-6702, www.fridayharbormarine.com) rents dinghies, runabouts, sailboats, kayaks, and stand-up paddleboards.

Located in Roche Harbor, **Island Boat Rentals** (360/317-6160, www.sanjuanislandboatrental.com) rents 21-foot aluminum boats with canvas enclosures.

Sailing

If you've ever dreamed of sailing the islands in a classic wooden boat, the highly recommended *Spike Africa* (360/378-2224, www.schoonersnorth.com) is the way to go. Based in Friday Harbor, the gorgeous 80-foot schooner has room for 33 guests. Built in 1974 and completely reconstucted in 2009, the boat has appeared in numerous TV shows and the Tom Hanks and Meg Ryan movie *Joe Versus the Volcano*. Schooners North offers a series of multiday adventures and groups can charter the boat for a special occasion. If you're just looking for a day of sailing, join a two-hour evening sail for $39 per person, a three-hour adventure for $75 per person, or an eight-hour all-day sail for $140 per person including lunch. Call ahead for reservations if possible, especially for the evening sails.

San Juan Classic Day Sailing (360/378-6700, www.sanjuanclassicdaysailing.com) has two beautiful and historic wooden boats in Friday Harbor. Day sails take place on the 42-foot *Iris*, built in 1934, and include morning mimosa cruises, afternoon trips, and sunset sails. A two-hour sail costs $95 per person, and evening sunset sails are $125 per person including wine and hors d'oeuvres. The more impressive *Dirigo II* is a gorgeous 72-foot schooner built in 1939 that has competed in international races. It is available for private charters from four hours ($950 for up to six people) to multiday trips around the San Juans.

Skipper David Howitt of **All Aboard Sailing** (360/298-1918, www.allaboardsailing.com) leads day sails around the San Juan Islands on his six-passenger *Peniel,* a 42-foot pilothouse sloop built in 1956. These cost $100 per person for three hours, $130 per person for a 4-5-hour sail, or $175 per person for an all-day trip. Most trips include an onboard naturalist.

Motorboats

Friday Harbor Marine (360/378-6702, www.sjimarine.com) rents skiffs, odd electric-propelled launches (perfect for cruising around nearby Turn Island if you don't mind looking a bit foolish), sailboats, and other craft from their waterfront location at the foot of Spring Street in Friday Harbor. In addition, the company provides sailing lessons and kayak rentals.

Friday Harbor Cruises (360/317-4321, www.fridayharborcruises.com) take place on the 12-passenger *Bee*. A variety of trips are available, starting with half-day cruises for $149 per person.

Marinas

Friday Harbor Marina (360/378-2688, www. portfridayharbor.org) is at the center of the Friday Harbor action. This 500-slip marina has space for 150 visiting boats, plus a chandlery. Just about anything else you might need can be found within a few blocks, from whale-watching to gallery snooping. Charter boats and fishing trips are available, along with showers, laundry, pump-out service, and a launch ramp. It is also a U.S. Customs port of entry and seaplane base.

Be sure to look for **Popeye the harbor seal.** He is often seen near Friday Harbor Seafood, where you can purchase small bags of herring to feed him. There's a sculpture of Popeye in the nearby park.

Busiest marina in the San Juans, **Roche Harbor** (360/378-2155 or 800/451-8910, www.rocheharbor.com) is a seasonal U.S. Customs port of entry for boaters arriving from Canada. Facilities include permanent and guest moorage for 350 boats, fuel, showers, laundry, and a launch ramp. Boat charters are through Adventure Charters Northwest. This full-service resort includes a grocery store, post office, restaurants, bar, hotel, cabins, and a swimming pool. Whale-watching tours and guided kayak trips are popular summertime diversions, and sit-on-top kayaks are available for rent through San Juan Outfitters (360/378-1962 or 866/810-1483, www.sanjuanislandoutfitters.com). There's also a free pump-out service called, creatively, the *M.V. Phecal Phreak,* whose motto is "We take crap from anyone."

feeding Popeye the harbor seal

FISHING

Charter fishing for salmon (king, silver, and sockeye) is best in August and September, with bottom fish available year-round. For fishing and other boat charters from Friday Harbor, contact **Outer Island Excursions** (360/376-3711, www.outerislandx.com), **Cedar Fishing Charters** (360/370-5017, www.cedarfishingcharters.com), or **North Shore Charters** (360/376-4855, www.orcasislandadventures.com). Expect to pay around $200 per person for a half-day fishing expedition.

Do-it-yourselfers can fish for trout at Egg Lake and Sportsmans Lake. Also popular is **Lakedale Resort** (4313 Roche Harbor Rd., 360/378-2350 or 800/617-2267, www.lakedale.com), where three lakes are stocked with largemouth bass, cutthroat trout, and rainbow trout. Fishing is $5 per person, and you might even land a lunker; the largest bass taken from the lake weighed 8 pounds.

DIVING

Scuba diving is popular in the cold but amazingly productive waters off San Juan Island. Right on the harbor, **Friday Harbor Dive** (360/378-6702, www.fridayharbordiveservices.com) provides air, nitrox, and rental gear. Boat rentals are available through Friday Harbor Marine (same owners and location, www.sjimarine.com), but the nearest full-service dive shops are in Anacortes and Bellingham.

HIKING AND BIRDING

The island's finest hiking trails are within San Juan Island National Historical Park and Lime Kiln Point State Park. Other areas open to hiking include **Roche Harbor Trails** on the forested lands near Roche Harbor Resort. The trails are privately owned, but the public is welcome to traverse them. These trails connect Roche Harbor with miles of National Park Service-maintained trails at English Camp and 320 acres of land at Mitchell Hill.

The **San Juan Island Trails Committee**'s helpful website (www.sanjuanislandtrails.org) has downloadable maps for parks and other public areas on the island. Copies of these maps are also available at the San Juan Island Chamber of Commerce Visitor Center (135 Spring St.) in Friday Harbor.

The **San Juan Islands Audubon Society** (www.sjiaudubon.org) has monthly birding walks on San Juan Island. See their Facebook page for the latest rare bird sightings. **Sea Quest Expeditions** (360/378-5767 or 888/589-4253, www.sea-quest-kayak.com), **San Juan Safaris** (360/378-1323 or 800/450-6858, www.sanjuansafaris.com), and **Austin Adventures** (800/575-1540, www.austinadventures.com) all lead custom birding tours in the San Juans.

BICYCLING

San Juan Island is very popular with cyclists, but it isn't as bike friendly as slower-paced Lopez Island. The terrain is varied, with quiet lanes through rolling farm country, densely forested areas, wide-open grasslands and gorgeous beaches at American Camp, and stunning shorelines fronting Haro Strait. The hilly western shore of San Juan (rising to 400 feet) is especially inviting, highlighted by a whale-watching stop at Lime Kiln Point State Park. Friday Harbor has a good bike shop and all the other travel amenities, but traffic can get congested and drivers distracted, so use caution, particularly around the ferry loading area. The **San Juan Island Trails Committee** website (www.sanjuanislandtrails.org) provides route information showing bike turnouts and roads with wide shoulders. If you need a lift, both **San Juan Transit** (360/378-8887 or 800/887-8387, www.sanjuantransit.com) and **San Juan Taxi & Tours** (360/378-8294, www.378taxi.com) will haul your bike along.

Bike Rentals and Tours

Rent bikes to cruise around San Juan Island from **Island Bicycles** (380 Argyle Ave., 360/378-4941, www.islandbicycles.com, 9am-6pm daily), a full-service shop just a few blocks from the ferry dock in Friday Harbor. Knowledgeable owner Paul Ahart has well-maintained, high-quality bikes, including mountain, hybrid, racing, tandem, and kids' bicycles. Adult hybrid bikes rent for $10 per hour, $60 per day, or $80 for three days, while electric-assist hybrids cost $15 per hour, $90 per day, or $120 for three days; helmets and other essentials are included. The shop also rents performance road bikes, tandems, children's bikes, bike trailers, Trail-A-Bikes, car racks, and baby strollers, and it is open year-round. Reservations are strongly recommended in the summer months. Rental bikes are not for use on trails and cannot be taken off San Juan Island, so bring your own for trips to Stuart or other islands.

Meat Machine Cycles (50 Malcom St., 360/370-5673, www.meatmachinebicycles.com) is located within Surina Business Park on a side street off Argyle Avenue in Friday Harbor. This full-service bike shop rents basic hybrid bikes for $40 per day, and carbon road bikes for $75 per day, with substantial discounts for multiday rentals.

Discovery Sea Kayaks (280 Spring St., 360/378-2559 or 866/461-2559, www.discoveryseakayak.com) rents road bikes ($30 for three hours or $50/day) and electric-assist bikes ($40 for three hours or $55/day) from its shop in downtown Friday Harbor.

Bike rentals are also available at the Roche Harbor office of **Susie's Mopeds** (360/378-5244 or 800/532-0087, www.susiesmopeds.com, late June-early Sept., $10/hour or $60/day); bikes are provided by Island Bicycles. Find them across from San Juan Island Sculpture Park as you come into Roche Harbor. The shop also rents mopeds and Scoot Coupes.

San Juan Outfitters (360/378-1962 or 866/810-1483, www.sanjuanislandoutfitters.com) rents hybrid bikes in Roche Harbor near the hotel. Hybrid bikes are $25 for four hours or $40 for all day. The company also guides cycle day tours.

For San Juan Island cycling tours, contact one of the following companies: **Terra Trek** (40 Spring St., 360/378-4223 or 888/441-2433, www.goterratrek.com), **Backroads** (510/527-1555 or 800/462-2848, www.backroads.com), **Bicycle Adventures** (425/250-5540 or 800/443-6060, www.bicycleadventures.com), or **Trek Travel** (608/441-8735 or 866/464-8735, www.trektravel.com).

HORSEBACK RIDING

Covering 66 acres off San Juan Valley Road, **Horseshu Ranch** (131 Gilbert Lane, 360/378-2298, www.horseshu.com) has 15 gentle horses and ponies. Even young children are welcome on the ponies (with parental help, of course). Hour-long rides through an old-growth forest cost $68, and Horseshu Ranch has an arena with riding lessons and horse boarding. This is a great family spot.

ZIPLINING

The zipline phenomenon has reached the San Juan Islands. Located halfway between Friday Harbor and Roche Harbor, **Zip San Juan** (1959 Egg Lake Rd., 360/378-5947, www.zipsanjuan.com) has eight cable ziplines suspended 15-50 feet above the ground in a forested setting. Tours last approximately three hours and cost $86 adults or $76 seniors and ages 8-15. Free round-trip transportation is provided from Friday Harbor.

SWIMMING AND FITNESS

Roche Harbor Resort (360/378-2155 or 800/451-8910, www.rocheharbor.com, $8 per person) has a large outdoor pool and children's wading pool with a lifeguard on duty. It's open to the public daily 9am-7pm early May-September. This is the only heated public outdoor pool on the island.

Fitness fanatics may want to take advantage of one-day memberships ($15) to **San Juan Fitness** (435 Argyle Ave., 360/378-4449, www.sanjuanislandfitness.com). Although privately owned, the fitness center is viewed by most locals as a community resource akin to a YMCA. Facilities include an indoor 25-yard swimming pool and wading pool, kids' gym with climbing wall, racquetball courts, coed sauna, steam room, and hot tub, plus a cramped weight room. A variety of classes—from yoga to swimming lessons—are included at no extra charge. Note that the lifeguard is only on duty one hour per day of family swim. Open daily year-round.

SPAS

Looking to indulge yourself? Relax in **Afterglow Spa** at Roche Harbor Resort (360/378-9888 or 800/451-8910, www.rocheharbor.com) or in Friday Harbor at **Lavendera Massage** (285 Spring St., 360/378-3637, www.lavenderamassage.com). Both offer couples massage, hydrotherapy, manicures, pedicures, and more. **Spa d Bune** (669 Mullis St., 360/370-5027, www.spadbune.com) has facials, therapeutic massage, and skin care.

GOLF AND TENNIS

The longest nine-hole course in the Northwest at 3,194 yards, the **San Juan Golf & Tennis**

Club (806 Golf Course Rd., 360/378-2254, www.sjgolfclub.com) overlooks Griffin Bay on the east side of San Juan Island. It's open to the public, with tennis and pickleball courts available. Nine holes of golf costs $35. Public **tennis courts** are next to the high school at 45 Blair Avenue.

PARKS AND PLAYGROUNDS

Head out Argyle Avenue to the San Juan County Fairgrounds, where you'll find a **skateboard park** that's popular with BMX bikers, along with a playground for younger kids. Much more impressive is the **playground** at Roche Harbor Resort, where the adjacent **outdoor pool** and wading pool ($8 per person) are very popular in the summer.

Just up from the harbor, **A Place to Play** (55 Spring St., 360/378-0378, www.aplace-toplay.biz) is designed for children ages 1 to 10 with all sorts of fun activities. A one-hour play session is $7.50 per child, and an all-day session costs $15 with in-and-out privileges. Adult supervision is required in general, but the center also has a summertime day camp where you can drop your child for $10 per hour (ages 2.5 to 10, max four hours). A Place to Play has free Wi-Fi.

Shopping

Downtown Friday Harbor is filled with interesting shops selling everything from Washington wines to bonsai trees. Browse the photos of homes for sale adorning the real estate offices, check out the toy shops for grandchild gifts, or sip a lavender tea at a coffee shop while surfing the web on your laptop.

In business since 1929, **Kings Market** (160 Spring St., 360/378-4505, www.kings-market.com, 7am-9pm daily) is Friday Harbor's version of Wal-Mart, with a big gift and clothing shop, plus an upstairs marine center stocked with fishing tackle, boating supplies, charts, outdoor gear, and sea kayaks.

Find recycled clothing and much more at **Thrift House** (667 Mullis St., 360/378-8483, 9am-4pm Mon.-Sat.).

The store at **Crystal Seas Kayaking** (40 Spring St., 360/378-4223 or 877/732-7877, www.crystalseas.com) has the best selection of local T-shirts, with designs by Jennifer Rigg.

GALLERIES AND STUDIOS

Friday Harbor is home to several excellent art galleries, most of which are within a few blocks of the ferry landing. Just walk the streets to see what appeals to your taste.

In addition to the galleries, you may want to drop by the library (1010 Guard St.) to see changing exhibits by local artists. During the **Artists' Studio Tour** (www.sanjuanisland-artists.com) in early June, 20 or so studios are opened to the public; it's a great way to meet the folks behind the art.

Friday Harbor's don't-miss place is **Waterworks Gallery** (315 Argyle Ave., 360/378-3060, www.waterworksgallery.com), a fine-arts gallery with contemporary paintings, prints, watercolors, and sculpture by island and international artists. New exhibits are unveiled monthly.

One of the largest galleries in the San Juans, **Island Studios** (270 Spring St., 360/378-6550, www.islandstudios.com) has works from more than 250 local artists. You'll find paintings, photography, stained glass, jewelry, pottery, and lots more jammed into every square inch of space here. It's a fun place to spend time, with a mix of fine art and pieces that cross the line into kitsch. Don't miss the wonderful pottery garden out back, complete with an impressive koi pond; the largest fish are more than 30 years old. An electric fence keeps raccoons from a sushi dinner. A few doors up the street is an amazing

Camperdown elm planted in the 1870s. These unique "weeping" trees are created when a cutting from the original tree in England is grafted to a Wych elm tree. The graft grows to form this unique shape naturally, but this 140-year-old mutant tree is unable to reproduce except through additional cuttings.

Arctic Raven Gallery (130 S. 1st St., 360/378-3433, www.arcticravengallery.com) features quality art by Northwest Coast and Alaska Native Americans, including wood carvings, bentwood boxes, baskets, soapstone carvings, masks, art prints, and more.

Harbor Song Gallery (180 1st St. S., 360/370-7037, www.harborsong.com) highlights original paintings by artist/owners Tom and Mary Garrels. Next door is **Ogle Fine Art Studio** (360/317-5163, www.oglearts.com), which has stylized wooden sculptures, paintings, and fiber arts by Terry Ogle and other artists.

BOOKSTORES

Friday Harbor has two good bookshops. **Griffin Bay Bookstore** (155 Spring St., 360/378-5511, www.griffinbaybook.com) is a book lovers' shop with both new and used books. Enjoy an espresso here and pull out your tablet or laptop for the free Wi-Fi.

Find an abundance of used titles—more than 50,000 books at last count—at the surprisingly well-organized **Serendipity Used Books** (223 A St., 360/378-2665). It's at the top of the ferry lanes.

Entertainment and Events

NIGHTLIFE

Friday Harbor's oldest bar—it opened in 1943—is **Herb's Tavern** (80 1st St., 360/378-7076). It has two pool tables, darts, a big selection of brews on draft, decent bar food, and live bands on summer weekends and karaoke Wednesday nights year-round. It's open till 2am most nights.

Rumor Mill (175 N. 1st St., 360/378-5555, www.rumor-millsanjuan.com) serves a menu that rambles from seafood to Greek specials, but is best known for the bar with 20-plus microbrews on tap, sports on the big-screen TVs, and live entertainment at least five evenings a week in the summer. It's a fun place to party late into the night.

The upstairs bar at **China Pearl Restaurant** (51 Spring St., 360/378-5254, www.chinapearldining.com) has pool tables, DJ tunes, karaoke, and a harbor vista from the outdoor deck.

Cask and Schooner (1 Front St., 360/378-2922, www.caskandschooner.com) re-creates an English pub setting with nine beers on tap, including Guinness. Drop by on a weeknight for happy hour specials, or belly up to the bar with the locals to watch a game on the telly.

Over in Roche Harbor, **Madrona Bar & Grill** (360/378-2155 or 800/451-8910, www.rocheharbor.com) has live music and dancing Friday and Saturday nights all summer.

Haley's Sports Bar & Grill (175 Spring St., 360/378-4434, 11am-10pm daily) has a big menu of appetizers, sliders, salads, wraps, fish tacos, and burgers, but the main attraction is sports on the TVs.

Watch first-run and art films in downtown Friday Harbor at the two-screen **Palace Theatre** (209 Spring St., 360/378-5666).

THEATER

The impressive **San Juan Community Theatre** (100 2nd St., 360/378-3210, www.sjctheatre.org) is a vital center for local performing arts, with year-round musical programs, plays, dance performances, chamber music, art shows, and more. Get your tickets early, as some events sell out. Local theater company **Island Stage Left** (360/378-5649, www.islandstageleft.org) puts on free **Shakespeare**

Under the Stars productions at the Roche Harbor amphitheater each July and August.

FESTIVALS AND EVENTS

One of the most popular weekly island events is the **San Juan Farmers Market** (360/378-6301, www.sjifarmersmarket.com, 10am-1pm Sat. Apr.-Oct.). It takes place at the Brickworks Building (Nichols St. at Sunshine Alley), with tents out back in the summer. The market features organic fruits, delicious finger food, baked goods, fresh oysters, vegetables, berries, flowers, jewelry, and more.

The first weekend of June brings the **Artists' Studio Tour** (www.sanjuanisland-artists.com) at 20 or so studios around the island, along with the **Celebrity Golf Classic** at San Juan Island Golf & Country Club (360/378-2254, www.sjgolfclub.com); it's the county's biggest annual fund-raising event.

Fourth of July features a variety of fun events, including a parade, "Rock the Dock" live music, the Pig War picnic, a 10K race, music, and dancing, plus evening fireworks above Friday Harbor. Over in Roche Harbor, the Fourth of July is the biggest event of the year, with a log-rolling contest, blind dinghy race, and other events, topped off by an impressive fireworks display.

The **Lavender Festival,** held the third weekend of July, includes tours, demonstrations, lavender-accented foods, and a big Saturday picnic dinner at Pelindaba Lavender Farm (www.pelindaba.com). Sailors should check out the **Shaw Island Classic,** a round-the-island race sponsored by the San Juan Island Yacht Club (www.sjiyc.com), held the first Saturday in August. Free **Music on the Lawn** concerts take place at the San Juan Historical Museum weekly in July and early August.

San Juan Island National Historical Park presents **Encampment** at English Camp (360/378-2240) the last weekend of July, when you'll meet 60 or so British and American "soldiers" and others in mid-19th-century period costume. Old-fashioned canvas tents are set up, and you can watch demonstrations on blacksmithing, small arms, black powder, woodworking, marching, and cookery, or join games of croquet, cricket, and 19th-century baseball. The highlight is a candlelight ball in the barracks building.

The four-day **San Juan County Fair** (360/378-4310, www.sanjuancountyfair.org) during the third week of August includes a sheep-to-shawl competition, chicken and rabbit races, music, livestock judging, and, of course, carnival rides.

Held at San Juan Vineyards on the last Sunday in August, **Concours d'Elegance** (www.sanjuanconcours.org) attracts vintage car enthusiasts, with 90 or so classic cars, some dating back before 1920.

Savor the San Juans (www.visitsan-juans.com/savor-san-juans) is a feast for the senses from late September to mid-November. Highlights include farm tours, a grape-harvesting festival at San Juan Vineyards, a fall farm parade, two film festivals, and all sorts of dining events.

In early November, the **Friday Harbor Film Festival** (www.fhff.org) showcases documentary films from around the globe, with more than 30 features and a dozen short films shown over three days. The opening-night gala is a big event with food, drinks, and an introduction to filmmakers in attendance.

Get ready for Christmas with an **Artisan's Holiday Marketplace** around Thanksgiving. The **Island Lights Fest** throughout December includes a tree lighting ceremony, caroling, and a lighted boat parade at Friday Harbor.

Food

San Juan Island has a wide range of restaurants and eateries, including some real gems. Unless otherwise noted, these restaurants are in the town of Friday Harbor.

FINE DINING

Dinner reservations are strongly suggested for any of San Juan Island's better restaurants, particularly on weekends and during the summer.

Mike's Café & Wine Bar (135 2nd St., 425/503-9906, www.mikescafeandwinebar. com, noon-9pm daily June-early Sept., 4pm-8pm Mon.-Thurs., 4pm-9pm Fri., noon-8pm Sat.-Sun. the rest of the year, $10-19) is the only vegan café in the San Juan Islands. The food is delicious, and even meat lovers will be pleasantly surprised by the flavors. Try the Szechwan Sizzle stir-fry, the Crabby Cakes, or the Chick'n Riesling—all made with veggies instead of meat. Even the pizzas are made with a nut-based substitute for cheese. There's a patio out front and backyard seating for a romantic summer meal beneath the stars. Owner Mike Sharadin creates his own wines (Northwest Totem Cellars), and always has 20 or so different wines available, along with six beers on tap.

Just two blocks from the ferry, ★ **Backdoor Kitchen** (400 A St., 360/378-9540, www.backdoorkitchen.com, 5pm-10pm Wed.-Sun., 11:30am-2:30pm Mon. June-Sept., 5pm-9pm Wed.-Sat., 11:30am-2:30pm Mon. Sept.-May, closed mid-Dec.-Feb., $24-38), is a hidden gem known to locals and wandering tourists who happen upon it (or read this book); find it behind a nondescript warehouse. Step through the gate into a small garden area with a handful of teak tables for open-air dining; there's additional seating inside the restaurant. Dinner includes inspired fare such as a Vietnamese duck and prawn platter, pork chops with a poblano goat cheese cream sauce, Mediterranean farro salad, and pan-seared sea scallops. The full bar serves unusual specialty drinks and a lighter menu, and be sure to try the coconut cream pie for dessert. The last seating is at 9pm and reservations are advised, especially for rainy days. In addition to evening meals, Backdoor Kitchen opens for lunch on Mondays, serving delicious noodle bowls with a variety of toppings for $11-15.

One of Friday Harbor's most romantic dining places, **Coho Restaurant** (120 Nichols St., 360/378-6330, www.cohorestaurant. com, 5pm-9pm Mon.-Sat. mid-June-Sept., 5pm-9pm Tues.-Sat. Oct. and Apr.-mid-June, 5pm-9pm Wed.-Sat. Nov.-Mar., closed Sun., $28-36) is housed in a cozy little side-street house. Reservations are recommended, not just because the restaurant only has nine tables, but more importantly because of its popularity with locals. The menu changes often, with a focus on farm-to-table Pacific Northwest cuisine, much of it from local sources. Everything is made on the premises, from bread and pasta to ice cream. Seafood is featured, but the menu also might include grilled octopus, beef tenderloin, stuffed red pepper, grilled Jidori chicken, and other adventurous dishes. The wine cellar is particularly notable. Try chef Bill Messick's tasting menu served 5pm-5:45pm daily; this three-course meal with a bottle of wine costs $70 for two people. Despite the upscale atmosphere the restaurant is perfect for families, so there's no need to dress up. The owners also operate the San Juan Inn Collection of lodging places.

Open for dinner only, **The Place Restaurant & Bar** (1 Spring St., 360/378-8707, www.theplacefridayharbor.com, 5pm-9pm daily, $28-41) gets rave reviews from locals who come here for the friendly service, from-scratch gourmet fare, and sophisticated atmosphere. The name should give you a clue to its location: on pilings over the water, with windows facing the ferry and marina. It's perfect for a warmly romantic evening. The menu changes seasonally but typically features a mushroom sauté appetizer with shiitake mushrooms and goat cheese, along with fresh Alaskan weathervane scallops, New Zealand lamb chops, and even a vegan stir-fry called Evil Jungle Prince. Be sure to save room for the warm chocolate pudding cake with toffee sauce. Get there for happy hour (weekdays beginning at 6pm) to taste locally famous Cuban pork sandwiches and small pizzas.

The Restaurant at Friday Harbor House (130 West St., 360/378-8455 or 866/722-7356, www.fridayharborhouse.com, 5pm-9pm Mon.-Fri., noon-9pm Sat.-Sun., $17-38) is another San Juan Island favorite. Chef Jason Aldous's menu emphasizes ultra-fresh local produce and seafood. Favorites include locally raised lamb, wild salmon with Swiss chard, and a delicious local beef burger with caramelized bacon-onion jam. Don't miss the crispy brussels sprouts appetizer. There's an extensive wine selection available by the glass, and tapas-style happy hour treats. The food is exquisite, and the setting is upscale and fashionable, with a central fireplace and tall windows overlooking the harbor. Call ahead to request a window table. Patio dining is available in the summer, and kids are welcome.

Vinny's Ristorante (165 West St., 360/378-1934, www.vinnysfridayharbor.com, 4pm-9:30pm daily June-Oct., 4pm-9pm Tues.-Sat. Nov.-May, $16-28) is a casually elegant Italian restaurant where the air is deliciously redolent and the tables are draped in white linen. The menu encompasses all the standard favorites, including veal marsala, shrimp scampi, and lasagna, along with "pasta from hell" for those who like it hot: pasta with garlic, pine nuts, raisins, mushrooms, and peppers in a fiery habanero and curry cream sauce. Unfortunately, the restaurant's hilltop vista is now obstructed by recently constructed penthouses.

Five miles north of Friday Harbor just off Roche Harbor Road, ★ **Duck Soup Inn** (50 Duck Soup Lane, 360/378-4878, www.

ducksoupinn.com, 5pm-10pm Tues.-Sun. July-early Sept., 5pm-10pm Fri.-Sun. spring and fall, closed Nov.-Mar., $28-37) specializes in superbly prepared local seafood and meats, along with a changing and eclectic menu with an international bent. Grilled duck breast is always on the menu, and recommended. The country setting and woodsy interior add to the relaxed and romantic atmosphere. This is where locals go for a celebration night. Reservations are recommended.

Three places serve meals at **Roche Harbor Resort** (www.rocheharbor.com). Busy **Madrona Bar & Grill** (360/378-7954, 11am-10pm daily, reduced winter hours, $16-30) has waterside patio dining with fish-and-chips, barbecue ribs, pastas, burgers, sandwiches, steaks, and much more, along with live music on summer evenings. The bar has a fine beer selection, along with wine by the glass, mojitos, and margaritas. Visit upscale **McMillin's Dining Room** (360/378-5757, 5pm-10pm daily, $27-47) for consistently good prime rib, seafood, steaks, and chicken. On the wharf, **Lime Kiln Café** (360/378-7954, 7am-8pm daily, $8-14) serves a breakfast and lunch menu with burgers, deli sandwiches, salads, and house-made soups. The real reason for a visit, however, is the justly famous donuts. They're made fresh each morning, and often sell out. Get a half dozen to go.

SEAFOOD

A tiny floating shop surrounded by the cruise and fishing fleet at the Friday Harbor Marina, **Friday Harbor Seafood** (360/378-5779, 10am-6pm Mon.-Sat., 10am-5pm Sun.) sells fresh salmon, halibut, and snapper, along with live mussels, clams, Dungeness crab, scallops, and prawns. The real attraction here is **Popeye,** a friendly little harbor seal who hangs around nearby docks for handouts. The shop sells bags of herring to feed Popeye.

North Sound Seafood (360/378-3904, www.northsoundseafood.com, 11am-6pm Mon.-Fri., 10am-6pm Sat.-Sun. June-Sept.) sells Dungeness crab (live or cooked), spot prawns, local oysters, salmon, halibut, and more from a little waterside tent at Roche Harbor.

★ **Westcott Bay Shellfish Co.** (904 Westcott Dr., 360/378-2489, www.westcottbayshellfish.com, 11am-5pm daily June-early Sept.) is a bit out of the way, but worth the detour. A rustic oyster farm stood along Westcott Bay for decades, but when it closed in 2012 locals feared the land would be sold to a wealthy individual who would put up a gate and build a waterfront mansion. Fortunately, the opposite happened when Erik and Andrea Anderson purchased the land and began the arduous process of reseeding the tidelands with Pacific oysters (a native species), Manila clams, and Mediterranean mussels. They rebuilt the decrepit 450-foot pier and added a beautiful timber-frame building that doubles as a packing shed and retail space. Westcott Bay oysters are served locally at Friday Harbor House, Roche Harbor, Cask and Schooner, and the San Juan Farmers Market. You can purchase the shellfish to go from the flow-through tanks, or buy them in the shop ($3/oyster). The shop also sells fresh bread from Bakery San Juan and provides shucking knives plus complimentary hot sauces. There is usually someone on hand to provide a quick shucking tutorial. Bring your own wine to enjoy lunch on the picnic tables out front. Louie the dog will saunter out to greet you. Parking is limited, and only for the oyster farm, not for the adjacent English Camp within San Juan Island National Historical Park. Stop by on Friday afternoons 1pm-4pm for barbecued oysters.

Directly across from the ferry, **Friday's Crabhouse** (360/378-8801, www.friday-scrabhouse.com, 11:30am-8pm daily late May-Sept., weekends only Apr. and May) is *the* place for finger-lickin' fish-and-chips, homemade crab cakes, fish tacos, popcorn shrimp, grilled salmon, or pan-fried local oysters, along with fajitas, hamburgers, and garden burgers—with most items priced under $13. Service is fast, making this an excellent last-minute stop. The multilevel eatery is primarily alfresco dining at picnic tables topped by big umbrellas, but a covered space is also available. There are plenty of specialty drinks too, including the Drunken Barnacle (Captain Morgan, Pepsi, and coconut rum).

Another simple family place is **Hungry Clam** (250 A St., 360/378-3474, 5am-7pm daily, $9-14), where you will find cheap, greasy, and quite good cod fish-and-chips served in a basket. The fries are fresh and crunchy. Also on the menu are such staples as clam chowder, Canadian bacon cheeseburgers, and grilled chicken sandwiches. The diner is open for the early ferry crowd, and breakfast is available till noon; blueberry pancakes are a favorite.

INTERNATIONAL AND PIZZA

Laotian owner Avon Mangala runs **Golden Triangle Thai Restaurant** (140 1st St., 360/378-1917, 11am-2:30pm and 5pm-8pm Mon.-Sat., closed Sun., $15-19), serving Thai coconut curry dishes and spring rolls, Laotian noodles, chicken satay, and other fast Asian treats in an eat-in or takeaway setting. Lunch is served in a casual cafeteria style with paper plates, but dinners are a sit-down affair.

Located upstairs above Cask and Schooner, **Tops'l Sushi and Seafood** (1 Front St., 360/370-7191, www.topslseafood.com, 5pm-9pm Wed.-Sat., $16-38) has a dark wood interior, windows facing the harbor, and a menu that blends traditional Japanese sushi, local seafood, and more. Entrées include Wagyu beef, troll-caught king salmon, oysters, udon noodles, and salads. Ultra-fresh sushi rolls, sashimi, and nigari are created by Japanese-trained master chef Kasu San; try the rainbow roll with fresh crab or the salmon avocado hand rolls. Tops'l is a bit pricey, but the sushi is delicious, and the location can't be beat. There's a good drink menu too.

A modest white house off the beaten path, **Tia's Tacos** (485 Ellsworth Ave., 360/378-8226, 11:30am-4pm Mon.-Fri., $6-11) attracts locals with affordable prices and an unpretentious setting. The taqueria's blackboard menu shows tacos, burritos, chimichangas, and quesadillas. The salsa bar has plenty of toppings, and you can eat inside or take it out to the backyard picnic tables.

Tiny **La Authentica Mexicana** (50 Malcom St., 360/317-5038, 11am-6pm Tues.-Fri., 10:30am-3:30pm Sat., $9) hides within Surina Business Park on a side street off Argyle Avenue. This very basic hole-in-the-wall serves authentic from-scratch Mexican food to go, with something different every day, including Wednesday enchiladas, Thursday chicken mole, and Saturday carnitas and posole. Most items are around $9, but you can also get tamales and carnitas by the pound and take home fresh homemade tortillas.

Van Go's Pizza (180 Web St., 360/378-0138, www.vangopizza.net, 4pm-8:30pm Mon.-Sat.) is popular with families for its thick homemade crusts and wide choice of toppings. The outdoor seating area is great on a hot summer afternoon, and kids love the gnome playhouse in the backyard. A 16-inch pizza costs $17-22.

PUBS

★ **Cask and Schooner** (1 Front St., 360/378-2922, www.caskandschooner.com, 11am-9pm Mon.-Fri., 10am-9pm Sat., 10am-8pm Sun., $13-39) occupies a busy corner at the base of Front Street right across from the harbor. Cask and Schooner is something of a cross between an English pub and the deck of an old schooner. The food and drink follow a similar nautical theme, with a menu featuring meat pie, fish-and-chips (the house specialty), bangers and mash, and other upscale pub grub. Fries are cut fresh daily, bread is baked in-house, and greens and meats are locally sourced when possible. The restaurant also has full dinners, from Dungeness crab with corn risotto to top sirloin steaks. There are not a lot of meat-free options, but the restaurant does serve a grilled eggplant sandwich and even a delicious gluten-free razor clam chowder (not vegetarian, of course). On draft are nine beers—including Guinness—along with martinis and a fair wine selection. Outside seating is also available.

Herb's Tavern (80 1st St., 360/378-7076, 11am-2am Mon.-Fri., 8am-2am Sat.-Sun., $9-18) serves burgers, fish-and-chips, hot wings, mini-pizzas, sandwiches, hot dogs, and other finger fare. It opens for weekend breakfasts, and stays open till 2am most nights. You'll find music on summer weekends, karaoke on Wednesdays, pool and dart games anytime, and yes, they do serve alcohol.

QUICK BITES

If you're in search of a great all-American burger, fries, onion rings, sandwiches, baskets, and shakes—mostly under $10—head up the hill to **Vic's Drive-In** (25 2nd St., 360/378-8427, www.vicsdriveinn.com, 11am-7pm Mon.-Fri., 8am-2pm Sat.). Breakfast is only available on Saturdays, and the drive-in is closed Sundays.

One of the newest restaurants in Friday Harbor, **Black Fish Bistro** (140 1st St., 360/317-1800, 5pm-11pm Wed.-Sun., $9-22) has an out-of-the-way location behind Golden Triangle Thai Restaurant. The limited menu features small plates of locally sourced food from the open kitchen and unusual drinks in the upstairs cocktail bar. Try the oyster po'boy, steak pommes frites, or softshell crab sandwich.

BREAKFAST AND LUNCH

A favorite of both locals and visitors, **Rocky Bay Café** (225 Spring St., 360/378-5051, 6:30am-2:30pm daily, $8-12) serves enormous portions in a simple all-American diner setting. This is the best breakfast in town. You'll find all the morning standards, plus chorizo burritos, corned beef hash, homemade donuts, and lunchtime French dip, Philly cheesesteak sandwiches, burgers (served with sweet potato fries), wraps, and daily specials. The café often has a long queue, so you may need to wait up to an hour on a summer weekend.

Tiny ★ **Market Chef** (225 A St., 360/378-4546, 10am-4pm Mon.-Fri., $6-11) is a fantastic deli next to the ferry lanes in Friday Harbor. Owner/chef Laurie Paul creates mouthwatering sandwiches (especially the roast beef), daily soups, and salads in the open kitchen. She uses island produce and meats whenever possible, and locals rave about the crab cakes—featured in *Gourmet Magazine*—and house-smoked meats. You can call a day ahead to reserve a boxed picnic lunch to go ($13-17), but you're probably better off picking your favorites from the day's creations in the deli case. Market Chef is closed on weekends (lots of weddings to cater).

A favorite little brunch spot, **Cynthia's Bistro** (65 Nichols St., 360/317-7178, www. cynthiasofcourse.com, 7am-3pm daily, $7-12) has a few tables inside and more on the covered front deck. House specials include Dutch baby deep-dish pancakes, avocado breakfast boat (poached eggs in baked avocados topped with bacon), and decadent French toast, along with chocolate silk pie and homemade pastries. The café serves a good selection of gluten-free items as well. Owner Cynthia Burke also runs Red Checkered Picnics at Lime Kiln State Park.

A standout lunch spot packed with locals, ★ **San Juan Island Cheese** (155 Nichols St., 360/370-5115, www.sjicheese.com, Wed.-Fri. 11am-3pm, Sat.-Sun. 10am-3pm, closed Jan.-Feb., $11-21) combines a little bistro and artisan cheese shop with wines from the Pacific Northwest and beers from Orcas Island. Start by sharing a "monger's choice" of three cheeses, crackers, and fruit. Lunch includes such treats as quiche du jour, grilled cheese panini with fresh pesto, French onion and rosemary ham tarts, and an amazing homemade mac and cheese. Everything is delicious and beautifully presented. Co-owners Sheri and Richard Daly are cheese connoisseurs; ask them about Washington's famous Cougar Gold, which comes in a can. Call ahead to reserve a table for the popular three-course Sunday champagne brunches ($35 per person; last seating at 2pm), which offer a choice of unusual items such as tuna confit, pastrami Italiano melt, shirred eggs, and coho lox quiche.

CAFÉS

San Juan Coffee Roasting Company (18 Cannery Landing, 360/378-4443 or 800/624-4119, www.rockisland.com/~sjcoffee, 9:30am-5pm daily) specializes in full- and dark-roasted coffees, and sells them from its shop next to the ferry terminal.

My favorite coffee spot—by far—is ★ **Crows Nest Coffee Shoppe** (70 Spring St., 360/317-8474, 6:30am-3pm daily, $4-9), where owner Jon Hurley, a fifth-generation resident of San Juan Island, uses Vivace beans. (They're considered by many the Rolls-Royce of Seattle coffee.) Jon worked as a barista for many years and attracts a loyal following of locals. This little hole-in-the-wall café also serves deli sandwiches, wraps, breakfast burritos, blended drinks, smoothies, and milk shakes.

The Bean Café (150 1st St., 360/370-5858, www.thebeancafe.com, 7am-5pm Sun.-Thurs., 7am-8pm Fri.-Sat. in summer, 7am-5pm daily in the off-season, $4-10) has big windows, free Wi-Fi, and a video monitor of the nearby ferry lanes so you can know when your ship comes in. Besides good espresso, the café serves breakfast burritos, salads, wraps, and baked goods. The same owners run the nearby **Far North Café** (85 Front St., 360/202-8885, 7am-5pm daily July-Aug., 7am-11am daily the rest of the year, $4-10), inside the white Queen Anne-style building adjacent to the ferry lines. This place also has a walk-up window so you don't miss the boat.

MARKETS, BAKERIES, AND SWEETS

For a real taste of the islands, head to the **San Juan Farmers Market** (360/378-6301, www. sjifarmersmarket.com, 10am-1pm Sat. Apr.-Oct.) at the Brickworks Building (Nichols St. at Sunshine Alley), with tents out back in the summer.

Kings Market (160 Spring St., 360/378-4505, www.kings-market.com, 7am-9pm daily) is the primary grocer on San Juan. You'll find fresh meats and fish, gourmet foods and wines, plus a fine deli with tasty made-to-order sandwiches. Also here is a gift shop and marine supply center.

Friday Harbor Market Place (515 Market St., 360/378-3238) is a larger grocery out near the airport. There's no sign out front and no deli—I'm surprised it isn't painted in camouflage. It's owned by Kings Market, but often has lower prices. Locals all know about it, but most travelers don't—except you, of course.

Dolled up in pink trim and flower boxes, **The Sweet Retreat & Espresso** (264 Spring St., 360/378-1957, $4-8) is a busy takeaway spot for ice-cream cones (dozens of flavors), sundaes, lemonade, malts, and ice-blended coffee drinks. Breakfast sandwiches here consist of a biscuit with egg, cheese, and bacon; surprisingly good lunches include sandwiches, Reubens, jumbo hot dogs, and burgers.

Friday Harbor's most popular ice cream shop is **Yo! Friday Harbor** (160 1st St., 360/378-2477, www.yofridayharbor.com). The location—next to the ferry landing—is perfect for a last-minute cone before your ship sails, and the shop gets packed most summer afternoons. It serves 30 flavors of ice cream from Lopez Island Creamery (a double scoop costs $4), along with shakes, Italian sodas, and baked goods.

You'll find excellent pastries at **Bakery Café Demeter** (80 Nichols St., 360/370-5443, 7am-3pm Tues.-Sat., under $10), but be prepared for a wait at this very popular bakery. Stop by to check out the fresh baguettes, bagels, and delicious breads, old-world-style pastries (brioche, Danish pastries, sweet cinnamon rolls, chocolate croissants, flaky turnovers, and more), along with soups, sandwiches, pizza slices, and fine espresso. There's free Wi-Fi too.

★ **Bakery San Juan** (775 Mullis St., 360/378-5810, www.bakerysanjuan.com, 8am-6pm Mon.-Sat. June-Aug., 8am-6pm Mon.-Fri. the rest of the year, $5-18) bakes several breads daily, and has key lime pie, butter apple tarts, chocolate mousse cakes, cheesecakes, sandwiches, and eight different types of pizza by the slice. It's definitely off the beaten path—the bakery is next to the airport south of town—but worth the drive or bike ride. Next to the bakery, **San Juan Island Food Co-Op** (360/370-5170, Mon.-Fri. 9am-6pm, Sat.-Sun. 10am-5pm) sells organic, local, and regional produce, fish, and dairy products.

WINE AND SPIRITS

Island Wine Company (360/378-3229 or 800/248-9463, 9:30am-7pm daily late

Yo! Friday Harbor is a popular ice cream shop.

May-early Sept., 10am-5pm daily the rest of the year) is a cozy shop in Cannery Landing, adjacent to the Friday Harbor ferry dock. Owners Dave Baughn and Kathryn Kerr have their own **San Juan Cellars** label, produced from eastern Washington grapes and bottled under contract, and you're welcome to sample any of their 10 wines, which are only available here. The riesling and reserve red are especially notable. In addition to these, the shop also has a range of upper-end Northwest wines, including vintages you won't find in Seattle wine shops. Grace, the resident black lab, loves to be petted.

San Juan Vineyards (3136 Roche Harbor Rd., 360/378-9463, www.sanjuanvineyards.com) is three miles from Friday Harbor on the way to Roche Harbor. The five-acre vineyard grows Madeleine Angevine and Siegerrebe grapes. The winery produces a limited bottling of these, plus several other wines from grapes harvested elsewhere in Washington.

A mile or so from Roche Harbor, **San Juan Island Distillery/Westcott Bay Cider** (12 Anderson an., 360/378-2606, www.westcottbaycider.com) produces award-winning hard cider, along with apple brandy and a dozen different gins. Visit the tasting room on Saturdays 1pm-4pm year-round and Sundays 1pm-4pm in the summer, or by appointment at other times. It is closed in January and February. You can purchase their products at Kings Market in Friday Harbor or select Seattle markets.

Accommodations

During the summer, it's a good idea to make reservations several months ahead of time to be assured of a bed on San Juan Island, particularly on weekends. All lodging prices quoted below are subject to an additional 10.1 percent in sales and lodging taxes.

Until recently there was no need for air-conditioning in local lodging places, but a few places have added it to their rooms in the past several years. At last check these included Discovery Inn, Friday Harbor House, Island Inn at 123 West, and even the budget-priced Orca Inn.

WEEKLY RENTALS

For weekly vacation rentals, **Vacation Rentals in the San Juan Islands** (360/378-3601 or 800/391-8190, www.vacation-rentalssanjuanislands.com), **San Juan Property Management** (360/378-2070 or 800/742-8210, www.sanjuanpm.com), and **Windermere Property Management** (50 Spring St., 360/378-8600, www.windermeres-jipm.com) all have big selections on San Juan Island. These range from bungalows to luxurious waterfront villas with space for eight guests. Most require a one-week minimum in July and August, or three or four nights at other times. Prices are lower by the week and in the off-season. Other companies offering vacation rentals include **Friday Harbor Vacation Rentals** (www.fridayharborvr.com) and **Friday Harbor Lights** (360/378-4317, www.fridayharborlights.com). Most of San Juan Island's resorts, inns, guesthouses, and cottages are also available on a weekly basis.

For dozens of additional weekly or nightly rentals on San Juan Island, browse **Airbnb** (www.airbnb.com), **VRBO** (www.vrbo.com), **Homeaway** (www.homeaway.com), **CouchSurfing** (www.couchsurfing.org), or **FlipKey** (www.flipkey.com).

HOSTEL

The only hostel on San Juan Island, **Wayfarers Rest** (360/378-6428, www.hostelsanjuan.com), has a convenient location just four blocks from the Friday Harbor ferry. It offers some of the most affordable lodging options on the island, with rooms spread over two nearby homes at 35 Malcolm Street and 60

Malcolm Street. The buildings are well maintained, the owners are friendly, and the backstreet location is quiet. One building contains a coed dorm room with six bunk beds ($40/person), four private rooms ($85-100 d), and two little cabins ($85) out back. Linens are included, and travelers in all these units share bathrooms, two kitchens, a living room, and dining room. Upstairs is a private apartment suite ($245 for up to six) with its own kitchen, deck, and bath. The second home has four additional private rooms ($100-135 for up to four guests) with shared baths and a full kitchen. Children are welcome, but older kids pay the same rates as adults (free for kids under five). Wi-Fi is available. The hostel is open year-round but is sometimes booked by groups in the summer, so make reservations as far ahead as you can, at least two weeks if possible for the peak of summer.

HOTELS
Friday Harbor Suites
The largest employer on the island, the sprawling **Friday Harbor Suites** (680 Spring St., 360/378-3031 or 800/752-5752, www.fridayharborsuites.com) is six blocks from downtown. The building was originally an assisted living center, and is a bit sterile compared to other local offerings. Fortunately, the 63 units are spacious, with well-maintained furnishings. This all-suites facility includes kitchenettes with full fridges, microwaves, and sinks, plus ceiling fans (no air-conditioning), Wi-Fi, and sitting rooms with large TVs; many also have gas fireplaces. Studio units are $225 d and one-bedroom suites cost $295 d; add $20 for each additional guest. Two-bedroom suites sleep up to six people for $350. All units have sliding glass doors leading to tiny patios or balconies. A couple of the rooms are wheelchair-accessible, and all guests are provided a filling hot breakfast and can relax in the covered hot tub or use the fitness center. Mi Casita Mexican restaurant is on the premises. Ride the free on-demand shuttle to the ferry, airport, or around town.

Bird Rock Hotel
Just a block from the water and right in the heart of town, **Bird Rock Hotel** (35 1st St., 360/378-5848 or 800/352-2632, www.birdrockhotel.com) is close to restaurants and shops. This trendy 15-room hotel is the latest incarnation of one of the island's oldest buildings, dating from 1891. Inside, find luxurious accommodations, all with private baths, a light breakfast, and Wi-Fi, plus afternoon lemonade and cookies. The smallest rooms ($143-153 d) have queen beds and a shared bath, or step up to larger standard rooms ($200-209 d) with private baths and deluxe units ($249-269 d) with king-size beds and jetted tubs. A deluxe two-bedroom suite ($309 for up to six people) is the top option. Borrow a cruiser bike to explore, or pull out your laptop to take advantage of the Wi-Fi. On-street parking only, but guests are welcome to park at Earthbox Hotel (same owners) a couple of blocks up the street and use the indoor pool, hot tub, Jacuzzi, and fitness center there. The rooms can be a bit noisy at night—a karaoke bar and a loading dock are not far away.

Discovery Inn
If you're looking for a moderately priced family-friendly place, it's hard to beat **Discovery Inn** (1016 Guard St., 360/378-2000 or 888/754-0034, www.discoveryinn.com, $169-199 d). This recently renovated two-story hotel is in a quiet part of town adjacent to the library. Rooms have one or two queen beds, fridges, microwaves, and Wi-Fi, plus access to a large outdoor hot tub (seasonal). The immaculate flower-filled grounds contain picnic tables, volleyball, bocce ball, and other lawn games. Discovery Inn is a 20-minute walk from the ferry, so you'll probably need a vehicle or taxi ride. This is one of the only places in Friday Harbor with air-conditioned rooms. The owners are helpful and friendly.

Earthbox Motel & Spa
This long-established 72-room motel underwent a transformation a decade or so back, reemerging as **Earthbox Motel & Spa** (410

Spring St., 360/378-4000 or 800/793-4756, www.earthboxmotel.com, $212-252 d). Don't let the rather bland exterior fool you; the rooms are stylish and trendy (larger rooms are your best bet), with the flair of a European boutique hotel. Beds and linens are top-end, and all units contain mini-fridges, microwaves, hardwood floors, and Wi-Fi. A central building houses a small pool, hot tub, exercise room, and sauna, and guests can borrow cruiser bikes to pedal around town. A separate two-bedroom Wind House ($433) is also available; it sleeps six, with a two-night minimum stay. Lavendera Day Spa is adjacent, with massage and other pampering.

Friday Harbor House

Located right along the harbor, **Friday Harbor House** (130 West St., 360/378-8455 or 866/722-7356, www.fridayharborhouse.com, $329-449 d) is a pleasant and romantic choice with 23 chic rooms, all with gas fireplaces, large jetted tubs, queen-size beds, flat-screen TVs, fridges, and Wi-Fi. Rooms range from non-view queens up to a luxurious suite. Most also feature ceiling-to-floor windows facing the harbor, and a homemade continental breakfast is served in the dining room. This is also one of the few local lodging places with air-conditioning. Friday Harbor House is popular for meetings, retreats, and wedding parties. A two-night minimum is required for summer stays.

Island Inn at 123 West

Friday Harbor's swankest hotel, ★ **Island Inn at 123 West** (123 West St., 360/378-4400 or 877/512-9262, www.123west.com) stairsteps up the hillside directly across from the harbor. Right in the heart of town, it encompasses four European-style guest rooms ($200-300 d), four suites ($300-380 d), and seven penthouse units ($380-600 d); add $30 per person for additional guests. Guest rooms are stylish, with luxurious beds, flat-panel TVs, and Wi-Fi. The small Euro rooms face the hillside (no view) and all have fridges. They share a comfortable lobby and a microwave. The larger suites (the inn calls them "sweets") all have king beds, fridges, and microwaves. Three of these have harbor views, and the largest has a private patio. Each penthouse has its own personality, but all include private decks, including three with rooftop decks. Other penthouse amenities are gourmet kitchens, space for up to six guests, and wonderful harbor vistas. Honeymooners and others looking for a romantic splurge will appreciate specialty packages that include in-room massage and champagne upon arrival. There's a two-night minimum for penthouses in the summer. Island Inn is one of the few hotels with air-conditioning. Kids are welcome in most of the rooms, and three units are pet friendly. The hotel does not have an elevator.

Orca Inn

Located near the airport in Friday Harbor, the 65-room **Orca Inn** (770 Mullis St., 360/378-2724 or 877/541-6722, www.orcainnwa.com, $80-120 d) has the lowest hotel rates on the island. The single-bed "micro" motel rooms with a double or queen bed are just 11x14 feet, making them barely wide enough to open the bathroom door without hitting the bed. Larger rooms are considerably nicer, with two queens or a king bed. Orca Inn is not at all fancy, but if you just want a clean and comfortable budget-priced room with fridges, microwaves, and air-conditioning it's a godsend. Free Wi-Fi throughout.

RESORTS
Lakedale Resort

A delightful and upscale place, ★ **Lakedale Resort** (four miles from Friday Harbor at 4313 Roche Harbor Rd., 360/378-2350, www.lakedale.com) sits on an 82-acre spread in the heart of San Juan Island. The rustically modern, 9,000-square-foot log lodge faces Neva Lake and features a great room with stone fireplace and a friendly staff. Inside are 10 immaculate guest rooms, each with a fireplace, jetted tub, and private deck. Most rooms face the lake, and one is wheelchair-accessible, while a second is set up specifically for the hearing-impaired. Lodge rooms are $295-305 d, with additional guests at $10 per person; the rate includes a delicious hot breakfast in the dining room with pancakes and made-to-order omelets. Mary Ann provides an informative introduction to the island during breakfast, and can help with planning your day. No kids under 16 are permitted in the lodge, and a two-night minimum is required.

Six log cabins, also recently built, are situated along a lake or set beneath tall second-growth Douglas firs. Each includes two bedrooms, two baths, a full kitchen with dishes, a loft (great for children), fireplace, covered back porch, and DVD players. The cabins sleep up to six (one hosts up to 10), and guests can use the central hot tub or head to the lake to swim or fish for trout and bass; they can also rent canoes, stand-up paddleboards, kayaks, and paddleboats. Games include bocce ball volleyball, table tennis, and a giant outdoor chess board. Cabins rent for $449 d, plus $10 per person for additional guests (kids free); there is no maid service at the housekeeping cabins. The most spacious option is a three-bedroom house with loft, kitchen, fireplace, and deck overlooking the lake; it rents for $625 for four guests. In addition to traditional cabins, the resort has "glamping" canvas cabins that provide a taste of the wild with the luxuries of a hotel; these go for $179 a night. Even nicer are the four-person canvas cottages (with chandeliers!) for $239.

Lakedale Resort does not have television reception and the video players are tiny, but there's a big library of movies in the office. There is no cell phone reception either, but the resort does have free Wi-Fi around the lodge. Call in January or February for peak-season reservations because Lakedale books up early.

Lonesome Cove Resort

This is what getting away from it all means. **Lonesome Cove** (416 Lonesome Cove Rd., 360/378-4477, www.lonesomecove.com) occupies the quiet north end of San Juan Island facing Spieden Channel. Get there by driving 0.5 mile down a narrow dirt road through tall trees before emerging onto the lovely grounds bordering Lonesome Cove and Spieden Channel—the passageway for ferries between Friday Harbor and Vancouver Island. The resort centers on an old apple orchard, small pond, and creek. Semi-tame deer wander through, and you're likely to see foxes and otters.

Lonesome Cove Resort is a favorite of the just-married crowd, but also remains popular with families. Guests stay in six charming waterfront log cabins, each with a double bed and futon, full kitchen with dishes, private bath, stone fireplace (firewood included), and large deck just 40 feet from the beach. There are no phones, Internet, or TVs to disturb your time here. Nightly rates are $190-215 d or $20 each for additional guests. A two-bedroom apartment suite sleeps six for $310.

Lonesome Cove is a delightful spot, but it was long ago discovered. You'll need to make reservations a year and a half in advance to be assured of space in the peak season; all the cabins are booked by the previous October! A five-night minimum is required June-August, with a two-night minimum at other times. During the summer, a 100-foot dock is available here, making this a fine base for boaters.

Roche Harbor Resort

Listed in the National Register of Historic Places, ★ **Roche Harbor Resort** (360/378-2155 or 800/451-8910, www.rocheharbor.com) features impressive 19th-century buildings juxtaposed with attractive modern structures. In addition to a wide range of lodging options, resort facilities include a restaurant and café, general store, seafood stand (fresh Dungeness crab, oyster, clams, and prawns), Wi-Fi, tennis and volleyball courts, bocce ball courts, a heated Olympic-size outdoor pool and wading pool, and a kids' playground (the best on San Juan Island), plus rentals of motorboats, bikes, mopeds, and sit-on-top kayaks. Whale-watching and sea-kayak tours depart from the harbor, a fascinating sculpture garden is just up the hill, and the lounge has live music and dancing on summer weekends.

Built in 1886, the classic **Hotel de Haro**—the oldest hotel in Washington—fronts a gracious formal garden and marina. The hotel's downstairs lobby is worth a look even if you aren't staying here, with historical photos and a big fireplace. Rates at the hotel start at $160 d for an old-fashioned room (bath down the hall and no TV) with a double bed, up to the presidential suite ($295 d) with its own fireplace, private bath, and veranda facing the harbor. This one really is a presidential suite: Theodore Roosevelt slept here in 1906 and 1907. John Wayne was also a frequent visitor (Wayne's room is $255 d). The building has settled over the decades, leaving floors with a distinctive slope. Times have changed, and today's visitor expects more than even presidents received a century ago, so the hotel is not for everyone. If you're accustomed to modern hotels with all the accompanying luxuries, this will definitely not be to your taste, but those who enjoy slipping into the past in a gorgeous setting will love it. Be sure to check out the extra-long custom tub provided specifically for John Wayne.

Employees of the Roche Harbor Lime Company once occupied the resort's nine **Company Town Cottages,** which are now rented out for $410-450 per night. All of these have two bedrooms, full kitchens, and gas grills, and the more expensive ones face the water. The price is the same for up to six guests here. Also available are a few gorgeous, newly built Victorian-style houses behind the hotel, starting at $750 nightly for a three-bedroom place, up to $1,200 for a 2,000-square-foot home with four bedrooms. Less attractive are the 1980s-era **Harbor View condos** that start at $285 for one-bedroom units, up to $375 for a two-bedroom condo. They're glaring eyesores in this historic and scenic place. One consolation: From their windows, you can't see them. A two-night minimum stay is required for the cottages, houses, and condos in the summer. Four **McMillin Suites,** located in an old harborside home, have wraparound covered decks, king-size beds, gas fireplaces, claw-foot tubs and radiant-heated floors in the bath, and tasteful furnishings. These cost $499 d and are a great splurge.

Luxurious accommodations can be found at a dozen **Quarryman Hall Suites,** each with 600 square feet of space (probably three times as much space as President Roosevelt's room!), heated tile floors, luxurious beds, separate sitting rooms with fireplaces, and

the pool at Roche Harbor Resort

private balconies facing the harbor for $395-415. A full-service spa is downstairs.

Snug Harbor Resort

Snuggled along protected Mitchell Bay, ★ **Snug Harbor Resort** (1997 Mitchell Bay Rd., 360/378-4762, www.snugresort.com) provides luxurious lodging in a beautiful setting. The resort was completely rebuilt in 2014, with 17 new cabins and three over-the-office suites, all with water views; some are just 50 feet from the shore. The cabins and suites are beautifully furnished, with 12-foot vaulted ceilings, big windows facing the bay, queen or king beds, sleeper sofas, gas fireplaces, TVs, private baths, kitchens stocked with cookware and utensils, and Wi-Fi, plus a gas grill and picnic table. Rates vary by the size of the room: one-bedroom cabins and suites sleep four people for $299, and two-bedroom units are $399-449 for up to six guests. A two-night minimum stay is required in the summer.

Guests can borrow stand-up paddleboards, canoes, kayaks, or bikes. There's even a pot to cook crab you catch (or purchase from the seafood stand at nearby Roche Harbor). Book a whale-watching or sea kayak tour at the private marina, fish from the dock, get light meals and espresso in the café, or borrow a board game to unwind and relax. Fire pits and free firewood are available for evening campfires, there's a fitness room in the main building, and both Roche Harbor and San Juan Island National Historical Park are a short drive away.

GUESTHOUSES AND SUITES

In addition to the places listed below, you should consider **Nichols St. Suites** (85 Nichols St., 360/378-2638 or 866/374-4272, www.lodging-fridayharbor.com, $175-195 d), **Ferry Landing Suites** (85 Front St., 800/391-8190, www.ferrylandingsuites.com, $325-450 d), **San Juan Suites** (360/378-2070, www.sanjuanislandsuites.com, $159-299 d), and **Courtyard Suites** (275 A St., 360/378-3033 or 800/378-1434, www. courtyardsuites-fridayharbor.com, $219-249 d). Most of these require a two-night minimum stay.

Etta's Place Suites

Etta's Place Suites (455 Argyle Ave., 360/298-2999, www.ettasplacesuites.com, $199-209 d) has suites and a motel-style room in an 1895 Victorian home just four blocks from the ferry. The two suites sleep up to four guests and have fully stocked kitchenettes. All units contain queen beds, private baths, and Wi-Fi. Dogs stay for an additional $50.

Friday Harbor Vacation Rentals

Friday Harbor Vacation Rentals (360/472-1050, www.fridayharborvacationrentals.com, $139-219 d) has five units in a restored historic downtown home called Acanthus Suites. The home was built in 1913 as a wedding gift for the daughter of a wealthy merchant, and the parlor and dining room retain the original fir flooring and woodwork. The units range from a cozy second-floor studio to a spacious two-room suite. All have kitchenettes, private baths, and Wi-Fi; most include electric fireplaces. There's a big backyard with a barbecue, koi pond, and big willow tree. Wedding parties often rent the entire house for $850/night; it sleeps 21 people. A two-night stay is required, and dogs are welcome in one of the suites.

The owners also offer a two-bedroom apartment over the Ace Hardware Store. This sleeps six, and has a full kitchen, private bath, and washer and dryer. It rents for $229/night, and is popular for longer-term stays.

Juniper Lane Guest House

Owner Juniper Maas took an eco-centric approach in constructing ★ **Juniper Lane Guest House** (1312 Beaverton Valley Rd., 360/378-7761 or 888/397-2597, www.juniperlaneguesthouse.com), a cheery country home built largely from salvaged and recycled materials. This is one of the best deals on the island, with comfortable, reasonably priced rooms and a welcoming ambience. The main house contains five guest rooms ($90-135 d, add $25 for each additional guest), private or shared baths, a stocked and stylish kitchen, and a relaxing common area, plus Wi-Fi throughout. Two rooms are perfect for families and groups, with a mix of queen- and twin-size beds. Wedding parties and groups can rent the entire house (it sleeps 15) for $745. A separate cabin ($225 d) has two bedrooms, a bath, and full kitchen, along with a deck looking across the grazing sheep and llamas in the fields of Beaverton Valley. Kids are welcome in the cabin, but no children under eight are allowed in the main house. There's a two-night minimum in the summer.

BED-AND-BREAKFASTS

The **Bed & Breakfast Association of San Juan Island** produces a lodging brochure with brief listings and a map showing bed-and-breakfast locations. Pick one up on board the ferry or in regional visitors centers. Call the hotline (360/378-3030 or 866/645-3030) for availability at 20 of the finest local bed-and-breakfasts, or head to www.san-juan-island.net for direct links to bed-and-breakfast homepages.

Friday Harbor Grand B&B

Named for the Steinway grand piano in the living room, ★ **Friday Harbor Grand B&B** (345 Blair Ave., 360/378-0442, www.fridayharborgrand.com, $195-325 d) is the most distinctive bed-and-breakfast on San Juan Island. Owner Farhad Ghatan has a long history of hosting lodging places, and when he took over this place several years ago it needed a massive amount of restoration. He added a second story to the historic home—built in the 1880s for San Juan County's first judge, John Bowman—and planted a big organic garden out back where kids enjoy holding the chickens. There's a pretty fountain with waterfall, along with a half-dozen spacious and impeccably clean rooms. One-bedroom suites are $235-375 d, and two-bedroom suites cost $400-450 d; add $25 per person for each

additional guest (including children). All rooms contain queen or king beds, private baths, TVs, and Wi-Fi, and several have kitchenettes, covered decks, and water views. The largest units sleep five people, and two units are dog friendly (additional charge). A two-night minimum stay is required.

Breakfast is extraordinary, with a changing multicourse menu of gourmet specialties, including shakshuka, an Israeli egg dish. Many items are gluten-free and from local sources. Freshly baked sourdough bread is always available, along with homemade jams and jellies. Breakfast is served on the veranda when the weather cooperates, or in the dining room on chilly mornings. Farhad is an accomplished amateur pianist, and performs a one-hour formal concert nightly at 7:30 pm on the Steinway grand piano. These classical performances include liner notes and wine. Freshly baked cookies are delivered to your room in the evening.

Argyle House B&B

A comfortable Craftsman-style home on an acre of land in Friday Harbor, **Argyle House** (685 Argyle Ave., 360/378-4084 or 800/624-3459, www.argylehouse.net) was built in 1910. Upstairs are three guest rooms ($200-220 d) with small private baths; two nicely appointed cottages ($250 d) provide more privacy. All guests have access to the backyard patio and hot tub. A filling hot breakfast is included, Wi-Fi is available, and children of all ages and dogs are welcome.

Hillside House B&B

A spacious contemporary dwelling, **Hillside House B&B** (365 Carter Ave., 360/378-4730 or 800/232-4730, www.hillsidehouse.com, $159-299 d) occupies an acre of wooded land less than a mile from the ferry. There are views of Friday Harbor, the islands, and Mount Baker from the deck, and the grounds feature an ornamental pond and atrium. Covering 4,000 square feet, this is one of the larger bed-and-breakfasts on San Juan, with seven guest rooms offering private baths and Wi-Fi.

One room (Eagle's Nest) takes up the entire third floor with a king-size bed, jetted tub, fireplace, and private balcony. A big buffet breakfast is offered each morning. Children under age 10 are not permitted. There is no minimum stay.

Inn to the Woods B&B

A luxurious hillside bed-and-breakfast, **Inn to the Woods B&B** (46 Elena Dr., 360/378-9501, www.inntothewoods.com, $180-280 d) is surrounded by tall Douglas firs four miles northwest of Friday Harbor and directly across the road from Sportsmans Lake. The four guest rooms have private baths, Wi-Fi, and filling breakfasts. Three of these rooms feature private outdoor hot tubs. The B&B isn't really for children.

Kirk House B&B

A lovely and romantic Craftsman home, **Kirk House B&B** (595 Park St., 360/378-3757 or 800/639-2762, www.kirkhouse.net, closed Oct.-Apr., $245-295 d) was built in 1907 as a summer retreat for industrialist Peter Kirk, the namesake of Kirkland, Washington. Four inviting guest rooms have private entrances and baths. The two nicest rooms each contain king-size beds; one room features a wood-burning fireplace, while the other has a big jetted tub. A full hot breakfast is included. No children under 14 are allowed.

Longhouse B&B

Located on the west side of the island, **Longhouse B&B** (2387 Mitchell Bay Rd., 360/378-2568, www.sanjuanlonghouse.com) is an eclectic, modern waterfront home with a fine view from the great room. Two spacious bedrooms ($145-155 d) are available, both with private baths. Co-owner Patty Rasmussen once owned a restaurant, and her kitchen skills come to the fore each morning with gourmet breakfasts. A quaint cabin ($165 d or $180 for three; breakfast not included) has a kitchen and a wraparound deck overlooking Mitchell Bay. Kids are allowed in the small cabin, which dates back almost 130

years. Guests can rent kayaks or take whale-watching trips from the adjacent Snug Harbor Marina. A two-night minimum stay is required in the summer.

Olympic Lights B&B

Located in the open meadows on the south end of the island, ★ **Olympic Lights B&B** (146 Starlight Way, 360/378-3186 or 888/211-6195, www.olympiclights.com, $165-185 d, June-Sept.) is one of the more remote bed-and-breakfasts on San Juan. Hosts Christian and Lea Andrale discovered the old Johnson farmhouse when they were on vacation in 1985 and opened it as a bed-and-breakfast the following year. This beautifully maintained Victorian home was built in 1895, and contains four guest rooms with king- or queen-size beds, down comforters, and private baths. A side garden becomes a riot of flowers in the summer, and the big lawn is a fine place for a game of croquet or to listen to singing birds.

Guests are served a full vegetarian breakfast that typically includes fresh eggs from resident hens, scones or biscuits, fruit juice smoothies, and more. The grassy parklands of American Camp are an easy after-breakfast walk, or you can saunter down to the shore at nearby Eagle Cove for a view of the Olympic Mountains. A two-night minimum is required, and children are not allowed.

San Juan Island Inn Collection

The **San Juan Island Inn Collection** consists of two adjacent properties—Harrison House B&B and Tucker House B&B—with space for 60 guests. Owners Anna Maria DeFreitas and David Pass also run Coho Restaurant, a popular fine-dining eatery in Friday Harbor.

One of the nicest Friday Harbor lodging choices, **Harrison House B&B** (235 C St., 360/378-3587, www.harrisonhousesuites.com) offers the perfect blend of privacy and comfort, and it's just two blocks from the ferry landing. The main house was built in 1905, with a cottage added in the 1930s. Today the buildings have been lovingly transformed into six spacious apartment suites, each with a private entrance and full kitchen and bath. The largest—1,600 square feet—encompasses 3 bedrooms, 1.5 baths with a jetted tub, hardwood floors, a piano, and stove, plus a large private deck and sunroom. It can sleep six adults and four kids and goes for $450 d. The other suites (one has its own hot tub) sleep 2-8 and rent for $230-375 d. Additional adults are $25 per person in any of the rooms. Guests will appreciate the three-course gourmet breakfasts, outdoor hot tub, and flower-filled grounds, plus use of mountain bikes and sea kayaks for no extra charge. Children are welcome and cribs are available, making this a fine option for families and wedding parties. Pets are accepted for an additional $25 fee. A two-night minimum stay is required on summer and holiday weekends.

Just a couple of blocks from the ferry, **Tucker House B&B** (260 B St., 360/378-3587, www.tuckerhouse.com) offers a variety of lodging options. A total of 11 units—most with jetted tubs—are located within a simple Victorian home built in 1898 and an adjacent home dating from 1910. Rooms rent for $280-320 d, and the six-person garden suite costs $425-450 d. Three cottages ($280-320 d) also contain kitchenettes and gas fireplaces, and welcome both kids and pets. One of these is rather plain, but the other is a modern and attractive log cabin that's perfect for families. Add $25 per adult for extra guests, $25 for pets. The B&B is adjacent to Harrison House Suites, and the two properties have the same owners, sharing a café for filling breakfasts. Guests from both can use the outdoor hot tub and borrow a bike or sea kayak.

Trumpeter Inn B&B

A contemporary two-story home, ★ **Trumpeter Inn B&B** (318 Trumpeter Way, 360/378-3884 or 800/826-7926, www.trumpeterinn.com, open Apr.-Oct., $199-259 d) overlooks five pastoral acres 1.5 miles southwest of Friday Harbor. Goats, alpacas, horses, and cattle graze in the adjoining fields. The pond is perfect for bird-watching; a small orchard has plum, apple, and pear trees; and the gardens are filled with summertime flowers. Six luxurious guest room are available (one is wheelchair accessible), all with private baths and Wi-Fi; the two nicest units include fireplaces and private decks. Owner Shaun Andres serves a gourmet breakfast each morning, along with her award-winning cookies each afternoon. No children under 12 are permitted, but dogs are okay with advance notice.

Wharfside B&B

One lodging place on San Juan Island isn't really on the island—it's in the water. **Wharfside B&B** (360/378-5661, www.slowseason.com) is a gracious 60-foot sailboat, the *Slow Season,* docked at the Friday Harbor Marina, slip K-13. Two staterooms rent for $195-215 d, including a hot breakfast. The larger forward stateroom includes a fireplace and full bath, while the aft cabin has lower ceilings and a sink, but no shower (public showers are just up the dock). Spending the night on a sailboat isn't for everybody; check online to determine if it's right for you. No kids under 12 are allowed, and there is no TV or Wi-Fi. Kenmore Air floatplanes land nearby, so travelers can fly from Seattle and step into their accommodations without even touching the shore!

CAMPING

Camping options on San Juan Island are limited and fill fast, so make reservations as far in advance as you can. Coin-operated **showers** ($1.50 for five minutes) are available at the Friday Harbor Marina and Roche Harbor Marina. **San Juan County Fairgrounds** (849 Argyle Ave., 360/378-8420, www.sjcfair.org) has eight RV sites (no tents) for $35 nightly with electricity, restrooms, and showers.

San Juan County Park

Pitch a tent at one of 20 campsites at the 12-acre **San Juan County Park** (360/378-8420, www.sanjuanco.com/parks, year-round,

$32-45), a mile north of Lime Kiln Point State Park along West Side Road. Cyclist or kayaker sites are $10 per person. Because this is essentially the only public campground on the island, you'll need to reserve months ahead for the summer season. Reservations ($7 fee) can be made between five days and three months ahead of time through the park website. You may find last-minute space on a summer weekday, but weekends are almost always fully reserved, especially in August. The park has a boat ramp, drinking water, ice, picnic tables and shelters, and flush toilets, but no RV hookups.

Griffin Bay Marine State Park

This small boat-in-only campsite is on the southeast end of the island just north of American Camp. The 15-acre **Griffin Bay Marine State Park** (360/378-2044, www. parks.wa.gov, $12) has four campsites, along with picnic tables and pit toilets. You'll need to bring your own water. Griffin Bay is a popular destination for quick overnight kayak trips out of Friday Harbor and has a pleasant gravel beach, but you're limited to the immediate area by fences that block access to adjacent private property. The park is a fine stopping point for kayakers circumnavigating San Juan or Lopez Islands. Note, however, that nearby Cattle Pass can be extremely treacherous under certain tide and wind conditions.

Lakedale Resort

Located in a peaceful setting with open fields, small man-made lakes, and forests, **Lakedale Resort** (4313 Roche Harbor Rd., 360/378-2350, www.lakedale.com, May-Sept.) has 65 attractive campsites along two small lakes near the center of San Juan Island, four miles from Friday Harbor. Car campers with tents pay $50-60, RV sites with full hookups are $67, and sites for hikers, bicyclists, and motorcyclists cost $37 d. Pets are allowed, but must be kept on a leash.

The resort also has surprisingly comfortable **canvas cabins,** complete with cots, chairs, and a table; they are $179 for four people (two-night minimum on weekends). There are even over-the-top canvas cottages with space for four at an over-the-top price of $239. Each has a king bed, fireplace, full bath, electricity, and even a chandelier! Canvas cabin guests also get a complimentary continental breakfast in the mess tent, making them perfect if you've never actually camped out. Also available are two vintage 1960s-motif

camping at San Juan County Park

Airstream trailers with space for four at $259-269; they share their own private dock.

All campers share a central bathhouse and porta-potties, and the well-stocked general store sells supplies, bathing suits, firewood, espresso, ice cream, fishing licenses, and s'mores kits. It also dishes out breakfast sandwiches, pancakes, hot dogs, salads, kebabs, panini, and quick homemade pizzas. The campground hosts all sorts of nostalgic family fun, from the giant chess set to tie-dye shirt making and birdhouse building. It's like summer camp for the whole family.

Reservations are advised, but there is usually space for tents (except over 4th of July weekend). The resort also has rooms and cottages and rents out boats of all types for $10/hour: rowboats, kayaks, stand-up paddleboards, canoes, and paddleboats. There are two beaches for summertime swimming. The lakes are stocked with rainbow trout, cutthroat trout, and bass, and fishing poles are available for rent. Wi-Fi is available around the lodge and store, but not in the campground. Your cell phone won't work at Lakedale.

Information and Services

Head to the friendly **San Juan Island Chamber of Commerce Visitor Center** (135 Spring St., 360/378-5240, www.sanjuan-island.org, 10am-4pm daily). Helpful private websites for San Juan Island are **San Juan Island Update** (www.sanjuanupdate.com) and **San Juan Island Directory** (www.sanjuandirectory.com). For other information, visit the **Town of Friday Harbor** offices (60 2nd St., 360/378-2810, www.fridayharbor.org).

LAUNDRY

Both **Sunshine Laundries** (80 Web St., 360/378-7223) and **Blue Sky Laundromat** (210 Nichols St., 360/317-5781) provide a fluff-and-fold service if you drop laundry off to be washed and folded. **Roche Harbor Marina** also has a laundry facility on the dock.

KID STUFF

Didn't bring along your stroller? **Island Bicycles** (380 Argyle Ave., 360/378-4941, www.islandbicycles.com) rents them and also has children's bikes and other cycling gear.

A Place to Play (55 Spring St., 360/378-0378, www.aplacetoplay.biz) is designed for children ages 1 to 10 and offers all sorts of fun activities. A one-hour play session is $7.50 per child, and an all-day pass costs $15 with in-and-out privileges. Adult supervision is required in general, but the center also has a summertime day camp where you can drop your child for $10 per hour (ages 2.5 to 10, max four hours). A Place to Play has free Wi-Fi.

LIBRARY AND INTERNET ACCESS

Spacious **San Juan Island Library** (1010 Guard St., 360/378-2798, www.sjlib.org, 10am-6pm Mon., Wed., and Fri., 10am-8pm Tues. and Thurs., 10am-5pm Sat., 1pm-5pm Sun.) is a pleasant rainy-day spot and a good place to check your email on the computers or use your laptop with Wi-Fi. Families will appreciate the lap-sit book sessions and pre-school story time.

Printonyx (270 Reed St., 360/378-2069, www.printonyx.com, 8:30am-5:30pm Mon.-Fri., 10am-2pm Sat.) has Internet access, copiers, and fax machines.

Pop open your laptop and you'll find free Wi-Fi hotspots around town, including **The Bean Café** (150 1st St., 360/370-5858, www.thebeancafe.com), **Blue Water Bar & Grill** (7 Spring St., 360/378-2245, www.bluewaterbarandgrill.com), **Griffin Bay Bookstore** (155 Spring St., 360/378-5511, www.griffinbaybook.com), and **China Pearl Restaurant** (51 Spring St., 360/378-5254, www.chinapearldining.com). **The Computer Place** (435 Argyle Ave., 360/378-8488, www.compplace.com, 9am-5pm Mon.-Fri., 10am-4pm Sat.) has computer rentals and Wi-Fi access for a fee.

BANKING AND MAIL

Friday Harbor's four banks all have ATMs: **Wells Fargo** (305 Argyle Ave., 360/378-2128, www.wellsfargo.com), **Islanders Bank** (225 Blair Ave., 360/378-2265 or 800/843-5441, www.islandersbank.com), **Key Bank** (95 2nd St. S, 360/378-2111, www.keybank.com), and **Whidbey Island Bank** (535 Market St., 360/370-5641 or 800/290-6508, www.wibank.com). You can also get cash back from an ATM purchase at Kings Market. Find other ATMs at Roche Harbor Grocery and Hotel de Haro in Roche Harbor, along with several Friday Harbor stores.

There are **post offices** in Friday Harbor (220 Blair Av., 360/378-4511) and in Roche Harbor (195 Reuben Memorial Dr., 360/378-2155), inside the Company Store. Head to **Post San Juan** (685 Spring St., 360/378-2400, www.rockisland.com/~postsanj) for FedEx, UPS, and other shipping needs.

MEDICAL CARE

Peace Island Medical Center (1117 Spring St., 360/378-2141, www.peacehealth.org/peace-island) is the only hospital on the San Juan Islands. Built in 2012 to stringent "green" standards, the building is said to be the nation's first carbon-neutral hospital. Services include primary care, critical care, a 24-hour emergency department, imaging and diagnostic equipment, and 10 beds for short-stay inpatient care; the hospital does not have surgery, obstetrics, and other complex medical services. The closest full hospital is in Anacortes.

San Juan Healthcare (689 Airport Center, 360/378-1338, www.sanjuanhealthcare.org) has two doctors and a physician's assistant on staff. You can fill prescriptions at **Friday Harbor Drug** (210 Spring St., 360/378-4421).

VETERINARY CARE

Take sick or injured pets to **Islands Veterinary Clinic** (850 Mullis St., 360/378-2333, www.islandsvet.com). **Animal Inn** (25 Boyce Rd., 360/378-4735, www.animalinnwellness.com) has a kennel for dogs, cats, birds, and other critters.

Getting There and Around

Friday Harbor has a serious parking problem in the summer, and the city *strictly* enforces a two-hour downtown parking limit. Get back to your car three minutes late and you'll probably have a $20 ticket pasted on your windshield. Meters are checked Monday-Saturday 8am-5pm, and officers stop marking cars after 3pm, so you're probably OK to park any time after that.

Eight-hour on-street parking is available at the north end of 1st Street near San Juan Community Theatre, and along Web Street (off Argyle Ave.). Seventy-two-hour parking spaces are up Spring Street beyond the junction with Argyle Avenue (a five-minute walk from the center of town).

If you are catching a ferry, you can park in the ferry line as soon as the previous ferry has sailed, but be sure to return to your car 20 minutes prior to departure. Doing this provides you with free parking, no worries about missing your boat, and the chance to walk around town an hour or two before heading out.

WASHINGTON STATE FERRIES

The Washington State Ferries (360/378-8665 for the Friday Harbor terminal, 206/464-6400 or 888/808-7977 for general information, www.wsdot.wa.gov/ferries) stop right in Friday Harbor. Find all the details—including current ferry wait times—on the website, or get a visual of the action at www.ferrycam. net/fridayhrbr.html.

Peak-season fares from Anacortes to Friday Harbor are $14 for passengers and walk-ons, or $64 for a car and driver. Bikes are $4 extra, and kayaks cost $21 more. There is no charge for eastbound travel by vehicles or passengers from Friday Harbor to Orcas, Shaw, Lopez, or Anacortes, but reservations are not available for these runs so you'll need to get in line well ahead of time. Vehicle reservations *are*, however, highly recommended if you're heading west on the runs from San Juan Island to Sidney, British Columbia. These one-way tickets to Vancouver Island cost $42 for a car and driver or $12 for passengers or walk-ons.

Anyone traveling in the summer from Anacortes to Friday Harbor or from Friday Harbor to Sidney should make a **Save A Spot vehicle reservation** online at www. wsdot.wa.gov/ferries/reservations. These can be made up to two months in advance. Passengers and walk-ons do not need reservations.

Some ferries start in Sidney, British Columbia, stop in Friday Harbor, and then continue to Anacortes. Because they originate in Canada, these ferries need to clear customs in Anacortes, adding a half-hour to the trip. So you can save some time by booking a ferry that originates in Friday Harbor, not Sidney, BC. (Ferries that run only from Friday Harbor to Anacortes don't need to go through customs since they do not start in Canada.)

PRIVATE FERRIES

Clipper Vacations operates the passenger-only *Victoria Clipper* (206/448-5000 or 800/888-2535, www.clippervacations.com, daily mid-May-early Sept., weekends only the rest of Sept.), a high-speed catamaran with day trips between Seattle and Friday Harbor. Rates vary with a convoluted schedule, including discounts on weekdays and if you book at least a day ahead. Adults pay $81-98 round-trip and kids are $41-49. You can combine transportation from Seattle with a 2.5-hour whale-watching trip for $25-30 extra. The company has a multitude of other travel options in the Northwest, including packages that add a night's lodging on San Juan Island, or a three-day/two-night visit to San Juan Island and Victoria. You can also use this as transportation to the islands from Seattle, traveling north one day and returning later.

Puget Sound Express (360/385-5288, www.pugetsoundexpress.com)

the *Victoria Clipper* in Friday Harbor

provides passenger-only service between Port Townsend and Friday Harbor. The boat leaves Port Townsend daily May-October, staying in Friday Harbor long enough for a brief two-hour visit, or you can overnight and return to Port Townsend later. The round-trip lasts eight hours and costs $104 adults, $65 kids ages 2-10, and $15 extra for bikes and kayaks. Although Puget Sound Express promotes this as a whale-watching tour, it is more of a ferry run that passes through waters where whales are often seen.

WATER TAXIS

Based in Friday Harbor, **San Juan Islands Water Taxi** (360/317-5475, www.sjiwatertaxi. net) can transport six passengers anywhere in the San Juan Islands. Captain Gunnar Wickman has sailed all over the world, and his boat spent many years fishing in Alaska. It isn't fast, but it is comfortable, with space for bikes or kayaks.

North Shore Charters (360/376-4855, www.orcasislandadventures.com) is based on Orcas Island, but can pick up passengers anywhere in the San Juans for an hourly rate. **Humpback Hauling** (360/317-7433, www. humpbackhauling.com) provides passenger and freight service throughout the San Juans on a large landing craft, with a smaller boat (Roche Harbor Water Taxi, www.rocheharborwatertaxi.com) also available.

AIR

Taking off from Lake Union in Seattle, **Kenmore Air** (425/486-1257 or 866/435-9524, www.kenmoreair.com) has year-round daily scheduled floatplane flights to Friday Harbor and Roche Harbor. The cost is $150-161 one way, with a 25-pound baggage weight limit. The company also offers wheeled-plane flights between Boeing Field in Seattle and **Friday Harbor Airport** (360/378-4724, www.portfridayharbor.org/airport) immediately south of town. Wheeled-plane flights have a 70-pound baggage limit. A shuttle van is available between Sea-Tac Airport and Lake Union ($15) or Boeing Field ($10).

Friday Harbor Seaplanes (425/277-1590, www.fridayharborseaplanes.com, May-Sept.) flies three times daily in the summer, departing from the south end of Lake Washington (Renton) and landing at Friday Harbor and Roche Harbor. These cost $139 adults or $109 kids one-way. The company provides a free shuttle van from Sea-Tac Airport to their base just south of Seattle. They also have 20-minute flightseeing tours from Friday Harbor for $99 adults or $89 kids.

San Juan Airlines (360/293-4691 or 800/874-4434, www.sanjuanairlines.com) has scheduled daily wheeled-plane service to San Juan Island from Anacortes and Bellingham, plus connecting service to Orcas, Lopez, and Blakely Islands from Friday Harbor and Roche Harbor. Air charters are available to the outer islands or to Victoria, Vancouver, or to Seattle.

Both **Island Air** (360/378-2376, www.sjiislandair.com) and **Westwind Aviation** (360/378-6991, www.westwindav.com) offer charter flights and flightseeing out of Friday Harbor Airport. Their experienced local pilots can take you virtually anywhere in the region, including north to British Columbia or south to Portland.

For unique flightseeing opportunities, **Aero Classic Aviation** (360/317-6276, www. aeroclassicaviation.com) has a beautiful red 1929 Waco biplane at the Friday Harbor Airport. A quick 15-minute loop around the island is $179 for two people, and a longer 35-minute flight that includes the lighthouse on Stewart Island is $299 for two. The owner also has a restored 1951 Piper PA-20 for flightseeing trips.

Friday Harbor Helicopter (360/435-3032, www.fridayharborhelicopter.com) has a Robinson R44 Clipper helicopter on floats, with space for up to three passengers.

BUSES AND TOURS

Island Airporter (360/378-7438, www.islandairporter.com) provides direct van service daily from Sea-Tac to San Juan Island. The bus departs the airport and heads straight

San Juan Island Mileage

	Friday Harbor	American Camp	English Camp	Roche Harbor	San Juan County Park	Lime Kiln Point State Park
American Camp	6					
English Camp	9	13				
Roche Harbor	10	16	4			
San Juan County Park	10	12	5	9		
Lime Kiln Point State Park	9	9	7	12	3	
Cattle Point	9	4	20	24	15	13

to the Anacortes ferry, where it drives on for San Juan Island, and then continues to Friday Harbor ($50) and Roche Harbor ($57). You'll need to add the ferry fare ($13), but it's approximately half the standard rate because you're on a bus. Vans operate once a day in each direction Monday-Saturday in summer and Monday-Friday in winter.

The **Friday Harbor Jolly Trolley** (360/298-8873, www.fridayharborjollytrolley. com, mid-June-mid-Sept.) circles the island four times daily, stopping at Lakedale Resort, Roche Harbor, English Camp, Krystal Acres Ranch, Snug Harbor, Lime Kiln Point State Park, Pelindaba Lavender Farm, and San Juan Vineyards. Riders can step off go dnjoy the sights and then catch a later trolley. All-day rates are $20 for adults or $10 for kids under age 11. The tour is narrated, and the trolley stays longer at some of the stops.

San Juan Transit

You really don't need a car to get around San Juan Island. **San Juan Transit** (360/378-8887, www.sanjuantransit.com) operates shuttle buses between the ferry landing in Friday Harbor and Roche Harbor, with stops at San

Juan Vineyards, Lakedale Resort, Krystal Acres Ranch, English Camp, American Camp, and the San Juan Island Sculpture Park. You can also get off or on anywhere along the route; just flag down the bus for a ride. The buses are dog friendly too.

Buses run mid-May-early September, with hourly service 10am-6pm every midsummer day, and with reduced service on weekends only for the first half of May and throughout September. The bus goes to American Camp only mid-June to early September. Charters are a year-round option. The buses can carry bikes and luggage, and fares are $5 each way ($3 for kids under 12), or $15 for an all-day pass ($10 kids). These passes are a great deal, letting you get off and on along the way. The San Juan Transit office is in the Cannery Landing building adjacent to the ferry dock.

CAR AND MOPED RENTALS

Rent cars from **M&W Auto Rentals** (725 Spring St., 360/378-2886 or 800/323-6037, www.sanjuanauto.com) near the airport. They'll pick you up from the airport or ferry terminal. Rentals are $60 per day for a compact or $70 per day for an SUV. If you just need a vehicle for a short time, M&W also provides four-hour rentals for $10 less.

Susie's Mopeds (125 Nichols St., 360/378-5244 or 800/532-0087, www.susiesmopeds.com, Mar.-mid-Oct.) rents all sorts of unusual vehicles, including mopeds (starting at $35/hour or $80/day), two-person Scoot Coupes ($70/hour or $160/day), four-person Chevy Trackers ($32/hour or $96/day), and Pedego electric-assist bikes ($30/hour or $70/day) from its shop at the top of the ferry lanes in Friday Harbor. Call a couple of days ahead for reservations on summer weekends.

Susie's also rents out mopeds, Scoot Coupes, and bikes from a facility next to the San Juan Island Sculpture Park in Roche Harbor late June-early September.

TAXIS
Call **Bob's Taxi & Tours** (360/378-6777, www.bobs-taxi.com), **Classic Cab Co.** (360/378-7519), **Friday Harbor Taxi** (360/298-4434, www.fridayharbortaxi.com), or **Rhode Trips Taxi & Tours** (360/298-6975, www.rhodetripstaxiandtours.com) for local rides and island tours. Taxi fare is $5 anywhere in Friday Harbor.

Orcas Island

Known as "The Gem of the San Juans," Orcas Island is considered by many the most beautiful island in the archipelago. It is definitely the hilliest. Visitors can drive, hike, or bike to the top of 2,409-foot Mount Constitution for a panoramic view from Vancouver, British Columbia, to Mount Rainier.

Orcas is the largest island in the San Juans, covering 57 square miles. It's home to around 4,500 people and has one of the only real towns in the archipelago, Eastsound. Locals jokingly refer to it as Orcapulco in the hectic summer season, or Orcatraz when winter doldrums make it an isolated rock. Orcas is home to a handful of celebrities who appreciate the relative anonymity of island life: cartoonist Gary Larson (creator of *The Far Side*), Richard Donner (director of *Free Willy, Lethal Weapon,* and *Superman*) and his wife, Lauren Shuler Donner (producer of *X-Men, Deadpool, Pretty in Pink, You've Got Mail,* and *Any Given Sunday*), Warren Miller (adventure filmmaker), author Richard Bach (*Jonathan Livingston Seagull*), astronaut Bill Anders (Apollo 8), and singer Susan Osborn (of Paul Winter Consort).

From the air, Orcas Island looks like either a giant horseshoe or a misshapen M, with two long inlets cutting in from the south. Washington State Ferries dock on the south end of the island at Orcas Village (also called Orcas Landing or simply Orcas), where you'll find a cluster of cafés and gift shops centering on a Victorian gem, the Orcas Hotel.

East Sound is the longest channel, nearly splitting the island into two pieces. The village of Eastsound (note that the village is rendered as one word, unlike the body of water) occupies the head of this sound and is 10 miles from the ferry. Although unincorporated, this is the primary village on the island, and the place to go for groceries, gas, and a wide choice of gift shops, cafés, and galleries. It also probably has more lounging cats per shop than any other town in the Pacific Northwest!

The easternmost lobe of Orcas Island delivers the most rugged terrain anywhere in the San Juans, including the half-mile-high summit of Mount Constitution within famous

---

Previous: horses on Orcas Island; Fishing Bay and Indian Island. **Above:** Doe Bay.

Look for ★ to find recommended
sights, activities, dining, and lodging.

Highlights

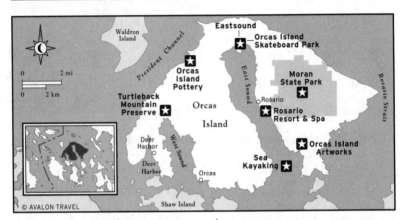

★ **Moran State Park:** Acclaimed as one of the best state parks in Washington, this one has it all: more than 5,200 acres of wild country, a road-accessible lookout tower atop 2,409-foot Mount Constitution, miles of hiking trails, abundant campsites, and a great swimming lake (page 168).

★ **Rosario Resort & Spa:** This well-known resort centers on the mansion built for industrialist Robert Moran a century ago (page 171).

★ **Eastsound:** The largest settlement on Orcas, Eastsound has the look and feel of coastal Maine. Its central location, good shopping, delectable meals, and upmarket lodging choices add to the appeal (page 173).

★ **Turtleback Mountain Preserve:** Some of the best hikes in the San Juans can be found on 1,519-foot Turtleback Mountain (page 173).

★ **Sea Kayaking:** The best kayaking destinations—including Jones, Sucia, Patos, and Matia Islands—are within a few miles of Orcas (page 178).

★ **Orcas Island Skateboard Park:** Most visitors are unaware that the island has one of the finest skateboard parks in the Pacific Northwest (page 182).

★ **Orcas Island Artworks:** This out-of-the-way cooperative art gallery is one of the oldest in the region (page 184).

★ **Orcas Island Pottery:** Step through the gate to discover hundreds of pieces of pottery strewn across a large lawn. Then enjoy a million-dollar view across President Channel (page 184).

Moran State Park. Not far away is Rosario Resort, an equally famous historic mansion and resort.

Smaller than East Sound, West Sound is home to the predictably named little settlement of West Sound. It is eight miles northwest of the ferry landing and has a marina, a homey little café, and a couple of lodgings. Approximately four miles west of here is another gathering place for boaters and others, Deer Harbor, with its substantial marina, plus bed-and-breakfasts, a restaurant, charter sailboats, and kayak rentals. It's appropriately named for the many black-tailed deer in the area (and throughout the San Juans).

PLANNING YOUR TIME

Because of its size, unusual shape, and rugged topography, Orcas Island takes longer to get around than other islands in the San Juans. It's approximately 25 miles by road from the easternmost end of the island to the western end at Deer Harbor, and that takes an hour or more to drive (if you don't speed). Yes, you can "see" the main sights in a single day, but why bother? If you can, plan to spend at least three or four days on Orcas.

Because of its central location and abundant amenities, many travelers choose the Eastsound area as their base. Even those staying at Doe Bay Resort or Deer Harbor, however, can easily get to the main island attractions if they set aside a bit of time. A pair of don't-miss sights are the legacy of Robert Moran: ostentatious **Rosario Resort** and nearby **Moran State Park,** with its winding road up Mount Constitution.

The beauty of Orcas Island has provided inspiration for countless artists, whose works are displayed in shops and galleries throughout the island. A few miles south of Moran State Park is a low building that houses one of the oldest artist-owned cooperatives in the Northwest, **Orcas Island Artworks.** North of the park and just before you reach Eastsound is **Lambiel Museum,** with hundreds of locally produced pieces on display.

Orcas Island Pottery—famous for its pottery-filled yard—hugs the western shore of the island, while **Crow Valley Pottery** lies in the heart of Eastsound.

The town of Eastsound is home to not just shops, restaurants, and lodgings, but also the surprising **Orcas Island Skateboard Park** along Mount Baker Road.

HISTORY

Orcas Island is apparently named for a viceroy of Mexico, Don Juan Vicente de Guemes Pacheco Pedilla Horcasitas y Aguayo, Conde de Revilla Gigedo. Fortunately, his name was shortened rather substantially, with "Horcasitas" becoming "Orcas." (Variations on his name also ended up on nearby Guemes Island and Padilla Bay, along with southeast Alaska's Revillagigedo Island.) The Spanish explorer Francisco Eliza named Orcas Island during his 1791 visit, and some scholars believe he actually named the island after his schooner of the same name. More imaginative folks claim the name came from the word *orca,* a Spanish term for the mammals still often seen here, killer whales or orcas.

Place names within West Sound highlight the area's sometimes violent history: Haida Point, Indian Point, Massacre Bay, Skull Island, and Victim Island. All of these names originated from Haida raids on the peaceful Coast Salish people who lived here for centuries. Many Salish men were murdered during these attacks, and surviving women and children were typically hauled away as slaves. Both Skull and Victim Islands are marine state parks.

Early white settlers on Orcas Island hunted deer, logged, farmed, and fished. Louis Cayou came to the island in 1859 as a market hunter for the Hudson's Bay Company, but he settled down with a Salish woman and raised a family. He is regarded as the first white settler. Other folks trickled in over the next 15 years, and by 1873 the island was home to 40 or so white settlers. Within a few years, the population grew rapidly as farmers discovered that Orcas was perfect for growing apples, pears, and Italian plums. In the 1880s and onward,

Orcas Island

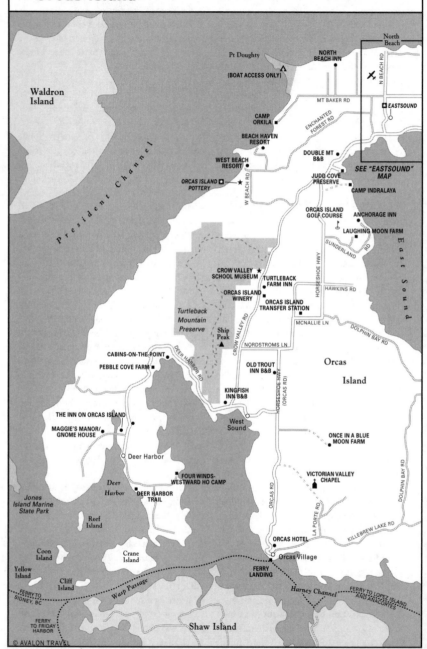

ORCAS ISLAND

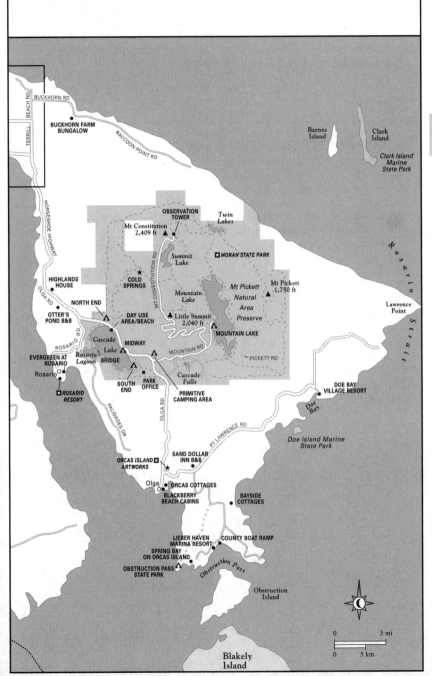

thousands of fruit trees were planted across the island for the Orcas Island Fruit Company. A major recession in 1890 forced the company into bankruptcy, but the trees kept producing and growers found other outlets. Competition from farmers in eastern Washington spelled the end to commercial fruit growing by the 1930s, but many of these small orchards still produce fruit more than a century after they were planted.

Sights

★ MORAN STATE PARK

Near Eastsound, 5,252-acre **Moran State Park** (360/376-2326, www.parks. wa.gov) is best known for its steep paved road to the 2,409-foot summit of **Mount Constitution.** The mountain is crowned by a 52-foot **stone observation tower** constructed by the Civilian Conservation Corps (CCC) in 1936 and patterned after the 12th-century watchtowers of Russia's Caucasus Mountains. This is the highest point anywhere in the San Juans and offers a commanding view, from Mount Rainier to British Columbia. The park is 14 miles by car from the Orcas ferry landing and occupies much of Orcas Island's eastern appendage. It is open year-round for both day use and camping. Get snacks from the little Airstream trailer (360/376-4665, www. orcasadventures.com, 11am-5pm daily June-Sept.) in the parking lot.

Moran State Park was the creation of Robert Moran—a shipbuilder, former mayor of Seattle, and builder of the mansion that is now Rosario Resort. Moran was working as chief engineer on an Alaskan steamer, the *Cassiar,* when he met famed naturalist John Muir. The two became close friends, and that friendship opened Moran's eyes to the natural world. In later years, Moran prospered financially, but this appreciation for nature inspired him to do something beneficial with his wealth.

In 1911, he tried to donate 2,700 acres on Orcas Island to establish a state park just uphill from his mansion at Rosario. The offer was turned down, and it wasn't until 1921 that the state finally accepted the land and created

forest in Moran State Park

stone observation tower on Mount Constitution

other information. You can also visit the park office (9am-5pm Tues.-Sat.) near the north end of Cascade Lake. The small **Summit Shop** (360/376-3111, 11am-4pm daily May-Sept., 11am-4pm Sat.-Sun. in the off-season), atop Mount Constitution, sells maps, books, postcards, and a few gifts. Parking requires a $10 day-use pass, or get an annual Discover Pass for all Washington parks for $30. Interested in helping the park's preservation efforts? Join the nonprofit **Friends of Moran State Park** (www.friendsofmoran.com).

Hiking Trails

Moran State Park has 38 miles of hiking trails, from short nature loops to remote and rugged out-of-the-way hikes. The CCC constructed most of these trails during the 1930s. Get a park map for details on the various routes, or see Ken Wilcox's *Hiking the San Juan Islands* (Northwest Wild Books).

The easiest path is 0.3-mile **Moran State Park Nature Trail,** which takes off from the day-use area along Cascade Lake, with signs identifying plants along the way. Only slightly more challenging is the 0.25-mile trail to **Cascade Falls,** where Cascade Creek plummets into a pool 75 feet below. The path begins from a parking area 0.25 mile up Mount Constitution Road and drops downhill to the falls, a 10-minute walk. Come here in spring for the most dramatic show. You can also continue downstream to two smaller waterfalls.

A longer path, the **Cascade Creek Trail,** begins near the park office on Cascade Lake and follows the creek uphill (with a detour to Cascade Falls) to the picnic area at Mountain Lake, a distance of three miles with a gain of 700 feet. You'll encounter enormous old-growth Douglas firs along the way. From the lake, you can hike back or catch a ride downhill along Mount Constitution Road.

Cascade Lake is a busy place in midsummer, with three oft-full campgrounds, a popular picnic area, rowboat and paddleboat rentals, and a great swimming beach. Orcas Road parallels its northeast shore. For a nearly level walk, follow the **Cascade Lake Loop**

Moran State Park. Eventually, Moran would donate nearly 4,000 acres for the park. He later constructed the distinctive concrete entrance arch and the road up Mount Constitution. During the 1930s, the CCC built most of the park's trails, bridges, shelters, and other structures, using sandstone from a local quarry and wood from area forests.

Moran State Park is a heavily wooded area, with old-growth forests of Douglas fir (some six feet in diameter), western hemlock, western red cedar, and Pacific yew in the lower elevations, plus hardy stands of shore pine (a subspecies of lodgepole) higher up the slopes. The windswept summit of Mount Constitution has grassy openings accented by lilies, asters, stonecrop, and other flowers in the summer. Black-tailed deer are relatively common, along with river otters, muskrats, raccoons, bald eagles, and many other species.

Park Information

Drop by the park registration booth (10:30am-9pm daily late May-early Sept.) for maps and

Trail for 2.7 miles around the lake, past tall trees drooping over the water and across a picturesque arched wooden bridge at Rosario Lagoon, known for good fishing. Several side trails offer tantalizing options, including one that switchbacks 300 feet uphill over 0.75 mile to **Sunrise Rock.** The vistas encompass Cascade Lake below, with the Cascades themselves in the distance on a clear day.

Another relatively easy round-the-lake hike is the **Mountain Lake Loop Trail,** a four-mile path that offers a chance to see black-tailed deer, particularly in the morning and early evening, and passes enormous old Douglas firs. Circle the lake counterclockwise for the best vistas.

The summit of **Mount Constitution** is readily accessible by car via a paved road, but to really appreciate the views, there's nothing like climbing it yourself. A number of trails ascend the mountain from various sides, but one of the best begins from Mountain Lake Landing (accessible by car). From here, you follow the lakeshore to the north end and continue uphill to **Twin Lakes.** Ascend sharply up a series of switchbacks to the summit, where you'll suddenly be surrounded by the masses who drove here. Finally, climb the old CCC viewing tower for a panorama of northern Puget Sound and the San Juans. It's 3.7 miles to the top of Mount Constitution from Mountain Lake. For variety on the way back, take the trail to **Little Summit,** which leads through stands of shore pine before dropping into dense forests of western hemlock and Douglas fir. The return is 3.3 miles, for a round-trip hike of seven miles, with a 1,500-foot elevation gain (and loss) en route. You can, of course, save your legs by catching a ride to the top and hiking downhill instead.

The western portion of Moran State Park encompasses **Mount Pickett Natural Area Preserve,** the largest contiguous tract of un-logged forest remaining in Puget Sound. It is closed to all off-trail hiking or other uses, but trails circle its margins, providing a woodsy 6.5-mile loop hike if you start at Mountain Lake Landing. Mount Pickett itself is a 1,750-foot summit with limited views from the trail.

Water Sports

During the summer, the beach at Cascade Lake is an exceptionally popular family destination, with a roped-off **swimming area** (no lifeguard) that has a shallow sandy bottom and relatively warm water June-August. There's a delightful playground, and the Sugar Shack snack bar (10am-6pm daily

The beach at Cascade Lake in Moran State Park

mid-June-early Sept.) sells Lopez Island Creamery ice cream on waffle cones, strawberry lemonade, iced coffees, hot dogs, grilled cheese, panini, sodas, microwave pizzas, other fast food, and ice. The store has swimsuits, sunscreen, and other supplies, and the boathouse (360/376-4665, www.orcasadventures.com) rents stand-up paddleboards, rowboats, kayaks, canoes, and paddleboats late May-early September. Rowboats, canoes, and kayaks are also available at Mountain Lake, but you'll need to reserve them at Cascade Lake. Both lakes have boat ramps, and motorboats are prohibited. Anglers have fun casting about for rainbow, cutthroat, and kokanee trout; Cascade Lake is stocked annually by the Washington Department of Fish and Wildlife.

Cycling

Moran is the most challenging cycling destination in the San Juans, with trails (and a paved road) leading from Cascade Lake to the summit of Mount Constitution, a gain of 2,100 feet in elevation. It's a fast and exhilarating ride back down! Eleven miles of park trails are open year-round to cyclists, and September 15-May 15, there are 25 miles open to mountain bike use. Before heading out, purchase a *Local Knowledge Trail Map* for Mount Constitution at Wildlife Cycles in Eastsound. This helpful map includes tips for the various trails and roads, along with difficulty ratings and seasonal closings. Cyclists must yield to hikers and horses. Never ride off-trail within the park.

Other Park Activities

The park has five kitchen shelters—most available on a first-come, first-served basis—plus a multitude of picnic tables. A spacious log kitchen shelter next to the Cascade Lake swim area can be reserved (888/226-7688, www.parks.wa.gov). It holds up to 100 people and includes a stone fireplace, wood grill, sink, electrical outlets, and lights.

Equestrians will appreciate the six miles of trails open to **horseback riding** within the park; see the park's official map for details.

★ ROSARIO RESORT & SPA

One of the most historic resorts in the San Juans, **Rosario Resort & Spa** (1400 Rosario Rd., 360/376-2222 or 800/562-8820, www.rosarioresort.com) is five miles south of Eastsound along the protected Cascade Harbor. This famous getaway is well worth a look even if you can't afford to stay here, with a picture-perfect setting that is popular for outdoor (and indoor) weddings.

Now listed in the National Register of Historic Places, the ostentatious mansion at Rosario Resort was built more than a century ago by Robert Moran, a shipbuilder and two-term Seattle mayor who—on doctors' orders—came here to retire.

Moran sold his mansion in 1938 to Donald Rheem, the son of Standard Oil Company founder William S. Rheem (and a major shareholder in Paramount Studios). Donald Rheem spent $400,000 improving the mansion, but it was his wife who is better remembered today. Some say he bought Rosario to keep her out of sight, but she certainly didn't stay out of sight on the island. Alice Goodfellow Rheem cut a wild swath, drinking and playing cards with the locals, zooming around the island on a motorcycle in a bright red nightgown, and playing host to military personnel while her husband was in California. She died in 1956 after falling from the library balcony into the Rosario music room below; some believed it was a suicide. Employees tell of a ghost who wears high heels and skimpy clothing, and of erotic moans coming from her old bedroom late at night. Aficionados say her presence is particularly strong around Christmas, when she died. After Alice's death, the mansion was sold a couple of times, and in 1960 it became Rosario Resort.

The historic mansion at Rosario Resort is open to the public. Visitors are welcome to tour the grounds and check out the antiques-filled rooms, distinctive furnishings, parquet floors crafted from Indian teak, and walls paneled in Honduran mahogany.

Head upstairs to the vaulted ballroom with

Robert Moran: Self-Made Man

Two of Orcas Island's most famous destinations—Moran State Park and Rosario Resort—were the creations of Robert Moran, a self-made millionaire who turned his back on success in the business world.

Born in 1857 to a New York family of 10 children, Moran left home at age 14 to become an apprentice machinist. Three years later, in 1875, he decided that his future lay westward and booked passage for San Francisco. Arriving amid an economic depression and failing to find a job, he spent his last $15 on a steerage ticket to Seattle.

Moran stepped into Seattle rain with just ten cents in his pocket. A hungry belly and the aroma of sausage and flapjacks led him to an eatery run by Big Bill Gross, offered him breakfast on credit, and later helped him get a job as a cook at a logging camp. Moran's cooking was so bad that the men threatened revolt and he hightailed it back to Seattle, where Gross found him another job, as a deckhand on a steamer. Finally, Moran was in his element. Over the next few years, he studied mathematics, drafting, and engineering under the tutelage of an experienced ship captain, gradually moving up the ranks to become chief engineer on the steamer *Cassiar*, sailing in southeast Alaska.

In 1881, Moran married Melissa Paul, and together they raised five children. He paid $500 for his mother, five younger brothers, and two sisters to sail from New York to Seattle. Moran and his brothers set up a marine repair shop and took over management of the adjacent Seattle Drydock and Shipbuilding Company. Within a few years, Moran was on the city council and elected mayor of Seattle. During his first year in office, a fire swept through downtown, leaving 30 city blocks in ruins—including the Moran brothers' machine shop. Moran rebuilt the city after the fire, and within six months, Seattle's population had doubled.

The 1897 discovery of gold in the Klondike transformed Seattle. Thousands of gold-crazed men flooded the town, intent on getting north as quickly as possible. Ships were needed to haul them there (and the gold out), and Moran Brothers began building stern-wheelers at a furious pace. Eighteen of these—each 175 feet long—were completed in 1898, and Robert Moran himself led the flotilla, starting at Roche Harbor on San Juan Island and sailing all the way to St. Michael at the mouth of the Yukon River, a distance of 4,000 treacherous miles. Only one of the 18 steamers was lost along the way, and it was insured. The Morans were on a roll. Their company established an international reputation. In 1900 the shipyard landed a contract to build the U.S.S. *Nebraska*, one of a new class of battleships. It was a huge event for Seattle; more than 55,000 people watched the launching ceremony. The ship became a favorite of naval officers and remained in service through World War I.

The Moran Brothers Company was sold in 1906 to, and later became part of, Todd Shipyards, a large Seattle operation that still flourishes. But the stresses of business took a severe toll on Moran, making him, in his own words, "a nervous wreck." Specialists from Europe told him that he was destined to soon gain "permanent residence in Lakeview Cemetery, Seattle, for the reason that they predicted that I had organic heart disease." He retired in 1905 at the age of 49, turning the shipyard over to his brothers. In 32 years, he had gone from a boy with one dime in his pocket to one of the wealthiest men in the Pacific Northwest. The next chapter in his life would take him to Orcas Island (for more of his story, see the sidebar on page 201).

its heavy doors, stained glass window, Tiffany chandelier, and ornate 1909 Steinway grand piano, which is dwarfed by the 1,972-pipe Aeolian organ. A horseshoe-shaped balcony hides the organ itself, which plays from musical rolls, much like a player piano. Moran had absolutely no musical talent, but he often pretended to play the organ and none of his guests were the wiser. The organ was later modified, adding a keyboard to allow it to be played.

Today, gifted local musician Christopher Peacock (he's also the resort manager) puts on one-hour performances that include music on the organ and piano, along with a slide show about the life of Moran and the resort's rich history. These free performances are open to the public and begin at 4pm Tuesday-Saturday mid-June-mid-September in the grand music room.

Also upstairs is a small free museum with original furnishings and Moran's impressive library just as he left it. Historical photos line the walls, and there's even a model of the U.S.S. *Washington,* one of the ships built by Moran's company. An upscale restaurant and lounge are downstairs, and the basement houses a gift shop, pool, and spa. Outside are manicured grounds and a veranda overlooking Cascade Harbor's bobbing boats. The anchor chain from the U.S.S. *Nebraska* and a beautifully carved figurehead from the clipper ship *America* are in front of the mansion. Lodging is available in newer buildings surrounding Moran's historic home, but not in the mansion itself.

★ EASTSOUND

Located at the north end of Orcas Island near its narrowest point, the settlement of Eastsound is the primary village on the island. Here you'll discover a mix of gift shops, top-end restaurants, comfortable inns, grocery stores, and kayak outfitters, not to mention the kids' science center, skateboard park, and historical museum.

Orcas Island Historical Museum

The Orcas Island Historical Society began in the 1940s as a small group of individuals dedicated to protecting and preserving the island's history. The organization's first museum consisted of artifacts displayed on the front porch of a pioneer family's home. In the 1950s and 1960s, island families donated six original homestead cabins built on Orcas between the 1870s and 1890s. Volunteers reconstructed and linked the structures to create the main museum building. These cedar cabins not only house the collections, but are considered important historical artifacts in themselves.

The collection at the **Orcas Island Historical Museum** (181 North Beach Rd., 360/376-4849, www.orcasmuseum.org, 11am-4pm Wed.-Sat. and noon-3pm Sun. mid-May-Sept., noon-3pm Wed.-Sat. in the off-season, closed January, $5 adults, $4 seniors, $3 students, free for kids under 13) has displays covering relics, life stories, and historical photos from 1880s farms and homesteads, early stores and post offices, fruit farming, and the Coast Salish people. Be sure to see the bison bones found at peat bogs around Orcas. Cut marks on the bones were caused by human hunters, providing evidence that people have been on the islands for nearly 14,000 years!

★ TURTLEBACK MOUNTAIN PRESERVE

This 1,576-acre preserve was purchased in 2006 after local citizens raised an astounding $18.5 million to prevent its development. Shaped like a tortoise—hence the name— **Turtleback Mountain** is accessed from trailheads on two sides. The north entrance is via a gravel road (look for the Turtleback Mountain sign) just south of Crow Valley Schoolhouse on Crow Valley Road. The south entrance is 2.4 miles west from West Sound along Deer Harbor Road. There is no sign for the preserve here, so look on the right (north) side for Wild Rose Lane. The south side trailhead is a few hundred feet up this lane.

Hiking trails loop for more than five miles through second-growth forests (logged in the 1920s and 1930s), with overlooks on both ends of the mountain; the best views are from the south side, where a path climbs 1.3 miles to 931-foot Ship Peak overlook, where you can stand atop rocky outcrops overlooking Crow Valley. The 1,519-foot summit of Turtleback Mountain is the second highest in the San Juan Islands (after Mount Constitution). Get additional info on the preserve—including a downloadable map—from the **San Juan County Land Bank** (360/378-4402, www.sjclandbank.org). The preserve is open for day use only, with no developed facilities or camping. Horses and bikes are allowed on north-end trailheads only, with bikes on even calendar days and horses on odd calendar days.

CROW VALLEY SCHOOL MUSEUM

Three miles southwest of Eastsound, the small **Crow Valley School Museum** (2274 Crow Valley Rd., 360/376-4260, noon-4pm Fri.-Sat. late May-early Sept.) is in a quiet spot surrounded by tall trees, and makes a pleasant stop during a cycling tour of the island. Built in 1888, the classic one-room school houses old desks and a collection of memorabilia that includes school photos, report cards, school clothes, toys, and other items from a bygone era.

ORCAS ISLAND WINERY

Located in a modern barn just south of the old Crow Valley School, **Orcas Island Winery** (2371 Crow Valley Rd., 425/314-7509, www. orcasislandwinery.com) is run by the friendly father-and-son team of Randy and Alexander Schemkes. This boutique winery planted its first grapevines in 2011, so it uses grapes from other parts of Washington in its wines. A $5 charge provides the opportunity to taste several of house wines, including riesling, chardonnay, cabernet sauvignon, merlot, and syrah. The location is peaceful and picturesque, with Turtleback Mountain as a backdrop.

VICTORIAN VALLEY CHAPEL

Hidden in an out-of-the-way part of the island, this picture-perfect chapel is surrounded by lush pastures and woods. From the Orcas ferry landing, drive north 1.5 miles on Orcas Road, turn right onto the easy-to-miss Victorian Valley Road (private), and continue 0.75 mile to the chapel. Built in 1974, **Victorian Valley Chapel** (360/376-3289, www.victorianvalleychapel.com) was intended as the centerpiece for a village of Victorian-style homes. (One local suggested the reason the Victorian village failed to

materialize was because they started with a church rather than a bar.) Although the village never materialized, the little white chapel, with its quaint setting, antique stained glass windows, and lovely wood interior, has become a favorite nondenominational place for candlelit weddings and other gatherings throughout the year. (Book well ahead for summer weddings.) A few steps away is a meditation garden surrounded by Douglas fir trees.

HISTORIC BUILDINGS

Both Deer Harbor and Olga contain buildings dating from the late 1800s, including the Olga Store, the former Deer Harbor Store (1893), and the Deer Harbor Post Office (1893). The last of these is worth a visit, if only for its blue-and-yellow stained glass windows. The quaint and beautifully situated **Emmanuel Episcopal Church** (242 Main St., 360/376-2352, www.orcasepiscopal.org) faces the water in downtown Eastsound. There's a labyrinth walk out front. Built in 1885 and modeled after an English country church, it is also the site for Wednesday and Thursday noontime Brown Bag Concerts all summer. The church was built on land that was originally intended for a saloon. The owner started clearing land here but was so harassed by temperance movement women that he finally gave up and left town. The land was later donated to the church.

LAMBIEL MUSEUM

Eccentric patron of the arts Leo Lambiel has spent more than three decades collecting hundreds of the finest works by 250 San Juan County artists. The collection is now on display at the **Lambiel Museum** (360/376-4544, www.lambielmuseum.org), where the pieces cover a wide array of media: paintings, drawings, sculpture, murals, glasswork, photography, and ceramics, with some works dating back to 1915. This private collection is housed in Lambiel's gracious home/museum, located 1.5 miles from Eastsound on Olga Road. The walls are lined with art, and you'll even find

Eastsound

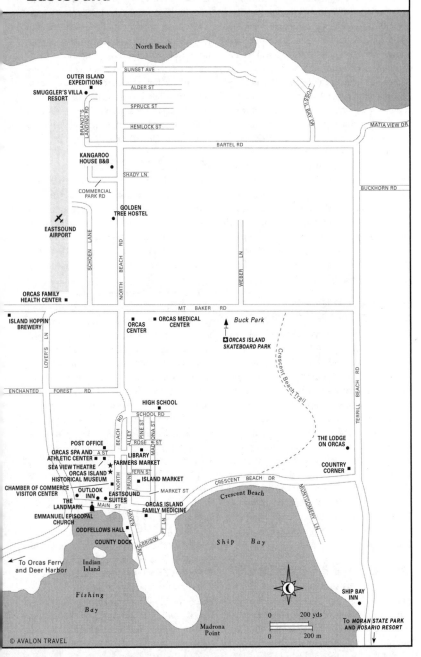

North Beach

SUNSET AVE

OUTER ISLAND
EXPEDITIONS

SMUGGLER'S VILLA
RESORT

ALDER ST

SPRUCE ST

HEMLOCK ST

BRANDT'S LANDING RD

FOREST BAY DR

MATIA VIEW DR

BARTEL RD

KANGAROO
HOUSE B&B

SHADY LN

BUCKHORN RD

COMMERCIAL
PARK RD

GOLDEN
TREE HOSTEL

EASTSOUND
AIRPORT

SCHOEN LANE

NORTH BEACH RD

WEBER LN

ORCAS FAMILY
HEALTH CENTER

MT BAKER RD

ISLAND HOPPIN'
BREWERY

LOVER'S LN

ORCAS
CENTER

ORCAS MEDICAL
CENTER

Buck Park

ORCAS ISLAND
SKATEBOARD PARK

Crescent Beach Trail

ENCHANTED FOREST RD

TERRILL BEACH RD

HIGH SCHOOL

SCHOOL RD

POST OFFICE

ORCAS SPA AND
ATHLETIC CENTER

SEA VIEW THEATRE
ORCAS ISLAND
HISTORICAL MUSEUM

CHAMBER OF COMMERCE
VISITOR CENTER

THE
LANDMARK

EMMANUEL EPISCOPAL
CHURCH

ALLEY

A ST

LIBRARY

FARMERS MARKET

FERN ST

ISLAND MARKET

OUTLOOK
INN

EASTSOUND
SUITES

ODDFELLOWS HALL

COUNTY DOCK

BEACH RD

PINE ST

ROSE ST

MADRONA ST

PRUNE

NORTH

HAVEN

MAIN ST

PT LN

HARRISON

MARKET ST

ORCAS ISLAND
FAMILY MEDICINE

CRESCENT BEACH DR

Crescent Beach

THE LODGE
ON ORCAS

COUNTRY
CORNER

MONTGOMERY LN

Ship Bay

To Orcas Ferry
and Deer Harbor

Indian
Island

Fishing

Bay

Madrona
Point

0   200 yds

0   200 m

SHIP BAY
INN

To MORAN STATE PARK
AND ROSARIO RESORT

pieces inside the closet doors! His collection includes 175 etchings by Helen Loggie (1895-1976), the best-known artist to emerge from the San Juans; her pieces are in both the Smithsonian and the Museum of Modern Art in New York. The collection also includes dozens of original paintings by artist/composer James Hardman, including one that is 27 feet across. On the grounds are various sculptures, along with a couple of fantasy structures: a three-room grotto (with humorous and grotesque pieces) and a "ruined" Greek Doric temple.

Exceptionally detailed two-hour tours of this nonprofit museum are given year-round for $20 per person. Call ahead for a reservation, especially in the busy summer season. Anyone with an appreciation for the arts will certainly enjoy a visit to this fascinating private museum. Lambiel is gregarious—he happily shares his views on art, culture, politics, and life on the island.

EASTSOUND WATERFRONT PARK

Eastsound Waterfront Park is a grassy little picnic area across from the intersection of Lovers Lane and Horseshoe Highway. At low tide, a sandy spit emerges, providing access to tiny **Indian Island.** Tidepools here are alive with fish, sea stars, crabs, anemones, mollusks, and marine creatures. When visiting the island, be careful where you step and avoid nesting birds. (Black oystercatchers on the island have not been able to fledge chicks in recent years, possibly due to human disturbance.) It's illegal to remove any animals or plants. The Chamber of Commerce Visitor Center in Eastsound has a very informative publication detailing the marinelife of Indian Island.

JUDD COVE PRESERVE

Judd Cove Preserve is a little jewel of a park covering just 11 acres along the western shore of East Sound. It is a bit over a mile south from Eastsound; look for the small sign along Orcas Road near the junction with Crow Valley Road, and turn onto Fowler's Way to the parking lot. A 0.5-mile loop trail leads down through fern-filled forests to the pretty cove, where you'll find the restored remains of an 1880s limekiln and quarry. Limestone was quarried from the hillside and heated in the wood-burning kiln to create lime, which was used in masonry construction. The kiln probably operated till 1902. Today, big leaf maples line the shore of Judd Cove, and at low tide the cobbled beach is filled with small crabs.

MADRONA POINT

Madrona Point is aptly named, with tall and colorful Pacific madrone (aka madrona) trees, along with graceful Douglas firs, framing the view across the water to Eastsound and the rest of Orcas Island. A meadow on the point contains camas plants; the bulbs of the purple great camas were a prized food source for the original inhabitants.

Located on Haven Road, Madrona Point was originally a burial ground for the Lummi Indians, and was later used as a graveyard by Orcas pioneers. In the 1980s the federal government bought it from developers who had planned condos for the site, but it was returned it to the Lummi under the condition that the public have access. The Lummi people have a different interpretation of the agreement, so Madrona Point has been officially closed to the public since 2007, but that situation may change. The sign says "Madrona Pt. is Closed. Please Do Not Enter. Violators are subject to trespass enforcement."

CRESCENT BEACH PRESERVE

Owned by the San Juan County Land Bank (360/378-4402, www.sjclandbank.org), the **Crescent Beach Preserve** includes shoreline along this shallow bay (popular with kayakers) and 140 acres of nearby woods. A nearly level 0.5-mile trail starts at Crescent Beach in Eastsound and continues through the woods to Mount Baker Road. A few parking spaces are available on both ends of this path. The usually placid bay at Crescent Beach is home to an oyster farm and a salmon hatchery.

OBSTRUCTION PASS STATE PARK

Obstruction Pass State Park (360/376-2326, www.parks.wa.gov) is an 80-acre park at the end of a one-mile dirt road off Obstruction Pass Road. It is approximately 2.5 miles southeast of Olga and 20 road miles from the ferry dock. A woodsy (and sometimes muddy) trail leads 0.5 mile from the parking lot to a small beach facing nearby Obstruction and Blakely Islands. Nine campsites are just back from the beach, and a side trail leads to a second beach looking west to Olga and the setting sun. Obstruction Pass is a favorite destination for sea kayakers, who can put in for free at the nearby county boat ramp and dock. No bikes are allowed on park trails.

DEER HARBOR TRAIL

The **Deer Harbor Trail** is a level 0.25-mile paved trail (formerly a road) located just south of Deer Harbor Marina. It's a great place to take in the bucolic scene of madrone trees bordering the water. Parking is nonexistent here, so walk down from the marina.

POINT DOUGHTY MARINE STATE PARK

Popular with kayakers, **Point Doughty Marine State Park** is on a small peninsula extending from the northwest edge of Orcas near YMCA's Camp Orkila. Access by larger boats is very difficult, and kayakers may contend with wind and waves at this exposed site. The point contains tall cliffs and a forest of Douglas fir and madrone. The nearby waters are a favorite of scuba divers, and harbor porpoises are common sights in rips just off the point.

Only the four acres at the very tip of Point Doughty are open to the public; the rest is a natural area preserve where trespassing is prohibited. There are no trails in this little park, and no easements to allow access from nearby roads, so you'll need a kayak to visit. Point Doughty's four primitive campsites are part of the Cascadia Marine Trail. No drinking water is available, but vault toilets are provided.

FRANK RICHARDSON WILDLIFE PRESERVE

Located close to Deer Harbor, **Frank Richardson Wildlife Preserve** is a 20-acre freshwater marsh and a premier birding area, with red-winged blackbirds, wood

madrona trees along the Deer Harbor Trail

ducks, hooded mergansers, Canada geese, mallards, wigeons, scaups, buffleheads, teal, rails, marsh wrens, and many other species. It is named for a University of Washington professor of zoology (and birder) who lived nearby. After his death in 1985, the land was saved through the efforts of the San Juan Preservation Trust. Get here by driving to Deer Harbor, turning right on Channel Road just before you reach the harbor itself. Cross the bridge and continue uphill for 0.75 mile. The marsh is on the right.

Recreation

WHALE-WATCHING

Two respected companies provide whale-watching trips from Orcas Island. Note, however, that killer whales are most often found in Haro Strait west of San Juan Island, so trips starting from Orcas require a bit more time en route than those out of Roche Harbor on San Juan Island. Reservations are advised.

Established in 1988 and highly recommended, **Deer Harbor Charters** (360/376-5989 or 800/544-5758, www.deerharborcharters.com) is the oldest whale-watching business on Orcas. Owner Tom Averna has a background in marine science and keeps professional naturalists aboard his two boats (one holds a maximum of 20, and the other up to 32 passengers). Four-hour trips depart from Deer Harbor Resort and Rosario Resort daily in the summer in search of orcas and minke whales, and cost $89 adults, $65 kids under 14. Rosario trips depart mid-June-mid-September, and Deer Harbor departures are available throughout the year. (Winter trips focus on wildlife viewing rather than whale-watching.) The company also has water taxi service to Sucia Island and day sailing from Rosario Resort

Orcas Island Eclipse Charters (360/376-6566 or 800/376-6566, www.orcasisland-whales.com, May-mid-Oct., $99 adults, $64 ages 3-12, $40 for tots) has a spacious 48-passenger boat with an upstairs deck and a heated cabin. Trips last 3.5 hours; they head out from Orcas Village (next to the ferry) and are timed to meet ferry departures, which is advantageous if you're in a hurry but might mean a shorter trip if you aren't. The company offers special lighthouse and history tours several times each summer; call for specifics. Book online for a 15 percent discount.

Former park ranger Beau Brandow runs **Outer Island Excursions** (360/376-3711, www.outerislandx.com), providing twice-daily trips ($99 adults, $89 seniors, $79 ages 12-17, $59 under age 12) that last 3-4 hours. The fast boat (top speed 45 knots) makes it possible to cover a lot of water in a short time. The boat is based in Brant's Landing on the north side of Orcas near Eastsound. The company also offers water taxi service, a ferry to Sucia Island, lighthouse tours, and charter fishing. Operated by Outer Island Excursions, **Orcas Wild** (217 Main St., 360/376-3711, www.orcaswild.com, 10am-6pm daily in summer, weekends in winter, free) is a little interpretive center with exhibits on orcas and other marine mammals.

★ SEA KAYAKING

Orcas Island is an excellent launching point for day trips and multiday paddles. Several of the most popular kayaking destinations—including Jones, Sucia, Patos, and Matia Islands—are within a few miles of Orcas.

Tours

Established in 1982, **Shearwater Adventures** (138 North Beach Rd., 360/376-4699, www.shearwaterkayaks.com) has a variety of kayak tours that depart daily from Rosario Resort, Deer Harbor Resort, West Beach Resort, and Doe Bay Resort & Retreat. Three-hour paddles—including popular sunset tours—cost $79 adults or $45 for kids under 13, and are led by experienced guides. All-day trips ($159) provide a chance to explore beautiful Sucia Island off Orcas at a leisurely pace. In addition, Shearwater staff members set up custom tours, and the Eastsound shop sells kayaks, along with quality paddling and camping gear, books, videos, and more.

Based at Smuggler's Villa Resort on the north side of Orcas, **Outer Island Excursions** (360/376-3711, www.outerislandx.com) provides kayak tours to beautiful Sucia Island. A six-hour trip ($159 adults or $99 ages 12-18) includes a water taxi to Sucia and guided kayaking in the convoluted bays of this unique island. A shorter three-hour paddle to Point Doughty on the northwest side of Orcas is $79 adults or $45 kids.

Located at the ferry landing, **Orcas Outdoors** (360/376-4611, www.orcasoutdoors.com) specializes in short paddles that entice folks waiting in line for the ferry. A two-hour trip is just $48 per person, with a three-hour tour going for $65. Longer trips—including overnights to Jones or Turn Island—are also available.

At **Spring Bay Kayak Tours** (360/376-5531, www.springbayonorcas.com), owners Carl Burger and Sandy Playa guide two-hour paddles around the waters of Obstruction Pass. Twice-daily tours are just $45 per person. The remote location, reasonable price, knowledgeable guides, and relatively protected waters make this an excellent option. There are no age limits and a triple kayak is available, making these trips perfect for families. Tours are offered for two or more people, and are limited to one group of people, making this a really private paddle.

Kayak and Paddleboard Rentals

Do-it-yourselfers can rent sea kayaks from several places on Orcas: **Outer Island Excursions** (360/376-3711, www.outerislandx.com, $75/day for doubles, $50/day for singles) from the north shore of Orcas, **West Beach Resort** (360/376-2240 or

877/937-8224, www.westbeachresort.com, $25/hour for doubles) on the west side of the island, **Orcas Kayaks** (360/376-2472, www.orcaskayaks.com, $40/day doubles, $30/day singles) at Lieber Haven Resort & Marina on the east side of the island, and funky **Crescent Beach Kayaks** (360/376-2464, www.crescentbeachkayaks.com, $18/hour per person or $50/person for a half-day, including a short lesson) in Eastsound. The last of these has all sorts of kayaks—including sit-on-top versions and kayaks with extra space for children.

Rent **stand-up paddleboards** for $25 per hour from West Beach Resort, Crescent Beach Kayaks, and **Orcas Boat Rentals** (360/376-7616, www.orcasboatrentals.com) at Deer Harbor Marina.

If you're planning on launching your own kayak, be forewarned that you may be subject to a **launching fee** ($5 at Deer Harbor, $10 at West Beach Resort) if you aren't on public lands, and may be charged for overnight parking. North Beach near Eastsound is the primary launch point for kayakers heading to the very popular trio of Sucia, Matia, and Patos Islands. Unfortunately, parking is limited and the spaces are quickly filled on summer weekends. You can also launch kayaks for free at the county dock (before your reach Madrona Point) in Eastsound. On the southern side of the island, kayakers put in at Obstruction Pass, where the county maintains the island's only public boat ramp. Across the road is Lieber Haven Resort & Marina (360/376-2472, www.lieberhavenresort.com), which has a wonderful beach that's open to the public and doesn't charge for launching kayaks.

BOATING
Marinas
Rattling calls of kingfishers fill the air and flowers drape the docks at picturesque **Deer Harbor Marina** (360/376-3037, www.deerharbormarina.com, 9am-5pm daily), located on the southwest end of Orcas Island. The small sandy beach is a great diversion for kids. It's a busy place in the summer,

with boat rentals and fishing (North Shore Charters), sailing charters, sea-kayak tours (Shearwater Adventures), whale-watching trips (Deer Harbor Charters), and nature tours (Gnat's Nature Hikes). Transit options include water taxis (North Shore Charters and Orcas Boat Rentals) and daily floatplanes to Seattle (Kenmore Air). Other services include a post office, bike rentals, showers, laundry, moorage, an ATM, Wi-Fi, boat gas and diesel (also for cars in an emergency), and a tiny year-round market. Just up the road is Deer Harbor Inn, with lodging and a restaurant. Along the shore beside the marina are cottages and suites rented by Worldmark Timeshares (www.worldmarktheclub.com).

On the other side of Deer Harbor at Cayou Quay Marina you may see the luxury yacht *Apogee,* owned by former astronaut Bill Anders. As the lunar module pilot for Apollo 8, he was on board the first spaceflight to leave Earth's orbit en route to the moon, and the first to see the entire sphere of the earth from outer space. *Earthrise,* a photo taken by Anders on Christmas Eve 1968, is one of most famous images ever taken; it shows a blue and white Earth rising over a desolate moonscape. The late photographer Galen Rowell called *Earthrise* "the most influential environmental photograph ever taken."

Historic Rosario Resort is the base for **Rosario Resort Marina** (360/376-2222 or 800/562-8820, www.rosarioresort.com), with moorage, fuel, showers, and a seasonal store with supplies on Cascade Bay near Moran State Park. There's direct Kenmore Air floatplane service to the marina from Seattle, and you can take sea-kayaking and whale-watching trips, go sailing with a pro, or go charter fishing. The resort itself houses a full-service spa.

Located three miles west of Eastsound off Enchanted Forest Road, **West Beach Resort** (360/376-2240 or 877/937-8224, www.west-beachresort.com) has a pier and summer-only marina. You can rent stand-up paddleboards, motorboats, canoes, fishing poles, and sea kayaks, or take a guided kayak tour through

Shearwater Adventures; a sunset tour costs $79 adults or $45 for kids under 13. If you aren't staying at the resort there's a $10 charge to use the launch ramp.

Orcas Island's largest marina is **West Sound Marina** (360-376-2314, www.west-soundmarina.net, year-round) on the northeast side of West Sound. Here you will find guest moorage, showers, a waste pump-out, fuel dock, marine repair facility, and chandlery.

Friendly **Lieber Haven Resort & Marina** (360/376-2472, www.lieberhavenresort.com) is a small marina where you can rent kayaks and rowboats or head out on whale-watching trips, sea-kayak tours, or fishing charters. They even have loaner fishing poles. A little store sells fishing supplies and snacks, and public moorage is available, along with free Wi-Fi. It is located along Obstruction Pass on the southeast end of the island. Across the road is the **Obstruction Pass Boat Ramp,** the only public ramp on Orcas.

Sailing

Deer Harbor (www.deerharbormarina.com) is the primary center for sailboat charters on Orcas Island, with four different companies offering day trips and longer sails.

Skipper Ward Fay of **Northwest Classic Day Sails** (360/376-5581, www.classicday-sails.com) sails a meticulously maintained cedar sloop, the 33-foot *Aura.* Three-hour trips depart Deer Harbor daily on this beautiful 1940s sailboat ($76 adults, $59 ages 7-12, $44 for younger kids).

Also based at Deer Harbor, **Emerald Isle Sailing Charters** (360/376-3472 or 866/714-6611, www.emeraldislesailing.com) has both six-hour day trips ($145 per person with a two-person minimum, snacks included) and multiday San Juan Islands skippered charter trips up British Columbia's Inside Passage. The boat, an immaculate 54-foot pilothouse ketch, is called *Nawalak,* a name that means "spirit of nature" in the Kwakwaka'wakw language. A commercial fisherman in Alaska for 19 years, captain Dave Lutz has a rich knowledge

sailing near Orcas Island

Motorboats

Located at Deer Harbor Marina, **Orcas Boat Rentals** (360/376-7616, www.orcasboatrentals.com, daily June-Sept.) rents a variety of boats, including 15-foot inflatables ($300/day) and 19-foot Habercrafts with 90-horse engines ($375/day). The staff provides water taxi service to nearby islands.

West Beach Resort (three miles west of Eastsound, 360/376-2240 or 877/937-8224, www.westbeachresort.com) rents 14-foot skiffs ($179/day), along with stand-up paddleboards, canoes, and sea kayaks ($25/hour).

Fishing

Fishing charters—primarily for salmon and halibut—are offered by **Outer Island Excursions** (360/376-3711, www.outerislandx.com), **Salt Rose Charters** (360/298-7353, www.saltrosecharters.com), and **North Shore Charters** (360/376-4855, www.orcasislandadventures.com). Expect to pay around $250 per person for an all-day fishing expedition. **West Beach Resort** (three miles west of Eastsound, 360/376-2240 or 877/937-8224, www.westbeachresort.com) rents fishing gear.

HIKING

The best hiking on Orcas is found within Moran State Park, but a handful of other trail options exist. Get a copy of *Hiking the San Juan Islands* by Ken Wilcox (Northwest Wild Books) or *San Juan Islands: A Guide to Exploring the Great Outdoors* by Dave Wortman (FalconGuides) for detailed descriptions of Orcas trails. **Olga Community Park** contains picnic tables and a playground next to the community hall in Olga.

Natalie (Nat) Herner of **Gnat's Nature Hikes** (360/376-6629, www.orcasislandhikes.com) leads morning nature walks that emphasize both human and natural history, along with wild edible and medicinal plants. The cost includes pickup and return to your hotel or bed-and-breakfast, plus two or three hours exploring Moran State Park trails. The pace is set to your abilities. She also offers customized half-day boat-and-hike trips to the

of both sailing (he bought his first boat at age 11) and the natural world.

Also based at Deer Harbor, **Kruger Escapes** (360/298-1023, www.krugerescapes.com) is operated by Karl and Jess Kruger, who offer day sails on the *Tomahawk,* a 50-foot ocean racer. A three-hour sail—including a picnic lunch—is $300 for up to four passengers or $450 for six people.

Rosario Sailing (360/376-5989 or 800/544-5758, www.rosariosailing.com) provides day sails from Rosario Resort on the *Simplicity,* a 43-foot gaff rigged sloop. A three-hour trip is $79 per adult, $59 for kids under 14, and free for children under four; there's a maximum of six people.

Skipper Ben Booth operates **Orcas Island Sailing** (360/376-2113, www.orcassailing.com) from Lieber Haven Resort & Marina on the east side of the island. Half-day sailing trips are $300 for up to six passengers. In addition to skippered charters, he provides sailing instruction and bareboat charters on board 19- to 27-foot boats.

marine state parks, including Jones Island and Yellow Island. There's a two-person minimum for the Moran hikes and a three-person minimum (and a six-person maximum) for the boat trips. Natalie has a background in environmental studies along with more than a decade of experience as a naturalist.

BICYCLING

Orcas has a great diversity of cycling options, from easy valley rides to a difficult five-mile climb (and worth it!) to the summit of Mount Constitution within Moran State Park. The island's 82 miles of county roads tend to be narrow, hilly, and winding, making this the most challenging of the islands for cyclists. Always travel in single file. Be sure to pull well off the road when you stop, and watch out for long lines of traffic heading up the road when a ferry has just docked at Orcas Village. Get a helpful cycling map of Orcas from Wildlife Cycles.

Rentals and Tours

Orcas Island's only bike shop, **Wildlife Cycles** (350 North Beach Rd., 360/376-4708, www.wildlifecycles.com, daily in the summer, Tues.-Sat. Sept.-Mar.) rents high-quality mountain/hybrid bikes ($40/day), road bikes ($60/day), baby joggers, trailers, panniers, and other biking gear. Electric-assist bikes may also be available for rent. This is where you'll meet the hard-core local cyclists for organized rides. Guided bike tours are available for groups heading to Moran State Park, and the store carries a map of park trails open to cyclists. You can also rent bicycles and electric bikes at **Deer Harbor Marina** (360/376-3037, www.deerharbormarina.com).

For Orcas Island **cycling tours,** contact **Backroads** (510/527-1555 or 800/462-2848, www.backroads.com) or **Trek Travel** (608/441-8735 or 866/464-8735, www.trek-travel.com).

★ ORCAS ISLAND SKATEBOARD PARK

Head out Mount Baker Road past the medical clinic and just before the cemetery (there must be a reason for their proximity) to **Orcas Island Skateboard Park** (www.skateorcas.org), recognized as one of the finest skate parks in the Northwest. It was funded in part by Warren Miller, the guru of extreme skiing, and contains 15,000 square feet of bumps and curving concrete that attract both locals and off-island skaters. No bikes are allowed, and helmets are required.

cyclists on top of Mt. Constitution in Moran State Park

The skateboard park is a part of **Buck Park,** which also contains tennis courts and baseball fields.

SWIMMING AND FITNESS

The YMCA's **Camp Orkila** (360/376-2678 or 206/382-5009, www.camporkila.org) has a large heated outdoor swimming pool open to the public for an hour on weekdays (1pm-2pm Mon.-Fri., late May-mid-September, free). The pool is for play, not lap swimming; an hour provides just enough time for fun in the water. The wonderful beachside location is two miles from Eastsound at the western end of Mount Baker Road. Families staying on Orcas for a week or more should be sure to get details on the Y's youth swim lessons, offered four days a week late June-mid-August.

Three Moran State Park lakes—**Mountain Lake, Cascade Lake,** and **Twin Lake**—are popular summertime swimming destinations, but there are no lifeguards. Cascade Lake is the center of the action and a favorite for families. It has a roped-off swimming area and shallow water that warms up to swimmable temperatures June-August. A snack bar is nearby, along with a playground and boathouse that rents rowboats and paddleboats. Rowboats are also available at Mountain Lake.

There are no public pools on Orcas, but you can pay $15 for a day pass and use the indoor pool at **Orcas Athletics** (188 A St., 360/376-6361 or 888/827-9262, www.orcasathletics.com) in Eastsound. This full-service athletic club also includes a hot tub, dry sauna, free weights, cardio machines, racquetball, and various classes.

Rosario Resort Spa (360/376-2222 or 800/562-8820, www.rosarioresort.com) includes outdoor and indoor pools, a children's pool, exercise facility, sauna, and hot tub. Pay $25 adults or $10 kids for an all-day pass to the spa and pools.

SPAS AND YOGA

Several places provide massage and other creature comforts on the island, including

Orcas Spa & Athletics (188 A St., 360/376-6361 or 888/894-8881, www.orcasspaandathletics.com), **Healing Arts Center** (453 North Beach Rd., 360/376-4002, www.healingarts.org), and **Island Massage Studio** (365 North Beach Rd., 360/376-1434).

Rosario Resort Spa (360/376-2152 or 800/562-8820, www.rosarioresort.com) is open to those who aren't staying at the resort. The day fee provides access to an indoor pool, an outdoor pool, hot tub, sauna, exercise equipment, towels, and showers. Day use is $25 for one person per day, or $40 per couple. A full range of spa options are also available, including fitness classes, professional massage, aromatherapy, body wraps, facials, manicures, and pedicures.

Doe Bay Resort & Retreat (360/376-2291, www.doebay.com, $15 for a day pass) has au naturel sauna and hot tubs. Children under six are not allowed and no minors are allowed after 6pm. The resort offers weeklong Ayurvedic yoga retreats throughout the year.

Orcas Mandala Yoga Studio (138 North Beach Rd., 360/298-0218, www.orcasmandala.com) has yoga classes most days for all levels of ability, and drop-ins are welcome.

GOLF AND TENNIS

Golfers will enjoy a round at **Orcas Island Golf Course** (360/376-4400, www.orcasgolf.com, Apr.-Oct., $30-33) a nine-hole, par-36 public course on Orcas Road southwest of Eastsound. Built in 1962, the course challenges with gently rolling hills, cantankerous water hazards, and a quaint setting. It's easily the most interesting course in the San Juans. The pro shop rents clubs, pull carts, and electric carts.

Buck Park, just north of Eastsound along Mount Baker Rd., has public tennis courts, baseball diamonds, and a big skateboard park.

HORSES AND ALPACAS

Orcas Island Trail Rides (360/376-2134, www.orcastrailrides.com) leads rides along trails within Moran State Park. These are for all abilities (ages 7 and up), starting with a

1.5-hour horseback ride ($79) that's perfect for novices. Their most popular trip lasts 2.5 hours and covers remote mountain terrain along the park boundary. Trail rides depart from a campground at the south end of Cascade Lake within the park. Call ahead for reservations.

A favorite of kids and weavers, **Orcas**

Moon Alpacas (329 Dolphin Bay Rd., 360/376-2707, www.orcasmoonalpacas.com, 10am-4pm Wed.-Sat. late May-early Sept.) has 20 or so of these adorable furry animals. Stop by to take a tour (donation) or feed the friendly alpacas and miniature donkeys. The farm stand sells produce, alpaca yarn, and eggs—all from this 20-acre farm.

Shopping

ART GALLERIES AND STUDIOS

Orcas Island has a well-deserved reputation as an arts mecca. Nearly 10 percent of locals list "artist" as their profession, and the island's diverse beauty is reflected in galleries dotting the landscape, selling everything from traditional oils to whimsical sculptures.

★ Orcas Island Artworks

The barnlike structure that houses **Orcas Island Artworks** (Horseshoe Hwy. and Doe Bay Rd., 360/376-4408, www.orcasartworks. com, 10am-5pm daily, reduced winter hours, closed Jan.-mid-Feb.) was built in 1938 and originally served as a processing plant for strawberries picked on nearby farms. The gallery has been here since 1982, making this one of the oldest artist-owned cooperatives in the Pacific Northwest. A disastrous fire (arson was suspected) in 2013 badly damaged the building, but it reopened two years later and is better than ever. More than 40 artists and craftspeople display their pieces on two levels (painter and musician James Hardman's works are featured upstairs), and one end houses the popular Catkin Café, open for breakfast and lunch. The gallery is approximately eight miles south of Eastsound and two miles beyond Moran State Park.

Studio 4:20

Head a mile east of Orcas Island Artworks to find **Studio 4:20** (1179 Point Lawrence Rd., 360/376-3622), a whimsical little spot

with glass, wind chimes, leather belts, jewelry, pot-inspired T-shirts, and an honor system for payment. In case you hadn't heard, the date 4/20—April 20—has become a marijuana holiday of sorts, and the shop's bumper stickers proclaim "Studio 420: We smoke the competition."

Crow Valley Gallery

Located in the heart of Eastsound, **Crow Valley Gallery** (296 Main St., 360/376-4260, www.crowvalley.com) fills several rooms with works by more than 100 local and regional artists. Inside, you'll find pottery, paintings, jewelry, sculpture, cards, baskets, and glass.

The gallery was originally an offshoot of Crow Valley Pottery, which was housed within an 1866 log cabin—the oldest building on the island—at 2274 Orcas Road. It operated from 1959 to 2016, at which time the artists/owners abruptly closed the shop and moved out of state. Locals are hopeful it will reopen soon, so take a look when you visit; it's along the main route connecting Orcas Village and Eastsound.

★ Orcas Island Pottery

This out-of-the-way studio should not be missed. The oldest pottery studio in the Northwest—it opened in 1945—**Orcas Island Pottery** (360/376-2813, www.orcasislandpottery.com) sits atop a high bluff overlooking President Channel and is a 0.25-mile drive through tall Douglas firs off West Beach Road. The inspiring setting alone makes it worth the side trip, but the wheel-thrown and hand-built pottery is equally notable. This is a laid-back and friendly place, and you're welcome to bring a picnic lunch and relax on the benches or have your kids climb into the treehouse or try out the swings with a million-dollar view. Two rustic log buildings feature the works of 15 potters—many of whom fire their pieces here—along with four bronze artists. Dozens of colorful plates and pots sit outside on the grounds, filling with water when it rains.

Olga Pottery

Located in a quiet corner of the island near the village of Olga, **Olga Pottery** (360/376-4648, www.olgapottery.com, open daily year-round) showcases the works of Jerry Weatherman. A potter since 1973, he exhibits a variety of styles that include colorful decorative porcelain. Drop by to watch him at work.

Other Galleries

As visitors approach Eastsound from the ferry, they are surprised to see a tall silvery sculpture twirling in the wind alongside the road. This is one of the many whimsical welded-metal mobiles and kinetic art pieces created by Tony Howe, a transplant from the New York art scene. His shop, the open-air **Howe Art Gallery** (360/376-2945, www.howeart.net) is now only open by appointment.

Other galleries worth a visit are **Peter C. Fisher Gallery** (138 North Beach Rd., 360/376-5955 or 800/920-8918, www.petercfisher.com) for fine art nature photos and **Jillery** (310 Main St., 360/376-5522).

BOOKS

Darvill's Bookstore (296 Main St. in Eastsound, 360/376-2135, www.darvillsbookstore.com, 8am-5:30pm Mon.-Sat., 8:30am-5pm Sun.) has the finest selection of books on Orcas, with a knowledgeable staff and many regional titles. And yes, they sell the *New York Times*. The little **coffee bar** in the back cranks out some of the finest espresso on the island.

Entertainment and Events

NIGHTLIFE

Anyone coming to Orcas for the nightlife will find slim pickings. **Random Howse** (365 North Beach Rd., 360/376-1111, www.randomhowse.com) has live music and events of all types, including dances, bands, plays, and Wednesday open-mic nights. **The Lower Tavern** (46 Prune Alley, 360/376-4848, www.lowertavern.com) has karaoke on Friday nights and open-mic Tuesdays, plus the occasional weekend band in the summer. Thursday night features open-mic sessions at **Doe Bay Café** (107 Doe Bay Rd., 360/376-2291, www.doebay.com), plus classical or piano music Sundays at **Deer Harbor Inn** (360/376-4110 or 877/377-4110, www.deerharborinn.com).

Token Herb (837 Crescent Beach Rd., 360/376-8420) is the only recreational cannabis dispensary on the San Juan Islands (so far). It's in the same building as Country Corner Grocery and Deli, so you can pick up your giant bags of chips and M&Ms at the same time. Other marijuana operators have been unable to get bank financing to open shops elsewhere in the San Juans.

PERFORMING ARTS

The **Orcas Island Performing Arts Center** (917 Mt. Baker Rd., 360/376-2281, www.orcascenter.org) hosts a variety of events year-round, from concerts by nationally known musicians like Taj Mahal or Wynton Marsalis to local theatrical performances and kid productions. Check out the latest movies at tiny **Sea View Theatre** (A St., 360/376-5724) in Eastsound.

EVENTS

In early October the four-day **Orcas Island Film Festival** (www.orcasfilmfest.com)

introduces 30 full-length and short films from around the world.

Don't miss the **Orcas Island Farmers Market** (360/317-8342, www.orcasisland-farmersmarket.org, 10am-3pm Sat. May-Sept.). It takes place next to the Orcas Island Historical Museum on North Beach Road. You'll find everything from locally grown flowers and fresh veggies to artwork and tempting food.

A **Summer Solstice Parade** takes place in Eastsound on the Saturday closest to June 21. Every Wednesday and Thursday at noon during July and August, head to the waterside Emmanuel Episcopal Church in Eastsound for a free **Brown Bag Concert.** The **Orcas Island Garden Tour** (www.orcasislandgardenclub.org) takes place the last weekend of June.

Eastsound has a fun parade on the Saturday nearest the **Fourth of July.** Other holiday weekend festivities include a community band concert, a pancake breakfast, and a salmon barbecue, plus fireworks at Eastsound on the 4th and at Deer Harbor on the 3rd of July.

The first weekend of August brings the popular **Eastsound Fly-In & Antique Car Show** (www.portoforcas.com) featuring many antique planes and a classic car show. It's followed on the second Saturday of August by the **Library Fair** (360/376-4985, www.orcaslibrary.org), a big arts and crafts fair and book sale.

In early August, **Doe Bay Fest** (www.doe-bayfest.com) features four days of live rock music from up-and-coming musicians. Held at Doe Bay Resort, it's limited to just 1,000 people and typically sells out within minutes of the official announcement in May. Good luck getting a ticket for this one—but if you do, you're in for a treat.

The always-sold-out **Orcas Island Chamber Music Festival** (360/376-6636 or 866/492-0003, www.oicmf.org) takes place over the last two weeks in August. You'll hear the works of Mozart, Bach, Schubert, Rachmaninoff, Gershwin, Copland, Brahms, Tchaikovsky, and others. It coincides with the **Orcas Island Artists' Three Day Studio Tour** (www.orcasartistsstudiotour.com), when 30 or so local artists open their studios.

Labor Day weekend brings the **Steve Braun Memorial Triathlon,** at Moran State Park. Also in early September, the **Wooden Boats Rendezvous** (360/376-3037, www.woodenboatsocietyofthesanjuans.org) exhibits handcrafted boats and features a sailing race and live music at Deer Harbor.

See the Orcas Island Chamber's website (www.orcasislandchamber.com) for more information on upcoming island events.

Summer Camps and Retreats

Orcas is a delightful spot for summer camps, with three very different options available. Camp Orkila and Four Winds-Westward Ho Camp are the definitive summer camps you probably remember from childhood, with a fun mix of activities and challenges. Each has its own advantages—Orkila is very reasonable but also large, while Four Winds-Westward Ho is chummier but more expensive. Camp Indralaya serves as a retreat center for members of the Theosophical Society, but the public is welcome. With its eco-ethics, we-are-all-one philosophy, and budget pricing, Indralaya is a place to get in touch with your spiritual center.

CAMP ORKILA

Operated by the Seattle YMCA, **Camp Orkila** (360/376-2678 or 206/382-5009, www.camp-orkila.org) covers 280 acres of forests and shoreline on Orcas Island. The camp opened in 1906, when 30 boys from Seattle spent a month on waterfront land belonging to Laurence Colman. The property was deeded to the Y in 1938. Located on the northwest shore of Orcas Island, with a spectacular sunset view across President Channel to the Gulf Islands of British Columbia, the camp is one of seven run by the Y in Washington. Forested grounds slope gently down to the water, with a half mile of private beach and an ideal setting for outdoor activities.

Featured camp attractions include a large heated outdoor pool, marinelife touch tanks, a 150-foot dock, sea kayaks, sailboats, rowboats, canoes, a 44-passenger boat, BMX track, large climbing tower, ziplines, high ropes courses, sports fields, a craft center, pottery studio, horses and a riding arena, and a vegetable garden. The Y also owns a mountain camp at Twin Lakes on the edge of Moran State Park, along with the 107-acre Satellite Island, a favorite overnight boating trip for campers.

Summer Camp

Camp Orkila is the ideal place for an old-time summer camp, available for youths in grades 3-12. Depending on their age and abilities, kids can join in a wide range of activities, including sports, crafts, swimming, nature study, archery, wilderness camping, skateboarding, high-ropes training, horseback riding, bicycling, rock climbing, canoeing, marine biology, and kayaking. Campers choose from a variety of skill clinics, sports, crafts, and activities each day. Younger kids take part in traditional summer camp sessions, while older youths enjoy more focused sessions.

Lodging is in rustic open-air Adirondack-style cabins with bathroom facilities a short walk away. Filling meals are served family style. Prices are on a three-tier system based upon your ability to pay; most camps run $830 per week for tier 1, up to $1,100 per week for tier 3. Camp spaces go fast, so make reservations early for your child—in January for the most popular programs.

Special teen expedition programs focus on building self-confidence and leadership skills through horse riding, biking, kayaking, and sailing treks. These last 1-4 weeks each and vary in cost, starting at $725-1,025 (depending upon family income) for a one-week camp.

Family Camps and Retreats

Camp Orkila isn't just for kids, offering both family camps and women's wellness retreats several weekends a year. The cost for family camps varies seasonally, with the highest rates over Labor Day: $294 for adults and $240 for ages 4-12; free for kids under four. Lodging is in rustic cabins that accommodate two or three families, with bathrooms a short walk away. Your fee includes lodging, meals, and activities for three days.

Family camp activities include hikes, archery, arts and crafts, pottery, rowboats, a climbing wall, campfires, games, horseback rides, swimming, and more. There's a small fee to use the sea kayaks or to try out the daredevil high-ropes course. The women's wellness weekends provide time away from husbands, kids, dogs, phones, and mortgages in mid-March and late October, with yoga, massage, kayaking, archery, climbing, pottery, and other activities. These cost $176-314; visit www.camporkila.org or call 360/376-2678 for complete details.

Day Camps

If you're bringing school-age children on vacation, this may be the hottest tip you'll find in this book. Camp Orkila operates an outstanding community day camp (8:45am-4:45pm Mon.-Fri. July-Aug., starting at $190 per week) that is open to anyone with kids in grades 1-6. The program includes swimming, arts and crafts, archery, games, field trips, and much more. Call 360/376-2678 several weeks ahead of your visit to Orcas to be assured of space in the day-camp program.

FOUR WINDS-WESTWARD HO CAMP

In 1927, a young teacher named Ruth Brown established Four Winds Camp for girls at Four Winds Bay on Orcas Island. Five years later, she created Westward Ho Camp for boys on the opposite side of the bay. She ran the camp for many years, and in 1967 deeded the 150 acres of land, facilities, and equipment to a nonprofit foundation called Four Winds Inc. (360/376-2277, www.fourwindscamp.org).

Camp Life

Today, all Four Winds-Westward Ho Camp activities are coed, but the boys and girls are still housed on separate sides of Four Winds Bay—to the relief of parents of teenage girls. The camp houses 170 kids at a time, with one counselor for every 4-6 children. Everyone wears a uniform (polo-style shirts and khaki shorts for the boys and decidedly old-fashioned middies and bloomers for the girls) to cut down on teen fashion jealousies and make it easier to manage the laundry. Girls live in simple cedar cabins and wall tents, while boys stay in wall tents.

During their stay, campers learn horseback riding (20 horses, and both Western- and English-style riding classes), sailing, tennis, archery, soccer, pickleball, basketball, photography, arts and crafts, poetry, and many other activities. No candy, cell phones, laptop or tablet computers, or electronic games are allowed, but music is a big part of camp life. In addition to dinghies and sailboats, the camp has a 61-foot yawl to train older kids in the art of sailing. The sailboat, canoes, and kayaks are used for multi-night trips away from camp as kids explore the San Juan Islands.

Two one-month sessions are offered each summer for kids entering grades 4-10, followed by a one-week session that introduces younger children (grades 2-5) to the wonders of camp life. These aren't cheap: $5,300 for the one-month sessions (June 24-July 21 and July 24-Aug. 20) or $1,250 for the one-week camp (Aug. 23-29). Families without that kind of money can apply for a scholarship, and the staff strives to make this a noncompetitive experience that brings together campers from various racial, economic, and social backgrounds. Approximately 20 percent of the kids attend on full or partial scholarships for low- and middle-income families. Most of those who attend Four Winds-Westward Ho

Camp come from San Francisco, Los Angeles, and Seattle—including quite a few children from famous families. Free transportation is provided from Sea-Tac Airport, Seattle, and Anacortes. In addition, a separate counselor-training program is available, giving young people the chance to take on greater responsibilities as they mature.

Four Winds-Westward Ho Camp is located along the southern end of West Sound, a mile from Deer Harbor.

CAMP INDRALAYA

This is a camp unlike any other in the San Juan Islands. The camp was founded in 1927 by members of the Theosophical Society (www.theosophical.org), a religion that shares philosophical similarities with Buddhism. The guiding principles of theosophy are that the universe and all within it are all one, and that everyone finds his or her own truth. There's a strong sense of community at this peaceful spot, where you might study therapeutic touch as a path of consciousness one week and Qigong and Tai Chi the next.

Camp Indralaya (360/376-4526, www.indralaya.org) is one of just four Theosophical retreat centers in America; the others are in Arkansas, California, and New York. The 78-acre camp is on the northwest end of East Sound, just two miles from the village of Eastsound. The name *Indralaya* is derived from Sanskrit and means "a home for the spiritual forces in nature." The setting is sublime, with 1.5 miles of shoreline, three miles of wooded hiking trails, and an abundance of deer, almost-tame rabbits, and other critters.

Many types of programs are offered, particularly in the summer, when the facilities are almost always busy. The camp is open to all, so you don't need to be a member of the Theosophical Society. Campers stay in simple rustic cabins, most of which have wood-burning stoves and separate bathhouses. Guests will need to provide their own sheets, blankets, pillows, sleeping bags, and towels (or rent them). Vegetarian meals are served in the dining hall, and all participants join in the cleanup. Indralaya also has a substantial metaphysical library and a small bookstore.

All sorts of classes and workshops take place here: silent meditations, deep singing, family gatherings, therapeutic touch classes, yoga, and much more. Program fees are amazingly inexpensive: lodging in simple cabins with a shared bathhouse is just $50 per person per night, $70 per person per night in cabins with baths, $77 per person per night in the Round House with seven rooms and three baths, or $40 per night if you stay in a tent, with discounts for anyone under 25. Amazingly, these rates include three substantial meals a day. Indralaya also welcomes volunteers willing to trade work for camping and meals. Day visitors can attend programs and activities at Indralaya for a small charge.

Food

Eastsound, the "big city" on Orcas, has the best choice of food on the island, though you'll find a scattering of fine restaurants and cafés elsewhere. For the nicer restaurants it's always wise to reserve a table ahead of time, and this applies not just on weekends but weekdays as well. Because of the abundance of Saturday summer weddings on Orcas it can sometimes be easier to get a table on a Saturday night than other times because meals are catered for weddings.

EASTSOUND AREA
Fine Dining
Ask locals where they go for special occasions and you're certain to hear one place at the top of everyone's list: ★ **Inn at Ship Bay** (326 Olga Rd., 360/376-5886, www.innatshipbay. com, 5:30pm-9pm or later Tues.-Sat., closed Dec.-mid-Feb., $21-34). Chef/owner Geddes Martin prepares a variety of fresh-from-the-sea specials—including Fanny Bay oysters harvested that morning—and uses fresh organic greens from the restaurant garden, along with plums, apples, and pears from the orchard out front. The emphasis is on fresh, local, and organic. The owners even have a pig or two to help recycle scraps, and you might find Mangalitsa pork on the menu later. The menu is updated frequently, and there's an impressive wine list. Located a mile east of Eastsound at an old farmhouse, this comfortably upscale restaurant is the sort of place where the knowledgeable staff stays year after year. Inn at Ship Bay has attracted the likes of Al Gore and Conan O'Brien in the past, so check nearby tables for a recognizable face, and be sure to call ahead for reservations. A bar menu includes lighter meals. The restaurant is closed December-mid-February and is always closed on Sunday and Monday.

Housed within Outlook Inn, ★ **New Leaf Café** (360/376-2200, www.outlookinn.com, 8am-11am and 5pm-9:30pm Mon., Thurs., and Fri., 7:30am-12:30pm and 5pm-9:30pm Sat.-Sun. June-Aug., 5:30pm-9pm Thurs., Fri., and Mon., 8am-1pm and 5:30pm-9pm Sat.-Sun. in the off-season, closed late Nov.-mid-Feb.) is easily one of the finest restaurants on Orcas. Killer brunches ($8-14) include Belgian waffles, duck confit hash, and a memorable smoked salmon Benedict. Pacific Northwest fusion seafood is the dinnertime focus ($18-42 entrées), including pan-seared Alaskan weathervane scallops, or grilled wild salmon with a pear-ginger glaze. Every seat has a water view, and the lounge's happy hour menu (4:30pm-5:30pm Mon., Thurs., and Fri.) features Wagyu beef sliders, duck mac and cheese, and shoestring truffle fries for $5-7. The "regional-centric" wine list has a fine choice of pinot noirs, and signature cocktails such as the New Leaf Manhattan are a treat. Reservations are recommended.

Head up a set of 22 narrow steps to **The Loft at Madrona** (310 Main St., 360/376-7173, www.madronaloft.com, 5pm-9pm Thurs.-Sun. and noon-4pm Sat.-Sun.

Apr.-Oct., closed Nov.-Mar., $18-34 dinner entrées, $14-24 lunches), where the little deck provides a sweeping view of the sound. Dinner favorites include New York strip steak, scallop and prawn fettuccini, and pan-seared halibut, along with lunchtime burgers, scallop sliders, and mahimahi tacos. Delicious desserts, including Greek yogurt crème brûlée, and a decadent bread pudding with whiskey sauce. The same owners run Madrona Bar & Grill, which is downstairs.

Burgers and Pizza

A good destination for finger food is **The Lower Tavern** (Prune Alley, 360/376-4848, www.lowertavern.com, 11am-10pm Sun.-Thurs., 11am-11pm Fri.-Sat. for food, till 2am for drinks, $9-14), where bar meals include the best fish-and-chips in town, along with specialty burgers (including a popular bacon cheeseburger) and soups. This is a tavern (10 beers on tap), so you must be 21 to enter. There's outside seating and a pool table, and the TVs are tuned to sports action, making this a popular rainy-day retreat.

At **Madrona Bar & Grill** (310 Main St., 360/376-7171, www.madronabarandgrill.com, 11:30am-9pm Sun.-Thurs., 11:30am-10pm Fri.-Sat. May-Sept., Sun.-Thurs. 11:30am-8:30pm, 11:30am-9pm Fri.-Sat. Oct.-Apr., $11-16), it's all about the location, with a large back deck right on Fishing Bay in downtown Eastsound. The big menu encompasses something for everyone, with steaks, seafood, chicken, pasta, sandwiches, burgers, and salads. The bar has a selection of microbrews and sports on the TVs; it's open weekdays till 11pm, and weekends till 1 am.

★ **Hogstone's Wood Oven** (460 Main St., 360/376-4647, www.hogstone.com, 5:30pm-9pm Wed.-Mon. July-Aug., 5:30pm-9pm Thurs.-Sun. in the off-season, $8-22) is the runaway hit on the Orcas Island food scene. In business since 2013, this tiny restaurant gets packed most nights. There's a backyard with picnic tables for summer evenings. Owner/chef Jay Blackinton was called one of the Seattle area's "culinary game changers under the age of 30" by Zagat, and a 2015 "Rising Star Chef of the Year" by the James Beard Foundation—heady stuff for a former vegan who now slaughters pigs, has tattoos down both arms, and spent years as a punk Seattle bike messenger. With few exceptions, he cooks exclusively using foods from Orcas Island; the oysters are raised exactly 344 yards from the restaurant. He co-owns Maple Rock Farm, where they raise not just hogs, but also organic produce, berries, and fruit. Because of this dependence on local items, the menu changes daily, with a mix of small-plate items and wood-fired pizzas. A 10-course tasting menu is also available for $85 per person, with wine parings for an additional $60; reservations are required for these. Note, however, that this is not a romantic and relaxing spot to enjoy such a meal, but it is fun to watch the chef at work as he prepares them. Personally, I'd share a pizza, a pint of local beer, and a small plate of artfully prepared greens. Come here to enjoy the show; you'll leave happy and full.

International

Get quick Asian-influenced takeaway fare—including hot and sour soup, wraps, pot stickers, fried tofu with sesame rice cakes, and teriyaki chicken—at **The Kitchen** (249 Prune Alley, 360/376-6958, www.thekitchenorcas.com, 11am-8pm Mon.-Sat. May-Sept., 11am-5pm Mon.-Fri. the rest of the year). Many items are under $12 (the "student special" chicken and rice is $8) at this tiny walk-up lunch spot popular with locals. Covered picnic tables sit next to a flower-filled yard, and indoor seating is also available at this casual eatery.

In the heart of Eastsound, **Majita's** (310 A St., 360/376-6722, 4pm-9pm Tues.-Sat., $14-22) serves excellent Mexican meals in a playful setting. House favorites include mesquite grilled carne asada, tacos al pastor, local oysters with tomatillo chili salsa, and daily specials, plus traditional desserts such as sopapillas and flan. The salsa is made in-house, a diversity of margaritas await, and there's an outdoor seating area accented by shade trees and handcrafted tables. Reservations are advised. Daily happy hour is 4pm-6pm in the courtyard.

Random Howse (365 North Beach Rd., 360/376-1111, www.randomhowse.com, 5pm-8:30pm Wed.-Sat., reduced winter hours, $9-16) is a local's place with very good Thai food plus live music and events of all types, including dances, live bands, plays, and Wednesday open mic nights. The menu is limited, but includes such favorites as tom kha soup, pad Thai, chicken satay, and Thai red curry and vegetables.

Breakfast and Lunch

Eastsound's old firehouse has been thoroughly transformed into a bright and delightful deli-restaurant called ★ **Roses Bakery Café** (382 Prune Alley, 360/376-4292, www.rosesbakerycafe.com, 8:30am-4pm Mon.-Sat. for the café, bakery till 6pm in summer, both closed Sun.). The café serves some of the best local espresso drinks and creative morning meals (served till 11am, $6-14), including rich and delicious baked eggs with gruyere, poached eggs on a potato nest, or a simple baguette with butter and jam—the perfect complement to a latte. Lunch (starting at 11:30am, $9-17) brings out the crowds for a menu that includes a pan-seared halibut sandwich, three daily soups, salads, and thin-crust pizzas from the wood-burning oven. The adjacent deli sells wines, rustic artisan breads (try the garlic parsley walnut), pastries, and gourmet cheeses, and has a freezer packed with homemade soups, three-cheese macaroni, potpies, and u-bake fruit pies to take home. You'll never go wrong with a meal at Roses!

Friendly Swiss owner Heinz Brand brings a European sensibility to **Enzo's Gallery Caffé** (365 North Beach Rd., 360/376-3732, 7am-6pm Mon.-Sat., 7am-4pm Sun., $8-11) in the heart of Eastsound. The café attracts a loyal following with made-to-order crepes (try the Italian sausage with spinach savory crepe or one with fresh strawberries and blueberries), bagels with lox and cream cheese, grilled panini, homemade gelato (a big hit with the kids), baked goods, and espresso, plus Wi-Fi and a guest computer. A few outside tables fill on sunny mornings.

Eastsound's best latte destinations are Roses, Enzo's, and **Darvill's Coffee Bar** (296 Main St., 360/376-2135, www.darvillsbookstore.com, 8am-5:30pm Mon.-Sat., 8:30am-5pm Sunday) inside the bookstore of the same name.

ORCAS ISLAND
FOOD

outdoor dining at The Kitchen

Island Skillet (325 Prune Alley, 360/376-3984, 8am-2pm daily, $7-12) is a popular place for breakfast and lunch. The setting is rather plain, but the food is dependably good, with huge portions. Skillet breakfast burritos, huevos rancheros, and the farmer's omelet are all good for breakfast, as are the sandwiches, burgers, and salads at lunch. Island Skillet is owned by the same folks who operate Deer Harbor Inn. Prices are reasonable, making this great for families. Also here is Island Scoop, serving ice cream cones, sundaes, banana splits, and milk shakes.

Sweets

Kathryn Taylor Chocolates (109 North Beach Rd., 360/298-8093, www.ktchocolates.com, 9am-5pm Mon.-Sat.) will send chocoholics into a coma. Whimsically decorated bonbons are filled with local pears, berries, plums, hazelnuts, lavender, rhubarb, and other flavors. Pastries, quiche, and fruit tarts change daily. Owned by accomplished chef Ted Taylor and his wife, Susan Taylor Aspinall, the shop is named for their daughter, Kathryn.

Enzo's Gallery Caffé (365 North Beach Rd., 360/376-3732, 7am-6pm Mon.-Sat., 7am-4pm Sun.) has homemade gelato in a variety of flavors. **Clever Cow Creamery** (209 North Beach Rd., 360/376-5222, 11am-10pm daily) offers 30 or so flavors of ice cream and sorbet, plus sundaes, shakes, malts, smoothies, and other treats.

Three miles west of Eastsound, the little café at **West Beach Resort** (360/376-2240 or 877/937-8224, www.westbeachresort.com) serves Lopez Island Creamery ice cream in homemade waffle cones, plus tasty milk shakes and mocha iced cappuccinos.

★ **Brown Bear Baking** (360/855-7456, 8am-5pm daily, under $10) has the perfect Eastsound location at the corner of Main Street and North Beach Road. The bakeshop sells artisan breads, peach pastries, wonderful pecan sticky buns, quiches, currant scones, berry bread pudding, chocolate muffins, lemon tarts, ham and Swiss croissants, delicious open-faced grilled sandwiches (croquet monsieur), and lattes. And yes, Brown Bear sells flaky bear claws. Gluten-free options are available. The shop gets exceptionally busy on summer weekends, so drop by early for the best selection.

Markets and Bakeries

For groceries and other essentials, stop by **Orcas Island Market** (469 Market St., 360/376-6000, www.orcasislandmarket.com, 7am-10pm Mon.-Sat., 8am-8pm Sun.). The largest market in the San Juans, it houses an in-store bakery, deli, ATM, and movie rentals.

Orcas Food Co-Op (138 North Beach Rd., 360/376-2009, www.orcasfood.coop, 8am-8pm Mon.-Sat., 10am-6pm Sun.) has natural foods and a deli with daily specials and salads, plus fresh crab and salmon in season. The deli case has lasagna, salads, breakfast burritos, daily soups, and tasty made-to-order sandwiches ($8).

The **Orcas Island Farmers Market** (360/317-8342, www.orcasislandfarmersmarket.org, 10am-3pm Sat. May-Sept.) takes place at Eastsound's Village Square, with local produce, flowers, crafts, photography, pottery, clothing, and tasty food. In October and November, the market moves indoors to the Odd Fellows Hall on Madrona Point and operates 11am-2pm Saturdays.

For the finest breads, cheeses, and gourmet deli foods, don't miss **Roses Bakery Café** (382 Prune Alley, 360/376-5805, www.rosesbakerycafe.com, 8:30am-4pm Mon.-Sat. for the café, bakery till 6pm, both closed Sun.).

Masquerading as a Chevron gas station/convenience store, **Country Corner Grocery and Deli** (837 Crescent Beach Dr., 360/376-6900, 6am-11pm daily, $7-20) is a surprisingly good deli with made-to-order deli sandwiches, take-out pizzas, and burgers. It's a good place to get an inexpensive lunch to go, and stays open late. Beer and wine are also sold, and **Token Herb** (360/376-8420)—the only pot dispensary on the San Juan Islands—is in the same building.

the porch at Orcas Hotel Café

Brewery

The only microbrewery in the San Juans, ★ **Island Hopping Brewery** (33 Hope Lane, 360/376-6079, www.islandhoppin-brewery.com, noon-9pm daily) always features seven of their beers on tap, available as flights or pints. The Old Madrona Imperial Red and Elwha Rock IPA are the flagship beers, and a taster flight of seven costs $15; add $1 for a basket of pretzels and peanuts. There are no official tours, but the friendly owners will be happy to talk about the brewing process. In addition to beers, the brewery serves snacks—there's no kitchen on the premises—and you're welcome to bring in food from elsewhere. This is a family-friendly place, with a Ping-Pong table and games inside, plus outdoor seating out back.

THE WEST END
Orcas Village

Stepping off the ferry at Orcas brings you face-to-face with the grand old Orcas Hotel. Inside is **Octavia's Bistro** (360/376-4300,

www.orcashotel.com, 5pm-9:30pm daily for dinner, breakfast 8am-noon Sun. Apr.-Sept., 5pm-8:30pm daily the rest of the year, $15-25 dinner entrées), where evening highlights include beer-battered fish-and-chips, mushroom risotto, beef tenderloin, ribs, and more. Outdoor seating is available, plus there's a seasonal Sunday brunch ($8-14). By the way, the restaurant is named for a one-time owner of the hotel whose ghost reportedly haunts the room where she died. Also here is the very popular **Orcas Hotel Café,** serving tasty breakfasts (baked goods, eggs and home fries, and croissant sandwiches) starting at 6am, along with lunchtime salmon fillet sandwiches, burgers, fish-and-chips, salads, and tuna melts. Everything is made in-house using local ingredients whenever possible. Eat inside or on the covered patio. A computer is available to check your email, and free Wi-Fi is also available.

Right next to the ferry landing is **Orcas Village Store** (360/376-8860, www.orcasvillagestore.com, 6am-8pm daily), with a good selection of groceries and a deli that makes premade and made-to-order sandwiches ($10), salads, clam chowder, lattes, u-bake pizzas, and entrées. Fresh pastries and cookies are baked daily, with homemade soups in winter. Stop here for a last-minute take-aboard lunch before walking on the ferry.

Deer Harbor

Housed in a 1915 farmhouse, **Deer Harbor Inn** (Deer Harbor, 360/376-4110 or 877/377-4110, www.deerharborinn.com, 5pm-9pm daily late May-early Sept., 5pm-8pm Fri.-Sun. the rest of the year) is a spacious and comfortable place with fine meals. It's a bit off the beaten path if you're staying near Eastsound, but it's worth the drive. You can get something as simple as freshly baked bread, salad, and homemade soup for $12, or choose a full dinner ($22-30 entrées) from the blackboard listing the day's specials. Meals come with a large soup, bread, all-you-can-eat salad, and veggies. There's always grilled seafood, steaks, house-smoked salmon, enormous salads (try the New York steak and blue cheese salad for $20), and a vegetarian choice, along with a full bar. Blackberry cobbler will be a hit, and late summer brings homemade apple pie à la mode made from apples picked in the century-old orchard out front. A large wraparound deck opens seasonally for al fresco dining, where you can hear classical or piano music on summer Sundays. Deer and rabbits are common sights in the field. Two generations of the Carpenter family have owned Deer Harbor Inn since 1982. Reservations are advised.

Homey ★ **West Sound Café** (4362 Crow Valley Rd., 360/376-4440, www.westsound-cafe.com, 5pm-9pm Wed.-Sun. late May-early Sept., 5pm-9pm Wed.-Sat. the rest of the year, $16-30) occupies a beautifully restored historic waterside building at the intersection of Crow Valley and Deer Harbor Roads. This is the real deal, with wonderful food, a classic setting, and friendly service. Chef Dirul Shamsid-Deen creates unusual tastes, including Dungeness crab spaghetti, an asparagus dish topped with goat cheese and egg, and grilled squid with toasted almonds and blood orange. The halibut fish-and-chips are always a hit, as is the big dinner burger with white cheddar, bacon, and garlic aioli. For dessert, try the New Orleans-style beignets or the butterscotch pot de crème. Dinner reservations are required, though you might get lucky without one if they have a cancellation. Outside seating is available on a little deck facing West Sound.

THE EAST END

Famous **Rosario Resort & Spa** (1400 Rosario Rd., 360/376-2152 or 800/562-8820, www.rosarioresort.com) has spectacular views and romantic dining in a historic building five miles south of Eastsound and close to Moran State Park. **The Mansion Restaurant** (breakfast 8am-11am, lunch noon-3pm, dinner 5pm-10pm daily, $22-40 dinner entrées) features a locavore menu that ranges from filet mignon to roasted rabbit to Moroccan spiced eggplant. The setting is elegant and formal, with great views from the deck. Reservations

are recommended, especially on Friday and Saturday nights. For something less formal, head to the marina, where **Cascade Bay Grill** (7am-9pm daily late May-early Sept.) has pizzas, burgers, and beer on draft.

Located at Doe Bay Resort & Retreat, ★ **Doe Bay Café** (107 Doe Bay Rd., 360/376-8059, www.doebay.com, 8am-2pm and 5pm-9pm daily June-Sept., 5pm-10pm Thurs., 5pm-9pm Fri., and 8am-2pm and 5pm-9pm Sat.-Sun. the rest of the year) serves delicious vegetarian, vegan, gluten-free, and seafood meals in an inviting, out-of-the-way location. Tables are set against large bayside windows at this peaceful spot. The organic garden produces much of the veggies used at Doe Bay, and eggs come from hens on the property. Brunch specials ($9-14) include brioche French toast, huevos rancheros, and coconut almond granola. Dinner entrées ($18-32) change often, so check the board for chef Jon Chappelle's daily specials or try the five-course tasting menu ($55-65). There's a good selection of wines, along with several beers on draft. After your meal, head up the creek for a soak in the clothing-optional saltwater hot tubs ($15 for a day pass if you aren't a guest). Thursday night attracts locals with open-mic music. Every second Thursday is 10-inch pizza night, with the intervening Thursdays scheduled for Indian, Thai, Spanish, sushi, or other fare. There's free Wi-Fi too.

Housed within Artworks Gallery at the intersection of Horseshoe Highway and Doe Bay Road, **Catkin Café** (360/376-3242, 9am-3pm Wed.-Sun., $5-15) serves breakfast and lunch all day. The atmosphere is warm and inviting, with a focus on locally grown produce and meats. Yummy favorites include baked eggs in tomato stew with herbed polenta, bratwurst on a homemade potato roll, and wonderful scones. Daily specials are always a good bet.

In business since the 1940s, **Buck Bay Shellfish Farm** (77 EJ Young Rd., 360/376-5280, www.buckbayshellfishfarm.com) grows Pacific oysters, Manila clams, and littleneck clams in netted bags on racks in this pretty bay near Moran State Park. Get a dozen to shuck and slurp on the picnic tables out front, and enjoy the organic farm where chickens are running around. Precooked Dungeness crab, smoked salmon, and spot prawns are available in season. Buck Bay is rustic, informal, and fun, and diners can bring their own beer or wine.

Accommodations

Anyone planning to stay on Orcas in the summer—particularly on weekends—should make reservations several months ahead of time. Note that all lodging prices quoted below are subject to an additional 10.1 percent tax.

The **Orcas Island Chamber of Commerce** website (www.orcasisland-chamber.com) provides an online listing of available lodging; just enter your dates to see what's available. The **Orcas Island Lodging Association** (www.orcas-lodging.com) has links to 11 bed-and-breakfasts, cottages, and inns.

WEEKLY RENTALS

If you plan to spend more than a few nights on Orcas, the best deal is often a vacation rental, especially for families needing space to spread out or folks looking to save money by cooking their own meals. **Cherie Lindholm Real Estate** (360/376-2204, www.orcashomes.com) offers 28 rental homes on Orcas Island. Most are two- or three-bedroom homes costing around $1,200-1,600 per week, but a number of modest places can be found for under $900 per week. The most elaborate waterfront mansions cost $2,600 or more weekly. Many homes go early, so book several months ahead if possible. Off-season (Sept.-May) rates are typically lower.

Windermere Vacation Doorways (360/378-3601 or 800/391-8190, www.vacationdoorways.com) typically has 30 or so homes on Orcas, plus additional rentals on San Juan and Lopez Islands. There's a one-week minimum mid-June-mid-September, and three nights at other times. The company's finest property, New Gedney Estate, is an elaborate seven-bedroom, 4.5-bath lodge on a 40-acre estate with two private lakes that rents for a mere $9,600 per week!

Many of the resorts, inns, cottages, and bed-and-breakfasts described in this section also offer weekly rates; call for specifics. For additional weekly rentals on Orcas, browse **Airbnb** (www.airbnb.com), **VRBO** (www.vrbo.com), **Homeaway** (www.homeaway.com), **CouchSurfing** (www.couchsurfing.org), or **FlipKey** (www.flipkey.com).

HOSTELS
Golden Tree Hostel

Now in the National Register of Historic Places, ★ **Golden Tree Hostel** (1159 North Beach Rd., 360/317-8693, www.goldentreehostel.com, closed Nov.-Mar.) began life as an 1890 Victorian farmhouse. It's actually much more than a hostel, with well-maintained and up-to-date facilities and all sorts of amenities. Golden Tree is centrally located on the north side of Eastsound, and has two dorm rooms ($48 per person), four private rooms ($130 d), an outside yurt-like geodesic dome ($135 d), two tepees ($130 d) for glamping, and a large loft ($205 for four, $275 for six guests; kids under five free). The private rooms, tepee, and yurt all have queen beds. The spa building contains a sauna, hot tub, laundry, outside kitchen, and bath (used primarily by guests in the loft, tepees, and dome). Five additional bathrooms are inside the main building. Golden Tree is a great place to meet fellow travelers, with a big central kitchen, covered porches, a game room with pool table and piano, living room, Wi-Fi, and a guest computer. There's a hot tub in the yard, a campfire for evening s'mores, a u-pick garden, century-old apple trees, and bike rentals ($20/day).

The Lodge on Orcas

Just a 20-minute walk from Eastsound, **The Lodge on Orcas** (32 Bracken Fern Lane, 360/622-6126, www.thelodgeonorcas.com) is something of a blend between a hostel and a lodge. Owner Dave Page provides a friendly and clean two-story house with six private rooms ($124 d or $144 for four people) that share three baths, along with a suite ($169 for three people) with a king bed, private bath, and sitting area. The adjacent bunkhouse ($99 d) has two bunks, and tent camping ($40 for up to four people) is also available. The two latter options include full access to the house, including the shared baths. There's a fully equipped kitchen and Wi-Fi, but the TV has been replaced by four aquariums. The grounds are something of a wildlife sanctuary, with 23 fruit trees and tall conifers. Hang out on the hammocks, fire up the barbecue, or just take in the quiet.

HOTELS AND INNS
Anchorage Inn

Anchorage Inn (249 Bronson Way, east of the Orcas golf course, 360/376-8282, www.anchorageonorcas.com, closed Oct.-late May, $195 d) is well out of the way, hidden among tall Douglas firs along East Sound at the end of a dirt road. Three modern town house-style units are available on a 16-acre parcel with a pebbly beach out front—perfect for launching kayaks—and a bluff-top hot tub to enjoy those romantic starry nights. Bald eagles nest close by, and you may also see herons, seals, deer, ospreys, otters, loons, and other critters. Each unit has a private stairway and entrance, queen-size bed, bath, fireplace, kitchenette, small cedar deck, and Wi-Fi. No children or pets are allowed, and a three-night minimum stay is required in the summer. Check in with owners Dick and Sandra Bronson, who live in the house next door.

Deer Harbor Inn

A variety of lodging options exist at **Deer Harbor Inn** (360/376-4110 or 877/377-4110, www.deerharborinn.com), located eight miles west of the ferry dock and just above Deer Harbor. The inn buildings surround an old apple orchard (Gravenstein and King varieties) and pear and plum trees that were planted in 1906. A contemporary log lodge contains eight comfy but rather small rooms ($159 d) with tables, chairs, queen beds, and other furnishings crafted from lodgepole logs. Each also has a fridge and private bath. There are no TVs in the rooms, but a central sitting area has sofas, a woodstove, and a television.

A two-bedroom suite ($299 d) contains king and queen beds, a private bath, kitchen, and a large deck with a hot tub and a fenced yard. Four attractive, modern cottages costing $249-350 d ($20 for additional guests) are also on the grounds. Each is a bit different: The largest (1,100 square feet, with room for eight people) has two bedrooms, a full kitchen, and a covered deck, while the other three units are smaller but have gas fireplaces, fridges, microwaves, TVs, log furnishings, and decks with private Jacuzzis. Pets are $25 extra in the cottages. Across the road is a small remodeled house ($385 for up to eight guests) with a king-size bed in one of the three bedrooms, plus a log fireplace, full kitchen, hot tub, and barbecue grill on the wraparound deck, and even a telescope for spying on boats in the harbor.

All guests at Deer Harbor Inn (including those staying in the lodge) can hop in the hot tub behind the lodge, but it can get a bit busy. Massage is also available, and all rooms have Wi-Fi. A two-night minimum stay is required in the summer, and no young kids are allowed in the lodge, though they're welcome in the cottages and house. Deer Harbor Inn is also home to a fine restaurant, run by the owners' sons and housed in a 1915 farmhouse.

Inn at Ship Bay

Just 1.5 miles out of Eastsound, **Inn at Ship Bay** (326 Olga Rd., 360/376-3933 or 877/276-7296, www.innatshipbay.com) houses one of the finest and most popular restaurants on Orcas. Behind the restaurant and facing the waters of East Sound are modern units containing nine comfortably large staterooms ($195 d) and an executive suite ($295 d), all with king beds, covered balconies, gas fireplaces, and fridges. One room is wheelchair-accessible. The busy restaurant brings considerable traffic most evenings, but mornings are quiet. Kids are welcome, but only three guests (including children) are permitted per room.

The Landmark

The Landmark (67 Main St., 360/376-2423, www.landmarkinn.net) has 15 modern, well-maintained condo units, all with private decks, fireplaces, kitchens, and Wi-Fi. Rates are $219-279 for two-bedroom units that can sleep four, and $289 d in three-bedroom town houses that can sleep six. Kids are welcome, pets are $25 extra, and a two-night stay is required in the summer.

Orcas Hotel

For classic lodging and a friendly staff, stay at **Orcas Hotel** (360/376-4300 or 888/672-2792, www.orcashotel.com), a 12-room Victorian inn overlooking the ferry landing in Orcas. Rates are just $169-189 d for small, nicely furnished old-style rooms with private baths. The two finest rooms ($225 d) have private decks and jetted tubs (one is wheelchair-accessible), and four tiny rooms with a bath down the hall are just $89-129 d. Room 9 on the third floor is reputed to be haunted by the ghost of Octavia Van Moorhem, who operated the hotel from its opening in 1904 until her death in 1933. The staff and visitors relate many tales of strange noises and ghostly appearances near this room. For ease of access, Orcas Hotel's location can't be beat; just step off the ferry and you're there. The hotel is also an extremely popular place for weddings, family reunions, and office parties, and it isn't always a quiet place due to the frequent ferry traffic. Wi-Fi is free and single-night stays are accepted. Because of the location, there's no need for a vehicle if you want to walk right off the ferry to your lodging. (If you want to explore the island you'll need to catch the shuttle bus or bring a bike.)

Orcas Hotel

Outlook Inn

★ **Outlook Inn** (360/376-2200 or 888/688-5665, www.outlookinn.com, closed Jan.) is a superbly restored 1888 hotel right in Eastsound with its own private beach. The historic main building features comfortable upstairs rooms with sinks and phones in the rooms (no TVs) and baths down the hall. They aren't spacious, but they do offer old-time hospitality for a budget price: $129 d. Larger rooms with private baths and TVs are $269 d, and the newest building contains 16 exceptional suites with king-size beds, jetted tubs, radiant floor heat, kitchenettes, small balconies overlooking the bay, and mini-bars for $339 d. Kids are welcome, and two rooms are wheelchair-accessible. New Leaf Café is on the premises, serving Northwest-style gourmet fare.

RESORTS
Beach Haven Resort

One of the hidden treasures in the San Juans, ★ **Beach Haven Resort** (684 Beach Haven Rd., 360/376-2288, www.beach-haven.com) has a peaceful setting, old-time cabins, and reasonable prices. Located on the northwest side of Orcas Island three miles from Eastsound, the resort consists of 11 log cabins—all built in the 1940s—along with a couple of newer units. Cabins front a long pebble beach (dramatic sunsets are a high point) and nestle beneath an old-growth forest of cedar and Douglas fir. Seals and Canada geese are common sights. Don't expect TVs, radios, phones, cell phone service, or the latest furnishings; the one- to four-bedroom cabins have rustic decor, full kitchens with dishes, woodstoves with firewood, private baths with showers, and decks with picnic tables and barbecues. Guests can get very limited Wi-Fi service at the office. There's a one-week minimum stay mid-June–early September, with a three-night minimum the remainder of September and winter holidays, and a two-night minimum October–mid-May.

One-bedroom cabins are $1,050 per week for two guests, two-bedroom cabins cost $1,295 per week for up to five guests, and three-bedroom cabins are $1,505 per week for up to eight guests. The resort's largest cabin (Beachcomber) holds up to 10 people in four bedrooms for $2,275 per week and has tall picture windows, a fireplace, and a large deck facing the bay. Also available is a modern honeymoon cottage ($1,050 d/week) with a jetted tub and heated tile floor, along with two apartments with waterfront decks. The smaller one sleeps two for $875 d per week, while the larger unit has space for six at $1,365 per week. Children are welcome in most of Beach Haven Resort's cabins, and they will love the delightful playground, Ping-Pong table, and beach. Guests can also rent canoes, rowboats, and sit-on-top kayaks, or hike the 1.5-mile wooded nature trail.

Don't tell anyone else about this place and maybe it'll stay a secret just between us. Sorry, but that was wishful thinking, since Beach Haven was discovered decades ago. Anyone looking for a cabin mid-June to mid-September should look elsewhere; families return each year and the resort doesn't even take reservations for July and August (they quit when the waiting list hits 100 people!). Space is, however, available at other times of the year, especially in the winter when prices are lower and fellow travelers are scarce.

Doe Bay Resort & Retreat

Located on a 30-acre spread along a peaceful cove, ★ **Doe Bay Resort & Retreat** (107 Doe Bay Rd., 360/376-2291, www.doe-bay.com) is 20 miles from the ferry terminal. Don't let the "Resort" in the name fool you; this is an unpretentious place with cabins (many of which are prefab units), yurts, and tent sites. The emphasis is on relaxation. Doe Bay attracts the NPR crowd; it's the sort of place you might see parodied in an episode of *Portlandia*, but it's also a fun spot for families and couples. You can sit inside the wood-fired sauna, gather around the communal fire pit, check out the big organic garden, and then head to one of three covered soaking tubs right on a pretty creek with a waterfall

hot tubs at Doe Bay Resort & Retreat

two guests in the cabins and yurts. The larger units book up far ahead of time, but there's often something available even at the last minute.

Resort headquarters is the historic Doe Bay General Store, built in 1908 and now home to a little store (open year-round with food, wine, beer, gifts, and toiletries), a game room/library, and the Doe Bay Café, serving mostly vegetarian fare three meals a day year-round. Join one of the yoga sessions each summer morning for $10. Free Wi-Fi is available throughout Doe Bay, along with a variety of outdoor activities: horseshoes, croquet, bocce, and volleyball. Guided sea-kayaking trips and massage are also available.

Lieber Haven Resort & Marina

A small, out-of-the-way place, **Lieber Haven Resort & Marina** (360/376-2472, www.lieberhavenresort.com) occupies a quiet and protected cove on the southern edge of Orcas Island near Obstruction Pass. A county boat ramp and dock are right across the road, and one of the only sandy beaches on the island is out front—it stretches for nearly a mile. Lodging is in nine simple units that are popular with families on a budget. This delightfully old-school resort opened in the 1950s and retains a frumpy, down-home feel that's certainly not for everyone. Ultra-friendly owners Dave and Kittie Baxter provide nightly beach fires in the summer along with a variety of lodging options. Most units have a small kitchen (with dishes, pots, and pans), queen-size bed, and sofa bed, along with a deck just a few steps from the water. Simple sleeping rooms (no cooking) cost $150 d, studio units are $160 d, apartments run $180 for up to four guests, and a two-bedroom cottage costs $220 for up to four; it's $15 for each additional guest, with a maximum of six. There's no minimum stay, and the owners welcome sailors and kayakers. A little store sells snacks, and you can check out the collection of nautical antiques and rent kayaks and rowboats at the marina (www.orcaskayaks.com). Free

that drops into Doe Bay. The clothing-optional sauna and saltwater soaking tubs are open daily 8am-10pm (11am-6pm for families; adults only after 6pm) and cost $15 if you aren't a guest.

At the budget end are summer-only tent spaces ($59-66 d), minuscule units ($100 d) with simple furnishings, and in-the-trees yurts and domes ($118-138 d; not recommended in winter due to the lack of heat). Located along the bay, the yurts provide the finest views from anywhere on the property, but they don't have running water and most lack electricity. Yurts and domes share a central shower house and communal kitchen. Somewhat nicer are 20 or so cabins ($215-336 d) with full baths and kitchens, and the two-story retreat house for groups ($723-804 for up to 22 guests). For something different, book the newly built Treehouse, a rustic two-room unit with a wraparound deck for $215-240 d. A two-night minimum stay is required at Doe Bay, and two units are wheelchair-accessible. Add $20 per person for more than

Wi-Fi is available, and the resort is open year-round.

North Beach Inn

A mile west of Eastsound, **North Beach Inn** (650 Gibson Rd., 360/376-2660, www.north-beachinn.com) is something of a misnomer, because this is actually a quaint family resort on a 90-acre spread where 13 housekeeping cottages face a very private beach. Most date from the 1930s and 1940s, and each unit contains a full kitchen, fireplace (with wood), Adirondack chairs, and a barbecue. North Beach Inn is rustic and unplugged, with no TVs or Wi-Fi to intrude. It's a pet-friendly place, and guests often bring dogs ($105/week).

Older studio and one-bedroom cabins are $1,186-1,282 d per week, and two-bedroom cottages cost $1,410-1,564 per week for four people. The resort has three more recently built, larger cottages—one even has a loft—that go for $1,940-1,989 per week for four guests. A separate three-bedroom vacation home is $1,750 per week for up to six guests.

Reserve far ahead for any of these popular cottages where many people return year after year; try to book in September for the following summer. A one-week minimum stay is required in July and August, but you might find a few shorter openings at the last minute. The resort is closed in December and January.

Rosario Resort & Spa

Built between 1905 and 1909 and now in the National Register of Historic Places, famous **Rosario Resort & Spa** (1400 Rosario Rd., 360/376-2222 or 800/562-8820, www.rosarioresort.com) is five miles south of Eastsound near Moran State Park. The striking mansion at the center of Rosario was once the home of Robert Moran, a shipping magnate, Seattle mayor, and philanthropist; he donated the land for nearby Moran State Park.

This is the largest lodging place on Orcas, with 55 guest rooms. Moran's grand white mansion serves as a centerpiece for the resort and is a fantastic place to explore even if you aren't staying here. Musician Christopher Peacock puts on free one-hour performances that include music on the organ and piano, along with a slide show on the resort and the life of Moran. These begin at 4pm Tuesday-Saturday mid-June-mid-September in the grand music room. You can take a self-guided mansion tour at other times.

The lush grounds and sprawling veranda, backdropped by boat-filled Cascade Bay, are popular for summer weddings. The mansion also houses a restaurant, along with a fascinating collection of historical items and photos. Downstairs is a full-service spa with massage, body wraps, facials, manicures, and pedicures, plus an indoor pool, hot tub, sauna, exercise equipment, and daily yoga and fitness classes.

On the 30 acres of lovingly manicured grounds and flower gardens, you'll find a large outdoor pool along the harbor and a separate pool for kids, plus tennis courts, horseshoes, croquet, shuffleboard, bocce, and other lawn games. Head to the marina for sea kayaking (through Shearwater Adventures), sailboat charters, and whale-watching trips (through Deer Harbor Charters). A concierge and gift shop are available. Scheduled floatplane flights directly to Rosario are provided by Kenmore Air out of Seattle's Lake Union.

Rosario rooms vary greatly in size and amenities, but visitors generally give the resort high marks. The least expensive rooms cost $169 d, while spacious hillside suites are $359-419 d. Other options include deluxe condos with kitchenettes ($239 d) and harborside suites ($269 d). The most distinctive options ($299 d) are the luxurious Cliffhouse honeymoon suite and the unique Roundhouse Suite. The latter was built as a playground for Thomas Moran's children and has a king sleigh bed, waterside location, and separate living room. All guests have free access to the pools, spa, and other facilities. Note that none of the Rosario mansion rooms are available for lodging. Instead, most Rosario lodging is in newer buildings surrounding and above the mansion.

The Birth of Rosario Resort

Self-made millionaire and one-time Seattle mayor Robert Moran retired in 1905 at the age of 49. During a pleasure cruise in the San Juans, he fell in love with Orcas Island, describing it as his paradise:

> In the lower reaches of Puget Sound and the Gulf of Georgia, looking out through the Strait of Juan de Fuca, toward the indles and lands of romance on the chief trade routes of the world's future commerce, lies a land unique and apart from anything else in the Western Hemisphere--the San Juan Islands!?.... It is a wonderful place in which to forget one's troubles and worries and get back to Nature in her happiest moods; a delightful place in which to regain health—physical, mental, and spiritual.

He purchased 7,800 acres on Orcas Island and began work on a retirement home he called Rosario, after nearby Rosario Strait. But this was no simple waterfront cottage. He hired the finest ship-wrights of the day to create a 54-room mansion covering 35,000 square feet. It cost $1.5 million and took four years to complete. Much of the ironwork—including butterfly hinges, nautical-style lamps, and door fasteners—was wrought at an on-site machine shop. Other touches included an indoor pool (with Italian marble) and bowling alley, a figure-eight-shaped lagoon, and a small hydroelectric plant (which still operates). The home was furnished in custom-made Mission-style pieces of teak and leather.

In 1932, at the height of the Great Depression, Moran put his estate up for sale. His wife had died two years earlier, his brothers and sisters had also passed away, and his children had other interests. Despite ads in prominent national magazines, there were no takers. The mansion was sold in 1938 to a wealthy Californian, Donald Rheem, who paid just $50,000 for the mansion and 1,339 acres of surrounding land. Moran moved to much simpler quarters near the Orcas ferry landing. He died on his beloved Orcas Island on March 27, 1943, at the age of 86. While he is buried in the same Lake View Cemetery in Seattle that the doctors had warned him about 37 years earlier, he probably outlived those doctors by many years.

For more on Robert Moran, see the sidebar on page 172. For his complete story, read *Rosario Yesterdays: A Pictorial History* by Christopher Peacock, sold at Rosario and in local bookstores.

ORCAS ISLAND
ACCOMMODATIONS

Smuggler's Villa Resort

Located on the north side of Orcas Island along Haro Strait, **Smuggler's Villa Resort** (360/376-2297 or 800/488-2097, www.smuggler.com, $299-349/night) consists of two-bedroom town houses and apartments with full kitchens, gas fireplaces, washers and dryers, large decks, and barbecues. Some units can sleep six for no additional charge. Amenities at Smuggler's Villa include a big year-round outdoor pool, hot tub, sauna, tennis and basketball courts, a playground, a guest marina, and a private pebble beach. Kids are welcome at this pleasant waterfront resort. A four-night minimum is required in the summer. No pets allowed.

West Beach Resort

A busy waterside spot, **West Beach Resort** (three miles west of Eastsound off Enchanted Forest Rd., 360/376-2240 or 877/937-8224, www.westbeachresort.com) opened in 1939 and remains popular with families today. Cabins face west along a gravelly beach, offering sunset vistas in a peaceful setting. Several types of cottages are available, and guests appreciate the central hot tub, general store, and free Wi-Fi.

Most of the 21 cottages are right along the shore—we're talking 20 feet to the water—and have one or two bedrooms with double beds, full kitchens, woodstoves, private baths with showers, hide-a-bed sofas, and covered porches with barbecue grills. Many of these are plain older units with a mismatched and funky decor that isn't for everyone, but several modern ones are nicer and have large decks. Cabins are available only on a weekly basis from late June to early September, with a two-night minimum in spring and fall, plus on weekends year-round. Call ahead, however, because one-night stays are occasionally available.

The cottages rent for $1,813-2,023 per week for up to four guests, plus $324 per week for each additional guest. A single studio cabin (number 16, $1,393 d/week) is the least expensive option, and two larger units (numbers 14 and 15, $1,673 d/week) are favorites of couples. Two modern cabins (numbers 18 and 19; $2,023-2,093/week) and a remodeled 1930s farmhouse ($2,443/week) are ideal for groups and family gatherings of six or more people. An adorable little honeymoon cottage (number 17; $1,673 d/week) faces a small pond, and the Madrona cabin ($2,023 d/week) is perfect for those looking for privacy. In addition, West Beach Resort has tent and RV spaces, along with upscale tent cabins.

Beachfront cabins lack TVs, but you can rent TV/VCRs to watch videos, and newer units away from the water have televisions. The store sells firewood, groceries, ice cream in homemade waffle cones, espresso, beer, local wines, and gas, while the marina rents skiffs, rowboats, canoes, and kayaks, and offers sea-kayaking tours through Shearwater Adventures.

West Beach Resort caters to families and offers an array of kid activities daily in the summer, along with evening bonfires. Cribs are also available, and pets are allowed in some of the cottages for an extra $324 per week. Thinking of boating at West Beach? Guest moorage is available ($28/night and up), along with a launch ramp. The resort is open year-round.

GUESTHOUSES, COTTAGES, AND SUITES

A number of bed-and-breakfasts also have guest cottages available, including Deer Harbor Inn and Old Trout Inn B&B.

All Dream Cottages

Consisting of five charming units scattered around the west side of Orcas Island, **All Dream Cottages** (360/376-2500, www. dreamstayorcas.com) are shoreside retreats from the stresses of life. Smallest is the romantic Isle Dream Cottage ($318 d), where a deck wraps around the cottage on three sides, and guests can follow the path to a private beach with a hammock and dock. Day Dream Farm Cottage ($288 d) has two bedrooms, an open floor plan, a queen-size bed along the bay window, and a small kitchen area. Sea Dream Cottage ($368 d) is a beachfront one-bedroom place with a magical location from which you can watch the sunset over an array of islands spreading across the horizon. Mariner's Dream Cottage ($368 d or $428 for four) has a dramatic waterside setting near the ferry terminal, along with a large deck, hot tub, woodstove, and full kitchen. Waveside Dream ($403 d or $483 for four) consists of two very private waterfront cottages, are perfect for families or two couples traveling together. A four-night minimum stay is required in summer (two nights in the off-season). Children are welcome at three of the cottages. Both Sea Dream and Isle Dream have been featured in national magazines.

Bayside Cottages

Bayside Cottages (65 Willis Lane, 360/376-4330, www.orcas1.com) consists of nine vacation cottages and houses on 14 waterfront acres at Obstruction Pass near the village of Olga. All include full kitchens and baths, with access to a private beach and fine views east to Mount Baker. The cottages range from a nicely appointed loft in the upper level of a converted barn ($225 d) to a recently built 2,000-square-foot three-bedroom home that sleeps six for $495. Also available is a small cottage ($225 for up to four) in the heart of Eastsound, and the least expensive option, a nicely restored 1950s-era four-unit motel in Eastsound ($145 d). Weekly rates are available, and kids are welcome. A four-night minimum is required in the summer.

Blackberry Beach Cabins

Located in tranquil Olga on the east side of the island, **Blackberry Beach Cabins** (360/376-2845, www.blackberrybeach.com) consists of two comfortable cabins, both with queen-size beds, private baths, and kitchens. The waterfront cabin ($200 d) has a picture window and an outdoor hot tub overlooking Buck Bay, and the modest garden cabin ($100 d) is a reasonably priced option. This is a place to kick back, so you won't find TVs, though Wi-Fi is available. Four-night stays are generally required in the summer (two nights in the off-season). No credit cards.

Buckhorn Farm Bungalow

If you're looking for a place that exemplifies island living, be sure to check out **Buckhorn Farm Bungalow** (17 Jensen Rd., 360/376-2298, www.buckhornfarm.com, $160 d, $10 each for additional guests), a cute one-bedroom cottage on the north side of Orcas near Eastsound. Step inside to find a full kitchen, woodstove, and private bath. Step outside to take in the peaceful orchard setting at this 10-acre farm. There's a three-night minimum in the summer, and kids are welcome, but book early for this popular spot. The cabin sleeps a maximum of five guests.

Cabins-on-the-Point

★ **Cabins-on-the-Point** (360/376-4114, www.cabinsonthepoint.com) consists of Cape Cod-style cabins facing Massacre Bay and West Sound from a rocky point of land. It's a wonderful spot for weddings or yoga retreats. Three cabins are available, each with a woodstove (wood provided) and full kitchen. The Heather Cabin ($275 d) is a premier choice, with windows just a few feet from the water (no TV here). Nearby, the Primrose Cabin ($250 d) features skylights, French doors into the sitting room, and a little garden. Willow ($295 d or $325 for up to four) is a two-bedroom cottage with a sun porch that fronts the bay. Guests at Heather and Primrose have access to the outdoor hot tub and free Wi-Fi, and all cabin guests can use a private

beach where kayaks are available at no additional charge. The trailhead for Turtleback Mountain Preserve is just a short walk from the cabins, and friendly deer and rabbits are frequent visitors.

Owner Jennifer Johnson is a good source for information and recommendations—she'll even set up restaurant reservations. Also offered are three family-friendly lodging options around Orcas. **Highlands House** is a large two-bedroom, two-bath hilltop home that includes an enormous great room with cathedral ceiling and stone fireplace, an open kitchen, and a deck affording stunning vistas across East Sound from the hot tub. The house is near Moran State Park and costs $325 for up to four guests. One of the most private places on the island, the house works well for two couples, **Sunset House** is a large waterside home close to Eastsound with three bedrooms and two baths, a big deck, floor-to-ceiling windows, and a full kitchen—all in a woodsy setting. It sleeps up to six comfortably for $420. **Westsound House** ($325 for up to four guests) is a 1940s-era home just 100 feet from the water. Amenities include a king bed, full kitchen, beach access, kayaks, French doors, Ping-Pong table, spacious lawns, and Wi-Fi.

These cabins and houses get repeat customers, so make reservations before March for a peak-season rental. Many guests book for a one-week stay, and a five-night summertime minimum is required at Willow, Highlands House, Westsound House, and Sunset House, with a three-night minimum at the Primrose Cabin. Off-season, there's a two-night minimum. Kids are welcome in the houses and cottages, and pets are also allowed in some units with prior arrangement.

Camp Moran Vacation House

Beneath tall trees on the south end of Cascade Lake within Moran State Park, **Camp Moran Vacation House** (360/360-4240 or 888/226-7688, www.parks.wa.gov) sleeps up to eight guests for an amazingly reasonable $135 per night. Inside this wheelchair-accessible structure are two bedrooms with a mix of full-size and bunk beds (bring your own linens and towels), a bathroom, a full kitchen with utensils, and a spacious living room with TV/VCR. Guests have access to a dock on the lake (not open to general park users). This is a fine base from which to explore the park, and can be reserved up to one year in advance. A two-night minimum stay is required.

Eagle Ridge Guesthouse

Eagle Ridge Guesthouse (503 Hidden Ridge Trail, 360/376-5634, www.eagleridgeguesthouse.com, $295) is a beautifully furnished, modern hillside home adjacent to Moran State Park. The home has space for three guests, with a bedroom and loft, full kitchen, hot tub, barbecue, Wi-Fi, and an enormous deck overlooking East Sound (perfect for sunset vistas). It's a 10-minute uphill drive from the town of Eastsound. A two-night minimum is required.

Eastsound Suites

Find luxurious rooms in the heart of town at **Eastsound Suites** (269 Main St., 360/376-2887, www.eastsoundsuites.com), with spacious and stylish one-bedroom studio apartments ($295 for up to four) that can be combined into a two-bedroom suite ($365 for up to six guests). Each has a gas fireplace, jetted tub, steam shower, full kitchen, washer/dryer, Wi-Fi, and a small deck facing the water. There is a two-night minimum stay, and kids are welcome. The suites are upstairs above Moon Glow Arts & Crafts.

Evergreen Cottage at Rosario

A recently built A-frame home with an open floor plan and high windows, **Evergreen Cottage at Rosario** (650/773-7296 or 415/806-9455, www.evergreenatrosario.com, $240 for up to six) sits beneath tall trees just a short drive from Moran State Park. Inside are two bedrooms, a full kitchen, living room, loft, two baths, and Wi-Fi, while the wraparound deck has a hot tub. A two-night minimum stay is required.

Laughing Moon Farm

On the shore of East Sound, and within walking distance of the golf course, **Laughing Moon Farm** (451 Osprey Lane, 360/376-7879, www.laughingmoonfarm.com) is a woodsy retreat with two recently constructed cottages. Each unit contains a full kitchen and bath, and the largest includes two bedrooms and a loft—plenty of space for a family gathering. Trout House cottage sleeps four and is available at $200 per night or $1,200 per week. The larger Gate House is $325 per night or $1,600 per week for up to seven people. A three-night minimum is required for both cottages. Guests always enjoy meeting the sheep and the llama, and watching the nesting eagles. No pets.

Once in a Blue Moon Farm

On the south end of Orcas, a couple of miles from the ferry dock, **Once in a Blue Moon Farm** (412 Eastman Rd., 360/376-7035, www.onceinabluemoonfarm.com) is a peaceful 35-acre farm featuring guest rooms with private baths and Wi-Fi. The farm has been here since the late 1800s, and a cabin from the farm has been moved to the Orcas Island Historical Museum. Once in a Blue Moon is popular with agritourists and families who appreciate the menagerie of horses, goats, alpacas, geese, ducks, turkeys, and chickens—not to mention the wild deer and rabbits. There's also an orchard with heirloom varieties of fruit (apple, plum, quince, cherry, kiwi, peach, and pear) and an organic garden that produces all sorts of berries, herbs, and flowers. Kids love to pet the animals and feed the chickens, and a brief farm tour is provided to arriving guests. Suite lodging rates are $225 d, or $325 for a four-person suite with two queen beds and a full kitchen. Pets are allowed for a fee. The owner also rents out Sleeping Sea, a home on the north side of Orcas.

Orcas Island Rentals

Orcas Island Rentals (360/376-4223, www.orcas-island-rentals.com) consists of three separate lodging places. **Maggie's Manor** is a pretty waterfront home on a 110-acre estate. The front porch and outdoor hot tub provide picture-postcard vistas of Deer Harbor, while inside are four bedrooms and two baths, a large kitchen, and a living room with a concert grand piano. The house rents for $2,370 per week and sleeps up to eight. Nightly stays are also available, starting at $395 d, with a three-night summer minimum.

Also on the estate is a unique little place called the **Gnome House,** a handcrafted cottage that looks like it belongs in a fairy tale. It's a delightful honeymoon spot. You'll find a spiral staircase, sleigh bed, sunken tub bath, full kitchen, and a bay window facing the surrounding flower gardens. Outside is a private hot tub. The Gnome House rents for $225 for up to four people or $1,350 per week. A three-night summertime minimum is required. The same owners offer **Grandma & Grandpa's Getaway,** a one-bedroom apartment with a full kitchen, bath, and private deck for $175 d. All three units have Wi-Fi and are located on Channel Road in Deer Harbor.

Rose Cottage

Right next to the busy Orcas ferry landing, **Rose Cottage** (360/376-4611, www.orcasislandboardwalk.com, $290 d) was built in the 1930s and has been nicely maintained. The one-bedroom cottage has a kitchen, living room with hide-a-bed, a private bath, and Wi-Fi. The big deck with leaning madrone trees provides a wonderful view of the ferry action.

Salish Seaside Escapes

Salish Seaside Escapes (327 Sunset Ave., 360/376-2234, www.the-salish.com) has six waterfront cottages on the north shore of Orcas Island, a mile from Eastsound. All have full kitchens, baths, and private hot tubs; the two largest have washers and dryers. A sauna is available for all guests, with beach and garden access. The cottages range from a unit that sleeps four people at $215 per night, up to a six-person cottage with two bedrooms and two baths for $265 per night.

Sea Star Lofts

Sea Star Lofts (344 Main St., 360/507-5444, www.seastarorcasisland.com, $185-275 d) has an ideal waterside location in the heart of Eastsound. The four apartments are large, modern, and beautifully furnished in "beachy elegance," with full kitchens and baths. One has a private patio, two share a balcony, and the fourth has a king-size bed, ADA accessibility, and plenty of room. The owners also rent out a charming four-bedroom home that sleeps up to 11 for $510 per night, and a more remote and peaceful cottage on a 25-acre farm adjacent to Turtleback Mountain Preserve. The latter sleeps up to four guests for $245 per night. A two-night minimum stay is required at all Sea Star lodging places, and all are booked through VRBO. Recommended.

Sleeping Sea Guest Home

Located on the north shore of Orcas 1.5 miles from Eastsound, **Sleeping Sea** (412 Eastman Rd., 360/376-7035, www.sleepingsea.com, closed Jan.-Feb., $225-350 d) has three suites, each with a queen bed, private bath, flat-screen TV, and Wi-Fi. A boardwalk extends over wetlands in front of the house to a lovely private beach. There's a two-night minimum stay. The entire house can be rented for weddings and other events. Owner Shana Lloyd also runs Once in a Blue Moon Farm.

Spring Bay on Orcas Island

A secluded waterside retreat adjacent to Obstruction Pass State Park, ★ **Spring Bay on Orcas Island** (360/376-5531, www.springbayonorcas.com, $250/night for up to three guests) provides comfortable accommodations in a gorgeous setting. The cabin is surrounded by 57 acres of private woods, with five miles of hiking trails and a covered deck a stone's throw from Spring Bay. There's even an active bald eagle nest nearby. The cabin has queen and twin beds, a kitchenette, barbecue grill, and bath, along with a waterside hot tub and kayaks. Former park rangers Carl Burger and Sandy Playa live just up the hill, bringing extensive knowledge of the outdoors to this slice of heaven. They lead daily **two-hour sea-kayak paddles**—all equipment provided—for $35/person ($45 for nonguests). A three-night minimum stay is required in the summer. Reserve far ahead for summertime stays. Wi-Fi is available, but cell phone service is limited (T-Mobile only). There is no TV reception, but you can watch DVD movies on the screen.

BED-AND-BREAKFASTS

Orcas has quite a few luxurious bed-and-breakfasts for discriminating travelers looking for a sanctuary from the hustle and bustle. Be sure to book several months ahead for summertime stays.

Double Mountain B&B

Enjoy a panoramic view of the San Juans from the deck of **Double Mountain B&B** (660 Double Hill Rd., 360/376-4570, www.doublemountainbandb.com), a contemporary home atop a 500-foot hill, two miles out of Eastsound. Inside are two guest rooms ($110-165 d) and a two-room suite ($175 d or $245 for four guests) with its own kitchen and entrance. All rooms have private baths, and a full country breakfast is served. No kids under 10 are permitted, and a two-night minimum is required in July and August.

The Inn on Orcas Island

Nestled along a marsh at the head of Deer Harbor, ★ **The Inn on Orcas Island** (114 Channel Rd., 360/376-5227, www.theinnonorcasisland.com) is one of the finest and most unusual lodgings on Orcas. Former owners of a Santa Barbara art gallery, John Gibbs and Jeremy Trumble have filled the walls of their elegant home with a remarkable collection of 19th- and 20th-century English paintings. Catering to couples in search of a romantic escape (no kids allowed), it's an art gallery masquerading as a luxury inn. Most rooms have gas fireplaces, and all include jetted tubs, indulgent beds, Wi-Fi, and balconies overlooking a pristine landscape. Borrow

a bike to pedal around Deer Harbor, or take the canoe out on the lagoon to watch birds. Guest are treated to a multicourse gourmet breakfast. Rates start at $225 d for a queen-size bed with water view, and go up to $285 d for a king suite. Two cottages ($305 d and $345 d) provide more private luxury; one has a full kitchen. A two-night minimum stay is required in the summer and on holiday weekends.

Kangaroo House B&B

Kangaroo House (just north of Eastsound, 360/376-2175, www.kangaroohouse.com, $175-209 d) was built in 1907 and purchased in the 1930s by sea captain Harold Ferris, who had picked up a young female kangaroo on one of his Australian voyages. The kangaroo is long gone, but the name remains on this attractive old home with a big fireplace, antique furnishings, decks, Wi-Fi, and a garden hot tub. The five guest rooms and suites all have king- or queen-size beds and private baths. There's a memorable multicourse organic breakfast each morning, and bird-watchers will appreciate the many species that come to the backyard feeders. A high fence protects the flower-filled gardens from deer. No children under age 12 are allowed. Owners Charles Toxey and Jill Johnson also manage **Artsmith** (www.orcasartsmith.org), a nonprofit literary organization that holds occasional writers' retreats and public readings at the B&B.

Kingfish Inn B&B

Built in 1902, **Kingfish Inn** (Deer Harbor and Crow Valley Rds., 360/376-2500, www.dreamstayorcas.com, $205-235 d) sits directly across the road from West Sound. The four small but luxuriously furnished guest rooms exhibit a Victorian charm. Each has a private bath, TV, and fridge, and two contain king beds. The building also houses the justifiably popular West Sound Café. The owners also operate the acclaimed All Dream Cottages (described above).

Apple Walnut Gorgonzola Omelet

This makes 1 serving.

1 ounce gorgonzola or blue cheese

1 tablespoon sour cream

2 tablespoons toasted walnuts, coarsely chopped and bounced around in a sieve to remove skin

2 eggs

2 drops Tabasco sauce

2 teaspoons cold water

4 or 5 thin slices of apple, about ¼ of an apple

2 teaspoons butter

2 tablespoons cooked crumbled bacon (1 piece per serving)

Mix the cheese, sour cream, and walnuts together to make the filling and set aside. Beat eggs with Tabasco and water until blended. Heat an 8-inch omelet pan, melt butter, and pour egg mixture into pan when butter is sizzling. When eggs begin to firm up, place apple slices along one side and cook at medium heat. When eggs are no longer liquid, add filling. Fold omelet in half and top with crumbled bacon.

Recipe courtesy of Otters Pond B&B

Old Trout Inn B&B

For a bit of France on Orcas, stay at **Old Trout Inn B&B** (5272 Orcas Rd., 360/376-7474, www.oldtroutinn.com), an elegant country home just three miles from the ferry dock. The pond out back attracts birds, and you can fish (catch-and-release only) for trout, carp, or bluegills. Inside the house are a large guest room ($185 d) with private bath, and a suite ($235 d) with private bath with sauna, a fridge, separate entrance, fireplace, wet bar, and huge deck, and a private hot tub overlooking the pond. Water's Edge Cottage ($215 d) is next door, with a full kitchen, gas fireplace, private bath, covered porch, and hot tub along the pond. Extra guests are $25 each. Owners Henri and Nicole de Marval once ran a French restaurant and offer two-night stays with a three-course dinner and two breakfasts for $335-480 d (depending upon the room). Because of the unfenced pond, young children aren't allowed.

Otters Pond B&B

A modern country home near Moran State Park, **Otters Pond B&B** (100 Tomihi Dr., 360/376-8844, www.otterspond.com) sits alongside a 20-acre pond. Five elegantly furnished rooms have private baths, access to the shoji screen-enclosed hot tub, and Wi-Fi. The more expensive rooms are quite spacious, with king-size beds and skylights; the Swan Room ($239 d) has a gas fireplace, claw-foot tub, and pond view, while the Goldfinch Room ($239 d) features a gas fireplace and a TV. The little Chickadee Room ($175 d) is equally popular, with a claw-foot tub and views of the pond. The tiny Blue Heron Room ($135 d) is fine for one person, but might be a bit claustrophobic for couples. Innkeepers Carl and Susan Silvernail are delightful hosts who create a five-course breakfast that's certain to please. Behind the home are a large deck, dahlia garden, and several bird feeders that attract a flittering crowd most mornings. The pond is home to nesting mallards and wood ducks in the summer, and migrating flocks at other times. Children are not allowed.

Pebble Cove Farm

Overlooking a grassy lawn along Massacre Bay, **Pebble Cove Farm** (3341 Deer Harbor Rd., 360/376-6161, www.pebblecovefarm.com) has three suites ($250-300 d) and a cottage ($350 d), each with private deck, bath, kitchenette, hardwood floors, barbecue grill, and

Wi-Fi. The cottage sleeps four and includes a separate bedroom. A tiny garden cabin ($160 d) provides simpler accommodations; there's no TV or Wi-Fi here. The farm has a private beach, a hot tub, and a four-acre organic garden, along with goats, miniature pigs, chickens, and Buddy the pony. Guest can collect eggs from the chickens or pick fresh vegetables from the garden to prepare meals in the kitchenettes. An organic continental breakfast is provided each morning. Take a swing in the hammocks, borrow the rowboat to head out to Skull Island, rent a kayak to paddle the protected waters of Massacre Bay, or join a private boat tour. A three-night minimum is required on weekends, and kids are welcome.

Sand Dollar Inn B&B

Sand Dollar Inn B&B (445 Point Lawrence Rd. near Olga, 360/376-5696, $115 d) is a 1920s home with three large upstairs rooms, all with private baths and sweeping views of Buck Bay, Lopez Island, and the Olympic Mountains. Orcas Island Artworks gallery is just up the road, and it's just a short drive farther to Moran State Park, making this a good base for hiking and biking. The house is furnished with Japanese antiques and woodblock prints; the owner lived in Japan for six years. A full breakfast is served, and Wi-Fi is available. No kids under 14 are allowed.

Turtleback Farm Inn

Orcas Island's most famous bed-and-breakfast, ★ **Turtleback Farm Inn** (1981 Crow Valley Rd., 360/376-4914 or 800/376-4914, www.turtlebackinn.com), began life as a simple 1910 farmhouse in the shadow of Turtleback Mountain. Innkeepers Susan and Bill Fletcher bought the run-down old farmhouse, restored and expanded the building, added hardwood floors, and then opened the doors to Orcas Island's first B&B. The inn is approximately six miles from the ferry landing near the center of Orcas, and its two-level back deck overlooks a bucolic pasture, part of this 80-acre farm. Cows and sheep graze

below, and a crowing rooster might wake you in the morning. Bird-watchers will enjoy exploring the farm's half-dozen ponds.

The farmhouse's seven guest rooms are furnished with a Victorian-inspired decor that deftly balances luxury and comfort. One minuscule room, The Nook, is barely big enough for the double bed and your shoes, but it's an inexpensive ($125 d) option and has a small private bath. The other rooms are substantially larger, with queen-size beds and claw-foot tubs in the private baths for $165-195 d. Nicest is the Valley View Room, with antique furnishings and a private deck overlooking the farm. The emphasis is on relaxation and getting away from it all, so there are no televisions or phones, but Wi-Fi is available. Kids over eight are welcome in the house. A substantial and delicious breakfast is served downstairs each morning, or on the deck when weather permits. End the day by sipping sherry or playing cards by the fireplace.

Adjacent to the historic farmhouse is the **Orchard House,** a cedar barnlike structure where the emphasis is on privacy. Each of the four plush guest rooms has a king-size bed, gas fireplace, private deck, sitting area, Wi-Fi, a bath with claw foot tub, and a separate shower. Breakfast is delivered to your room, making this spot popular with couples who just want to be alone for a quiet morning. It's perfect for honeymooners, but families with children are also welcome. One of the rooms has been set up to accommodate travelers with disabilities; it's the most popular room. Orchard House rooms go for $265 d. All rooms at Turtleback Farm require a two-night minimum in the summer and on many weekends and holidays at other times.

CAMPING

Orcas Island has the vast majority of public campsites on the San Juans, nearly all of which are in Moran State Park on the east end of the island. Find **showers** in Moran State Park and the marinas at Deer Harbor, Rosario, and West Sound.

Warm Chocolate-Espresso Pudding Cakes

¾ cup butter or margarine

6 ounces bittersweet chocolate, chopped

2 teaspoons freeze-dried espresso powder, or 2 tablespoons hot espresso

½ tablespoon unbleached white flour

2 tablespoons unsweetened cocoa

5 large eggs, separated

⅓ cup sugar

½ tablespoon Kahlua

½ teaspoon vanilla

Preheat oven to 375°F.

In a small pan, combine butter and chocolate. Heat over low flame until melted and smoothly mixed. Add espresso and mix. Mix together flour and cocoa. In a large bowl, beat the 5 egg whites until they become white. Beat in sugar, 1 tablespoon at a time, until the eggs hold stiff and shiny, but not dry, peaks.

Blend together the yolks, liqueur, vanilla, and the cocoa and flour mixture, and then add the chocolate and butter mixture. Gently fold in the egg whites.

Pour about ½ cup batter into each of 8 buttered ramekins or custard cups. For ease of handling, place the ramekins on a cookie sheet before placing in the oven to bake. Bake until the edges begin to firm but the center is still soft when pressed, 11-12 minutes. Let cool for a few minutes, then invert onto serving plates. Serve with coffee ice cream.

Recipe courtesy of Turtleback Farm Inn

ORCAS ISLAND
ACCOMMODATIONS

Moran State Park

One of the most popular camping areas in Washington, ★ **Moran State Park** (360/376-2326, www.parks.wa.gov) has 151 campsites scattered across three campgrounds along Cascade Lake, with a fourth along Mountain Lake plus a separate bike-in area. These represent some of the finest camping opportunities in the San Juans, and they fill early during July and August. Tent sites cost $20-30 (maximum eight people/site), including hot showers. There are no RV hookups, though there is a dump station. The four standard campgrounds all accommodate trailer campers and RVs, but some campsites will not fit large motor homes. Camping is not allowed outside established park campgrounds.

North End Campground is across the road from the swimming beach area, and several of these sites are quite private. **Midway Campground** is near the Cascade Lake boat launch, and its most popular sites are right on the lakeshore (but also next to the sometimes noisy road). **South End Campground** is the park's most popular (and justly so), with almost all the sites right along the shore. This premier area has a wheelchair-accessible campsite and restroom. **Mountain Lake Campground** is one mile up Mount Constitution Road on the shores of Mountain Lake, the park's largest lake. In addition, for those who arrive by bicycle or on foot, 15 primitive campsites ($12) are located in a small site on the road to Mount Constitution.

Due to Moran State Park's popularity, camping reservations are highly advised in July and August, when the sites are perpetually full seven days a week. (You may find a space without a reservation, but get there early if you want to risk it.) All sites are preassigned in the summer, so check in at the pay station across from Cascade Lake when you arrive. Campground reservations can be made as little as two days in advance, or as much as nine months ahead. Make reservations ($10 extra) at 888/226-7688 or the park website, which also includes a campsite availability map. Mid-September-mid-May, camping is on a first-come, first-served basis with no reservations. At least one of the campgrounds remains open year-round.

For something more comfortable, the park now has seven **glamping tents** located next to the South End Campground. These canvas tents have queen beds, attractive furniture, bedding and linens, picnic tables, Adirondack chairs, and nearby bathrooms and showers. They are popular with people who either want the experience of camping without the hassles of bringing all the camping gear, or are physically unable to sleep in a sleeping bag on the hard ground. These luxury tents are available mid-April-early October, and are not cheap. Five of the sites have one tent; these cost $159-179 for up to four people. Glampsites with two tents on the same site are $249-259 for up to four guests. (Yes, you read that correctly. People are willing to pay more for these luxury campsites than for many upscale B&B lodging places on Orcas Island!) Glamping sites in Moran State Park are maintained and reserved through **Leanto** (360/298-1684, www.stayleanto.com). A two-night minimum is required for most sites.

Obstruction Pass State Park

Eighty-acre **Obstruction Pass State Park** sits on the south end of Orcas Island, 2.5 miles southeast of Olga and 17 road miles from the ferry dock. A 1-mile dirt road heads off Obstruction Pass Road and ends at a parking lot where a pleasant 0.5-mile hike takes you to four campsites (360/376-2326, www.parks.wa.gov, $20) with pit toilets. The location is very scenic, with sites facing nearby Obstruction and Blakely Islands, but there's no vehicle access, reservations, or potable water. Campsites fill fast, and it's illegal to camp elsewhere nearby, so get there early on summer weekends to be sure of a space following your hike. Avoid the crowds by coming in midweek or the off-season. A county boat ramp is available at Obstruction Pass, and it's just a short paddle to privately owned Obstruction Island.

Point Doughty Marine State Park

Located on the northeast end of Orcas, 60-acre **Point Doughty Marine State Park** has four primitive water-accessible Cascadia Marine Trail campsites ($12). There's no drinking water, but vault toilets are provided. You'll need a kayak to camp here because there's no road or trail access. The point faces west to British Columbia's Gulf Islands, making for magnificent sunsets. Only the four acres at the very tip of Point Doughty are open to the public.

Doe Bay Resort & Retreat

Funky **Doe Bay Resort** (107 Doe Bay Rd., 360/376-2291, www.doebay.com, open for year-round camping, $66 d weekends, $59 d weekdays) is a couple of miles east of Olga and 20 miles from the ferry terminal. It has tent sites (no RV hookups) with access to a guest kitchen and bathhouse. Drive-up sites are in a field, but walk-in tent spaces sit atop a wooded bluff overlooking Doe Bay. Campers can join other resort guests in the popular creekside hot tubs at no extra charge, take a kayak tour, or enjoy a fine vegetarian meal in the on-site café. A two-night minimum stay is required at the campground. There is free Wi-Fi.

West Beach Resort

A cozy family place, **West Beach Resort** (three miles west of Eastsound off Enchanted Forest Rd., 360/376-2240 or 877/937-8224, www.westbeachresort.com) has both lodging and campsites in a setting that serves up great sunsets over President Channel. Tent spaces are $45 for up to three people, while RV sites with water and electricity cost $49 for up to three. Nine canvas tent cabins ($139-179 d; $7 each for extra guests) are furnished with queen beds, futons, and tables and chairs, plus small decks and picnic tables (but no water, and some lack electricity). A shower house is nearby, and pets are an extra $7. Kid activities are offered most days, and parents will appreciate the big hot tub ($5/person; free if you're staying in the tent cabins), along with Wi-Fi.

The store sells firewood, groceries, ice cream in homemade waffle cones, espresso, and limited supplies, while the marina rents motorboats, stand-up paddleboards, canoes, kayaks, and fishing gear, along with sea kayaking tours. Guest moorage is available ($28 and up) for campers. Reservations are highly advised for July and August and on holidays and busy weekends. If you show up without a reservation in the peak summer season, you may well be out of luck. Call two weeks ahead of your visit if you're bringing an RV, and a year ahead for the ocean-view sites near the beach! The tent cabins are open April-September, while the RV and tent spaces are available year-round (but the shower house is closed in winter).

Information and Services

Get island information from the helpful **Orcas Island Chamber of Commerce Visitor Center** (360/376-2273, www.orcasislandchamber.com, 10am-3pm Mon.-Sat. year-round), located in Eastsound at 65 North Beach Road. **Orcas Issues** (www.orcasissues.com) is a good online-only news site for the island.

KID STUFF
Weekday childcare is available on a drop-in basis at **Orcas Island Children's House** (36 Pea Patch Lane, 360/376-4744, www.oich.org) and **Kaleidoscope Preschool and Childcare Center** (1292 North Beach Rd., 360/376-2484, www.ourkaleidoscopekids.org). You'll need to provide a copy of your child's immunization records. Call ahead for age requirements and to make sure they have space.

LIBRARY
Eastsound is home to the attractive **Orcas Island Library** (500 Rose St., 360/376-4985, www.orcaslibrary.org, 10am-7pm Mon.-Thurs., 10am-5pm Fri.-Sat., noon-3pm Sun.), a great place to relax on a drizzly afternoon. The public is welcome at the preschool story hour every Thursday and Saturday. A half-dozen computers are available to surf the web or check your email, but you may need to wait for a machine. Nonlocals can pay $10 for a 30-day library card if you want to check something out. Wi-Fi is free, and it's even available if you're sitting outside the library when they're closed!

COMMUNICATIONS
In addition to the free computers and Wi-Fi at the library, **Orcas Online** (109 North Beach Rd., 360/376-4124, www.orcasonline.com, $5 for 30 min.) lets you surf the web and use the printer and scanner.

Cell phone service can be surprisingly spotty on the east side of Orcas Island, and from the west side your phone may use Canadian cell towers; this could potentially add a roaming charge to your bill.

BANKING AND MAIL
Find ATM machines at **Islanders Bank** (475 Fern St., 360/376-2265 or 800/843-5441, www.islandersbank.com), **Washington Federal Credit Union** (35 Main St., 360/376-2218, www.washingtonfederal.com), and **Key Bank** (487 Main St., 360/376-2211, www.keybank.com). Machines are also inside the Orcas Island Market and Ray's Pharmacy in Eastsound, at Deer Harbor Marina, Rosario Resort, and Doe Bay Resort & Retreat, and the Orcas Village Store at the ferry landing.

Post offices can be found on A Street in Eastsound (360/376-4121), and at Deer Harbor (360/376-2548), Olga (360/376-4236), and Orcas (360/376-4254).

MEDICAL CARE

Several options are available if you need medical care while on the island: **Orcas Medical Center** (7 Deye Lane, 360/376-2561, www.orcasmedicalcenter.com), **Orcas Island Family Medicine** (33 Umer St., 360/376-4949), and the nonprofit **Orcas Family Health Center** (1286 Mt. Baker Rd., 360/376-7778, www.orcasfamilyhealthcenter.org). All three facilities can provide urgent care and lab tests and are open weekdays, with a physician on call after hours. Orcas Island has a paramedic system, but the closest hospital is in Anacortes, and serious medical problems require a Medevac flight to Seattle. Get prescription medicines from **Ray's Pharmacy** in Eastsound (68 North Beach Rd., 360/376-2230, 10am-4pm Mon.-Sat.).

For a new age take on health—including massage therapists, acupuncture, herbal remedies, and counseling—visit **Healing Arts Center** (453 North Beach Rd., 360/376-4002, www.healingarts.org).

VETERINARY CARE

Take sick or injured pets to **Orcas Veterinary Service** (429 Madrona St., 360/376-6373, www.orcasvets.com) or board your dog or cat at **Eastsound Kennels** (186 Dolphin Bay Rd., 360/376-2410, www.eastsoundkennels.com). **Pawki's Pet Boutique** (199 Main St., 360/376-3648, www.pawkis.com) sells pet supplies in Eastsound.

LAUNDRY AND WASTE DISPOSAL

Country Corner Laundry (837 Crescent Beach Dr., 360/376-6900) is a half mile east of Eastsound. Additional washers and dryers are at Rosario Resort Marina and Deer Harbor Marina, and both have **showers** ($2).

If you're staying in a rental house on the island, you'll need to haul garbage to the **Orcas Island Transfer Station** (3398 Orcas Rd., 360/376-4089, www.exchangeorcas.org, 10am-4pm Thurs.-Mon.) on the west side of the island. You can recycle many items here, including mixed paper, tin cans, aluminum, plastic bottles, cardboard, and newspapers, but don't bother to sort your recyclables; they all go in one bin to be sorted later. Dumping garbage costs $12 per bag.

Getting There and Around

WASHINGTON STATE FERRIES

Washington State Ferries (360/376-6253 for the Orcas ferry terminal, 206/464-6400 or 888/808-7977 for general info) dock at Orcas Village on the south end of the island. Find all the details—including current ferry wait times—at www.wsdot.wa.gov/ferries, or view ferry cams at www.ferrycam.net/orcas.html.

Peak-season fares from Anacortes to Orcas are $14 for passengers and walk-ons, or $54 for a car and driver. Bikes are $4 extra, and kayaks cost $19. The fare for a car and driver from Orcas westbound to Friday Harbor is $28; walk-ons and passengers ride free. Vehicles and passengers traveling east from Orcas to Shaw, Lopez, or Anacortes do not need tickets and there is no charge. There are no direct sailings from Orcas westward to Sidney, British Columbia, but you can take a ferry from Orcas to San Juan Island and then connect with a ferry to Sidney.

Anyone traveling from Anacortes to Orcas in summer should make **Save A Spot vehicle reservations** online at www.wsdot.wa.gov/ferries/reservations. These can be made up to two months in advance, but are not available for interisland ferries. Passengers and walk-ons do not need reservations.

Reservations are not taken for eastbound travel, and during the summer, visitors try to catch the 11am Sunday sailing from Orcas to Anacortes. Unfortunately, many of them arrive too late, leading to a long delay till the

Orcas Island Mileage

	Orcas Village Ferry Dock	Deer Harbor	Doe Bay	Eastsound	Moran State Park	Olga
Deer Harbor	8					
Doe Bay	20	22				
Eastsound	9	11	11			
Moran State Park	14	15	7	4		
Olga	17	18	3	8	4	
West Sound Marina	4	4	18	7	12	15

5pm ferry. This provides plenty of business for the Orcas Hotel Café (and it's a pleasant place to hang out), but makes for a long wait. If you're heading back to Anacortes from a weekend adventure and want to catch the 11am ferry, be sure to arrive at the Orcas ferry terminal at least an hour ahead of time.

WATER TAXIS

North Shore Charters (360/376-4855, www.orcasislandadventures.com) provides water taxi service to state marine parks on Stuart, Sucia, Matia, Patos, and other islands—even to Victoria, Vancouver, and the Gulf Islands in Canada. The boat departs from Deer Harbor Marina, and has space for kayaks and bikes. Rates are based on distance and the number of passengers; it costs $20-25 one-way to Jones Island.

Based on the north side of Orcas near the Eastsound Airport, **Outer Island Excursions** (360/376-3711, www.outerislandx.com) leads daily summertime shuttles to nearby Sucia Island ($45 adults, $35 kids round-trip), where they also have kayaks available for rent. In addition, Outer Island Excursions has lighthouse tours to Stuart and Patos Islands, water taxi service throughout the San Juans and to Bellingham

and Anacortes, and whale-watching, charter fishing, and guided kayak trips.

Deer Harbor Charters (360/376-5989 or 800/544-5758, www.deerharborcharters.com) has water taxi service to Sucia Island for $65 per person, providing approximately three hours on the island. Sucia Island trips depart from West Beach Resort on the west side of Orcas, and are offered mid-May-mid-September.

AIR

Operating out of Lake Union in Seattle, **Kenmore Air** (425/486-1257 or 866/435-9524, www.kenmoreair.com) has daily scheduled floatplane flights for $150-161 one-way to Rosario Resort, Deer Harbor, and West Sound Marina on Orcas Island. A 25-pound baggage weight limit is in effect on these flights. They also fly wheeled planes between Seattle's Boeing Field and Eastsound Airport daily; there's a 70-pound weight limit on these flights.

San Juan Airlines (360/376-4176 or 800/874-4434, www.sanjuanairlines.com) has daily scheduled wheeled-plane service to Eastsound Airport from Anacortes and Bellingham, plus connecting service to San Juan, Lopez, and Blakely Islands. Flightseeing and charters are also available to Victoria, Seattle, Vancouver, or other destinations.

SHUTTLE BUS

San Juan Transit (360/378-8887, www.sanjuantransit.com) operates shuttle buses between the Orcas ferry landing and Rosario Resort, with stops at West Sound, Turtleback Mountain Trailhead, Deer Harbor, Orcas Island Golf Course, Eastsound (Island Market), and Moran State Park (Cascade Lake). Buses operate 9am-1pm Friday-Sunday mid-June through Labor Day in early September. The buses can carry bikes and luggage, and fares are $5 each way ($3 for kids under 12), or $15 for an all-day pass ($10 kids). These passes are a great deal, letting you get off and on along the way.

CAR RENTALS

Orcas Island Rental Car (360/376-7433, www.orcasislandshuttle.com) rents a variety of cars, starting at $65 per day for a sedan. They provide free pickup and delivery of cars anywhere on Orcas with a 24-hour notice. Cars cannot be driven off the island.

Gas is available at two stations east of Eastsound along Crescent Beach Drive, but prices are slightly cheaper at the hardware store at the junction of West Beach Road and Crow Valley Road. In a pinch, you can also get fuel from the various boat harbors, including West Beach Resort and Deer Harbor Marina. Fuel prices are exorbitant on Orcas, so fill up on the mainland before you get on the ferry or get ready to add at least $1 a gallon.

Don't have a rental car and the shuttle isn't available? It's relatively easy to **hitchhike** on Orcas, and a good way to meet the locals.

TAXIS

Orcas Island Taxi (360/376-8294, www.orcasislandtaxi.com) and **New Orcas Taxi Tours** (360/298-1639) provide service from the ferry terminal to Eastsound ($30), Moran State Park ($40), Rosario Resort ($40), Doe Bay ($60), Deer Harbor ($30) and other places on the island. Rates are for two people; add $5 each for additional people.

Lopez Island

Look for ★ to find recommended
sights, activities, dining, and lodging.

Highlights

★ **Lopez Village:** This little business center has a small museum, galleries, good food, and more (page 219).

★ **Lopez Island Vineyards & Winery:** This six-acre farm eschews pesticides in the production of its Madeleine Angevine and Siegerrebe wines. Locals pick the grapes each fall in a harvest party (page 220).

★ **Spencer Spit State Park:** Excellent camping, kayaking, beachcombing, and clamming attract crowds to this park on the east side of Lopez (page 221).

★ **Iceberg Point:** An easy half-mile hike leads through forest and grasslands to this rugged, rocky point (page 222).

★ **Watmough Head:** This out-of-the-way spot on the south end of Lopez features a pebbly beach facing the snowy summit of Mount Baker (page 224).

★ **Biking:** Cycling the 30-mile loop is a perfect way to explore the farms, fields, forests, and bays of Lopez (page 226).

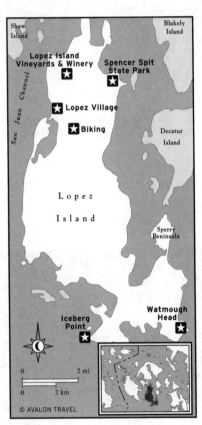

O ften called "The Friendly Isle" or "Slowpez," Lopez Island is an easy-going place with gently rolling terrain, old farms in various states of disrepair, shaggy black dogs, and a famously friendly populace. Waving to passing cars and bicycles is a time-honored local custom. Failure to wave back will label you a tourist as surely as a camera around your neck and rubber flip-flops. Befitting the slow pace, you'll discover spotty cell phone service around the island—so put that phone away and relax.

If you're venturing out to the San Juans from Anacortes, Lopez Island (population 2,400) is the first place the ferry stops. The third-largest island in the archipelago, it covers almost 30 square miles. Pastoral farmland and water vistas predominate, especially on the southern end of the island.

Because of its lack of both steep hills and traffic, Lopez is popular with cyclists, including many groups of touring bikers. The roads are mostly paved, and views of the surrounding islands and mountains to the east and west jut out from every turn.

Along the west side of Lopez just north of Fisherman Bay is the island's quaint business center, little Lopez Village. Here you'll find a scattering of cafés and shops; a museum, grocery store with gas, post office, pharmacy, and medical clinic; and a few real estate offices. South End General Store is on the south end of the island, and a few more businesses cluster along pretty Fisherman Bay, filled with sailboats and other craft, but the rest of Lopez Island is rural. Many Lopez businesses are shuttered during the winter.

Lopezians are an odd amalgamation of carpenters, retirees, back-to-the-land organic farmers, commercial fishers, artists and musicians, bed-and-breakfast owners, and more than a few eccentrics. Microsoft billionaire Paul Allen owns a guarded estate on Sperry Peninsula.

HISTORY

Lopez is named in honor of Lopez Gonzales de Haro, the first European to discover the San Juans. He served as sailing master during

Previous: sailboats in Fisherman Bay; Center Church. **Above:** wooded road.

Lopez Island

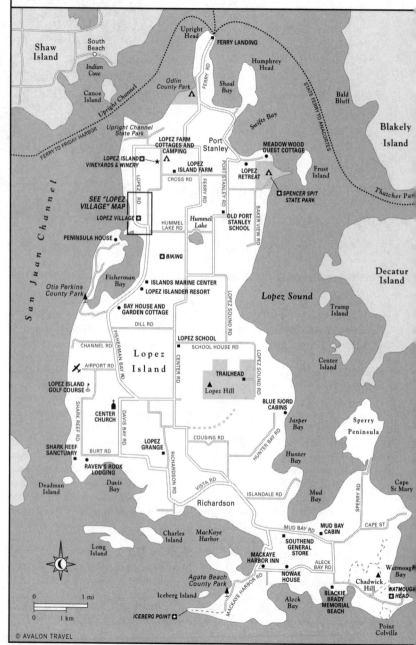

Shaw Island

South Beach

Indian Cove

Canoe Island

Upright Head

FERRY LANDING

Humphrey Head

Shoal Bay

Swifts Bay

Bald Bluff

Blakely Island

Thatcher Pas

Odlin County Park

Upright Channel

Upright Channel State Park

FERRY TO FRIDAY HARBOR

LOPEZ FARM COTTAGES AND CAMPING

LOPEZ ISLAND VINEYARDS & WINERY

LOPEZ ISLAND FARM

Port Stanley

MEADOW WOOD GUEST COTTAGE

Frost Island

STATE FERRY TO ANACORTES

CROSS RD

FERRY RD

PORT STANLEY RD

LOPEZ RETREAT

SPENCER SPIT STATE PARK

BAKER VIEW RD

SEE "LOPEZ VILLAGE" MAP

LOPEZ VILLAGE

HUMMEL LAKE RD

Hummel Lake

OLD PORT STANLEY SCHOOL

San Juan Channel

PENINSULA HOUSE

BIKING

Fisherman Bay

Otis Perkins County Park

ISLANDS MARINE CENTER

LOPEZ ISLANDER RESORT

BAY HOUSE AND GARDEN COTTAGE

DILL RD

Lopez Sound

Trump Island

Decatur Island

Center Island

CHANNEL RD

FISHERMAN BAY RD

Lopez Island

LOPEZ SCHOOL

SCHOOL HOUSE RD

LOPEZ SOUND RD

AIRPORT RD

CENTER RD

LOPEZ ISLAND GOLF COURSE

CENTER CHURCH

DAVIS BAY RD

TRAILHEAD

Lopez Hill

BLUE FJORD CABINS

Jasper Bay

Sperry Peninsula

SHARK REEF RD

SHARK REEF SANCTUARY

LOPEZ GRANGE

RAVEN'S ROOK LODGING

BURT RD

COUSINS RD

RICHARDSON RD

Hunter Bay

HUNTER BAY RD

Deadman Island

Davis Bay

VISTA RD

ISLANDALE RD

Richardson

Mud Bay

SPERRY RD

CAPE ST

Cape St Mary

Long Island

Charles Island

MacKaye Harbor

MUD BAY RD

MUD BAY CABIN

SOUTHEND GENERAL STORE

ALECK BAY RD

Watmough Bay

MACKAYE HARBOR INN

MACKAYE HARBOR RD

NOWAK HOUSE

Chadwick Hill

WATMOUGH HEAD

Agate Beach County Park

Iceberg Island

BLACKIE BRADY MEMORIAL BEACH

Aleck Bay

Point Colville

ICEBERG POINT

0   1 mi

0   1 km

© AVALON TRAVEL

the 1791 expedition of explorer Francisco Eliza. Haro Strait is another of his namesakes.

The Coast Salish people occupied Lopez Island for thousands of years, and the coastline is littered with archaeological sites. Whites first settled the island in the 1850s. They found incredible forests covering a rich land that would prove perfect for farming, a heritage that continues today. By the middle of the 20th century, Lopez was known as the Guernsey Island, and more than 130 farms produced milk, eggs, poultry, veal, pork, peas, vetch, oats, barley, and wheat. Nearly all the big farms are gone, but agriculture is still important. Today, the farms are smaller and more specialized, offering everything from organic beef to cut flowers.

PLANNING YOUR TIME

Lopez reaches 17 miles north to south, and approximately 4 miles across. Flat or gently rolling terrain, open country, and relatively straight roads make it easy to cover the island in a day—even on a bike. It's the first ferry stop heading west from Anacortes and has a couple of campgrounds near the ferry landing on the north end, making it perfect for relatively short visits, such as a weekend.

Because it's so easy to get around, you can stay almost anywhere on the island and still be just a few miles from the main settlement of **Lopez Village.** There aren't a lot of "sights" to discover, but this rural island is a perfect place to explore by bicycle. Most of the land is privately owned, but a handful of small parks and preserves remain in public hands, including **Spencer Spit State Park** on the northern end of the island. This park is popular not only for beachcombing, camping, and picnicking, but also as a launching point for sea kayaks. A number of mooring buoys are just offshore. **Iceberg Point** is an especially scenic spot on the south end of the island. Other small but interesting wild areas include Hummel Lake Preserve, Shark Reef Sanctuary, Odlin County Park, and Agate Beach County Park.

Sights

Lopez's main attraction is its pastoral countryside. The long stretches of hills, fields, orchards, and woods could just as well be rural Vermont, complete with contented cows. You might even see flocks of sheep being driven along local roads. Bucolic Lopez Island is a delightful place to explore, but unfortunately, much of the shoreline and many of the beaches are privately owned and closed to the public.

Picturesque **Fisherman Bay** is the boating center for Lopez, with two marinas and a small fleet of commercial fishing boats, including a few distinctive reefnet boats unique to this area.

★ LOPEZ VILLAGE

This small settlement near Fisherman Bay is as developed as things get on Lopez, with all the "necessities" of life: restaurants, fresh baked goods, espresso, video rentals, art galleries, books, a farmers market, and hot dogs. Like the rest of the island, it's laid-back, and stores may or may not open at the posted hours.

Lopez Historical Museum

The **Lopez Historical Museum** (Weeks Rd., 360/468-2049, www.lopezmuseum.org, noon-4pm Wed.-Sun. May-Sept., by appointment only Oct.-Apr., $2) contains local flotsam and jetsam: old farm equipment, a stuffed albino red-tailed hawk, historical photos, and changing exhibits. Outside, find a reefnet fishing boat, a gillnetter, and an aging tractor.

Historic Buildings

Several buildings around the island are worth

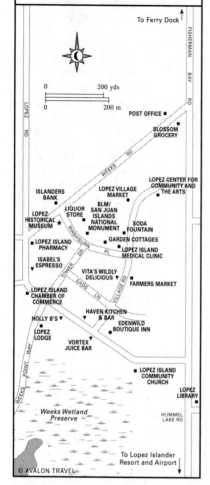

Lopez Village

To Ferry Dock

FISHERMAN BAY RD

LOPEZ RD

0   200 yds
0   200 m

POST OFFICE ■

■ BLOSSOM
GROCERY

WEEKS RD

LOPEZ CENTER FOR
COMMUNITY AND
THE ARTS

ISLANDERS
BANK ■

LOPEZ VILLAGE
MARKET ■

BLM/
SAN JUAN
ISLANDS
NATIONAL
MONUMENT ■

LIQUOR
STORE ■

LOPEZ
HISTORICAL
MUSEUM ★

SODA
FOUNTAIN

WASHBURN PL

■ LOPEZ ISLAND
PHARMACY

GARDEN COTTAGES ■

TOWER DR

LOPEZ ISLAND
MEDICAL CLINIC

ISABEL'S
ESPRESSO ■

VITA'S WILDLY
DELICIOUS ▼

EADS LN

VILLAGE RD

■ FARMERS MARKET

■ LOPEZ ISLAND
CHAMBER OF
COMMERCE

HAVEN KITCHEN
& BAR ▼

HOLLY B'S ▼

EDENWILD
BOUTIQUE INN

■ LOPEZ
LODGE

VORTEX ▼
JUICE BAR

WEEKS POINT WAY

■ LOPEZ ISLAND
COMMUNITY CHURCH

LOPEZ
LIBRARY ■

*Weeks Wetland
Preserve*

HUMMEL
LAKE RD

To Lopez Islander
Resort and Airport

© AVALON TRAVEL

a gander. Pick up a historical landmark tour brochure from the museum for all the details. The white New England-style **Lopez Island Community Church** in Lopez Village was built in 1904 and is notable for its steeple, which splits into four cupolas. **Center Church,** built in 1887, is a simple white structure surrounded by a picket fence and next to a hilltop cemetery. The church is home to both Catholics and Lutherans (what would Martin Luther say?) and is about two miles south of Lopez Village on Fisherman Bay Road. It's a favorite spot for island weddings.

The **Lopez Library** (just east of Lopez Village) is housed in a bright red-and-white building that began life in 1894 as a schoolhouse. Built in 1917 and used until 1940, the restored **Port Stanley School** is on Port Stanley Road near Hummel Lake; call the museum at 360-468-2049 for tours. Also of interest is the **Lopez Grange** (built in 1908) on the south end of the island along Richardson Road.

★ LOPEZ ISLAND VINEYARDS & WINERY

Head a mile north of Lopez Village on Fisherman Bay Road to **Lopez Island Vineyards & Winery** (724 B Fisherman Bay Rd., 360/468-3644, www.lopezisland-vineyards.com), a family operation that grows pesticide-free grapes on six acres of land. The grapes grown here are Madeleine Angevine (a white-wine grape from the Loire Valley of northern France) and Siegerrebe (a cross between Madeleine Angevine and Gewürztraminer). In addition to producing award-winning wines from local grapes, winemaker Brent Charnley, trained in enology at the University of California, Davis, uses grapes from Washington's hot and dry Yakima Valley for his chardonnay, merlot, and cabernet sauvignon-merlot wines. Lopez Island Winery also produces several fruit wines—primarily from locally grown organic fruits—including raspberry, blackberry, and apple-pear wines. Lopezians harvest all the grapes by hand at a community picking party in early October.

The winery's **tasting room** is in Lopez Village (265 Lopez Rd., 360/468-4888, noon-6pm Wed.-Sun. July-Aug., reduced hours in fall and spring, closed Jan.-Mar.) across from Isabel's Espresso. The vineyards themselves are open during twice-weekly events in July and August, with classical music on Saturday afternoons and jazz on Thursday evenings. There's a large tent for inclement weather or to get out of the sun. Buy a glass or bottle of wine and bring your picnic lunch to enjoy surrounded by landscaped gardens. See Lopez Island Vineyards' Facebook page or website for upcoming music and events.

FARMS

Several dozen farms dot the Lopez Island landscape, producing such specialty products as blackberry jams, mohair yarn, Asian pears, organic garlic, Nubian goats, heirloom tomatoes, Kobe beef, and cut flowers, and even Navajo Churro sheep. One of the most interesting is **Horse Drawn Farm** (2823 Port Stanley Rd., 360/468-3486), where vegetables, lambs, hogs, and cattle are raised—primarily with animal power. You might even see someone plowing a field with oxen. Tours are available by appointment. Also worth a visit is **Lopez Island Farm** (193 Cross Rd., 360/468-4620, www.lopezislandfarm.com), raising sheep and pasture-raised pigs.

For a complete list of island farms, pick up the **_Lopez Island Farm Products Guide_** at the museum or chamber of commerce office. Farm stands pop up in the summer, and many local farm products are sold at the Lopez Island Farmers Market, held on summer Saturdays in Lopez Village.

PARKS

Created by President Obama in 2013, **San Juan Islands National Monument** (360/468-3754, www.sanjuanislandsnca.org) covers 1,000 acres of land in a multitude of locations, including three places on Lopez Island: Iceberg Point, Point Colville, and Watmough Bay; all three are described below. The national monument is maintained by the Bureau of Land Management, operating from a tiny office next to the liquor store in Lopez Village. The one lonely staff person is often out working on trails, so hours can be haphazard, but there's a rack out front with maps and brochures describing the monument.

San Juan Islands Preservation Trust (360/468-3202, www.sjpt.org) has an office on Fisherman Bay Road. The **Lopez Bicycle Alliance** (www.members.shaw.ca/lopezbeaches) produces a helpful map that details publicly accessible beaches on Lopez; paper copies are available at the chamber of commerce.

★ Spencer Spit State Park

On the east side of Lopez Island, the 130-acre **Spencer Spit State Park** (360/468-2251, www.parks.wa.gov, Mar.-Oct.) has a half-mile beach with good clamming, beachcombing,

farm on Lopez Island

hiking, and picnicking. The sandy shoreline is strewn with driftwood, and a reconstructed cabin—part of an old homestead belonging to the Spencer family—sits at the end of the spit. The spit points like an arrow to nearby **Frost Island,** less than a hundred feet from its tip. Frost is private and rocky, with a handful of homes. Spencer Spit hems in a brackish lagoon that frequently hosts ducks, herons, gulls, and shorebirds. Rabbits and black-tailed deer are common evening sights in the park. Day use of the park costs $10 per vehicle.

Spencer Spit State Park has excellent campsites, but if you're pitching a tent here, you won't be the first person to do so. Not only is it a very popular destination today, but the Coast Salish people also used it for at least 3,000 years as a seasonal fish camp. In addition to camping, park facilities include 12 very popular mooring buoys ($15), drinking water, restrooms, and an RV dump station. Spencer Spit doesn't have a boat ramp or dock, but the beach is a launching spot for sea kayaks; ask at the park office for access via a service road so you don't have to carry your kayaks and gear too far. Kayak and bike rentals are available from a beachside kiosk. Kayakers heading out overnight will need to get a parking permit ($10/day).

Odlin County Park

Located on the north end of Lopez just a mile from the ferry landing, **Odlin County Park** (360/468-2496, www.co.san-juan.wa.us/parks) has a sandy beach along Upright Channel with views of nearby Shaw Island. Two short paths provide a bit of diversion here: **Big Tree Trail** leads through a stand of giant old-growth Douglas firs and **Little Bird Trail** offers up bluff-top viewpoints. Campsites, picnic areas, a boat launch, and a baseball field are also in the park, and the abundant rabbits are a treat for kids.

Upright Channel State Park

The 20-acre **Upright Channel State Park** is accessible from a parking area on Military Road. A short, wooded walk takes you to four picnic tables on the beach, but public access is limited to the immediate area because adjacent beaches are private property. Four mooring buoys are just offshore.

Agate Beach County Park

Very few of Lopez's beaches are open to the public. One exceptional exception is **Agate Beach County Park,** on the south end of the island at the end of MacKaye Harbor Road. Across the road from the beach are a few parking spaces, a picnic area, and outhouses. The pebbly beach is filled with colorful wave-rounded stones. I've never found agates here, but persistent rock hounds might find a few. At low tide you can walk to the tiny island just offshore.

★ Iceberg Point

Located on the southern end of the island, picture-perfect **Iceberg Point** is accessed from the parking lot at Agate Beach County Park. Walk south up MacKaye Harbor Road past signs noting End of County Road and Private Road (ignore the No Trespassing signs) for 100 yards or so, before turning right at the small Iceberg Point sign. A trail (no bikes) leads 0.5 mile through the bird-filled forest (look for salmonberries in early summer) to open grassy slopes and rocks at the end of the point. On a clear day you'll be treated to vistas of Mount Baker and the Cascade Range to the east, with the Olympics rising to the southwest. The land is managed by the Bureau of Land Management; get a map from its Lopez Village office to make sure you're not trespassing. Do not drive on the private road. The **Iceberg Point Project** (www.iceberg-pointproject.org) is conducting ongoing bird studies here.

Lopez Hill

Managed by the San Juan County Land Bank (360/378-4402, www.sjclandbank.org), **Lopez Hill** is a 400-acre parcel of wooded land near the center of the island with parking at a trailhead off Lopez Sound Road. A maze of trails provides several miles of fun hiking, horseback riding, and mountain biking beneath tall Douglas fir trees. The hill has many small wetlands where you may see salamanders, frogs, and newts, and there are some open rocky bald areas. The **Friends of Lopez Hill** produces a helpful map showing hiking trails and access; get a copy from the chamber of commerce or download one at www.lopezhill.org.

Shark Reef Sanctuary

Shark Reef Sanctuary is a fine small natural area at the end of Shark Reef Road on the southwest side of Lopez. An easy 0.5-mile path takes you through one of the few old-growth stands of trees (including Douglas fir, lodgepole pine, and Pacific yews) left on the island. It ends at a rocky coastline, a good place to look for harbor seals and sea lions sunning on nearby rocks, while bald eagles wheel through the sky and black oystercatchers call from the rocks. Less than a mile away is the southern end of San Juan Island, with the grassy slopes of American Camp capped by Cattle Point Lighthouse. The narrow passage frequently develops turbulent flows when the tide is changing. Tiny **Deadman Island**—just offshore south of Shark Reef—is owned by the Nature Conservancy

(206/343-4344, www.tnc-washington.org); no public access is permitted.

Weeks Wetland Preserve

This 22-acre saltwater marsh that comprises **Weeks Wetland Preserve** is on the north end of Fisherman Bay and adjacent to Lopez Village. A short loop trail leads to an observation deck overlooking this important resting area for migrating birds, and interpretive signs describe the animals and plants that live here.

Otis Perkins County Park

The scenic beach at **Otis Perkins County Park**—one of the longest on the islands—is located along Bayshore Road on the south end of Fisherman Bay. The west-facing location makes this a fine sunset stroll, with San Juan Island and the Olympic Mountains accenting the horizon. A couple of picnic tables are also here. The beach (day use only) is public north from the parking area, but to the south it becomes private property.

Fisherman Bay Preserve

The north end of the peninsula is the 29-acre **Fisherman Bay Preserve,** also known as **The Spit.** Get here by continuing north on

SIGHTS

Shark Reef Sanctuary

Bayshore Road and then taking a right on Peninsula Road. Stay right where the county road ends and continue to a parking area. Trails cut through tall grass and past remains of an old home to a point of land overlooking bucolic Fisherman Bay and Lopez Village.

★ Watmough Head

The Bureau of Land Management owns several easily accessible natural areas on the southeast end of Lopez Island off Watmough Head Road. Access to this area is confusing, and local landowners sometimes have No Trespassing signs posted on public land, so contact the BLM office in Lopez Village for a detailed map and specific directions. No motorized vehicles or camping are allowed, and please follow the leave-no-trace ethic to preserve these environmentally significant places.

The most accessible area is **Watmough Bay;** look for the Watmough Bay sign on the left at the bottom of a hill in the woods. The road leads to a parking area where a 0.25-mile trail continues to a protected beach, hemmed in by rocky cliffs, a marsh, and dense woods. On a clear day, Mount Baker stands front-and-center from the pebbly shore. Don't be surprised if you also see a bit of skin; nobody seems to care at this de facto nude beach. Take the trail south from the east end of the beach to a wooded ridge along **Watmough Head,** or scramble up steep slopes to nearby **Chadwick Hill** (470 feet). The hill can also be accessed from an unmarked trail off Watmough Head Road.

Point Colville is farther out Watmough Bay Road (a rough dirt road), and a bit tricky to find. Drive 0.25 mile past the End of County Road sign. There's a small parking area in front of the gate marked "Private." The Point Colville trail heads into the woods on the right side, and a short distance down is a trailhead sign. The path continues through the woods for a one-mile loop south to a cove and beach along the Strait of Juan de Fuca.

Hummel Lake Preserve

The 79-acre **Hummel Lake Preserve** is one of many areas protected by the San Juan County Land Bank (360/378-4402, www.sjclandbank.org). A pleasant trail passes through the woods to a tiny dock along this lake near the middle of Lopez. The path starts off Center Road, where you'll find picnic tables and an outhouse.

Blackie Brady Memorial Beach

The little county-owned **Blackie Brady Memorial Beach** is a fine, out-of-the-way place to escape. Find it on the south end of Lopez along Hughes Bay; turn right on Huggins Road off Aleck Bay Road. Huggins ends at a couple of parking spaces with stairs leading to this gorgeous cove.

Recreation

The **Lopez Island Family Resource Center** (360/468-4117, www.lifrc.org) puts on a wide range of activities open to the public, from sailing lessons to kayaking and watercolor classes.

SEA KAYAKING

If you're taking your kayak on the ferry to Lopez, note that you can't access the water near the ferry terminal. The closest put-in is Odlin County Park, a mile away. Other commonly used places to put your kayak in the water include Spencer Spit State Park, the marinas on Fisherman Bay, and boat ramps at MacKaye Harbor and Hunter Bay.

On the grounds of Lopez Islander Resort, **Lopez Kayaks** (130 Normandy Lane, 360/468-2847, www.lopezkayaks.com, late May-Sept.) rents and sells sea kayaks from its beach location along Fisherman Bay. Double plastic kayaks go for $60 per day ($80/day for fiberglass touring doubles or triples). Lopez

Bicycle Works has a shop right next door; the shops are father-and-son operations.

The **Outdoor Adventures Center** (425/883-9039 or 800/282-4043, www.outdooradventurecenter.com) rents sea kayaks and bikes from a kiosk at Spencer Spit State Park. It's open daily late May to early September, with singles, doubles, and triples available by the hour. Rent a stand-up paddleboard or kayak to paddle across to James Island or to explore the nearby shoreline. The company also has various tours from Spencer Spit, from a three-hour guided paddle ($89) up to three-night explorations of the San Juan Islands.

BOATING, FISHING, AND WHALE-WATCHING

Lopez's two marinas are next to each other along Fisherman Bay. Both offer guest moorage, boat-launching ramps, and restrooms with showers. It's less than a mile from the marinas to "downtown" Lopez Village. **Islands Marine Center** (360/468-3377, www.islandsmarinecenter.com) has a 100-slip marina and the largest marine repair operation in the San Juans, plus a chandlery, marine supplies, fishing licenses, boat-launch ramp, showers, and apartment

rentals. Immediately to the south is **Lopez Islander Resort and Marina** (360/468-2233 or 800/736-3434, www.lopezfun.com), with a 64-slip marina, boat fuel, propane, laundry, and groceries, plus a small resort with lodging, camping, RV sites, a restaurant, gift shop, and lounge. Just down the road is a dock and transient slips for boaters visiting Galley Restaurant and Lounge.

Patrick Cotton of **Harmony Charters** (360/468-3310, www.harmonycharters.com) rents a luxurious 65-foot motor yacht, the *Countess*, for $375 per person per day including meals and crew. The boat is based in Fisherman Bay, and there's a four-person minimum, with a maximum of six.

You'll find public boat-launch ramps at Odlin County Park on the north end of the island, and at MacKaye Harbor and Hunter Bay on the south end.

Fishing charters—primarily for salmon and halibut—are offered by **Outer Island Excursions** (360/376-3711, www.outerislandx.com) and **North Shore Charters** (360/376-4855, www.orcasislandadventures.com). Expect to pay around $250 per person for a four-hour fishing expedition. Join Outer Island for a three-hour **whale-watching** tour; these depart Lopez Islander Resort and

kayaks along Fisherman Bay

cost $109 adults, $99 seniors, $89 ages 12-16, and $69 for younger kids.

Anglers may want to drop a line at **Hummel Lake,** just a mile east of Lopez Village along Hummel Lake Road. The largest freshwater lake on Lopez, this is also a pleasant spot for a picnic lunch if you're cycling around the island. A trail leads into a small cedar grove and eventually winds up at the floating dock.

★ BIKING

A favorite local activity is pedaling the 30-mile loop around Lopez Island. Once you get beyond the steep initial climb from the ferry dock, the rest of the island consists of gently rolling hills, making Lopez ideal for family rides. Center Road is relatively busy and best avoided, but most of the other roads don't see a lot of traffic. Before heading out, pick up biking maps from the chamber of commerce office or bike shops showing recommended routes, roads that get heavy traffic, and loop rides on Lopez.

Village Cycles

In business since 1978, **Lopez Bicycle Works** (at Lopez Islander Resort, 2847 Fisherman Bay Rd., 360/468-2847, www.lopezbicycleworks.com) is the oldest bike shop on the San Juans. Road and mountain bikes rent for $7 per hour or $30 per day, including a helmet. Tandem, road bikes, children's bikes, recumbent bikes, tagalongs, trailer carts, car bike racks, and panniers are also available. Reservations are recommended, especially for midsummer weekends. The shop is open daily late May-early September, but bikes may be available in the off-season if you call ahead. The shop can drop off or pick up bikes at the ferry landing for $5. No tours are offered, but cycling the island is easy enough for almost anyone, and it's hard to get lost.

A full-service bike shop in the heart of Lopez Village, **Village Cycles** (214 Lopez Rd., 360/469-4013, www.villagecycles.net, Mar.-Oct.) rents hybrids, road, and electric bikes, plus child bikes, and tagalongs.

Hybrid bikes are at $7 per hour or $30 per day; add $5 for delivery to the ferry terminal. Electric-assist bikes are $16 per hour and performance bikes cost $13 per hour. Tours start at $60 for a two-hour ride ($85 with an electric-assist bike), everything provided.

Seasonal mountain bike rentals are also available from a small kiosk within Spencer Spit State Park operated by **Outdoor Adventures Center** (425/883-9039 or 800/282-4043, www.outdooradventurecenter.com) for $25 per day.

For Lopez Island cycling tours, contact one of the following companies: **Terra Trek** (40 Spring St., 360/378-4223 or 888/441-2433, www.goterratrek.com), **Backroads** (510/527-1555 or 800/462-2848, www.backroads.com), **Bicycle Adventures** (425/250-5540 or 800/443-6060, www.bicycleadventures.com), or **Trek Travel** (608/441-8735 or 866/464-8735, www.trektravel.com).

GOLF AND FITNESS

Lopez Island Golf Club (360/468-2679, www.lopezislandgolf.com, year-round, $20-25) is a nine-hole, par-35 public course along Airport Road.

Housed within Lopez Islander Resort, **Lopez Islander Gym** (2864 Fisherman Bay Rd., 360/468-4911, www.lopezfun.com) has exercise equipment and tanning booths. A $6 day pass includes access to the seasonal outdoor pool and year-round hot tub; $10 also gets you in the gym.

If you have teens, be sure to check out **Lopez Skate Park** next to the community center in Lopez Village. The park was a gift from Skatelite.

Shopping

Note that many Lopez businesses are closed Monday (and some also on Tuesday) in the summer and some aren't open at all in the winter.

The **Lopez Artist Guild** website (www.lopezartistguild.com) provides descriptions of local artists. The Lopez Island Studio Tour over Labor Day weekend in early September encompasses more than 30 artists. Don't miss **Chimera Gallery** (Lopez Village Plaza, 360/468-3265, www.chimeragallery.com), a cooperatively run gallery with unusual blown-glass pieces, etchings, ceramics, watercolors, pottery, sweaters, cedar baskets, and jewelry.

Christa Malay Studio (341 Shoal Bay Lane, 360/468-2159, www.christamalay.com), on the north end of the island, exhibits the artist's bright watercolor, oil, and pastel paintings; it's open by appointment only. Renowned painter Steven Hill exhibits his pastels at **Windswept Studios** (783 Port Stanley Rd., 360/468-2557, www.windsweptstudios.com).

Get new and used books along with cards from cozy **Lopez Bookshop** (211 Lopez Rd. in Lopez Village, 360/468-2132, www.lopezbookshop.com). **Paper Scissors on the Rock** (131 Weeks Rd., 360/468-2294) is a stationery and arts and crafts shop that also has a good selection of cards, gifts, and toys.

For fashion on the cheap, head to the **Lopez Thrift Shop** at 83 Weeks Point Way.

Entertainment and Events

The modern **Lopez Center for Community and the Arts** (204 Village Rd., 360/468-2203, www.lopezcenter.com) was built entirely with local funding and is used for concerts, art exhibitions, theatrical productions, and other activities. Outdoor pavilion concerts are a staple in the summer months here.

Located at Lopez Islander Resort (2864 Fisherman Bay Rd., 360/468-2233, www.lopezfun.com), **Tiki Cocktail Lounge** has pool tables and live music on summer weekends. Just up the road, **Galley Restaurant and Lounge** (3365 Fisherman Bay Rd., 360/468-2713, www.galleylopez.com) has a pool table and live music on an irregular basis. It's the locals' hangout.

Held the last Saturday of April, the **Tour de Lopez** is a noncompetitive 5-, 10-, 18-, or 31-mile ride around the island, with a big community barbecue lunch afterward. This is a great family event with a maximum of 900 people. Register online at www.lopezisland.com/tourdelopez.htm by mid-March to be assured of a space.

The big event in Lopez Village comes, not surprisingly, on the **Fourth of July,** with a corny parade, fun run, live music, arts fair, library book sale, and a big display of fireworks (www.lopezfireworks.com) over Fisherman

Bay. It's said to be the largest private fireworks display in Washington, attracting multitudes of people to the island.

The popular **Lopez Island Studio Tour** (www.lopezstudiotour.com) takes place over Labor Day weekend, with over 30 artists participating.

You can also join in the fun at the annual **Harvest Festival** at Lopez Island Vineyards & Winery (360/468-3644, www.lopezislandvineyards.com) in early October. It's a combination party and community grape harvest. Held the Friday after Thanksgiving, **Winter Village Gathering** (www.lopezisland.com/winter.htm) brings holiday lights, decorations, bonfires, Christmas carols, and other traditions.

Food

Dining choices on Lopez are good but a bit limited, particularly in the winter when many places are shuttered. (Get there on a Tuesday evening in November and you'll find only a couple of places open.) In addition, local restaurants have a tough time finding workers, so some places may not be open for breakfast and lunch.

FINE DINING

★ **The Bay** (9 Old Post Rd. in Lopez Village, 360/468-3700, www.bay-cafe.com, dinner 5pm-9pm Thurs.-Tues., lunch noon-4pm Fri.-Sun. June-Sept., dinner 5pm-9pm Wed.-Sun., lunch noon-4pm Sat.-Sun. the rest of the year, $17-40) is Lopez Island's four-star restaurant, with a wonderful bayside location. All seats face Fisherman Bay, and the deck opens when the weather approves. Enjoy relaxing water views as you savor Northwest cuisine that includes seafood, local produce, wonderful salads, and grilled meats. Try the warm brie and onions appetizer, the Dungeness crab cakes, pork tenderloin, or the daily fish specials. The Bay opens for lunch and dinner all summer or weekend lunches at other times; reservations are essential.

In the heart of Lopez Village, ★ **Haven Kitchen & Bar** (210 Lopez Rd., 360/468-3272, www.lopezhaven.com, noon-9pm Wed.-Sun. in summer, noon-3pm and 5pm-8pm Wed.-Sat. the rest of the year, $12-15) is casually eclectic, with something to please any taste, from Thai fresh rolls and gado-gado tofu to pulled pork sliders and Native American fry bread. There are plenty of vegetarian options, including a "hot Mexican mess" quesadilla, packed with soy-chorizo, black beans, caramelized onions, fried eggs, pico de gallo, avocado, sour cream, salsa, and cotija cheese. Haven bakes deliciously decedent pastries too. Prices are reasonable, and there's a pleasant deck with large umbrellas. Because of its popularity, the restaurant often has a lengthy wait on weekend summer evenings.

BAR & GRILLS

In business since 1971, **Galley Restaurant and Lounge** (3365 Fisherman Bay Rd., 360/468-2713, www.galleylopez.com, $11-29) is right across the street from Fisherman Bay; there's even a dock for customers' boats. The working-class restaurant is open three meals daily, covering the basics with seafood, steaks, pasta, Mexican specialties (especially the chimichangas), fish-and-chips, and double-size bacon cheeseburgers. The food is surprisingly consistent, hence the always-packed parking lot out front. There's a bar with a half-dozen beers on tap, along with a pool table and sports on the television. The restaurant is open daily 8am-9pm, but the bar stays open much later. There's free Wi-Fi too. If you visit Lopez on a weekday in the off-season, this may be the only restaurant open in the evening.

Housed within Lopez Islander Resort, **Islander Bar & Grill** (2864 Fisherman Bay Rd., 360/468-2233 or 800/736-3434, www.lopezfun.com, 11:30am-9pm Mon.-Fri., 10am-9pm Sat.-Sun., $15-30) serves prime rib and seafood dinners, but it also opens for breakfast and lunch daily. The main attraction here isn't so much the food as it is the view from the harborside patio out back. It's a fine spot for a sunset drink, and the Tiki Lounge has pool tables and live music some weekends.

QUICK BITES

Located in the Homestead Building within Lopez Village, **Vortex Café and Juice Bar** (135 Lopez Rd., 360/468-4740, www.vortexonlopez.com, 10am-7pm Wed.-Sat. in summer, 10am-3pm Wed.-Sat. in winter, $5-12) serves healthy food using organic produce and ingredients whenever possible. On the menu are burritos, wraps, rice and bean bowls, salads, quesadillas, soups, smoothies, housemade chai tea, and a big choice of fruit and vegetable juice combinations. Faves include the black beans and corn wrap, and the smoked salmon, cream cheese, and feta version. For something different, try Vortex's green juice, blended from greens, celery, cucumber, and parsley. There are a few indoor seats, plus a couple of tables outside on the deck facing the old apple orchard.

Open for wildly delicious lunches and dinners to go, ★ **Vita's Wildly Delicious** (77 Village Rd., 360/468-4268, www.vitasonlopez.com, 11am-5pm Tues.-Sat., till 9pm Tues., till 8pm Fri., May-Sept., café closed Oct.-Apr., $5-11) is right across from the farmers market on Village Road North. Check the chalkboard for today's gourmet panini, or scan the deli for daily specials and such favorites as chicken satay, meatloaf, shrimp cakes with chipotle sauce, Lopez lamb pies, salads, and a delectable green-chili chicken breast. Drop by Vita's for Taverna Tuesdays 5pm-9pm, with very popular wood-fired pizzas. One side of the shop is devoted to an extraordinary selection of organic wines and small-production wines you'll never find at Safeway. Join locals for Friday evening wine tastings with music on the patio; it's $7 for three wines. Seating is limited inside, but colorful picnic tables are on the front patio. Service can be slow, so don't come here in a hurry. The wine shop at Vita's is open in winter, but no food is served.

BAKERIES, CAFÉS, AND SWEETS

★ **Holly B's Bakery** (Lopez Village, 360/468-2133, www.hollybsbakery.com, 7am-5pm Wed.-Mon. in summer, 7am-5pm Fri.-Sat., 7am-4pm Sun. Oct.-Nov., closed Dec.-Mar., $4-10) is *the* place to go for great breads (including a caramelized onion brie French bread), cookies, almond butterhorns, raspberry scones, gruyere croissants, and world-famous cinnamon rolls, plus focaccia and pizza by the slice.

The village hosts two good espresso joints a short walk from each other. **Lopez Coffee Shop** (360/468-3533, www.lopezcoffeeshop.com, 6:30am-5pm daily) is adjacent to Holly B's, while **Isabel's Espresso** (360/468-4114, 7:30am-5pm daily) is a relaxed hangout with an outdoor deck that attracts locals.

Also in the village—and just steps from Holly B's—is **Bucky's Lopez Island Grill** (360/468-2595, 11:30am-8pm daily Apr.-Sept., $9-11). Check the board for today's lunch or dinner specials, or try one of the justly famous fish tacos. The black 'n bleu burger (with Cajun spices and blue cheese) is another favorite. Dine inside, or on the (dog-friendly) waterside deck out back.

The **Just Heavenly Fudge Factory** (9 Old Post Rd., 360/468-2439, 10am-6pm daily in summer, $4-10) has 100 or so different fudges, including a heavenly salted caramel version. The shop also serves ultra-creamy ice cream by the cone, plus sundaes, root beer floats, milk shakes, and more. (The Lopez Island Creamery started here in 1993, but in 2010 moved to Anacortes to be closer to regional markets and reduce its carbon footprint). Try the unique "Lopezian" milk shake made from Chicoaji chili sauce and local blackberry jam.

MARKETS

The popular **Lopez Island Farmers Market** (www.lopezfarmersmarket.com, 10am-2pm

Sat. May-Sept.) in the village has fresh garden produce, flowers, preserves, plants, and eggs, along with arts and crafts.

Get groceries and general merchandise from **Lopez Village Market** (162 Weeks Rd., 360/468-2266, www.lopezvillagemarket. com, 7:30am-7pm daily year-round). The store moved and greatly expanded several years ago, and now features a deli, bakery, ATM, fresh produce, seafood, meats, bulk foods, wine, beer, firewood, and other supplies. The deli serves everything from fried chicken and burgers to pizza slices and pies.

In the heart of Lopez Village, **Blossom Grocery** (295 Village Rd., 360/468-2204, www.blossomgrocery.com, 9am-7pm daily) focuses on organic fare, including cheeses, milk, bulk foods, nuts, herbs, and local produce, along with island-raised lamb, beef, and pork.

On the south end of the island, the **South End General Store and Restaurant** (3024 Mud Bay Rd., 360/468-2315, www.southend-generalstoreandrestaurant.com, 7am-9pm Mon.-Fri., Sat.-Sun. 8am-9pm) has a fair choice of groceries, supplies, beer, wine, and gas. The restaurant cranks out cheeseburgers, fish tacos, deli sandwiches, wraps, evening steak and pasta, and Sunday brunches. The back deck and lawn are fun on a summer afternoon.

Lopez Liquor Store (Lopez Village, 360/468-2407, Tues.-Sat.) sells the hard stuff, along with beer and wine.

Accommodations

Only 80 or so rooms are available on Lopez Island, so it's a good idea to make reservations a month or more ahead of time to be assured of a space, particularly on summer weekends. If you want to stay at a specific place, make reservations in January or February for a mid-summer date. Many of the resorts, inns, and cottages also offer weekly rates. The Lopez Chamber of Commerce website (www.lopez-island.com) has links to local lodgings. All lodging prices quoted below are subject to an additional 10.1 percent tax.

WEEKLY RENTALS
For furnished homes on a weekly basis, contact **Lopez Village Properties** (360/468-5055, www.lopezisproperties.com) or **Windermere Lopez Island** (360/468-3344, www.wrelopez.com). Together they list more than 30 vacation rental properties on Lopez. These vary greatly, starting at $700 per week for a cozy cabin to $5,100 weekly for a spectacular five-bedroom waterfront estate with a private beach. Some of these may be available for shorter (three days and up) rentals. **Lopez Islander Resort** (360/468-2233,

www.lopezfun.com) also has weekly rentals around Lopez.

For additional weekly and nightly rentals on Lopez, browse **Airbnb** (www.airbnb. com), **VRBO** (www.vrbo.com), **Homeaway** (www.homeaway.com), **CouchSurfing** (www.couchsurfing.org), or **FlipKey** (www. flipkey.com).

RESORTS AND INNS
Lopez Islander Resort
Less than a mile south of Lopez Village, **Lopez Islander Resort** (2864 Fisherman Bay Rd., 360/468-2233, www.lopezfun.com) is an unpretentious, family-friendly waterside place where all units include mini-fridges and microwaves. A one-story building houses small motel-style rooms ($149 d Fri-Sat., $129 Sun.-Thurs.) with a queen bed in each. The larger two-story building has views of the bay from private decks, especially from the upper-level rooms. These units have one queen ($159 Fri.-Sat., $139 Sun.-Thurs.), two queen beds ($199 Fri.-Sat., $169 d F Sun.-Thurs.), or a king ($199 Fri.-Sat., $179 Sun.-Thurs.); the larger upstairs rooms are your best bet.

There's a two-night minimum on summer weekends, or three nights over holiday weekends. Also available are two modern and spacious family suites with three bedrooms, full kitchens (with dishes, utensils, and pans), and gas fireplaces for $279-299 per night or $1,475 per week for up to eight guests. A three-night minimum is required for the suites. Three nearby guesthouses provide plenty of room for families and groups; they run $245-349 per night or $1,195-1,995 per week. Pets are allowed in some rooms for an extra $20. Also at the resort are a very popular seasonal outdoor pool (the only one on the island), a year-round hot tub, a volleyball court, horseshoes, and a marina, restaurant, and lounge. Wi-Fi is available in the main building and restaurant, but not in guest rooms. Catch the free shuttle from the ferry or airport; it's the only taxi service on Lopez. This is a favorite place for boaters to pull in and dry out for a while, and Kenmore Air has direct floatplane flights from Seattle to the harbor.

Edenwild Boutique Inn

An elegant Victorian-style hotel in the heart of Lopez Village, ★ **Edenwild Boutique Inn** (132 Lopez Rd., 360/468-3238, www.edenwildinn.com, $190-270 d) is surrounded by floral gardens and rose arbors. The modern home features nine spacious and distinctive rooms, all with private baths. One room is wheelchair-accessible, and three of them have fireplaces that actually burn wood (a rarity in our turn-on-the-gas era). Most rooms have pullout sofas, and Room 8 ($270 for four people) has both a king and a queen bed. Kids are welcome at no additional charge, and there is no minimum stay. House-baked pastries and locally roasted coffee are available in the morning. There are no TVs in the rooms, but Wi-Fi is available.

The inn was purchased in 2013 by Anthony and Crystal Rovente, an energetic young couple with four children. They have transformed this B&B into a place where the focus is on adventure and romance. Guests can rent bikes or kayaks, join kayak tours, whale-watch on a sailboat, or take a guided hike led by the inn. There's even a free Edenwild Insider app to help visitors explore the island.

GUESTHOUSES, COTTAGES, AND SUITES
Nowak House and Cedar Ridge

Unique among the lodging places on Lopez Island, **Nowak House** (109 McBarron Lane, 206/329-3654, www.nowakhouse.com, $198

Edenwild Boutique Inn

d) was built in 2008 by Seattle glass artist James Nowak. Given its heritage, the enormous front windows shouldn't be a surprise, and the interior has a European elegance accented by the artist's blown-glass pieces. There's a loft bedroom, modern kitchen, living room with gas stove, bath with Italian tiles, flat-screen TV, Wi-Fi, and a large patio. The contemporary house faces a big meadow and MacKaye Harbor.

The same owner and contact information applies for **Cedar Ridge,** a large handcrafted log home just a half mile from the ferry landing. The two-story home has a bedroom with queen bed, kitchen, and stone fireplace. Both Nowak House and Cedar Ridge have the same rate: $198 d, with a three-night minimum in the summer. No kids or pets allowed.

Bay House and Garden Cottages

Two options are available at ★ **Bay Houses and Garden Cottages** (360/468-2259, www.interisland.net/cc). Two beautiful two-bedroom houses ($210-225 d, $25 for each additional guest) on Fisherman Bay have full kitchens and baths, with outside decks facing across the channel to San Juan Island. Two guest cottages ($160 d, $25 for each additional guest) are right in the heart of Lopez Village on a beautifully accented and flower-filled yard. The owners are professional landscapers, and the grounds reflect their aesthetics. Cottages include a queen-size bed, skylights, a kitchen, and a woodstove. Dogs ($35) are welcome at any of the units.

Islands Marine Center

Islands Marine Center (360/468-3377, www.islandsmarinecenter.com, $150 d) is the boating hub for Lopez, but it also rents out an apartment over the store, right across the road from Fisherman Bay. It has a full kitchen with dishes, private bath, woodstove, and TV. A second room can be added to the apartment for $50, and extra guests are $10 each. This is a good deal for families and groups: There is space for seven

people. A barbecue pit and picnic tables are out front, and Lopez Islander Resort is next door.

Islands View Village House

Right in the heart of Lopez Village, **Islands View Village House** (337 Lopez Rd., 360/468-2191, www.cowan.us.com) is right on the water, with gorgeous sunsets from the deck. The three-bedroom home sleeps six for $300 per night with a three-night summer minimum stay (two nights the rest of the year). It is nicely furnished, with a full kitchen, two baths, and a back deck, and it's steps away from the beach. Lopez Village restaurants and shops are just a short walk away.

Lopez Lodge

Three options are available at **Lopez Lodge** (Weeks Point Rd., 360/468-2816, www.lopezlodge.com) in the heart of Lopez Village: a studio apartment and two motel-style rooms with Wi-Fi and TVs. The studio ($155 for up to four) includes two queen-size beds and a full kitchen and bath, while the rooms ($85-115 d) are simpler, each with a bath, fridge, and microwave.

Lopez Retreat

A charming two-bedroom vacation home, **Lopez Retreat** (1795 Port Stanley Rd., 360/410-9149, www.lopezretreat.com) faces Swifts Bay close to Spencer Spit State Park. You'll find all the amenities, including a full kitchen, two baths, a wraparound deck, tall windows, a washer and dryer, Wi-Fi, and even a mooring buoy. This attractive home is primarily offered on a weekly basis ($1,200), but space may be available for shorter stays ($200/night with a three-day minimum). Book early if you plan to visit in July and August.

Meadow Wood Cottage

Set on a quiet five-acre spread near Spencer Spit, **Meadow Wood Cottage** (252 Coyote Lane, 360/468-4023 or 406/728-1777, www.

Finnish Pancakes

8 eggs
¼ cup honey
½ teaspoon salt
2 ½ cups milk
⅔ cup flour
4 tablespoons butter

Blend all ingredients except butter in a blender, alternating flour and milk last. Melt 4 tablespoons of butter in a large baking dish or pan (9 by 13 inches). Pour blended mixture into this dish and bake at 425°F for 20-25 minutes until puffed and golden. Drizzle with hot jam or sprinkle with nutmeg or powdered sugar. Serves 6-8 people. This recipe is almost like having custard for breakfast—something gentle for the awakening tummy and tongue.

Recipe courtesy of MacKaye Harbor Inn

rockisland.com/~joann, $175 d) is a two-bedroom, two-bath home with a full kitchen and deck. There's a four-night minimum stay in summer, three nights in winter.

Mud Bay Cabin

A fine budget option on the south end of the island, **Mud Bay Cabin** (4055 Mud Bay Rd., 360/468-3726, www.interisland. net/kpatrick, $120 d) has a cozy bedroom, kitchenette, and bath. Outside is a deck with gas barbecue plus a little hillside garden. The cabin is in the woods, but not far from the beach at Mud Bay. A two-night minimum is required.

Raven's Rook Lodging

A unique in-the-trees option, **Raven's Rook Lodging** (58 Wild Rose Ln., 360/468-2838 or 877/321-2493, www.ravensrooklodging.com) is just a short hike from Shark Reef Sanctuary on the south end of Lopez. Inside this post-and-beam cabin ($155 d) you'll find skylights, two queen-size beds, and a full kitchen and bath. A two-night minimum stay is required. Families are welcome, but no toddlers or pets are permitted.

BED-AND-BREAKFASTS
Lopez Farm Cottages and Tent Camping

For delightful in-the-country lodging, stay at the fairy-tale ★ **Lopez Farm Cottages** (607 Fisherman Bay Rd., 360/468-3555, www. lopezfarmcottages.com) just up the way from Lopez Island Vineyards. These four immaculate little cottages ($185 d) include queen beds, kitchenettes, gas fireplaces, a continental breakfast basket, and private baths with dual showerheads, and they share a delightful outdoor hot tub. Guests walk in the last 100 yards or so, and the intentional lack of phones or TVs—not to mention children (kids must be 14 or older)—helps preserve the quiet character. The adjacent pasture has several sheep, and you're almost guaranteed to see rabbits hopping around the grounds in the morning. Also here is a fifth cottage ($245 d) that is larger and more luxurious, with a king-size bed and private outdoor hot tub. You can drive up to this one, and it's wheelchair-accessible. Lopez Farm Cottages are especially popular with honeymooners and couples celebrating anniversaries. Wi-Fi is available at the cottages.

MacKaye Harbor Inn

This stately white farmhouse sits near the southern end of Lopez, directly across the road from protected Barlow Bay. Originally constructed in 1904, **MacKaye Harbor Inn** (949 MacKaye Harbor Rd., 360/468-2253 or 888/314-6140, www.mackayeharborinn.com) was the first place on Lopez to have electric lights. Today, four guest rooms ($185-245 d) and a lovely suite ($265 d) are available, all with private baths. The suite features a fireplace, private covered deck facing the setting sun, antique Italian furnishings, and a bath. The inn is just a stone's throw from a sandy beach where seals, otters, and eagles are common sights. Rent sea kayaks ($25/day) to explore nearby waters, or borrow a mountain bike to ride around the island. Guests are served a filling hot continental breakfast, along with port and chocolates in the evening.

Children 12 and up are welcome, and Wi-Fi is available. The inn is a dozen miles from the restaurants in Lopez Village, though the South End General Store is relatively close for groceries and meals.

CAMPING

Camping is available at four places on Lopez, but the two public campgrounds do not have showers. Coin-operated showers are available at the public restrooms near Lopez Village Market and the marinas on Fisherman Bay.

Odlin County Park

Just a mile south of the ferry landing, **Odlin County Park** (360/378-8420, www.sanjuanco.com/parks) has year-round waterfront campsites ($27), wooded sites ($22), and walk-in ($20) or shared hike-in/bike-in sites ($10). There are no RV hookups or showers, but the park does have a boat ramp, mooring buoy ($10), a sandy beach, and hiking trails. Make reservations ($7 extra) online only through the park website. Reservations are available April-October, and can be made five days to three months ahead; they're a wise idea on summer weekends.

Spencer Spit State Park

★ **Spencer Spit State Park** (360/468-2251, www.parks.wa.gov, open Mar.-Oct.), five miles from the ferry landing on the east end of Baker View Road, has standard campsites ($25-35) and bike-in/hike-in sites ($12), along with Adirondack-style shelters for groups. There are no showers or RV hookups, but there are restrooms and a dump station. The delightful sandy spit is a short walk from the campground. All sites fill early on summer weekends, so make reservations in advance ($10 fee) at 888/226-7688 or http://washington.goingtocamp.com. The separate Cascadia Marine Trail campsite ($12)

within the park is accessible by kayak or other beachable boat only.

Lopez Farm Cottages and Tent Camping

Located on a 27-acre spread, ★ **Lopez Farm Cottages and Tent Camping** (607 Fisherman Bay Rd., 360/468-3555, www.lopezfarmcottages.com, $48-52 d, $10 for each additional guest, closed Oct.-May) has 16 nicely designed walk-in "gourmet" campsites in the woods with hammocks, Adirondack chairs, and bocce ball. The central building contains, bathrooms, showers, a fireplace, picnic tables, charcoal barbecues, and a microwave. Firewood is available. Tent sites are ideal for couples and single travelers; the sites do not allow kids under age 14, and no trailers, RVs, or pets are permitted. Don't want to bring a tent and sleeping bags? Two "glamping" sites ($98 d) have a tent on a carpeted platform, with a queen-size futon bed made up inside and a cooler and chairs outside. All you need is a toothbrush and bath towel. Parking is in a separate location to cut down on noise and nighttime headlights.

Lopez Islander Resort

Less than a mile from Lopez Village, centrally located **Lopez Islander Resort** (2864 Fisherman Bay Rd., 360/468-2233 or 800/736-3434, www.lopezfun.com) has an abundance of in-the-open tent sites ($32 d) on the lawn, along with woodsy RV sites ($42 d with water and electricity). The shower house is next to a seasonal pool and year-round hot tub ($5 for a day pass), volleyball, and horseshoes. Kayak and bike rentals are available at the resort, which also has a full-service marina, motel, and restaurant. There's no Wi-Fi at the campground, but it's free at the main resort building that houses the restaurant and lounge.

Information and Services

Get local information at the helpful **Lopez Island Chamber of Commerce** (265 Lopez Rd., 360/468-4664, www.lopezisland.com, 10am-3pm Tues.-Sat. June-early Sept., 11am-3pm Wed.-Sat. in the off-season). It's in Lopez Village across from Isabel's. Be sure to pick up the free *Map and Guide of Lopez Island* here.

Quaint **Lopez Island Library** (Fisherman Bay and Hummel Lake Rds., 360/468-2265, www.lopezlibrary.org, 10am-5pm Mon. and Sat., 10am-6pm Tues., Thurs., and Fri., 10am-9pm Wed., closed Sun.) is close to Lopez Village. Use the computers here to check your email or surf the web; there's also free Wi-Fi. This library gets more usage per capita than any other in Washington.

LAUNDRY

Wash clothes at the self-service **Keep It Clean Laundry** (865 Fisherman Bay Rd., 360/468-3466), a mile north of Lopez Village; it's open daily. A second public laundry is inside **Lopez Islander Resort and Marina** (360/468-2233 or 800/736-3434, www.lopezfun.com).

KIDS STUFF

Lopez Elementary School has a **playground** and **Lopez Children's Center** (160 Village Rd., 360/468-3896, www.lopezchildrenscenter.com) provides day care on a space-available basis in a wonderful setting.

BANKING AND MAIL

Get cash from ATMs at **Islanders Bank** (45 Weeks Rd., 360/468-2295 or 800/843-5441, www.islandersbank.com) or **Lopez Village Market** (162 Weeks Rd., 360/468-2266, www.lopezvillagemarket.com).

Take care of your mailing needs at the **Lopez Post Office** (Weeks Rd., 360/468-2282) in Lopez Village.

MEDICAL AND VETERINARY CARE

Lopez Island Medical Clinic in Lopez Village (157 Village Rd., 360/468-2245, www.lopezislandmedical.org, 9am-5pm Mon.-Fri.) has a physician or nurse practitioner on duty, along with a lab and X-ray services. The clinic is open for primary care and emergencies, but the closest hospital is in Anacortes. Fill your prescriptions at **Lopez Island Pharmacy** (352 Lopez Rd., 360/468-2616 or 888/325-3269, www.lopezislandpharmacy.com, 9am-6pm Mon.-Fri.).

For pet care, contact **Ark Veterinary Clinic** (262 Weeks Rd., 360/468-2477).

Getting There and Around

San Juan Transit (360/378-8887, www.sanjuantransit.com, 10am-6pm Fri.-Sun. mid-June-early Sept.) has a summer-only weekend shuttle schedule on Lopez Island. Buses stop at the ferry dock, Odlin Park, Lopez Farm Cottages, Lopez Village Park, Fisherman's Bay, the golf course, Shark Reef Park, South End General Store, Lopez School, Hummel Lake, Spencer Spit State Park, and Lopez Village Market. The cost is $5 each boarding for adults, $3 for kids under 13, or get a day pass for $15 adults or $10 kids.

There are **no car rentals or taxi service** on Lopez, but Lopez Island Resort may be able to provide a shuttle for families willing to pay $5 a mile (free for resort guests) from the ferry.

Hitchhiking is not uncommon on Lopez Island, but you might end up in the back of a pickup atop a load of hay. It's relatively easy to

Lopez Island Mileage

	Ferry Landing	Spencer Spit State Park	Lopez Village	Agate Beach	South End General Store
Spencer Spit State Park	3				
Lopez Village	4	4			
Agate Beach	15	10	11		
South End General Store	14	15	12	7	
Shark Reef	9	19	6	5	5

get a ride from the ferry to Lopez Village if a ferry is off-loading.

WASHINGTON STATE FERRIES

Washington State Ferries (360/468-4095 for the Lopez ferry terminal, 206/464-6400 or 888/808-7977 for general info) dock at the north end of Lopez Island at Upright Head, about four miles from Lopez Village. Find all the details—including current ferry wait times—at www.wsdot.wa.gov/ferries. The ferry terminal has a couple of vending machines, but no food service.

Peak-season fares from Anacortes to Lopez are $14 for passengers and walk-ons, or $45 for a car and driver. Bikes are $4 extra, and kayaks cost $17 more. The fare for a car and driver to any of the other islands is $28; walk-ons and passengers ride free between the islands. There are no direct sailings from Lopez westward to Sidney, British Columbia, but you can take a ferry from Lopez to Friday Harbor and then connect with sailings to Sidney.

Lopez Island ferry dock

Tickets are needed if you're heading west from Lopez to Shaw, Orcas, or San Juan Islands, but not for travel east to Anacortes (even with a vehicle). Reservations are not taken for eastbound travel, but they do have quotas for the number of vehicles leaving Lopez bound to Anacortes, so get there at least an hour before your ferry departs.

Anyone traveling west from Anacortes to Lopez during a busy time of year should make **Save A Spot vehicle reservations** online at www.wsdot.wa.gov/ferries/reservations. Reservations can be made up to two months in advance, but they're not needed for passengers or walk-ons. No reservations are required for interisland runs (such as between Lopez and Orcas); just get in line and wait.

Here's a somewhat confusing tip that isn't widely publicized: If you're planning a short stop on Shaw Island or Orcas Island and then continuing westward to another island within 24 hours, request a **free vehicle transfer** before leaving the Lopez terminal. This is useful if you're on Lopez and heading to Friday Harbor (free stops at Shaw and Orcas), or going from Lopez to Orcas (free stop at Shaw). It saves you $28 for each stop, but you must ask for it on Lopez. Note that you cannot stop for more than 24 hours when using a vehicle transfer.

WATER TAXIS

Three companies are available for water taxi service from Lopez, but none are based on the island. These include **Paraclete Charters** (360/293-5920 or 800/808-2999, www.paracletecharters.com) and **Island Express Charters** (360/299-2875 or 877/473-9777, www.islandexpresscharters.com) in Anacortes and **North Shore Charters** (360/376-4855, www.orcasislandadventures.com) from Orcas Island.

AIR

Lopez Airport (www.portoflopez.com) is three miles south of Lopez Village.

San Juan Airlines (360/293-4691 or 800/874-4434, www.sanjuanairlines.com) has scheduled daily service to the airport from Anacortes and Bellingham, with connecting flights to San Juan, Orcas, and Blakely Islands. Flightseeing and air charters are also available.

Operating out of Lake Union in Seattle, **Kenmore Air** (425/486-1257 or 866/435-9524, www.kenmoreair.com) has daily scheduled floatplane flights for $150-161 one-way to Lopez Islander Resort Marina. A 25-pound baggage weight limit is in effect on these flights.

Other Islands

The San Juan archipelago contains a myriad of smaller islands, including some islets that only appear at low tide. Shaw Island is served by the ferry system but has limited services. Lummi Island is just a short distance from the mainland

and is served by an hourly ferry. Of the remaining islands, only Blakely has a store.

Beyond these islands are the various marine state parks and private islands, places often called the "outer islands." Even though these islands are not widely known outside the region, many still see large numbers of boat-in visitors, especially on summer weekends. This is particularly true for the marine state parks on Clark, James, Jones, Matia, Patos, Stuart, Sucia, and Turn Islands, where the campsites fill quickly and protected coves are dotted with motor yachts and sailboats.

San Juan Islands National Wildlife Refuge encompasses 83 islands, islets, and reefs within the archipelago. The largest, Matia Island, covers 145 acres, while many more are just tiny rocky points. These islands are vital nesting areas for bald eagles and seabirds, including pelagic and double-crested cormorants, pigeon guillemots, rhinoceros auklets, black oystercatchers, and glaucous-winged

gulls. Tufted puffins are also present in these waters, but they only breed on one undisclosed island in the San Juans. The NWR islands are also used as haul-outs for harbor seals, California and Steller sea lions, elephant seals, and other animals.

Boaters—including sea kayakers—must stay at least 200 yards offshore from these islands, and no landings are permitted except at designated areas on Turn and Matia Islands. The U.S. Fish & Wildlife Service office (Port Angeles, 360/457-8451, http://pacific.fws.gov) manages the refuge and can provide a small map of the islands. Marine navigation charts also denote islands within the refuge.

PLANNING YOUR TIME

Most travelers to the San Juans don't get beyond the three main islands of San Juan, Orcas, and Lopez, but the lesser-known islands also have much to offer, especially for those who love wild places. These less-visited

Previous: quiet road on Lummi Island; beach on the west end of Shaw Island. **Above:** Scottish Highlands bull at Our Lady of the Rock Monastery on Shaw Island.

Look for ★ to find recommended
sights, activities, dining, and lodging.

Highlights

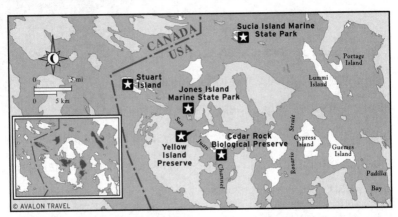

© AVALON TRAVEL

★ **Cedar Rock Biological Preserve:** Owned by the University of Washington, this little-known gem is located on the south side of Shaw Island (page 247).

★ **Jones Island Marine State Park:** A quick water taxi ride from Orcas Island, this easily accessible marine park has fun hikes, tall trees, and a gorgeous shoreline (page 257).

★ **Stuart Island:** Take a water taxi from Friday Harbor to this island, where you can hike to one of the most picturesque lighthouses in the San Juans (page 262).

★ **Sucia Island Marine State Park:** An exceptionally popular marine park, this diverse island is a favorite of kayakers, sailors, campers, and hikers (page 266).

★ **Yellow Island Preserve:** The Nature Conservancy allows daytime access to this 11-acre jewel, where more than 150 species of flowers bloom each spring (page 274).

islands are scattered across the archipelago and include a mix of public and private lands.

Best known of these "other islands"—and the only one visited by the state ferry system—is **Shaw Island,** home to a little country store, many well-heeled landowners, and a couple of natural areas: **Cedar Rock Biological Preserve,** which allows day use only, and **Shaw Island County Park,** with a handful of campsites.

Lummi Island is just west of Bellingham, with access via a county-run ferry. The island has very little public land, but comfortable lodging and cafés are available.

Quite a few of the more remote islands in the San Juans are marine state parks. They are popular with boaters, kayakers, campers, and day hikers, and are accessible by water taxi from the main islands, Anacortes, or Bellingham. **Jones Island Marine State Park** is a short boat ride from Deer Harbor on Orcas Island and features good mooring, camping, and easy hikes. **Stuart Island** lies

northwest of San Juan Island. Much of the island is privately owned, but the main harbors are public, and a pleasant day hike takes you to a lighthouse overlooking Boundary Pass.

Sucia Island Marine State Park is north of Orcas Island, with protected coves, miles of hiking and biking trails, good campsites, and a couple of sandy beaches. It's an especially popular place for sailboats to drop anchor.

A scattering of islands in the San Juans are privately owned or have only limited public access. Two of the islands (Canoe and Johns) have summer camps open to the public, and two others (Blakely and Decatur) have general stores and limited access or lodging. Sinclair Island has a boat dock and dirt roads leading to a 35-acre public park. The Nature Conservancy owns several San Juan Islands, the best known being tiny **Yellow Island,** a short water taxi ride from Friday Harbor or Orcas Island. It's famous for springtime floral displays and is open to the public during the day.

Shaw Island

The smallest and least visited of the ferry-served islands, Shaw is a primarily residential island where locals jealously guard their privacy. Around 200 people live here year-round, with two or three times that in the summer. Covering a bit less than eight square miles, it is the fifth largest of the San Juans (after Orcas, San Juan, Lopez, and Cypress). It sits at the center of the San Juan archipelago, with the Orcas ferry landing just 1.5 miles away from the Shaw ferry dock. A number of well-known and wealthy business leaders have homes on the island, including Bill Gates Sr., members of the Kaiser family, and executives from Boeing and the *Seattle Times.* Bill Gates Jr. also owns hundreds of acres of land on Shaw and may or may not have a house here.

Shaw Island received its appellation during the 1841 Wilkes Expedition. It was named for U.S. naval captain John Shaw, who fought

against the Barbary pirate states in 1815. The island was home to the Coast Salish people for thousands of years; one archaeological site at Blind Bay is 9,000 years old. The island supported far more people than now live here, with almost 750 Native Americans living here in the 1700s. Many of them died from diseases brought by Europeans or from raids by the Haidas, but some remained on the island. A few Salish women married American settlers.

Shaw Island remains essentially undeveloped, with second-growth forests, old orchards, and pastures covering most of the land. Prominently posted No Trespassing signs limit access to all but a few beaches. To outsiders, Shaw Islanders appear insular and anxious to keep the rest of the world away (which shouldn't be surprising). Shaw Islanders really don't care what the rest of the world does: They relish their peaceful

Other San Juan Islands

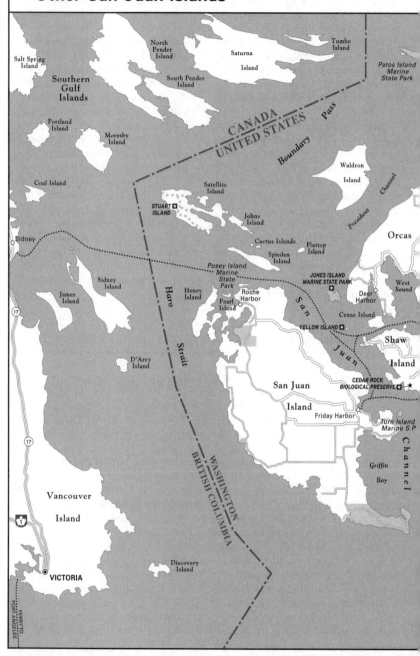

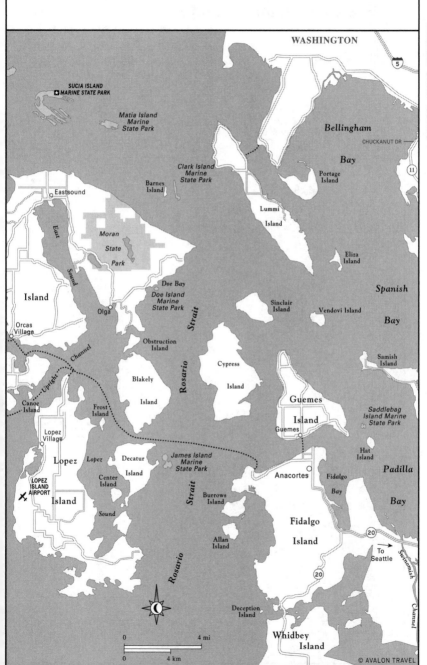

WASHINGTON

SUCIA ISLAND
MARINE STATE PARK

*Matia Island
Marine
State Park*

*Clark Island
Marine
State Park*

Bellingham

CHUCKNUT DR

Bay

*Barnes
Island*

Eastsound

Portage
Island

Lummi

Island

*Moran
State
Park*

East
Sound

Eliza
Island

Island

Doe Bay
*Doe Island
Marine
State Park*

Spanish

Olga

Sinclair
Island

Vendovi Island

Orcas
Village

Bay

Rosario
Strait

Obstruction
Island

Samish
Island

Channel

Cypress

Guemes

Upright

Blakely

Island

Island

*Saddlebag
Island Marine
State Park*

Canoe
Island

Frost
Island

Guemes

Hat
Island

Padilla

Lopez
Village

*James Island
Marine
State Park*

Anacortes

Fidalgo

Lopez

Decatur

Bay

Bay

LOPEZ
ISLAND
AIRPORT

*Center
Island*

Island

Rosario
Strait

Burrows
Island

Island

Fidalgo

To
Seattle

Sound

Allan
Island

Island

20

Swinomish Channel

Rosario
Strait

20

Deception
Island

Whidbey
Island

0   4 mi

0   4 km

© AVALON TRAVEL

Shaw Island and Vicinity

© AVALON TRAVEL

0   0.5 mi
0   0.5 km

Friday Harbor

San Juan
Island

San Juan Channel

FRIDAY HARBOR FERRY

YELLOW ISLAND
PRESERVE

Wasp
Islands

Low Island

Northwest McConnell
Rock State Park

McConnell
Island

Coon
Island

Nob Island

Neck
Point

Cliff
Island

NECK

Tilt Rocks

Point
Caution

Point
George

Parks Bay

POINT

BEN

NEVIS

RD

PRIVATE ROAD

Crane
Island

Wasp Passage

Reef
Island

Jones
Island

JONES ISLAND
MARINE STATE PARK

Steep
Point

Orcas
Island

Fawn
Island

Deer Harbor

Orcas
Island

Caldwell
Point

Broken
Point

Double
Island

Allegria Island

Vaclui
Island

West
Sound

Hoffman Cove

CEDAR ROCK
BIOLOGICAL PRESERVE

HOFFMAN   COVE   RD

OUR LADY OF THE
ROCK MONASTARY

LITTLE RED
SCHOOLHOUSE

SHAW ISLAND
HISTORICAL
MUSEUM

BLIND

SMUGGLERS COVE RD

BAY

Blind Island
Marine
State Park

FERRY
DOCK

Orcas

SQUAW BAY RD

Squaw Bay

Indian
Cove

SHAW ISLAND
COUNTY PARK

PRIVATE
ROAD

Blind
Bay

SHAW GENERAL
STORE

Harney Channel

Orcas
Island

CANOE ISLAND
FRENCH CAMP

Canoe
Island

Picnic Point

BAY

RD

Shaw
Island

LOPEZ ISLAND AND
ANACORTES FERRY

Flat Point

Upright Channel

Lopez Island

Hankin
Point

and slow-paced life, the lush landscape, and a grade school where the teacher-to-student ratio is 1:6. The island has a general store, one lodging place, a little post office, and two private airstrips, but no medical facility. The only other commercial business headquartered on Shaw Island is **Northwest Marine Technology** (www.nmt.us), the manufacturer of fish tags used all over the world.

There are no bike rental shops, kayak companies, B&Bs, or galleries on Shaw, and none are likely to appear. When kayakers started launching from a dock next to the ferry landing, Shaw Islanders purchased the land and posted signs to keep commercial kayak companies away. Sky-high land prices, minimal turnover, and locals who snatch up whatever comes on the market make it virtually impossible to buy property or a house on Shaw.

Independence Day on July 4th brings a little parade across the island and a potluck dinner. In early August, the **Round Shaw Row** (www.soundrowers.org) hosts rowboats, kayakers, and canoeists in a fun race around the island; the record is 1 hour and 39 minutes. On the first Saturday of August, a popular sailing race circumnavigates the island, the **Shaw Island Classic** (www.sjiyc.com).

SIGHTS AND RECREATION

Besides the preserve and county park, nearly all of Shaw is a look-only place. Despite this, the roads are quiet and the countryside is very scenic, making Shaw a wonderful place to explore by bicycle. You'll find old orchards, some beautiful homes, and peaceful vistas of nearby islands. From the ferry, Blind Bay Road follows the shore of this pasture-and-forest-bordered bay, with **Blind Island Marine State Park** in the middle. The westernmost end of Shaw Island, **Neck Point,** is especially picturesque, with the road passing over a slender peninsula where waves lap on both sides.

Shaw General Store

"Downtown" Shaw consists of the ferry dock, the **Shaw General Store** (360/468-2288,

www.shawgeneralstore.com, 9am-5pm Mon.-Thurs., 9am-6pm Fri.-Sun. May-Sept., closed Oct.-Apr.), and a couple of adjacent buildings. For almost three decades, the island's claim to fame was the Franciscan Catholic nuns who operated the ferry dock and store. The nuns left in 2004 when they grew too aged to continue their work. Today, the store and adjacent ferry terminal are run by friendly Steve and Terri Mason and their kids. Step inside the store for basic supplies and gifts, local produce and eggs, and ice cream cones and coffee, along with items made at Our Lady of the Rock Monastery: raw milk cheese, Mother Prisca's hot mustard, infused vinegars, herbal teas, and spice blends. Picnic tables and restrooms are nearby, and the little marina has a couple of slots for guest mooring.

The owners of Shaw General Store rent out the charming 1900s **Silver Bay Cottage** close to the ferry dock; find it at www.vrbo.com/334848. This nicely restored two-bedroom, one-bath cottage with a full kitchen, Wi-Fi, a glassed-in "wheelhouse," and a magnificent location along Harney Channel sleeps up to six guests for $175 per night; call 360/468-2288 for details. A two-night minimum stay is required. This is the only lodging place available on Shaw Island.

Our Lady of the Rock Monastery

Founded in 1977, **Our Lady of the Rock Monastery** (360/468-2321, www.olrmonastery.org) is home to eight Benedictine Catholic nuns who live on an immaculate 300-acre spread of forests and farmland. The nuns are sometimes called the "spinning nuns," and you might see them spinning and weaving hand-dyed yarn on the ferry to Shaw. Guest mistress Mother Hildegard George has a Ph.D. in child and adolescent psychology and is a leader in the field of animal-assisted therapy. Not surprisingly, the priory raises long-haired Scottish Highland cattle, black Cotswold sheep, Kerry cattle, llamas, alpacas, and a menagerie of pigs, turkeys, chickens, geese, ducks, peacocks, and other critters—all of which have names. The farm's state-licensed raw milk cheese is sold in the Shaw General Store and the Orcas Farmers Market. Tours of Our Lady of the Rock may be available, but call a day in advance. The order also has a small guesthouse for religious retreats. Call ahead before visiting the monastery; they are not welcoming of strangers who show up unannounced.

Shaw Island Historical Museum

Tiny **Shaw Island Historical Museum** (360/468-4068, 2pm-4pm Tues., 11am-1pm Thurs., 11am-1pm and 2pm-4pm Sat., free) is housed in a log cabin two miles from the ferry landing at the intersection of Blind Bay and Hoffman Cove Roads. Inside are historical photos and various farming and fishing implements, along with arrowheads and other Coast Salish artifacts. Out front is a reefnet fishing boat like those still used to fish for salmon in nearby waters. Next door is **Shaw Island Library** (360/468-4068), which keeps the same hours. If the museum is locked, ask for a key from the librarian.

Little Red Schoolhouse

Across the intersection from the museum and library is the one-room **Little Red Schoolhouse** (www.shaw.k12.wa.us), which is listed in the National Register of Historic Places. It's still in use today, with 15 or so students in grades K-8; a second building has been added in the back. Shaw's count-them-on-one-hand high school students commute by ferry to Orcas or San Juan Islands. If you have kids in tow, the school playground will be a required stop.

Shaw Island County Park

The 65-acre **Shaw Island County Park** (360/378-8420, www.sanjuanco.com/parks), also known as South Beach County Park, is one of the few public spots on the Shaw shoreline. It is two miles south of the ferry landing off Squaw Bay Road and faces Canoe Island, home to a French-language summer camp. The park is best known for its beautiful sandy beach—one of the best in the islands—where you'll sometimes find sand dollars. By midsummer, the shallow waters of Indian Cove are warm enough for a swim, and a picnic area and boat launch are available, along with outhouses.

The park includes six waterfront ($20) and five in-the-trees ($15) campsites, along with a shared hiker/biker site ($6 per adult), and

Shaw Island Historical Museum

Cedar Rock Biological Preserve

one Cascadia Marine Trail site for kayakers ($12). The campground has a cooking shelter and seasonal drinking water, but no showers. There are no other camping options on Shaw, so reserve ahead for peak-season weekends unless you want to catch the next ferry back to Anacortes. Visit the park website for online campground reservations ($7 extra); you can reserve from 5 days to 90 days in advance. The campground is open year-round.

★ Cedar Rock Biological Preserve

The University of Washington's **Cedar Rock Biological Preserve** (owned by the University of Washington Friday Harbor Laboratories, 360/378-2165, http://depts. washington.edu/fhl) is a quiet, off-the-beaten-path place on the south side of Shaw along Hoffman Cove. Open to the public, it comprises approximately 370 acres of rocky shorelines and forests dominated by stately Pacific madrones and Douglas firs. (The land was donated by Robert Ellis, and an adjacent

579-acre parcel was set aside by his brother Frederick and his wife, Marilyn. The latter portion—on the west side of the road—is for preservation and biological research only, with no public access.)

Get to Cedar Rock from the ferry by following Blind Bay Road to the schoolhouse and turning left (south) on the gravel Hoffman Cove Road. The road ends near the water's edge at the preserve, but parking is almost nonexistent, so bikes are a better way to get here. Sign in at the entrance box and head up the path to an old field with several homestead buildings and out to a small rocky point. Stop awhile to soak up the view across San Juan Channel and to watch the ferries steaming into Friday Harbor. From here, a rough path continues east along the shore to small coves with gravelly beaches, through pristine forests with periodic openings, and up rocky knolls. The route dwindles away, becoming little more than a game trail, but ambitious hikers could continue along the shore 1.5 miles to Squaw Bay, where you run into private land again. Most folks turn back before this, but even a short hike at Cedar Rock offers a relaxing respite. You may want to time your hike to coincide with low tide, making it easier to walk the beaches.

Kayaking, Boating, and Biking

The relatively protected waters and undeveloped shores of Shaw Island are very popular with sea kayakers. Randel Washburne's *Kayaking Puget Sound, the San Juans, and Gulf Islands* (The Mountaineers, www.mountaineers.org) has details on a 14-mile circumnavigation of Shaw Island. Unfortunately, you can't launch sea kayaks from the Shaw Island ferry landing; the closest place to do so is Shaw Island County Park, two miles away, or from Odlin County Park on Lopez Island.

The island's shoreline is also popular with sailors and motorboaters, and each August the **Shaw Island Classic** (www.sjiyc.com) yacht race circles the island.

Shaw Island, with its paved roads, bucolic country, and paucity of cars, is a delight for cyclists. Unfortunately, even Shaw can get busy in midsummer, particularly when large touring groups of cyclists roll off the ferry. Because of the island's small size, some cyclists just spend a half-day here, arriving in the morning to pedal around, then take a lunch break and head off to another island to pitch their tents.

GETTING THERE

Washington State Ferries (360/468-2142 for Shaw ferry terminal, 206/464-6400 for general info, or 888/808-7977 in Washington and British Columbia, www.wsdot.wa.gov/ferries) ply the waters around Shaw almost constantly, en route to Anacortes, Lopez Island, Orcas Island, Friday Harbor on San Juan Island, or Vancouver Island. Quite a few of these also stop at Shaw Island's little dock.

Peak-season summertime fares from Anacortes to Shaw are $14 for passengers and walk-ons, or $54 for a car and driver. Bikes are $4 extra, and kayaks cost $19 more. The fare for a car and driver from Shaw to Orcas Island or Friday Harbor is $28. Eastbound service from Shaw to Lopez or Anacortes is free, and there's never a charge for walk-on passengers traveling between the islands. There are no direct sailings from Shaw westward to Sidney, British Columbia, but you can take a ferry from Shaw to Friday Harbor and then connect with a ferry to Sidney.

If you're on Shaw and want to look around Orcas Island before continuing to Friday Harbor, be sure to request a **free vehicle transfer.** These are good for up to 24 hours, and getting one saves you $28, but you must ask for it on Shaw Island before getting on the ferry.

Anyone traveling from Anacortes to Shaw during the peak of summer should make **Save A Spot** vehicle reservations online at www.wsdot.wa.gov/ferries/reservations. Reservations can be made up to two months in advance, but aren't needed for passengers or walk-ons.

Lummi Island

Lummi (pronounced LUM-ee, as in tummy) is only an eight-minute ferry ride from the mainland, but since it is some distance from the other islands in the San Juans, it doesn't get a lot of attention. Lummi Island lies within Whatcom County, not San Juan County, and many people do not consider it part of the archipelago. At the peanut-shaped island's southern end is a steeply wooded mountain that slopes down abruptly to flatter land on the north end, which is where nearly all the residents live. The 800 or so locals are a diverse lot, with tony homes and dramatic waterside vistas just up the road from hardscrabble mobile homes where rusting trucks serve as lawn ornaments.

Lummi is a quiet island, home primarily to artists, weekenders, and a few salmon fishers, some of whom fish with reefnets. Most of the island is private property with no public access, and the undeveloped mountainous southern end of the island is off-limits, but you can ride the roads to public areas in front of the Beach Store Café just north of the ferry dock, and along a side road off West Shore Drive. Stop for a photo of reefnet boats along Legoe Bay and the charming **Lummi Island Congregational Church** (www.lummi-church.com) just up the road. The church has been here since 1903.

The Lummi people were the first inhabitants of the island, but they abandoned it after Haidas raided their village to capture slaves. By the time the first whites arrived in the 1870s, the Lummi had moved to the mainland. Today, 600 Lummi people live in scattered homes on the 13,000-acre Lummi Reservation at Gooseberry Point, where the ferry departs for the island.

The little **Lummi Island Library** (2144 S.

Nugent Rd., 360/305-3600) is open 2pm-8pm Tuesday and Thursday, 10am-5pm Saturday.

RECREATION

Bike rentals are not available on Lummi, so bring one over from Bellingham. Traffic is minimal, but roads are narrow and winding, with no shoulders—not the best for cyclists.

Beach access is very limited on Lummi Island, with a small public beach in front of the Beach Store Café and another near the Willows Inn. A large rock at the latter (visible at low tide) has a petroglyph depicting Tsagaglalal, or "She Who Watches." The private beach behind the Lummi Island Congregational Church is also open to the public.

The nonprofit **Lummi Island Heritage Trust** (3560 Sunrise Rd., 360/758-7997, www.liht.org) works to preserve land on the island, and now protects some 983 acres in several parcels. Its headquarters are in an old farm building at **Otto Preserve,** a 70-acre site near the center of the island on Sunrise Road. An easy 1.4-mile trail loops through the woods and wetlands.

Curry Preserve (2449 N. Nugent Rd.) occupies 42 acres on the north end of the island, with an old apple orchard, community garden, and footpaths through forests and fields.

The **Baker Preserve** contains 80 acres of public lands, along with another 1,000 acres protected by conservation easements. A steep trail climbs more than 1,000 feet in elevation over just 1.6 miles, ending at an overlook with extraordinary views west across Rosario Strait to the San Juan Islands.

West Shore Marine (360/303-1672, www.westshore-marine.com) provides whale watching trips and custom charters from Lummi Island. A personalized three-hour trips costs $285 for up to five people on a 22-foot rigid hull inflatable Zodiac. Float coats are provided, and picnic lunches are available.

ENTERTAINMENT AND EVENTS

One corner of the Islander grocery store houses **Sisters Bountiful Mercantile** (2106 South Nugent Rd., 360/758-2190, www.islandergrocery.com, 6am-10:30pm daily), selling island arts and crafts. Pick up a copy of the Lummi Island Artist Studios Self-Guided Tour map

Also check out **Good Thunder Arts** (2307 Tuttle Ln., 360/758-7121) for beautiful pottery. Call ahead to see one of the more interesting local places, **Sculpture Woods** (3851 Legoe Bay Rd., 360/758-2143, www.sculpturewoods.

Lummi Island Congregational Church

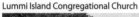

Lummi Island

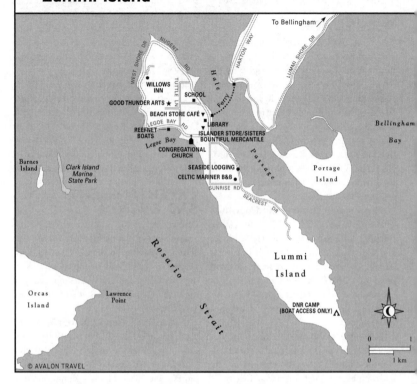

com), where Ann Morris has positioned 16 large bronze pieces that appear to be emerging from the earth. **Lummi Island Artists' Studio Tours** (360/758-7121) are popular events over Memorial Day and Labor Day weekends, and in mid-November.

Held on the Lummi Reservation, the **Lummi Stommish Water Festival** (360/384-1489, www.stommish.com) in mid-June features competitive war-canoe races over a five-mile course, with up to 11 people per canoe. Other activities include arts and crafts sales, Native American dancing, and a salmon bake.

FOOD

Foodies already know about ★ **The Willows Inn** (2579 W. Shore Dr., 360/758-2620 or 888/294-2620, www.willows-inn.

com, Wed.-Sun., closed Jan.-mid-Mar.), one of the most acclaimed restaurants in the state. Under the direction of chef Blaine Wetzel, the restaurant has gained national acclaim, and was ranked the top Northwest restaurant by the James Beard Foundation in 2015. A few years before that, the *New York Times* labeled it "One of 10 restaurants in the world worth a plane ride." A single seating at 7pm (6:30pm in winter) is available for the astounding 20-course prix fixe chef's tasting menu ($195 per person, $90 wine pairing). Guests linger over a 3.5-hour meal of locally sourced seafood and vegetables—from smoked mussels to pumpkin seed fudge and cordial. With just 25 seats, the restaurant books up far ahead of time. Most people dining at The Willows are lodging guests as well, and they make restaurant reservations when

Reefnet Fishing

When we went out there and put in those reef nets, we caught fish right off starting the first day and the white fishermen never had one to eat. They didn't know how to catch them. They didn't know how to use a reef net. Every night when we'd go home, you could go down and sit on the beach and see them out there measuring our reef net and copying it.

Herman Olsen, *Lummi Elders Speak,* edited by Ann Nugent

This unique and ingenious way to catch salmon originated with the Coast Salish people around the San Juans. Today, fewer than a dozen commercial reefnet operations remain in Washington, all run by non-Native Americans. Each summer, salmon return from the Pacific Ocean to spawn in British Columbia's Fraser River. Their migration takes them past the San Juan Islands, where reefnet fishers work from a pair of small scows with a net strung between them. (The Salish originally used large dugout canoes for this purpose.) Salmon are directed into the net through an artificial reef covered with plastic ribbons that simulate reef grasses. The open end of the "reef" is held on the bottom by heavy concrete anchors, and at the back is a 50-foot-long windsock-shaped net.

Each boat has a tall ladder that allows spotters to see salmon as they enter the net and to alert crew members below to close the net. Timing is tricky, and precautions must be taken to keep from spooking the salmon. Within 15-30 seconds the net is winched up, pulling the boats together and forcing the fish into a pocket. The fish are lifted onboard and dumped into a water-filled tank called a live box. They remain in the tank until sold to a fish buyer, who selects the salmon he wants and immediately puts them on ice. Everything else in the live box is released back into the sea. Reefnet fishing results in the highest-quality fish, since the netted salmon stay alive longer and are kept in much better condition than those caught using other fishing methods. In addition, there is no bycatch (taking of unwanted or prohibited species of fish).

You'll see reefnet boats anchored or in use at a couple of places around the San Juans. The little Shaw Island Historical Museum (360/468-4068) has one out front, and others are often visible in Fisherman Bay on Lopez Island, in Reid Harbor on Stuart Island, and along Lummi Island's Legoe Bay. Find out more online at www.lummiislandwild.com.

---

they set up accommodations (up to a year in advance). If you aren't a guest at the inn, dinner reservations are only available two weeks in advance and are difficult to get, especially in the busy summer season. For something a bit more proletarian, The Willows Inn serves a preset breakfast ($25 per person, 8:30am-10:30am) and lunch ($5-25 items, noon-4pm Thurs.-Sun. May-mid-Dec.); reservations not needed for these.

Just south of the ferry dock, **The Islander** (2106 South Nugent Rd., 360/758-2190, www.islandergrocery.com, 6am-9:30pm Mon.-Fri., 6am-10:30pm Fri.-Sat. late May-early Sept., 6am-9:30pm daily the rest of the year) has beer, soda pop, ice cream, and other necessities of life. There's a chessboard to while away the time, along with free Wi-Fi. A small

farmers market takes place next door 10am-1pm Saturday May-September.

Adjacent to The Islander is the **Sauseburger Stand** (360/319-0155, www.sauseburger.com, 11:30am-5:30pm Fri.-Sun., $6-12) serving Belgian waffles, huevos rancheros, and other breakfast items, along with lunchtime sandwiches, sausages, and burgers.

North of the dock, ★ **Beach Store Café** (360/758-2233, www.beachstorecafe.com, noon-9pm Mon., Thurs., and Fri., 9am-9pm Sat.-Sun. in summer, 4pm-8pm Mon., Thurs., and Fri., 9am-8pm Sat.-Sun. in winter, $14-29) is a casual bistro with steamed local mussels, roasted chicken, gluten-free fish-and-chips, and wood-fired pizzas. For breakfast (weekends only), get the corned beef hash or a Ferryman omelet. Sit on the front deck to take in snowy Mount Baker when the skies cooperate. There's free Wi-Fi, along with live music in the beer garden on Friday evenings, plus Monday-night trivia sessions. Try the shrimp and grits happy hour special. You'll find the only espresso on Lummi, along with a surprising choice of French and Spanish wines (but almost nothing from Washington State!).

ACCOMMODATIONS

On the west side of the island, ★ **The Willows Inn** (2579 W. Shore Dr., 360/758-2620 or 888/294-2620, www.willows-inn.com) has eight lovely rooms at the inn for $230-450 d, plus eight houses on other parts of the island for $400-700 per night. All guests at Willows Inn have access to an outdoor hot tub, and virtually everyone who stays here books a dinner at the inn. Make reservations far ahead to stay here—at least four months ahead for summer visits. The Willows Inn Spa is popular with guests, and you can also book whale-watching, kayaking, and sailing trips.

Beachwood (360/758-7064 or 888/758-7064, www.seasidelodgingnorthwest.com) is a spacious home on the east side of Lummi Island that sleeps up to six guests for $375 nightly. The Cape Cod-style waterfront home has French doors opening to landscaped grounds, a modern kitchen, wood-burning fireplace, and hot tub, plus luxurious bedding,

granite countertops, and bath supplies you'd expect in a high-end hotel. A five-night minimum is required.

The **Washington Department of Natural Resources** (360/856-3500, www.dnr.wa.gov) maintains a free kayak-accessible **campground** near the south end of the island. This delightful spot is the only place to camp on Lummi Island.

Also check out **Airbnb** (www.airbnb.com) and **VRBO** (www.vrbo.com) for vacation rentals on Lummi Island; the last time I looked there were more than 30 places available.

GETTING THERE

From I-5, take Exit 260 and travel four miles west on Slater Road to Haxton Way (location of Silver Reef Casino) on the Lummi Reservation, and follow it seven miles to the **ferry landing.** The county-owned *Whatcom Chief* ferry (360/676-6876) makes eight-minute trips between Gooseberry Point on the mainland to Lummi Island every hour from 6am to midnight (every 20 minutes during the morning and evening commute periods). Round-trip cost is $13 for a car and driver, $7 for passengers and walk-ons, and $7 for bikes. Kids ride free.

Whatcom Transportation Authority (360/676-7433 or 866/989-4287, www.ridewta.com) provides bus service from Bellingham to the Lummi Island ferry landing.

Marine State Parks

Many of the smaller islands in the San Juan archipelago are preserved as marine state parks. Locals often refer to these islands as the **outer islands,** and the parks are very popular with boaters and sea kayakers looking for a summertime escape. In addition to these, the Nature Conservancy's Yellow Island is also open to the public. **San Juan Islands National Wildlife Refuge** is made up of 83 islands, almost all off-limits. Be sure to avoid these refuge islands, as they provide

vital breeding and resting areas for birds and marine mammals. Boaters—including kayakers—must stay at least 200 yards away.

Several small island state marine parks are closed to the public to protect them from being damaged. Three of these undeveloped parks are offshore from Orcas Island: **Freeman Island State Park** near Point Doughty, **Skull Island Marine State Park** at the head of Massacre Bay, and **Victim Island Marine State Park** in West Sound. Another closed area, **Iceberg Island State Marine Park,** sits near the southwest end of Lopez Island just off Iceberg Point.

CAMPING AND MOORING

Most marine state parks have primitive campsites for $12 a night, available on a first-come, first-served basis. At the most popular parks—Clark, James, Jones, Matia, Patos, Stuart, Sucia, and Turn Islands—campsites often fill on weekends between mid-July and mid-August or over summer holiday weekends. There's generally space midweek.

Kayakers and canoeists will find **Cascadia Marine Trail** campsites ($12) on Blind, Burrow, Cypress, James, Jones, Lopez, Posey, Strawberry, and Stuart Islands. Park rangers try to prevent overcrowding but won't make folks move off-island if the sea conditions are unsafe. Campsite reservations are only available for group sites on Clark, Jones, Posey, and Sucia Islands; all the other sites are on a first-come, first-served basis. The nonprofit **Washington Water Trails Association** (206/547-0350, www.wwta.org) has additional information on Cascadia Marine Trail campsites, but the areas are managed by Washington State Parks.

Most marine parks contain relatively protected coves with mooring buoys ($15). Other attractions include hiking trails and picnic tables, while some islands also have drinking water, docks, or floats. Most islands have outhouses, but you'll need to haul out any garbage. Pets are allowed in the marine parks but must be on a leash at all times.

SEA KAYAKING

Quite a few companies lead sea kayaking trips of varying lengths to the marine state parks. Most operate from San Juan or Orcas Islands.

Companies based on San Juan Island are **Discovery Sea Kayaks** (360/378-2559 or 866/461-2559, www.discoveryseakayaks.com), **Outdoor Odysseys** (360/378-3533 or 800/647-4621, www.outdoorodysseys.com), **Sea Quest Expeditions** (360/378-5767 or 888/589-4253, www.sea-quest-kayak.com),

and **San Juan Kayak Expeditions** (360/378-4436, www.sanjuankayak.com).

Orcas Island-based kayak companies are **Shearwater Adventures** (360/376-4699, www.shearwaterkayaks.com) and **Outer Island Excursions** (360/376-3711, www.outerislandx.com). **Moondance Sea Kayaking Adventures** (360/738-7664, www.moondancekayak.com) leads sea kayak tours from Bellingham, while **Anacortes Kayak Tours** (360/588-1117 or 800/992-1801, www.anacorteskayaktours.com) has trips out of Anacortes.

Sea kayaks are a popular island-hopping mode of transportation, but since some of the smaller islands are several miles out, be careful not to overestimate your ability. If you're planning a kayak trip to the islands, get a copy of Randel Washburne's *Kayaking Puget Sound, the San Juans, and Gulf Islands* (The Mountaineers, www.mountaineers.org). It contains information on destinations, safety, difficulty ratings, and launching points.

MOUNTAIN BIKING

Mountain bikes are allowed year-round on all marine state park trails, but cyclists need to avoid conflicts with other users. This means staying on trails, looking out for others, and riding slowly around camping areas. Bikes aren't allowed on piers, ramps, or floats. Local water taxis will transport bikes, and bike rentals are available from the three main islands of Orcas, Lopez, and San Juan, but the bike shop on San Juan Island will not allow bikes to be taken to the outer islands due to salt damage.

INFORMATION

For additional information on the marine parks, call 360/376-2073 or visit the state park website (www.parks.wa.gov) See Ken Wilcox's *Hiking the San Juan Islands* (Northwest Wild Books) or Dave Wortman's *San Juan Islands: A Guide to Exploring the Great Outdoors* (FalconGuides) for details on marine state park hiking trails.

Boaters heading out on their own to these smaller islands will want to pick up one of the cruising guides to the islands. *Gunkholing the San Juans* by Jo Bailey and Carl Nyberg (San Juan Enterprises) is packed with details on all the islands in the archipelago, and is interesting even if you don't have a boat or kayak.

GETTING THERE

The state ferry does not stop on any of the marine state parks; access is limited to water taxi, airplane, private boat, or sea kayak.

Water Taxis

Several companies provide water taxi service to the outer islands. Most operate seasonally, but **Paraclete Charters** (360/420-5187, www.paracletecharters.com) provides year-round service. In business since 1992, the company runs three boats (the largest can carry 64 passengers) from Anacortes to anywhere in the San Juans. They serve homeowners on islands not on the ferry system, along with other folks wanting to reach the islands. Prices depend on your destination and number of people, but you don't need to charter an entire boat, and they have room for kayaks, bikes, and pets. As an example, Anacortes to Clark Island costs $136 for one person round-trip; add $10 round-trip for bikes or $20 for kayaks.

Based at Skyline Marina in Anacortes, **Island Express Charters** (360/299-2875 or 877/473-9777, www.islandexpresscharters.com, open year-round) has two high-speed landing craft with space for kayaks, bikes, and gear. Water taxi rates vary depending upon your destination. Most trips require at least two passengers.

Based at Deer Harbor on Orcas Island, **North Shore Charters** (360/376-4855, www.orcasislandadventures.com) offers day trips to and drop-offs at state marine parks on Jones, Stuart, Matia, Patos, Sucia, and other islands. Owner Marty Mead has years of experience in local and Alaskan waters and was also the engineer on a 2007 crossing of the Pacific by *Earthrace*, a wave-piercing trimaran that set the record for the fastest crossing time by a biodiesel-powered boat.

Also at Deer Harbor Marina, **Orcas Boat Rentals** (360-376-7616, www.orcasboatrentals.com) has boat rentals if you want to head out on your own.

Based on the north side of Orcas Island, **Outer Island Excursions** (360/376-3711, www.outerislandx.com) provides water taxi service to Stuart, Sucia, Jones, Matia, and Patos Islands, as well as most other islands.

Humpback Hauling (360/317-7433, www.humpbackhauling.com) provides passenger and freight service throughout the San Juans on a large landing craft. Owner Bob Miller—a highly experienced captain—also operates a smaller boat under the name Roche Harbor Water Taxi.

Based in Friday Harbor, **San Juan Islands Water Taxi** (360/317-5475, www.sjiwatertaxi.net) can transport six passengers anywhere in the San Juan Islands. Captain Gunnar Wickman has sailed all over the world, and the boat spent many years as a fishing vessel in Alaska. It's not fast, but the boat is comfortable, with space for bikes or kayaks.

Air

San Juan Airlines (360/293-4691 or 800/874-4434, www.sanjuanairlines.com) has scheduled daily wheeled-plane service from Anacortes and Bellingham to San Juan, Orcas, Lopez, and Blakely Islands; it will stop at most other island runways, including Center, Crane, Eliza, Sinclair, Stuart, and Waldron Islands on a charter basis.

Based at San Juan Island Airport, **Island Air** (360/378-2376 or 888/378-2376, www.sanjuan-islandair.com) provides charter flights to most islands.

Kenmore Air (425/486-1257 or 866/435-9524, www.kenmoreair.com) has charter floatplane flights from Lake Union in Seattle to many of the remote San Juan Islands, including Cypress, Blakely, Jones, Stuart, Henry, Sucia, and Decatur.

BLIND ISLAND MARINE STATE PARK

Blind Island (360/378-2044, www.parks.wa.gov) is a grassy three-acre island within

Blind Bay on the north side of Shaw Island. It's a great place to watch the ferries pass, with the Shaw ferry dock just 0.25 mile away, and Orcas Village less than a mile away. Facilities are limited to four mooring buoys, picnic tables, fire pits, and a composting toilet. Bring your own water. The island's four primitive campsites ($12) are part of the Cascadia Marine Trail and are available only for use by sea kayakers.

In the early 1900s, Blind Island was occupied by a squatter family who built several buildings and rock cisterns and had a garden. The buildings are long gone, but you can see the cherry, apple, and hazelnut trees they planted.

Blind Island is a part of **San Juan Island National Monument** (360/468-3754, www.sanjuanislandsnca.org), created by President Obama in 2013. The monument, overseen by the Bureau of Land Management, covers public lands in many locations throughout the San Juan Islands.

CLARK ISLAND MARINE STATE PARK

Two miles northeast of Orcas Island, **Clark Island** (360/376-2073, www.parks.wa.gov) is a narrow 55-acre island. It's relatively close to the western shore of Lummi Island, making it a destination for sea kayakers and boaters. The island has pretty sand and gravel beaches for walking, sunbathing, fishing, or scuba diving, plus a 100-foot-high hill in the middle. Droopy madrone trees line the water, framing dramatic views of the Cascades to the east, or Georgia Strait and the setting sun to the west. Short paths connect the two sides of the island, but the once-popular south-end trail has been closed to protect nesting seabirds.

Currents can be strong on the west side of the island, and storms often bring big waves and powerful currents that create hazardous conditions. The island is popular for day use, but it's not advisable if the wind is blowing. In addition, there's heavy tanker traffic in the channel east of Clark Island.

Nearby is privately owned **Barnes Island,** with a few homes, plus a cluster of rocky islets just southeast of Clark Island called **The Sisters Islands.** These are frequently crowded with nesting gulls, cormorants, and other seabirds. Two of them lie within San Juan Islands National Wildlife Refuge, and boaters must stay 200 yards away.

Camping and Mooring

Clark Island has nine primitive campsites ($12) with pit toilets but no water. Groups can reserve one of the campsites by calling the park at 360/376-2073. Mooring buoys ($15) are available on both sides of Clark Island, but buoys on the west side are exposed.

Getting There

Paraclete Charters (360/420-5187, www.paracletecharters.com, $136 per person round-trip, add $10 for bikes or $20 for kayaks) provides water taxi service to Clark from Anacortes.

Also based in Anacortes, **Island Express Charters** (360/299-2875 or 877/473-9777, www.islandexpresscharters.com, $184 per person round-trip to Clark, plus $20 for bikes or $30-40 for kayaks) has high-speed landing craft with plenty of room for kayaks, bikes, and gear.

Outer Island Excursions (360/376-3711, www.outerislandx.com, $300 round-trip for up to six people) provides water taxi service to Clark from Orcas Island.

CYPRESS ISLAND

The fourth-largest island in the San Juans, Cypress is just three miles northeast of Anacortes. It is surprisingly wild, with excellent recreational opportunities and beautifully rugged scenery. Featured attractions include tall stands of old-growth trees and more than 25 miles of hiking trails, along with campsites, pretty beaches and coves, a couple of small lakes, abundant wildlife, and some stunning hilltop viewpoints.

There are no cypress trees on Cypress Island. Captain George Vancouver named the island in 1792 but misidentified the trees; they're actually Rocky Mountain junipers. Coast Salish people once occupied the island seasonally, and several archaeological sites have been identified. American settlers came to homestead, farm, log, fish, or mine, but most of them gave up almost a century ago. In the 1970s, local environmentalists prevented the island from being developed into a planned resort and residential area. Today, the 4.5-mile-long island is mostly in public hands and managed as a natural area by the Washington Department of Natural Resources (360/856-3500). Download Cypress Island trail maps from the DNR website (www.dnr.wa.gov).

Hiking

For an incredible view, climb to the 800-foot summit of **Eagle Cliff** on the northern end of Cypress Island. The shortest trail begins from Pelican Beach and is a bit less than three miles round-trip. As might be surmised from the name, this is a bald eagle nesting area. To protect them, the trail is closed February-mid-July. Other trails and dirt roads lace the island, going all the way from Pelican Beach to the southern tip of Cypress Island. Mountain bikes and motorized vehicles are not allowed on any of these. See Ken Wilcox's *Hiking the San Juan Islands* (Northwest Wild Books) or Dave Wortman's *San Juan Islands: A Guide to Exploring the Great Outdoors* (FalconGuides) for complete details on Cypress Island hikes.

Camping

Free campsites are located at **Cypress Head DNR Recreation Site** on the east side of the island, where you will also find five mooring buoys and outhouses, but no drinking water—so bring plenty with you. The bay at Cypress Head is peaceful and gorgeous. **Pelican Beach DNR Recreation Site** is another picturesque place, with six mooring buoys, free campsites, a shelter, picnic tables, and outhouses, but no water. It is located on the northeast side of Cypress. Camping is only allowed in designated campsites.

Getting There

Kayakers and boaters typically head to Cypress from Anacortes, but small vessels need to take precautions due to difficult currents and tide rips in Bellingham Channel.

Based in Anacortes, **Island Express Charters** (360/299-2875 or 877/473-9777, www.islandexpresscharters.com, $90 per person round-trip to Cypress, add $20 for bikes or $30-40 for kayaks) has high-speed landing craft with plenty of room for kayaks, bikes, and gear.

Paraclete Charters (360/420-5187, www.paracletecharters.com, $76 per person round-trip, add $10 for bikes or $20 for kayaks) provides water taxi service to Cypress from Anacortes.

Kenmore Air (425/486-1257 or 800/543-9595, www.kenmoreair.com) has charter floatplane flights from Lake Union in Seattle to Cypress Island.

DOE ISLAND MARINE STATE PARK

Doe Island (360/376-2073, www.parks.wa.gov) is a delightful six-acre escape. The secluded island is heavily forested and has both rocky shorelines and a gravel beach. It is located just southeast of Orcas Island, less than a 0.5-mile kayak paddle from the hot tubs at Doe Bay Resort & Retreat on Orcas. There are no mooring buoys, but a seasonal float extends from the north shore. Hiking trails circle and cross the island, and five simple campsites ($12) are available. No drinking water is available, but there are picnic tables and pit toilets. Be sure to check out the archaeological site in a little pocket cove on the north side; you can still see the place where the Lummi cleared rocks to beach their canoes.

Shearwater Adventures (360/376-4699, www.shearwaterkayaks.com) guides kayak trips to Doe Island from Doe Bay Resort & Retreat daily in the summer. A three-hour paddle costs $79 adults or $45 for kids under 13. The closest access point for boaters and kayakers heading to Doe Island is the county's Obstruction Pass boat ramp on Orcas Island.

JAMES ISLAND MARINE STATE PARK

Less than a half mile east of Decatur Island and just four miles from the Anacortes ferry terminal along Rosario Strait, **James Island** (360/376-2073, www.parks.wa.gov) is a cliff-faced and scenic little place. The island was named for an American sailor, Reuben James, who died during a naval battle in Tripoli while saving the life of Stephen Decatur. It was one of many places named during the 1841 Wilkes Expedition.

Covering 114 acres, James Island is shaped like an hourglass, with coves and mooring buoys ($15) on both sides of the "waist." The east cove offers a better anchorage for boats if the buoys are already taken, and the west cove has a floating dock. Beaches on both sides are steep. Kayakers need to be especially cautious in the waters north of the island, where deadly rip currents can form.

Two Anacortes-based companies provide transport to James Island: **Island Express Charters** (360/299-2875 or 877/473-9777, www.islandexpresscharters.com, $90 per person round-trip, add $20 for bikes or $30-40 for kayaks) and **Paraclete Charters** (360/420-5187, www.paracletecharters.com, $136 per person round-trip, add $10 for bikes or $20 for kayaks).

Camping

Pitch a tent ($12) at one of 13 primitive campsites, or at the Cascadia Marine Trail campsite if you're in a kayak. The island has the usual complement of deer, birds, and raccoons, the last of which can be real pests when the sun goes down. You'll need to bring your own water. Picnic tables, a shelter, and pit toilets are present, however, and a network of short trails traverses the forests and twin 200-foot-high hills of James Island.

★ JONES ISLAND MARINE STATE PARK

One of the most heavily visited of the San Juan marine parks, **Jones Island** (360/376-2073, www.parks.wa.gov) is a 188-acre island just a mile from the southwestern tip of Orcas Island, or a two-mile boat ride from Friday Harbor. The island is named for Jacob Jones, an American naval captain during the War of 1812, and is yet another place named during the 1841 Wilkes Expedition. It is a wonderful destination, either as a day trip or a multi-night family adventure. Two coves provide boat anchorage and access to the island's pleasures, and boaters can tie onto one of seven mooring buoys ($15). North Cove is a better anchorage and has both a dock and a seasonal moorage float. Local boaters recommend avoiding North Cove in high-pressure conditions, when winds blow from the north; avoid South Cove during low-pressure systems, when winds are reversed.

Jones Island has a mixture of old-growth forests (some of which were flattened in a fierce 1990 windstorm); stands of stately madrone, oak, and juniper trees; and grassy meadows. The shoreline is equally diverse, containing both rocky stretches and sandy beaches in pocket-size coves. Two unusual plants—prickly pear cactus and Garry oak—are present in protected areas on Jones Island.

A wide, nearly level 0.5-mile path leads through the forest from North Cove to South Cove, passing an old apple orchard along the way. South Cove is actually composed of two adjacent small bays, each with a fine sandy beach—perfect for Frisbees, sunbathing, a picnic lunch, or just hanging out. A second trail follows the western shore of the island from South Cove, leading past interesting tidepools and up rocky slopes where you can watch sailboats and kayakers plying San Juan Channel. The trail continues to the north end of the island, where vistas extend to British Columbia's Gulf Islands.

Camping

Jones Island Marine State Park has 24 primitive campsites ($12) with picnic tables, pit toilets, and potable water. Two Adirondack shelters ($25) at the South Cove have bunk beds; North Cove has a large kitchen shelter. Jones Island is often crowded. Camping is

Jones Island Marine State Park

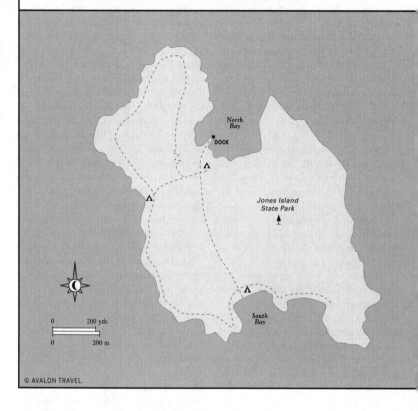

North Bay

DOCK

Jones Island State Park

South Bay

0   200 yds

0   200 m

© AVALON TRAVEL

only allowed at designated sites, and these fill quickly on summer weekends. Reservations are available only for a group campsite and the Adirondack shelters on Jones Island; call 360/378-2044 for details. Kayakers will find two Cascadia Marine Trail campsites ($12) on a gorgeous southwestern beach facing San Juan Channel.

Getting There

Jones Island is exceptionally popular with boaters, sailors, and sea kayakers. Several water taxi companies are happy to get you to the island. Located at Deer Harbor Marina, **Orcas Boat Rentals** (360/376-7616, www.orcasboatrentals.com) has skiff rentals; it's just a 10-minute boat ride to Jones Island.

Other water taxis providing service to the island include **Island Express Charters** (360/299-2875 or 877/473-9777, www.island-expresscharters.com, $194 per person round-trip, add $20 for bikes or $30-40 for kayaks) and **Paraclete Charters** (360/420-5187, www.paracletecharters.com, $136 per person round-trip) from Anacortes, and **North Shore Charters** (360/376-4855, www.orcasislandadventures.com, $50 per person round-trip) from Deer Harbor on Orcas.

Black Fish Whale & Wildlife Tours (360/370-5696, www.sanjuanislandwhales.com) runs four-hour trips to Jones Island from Friday Harbor for $139 per person. These include lunch and a naturalist-guided tour.

Gnat's Nature Hikes (360/376-6629, www.orcasislandhikes.com) leads boat-and-hike trips to Jones Island in the spring from Orcas Island. There's a three-person minimum and a six-person maximum.

Kenmore Air (425/486-1257 or 800/543-9595, www.kenmoreair.com) has charter floatplane flights from Lake Union in Seattle to Jones Island.

MATIA ISLAND MARINE STATE PARK

Located three miles northeast of Orcas Island and a mile from Sucia Island, **Matia Island** (pronounced ma-TEE-uh by some folks, MAY-shuw by others; 360/376-2073, www.parks.wa.gov) is a mile long and covers 145 acres. Sandstone bluffs line the shore, and tall old-growth forests of Douglas fir, western hemlock, and western red cedar fill the center of the island. It's a beautiful and essentially undeveloped place. Matia received its name from the 1791 expedition of Francisco Eliza; in Spanish, the word means "no protection."

Matia was for decades the quiet home of a Civil War veteran, Elvin Smith, who got a regular workout rowing the three miles to Orcas and walking another two miles to Eastsound to buy his groceries. On his last trip in 1921, he and an elderly friend headed out from Eastsound in seas that suddenly turned rough. Pieces of the boat were later discovered near the Canadian border, but the two men were never found.

Most of Matia Island lies within **San Juan Islands National Wildlife Refuge,** but the five-acre **Matia Island Marine State Park** centers on Rolfe Cove on the western end. Here you'll find a seasonal dock (generally Apr.-Sept.), two mooring buoys ($15), six primitive campsites ($12), and a composting toilet. No water is available, and wood fires aren't allowed on Matia, though you can use charcoal briquettes in the fire stands.

A scenic one-mile **hiking trail** starts at Rolfe Cove and loops across the island, passing scattered remnants of Smith's old homesite and taking you through dense forests and along rocky shores. This is all part of the national wildlife refuge, so stay on the trails to protect the land and wildlife. Pets are not allowed on Matia Island trails. Boaters cannot approach Matia closer than 200 yards, except at the state park.

Immediately east of Matia is **Puffin Island,** with an active eagle nest, various nesting seabirds, and seals and sea lions.

kayakers off Jones Island

Patos, Sucia, and Matia Islands

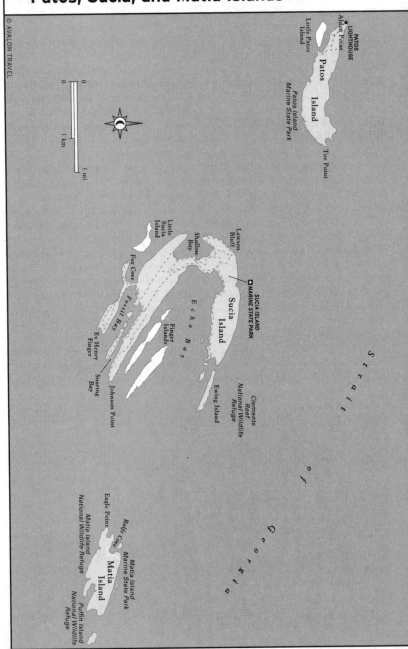

© AVALON TRAVEL

Little Patos Island

PATOS LIGHTHOUSE
Alden Point

Patos Island

Patos Island Marine State Park

Toe Point

0 — 1 km
0 — 1 mi

Little Sucia Island

Fox Cove

Fossil Bay

Ev Henry Finger

Snoring Bay

Johnson Point

Shallow Bay

Lawson Bluff

Finger Islands

Echo Bay

Sucia Island

SUCIA ISLAND MARINE STATE PARK

Clements Reef National Wildlife Refuge

Ewing Island

Strait of Georgia

Eagle Point

Rolfe Cove

Matia Island National Wildlife Refuge

Matia Island

Matia Island Marine State Park

Puffin Island National Wildlife Refuge

Puffins no longer nest there, though they apparently did in the past.

Getting There

Matia Island is popular with kayakers and boaters but has potentially treacherous currents. The closest water taxi service is through **Outer Island Excursions** (360/376-3711, www.outerislandx.com), based on the north side of Orcas Island.

North Shore Charters (360/376-4855, www.orcasislandadventures.com, $150 per person round-trip) provides day trips and drop-offs to Matia Island from Deer Harbor on Orcas Island.

Paraclete Charters (360/420-5187, www.paracletecharters.com, $190 per person round-trip, add $10 for bikes or $20 for kayaks) provides water taxi service to Matia from Anacortes.

Also based in Anacortes, **Island Express Charters** (360/299-2875 or 877/473-9777, www.islandexpresscharters.com, $210 per person round-trip, add $20 for bikes or $30-40 for kayaks) has a high-speed landing craft with plenty of room for kayaks, bikes, and gear.

PATOS ISLAND MARINE STATE PARK

Northernmost of the San Juan archipelago, **Patos Island** (usually pronounced PAY-tohs; 360/376-2073, www.parks.wa.gov) covers 208 acres and is six miles north of Orcas Island or two miles northwest of Sucia Island. The Southern Gulf Islands of British Columbia are only a few miles away. Wild, remote, and quiet Patos Island was named during a Spanish expedition in 1792. The name means "duck" and may have possibly come from a rock formation on the east side of the island that resembles the head of a duck. Patos is part of **San Juan Island National Monument** (www.sanjuanislandsnca.org).

The lack of a dock on Patos limits access, but you can anchor at two mooring buoys ($15) in **Active Cove.** Located on the southwestern side of Patos, it's sheltered behind **Little Patos Island.** During high-pressure

systems, the moorage is exposed to winds blowing down the Strait of Georgia, creating a rough anchorage; otherwise, it's fairly protected.

Seven primitive campsites ($12) on Patos have picnic tables, fire pits, and outhouses, but no water. A 1.5-mile loop trail circles the western side of the island, passing through dense forests before opening onto the barren northwest tip at Alden Point. A 0.25-mile spur leads to picturesque **Patos Lighthouse.** Built in 1893 and now automated, the lighthouse sits atop a rocky bluff. **Keepers of the Patos Light** (www.patoslightkeepers.org) works with the Bureau of Land Management (which owns the site) to preserve this historic structure.

For a lovingly written reminiscence of growing up on Patos in the early 1900s, see *Light on the Island* by Helene Glidden (San Juan Publishing). The author was a lighthouse-keeper's daughter and tells of her adventures with scoundrels, native people, and even Teddy Roosevelt.

Getting There

Patos is not the place for novice kayakers or folks in small boats. There are few areas offering any protection, and the currents and riptides can be treacherous. Kayakers typically head to Patos from Sucia Island, rather than attempting the four-mile open-water crossing from Point Doughty on Orcas Island.

Based on the north side of Orcas Island, **Outer Island Excursions** (360/376-3711, www.outerislandx.com) has 2.5-hour trips ($89/person) to nearby Patos Island. The trip includes a guided 0.5-mile hike to the lighthouse and the chance to see porpoises and other wildlife. The water taxi rate to Patos is $300 round-trip for up to six people.

Orcas Island Eclipse Charters (360/376-6566 or 800/376-6566, www.orcasisland-whales.com) leads informative lighthouse tours to all four lighthouses in the San Juan Islands. These take place several times each summer and are on the water only; call for details. They depart from the ferry landing on Orcas Island.

North Shore Charters (360/376-4855, www.orcasislandadventures.com, $150 per person round-trip) provides water-taxi service to Patos Island from Deer Harbor on Orcas Island.

Based in Anacortes, **Island Express Charters** (360/299-2875 or 877/473-9777, www.islandexpresscharters.com, $240 per person round-trip, add $20 for bikes or $30-40 for kayaks) has a high-speed landing craft with plenty of room for kayaks, bikes, and gear.

Paraclete Charters (360/420-5187, www.paracletecharters.com, $190 per person round-trip, add $10 for bikes or $20 for kayaks) provides water taxi service to Patos from Anacortes.

POSEY ISLAND MARINE STATE PARK

This pinprick of an island covers just one acre and is located a quarter mile north of San Juan Island's Roche Harbor. **Posey Island** (360/378-2044, www.parks.wa.gov) is named for the small and abundant wildflowers that carpet the ground in midsummer. Shallow waters and two Cascadia Marine Trail campsites ($12) make this a favorite spot for folks in kayaks and canoes in search of their own island. It's a great place to watch the parade of boats heading into or out of busy Roche Harbor. Campsite reservations ($10 extra, call 360/378-2044) are taken for mid-May to mid-September and must be made at least seven days in advance. Call early in the year (reservations open in Jan.) to be sure of a peak-season campsite on the island. In the off-season, campsites are available on a first-come, first-served basis.

The island sees heavy daytime use by kayakers, and camp spaces fill quickly. A two-night maximum is allowed, but try to limit your stay to one night to give someone else a chance. Because of its location close to numerous summer homes and the harbor entrance, you shouldn't expect a quiet night during the summer. No water is available on the island, but picnic tables and a composting toilet are here. A maximum of 16 people are allowed to camp on Posey, which is far too many for such a tiny spot.

SADDLEBAG ISLAND MARINE STATE PARK

This 24-acre island in Padilla Bay is just two miles northeast of Anacortes and half a mile east of Guemes Island. It might be a stretch to call **Saddlebag Island** part of the San Juan archipelago, but the island is a marine state park (360/757-0227, www.parks.wa.gov). Facilities include five primitive campsites ($12) and an outhouse; there is no drinking water, and buoys and floats are not available. A Cascadia Marine Trail campsite ($12) is available for kayakers. The southeast corner of Saddlebag Island almost touches tiny **Dot Island,** part of San Juan Islands National Wildlife Refuge. To protect nesting sites for seabirds, boaters aren't allowed within 200 yards of Dot Island. **Hat Island,** a larger island southeast of Saddlebag, is also closed to the public to protect wildlife.

★ STUART ISLAND

Stuart Island, five miles northwest of San Juan Island's Roche Harbor, has two bucolic harbors just a stone's throw apart, along with a densely forested, hilly landscape and a classic old lighthouse. The island sits in the middle of Haro Strait, where killer whales are a common summertime sight. Canadian waters are less than a mile from the western end of Stuart Island. The three-mile-long island is predominately private, but **Stuart Island Marine State Park** (360/378-2044, www.parks.wa.gov) covers 85 prime acres, including 33,000 feet of shoreline. There are no stores of any kind on the island, so bring whatever you need when you come.

The island's two large and well-protected harbors—both within the state marine park—are favorites of boaters. Located on the southeast end of Stuart Island, **Reid Harbor** has 15 mooring buoys, linear moorage, and a dock,

Stuart Island

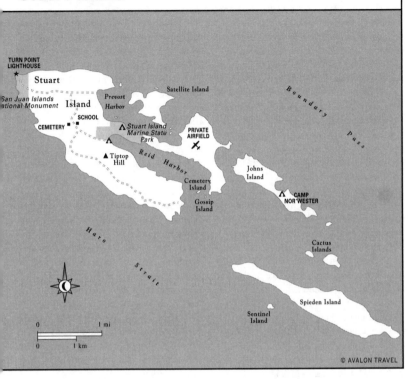

Map labels:
TURN POINT LIGHTHOUSE
Stuart
San Juan Islands National Monument
Island
CEMETERY
SCHOOL
Satellite Island
Prevost Harbor
Stuart Island Marine State Park
PRIVATE AIRFIELD
Tiptop Hill
Reid Harbor
Cemetery Island
Gossip Island
Johns Island
CAMP NOR'WESTER
Boundary Pass
Haro Strait
Cactus Islands
Spieden Island
Sentinel Island
0   1 mi
0   1 km
© AVALON TRAVEL

along with two floats at the head of the bay and a marine pump-out station. The 640-foot summit of Tiptop Hill (no public access) rises to the south, with a narrow dirt road providing access to other parts of the island. A trail connects Reid Harbor with **Prevost Harbor,** with seven mooring buoys, linear moorage, and a dock. It's an easy 200-yard walk, but boats enter Prevost Harbor from the north side of Stuart Island.

The 1841 Wilkes Expedition named Stuart Island for the captain's clerk, Fredrick D. Stuart. Loggers, fishermen, and a few farmers later settled the island. Today, Stuart is home to 20 or so year-round residents, augmented by another 150 folks with summer homes. Privacy is a priority here, and many areas are posted with No Trespassing signs. Fortunately, some of the most interesting

sights are accessible by public trails or county roads, including Stuart Island Marine State Park and a beautiful lighthouse on the island's westernmost end.

Several relatively short trails—the longest is three miles—cut through the marine state park, offering ridge-crest views; open forests of madrone, cedar, and Douglas fir; and rocky shorelines along the way. Check the information kiosks at either harbor for details. For something a bit more ambitious, head up the county road that begins on public land at the head of Reid Harbor. This dirt road climbs uphill for 0.75 mile to a white one-room **schoolhouse.** Built in 1902, it now serves as a library and museum. Adjacent is a newer school that closed in 2007 after the number of students dwindled. It was one of the last American public schools without electricity or flush toilets. Take a gander at the quaint **Treasure Chest,** a big wooden box filled with locally printed T-shirts available on an honor system basis, including some fun pirate ones for kids.

Continue just past the school to a road junction and turn right. A short distance beyond is an unmarked road on the left leading to the **Stuart Island Cemetery,** with graves dating to 1904. Look for the distinctive headstone of Little Wolf, a local character who crafted copper bracelets that supposedly offered medical benefits. Back on the main road, you'll meet placidly grazing cows and horses at the next road junction. Turn right to Prevost Harbor, or left at the sign and pass an airstrip before continuing another 1.5 miles to **Turn Point Lighthouse.** The last portion of this hike is delightful, and the trail eventually emerges atop a tall cliff (stay away from the edge) where the panorama encompasses Haro Strait, the Southern Gulf Islands, and Vancouver Island. You'll see a parade of freighters, tankers, and smaller boats, and you might even spot a pod of killer whales. It's a fantastic picnic spot.

Completed in 1893, the lighthouse has been automated since 1974. The lighthouse and surrounding 53 acres are owned by the Bureau of Land Management, which allows day use

only. Turn Point is a part of **San Juan Island National Monument** (360/468-3754, www. sanjuanislandsnca.org).

The nonprofit **Turn Point Lighthouse Preservation Society** (360/376-5246, www.tplps.org) assists in preserving this historic site. Their docents are on site 11am-4:30pm Tuesday-Saturday July through early September, and provide tours of the renovated and furnished keeper's quarters several times a day. The old fog signal building now houses a small museum with artifacts, photos, and a 20-minute video about the lighthouse, and the former oil storage building has interesting exhibits on orcas. Just uphill from the lighthouse are large solar panels used to power the lighthouse. A pump at the lighthouse provides water, but it is not potable, so bring water with you when you visit.

Turn Point marks the transition between Haro Strait to the south and Boundary Pass to the north. Large ships threading these channels must make a sharp turn here, and so do the often-turbulent tidal currents. The boundary waters are the deepest in the San Juan archipelago, reaching a maximum of 1,200 feet. It's a 6-mile round-trip hike from Reid Harbor to the lighthouse, or 3.5 miles round-trip from Prevost Harbor.

Turn Point Lighthouse

Tours

Based on the north side of Orcas Island, **Outer Island Excursions** (360/376-3711, www.outerislandx.com) has 4-hour trips ($89/person) to Stuart Island. The trip includes a guided hike to the lighthouse. The water taxi rate to Stuart Island is $500 round-trip for up to six people.

Orcas Island Eclipse Charters (360/376-6566 or 800/376-6566, www.orcasisland-whales.com) leads informative lighthouse tours to all four lighthouses in the San Juan Islands. These take place several times each summer and are on the water only; call for details. They depart from the ferry landing on Orcas Island.

Boating and Kayaking

Powerful currents and tidal rips make the waters around Stuart Island challenging for small boats and kayaks; paddling here is not for beginners or the faint of heart. The closest access is Roche Harbor on San Juan Island, but you'll need to pass through the frequently swirling flows of Spieden Channel. For details on the best way to proceed, see Randel Washburne's *Kayaking Puget Sound, the San Juans, and Gulf Islands* (The Mountaineers, www.mountaineers.org).

Camping

Stuart Island Marine State Park straddles the isthmus between Prevost and Reid Harbors, and includes 18 campsites ($12), picnic tables, seasonal drinking water, fireplaces, and pit toilets. Drinking water is limited and the system often runs dry by mid-July, so call ahead to make sure it's available. Four Cascadia Marine Trail campsites ($12) are available for sea kayakers on the east side of Reid Harbor.

Getting There and Around

North Shore Charters (360/376-4855, www.orcasislandadventures.com, $130 per person round-trip) provides day trips and drop-offs to Stuart Island from Deer Harbor on Orcas Island.

Based in Anacortes, **Island Express Charters** (360/299-2875 or 877/473-9777, www.islandexpresscharters.com, $290 person round-trip to Stuart) has high-speed landing craft with space for kayaks ($30-40 extra), bikes ($20 extra), and gear.

Paraclete Charters (360/420-5187, www.paracletecharters.com, $190 per person round-trip, add $10 for bikes or $20 for kayaks) provides water taxi service to Stuart from Anacortes.

Based on the north side of Orcas Island, **Outer Island Excursions** (360/376-3711, www.outerislandx.com) has four-hour trips to Stuart Island ($189 per person). The trip includes a guided 1.5-mile hike to the lighthouse and the chance to see orcas and other marine mammals. Water taxi service to Stuart is also available ($250 one-way for up to six people).

Outdoor Odysseys (360/378-3533 or 800/647-4621, www.outdoorodysseys.com) has three-day sea-kayak tours ($599) that depart San Juan Island for Stuart Island, and more leisurely four-day paddles ($799) to Stuart, Jones, and other islands.

San Juan Airlines (360/293-4691 or 800/874-4434, www.sanjuanairlines.com) will fly to Stuart Island on a charter basis. **Kenmore Air** (425/486-1257 or 800/543-9595, www.kenmoreair.com) has charter floatplane flights from Lake Union in Seattle to Stuart Island.

Nearby Islands

Johns, Satellite, Sentinel, and Spieden Islands are nearby, and **Cactus Island** and several surrounding tiny islets are within the San Juan Islands National Wildlife Refuge. Boats aren't allowed within 200 yards of refuge islands to protect habitat for seals, sea lions, and seabirds. Cactus Island, along with a few other places in the San Juans, has Puget prairie vegetation, with native grasses and various rare plants, including the prickly pear cactus—the only species of cactus native to western Washington. You'll also find these unusual conditions at minuscule **Gossip Island** and **Cemetery Island,** near the mouth of Reid

Harbor. These two islands are undeveloped state parks with day use only allowed and no picnics. There's a pretty white beach at Gossip Island.

★ SUCIA ISLAND MARINE STATE PARK

Sucia Island (commonly pronounced SUE-sha, but you may occasionally hear the original Spanish pronunciation, sue-SEE-uh; 360/376-2073, www.parks.wa.gov) is the gold standard for Washington's marine state parks, with something for almost everyone. The shoreline has delightful sandy beaches for sunbathing, exploring, clamming, and crabbing, plus bizarre water-carved sandstone formations and lounging seals. Offshore, you can scuba dive on an artificial reef created by three sunken wrecks. Hikers and mountain bikers will find 10 miles of scenic trails, campers revel in the many primitive campsites, and boaters tie up at buoys, linear moorage, or docks in a half-dozen small bays. Picnic tables and shelters dot the coves.

Shaped like a horseshoe, Sucia Island is 2.5 miles north of Orcas Island, almost reaching the Canadian border. In addition to the main island of Sucia, nine smaller islands (some privately owned) are adjacent, including the Finger Islands, Little Sucia Island (closed to public access when bald eagles are nesting here), Justice Island, and Ewing Island. Altogether, the islands cover almost 750 acres. Two other popular marine destinations are nearby: Patos and Matia Islands.

Sucia Island is the largest and one of the most popular marine state parks in Washington, with more than 100,000 boaters visiting annually. Don't expect to be the only visitor on Sucia Island; on a summer weekend, the waters around the island are jam-packed with U.S. and Canadian vessels of all descriptions. You can avoid some of the mob scene in midweek or during the slower spring and fall months.

The first European to discover Sucia Island was explorer Francisco Eliza in 1791. He named it for the Spanish word that means "dirty" or "foul," a nautical reference to the shoal-filled waters surrounding Sucia.

The San Juans have long been a haven for smuggling, and Sucia Island's multitude of coves and sculpted sandstone rocks made it a center for everything from illegal booze during Prohibition to Chinese laborers in the late 19th century. During the early 1900s, sandstone quarried from Sucia was used to pave Seattle's streets. In the 1950s, a wealthy

Sucia Island

Californian prepared to buy Sucia Island from its local owners, intending to subdivide it for vacation homes. Word quickly spread in the Puget Sound yachting and boating community, and a drive was mounted to raise $25,000 to purchase the island. In 1960, the Puget Sound Interclub Association donated Sucia to the state of Washington, thus preserving this marvelous island for the public.

Mooring

Sucia Island wraps its two long arms around **Echo Bay,** where you'll find 17 mooring buoys and two sets of linear moorage ($15). **Shallow Bay** is right across a narrow isthmus from the head of Echo Bay and has a pleasant beach, eight buoys, and colorful sunsets. An eroded sandstone cliff, filled with many small nooks and crannies, borders the northeast side of Shallow Bay. Known as **China Caves,** these niches were supposedly used by 19th-century smugglers to hide illegal Chinese laborers from immigration officials. It's a good tale, but probably apocryphal.

On the southern end of the island is **Fossil Bay**—named for marine fossils scattered along the beach—with 16 buoys, two docks, and a ranger station. Families have fun finding the fossils, but it's illegal to take them. A low, sandy isthmus (great for hanging out on a sunny day) separates the bay from **Fox Cove,** which has four buoys. **Snoring Bay,** with two buoys, is near the south end of the island, while **Ewing Cove,** with three buoys, occupies the northeast end of the island facing Ewing Island.

Hiking and Biking

Despite the abundance of summertime boaters in Sucia, it is easy to escape the crowds by simply heading inland on one of the trails that lace the island. The land is surprisingly diverse, with a variety of forests—including Douglas fir, shore pine, Pacific madrone, and Rocky Mountain juniper—along with sea cliffs (use caution when hiking with small children), sandy beaches, odd rock formations, and all-encompassing seascapes.

Trails start from all the popular bays and coves, offering options of varying lengths. If you were to hike from Johnson Point on the southern end of the island to Ewing Cove on the northern end, it would be a round-trip walk of nine miles. Of note is the one-mile hike from Fossil Bay to the end of **Ev Henry Finger,** a narrow peninsula with steep cliffs and killer views of Orcas Island and points south. The hike to **Ewing Cove** is another delightful option, with a wooded trail that follows the shoreline to this beautiful and out-of-the-way cove. There are some steep drops along the way, so watch your step.

These trails are also open to mountain bikers, and biking the main roads is quite easy, but it's best to leave the narrower trails to hikers.

Camping

A total of 60 primitive campsites ($12) are located at Echo Bay, Fossil Bay, Shallow Bay, Fox Cove, Ewing Cove, and Snoring Bay. Picnic shelters, fireplaces, firewood, and composting toilets are all available at the various campgrounds. Drinking water is available early in the season; call ahead to check availability, or bring your own. Camping is only allowed at designated sites. The campsites at Ewing Cove and Snoring Bay are a bit more isolated and may be a better choice in the peak summer season when the island is a frenzy of activity. Reservations are available for three group campsites and an Adirondack shelter on Sucia Island; call 360/376-2073 for details. Groups can also reserve a picnic area along Fossil Bay.

Getting There and Around

It's relatively easy to get to Sucia via sailboat or motorboat, and many others paddle kayaks from North Beach or Coho Lodge on Orcas Island. A number of regional kayak companies offer guided trips to Sucia for those who prefer a knowledgeable guide when crossing these sometimes-difficult waters filled with odd currents, sudden winds, and dangerous reefs. Don't take chances!

Outer Island Excursions (360/376-3711, www.outerislandx.com) operates the **Sucia Island Ferry,** with round-trip service to Sucia from a small harbor just north of Eastsound on Orcas Island. The cost is $45 for adults and $35 for youths, plus $10 to bring along a bike or $30 for a kayak.

Two companies offer sea kayak day trips from Orcas to Sucia: **Shearwater Adventures** (360/376-4699, www.shearwaterkayaks.com) and **Outer Island Excursions** (360/376-3711, www.outerislandx.com). A five-hour trip includes a water taxi to Sucia and guided kayaking in the protected bays ($159 adults, $99 teens). Both companies use the water taxi from Outer Island Excursions, based on the north side of Orcas and just a 15-minute ride to Sucia. These tours are highly recommended.

North Shore Charters (360/376-4855, www.orcasislandadventures.com, $140 per person round-trip) provides day trips to and drop-offs at Sucia Island from Deer Harbor on Orcas Island.

Black Fish Whale & Wildlife Tours (360/370-5696, www.sanjuanislandwhales.com) runs day trips to Sucia Island from Friday Harbor. The six-hour boat-and-hike trip costs $239 per person, including lunch and a naturalist-guide.

Operating out of Bellingham, **San Juan Cruises** (360/738-8099 or 800/443-4552, www.whales.com, $89 adults, $45 kids, free for under 6) offers Sunday-only trips to Sucia Island that include 2.5 hours to explore the island and a picnic lunch on the beach.

Based in Anacortes, **Island Express Charters** (360/299-2875 or 877/473-9777, www.islandexpresscharters.com, $210 per person round-trip to Sucia) has high-speed landing craft with space for kayaks ($30-49 extra), bikes ($20 extra), and gear.

Paraclete Charters (360/420-5187, www.paracletecharters.com, $190 per person round-trip, add $10 for bikes or $20 for kayaks) provides water taxi service to Sucia from Anacortes.

Kenmore Air (425/486-1257 or 800/543-9595, www.kenmoreair.com) provides charter floatplane flights to Sucia Island.

TURN ISLAND MARINE STATE PARK

Just a quarter mile from San Juan Island's east shore, **Turn Island** (360/378-2044, www.parks.wa.gov) is within easy kayaking distance of Friday Harbor. The 35-acre island is both a marine state park and a part of San Juan Islands National Wildlife Refuge. The island was named by the British in 1858 to denote the abrupt change in course required when navigating the San Juan Channel here.

For such a little place, Turn Island has more than its share of attractions, including three mooring buoys ($15), two pebbly beaches, camping, nearby scuba diving, and three miles of hiking trails. One path completely circles Turn Island, with another cutting through its densely forested center.

Campers can pitch a tent at one of 12 primitive campsites ($12), which fill quickly. The island has picnic tables and compost toilets, but no water. Campfires and charcoal grills are not allowed, so bring your cookstove and fuel. The proximity to Friday Harbor makes this island both easy to reach and close to the noises caused by all that summertime activity, resulting in something less than a wilderness experience.

Getting There

Turn Island is a very popular place for day-use picnickers and hikers who arrive by small boat or sea kayak. The closest access is from a little parking lot on Turn Point Road just 1.5 miles east of Friday Harbor; it is locally called Pinedrona Cove. From here, it's 0.2 mile to the island. Note, however, that the channel between Turn Island and San Juan Island can have strong currents and wakes from passing ferries. You can also put in at the Friday Harbor dock.

Private Islands

Scattered across the San Juans are islands that are predominately—or entirely—owned by private individuals or nonprofit organizations. Not all of these islands are restricted to landowners, however, and a number of these have at least some publicly accessible areas.

Some islands have only a single home; others host a few dozen residences and an unpaved airstrip. None have more than 80 or so people. Privacy is closely guarded on many of these islands, and visitors—particularly those who trespass on private land—are not appreciated.

Anyone interested in buying their own island should look over local real estate publications or a website such as www.privateislandsonline.com. When I last checked, four islands were available, including 29-acre **Trump Island** (off Decatur Island) for the bargain price of $8.7 million. It includes a 7,000-square-foot, six-bedroom home, deepwater dock, and helipad. And no, it isn't (yet) owned by Donald Trump.

Note that even those islands that are entirely in private hands may have beaches and tidelands that are accessible to the public if you arrive by boat. The Washington Department of Natural Resources (360/856-3500, www.dnr.wa.gov) produces detailed State Public Lands Quadrangle Maps showing public beaches in the San Juans and elsewhere.

BLAKELY ISLAND

As the state ferry heads west from Anacortes to the San Juans, it threads its way between two large and privately owned islands, Blakely and Decatur. Blakely is the namesake of Johnston Blakely, a U.S. naval commander in the War of 1812, and was named during the 1841 Wilkes Expedition. Today, Blakely is sometimes called the "Flying Island." Many residents are pilots whose homes are adjacent to the airstrip; they taxi right up their driveways and park.

Blakely has a heavily wooded interior (all second-growth forests from logging in the 1950s), two lakes, a 100-foot-high waterfall, several large hills (one is 1,042 feet), and miles of private roads. A public marina is located on the northern tip of Blakely across from

Blakey Island

Obstruction Island. Visitors are welcome here, and guest moorage is available, along with a post office, picnic tables, a barbecue shelter, fuel, showers, and washers and dryers. A good little general store (360/375-6121) has food, basic supplies, ice, and even espresso. Beyond this, almost the entire island is private and completely off-limits. A handful of locals live on the island year-round, with more flying or boating in seasonally. In addition, Seattle Pacific University (360/375-6224, www.spu. edu) owns 967 acres on Blakely and operates the Blakely Island Field Station, which it uses for marine biology and ecological research; there is no public access.

Getting There

You can't stay on Blakely without permission, but you can at least get there and check out the marina. **Paraclete Charters** (360/420-5187, www.paracletecharters.com, $76 per person round-trip, add $10 for bikes or $20 for kayaks) provides water taxi service to Blakely from Anacortes. Also based in Anacortes, **Island Express Charters** (360/299-2875 or 877/473-9777, www.islandexpresscharters.com, $60-80 per person round-trip) has high-speed landing craft with space for kayaks ($30-40 extra), bikes ($20 extra), and gear. **San Juan Airlines** (360/293-4691 or 800/874-4434, www.sanjuanairlines.com) has daily scheduled flights to Blakely Island from Anacortes and Bellingham. **Kenmore Air** (425/486-1257 or 800/543-9595, www.kenmoreair.com) provides charter floatplane flights to Blakely.

CANOE ISLAND

Halfway between Shaw and Lopez Islands is this privately owned 50-acre island, home to the **Canoe Island French Camp** (360/468-2329, www.canoeisland.org), a nonprofit language and culture summer camp that attracts children from around the nation. The coed camp opened in 1969 and is staffed by French speakers who work with the 45 campers, ages 9-16. Kids don't need to know any French to attend, and there's a 1:3 staff-to-camper ratio.

All counselors are fluent in French, and many come from France and other French-speaking countries.

Campers stay in tepees, and mornings are filled with French-language classes and activities, such as theater, fencing, music, and French cooking. Afternoons include games, kayaking, swimming, sailing, and boating. Four sessions are offered each summer, each lasting two or three weeks, and rates start around $2,100 for a two-week session. Three-day family camps ($200-300/person) take place over Memorial Day and Labor Day weekends, providing a great intro for younger kids. The program is semi-immersion, in which the campers are encouraged to use French as much as possible. The island is not open to the public, though the tidelands are public below the mean high tide line.

DEADMAN AND GOOSE ISLANDS

These two little islands are sandwiched between Lopez and San Juan Islands and are owned by the Nature Conservancy (206/343-4344, www.nature.org). **Deadman Island** is just west of Shark Reef along Lopez, while **Goose Island** is a grassy isle off Cattle Point on San Juan Island. They are not generally open to the public, but access may be allowed if you contact TNC in advance. Deadman is used by the University of Washington Friday Harbor Laboratory for marine research.

The conservancy also owns the publicly accessible **Chuckanut Island** within Chuckanut Bay just south of Bellingham. This five-acre island is popular with kayakers and features graceful madrone trees and a short trail.

DECATUR AND CENTER ISLANDS

Decatur Island is just east of Lopez Island and immediately south of Blakely Island. This large island is privately owned and home to 60 or so people year-round and hundreds more seasonally. The island has a post office, grade school (the smallest one in Washington,

Gumdrop Islands

Boats for the San Juans leave the Quackenbush Dock in Bellingham at seven. On a Puget Sound morning in winter, seven is pitch-dark night. In summer, it has been full day for two hours or more. In the fall and spring, it is pale dawn. That is how it was on this September day, but fresh and clear, as though the world had got up on the right side of the bed.

Little fishing boats rolled sleepily against their moorings. Another passenger-and-freight boat was loading. It left just before us. I watched its keel rip open the bright silk of the bay.

Later, I learned the names of the dark green islands we passed, but that morning they were mysterious and dreamlike. Eliza slipped behind. Lummi Island, elephant-big, reared up on its haunches in front of the boat, but we side-stepped it and went on. Eagle Cliff on Cypress, Blakely Island, Lopez, Shaw, Orcas, Deer Harbor, Waldron, Stuart Island.

From the narrow channel between Johns and Stuart, we saw a tall, long, lovely island just ahead.

"That's Spieden," the captain said. "Ed Chevalier lives there. His wife's father homesteaded part of it, and Ed has gradually got it all. Just on the other side of Spieden is the little island you are looking for."

Across another channel, seagulls screaming. Around the immense hip of Spieden—and there was Sentinel Island, like a green gumdrop, fir trees lifting their beautiful crowns into the sky, sedum-covered bluffs shearing straight down into the rich, green-blue water.

from June Burn's *Living High,* an autobiography published by Griffin Bay Bookstore on San Juan Island.

with 4-6 students), boat launch, and airport, plus miles of scenic county roads open to the public. The island's only business—a country store—has closed, there are no lodgings, you can't get off the roads to explore the private lands, and the beaches are not readily accessible. So it's no surprise that the island is not on most travelers' agendas. Experienced kayakers sometimes visit pretty **White Cliff Beach** on the southeastern side of Decatur, walking the public tidelands. Island rentals are sometimes available via **VRBO** (www.vrbo.com).

Decatur Island received its name during the 1841 Wilkes Expedition and is named for Stephen Decatur, a famous U.S. naval officer who served during the War of 1812 and in various skirmishes in northern Africa. He is best known for the maxim, "Our country, right or wrong." Decatur was killed in a duel with a fellow captain at the age of 40.

Nearby **Center Island** is a 222-acre private island sandwiched between Decatur and Lopez Islands. It has quite a few summer homes and an airstrip.

Getting There

Paraclete Charters (360/420-5187, www. paracletecharters.com, $38 per person round-trip, add $10 for bikes or $20 for kayaks) provides service to Decatur and Center Islands from Anacortes. Also based in Anacortes, **Island Express Charters** (360/299-2875 or 877/473-9777, www.islandexpresscharters. com, $90 per person round-trip to Decatur or Center Islands) has high-speed landing craft with space for kayaks ($30-40 extra), bikes ($20 extra), and gear. **San Juan Airlines** (360/293-4691 or 800/874-4434, www.san-juanairlines.com) has chartered flights to Decatur from Anacortes or Bellingham. **Kenmore Air** (425/486-1257 or 800/543-9595, www.kenmoreair.com) lands at Decatur Island on a charter basis.

JOHNS ISLAND

A little more than a mile long, this privately owned island has a mixture of rocky bluffs and quiet beaches, but no public facilities—unless you count the popular summer camp

(Camp Nor'wester). The island lies immediately east of Stuart Island and north of Spieden Island.

Johns Island is the home of **Camp Nor'wester** (425/670-1935, www.norwester. org), a coed summer camp for ages 9-16. The camp has been in existence since 1935, though it only recently moved to the beautiful 135-acre Johns Island site from Lopez Island; billionaire Paul Allen bought the old camp property. Kids take part in such traditional summer-camp activities as camping, sailing, kayaking, canoeing (on a 35-foot Haida-style canoe), and natural history, along with a ropes course, biking, and arts and crafts. The emphasis is on working with peers to develop friendships and to learn together rather than independently. Sessions include a maximum of 170 campers with a staff of 75. The camp has a three-tier pricing system based on parental income, and four-week sessions for ages 11-16 cost $4,025-4,475, while two-week camps for ages 9-10 are $2,075-2,525; prices include transportation to and from Seattle. In late August, a special four-day "preview session" provides an introduction for parents and kids. The cost is just $325 per person, including transportation from Anacortes. This is a great way to introduce your child to summer camp.

Getting There

Two Anacortes-based companies provide water taxi service to the island: **Island Express Charters** (360/299-2875 or 877/473-9777, www.islandexpresscharters.com, $290 per person round-trip) and **Paraclete Charters** (360/420-5187, www.paracletecharters.com, $190 per person round-trip, add $10 for bikes or $20 for kayaks).

OBSTRUCTION ISLAND

This triangular island is wedged between Blakely and Orcas Islands. The state park campsites at Obstruction Pass on Orcas are less than 400 yards away. Entirely private, Obstruction Island has rocky shores, tiny beaches, and a dozen or so homes. Public access is not allowed. The island covers 217 acres and is heavily forested. Even though you can't go ashore, kayakers often put in at Obstruction Pass and paddle around the island.

SATELLITE ISLAND

The Seattle YMCA's **Camp Orkila** (206/382-5009, www.seattleymca.org) owns 107-acre Satellite Island, located just off the north side of Stuart Island at Prevost Harbor. The island was named for the H.M.S. *Satellite,* a steamship used for surveys by the British during the Pig War. Satellite Island has no permanent structures and is not open to the public, though Camp Orkila uses it for adventure trips. (The only exceptions are areas below mean high tide line, which are publicly accessible at low tides.)

SENTINEL ISLAND

Owned by **The Nature Conservancy** (206/343-4344, www.nature.org), Sentinel Island is a 15-acre forested island immediately south of Spieden Island. The island is preserved as habitat for eagles, black oystercatchers, and glaucous-winged gulls today, but it was once the home of June and Farrar Burn, who homesteaded here in 1940. June went on to write about life here in the autobiographical *Living High* (Griffin Bay Bookstore) and described their adventures sailing around the San Juans in *100 Days in the San Juans* (Long House Printcrafters & Publishers). Both books make for interesting reading if you're looking for a taste of a quieter era. Sentinel Island is not generally open to the public, but access may be allowed if you contact TNC in advance.

SINCLAIR ISLAND

Sinclair Island was named during the Wilkes Expedition of 1841 for Arthur Sinclair Sr., a U.S. naval captain during the War of 1812. During his heyday as a smuggler, Larry Kelly owned a third of Sinclair Island.

This small and mostly private island is less than a mile northeast of Cypress Island.

A county dock extends from the southwest end of the island, providing access to the little village called Urban and to the dirt roads that crisscross Sinclair. It's a 0.7-mile walk to **Sinclair Island Natural Wildlife Area,** a 35-acre beachfront parcel on the southeast end of the island. By combining beach walks with the island's quiet back roads, you can spend an enjoyable afternoon wandering the island while remaining on public lands.

Getting There

Paraclete Charters (360/420-5187, www. paracletecharters.com, $38 per person round-trip, add $10 for bikes or $20 for kayaks) provides service to Sinclair Island from Anacortes. Also based in Anacortes, **Island Express Charters** (360/299-2875 or 877/473-9777, www.islandexpresscharters.com, $90 person round-trip to Sinclair) has high-speed landing craft with space for kayaks ($30-40 extra), bikes ($20 extra), and gear. **San Juan Airlines** (360/293-4691 or 800/874-4434, www.sanjuanairlines.com) will fly to Sinclair Island on a charter basis.

SPIEDEN ISLAND

Located between Stuart and San Juan Islands, Spieden (pronounced SPY-den) Island covers 480 acres and is privately owned with no public access. The island is informally known as John Wayne Island. In the early 1970s, Wayne and two taxidermists bought the entire island and began importing exotic animals for wealthy trophy hunters to bag. Environmentalists protested the sham, and locals feared stray bullets would be a hazard for people on nearby San Juan Island. After three years, the game farm closed. Most of the axis deer, Japanese sika deer, Spanish goats, Corsican mouflon sheep, Barbary sheep, Indian blackbuck, and other animals gradually disappeared, though mouflon sheep and sika deer may be seen grazing in the distinctive open grasslands lining the south side of Spieden. Forests carpet the north side of the island, and Steller sea lions are sometimes seen on rocks off the eastern end of Spieden.

The island is now owned by billionaire James Jannard, founder of Oakley Sunglasses and creator of the RED digital cinema camera; it's said he paid $20 million for the island. You'll hear all sorts of wild rumors from locals about the island, including ones of high-tech surveillance equipment to keep intruders away.

WALDRON ISLAND

This large, mostly private island is 1.5 miles northwest of Orcas. The locals don't generally take kindly to outsiders, but the roads are open to the public, along with the dock at Cowlitz Bay. There are no stores, electricity, or phone service on the island, though it does have a small post office, cemetery, grade school, and landing strip. The year-round population is around 100, but it doubles when summer residents show up. Waldron Island was named for two members of the 1841 Wilkes Expedition: Thomas W. Waldron and R. R. Waldron.

Much of Waldron Island is flat and marshy, though the south end rises to 600 feet at Disney Mountain. **Waldron Island Preserve** encompasses 478 acres along Cowlitz Bay and Disney Mountain. These lands are jointly managed by the Nature Conservancy (206/343-4344, www.nature. org) and the San Juan Preservation Trust (www.sjpt.org), with only day use allowed. The conservancy has a steward on the island; call for access information.

Waldron gained a measure of infamy in 1997 when drug enforcement officers swarmed across the island in search of marijuana growing operations. Several residents were arrested, and 886 plants were seized. The operation led to finger pointing in all directions, and still leaves a bad taste with islanders who cherish their leave-me-alone privacy.

Getting There

Outer Island Excursions (360/376-3711, www.outerislandx.com, $240 round-trip for up to six people) provides water taxi service to Waldron from Orcas Island. **Paraclete Charters** (360/420-5187, www.

King of the Smugglers

Smuggling along the U.S.-Canadian border has always been a fact of life, and the items transported back and forth have always been the same: liquor (particularly during the United States' foray into prohibition), illegal drugs, illegal Chinese immigrants, and even Canadian wool and silks.

An Irishman named Larry Kelly was the most infamous of all the smugglers, though perhaps not the most successful at staying away from the law. Kelly arrived in America simply by jumping ship in New Orleans. He fought in the Civil War on the Confederate side. Not long after the war, he arrived in Seattle. He had heard about the "hole in the fence," meaning the easy smuggling across the Canadian border—especially through Puget Sound—of liquor, opium, and Chinese laborers.

Kelly bought an old sailboat in 1872 and sailed north to Guemes Island, where he set up shop. He learned it was easy to hide from the revenue cutters because they ran on a set schedule. Kelly made a nice profit smuggling opium, which he bought at $15 a pound from factories in Victoria and sold for three times that in Seattle. The opium was packed in watertight tin cans, and to each can Kelly tied a chunk of salt as a sinker in case he was caught and had to dump the opium. After the salt dissolved, the can would float to the surface so Kelly could go back out and retrieve it.

Kelly charged about $50 for smuggling a Chinese laborer out of Canada and into the United States. Although he denied ever killing one, other smugglers weren't averse to chaining a boatload of immigrants together and dumping them overboard to drown if a revenue cutter approached. It is likely he did some of the things common among his fellow smugglers, such as putting laborers down on a beach in British Columbia and telling them they were in America.

Kelly was caught in 1882 with 40 cases of Canadian whisky and fined. He wasn't caught again for another four years, but that time he had 567 tins of opium. For this he was sent to McNeil Island Federal Penitentiary. In 1891 he was caught for the final time, on a train with opium in his traveling bag. He was put away again, and while in prison he decided to change his life. He wrote to the Louisiana Chapter of the Daughters of the Confederacy to see if any of his old friends from the Civil War were still alive. He found some in a Confederate old soldiers' home in New Orleans, and it was there he went on his release from prison, never to smuggle again.

At least, he was never caught at it.

---

paracletecharters.com, $190 per person round-trip, add $10 for bikes or $20 for kayaks) provides service to Waldron Island from Anacortes. Also based in Anacortes, **Island Express Charters** (360/299-2875 or 877/473-9777, www.islandexpresscharters.com, $240 per person round-trip, add $20 for bikes or $30-40 for kayaks) has two high-speed landing craft. **San Juan Airlines** (360/293-4691 or 800/874-4434, www.sanjuanairlines.com) will land at the Waldron Island airstrip on a charter basis.

★ YELLOW ISLAND PRESERVE

This 11-acre slice of paradise is virtually equidistant from San Juan, Shaw, and Orcas Islands. Owned by the **Nature Conservancy** (206/343-4344, www.nature.org), Yellow Island is famous for its lush wildflower displays that peak mid-April-early June, when more than 50 species are in bloom. Long and thin, Yellow Island has sand spits and grassy meadows on both ends, with a swath of evergreens across the middle. The lack of deer and strong preservation efforts keep the island in a pristine state.

Yellow Island was home for many years to Lewis and Tib Dodd, who lived a life that followed Henry David Thoreau's philosophy of self-sufficiency and harmony with nature. Lewis died in 1960, and Tib continued to spend summers on the island for many more years before donating the land to The Nature Conservancy in 1980. The simple driftwood-and-rock cabin built by the Dodds now serves as the caretaker's seasonal home.

Yellow Island is managed as an ecological

preserve with a very stringent set of regulations. Visitors can only visit between the hours of 10am and 4pm daily and will generally need to land their kayak or small boat on the southeast beach. No camping or overnight mooring is allowed, and you can't bring pets, food, or beverages onto the island. Groups larger than six people will need written permission to visit. A 0.5-mile trail rings the small island; pick up an interpretive brochure before heading out.

Getting There

Most visitors to Yellow Island arrive by sea kayak or motorboat from Deer Harbor on Orcas Island or Friday Harbor on San Juan Island. Located at Deer Harbor Marina on Orcas, **Orcas Boat Rentals** (360/376-7616, www.orcasboatrentals.com) has skiff rentals. It's a short 15-minute ride to Yellow Island.

Also timed for the peak of the flowers, **Shearwater Adventures** (360/376-4699, www.shearwaterkayaks.com, $89 per person) guides springtime kayak day trips to Yellow Island from Deer Harbor Marina.

Gnat's Nature Hikes (360/376-6629, www.orcasislandhikes.com) leads boat-and-hike trips to Yellow Island in the spring from Orcas Island. There's a three-person minimum and a six-person maximum.

Other Wasp Islands

Yellow Island is one of the Wasp Islands. Others in the group include Bird Rock, Cliff, Coon, Crane, Low, McConnell, Nob, and Shirt Tail Reef. Crane Island is the largest of these, covering 222 privately owned acres. McConnell Island is also private, but a tombolo (narrow sandy strip) links it to diminutive **Northwest McConnell Rock State Park,** a popular lunch spot for kayakers. Look along the shore of McConnell for remains of an old miniature railroad that was once used to entertain kids.

Background

The Landscape

ISLAND NAMES

A look at a map of northern Puget Sound will reveal a mélange of Spanish, British, and American names. None of the original Native American names remain in the San Juans, though surrounding areas kept a few indigenous terms, including Lummi Island, Samish Bay, and Skagit Island.

The Strait of Juan de Fuca is named for Apostolos Valerianos, a Greek who sailed for Spain under the alias of Juan de Fuca. The first European to sail the northwest coast of the United States and Canada, he entered Puget Sound in 1592, believing that he had found the fabled Northwest Passage. The Spaniard Francisco de Eliza and his assistant, Lopez Gonzales de Haro, explored these waters more thoroughly in 1791 and 1792, labeling the San Juan Islands, Haro Strait, Rosario Strait, and Orcas, Lopez, Eliza, Sucia, Patos, Matia, Guemes, and Fidalgo Islands.

Many regional landmarks—including Vancouver Island, Puget Sound, Georgia Strait, Cypress Island, Whidbey Island, Possession Sound, Mount Baker, and Mount Rainier—were named during English expeditions by Captain James Cook in 1778 and Captain George Vancouver in 1792.

Another major player in the naming game was Lieutenant Charles Wilkes of the U.S. Navy, who sailed through the San Juans on an 1841 scientific expedition. Wilkes applied the names of his naval heroes (along with several crewmembers) to everything in sight: Allan Island, Barnes Island, Blakely Island, Burrows Island, Clark Island, Decatur Island, Frost Island, Henry Island, James Island, Jones Island, Shaw Island, Sinclair Island, Spieden Island, Stuart Island, and Waldron Island. He also tried to rename the main islands of Orcas, San Juan, and Lopez, but his choices didn't stick.

THE SALISH SEA

In recent years, biologists have begun using the name Salish Sea for the waters surrounding the San Juan Islands. This great inland sea—named for the Coast Salish people who first made this their home—encompasses Puget Sound, the Strait of Juan de Fuca, and the Strait of Georgia off the west side of Vancouver Island. Enormous glaciers carved out the basin that became the Salish Sea more than 14,000 years ago.

The Salish Sea is a fertile place, with twice-daily tides that sweep massive amounts of water upwards over submerged ridges, thus bringing nutrients to the top layers and surface oxygen to lower depths upon tidal retreat. Rivers and streams supply additional nutrients to the mix, and the temperate climate supports a diverse ecological web. The result is an incredibly productive environment for all forms of marinelife. Steve Yates's *Orcas, Eagles, and Kings* provides an in-depth introduction to the Salish Sea.

GEOLOGY

The San Juan Islands are composed of a complex and jumbled assemblage of rocks that were laid down in ancient oceanic trenches and then pushed up into mountains by tectonic forces. Over the last three million years, they were further shaped by a series of enormous glaciers that pushed southward from Canada and bulldozed everything in their path. The land that would later become the San Juans was buried several times beneath hundreds of feet of ice. When the last of the glaciers retreated around 12,000 years ago,

---

Previous: homes on the shore of San Juan Island; red fox on San Juan Island.

they left behind evidence of their passing, including glacial erratics (large boulders that were carried atop the ice) and bedrock that shows the scratches and gouges of glaciers.

Other unusual rocks found on the islands include marine fossils on Sucia Island (in Fossil Bay, of course), impressive pillow basalts (created when lava flowed under the Pacific Ocean) along San Juan's west coast and Lopez's south side, and substantial limestone deposits on the north end of San Juan Island. This limestone was mined extensively in the early 1900s and used to produce Portland cement. The old limekilns are still visible at Roche Harbor Resort and Lime Kiln Point State Park. For a more detailed look at San Juan Islands geology, pick up *Roadside Geology of Washington* by David Alt and Donald Hyndman.

CLIMATE

Noting their location—in the middle of northern Puget Sound—one might assume that the San Juan Islands suffer from Washington's notoriously wet weather. Fortunately, such is not the case. Mountains on the Olympic Peninsula and Vancouver Island force clouds to drop much of their moisture before they reach the San Juans, creating a rain shadow.

Summertime visitors are pleasantly surprised by the warm and sunny weather that predominates. Winters are typically overcast and rainy, though still drier than many other parts of Washington.

The San Juans do most of their tourist business between Memorial Day and Labor Day, when the weather is delightful. For locals, September and October are the best months of the year: The tourists are gone, and the weather is still warm and relatively dry, with highs in the 60s and lows in the 40s or 50s.

Rain, Fog, and Wind

Rainfall amounts to around 29 inches per year on the San Juans, compared with 37 inches in Seattle. Precipitation varies across the islands, with the driest areas closer to Anacortes or southern Lopez and the wettest on the northwestern end of San Juan Island.

The sun shines an average of 247 days a year, much of that during the summer months; July and August each average only an inch of rain per month. May, June, and September are also relatively dry. November, December, and January make up the rainiest season, with more than four inches of precipitation typically falling each month. Snow is

the Salish Sea

uncommon in the San Juans—only around seven inches fall per year—and it rarely stays around for more than a few days. The one exception is the summit of Mount Constitution, half a mile up on Orcas Island, where snow occasionally gets two feet deep before a warm spell melts it again.

Fog can get thick around the islands at times, particularly in late summer. Fortunately, it is generally gone by early afternoon.

Winds are typically mild in the San Juans, but passes often funnel them, causing very different conditions depending on your location around an island. Sailors take advantage of these winds, which often top 20 knots in open straits and channels. Those in small boats—particularly sea kayaks—need to avoid such areas when the winds are blowing. Occasional winter storms can bring extreme events, such as the December 1990 nor'easter that flattened thousands of old-growth trees, particularly on Jones Island.

Temperatures

Temperatures on the islands are generally quite comfortable. Midsummer days are typically in the upper 60s and low 70s, and only rarely top 85°F; the record high was 92°F on July 17, 1941. Nighttime lows in the summer average 50°F.

The record low for the San Juans was 8°F on January 13, 1950, but most winters the thermometer doesn't even come close to zero. In January (the coldest month), daytime highs are typically in the low to mid-40s, with nighttime minimums a few degrees above freezing. The thermometer dips below freezing approximately 34 days a year.

Weather Updates

Get current weather and marine forecasts for the San Juan Islands—and anywhere else in America—from the National Weather Service's website (http://weather.noaa.gov). Another useful web source for weather is linked through the *Journal of the San Juans* (www.sanjuanjournal.com). Boaters can also get the latest forecast on their VHF radios (channels 1, 2, and 8); weather reports are broadcast continuously.

Water

Water—or the lack thereof—is a serious problem on the San Juan Islands, particularly during the all-too-frequent drought years. Relatively low annual precipitation, limited underground aquifers, and the presence of only a handful of year-round creeks and lakes make water a scarce commodity. As the population increases and development grows, the demands for water escalate. Old wells are drying up, and new ones are often contaminated by saltwater intrusion as the underground aquifers are drained. Most bed-and-breakfasts and other lodgings use low-flow showerheads and other means to conserve water. Do your part by not wasting a drop. This means avoiding long showers, not leaving the water running while brushing your teeth or shaving, and not flushing the toilet as often.

PUBLIC LANDS
State Parks

Numerous state parks (360/902-8844, www.parks.wa.gov) are scattered across the San Juans. **Moran State Park** on Orcas Island is the biggest and most famous of these, covering more than 5,200 acres of heavily forested terrain. It includes the islands' highest point, 2,409-foot Mount Constitution. A paved road leads to the summit, and the park offers camping, swimming, boating, fishing, and more than 30 miles of hiking trails. Smaller parks are **Spencer Spit State Park** on Lopez Island, a popular camping spot; **Lime Kiln Point State Park** on San Juan Island, a day-use-only park famous for views of killer whales from shore; and two small places on Orcas Island: **Obstruction Pass State Park** and **Point Doughty Marine State Park.**

Several smaller islands contain **marine state parks** that are open to hiking and camping and are accessible only by boat or floatplane. These include Blind, Clark, Doe, Jones, James, Matia, Patos, Posey, Stuart, Sucia, and

Preserving the San Juans

To vacationers, the San Juans may seem like a recreational playground, but for island inhabitants, they provide sustenance. Puget Sound is becoming increasingly developed as the population spirals upward, leaving the islands as a place to rediscover the natural world. But the islands themselves are also under pressure as new homes encroach on old farms or carve openings into remote shorelines, as public areas are closed off because the access trails cross private lands, and as increasing use impacts the natural areas. It's yet another case of wild places being loved to death. Several nonprofit organizations are working to protect the San Juans through land purchases and environmental action.

SAN JUAN PRESERVATION TRUST

In existence since 1979, the **San Juan Preservation Trust** (360/468-3509, www.sjpt.org) works with local landowners to protect special features of their lands for future generations through conservation easements and donations. Over the years the trust has protected more than 9,300 acres of land, including working farms, forests, picturesque shorelines, and wildlife-rich wetlands. Most of the property preserved by the trust remains in private hands, with public access by permission only.

SAN JUAN COUNTY LAND BANK

Established by a 1990 ballot measure, the **San Juan County Land Bank** (360/378-4402, www.sjclandbank.org) is a public program funded by a 1 percent real estate transfer tax. These taxes raise $1 million-2 million annually (depending upon the real estate market) to acquire land or conservation easements. More than 3,500 acres have been protected in natural areas, including such places as Hummel Lake and Upright Head Preserves on Lopez, Crescent Beach and Turtleback Mountain Preserves on Orcas, and Westside and Limekiln Preserves on San Juan.

FRIENDS OF THE SAN JUANS

Based in Friday Harbor, **Friends of the San Juans** (650 Mullis St., 360/378-2319, www.san-juans.org) is a local environmental group with nearly 2,000 members. The organization focuses on land-use issues and beach research, and pushes for shoreline and Salish Sea preservation throughout the islands.

THE NATURE CONSERVANCY

An international organization, **The Nature Conservancy** (206/343-4344, www.nature.org) owns Deadman, Goose, Sentinel, and Yellow Islands and has 480 acres on Waldron Island. Only Yellow Island is readily accessible to the public.

Turn Islands. Small marine state parks are also located on Orcas and San Juan Islands.

National Wildlife Refuge

San Juan Islands National Wildlife Refuge encompasses 83 islands and islets, most of which are off-limits to tourists, to protect birds and other animals. These islands provide vital nesting spots for bald eagles and seabirds, and the rocks are used as haul-out areas for harbor seals, California and Steller sea lions, and elephant seals.

Boaters (including sea kayakers) must stay at least 200 yards offshore from these islands. Landing is permitted only at two designated areas, on Turn and Matia Islands. The refuge is managed by the U.S. Fish & Wildlife Service (360/457-8451, www.pacific.fws.gov), which is based in Port Angeles; contact the agency for a small map of the islands. Marine navigation charts also show which islands are within the national wildlife refuge.

San Juan Island National Historical Park

The so-called Pig War is memorialized in the 1,750-acre **San Juan Island National Historical Park** (headquarters: 640 Mullis St., Friday Harbor, 360/378-2240, www.nps. gov/sajh). Established in 1966, the park is divided into two sections. American Camp occupies a beautiful grassy peninsula on the southeast end of the island, while English Camp is in a wooded, peaceful cove on the opposite side of San Juan. Both areas are worth a visit, not only for the handful of historic buildings but also for excellent hiking trails and gorgeous beaches.

San Juan Islands National Monument

Created by President Obama in 2013, **San Juan Islands National Monument** (360/468-3754, www.sanjuanislandsnca. org) covers 1,000 acres of land spread across a multitude of locations. The most notable of these are Blind Island off the north shore of Shaw Island, Patos Island north of Orcas Island, Turn Point on Stuart Island, Cattle Point on San Juan Island, and three places on Lopez Island: Iceberg Point, Point Colville, and Watmough Bay. The national monument also encompasses dozens of smaller islands and rocks, from Chuckanut Rock off Bellingham to Pudding Island near the Canadian border. San Juan Islands National Monument is maintained by the Bureau of Land Management, based on Lopez Island.

Other Public Lands

Seven **San Juan County parks** (360/378-8420, www.co.san-juan.wa.us/parks) are on the ferry-served islands: Agate Beach, Blackie Brady Memorial Beach, Odlin, and Otis Perkins County Parks on Lopez Island; Ruben Tarte and San Juan County Parks on San Juan Island; and Shaw Island County Park on Shaw Island. Camping is available at Odlin, San Juan, and Shaw Island County Parks; the others are for day use only.

The **Washington Department of Natural Resources** (DNR, 360/856-3500, www.dnr.wa.gov) has considerable land on Cypress Island, with primitive campsites, hiking trails, and protected moorages. It also manages a campsite on Lummi Island.

The **San Juan County Land Bank** (360/378-4402, www.sjclandbank.org) has acquired more than 3,100 acres in 13 natural areas scattered around the islands. These are open to the public for day use only.

The Nature Conservancy (206/343-4344, www.nature.org) owns several small San Juan islands, plus 480 acres on Waldron Island, but only Yellow Island is readily accessible to the public.

The **University of Washington**'s Friday Harbor Laboratories (360/378-2165, http://depts.washington.edu/fhl) manages several natural areas around the San Juans, but only Cedar Rock Biological Preserve on Shaw Island is open to the public.

Plants and Animals

Plant and animal communities on the San Juans reflect local topographic and weather conditions. Forests dominate in many areas, but the islands also contain broad expanses of grassland, open meadows and fields, rich marine areas, marshes and lagoons, and a long and diverse shoreline that includes rocky cliffs, sheltered bays, and sandy beaches. There are even islets so dry that cacti grow.

HABITATS
Forests

Dense coniferous forests (or ones regenerating after logging) cover large portions of the islands, and are typically dominated by Douglas fir, western hemlock, and western red cedar. Common understory plants include salal, Oregon grape, red elderberry, thimbleberry, salmonberry, blackberry, wild roses, and various ferns. Dry, rocky sites commonly have picturesque groves of Pacific madrone (madrona), particularly along island shores. At higher elevations and on exposed ridges, shore pine often grows.

Forests are home to Columbian black-tailed deer, raccoons, beavers, mink, river otters, bats, shrews, and various introduced species of squirrels, along with such birds as ravens, woodpeckers, winter wrens, and owls. Good places to explore island forests include Moran State Park and Madrona Point on Orcas Island, English Camp and Jackle's Lagoon on San Juan Island, Odlin County Park on Lopez Island, Cedar Rock Biological Preserve on Shaw Island, and the boat-accessible marine state parks on Jones, Matia, and Sucia Islands.

Meadows

Meadows may be either natural grasslands, hilltops, and mountain slopes, or spaces created by the clearing of land for agriculture. Some of the best grasslands to explore include American Camp and the top of Mount Young on San Juan Island, Mount Constitution on Orcas Island, the wonderful floral displays on the Nature Conservancy's Yellow Island, and fallow agricultural land on all four of the main islands.

Animals commonly seen in island meadows include nonnative European rabbits, voles (meadow mice), shrews, alligator lizards, red foxes (a nonnative species on San Juan Island), and small birds, such as vesper sparrows, savannah sparrows, and American goldfinches. Overhead you might see birds of prey, such as bald and golden eagles or northern harriers. A few small islands (including Cactus, Gossip, and Cemetery Islands) contain areas called **Puget prairies,** with distinctive plants like the lance-leafed stone and even prickly pear cactus—the only species of cactus native to western Washington.

Wetlands

Swamps, lagoons, marshes, ponds, and other wetlands are vital areas for wildlife on the islands and are home to river otters, muskrats, beavers, raccoons, garter snakes, red-legged frogs, Pacific tree frogs, rough-skinned newts, red-winged blackbirds, great blue herons, Canada geese, belted kingfishers, and many species of ducks. Good places to find wetlands include Jackle's Lagoon and Egg Lake on San Juan Island, the Frank Richardson Wildlife Preserve on Orcas Island, and Spencer Spit Lagoon on Lopez Island.

Shorelines

San Juan County contains more than 375 miles of shoreline—the most of any county in the lower 48 states. This coast varies widely, from rocks to sand to mud, and supports an equally varied population of animals. Intertidal areas are particularly productive.

Beautiful **sandy beaches** are found on all the larger islands, with some of the best at American Camp on San Juan Island, Obstruction Pass State Park on Orcas Island,

madrone tree on Orcas Island

here include minke whales, harbor porpoises, Dall's porpoises, California sea lions, Steller sea lions, harbor seals, and elephant seals. Of course, these waters also contain many species of fish and other creatures. Divers are attracted to the vibrant undersea world of the San Juans, commercial whale-watching trips are a summertime staple, and fish are caught commercially and for sport.

One of the best ways to see killer whales—without impacting them in any way—is by viewing from the shore at Lime Kiln Point State Park on San Juan Island. Folks riding the Washington State Ferries are certain to see gulls and various seabirds along the way and may also spot bald eagles and the occasional whale. San Juan Islands National Wildlife Refuge covers 83 islands and rocky points, providing protected breeding and resting areas for an incredible array of seabirds and mammals.

TREES

The most distinctive and photogenic tree species on the San Juan Islands is the **Pacific madrone,** commonly called madrona or arbutus. These trees grow on rocky sites and are conspicuous as they angle out over the shoreline. Madrones are characterized by dark and leathery evergreen leaves and peeling reddish-orange bark that exposes a smooth underskin. Pacific madrone grows from California to British Columbia.

Washington's state tree, the **western hemlock,** is common in dense, shady forests throughout the archipelago. These trees can reach 500 years old, topping out at 200 feet. Look for the droopy crowns of western hemlock to distinguish them from other trees at a distance.

Western red cedar has distinctive flat sprays and a stringy bark. The Coast Salish people prized this tree, using it for dugout canoes and splitting the wood for planks to build their houses. The sweet-smelling wood is resistant to decay. Western red cedar is a member of the cypress family and is not a true cedar.

One of the most important trees on the San Juans, **Douglas firs** can grow to six

Spencer Spit State Park and Agate Beach County Park on Lopez Island, Shaw Island County Park on Shaw Island, Pelican Beach on Cypress Island, and Shallow Bay on Sucia Island.

Rocky shores are ubiquitous in the San Juans and are welcoming areas for wildlife, including many species of birds. Good places to find them include San Juan County Park and Lime Kiln Point State Park on San Juan Island, Madrona Point and Point Doughty on Orcas Island, Shark Reef Park and Point Colville on Lopez Island, Cedar Rock Biological Preserve on Shaw Island, Eagle Cliff on Cypress Island, Doe Island Marine State Park, Turn Point on Stuart Island, and Ev Henry Finger on Sucia Island.

Marine Areas

The rich waters around the San Juan Islands abound with marinelife. The area is justly famous for killer whales, and a surprisingly large business has grown up around whale-watching. Other marine mammals spotted

Slugs

If western Washington had an official creature, it could easily be the common slug; the region is famous for them. The damp climate is just what slugs need to thrive: not too wet, because slugs aren't waterproof (they will absorb water through their outer membranes until their bodily fluids are too diluted to support them), and not too dry, because insufficient humidity makes them dry up and die. Optimum humidity for slugs is near 100 percent, which is why you'll see them crossing the sidewalk very early in the morning, at dusk, or on misty days.

During the dry parts of the day, slugs will seek refuge under the pool cover you casually tossed onto the lawn, or under the scrap lumber piled in the back of your lot.

Slugs look like snails that have lost their shells, or like little green or brown squirts of slime about 3-5 inches long. Though more than 300 species of slugs exist worldwide, the Northwest is home to little more than a dozen. The native **banana slug,** light green or yellowish with dark spots, has been rapidly outnumbered by the imported European **black slug,** which is now far more common in area gardens than the native variety. Slugs can curl up into a ball to protect themselves, or flatten and elongate themselves to squeeze into tight places. They move on one long foot by secreting mucus that gets firm where the foot must grab hold and stays slimy under the part that must slide. They see (probably just patterns of light and dark) with eyes at the ends of a pair of tentacles; they have a mouth and eat primarily plants and mushrooms.

Getting rid of slugs is no easy matter. Traditional home remedies include salt shakers and beer traps; both require a strong stomach. Most residents just try to avoid stepping on them.

feet in diameter. They are commonly found with western hemlock and western red cedar. Heavy ridges mark the bark of mature Douglas firs, and lower limbs fall off as the tree grows, making them a favorite of loggers who appreciate the knot-free wood.

Pacific yew has sharply pointed needles and grows in moist areas, particularly along streams. Yews are slow growing and never get very tall. The Coast Salish used the dense wood to carve paddles and bows. Today, the tree is best known as the source for a potent anti-cancer chemical, taxol.

Big-leaf maples are distinguished by—you got it—their big leaves, which can reach a foot in width. The trees can grow quite large (to 100 feet high), with spreading trunks. One of the largest is on the grounds of English Camp on San Juan Island. The yellow leaves of maples are particularly beautiful in the fall. Two other related (but smaller) species are also present on the islands, the **vine maple** and **Douglas maple.**

Shore pines are a subspecies of lodgepole pine and are generally found on high, wind-swept bluffs, such as the summit of Mount Constitution on Orcas Island. Most are relatively stunted in height. The trees are well adapted to fire, with some cones that only release seeds when heat melts the sticky covering.

The **Rocky Mountain juniper** is commonly found in the Rockies, but also exists on the San Juans and nearby islands. The trees are stunted, rarely topping 20 feet in height. Cypress Island was misnamed by Captain George Vancouver when he sailed past it in 1792; the "cypress" he saw were actually Rocky Mountain junipers.

Other common trees on the San Juans include **grand firs,** recognizable by their long, flat needles with white undersides; **Sitka spruce,** which grows fast and tall and is common near the shore; and **red alder,** a common, fast-growing plant in moist areas.

MARINE LIFE
Whales and Dolphins

The most famous local mammal—the **killer whale**—attracts more than half a million visitors to the San Juans each summer. An excellent source for information about these strikingly marked and social animals, as well as other marine mammals around the islands, is the Whale Museum's website (www.whalemuseum.org).

Minke whales are gray or brownish in color, with diagonal white bands on their pectoral fins. They are generally seen as solitary individuals, moving slowly and with a blow that is often inconspicuous. Minke are the most numerous of the world's baleen whales and are frequently seen around the San Juans in the summer, but not at other times of the year. Minke whales feed by driving schools of small fish to the surface and then opening wide to engulf them. They also take advantage of clusters of fish that have been schooled together by other fish or birds; minkes pop to the surface through this ball of fish, sometimes scattering gulls and other birds when they emerge. Minke whales can reach 30 feet long, and the larger females may weigh up to 10 tons.

Gray whales are bigger than minkes and lack a dorsal fin. They have a mottled gray body and are often covered with patches of barnacles, especially on the head. They are generally seen in shallow coastal areas and migrate some 9,000 miles, from Alaska to Baja. In recent years, a few gray whales have stayed in the waters of northern Puget Sound through the summer, but they are not commonly seen.

Humpback whales can reach up to 55 feet long and are slate gray or black, with irregular knobs on the head and jaw and a short dorsal fin. Their blows are strong and obvious. Humpbacks are rarely seen around the San Juans, but are fairly common in more northern waters.

Other species of cetaceans sometimes seen around the San Juans include **false killer whales,** a relatively small whale that is mostly black; and **Pacific white-sided dolphins,** with a gray-black upper body accented by a white belly and grayish sides.

Porpoises

Visitors often think that the black-and-white sea creatures riding the bow waves of their tour boat are baby killer whales, but these playful characters are **Dall's porpoises.** They feed primarily on squid and small fish and can reach lengths of 6.5 feet and weights of up to 330 pounds.

The **harbor porpoise** is Puget Sound's smallest cetacean, growing to nearly six feet long and 150 pounds. Although similar in appearance to the Dall's porpoise, the much shyer harbor porpoise is rarely spotted in the wild. Accurate counts are impossible, but the

killer whale

population around the San Juan Islands has been estimated at fewer than 100.

Seals and Sea Lions

Harbor seals are the most abundant marine mammals in the San Juans. They can be seen at low tide sunning themselves on rocks in isolated areas, but they will quickly return to the water if approached by humans, particularly kayakers. Though they appear clumsy on land, these 100- to 200-pound seals (some males can reach 800 pounds!) are poetry in motion underwater; they flip, turn, and glide with little apparent effort, staying underwater for as long as 20 minutes. Harbor seals have a bad reputation with area salmon anglers, although studies of the seals' stomach contents and fecal material indicate that they feed primarily on flounder, herring, pollock, cod, and rockfish, as well as some mollusks and crustaceans.

The **California sea lion** is a seasonal visitor to northern Puget Sound. These dark-brown sea lions breed off the coast of California and Mexico in the early summer, and then some adventurous males migrate as far north as British Columbia for the winter.

The lighter-colored **Steller sea lions** are often seen in the spring around the San Juan Islands, particularly Spieden Island. Males of the species are much larger than the females, growing to almost 10 feet in length and weighing over a ton, while the females are a dainty six feet long and 600 pounds.

Recent years have seen an increased population of the **northern elephant seal** in waters around the San Juans. Adult males have a large elephantine snout, and the biggest may weigh upward of four tons. Females are much smaller. Both have a brownish-gray color and occasionally haul out on local beaches.

If you come upon a stranded seal, sea lion, whale, or other marine mammal, do not handle it; instead, immediately call the **Stranded Marine Mammal Hotline** at 800/562-8832.

LAND MAMMALS

European rabbits were brought to the islands in the late 19th century as caged meat

Wolf Hollow

Located on San Juan Island, north of Friday Harbor, **Wolf Hollow Wildlife Rehabilitation Center** (360/378-5000, www.wolfhollowwildlife.org) is a nonprofit organization that works with injured, sick, or orphaned wild animals. Most of these animals were injured by human activities. Since its founding in 1983, Wolf Hollow has treated more than 200 species—from hummingbirds to seals—and has a songbird aviary, raccoon pen, and eagle flight cage. It offers educational programs at local schools and parks, but the facilities are not open to the public. If you find an injured or orphaned animal on the San Juan Islands, call Wolf Hollow; the staff is available 24 hours a day.

animals but were released when the breeders ran out of money. The rabbits are now common in grassy parts of San Juan and Lopez Islands and also occur on other islands in the San Juans. Most of them remain underground during the day, emerging at dusk. Bald and golden eagles, red-tailed hawks, northern harriers, and red foxes all feed on them.

Columbian black-tailed deer are found almost everywhere on the San Juans and may even be seen swimming between the islands. The deer are quite small, generally under three feet high and only rarely more than 200 pounds. Keep your eyes open for them in old fields and orchards or in brushy areas. During the summer, deer are commonly seen early in the morning or late in the day, when temperatures are cooler.

Other island mammals include raccoons, beavers, mink, river otters, vagrant shrews, white-footed (deer) mice, Townsend's voles, and several species of bats. Flying squirrels were recently discovered on San Juan Island and are presumably native. Introduced species include muskrats, Norway rats, and house mice, plus Townsend's chipmunk on Lopez Island and red foxes and European ferrets on San Juan Island. Three types of squirrels—eastern gray squirrels, eastern fox squirrels, and Douglas squirrels—have been introduced. Surprisingly, skunks, porcupines, and coyotes are not found on the San Juans. Elk were once found on the islands, but 19th-century market hunters killed off the last of them.

REPTILES AND AMPHIBIANS

There are no poisonous snakes on the San Juans, but you might encounter three species of garter snakes (the double-striped common garter is most often seen). Other regional species include northern alligator lizards, Pacific tree frogs, red-legged frogs, northwestern toads, and rough-skinned newts, whereas bullfrogs and western painted turtles were introduced.

BIRDS

More than 200 species of birds live on or travel through the San Juans, including large numbers of shorebirds in the spring and fall, nesting seabirds, great blue herons, trumpeter swans, Canada geese, wild turkeys (introduced in the 1970s), belted kingfishers, common ravens, rufous hummingbirds, and such predators as bald eagles, red-tailed hawks, sharp-shinned hawks, northern harriers, turkey vultures, and great horned owls. San Juan Island National Historical Park and local bookstores sell a nicely designed *Wildlife of the San Juan Islands* checklist that includes all these birds, along with local mammals, reptiles, and amphibians.

The **National Audubon Society**'s Washington state office (http://wa.audubon.org) has detailed information on birds and birding in the state. Call its rare bird alert line (425/454-2662) for unusual sightings in the San Juans and elsewhere. The **San Juan Islands Audubon Society** (www.sjiaudubon.org) has monthly birding walks on San Juan Island. See their Facebook page for the latest rare bird sightings.

Both **Sea Quest Expeditions** (360/378-5767 or 888/589-4253, www.sea-quest-kayak.com), **San Juan Safaris** (360/378-1323 or 800/450-6858, www.sanjuansafaris.com), and **Austin Adventures** (800/575-1540, www.austinadventures.com) all lead custom birding tours in the San Juans. Bellingham-based **San Juan Cruises** (360/738-8099 or 800/443-4552, www.whales.com) leads birding trips to see Smith Island puffins and seabirds around Sucia and Patos Islands; these take place several times each summer.

The San Juan Islands are home to the largest year-round population of **bald eagles** outside Alaska. They are common sights soaring over the bays and channels or riding the thermals atop Mount Constitution on Orcas Island or Mount Findlayson and Mount Dallas on San Juan Island.

In the past, bald eagles were often blamed for the deaths of sheep and other domestic animals. Actually, eagles much prefer dead and dying fish to anything running around on hooves; their common fare, aside from dead salmon, is sick or injured waterfowl or rabbits that didn't make it across the road. An aggressive bird, the eagle will often purloin the catch of an osprey or other bird in favor of finding its own. The large nests of bald eagles, sometimes measuring more than 8 feet wide and 12 feet high, are often found in old-growth spruce and fir snags (standing dead trees).

The adult bald eagle's distinctive white head and tail make it easy to spot. But it takes four years for it to acquire these markings, making the immature eagle difficult to identify, as it may show whitish markings anywhere on its body. In contrast, the somewhat similar golden eagle has distinct white patches on its tail and underwings.

Another large bird seen throughout the San Juans is the **great blue heron,** a long-legged bird that wades in shallow bays and marshes. Their diet consists of frogs, small fish, snakes, crabs, and other creatures. Look for them in places such as the Frank Richardson Wildlife Preserve on Orcas Island, English Camp on San Juan Island, or Weeks Wetland on Lopez Island; the long legs, slate-blue coloration, yellow bill, and ornate black plumes are distinctive.

History

North America has been inhabited for a very long time. Low ocean levels during the Pleistocene epoch (some 30,000-40,000 years ago) offered the nomadic peoples of northeastern Asia a walkable passage across to Alaska. One of the earliest records of humans in the Americas is a caribou bone with a serrated edge found in northern Yukon Territory. Almost certainly used as a tool, the bone has been placed at 27,000 years old by carbon dating. As the climate warmed and the great ice sheets receded toward the Rocky Mountains and Canadian Shield, a corridor opened down the middle of the Great Plains, allowing movement farther south. Recent scientific evidence suggests that ancient peoples also sailed or paddled along the coast from Asia to North America.

THE COAST SALISH

Humans have occupied the San Juan Islands for thousands of years. Recent discoveries of bison bones in Orcas Island peat bogs revealed cut marks on the bones caused by human hunters, providing evidence that people have been on the islands for nearly 14,000 years. When the first European explorers sailed around the San Juan Islands, they found them populated primarily by the Lummi and Samish tribes, though the Songhees and Saanich were present on parts of the western and northern islands. These closely related tribes are all considered Strait Coast Salish people. Lummi legends tell of a man named Swetan who landed on San Juan Island where he built a home, probably at Garrison Bay. His descendants became the various family groups that settled the islands and surrounding shores. Nobody knows exactly when Swetan arrived, but he may represent the earliest influx of people to the area. The Salish culture underwent changes over the eons as people developed better ways to catch and preserve fish and shellfish.

Although the Coast Salish were a peaceable people, their Haida and Kwakiutl neighbors to the north were infamously aggressive, and the Salish found themselves under periodic threat from marauding parties that swept through the islands in 50-man war canoes. Salish men were often killed in these attacks, while the women and children were taken away as slaves. Once captured, a slave's only hope was to run away, since he or she could never marry a nonslave and was treated as property. To defend their territory against such raids, the Salish constructed rock stockades and armed themselves with whalebone clubs; these ancient fortifications are still visible on Lopez Island. Unfortunately, the northern tribes were some of the first to obtain firearms from Russian traders, making life even more difficult for the Salish. By the middle of the 19th century, the raiders were attacking not only the Salish but also white settlers in the region.

The Cycle of Life

Strait Coast Salish life revolved around access to foods such as salmon, clams, and edible plants. The arrival of summer meant the return of salmon, and the Salish prepared by moving their families to temporary camps on the islands where they would be close to the migrating schools of fish. The salmon were caught in reefnets suspended from dugout canoes, and the fish were then preserved by air drying or smoking over a fire. Reefnets are still used today in the islands. Other important foods included clams, cockles, oysters, sea cucumbers, crabs, sea urchins, chitons, snails, barnacles, mussels, and various species of fish. Edible plants included wild strawberries, blackberries, gooseberries, huckleberries, purple great camas bulbs, horsetails, and tiger lilies. The Coast Salish used nets to catch black-tailed deer and ducks.

Men had the primary responsibility for fishing, hunting, house building, and carving canoes, while the women gathered, cooked, and preserved the food and made clothing, wove mats, and coiled baskets. Clothes were woven using processed cedar bark or roots, duck down, nettle fiber, wool, animal skins, and other materials. In the summer, Coast Salish people often went naked. After the busy summer season of hunting and gathering, the families returned to their winter village, which might be on the islands or the mainland. Fall was often a time for big potlatches. Guests were invited from throughout the region, and the festivities always included games, canoe races, mock battles, intertribal marriages, and an elaborate potlatch ceremony in which the host gained prestige by giving away gifts.

Winter quarters—cedar plank houses and enormous longhouses used for potlatches— were built along protected beaches. A number of families lived inside each plank house. Sleeping platforms lined the outside walls, and mats hung from the rafters as partitions and to insulate from the cold. Families cooked over a central fire that also heated the house; smoke escaped through a hole in the roof. Western red cedar was important not just for the Salish homes but also in their carvings and dugout canoes, some of which reached 30 feet in length.

Death of a Culture

The Pacific Northwest tribes were introduced to the by-products of the white man's culture, such as knives, guns, and the deadly smallpox virus (to which they were not immune), before ever laying eyes on a white explorer. The first disease outbreak in this era of death swept through in 1782, followed by additional plagues in the 1830s and early 1850s. Over this 75-year period, some 80-90 percent of the Coast Salish died from disease. They were not the only ones; the population of Native Americans in the entire Pacific Northwest may have numbered one or even two million before the diseases struck, but their numbers plummeted to 180,000 by the time Europeans arrived. Smallpox Bay on San Juan Island is named for an incident in the 1860s when many Salish died after two sick sailors were forced ashore from an unknown ship to keep them from contaminating other sailors.

It wasn't just disease that killed the Coast Salish. Alcohol took a deadly toll, and San Juan Island became known far and wide for its saloons, where drunkenness and violence were the norm at any time of the day or night. And direct conflicts with whites pushed the Salish from areas they had inhabited for thousands of years. This combination of diseases, repeated raids by northern tribes, alcohol, and aggressive white settlers decimated the Coast Salish. By the 1840s, the San Juan Islands had no year-round residents; the survivors had moved to the Washington mainland or Victoria. The **Point Elliott Treaty** of 1855 established the Lummi Indian Reservation near Bellingham. The book *Lummi Elders Speak*, edited by Ann Nugent, has an insightful quote from one village elder, Herman Olsen. Describing Mitchell Bay on San Juan Island, he said:

A white fellow moved in there. They homesteaded the whole thing. They just plain homesteaded it wrong and everything. Then on the other side of the bay, what there was left, the Lummis moved across, just a stone's throw across the bay; they had two great big houses there. Then they had some more small houses, cabin-like, that they stayed in that got homesteaded so the Lummis just lost out there too. White people came and homesteaded the darn place and never even left their ground for the Lummis.

For additional information on the original San Juan settlers, read Julie K. Stein's *Exploring Coast Salish Prehistory: The Archaeology of San Juan Island* (University of Washington Press, www.washington.edu/uwpress). The book details excavations at a seasonal camp near American Camp and Salish winter quarters at English Camp. Both camps were used for thousands of years, and

English Camp may have been in use up until just before the English soldiers showed up in 1859. There are literally hundreds of other archaeological sites on the islands. Also worth a read is *San Juan Island Indians,* a self-published work by Gary J. Morris that's available in local libraries.

THE EUROPEANS ARRIVE
Spanish Explorers

In 1592, exactly a century after Columbus made his landfall in the Caribbean, a Greek explorer using the Spanish name **Juan de Fuca** sailed along Washington's coast and claimed to have discovered the fabled "Northwest Passage," an inland waterway crossing North America from the Pacific to the Atlantic. Later explorers did find a waterway close to where de Fuca indicated, but it led only into today's Puget Sound, not all the way to the Atlantic Ocean.

Spain, hoping to regain some of its diminishing power and wealth, sent out several expeditions in the late 1700s to explore the Pacific Northwest coast. In 1774, Juan Perez explored as far north as the Queen Charlotte Islands off Vancouver Island and was the first European to describe the Pacific Northwest coastline and Olympic Mountains before being forced to turn back by sickness and storms.

In 1775, a larger Spanish expedition set out, led by **Bruno de Heceta** and **Juan Francisco de la Bodega y Quadra.** Heceta went ashore at Point Grenville, just north of Moclips on the Washington coast, and claimed the entire Northwest for Spain. Farther north, at an island off the Olympic Peninsula, Bodega y Quadra sent seven men ashore in a small metal craft for wood and water; they were quickly killed and their boat torn apart in the whites' first encounter with coastal Native Americans. The two ships sailed away without further incident; Quadra named the island Isla de Dolores (Isle of Sorrows), today known as Destruction Island. Quadra continued his explorations as

far north as present-day Sitka, Alaska, while Heceta sailed north to Nootka Sound. Heceta failed to note the Strait of Juan de Fuca, but he did come across "the mouth of some great river," presumably the Columbia, though the death or illness of much of his crew prevented further exploration and robbed Spain of an important claim.

It was not until 1791 that the first Europeans finally saw the San Juan Islands up close. In that year the Spanish explorer **Francisco Eliza** sent his schooner *Santa Saturnina* into what his pilot, **Lopez Gonzales de Haro,** described as "an indescribable archipelago of islands, keys, rocks, and big and little inlets." The Spaniards returned to the San Juans the next summer, this time better equipped to explore the islands in depth. But when they arrived, they found two other ships already present, the *Discovery* and *Chatham,* captained by their English competitors under George Vancouver. Despite the often-hostile relations between the Spanish and English, the two decided to work together as they explored the area. This cooperation may have been an augury of the later Pig War on San Juan Island, in which two nations chose cooperation over conflict.

English Explorations

England was *the* force to be reckoned with in the battle for the Northwest. In 1776, Captain **James Cook** took two ships and 170 men on an expedition that brought him to the Hawaiian Islands, the Oregon coast, and Vancouver Island's Nootka Sound. Though he charted the coastline from Oregon to the Bering Sea, he made no mention of the Strait of Juan de Fuca. Hostile Hawaiians killed Cook in a 1779 dispute over a boat, and his crew returned to England.

Other English sailors continued in Cook's footsteps, and in 1787, Charles Barkley and his wife, Frances, explored and named the Strait of Juan de Fuca. Best known today, however, is the expedition led by **George Vancouver** in 1792. His goal was to explore the inland waters and make one last attempt at finding the

Northwest Passage. The names of Vancouver's lieutenants and crew members read like a list of Washington place-names: Baker, Rainier, Whidbey, and Puget. (Many of the place-names were attached to curry political favor back home; almost anyone in a position of power had his name stuck on something.) The expedition carefully charted and thoroughly described all navigable waterways and named every prominent feature. Vancouver's survey crew reached the Strait of Juan de Fuca in May 1792, and one of his boats landed at Blind Bay on Shaw Island, where they found a Coast Salish settlement. Some of the Coast Salish people paddled canoes out to trade with the Englishmen, providing them with three freshly killed deer and a live fawn for venison.

American Explorations

An American, **Robert Gray,** sailed out of Boston to explore and trade along the Northwest Coast in 1792. Stopping first at Nootka Sound—the hot spot to trade on Vancouver Island—Gray worked his way south and spent three days anchored in today's Grays Harbor. Continuing south, Gray discovered the mouth of the Columbia River and traded there with the Chinook before heading home without finding Puget Sound and the San Juans. His explorations helped establish American claims to the Pacific Northwest.

The first American survey of the San Juan archipelago took place in 1841 under the leadership of Lieutenant **Charles Wilkes.** The surveyors were only in the islands for three days in July but managed to see much of the country and to apply American names to virtually everything in sight. The predictable choices were American naval heroes from the War of 1812 or Tripoli, along with members of the expedition itself, including Stuart Island for Wilkes's clerk, Fredrick D. Stuart, and Waldron Island for two of his crewmembers. Some of his other name choices—Navy Archipelago instead of the San Juan Islands, Hulls Island instead of Orcas, Rodgers Island instead of San Juan Island, and Chauncys

Island instead of Lopez—were later rejected. Wilkes's charts of the islands did, however, later prove vital in the designation of the San Juans as American, rather than British, property.

SETTLING THE ISLANDS

During the time between the early exploration and the permanent settlement of the Northwest, British and American trading posts emerged to take advantage of the area's abundant supply of beaver and sea otter pelts. Two English companies, the North West Company and Hudson's Bay Company, merged in 1821; American fur-trading outfits included many small, independent companies as well as John Astor's Pacific Fur Company and the Rocky Mountain Fur Company.

The most influential of them, the **Hudson's Bay Company,** built its temporary headquarters on the north shore of the Columbia, 100 miles inland at Fort Vancouver. The settlers planted crops, raised livestock, and made the fort as self-sufficient as possible. At its peak, 500 people lived at or near the fort. When settlers began arriving in droves and the beaver population diminished in the late 1840s, the Hudson's Bay Company was crowded out and moved its headquarters north to Fort Victoria on Vancouver Island.

Manifest Destiny

In the 1840s, the United States and England jointly occupied "Oregon Country," the land north of the 42nd parallel. It included lands that today make up Washington, Oregon, Idaho, and parts of Montana, Wyoming, and British Columbia. The westward movement gained momentum when a New York editor coined the phrase "Manifest Destiny" to symbolize the idea that all the land west of the Rockies rightfully belonged to the United States.

Between 1840 and 1860, more than 50,000 American settlers moved west to Oregon Country to take advantage of the free land they could acquire through the Organic Act of 1843 and the Donation Land Law of 1850.

Under the Organic Act, each adult white male could own a 640-acre section of land (one square mile) by simply marking its boundaries, filing a claim, and building a cabin on the land. The Donation Land Law put additional restrictions on land claims: 320 acres were awarded to each white or half-white male who was an American citizen and had arrived prior to 1851; another 320 acres could be claimed by his wife.

The promise of free land fueled the "Great Migration" of 1843, in which almost 900 settlers traveled to Oregon Country, six times the number of the previous year. More pioneers followed: 1,500 in 1844 and 3,000 in 1845. Most settlers came by way of the Oregon Trail from St. Joseph, Missouri; they followed the North Platte River across Nebraska and into southern Wyoming, and then traveled across southern Idaho and into Oregon before heading north to the Columbia River. Soon the route looked like a cleared road; traces of it can still be seen where the wagons dug ruts in stone and where wheels packed the ground so hard that grass still cannot grow.

Divvying up the Northwest

Britain regarded the westward expansion with dismay, watching as the lands it claimed were increasingly populated by Americans. The Oregon Treaty of 1846 settled the dispute, giving possession of all lands south of the 49th parallel to the United States. Although the problem appeared resolved, the treaty failed to adequately describe the boundary through upper Puget Sound, causing both the United States and Britain to claim the San Juan Islands. Over time this issue came back to haunt both nations. Thirteen years after the treaty signing, an incident involving a potato-loving pig and an angry settler on San Juan Island nearly precipitated a war. The issue would not be finally resolved until 1872, when an arbitrator awarded the islands to the United States.

Smuggling Takes Hold

Smuggling was an important part of life on the San Juans for many years, and some of the earliest businesses were illegal booze joints catering to soldiers, settlers, and Native Americans. Around 1880, large numbers of Chinese laborers began arriving on San Juan Island, working both in local potato fields and at the limestone operation along Roche Harbor. Smuggling of Chinese workers from Vancouver Island through the San Juans to Seattle became a big business. An even more lucrative one was (and still is) illegal drugs. The drug of choice at the time—primarily for Chinese workers in the United States—was opium. Legal in British Columbia, it was refined in factories there. Opium smuggling became an important source of income for many island folks, including the best-known smuggler, Larry Kelly.

During Prohibition, the islands were a way station for booze destined for Seattle speakeasies, and a new generation of profiteers emerged. Today, there are still occasional busts of people attempting to transport drugs through the islands, and a few folks have even been caught with drug-packed sea kayaks.

THE 20TH CENTURY

Once the Americans had successfully ejected the English from the San Juans, one of their first actions was a tax revolt. When Whatcom County imposed a tax, the locals managed to get the legislature to carve out a separate San Juan County for the 200 or so settlers on the islands. The initial seat of power was a ragtag and boozy settlement called Old Town that was located near American Camp on the south end of San Juan Island. Eventually, the more civilized town of Friday Harbor became the island's primary settlement, and it remains so to this day.

In the late 1800s and early 1900s, Roche Harbor on San Juan Island developed into one of the world's largest limestone mining operations under the leadership of "boss" John S. McMillin. Another industrialist, Robert Moran, had a more lasting impact, however. A shipbuilder and former Seattle mayor, Moran retired early on Orcas Island, built a mansion (today's Rosario Resort), and donated thousands of acres of land for Moran State Park, one of the finest parks in Washington.

One surprising product of the islands from the 1890s through World War I was fruit, particularly apples, plums, and pears. Orcas Island was the primary fruit producer, but orchards spread across Lopez, Shaw, and San Juan as well. Insect infestations and competition from fruit growers in eastern Washington eventually doomed growers on the San Juan Islands, but many of these trees still produce today, more than a century after they were planted. In recent years, as the grow-local movement has caught on, fruit trees are again being planted on farms throughout the archipelago. Fresh apples are sold in weekend farmers markets, and one business on San Juan Island is even producing traditional hard cider, gin, and apple brandy.

Cars and Ferries

Early in the 20th century, the San Juan Islands were home to a rough mix of farmers, fishers, miners, loggers, and smugglers. Tourism remained of minor importance on the San Juans until the middle of the century, when cars and ferries made the islands increasingly accessible to the masses.

Washington's ferry system had its origins in the early 1900s when a number of companies sailed Puget Sound waters in small steamers known as the Mosquito Fleet. Competition and consolidation forced most of these companies under, and by 1935 only one remained: the Puget Sound Navigation Company, better known as the Black Ball Line.

That same year, the first auto ferry linked the islands with Anacortes and Sidney, British Columbia. As automobiles became an increasingly important part of the transportation mix in Puget Sound, Black Ball ferries acted as a link across the wide expanses of water. Prior to the ferries, steamers had sailed out of Seattle or Bellingham to deliver freight and passengers around the islands.

The state of Washington jumped into the ferry business in 1951 when it bought out Black Ball's ferries, terminals, and most other assets. The state ferry system was originally intended to be a temporary measure until bridges could be built across Puget Sound, but the legislature rejected that idea in 1959. Since then, Washington State Ferries has become the largest ferry system in the nation (Alaska's is vastly longer, however), with 20 ports of call served by 22 vessels, the largest of which can carry 2,500 passengers and more than 200 vehicles. Today, Washington ferries transport

Lummi Island ferry

more than 11 million vehicles and 23 million people annually around Puget Sound. The run from Anacortes to Lopez, Shaw, Orcas, and San Juan Islands and then on to Sidney, British Columbia, is not only extremely popular but also the most scenic of all the cross-sound sailings.

DESTINATION ISLES

For the last 50 years or so, the San Juans have increasingly been a place of recreation and relaxation rather than industry. Small farms and pastures are still important, particularly on Lopez Island, and commercial fishers call the islands home, but the real engines driving the economy are tourism and retirement. In the last decade or so, the islands have attracted national attention as a place to retire, and as a spot for affluent young professionals who work out of their homes. During the 1990s, San Juan County had the second fastest-growing population in Washington.

As the population grew, development pressure led to water shortages, the loss of public access to island shorelines, and overpriced housing. Despite these troubles, the San Juan Islands remain an eminently livable place where the natural world still dominates. After all, even with a 45 percent increase in the last 30 years, the total population on the islands is still just 16,000 people. The per capita income is more than $38,000 (higher than most other counties in Washington State), but much of this is due to wealthy retirees.

Essentials

Transportation

There are no bridges to the San Juan Islands, but ferries ply these waters, scheduled air service is available, and the islands are popular with boaters and kayakers who head out on their own. The main regional airports are Seattle's Sea-Tac International Airport and Vancouver International Airport. From either of these, you can rent a car and drive to Anacortes, where the Washington State Ferries depart for the islands. Shuttle buses also run from Sea-Tac directly to the Anacortes ferry dock. Scheduled flights connect the islands with Seattle, Anacortes, Bellingham, and Victoria.

WASHINGTON STATE FERRIES

If you can only take one ride aboard a **Washington State Ferry** (206/464-6400 or 888/808-7977, www.wsdot.wa.gov/ferries), the trip from Anacortes to the San Juans should be the one. The scenery is so beautiful that even point-and-shoot photographers can get spectacular sunset-over-the-islands shots. In the summer, ferries leave Anacortes at least a dozen times a day, 4:30am-12:15am, stopping at the north end of Lopez Island, on Shaw Island, at Orcas Village on Orcas Island, and finally at Friday Harbor on San Juan Island. It takes roughly two hours to ferry from Anacortes to Friday Harbor. Not every ferry run stops on each island, but nearly all of them pull into Friday Harbor.

Ferries between **Anacortes** and **Sidney, British Columbia,** run twice a day in the summer and once daily in fall and spring; there's no service January-March. When boarding a ferry and returning to the U.S. mainland from the islands, try to avoid sailings that start in British Columbia; these all must clear **customs** in Anacortes, and the process can cause substantial delays.

Vehicle reservations are *highly recommended*. Make a **Save A Spot vehicle reservation** at www.wsdot.wa.gov/ferries/ reservations. Use your credit card to hold space for standard vehicles on ferries up to two months prior to your sailing to the islands. You'll receive a confirmation email, but won't be billed for travel till you board. You can change or cancel reservations until 5pm on the day prior to travel. Bring the bar code printout or your reservation confirmation number.

If you have not made a reservation, arrive at least **two hours early** on Friday and Saturday, or an hour early on weekdays. **Avoid crowds** by traveling midweek, early in the morning, late in the evening (except Friday evenings), or better yet, by foot, kayak, or bike. Leave your car in the lot at the terminal ($25 for three days) and stroll aboard; there's always space for walk-on passengers.

There are no ferry reservations for travel heading eastward from the San Juan Islands to Anacortes, so get to the ferry terminal 1.5 or 2 hours in advance for these sailings. You can find **current wait times** and **ferry lane webcams** at www.wsdot.wa.gov/ferries.

Anacortes to the Islands

For travel to the San Juan Islands, the state ferries charge higher rates in summer (May-Sept.) than in the off-season. Peak-season summertime fares from Anacortes to Friday Harbor—the last American stop—are $14 for adult passengers in a vehicle and walk-ons, or $64 for a standard car and driver. Bikes are $4 extra, and kayaks cost $21 more. Summertime fares from Anacortes to the other islands are

---

Previous: floatplane landing at Friday Harbor on San Juan Island; sailboats anchored off Orcas Island.

$14 for passengers or $45 for a car and driver to Lopez Island, and $14 for passengers or $54 for a car and driver to Orcas or Shaw Islands.

Ferry travelers heading to the San Juans are **only charged in the westbound direction.** Eastbound travel within the islands—such as from Orcas to Lopez, or from San Juan Island to Anacortes—is free, with no tickets required. If you're planning to visit all the islands, save money by heading straight to Friday Harbor (the most westward of the islands) and then work your way back through the others at no additional charge. This does not, however, apply to ferry travel to Sidney, British Columbia, from either Anacortes or the San Juan Islands; you'll need to pay in both directions for these trips.

Interisland Ferries

Once you're on the San Juans, there is never a charge for passengers, walk-ons, or bikes to travel to another island in either direction. Also, there's no charge for cars heading east within the islands (such as from Friday Harbor to Orcas or Orcas to Lopez), but the westbound charge is $28, whether it is just across the waterway from Shaw to Orcas, or all the way from Lopez to Friday Harbor. Rates are lower in the off-season.

Here's a tip that isn't widely publicized: If you're planning a short stop on one of the islands and then continuing westward to another island within 24 hours, request a **free vehicle transfer.** This is useful if you're on Lopez and heading to Friday Harbor (free stops at Shaw and Orcas), or going from Lopez to Orcas (free stop at Shaw). It saves you $28 for each stop, but you must ask for it on your departure island. Note that you cannot stop for more than 24 hours when using a vehicle transfer.

To Sidney, British Columbia

Washington State Ferry (206/464-6400 or 888/808-7977, www.wsdot.wa.gov/ferries) service connects Anacortes with Sidney, British Columbia. Sidney is just 20 miles from the beautiful city of Victoria, and BC Ferries head east from Sidney to the Gulf Islands and Tsawwassen (near Vancouver). Service between Anacortes and Sidney is twice daily in the summer (mid-June-Sept.), and once daily in the fall (Oct.-Dec.) and spring (Mar.-mid-June), with no ferries at all in the winter (Jan.-Mar.). One-way tickets cost $20 for passengers and walk-ons, or $67 for a car and driver. The charge is the same in the opposite direction (Sidney to Anacortes) or from

Washington State Ferries

Sidney to Friday Harbor, but if you stop in Friday Harbor, there are no additional charges to continue east all the way to Anacortes.

Once a day, the Anacortes-Sidney ferry stops at Friday Harbor in both directions. If you get on in Friday Harbor, the passage westward to Sidney costs $12 for passengers or $42 for a car and driver. **Save A Spot vehicle reservations** (www.wsdot.wa.gov/ferries/reservations) are highly recommended.

When crossing between the United States and Canada, adults of either country will need a passport. All baggage is subject to inspection.

PRIVATE FERRIES AND DAY CRUISES
From Seattle

The passenger-only *Victoria Clipper* (206/448-5000 or 800/888-2535, www.clippervacations.com) runs high-speed catamaran day trips between Seattle and San Juan Island. Rates vary with a convoluted schedule, including discounts on weekdays and if you book at least a day ahead. Adults pay $81-98 round-trip and kids are $41-49. Combine transportation from Seattle with a 2.5-hour whale-watching trip for $25-30 extra. The company has a multitude of other travel options in the Northwest, including packages that add a night's lodging on San Juan Island, or a three-day/two-night visit to San Juan Island and Victoria. You can also use this as transportation to the islands from Seattle, traveling north one day and returning later. In addition, the *Victoria Clipper* has year-round service between Seattle and Victoria for $154 round-trip (less if purchased in advance).

From Port Townsend

Puget Sound Express (360/385-5288, www.pugetsoundexpress.com) provides passenger-only service between Port Townsend and Friday Harbor. The boat leaves Port Townsend daily May-October, staying in Friday Harbor long enough for a brief two-hour visit, or you can overnight and return to Port Townsend later. The round-trip lasts eight hours and costs $104 adults, $65 kids age 2-10, and $15 extra for bikes and kayaks. Although Puget Sound Express promotes this as a whale-watching tour, it is more of a ferry run that passes through waters where orcas are often seen.

From Bellingham

San Juan Cruises (360/738-8099 or 800/443-4552, www.whales.com, Fri.-Sat. May-Sept.) departs Bellingham for all-day cruises to the San Juan Islands on the 149-passenger *Victoria Star 2*. These trips combine a two-hour stop in Friday Harbor with a three-hour whale-watching voyage and lunch; fares are $109 adults, $55 ages 6-17, free for younger kids. Special birding trips to see Smith Island puffins and seabirds around Sucia and Patos Islands take place several times each summer. Sunday-only trips to Sucia Island State Park ($89 adults, $45 kids, free for under 6) includes 2.5 hours on the island and a picnic lunch on the beach.

WATER TAXIS

Water taxis provide a quick and easy way to reach a specific place in the islands without dealing with ferry lines or vehicles.

Operating out of Anacortes, **Paraclete Charters** (360/293-5920 or 800/808-2999, www.paracletecharters.com) has been in business since 1992 and has a very experienced crew. They run three passenger boats—the largest is 58 feet long and can carry 64 passengers—to any place in the San Juans. This is the place to go for transportation to destinations off the route of the state ferry system, including the private islands. Rates depend on the destination and number of passengers. As an example, Anacortes to Clark Island costs $136 for one person round-trip; add $10 round-trip for bikes or $20 for kayaks. In addition to passengers, Paraclete will haul anything from motorcycles and appliances to furniture and construction material. There's no charge for pets, and kids get discounted rates. The boats are designed for all weather conditions and even provide 24-hour emergency transportation when planes are grounded.

Also based in Anacortes, **Island Express Charters** (360/299-2875 or 877/473-9777, www.islandexpresscharters.com) has two high-speed landing craft (one can carry 42 passengers) with plenty of deck space for kayaks, bikes, and gear. Water taxi rates vary depending on your destination. Most trips require at least two passengers.

Based at Deer Harbor on Orcas Island, **North Shore Charters** (360/376-4855, www.orcasislandadventures.com) offers day trips to and drop-offs at state marine parks on Jones, Stuart, Matia, Patos, Sucia, and other islands.

Based on the north side of Orcas Island, **Outer Island Excursions** (360/376-3711, www.outerislandx.com) provides water taxi service to Stuart, Sucia, Jones, Matia, Patos, and most other islands. **Humpback Hauling** (360/317-7433, www.humpbackhauling.com) provides passenger and freight service throughout the San Juans on a large landing craft.

Based in Friday Harbor, **San Juan Islands Water Taxi** (360/317-5475, www.sjiwatertaxi.net) can transport six passengers anywhere in the San Juan Islands. Captain Gunnar Wickman has sailed all over the world, and the boat spent many years as a fishing vessel in Alaska. It's not fast, but the boat is comfortable and has space for bikes or kayaks.

MULTIDAY CRUISES

Operating from Bellingham, the **Northwest Navigation Co.** (360/201-8184 or 877/670-7863, www.northwestnavigation.com) operates the six-passenger *David B*, a distinctive and lovingly maintained 1929 wooden vessel. Travelers can join multi-night San Juan trips or kayak mothership trips.

Based on Orcas Island, **Emerald Isle Sailing Charters** (360/376-3472, www.emeraldislesailing.com) has multiday San Juan Islands charter trips onboard a gorgeous 54-foot pilothouse ketch.

Sail the San Juans (360/671-5852 or 800/729-3207, www.sailthesanjuans.com) offers six-day fully crewed charters around the islands, departing from Bellingham. The 50-foot *Northwind* comfortably accommodates six guests.

FLYING INTO SEATTLE

Anyone flying into western Washington State will almost certainly be landing at **Sea-Tac International Airport** (206/787-5388 or 800/544-1965, www.portseattle.org/seatac), 12 miles south of Seattle. The airport has undergone a significant upgrade in the last few years and is a pleasant place to spend a couple of hours in transit. The central terminal has enormous windows facing the runways and a good selection of reasonably priced dining choices. All major domestic, and many international, airlines operate out of Sea-Tac, and foreign travelers can change money in the main terminal. A **Visitor Information Booth** (open daily May-Sept., brochures available anytime) is close to the baggage claim area.

The fastest and least expensive way to reach downtown Seattle from the airport—just $3—is aboard a **Link Light Rail Train,** operated by Sound Transit (206/398-5000 or 800/201-4900, www.soundtransit.org). These trains run every 6 to 15 minutes daily 6am-11pm and take you directly to Pioneer Square, University Street, and Westlake (near Pike Place Market) downtown, before continuing to Capitol Hill and the University of Washington. City buses provide connections to other parts of Seattle.

The San Juan Islands are 65 air miles northeast of Seattle, with access by air, boat, shuttle van and ferry, or car and ferry.

Car Rentals

All the major national car rental companies operate from the new **Sea-Tac Rental Car Facility,** a five-minute shuttle ride from the air terminal. Catch a free shuttle from outside the baggage claim area. I've found the best rates with an Internet search at www.travelocity.com, www.expedia.com, or www.orbitz.com. AAA or Costco members should be sure to ask about any additional discounts. **Thrifty Car Rental** (www.thrifty.com) and **Payless** (www.paylesscarrental.com) often have some of the lowest rates and provide a starting point for price comparisons.

Shuttle Vans

Getting to the islands from Sea-Tac is easy. **Airporter Shuttle** (360/380-8800 or 866/235-5247, www.airporter.com) makes connections between Sea-Tac and the ferry terminal at Anacortes, and it also goes to Bellingham and points north all the way to Vancouver. Fares are $40 one-way ($34 kids) to the ferry terminal. Vans run a dozen times or so a day and the trip generally takes three hours.

SeaTac Direct (360/733-3666, www.seatacdirect.com) has bus connections between Sea-Tac and Bellingham three times a day for $50 one-way with a four-person minimum. **Quick Shuttle Service** (604/940-4428 or 800/665-2122, www.quickcoach.com) has service to Vancouver, British Columbia, for $59 one-way ($20 kids).

Island Airporter (360/378-7438, www.islandairporter.com) provides direct van service daily from Sea-Tac to San Juan Island. The bus departs the airport and heads straight to the Anacortes ferry, where it drives on for San Juan Island, and then continues to Friday Harbor ($50) and Roche Harbor ($57). You'll need to add the ferry fare, but it's approximately half the standard rate because you're on a bus. Vans operate once a day in each direction Monday-Saturday in summer and Monday-Friday in winter.

Trains and Buses

Amtrak trains serve Seattle from the King Street Station (3rd Ave. S and S. King St., 206/464-1930 or 800/872-7245, www.amtrakcascades.com). The Amtrak *Cascades* train connects Seattle with Vancouver, British Columbia, stopping at Mount Vernon and Bellingham twice a day in each direction. Trains do not stop in Anacortes (where Washington State Ferries depart for the San Juan Islands); the closest station to the ferry terminal is 18 miles away in Mount Vernon.

Greyhound (206/628-5526 or 800/231-2222, www.greyhound.com) has daily bus service throughout the Lower 48 and to Vancouver, British Columbia, from its Seattle terminal at 9th and Stewart. It's the same story here as for Amtrak: Greyhound's closest stop is the town of Mount Vernon, 18 miles from the ferry terminal in Anacortes.

BoltBus (877/265-8287, www.boltbus.com) travels the I-5 corridor from Seattle north to Bellingham and Vancouver, and south to Portland. Fares are very reasonable and the buses all have Wi-Fi, reserved seating, and ample legroom.

Car

If you're driving from Seattle, it's 80 miles (92 miles from Sea-Tac) to Anacortes, where you catch the Washington State Ferries to the San Juans. The ride is very straightforward: Follow I-5 north to Mount Vernon, take Exit 230, and turn west onto Highway 20, which goes straight into Anacortes. The ferry terminal is three miles west of downtown Anacortes via 12th Street.

Be sure to fill your tank in Anacortes before driving on to the ferry. Because of the extra cost of shipping fuel (and because they can get away with it), gas stations on the islands charge at least 30 percent more than those on the mainland.

Flying to the Islands

The quickest way to reach the islands is by air, but there are no direct flights from Sea-Tac Airport. You'll need to take a free shuttle to Seattle's Lake Union or Boeing Field to connect with Kenmore Air flights.

The San Juans are served by a legendary floatplane company, **Kenmore Air** (425/486-1257 or 800/543-9595, www.kenmoreair.com). In business since 1946, it is the world's largest full-service seaplane operation, with two dozen planes and a summertime staff of more than 200. Kenmore is best known for its De Havilland Beavers (a workhorse of Alaskan bush pilots), but also flies larger turbine Otters and Cessna Caravans. The company's yellow-and-white floatplanes are a familiar sight on Lake Union in Seattle and nearby Lake Washington in Kenmore.

Kenmore Air has daily scheduled flights from Lake Union and Lake Washington to Friday Harbor and Roche Harbor on San Juan Island; Fisherman Bay on Lopez Island; and Rosario Resort, Deer Harbor, and West Sound on Orcas Island. They also fly daily to various places along British Columbia's Inside Passage, including Victoria and the Gulf Islands. A free shuttle provides transport to Lake Union from Sea-Tac. Pack light for your trip: a 25-pound baggage weight limit is in effect.

Kenmore also offers flightseeing trips and charter service to other destinations in the San Juans, including Cypress, Sucia, Stuart, and Jones Islands. Wheeled-plane flights take place between Boeing Field in Seattle and airports on San Juan, Orcas, and Whidbey Islands. The baggage weight limit for these is 70 pounds.

San Juan Airlines (360/293-4691 or 800/874-4434, www.sanjuanairlines.com) has scheduled daily wheeled-plane service to the San Juans from Anacortes and Bellingham, stopping at San Juan, Orcas, Lopez, and Blakely Islands on a scheduled basis. Flightseeing and air charters are available to other airports on the San Juans, including those on Center, Crane, Decatur, Eliza, Sinclair, Stuart, and Waldron Islands. **Charter flights** to the San Juans can be cheaper than scheduled flights if you have four or more passengers. San Juan Airlines and **Island Air** (360/378-2376 or 888/378-2376, www.sanjuan-islandair.com) on San Juan Island provide charter flights throughout the region, including to Boeing Field in Seattle.

FLYING INTO BRITISH COLUMBIA

The city of Vancouver is the primary air hub for southwestern Canada, though there are also quite a few flights into nearby Victoria on Vancouver Island. There are no airport shuttles between **Vancouver International Airport** (www.yvr.ca) and Anacortes, but car rentals at the Vancouver airport are an option if you want to drive south across the border to Anacortes and then catch the Washington State Ferries to the islands.

If you are flying into **Victoria International Airport** (www.victoriaairport.com), take a taxi to the town of Sidney, where the Washington State Ferries depart for the San Juans.

GETTING AROUND ON THE ISLANDS

You can avoid the lengthy summertime ferry waits by parking at the Anacortes ferry terminal, walking on board the ferry, and renting a car once you reach the San Juans. On Orcas Island, rentals are available through **Orcas Island Rental Car** (360/376-7433, www.orcasislandshuttle.com), with free pickup and delivery of cars anywhere on Orcas.

On San Juan Island, contact **M&W Auto Rentals** (360/378-2886 or 800/323-6037, www.sanjuanauto.com). Rates start around $60 per day for a compact or $70 for an SUV. Rental vehicles are allowed off the islands to the Washington mainland and Canada (with restrictions). **Susie's Mopeds** (360/378-5244 or 800/532-0087, www.susiesmopeds.com) rents mopeds and Scootcoupes in Friday Harbor.

If you're flying to Sea-Tac and then heading to the islands for a week or more, you're probably better off renting a car at the airport, where rates are lower than on the islands.

San Juan Transit (360/378-8887, www.sanjuantransit.com) operates shuttle buses on San Juan Island, Orcas Island, and Lopez Island in the summer, providing a reasonable way to reach the most-visited points. The buses can also carry bikes and luggage.

Taxis are available on San Juan and Orcas Islands, but not on Lopez.

Recreation

The San Juans abound with outdoor pleasures: cycling, sea kayaking, camping, hiking, bird-watching, scuba diving, boating, sailing, whale-watching, skateboarding, and fishing, to name a few.

BICYCLING

The San Juans are a very popular cycling destination, offering up mild weather, a wide diversity of terrain, gorgeous scenery, excellent facilities, and little traffic. If you have a family in tow or aren't in great shape, head to slow-paced Lopez with its pastoral countryside, good camping, comfortable inns, and friendly locals. Shaw is small but fun to explore, with quiet roads that are fine for families; there's no lodging, but there is a campground. Orcas has the most rugged rides—including a tough haul to the top of 2,409-foot Mount Constitution—and the most challenging roads, but the diversity and beauty make it unique. San Juan offers varied terrain, the most services (especially at Friday Harbor), and wide shoulders, but also the heaviest traffic.

You won't find any separate bike paths on the islands, and some roads can be narrow and winding with minimal shoulders. Use common sense when riding. Local bike shops carry maps that denote routes with problems (such as heavy traffic or narrow and winding roads), and they also offer travel tips. The **San Juan Island Trails Committee** website (www.sanjuanislandtrails.org) also has details on San Juan Island bike routes.

Bikes on Ferries and Buses

You can bring your own bike on the ferry for an extra $4 round-trip (far cheaper than hauling your car, and you won't have to wait). Ferry loading procedures vary, so be sure to follow the instructions of terminal personnel. Be sure to walk your bike on and off the ferry. Space is always available for bikes.

San Juan Transit (360/378-8887 or 800/887-8387, www.sanjuantransit.com) serves San Juan, Orcas, and Lopez, and can transport bikes on board their vans, providing an easy way to get around if your legs begin to tire.

cyclists boarding the ferry

Bike Rentals

Bike rentals are available on the three major islands by the hour, day, or week. Most shops rent touring and hybrid bikes for around $60 per day or $80 for three days, including bike helmets. Specialized equipment, such as tandems, racing bikes, kids' bikes, panniers, child carriers, and bike trailers are also generally available, but it's wise to reserve ahead. Electric-assist bikes are increasingly available at island bike shops.

Bike Tours

Several companies guide multiday cycling tours of the San Juans, with food, lodging, and a support vehicle included in the rate. Bike rentals are also available, and you can choose your own pace on these relatively leisurely tours. These tours differ in routing, amenities, and the number of participants, so view each company's catalog or website to see which one works for you. Note that cycling trip prices are often substantially higher if you are a single traveler looking for a private room.

Operating from San Juan Island, **Terra Trek** (40 Spring St., 360/378-4223 or 888/441-2433, www.goterratrek.com) leads both inn-to-inn tours and bike-camping trips. These range from a two-day/one-night camping trip for $500 up to a six-day/five-night luxury bike and lodging tour that covers three islands for $2,580 per person.

Based in Redmond, Washington, **Bicycle Adventures** (425/250-5540 or 800/443-6060, www.bicycleadventures.com) leads a variety of cycling tours around the San Juans, starting at $2,240 for a four-day tour that includes biking, hiking, and kayaking, with lodging at island inns. They also lead seven-day loop tours starting in Seattle and going to Anacortes, Lopez Island, San Juan Island, Victoria, Port Angeles, and Port Townsend. These include cycling, kayaking, and other activities, plus luxury lodging and fine dining for around $4,000.

California-based **Backroads** (510/527-1555 or 800/462-2848, www.backroads.com) has cycling, multisport, and hiking tours of the San Juans approximately 40 times a year. All sorts of options are available, including five- or six-day trips with lodging in casual or luxurious accommodations, multisport adventures with lodging or camping, family multisport camping trips, and hiking trips. Multisport trips are especially popular, mixing cycling with kayaking, hiking, and other activities. These six-day trips are available with camping—guides set up and take down the tents—and meals included for around $2,000. At the luxury end, you'll pay $3,100 for a six-day multisport trip that includes upscale lodging and meals.

Based in Wisconsin, **Trek Travel** (608/255-8735 or 866/464-8735, www.trektravel.com) offers six-day San Juan bike treks for $2,900, lodging included. In addition, the YMCA's **Camp Orkila** (360/376-2678 or 206/382-5009, www.camporkila.org) leads a seven-day cycling program for teens that covers the San Juan Islands.

Bike Safety

Common-sense precautions are wise for anyone heading out on a bike in the San Juans:

- Always wear a helmet, even for short trips.

- Be especially cautious near ferry docks, particularly when a ferry has just disgorged its load of vehicles. Get off the road to let the traffic pass safely.

- Watch out for long lines of traffic heading up the road when a ferry has just docked.

- Always keep to the right and ride in single file.

- Ride straight ahead and avoid weaving into traffic.

- Keep your groups small, with three or four riders together spaced widely apart. Larger groups should divide up to make it easier and safer for cars to pass.

- Pull well off the road whenever you stop, particularly when visibility is poor, such as at hilltops or on corners.

- Stay off roads posted as private property.

Festivals and Events

Some of the biggest island celebrations take place over the **Fourth of July** weekend, when parades, fireworks, barbecues, street dances, and other events draw locals and tourists to Friday Harbor, Roche Harbor, Lopez Village, and Eastsound. **Memorial Day** in late May is another time for play, with a parade, artist studio open houses, the Spring Celebration on San Juan Island, and the Bite of Orcas restaurant sampling at Eastsound. The **Celebrity Golf Classic** on San Juan in early June is the county's top fundraising event. San Juan Island National Historical Park puts on an impressive **Encampment at English Camp** in August, with British and American "soldiers" and others in 19th-century costume.

The islands burst with musical performances all summer, including classical and rock music festivals on Orcas Island, weekly brown-bag concerts in Eastsound, musical weekends at the Lopez Center, and weekly concerts on the lawn in Friday Harbor.

Don't miss the premier playtime of the year, the **San Juan County Fair,** held on the third week of August in Friday Harbor. Other popular events include the **Lavender Festival** in July on San Juan, **Orcas Island Fly-In** in August, **Tour de Lopez** bike ride in April, and **Shakespeare Under the Stars** in July and August at Roche Harbor. San Juan, Orcas, and Lopez all have holiday arts-and-crafts fairs a couple of weeks before Christmas.

Boaters take part in **Whidbey Island Race Week** in mid-July, the **Round Shaw Row** in early August, and the **Shaw Island Classic** yacht race the first weekend of August.

- Avoid riding at night, and be cautious when roads are slick from recent rain.
- Wear reflectors and use strobes to show your presence when light conditions are poor.

HIKING

Hiking trails in the San Juans are somewhat limited, and there are no overnight backpacking routes anywhere on the islands. The longest and best trails are on Orcas Island within Moran State Park and at Turtleback Mountain Preserve. Other pleasant day hikes can be explored within San Juan Island National Historical Park, on Mount Grant, and at smaller state and county parks and other public lands on San Juan, Orcas, Lopez, Shaw, and Cypress Islands. Many of the marine state parks have trails, including delightful paths to old lighthouses or remote beaches; especially notable are those on Stuart and Sucia Islands.

Ken Wilcox's *Hiking the San Juan Islands* (Northwest Wild Books) and Dave Wortman's *San Juan Islands: A Guide to Exploring the Great Outdoors* (FalconGuides) are authoritative sources for anyone planning a hike on the islands. They cover not just the main islands in the archipelago, but also marine state parks, private islands, and trails on Whidbey, Camano, and Fidalgo Islands.

Although best known for its cycling trips on the San Juans, **Backroads** (510/527-1555 or 800/462-2848, www.backroads.com) also guides six-day hiking-focused adventures for $3,200-3,600 including transportation, meals, and lodging. These begin in Anacortes and include time exploring sights on Orcas and San Juan Islands before ferrying on to Victoria and Olympic National Park, after which they return to Seattle.

REI Adventures (800/622-2236, www.rei.com/adventures) also leads five-day family-friendly adventure trips in the San Juan Islands for $2,400. These include hiking, biking, whale-watching, and an overnight kayak tour to Jones Island.

Natalie (Nat) Herner of **Gnat's Nature Hikes** (360/376-6629, www.orcasislandhikes.com) guides trips in Moran State Park on Orcas Island and leads boat-and-hike treks to the marine state park on Jones Island and The Nature Conservancy preserve on Yellow Island. She has a background in environmental studies along with more than a decade of experience as a naturalist.

HORSEBACK RIDING

The rolling farm country in rural parts of the San Juans is perfect for horses and riding. Two outfits provide trail rides on the islands: **Horseshu Ranch** (360/378-2298, www.horseshu.com) on San Juan Island and **Orcas Island Trail Rides** (360/376-2134, www.orcastrailrides.com) on Orcas. In addition to rides, Horseshu also has riding lessons and horse boarding.

SEA KAYAKING

The relatively protected waters, diverse landscapes, abundant wildlife (including killer whales), and myriad bays and coves make the San Juans a marvelous place to explore by sea kayak. This is one of the finest ways to see the islands, as more and more folks are discovering each year. A number of companies offer guided trips, and several will also rent kayaks to experienced paddlers. No kayaking experience is necessary on any of the guided tours, but it certainly helps to be in good physical condition. All necessary instructions and paddling gear are provided, and you'll typically use a stable two-person kayak.

Guided Trips

Kayaking companies on San Juan, Orcas, Lopez, and Whidbey Islands, as well as in Anacortes and Bellingham, offer guided trips of varying lengths. Any of the listed outfitters will do a good job on a day trip, but for longer paddles you may want to look around to find a company that best meets your needs. One of the most professional is **Shearwater Adventures** (360/376-4699, www.shearwaterkayaks.com), based on Orcas Island. In addition to day trips, guides teach kayaking classes, set up custom tours, and have a shop that sells paddling gear and kayaks. Other Orcas kayak companies are **Outer Island Excursions** (360/376-3711, www.outerislandx.com), **Spring Bay Kayak Tours** (360/376-5531, www.springbayonorcas.com),

and **Orcas Outdoors** (360/376-4611, www.orcasoutdoors.com).

On Lopez Island, **Outdoor Adventures Center** (425/883-9039 or 800/282-4043, www.outdooradventurecenter.com) leads day trips and multi-night sea kayak trips.

Several San Juan Island-based kayak companies offer multiday trips, including **Discovery Sea Kayaks** (360/378-2559 or 866/461-2559, www.discoveryseakayaks.com), which has a kayak shop in Friday Harbor. Other operators include **Outdoor Odysseys** (360/378-3533 or 800/647-4621, www.outdoorodysseys.com), **San Juan Kayak Expeditions** (360/378-4436, www.sanjuankayak.com), **Sea Quest Expeditions** (360/378-5767 or 888/589-4253, www.sea-quest-kayak.com), and **Crystal Seas Kayaking** (360/378-4223 or 877/732-7877, www.crystalseas.com).

Moondance Sea Kayaking Adventures (360/738-7664, www.moondancekayak.com) is a Bellingham-based kayak company. Seattle-based **REI Adventures** (800/622-2236, www.rei.com/adventures) also leads sea kayak and multisport trips to the San Juans.

On Your Own

From a ferry, the waters around the San Juan Islands often appear tranquil, and sea kayaking seems to simply involve getting in and paddling. Beginners may be fine on a calm day in a protected cove, but conditions can quickly turn treacherous in the more exposed channels; a simple rollover can become a life-and-death situation. Particularly deadly are situations where strong tidal currents are pulling one way while winds are pushing in the opposite direction, creating large waves. Even experienced paddlers are wise to start by taking a trip through a San Juan Islands-based sea kayak company where they can learn details of the local conditions before heading out on their own.

SeaTrails produces excellent waterproof maps covering the San Juans; they're available in local kayak shops. The Canadian Hydrographic Service's (www.charts.gc.ca)

Tide and Current Tables book is very useful for kayakers; find it in local marinas or bookstores. Randel Washburne's detailed *Kayaking Puget Sound, the San Juans, and Gulf Islands* is packed with information on destinations, tide rips, current and wind problems, difficulty ratings, and launching points and includes itineraries for paddling trips. Kayakers heading out on their own should probably read this book first.

Minimizing Impact

Sea kayakers can be particularly damaging to the environment even while attempting to have minimal impact. Many sailors and some motorboaters "camp" in their boats, while San Juan Islands kayakers always depend on the fragile islands for a campsite. This can mean lots of trampled plants, and camping can impact the animals that live there as well. A park ranger told me of once seeing 72 kayak campers on Posey Island Marine State Park (near Roche Harbor). The island covers a total of one acre, so the campers' "wilderness experience" was more like a crowded tenement with just one outhouse for everyone.

Kayakers also can have surprising effects on wildlife, particularly seals and sea lions

hauled out on the rocks. To a snoozing seal, a paddler and kayak may look like a cruising killer whale scoping them out for a meal. Don't get too close to marine mammals, particularly at San Juan Islands National Wildlife Refuge islands, where all boats are legally required to stay 200 yards offshore. The Whale Museum's Soundwatch program (360/378-4710 or 800/946-7227, www.whalemuseum. org) recommends other precautions for kayakers heading out to watch killer whales; pick up the *Be Whale Wise* viewing guidelines from the museum in Friday Harbor or download a copy from its website. Also on the website and at the museum is a pamphlet detailing **responsible kayaker code** guidelines to help protect marine wildlife. Important ones include having a trip plan, not positioning yourself in the path of whales or paddling into a group of whales, and staying 100 yards or more away from seal haul-outs and nesting bird sites.

If you come upon a stranded seal, sea lion, or other marine mammal, do not handle it, but instead immediately call the **Stranded Marine Mammal Hotline** at 800/562-8832 or visit the NOAA website, www.westcoast. fisheries.noaa.gov.

kayakers

Cascadia Marine Trail

The Cascadia Marine Trail covers water-accessible campsites throughout Puget Sound, including more than a dozen in the San Juan Islands. These campsites ($12) are only open to those in sea kayaks and other small and beachable human- or wind-powered craft—no sailboats with motors or motorboats where you row ashore in a dingy. All permit money goes to marine trail maintenance and expansion. Designated Cascadia Marine Trail campsites are not just for one tent, and you may have quite a few neighbors during the peak season. Limits, however, are placed on the number of campers at the most popular marine state parks in the San Juans.

The nonprofit **Washington Water Trails Association** (WWTA, 206/545-9161, www.wwta.org) works to protect waterfront areas for public use, and its website provides detailed information on Cascadia Marine Trail campsites. The parks are managed by Washington State Parks, not the WWTA.

The following marine state parks, county parks, and Washington Department of Natural Resources lands in the San Juans contain designated Cascadia Marine Trail campsites: Blind Island, Burrows Island, Cypress Head (Cypress Island), Griffin Bay (San Juan Island), James Island, Jones Island, Lummi Island, Obstruction Pass (Orcas Island), Odlin County Park (Lopez Island), Pelican Beach (Cypress Island), Point Doughty (Orcas Island), Posey Island, Saddlebag Island, San Juan County Park (San Juan Island), Shaw County Park (Shaw Island), Spencer Spit (Lopez Island), Strawberry Island, and Stuart Island. On Whidbey Island, Cascadia campsites are located at Deception Pass State Park, Joseph Whidbey State Park, Fort Ebey State Park, and Windjammer Park (Oak Harbor).

Water Taxis

Several companies provide transportation to the more remote islands in the San Juans. All of them will transport your kayak ($20-40 extra round-trip), and prices vary depending on the destination and number of people. Anacortes-based **Paraclete Charters** (360/293-5920 or 800/808-2999, www.paracletecharters.com) has been in business since 1992 and operates three boats. Also operating out of Anacortes is **Island Express Charters** (360/299-2875 or 877/473-9777, www.islandexpresscharters.com), with two high-speed landing craft. From Orcas Island, hop aboard **North Shore Charters** (360/376-4855, www.orcasislandadventures.com), with a shallow-draft landing craft for service to Sucia, Patos, Matia, and other state marine parks popular with kayakers.

WHALE-WATCHING

The waters around the San Juans are famous for whales, particularly the exciting killer whales, or orcas, that pursue migrating salmon. Other marine mammals commonly seen around the islands include minke whales, harbor porpoises, Dall's porpoises, harbor seals, California and Steller sea lions, and even elephant seals. The best time to see orcas is mid-June to mid-July, but they are periodically visible anytime from mid-May to mid-September. Three resident pods, or families, of orcas are frequently spotted. For more information, see the San Juan Island chapter.

BOATING

The San Juan Islands are one of the top three sailing destinations in the nation and are equally popular with power yachts. Boat charters are available at San Juan, Orcas, and Lopez Islands and from marinas throughout the area, particularly in Anacortes and Bellingham. Two types of charters are offered. For **bareboat charters,** the company provides the boat and you do everything else, from captaining to swabbing the decks. You'll be required to show navigational and on-the-water skills in advance or the charter company won't let you take the boat. (Some companies also offer learn-to-cruise classes for landlubbers.) **Skippered charters** are for those who either lack the knowledge to head out on their own or want someone else doing the work. These cost considerably more, of course, and typically include an experienced local skipper and three meals a day. Much to the relief of those who appreciate peace and quiet, **Jet Skis** and similar personal watercraft are prohibited anywhere in San Juan County waters. Take precautions not to disturb killer whales when boating in their vicinity.

Charter Companies

Anacortes is home to one of the largest concentrations of bareboat charters in North America, with more than 350 power yachts and sailboats available. If you don't have boating skills, these companies can also provide a qualified skipper and a cook for absolute luxury. The largest Anacortes charter companies are **ABC Yacht Charters** (360/293-9533 or 800/426-2313, www.abcyachtcharters.com), **Anacortes Yacht Charters** (360/293-4555 or 800/233-3004, www.anacortesyachtcharters.com), **Crown Yacht Charters** (800/426-2313, www.crownyachtcharters.com), and **Ship Harbor Yacht Charters** (360/299-9193 or 877/772-6582, www.shipharboryachts.com).

Bellingham is another major center for boaters heading to the islands, with the following companies offering powerboat or sailing charters: **Bellhaven Charters** (360/733-6636 or 877/310-9471, www.bellhaven.net), **Bellingham Yachts Sales and Charters** (360/671-0990 or 877/310-9446, www.bellinghamyachts.com), **Northwest Explorations** (360/676-1248 or 800/826-1430, www.nwexplorations.com), **San Juan Sailing** (360/671-4300 or 800/677-7245, www.sanjuansailing.com), and **San Juan Yachting** (360/671-4300 or 800/670-8089, www.sanjuanyachting.com).

Nearly all bareboat sailing charters in the San Juans start from Anacortes, Bellingham, or other ports, but a few island companies have a limited number of sailboats for experienced yachtsmen. On Orcas, contact **Orcas Island Sailing** (360/376-2113, www.orcassailing.com); sailboat charters are available at **Deer Harbor Marina** (360/376-3037, www.deerharbormarina.com) and **Rosario Resort Marina** (360/376-2222 or 800/562-8820, www.rosarioresort.com). Companies on San Juan, Orcas, and Lopez Islands offer skippered sailing trips for an afternoon or a week.

On Your Own

Boaters heading out on their own will want to pick up one of the cruising guides to the islands. Recommended is the oddly named ***Gunkholing the San Juans*** by Jo Bailey and Carl Nyberg. It's out of print but still readily available. ("Gunkhole" is slang for a protected anchorage.) Also look over the ***Waggoner Cruising Guide*** (www.waggonerguide.com) for coverage from Puget Sound all the way to Prince Rupert, British Columbia. Regional visitors centers have copies of ***SunCruiser Magazine*** (www.suncruiser.ca), a free boating publication covering northern Puget Sound and the Strait of Georgia.

Boaters need to avoid most of the 83 islands within **San Juan Islands National Wildlife Refuge** (360/457-8451, www.fws.gov/refuge/san_juan_islands). To preserve vital wildlife habitats, you are not allowed closer than 200 yards from these; the only exceptions are portions of Turn and Matia Islands. The refuges are marked on nautical charts.

The **San Juan Island Yacht Club** (360/378-3434, www.sjiyc.com) sponsors a dozen or so local cruises annually, along with the biggest sailing event of the year—the Shaw Island Classic—held the second Saturday of August.

Boaters heading out on their own should pick up the ***Be Whale Wise*** viewing guidelines from the Whale Museum or download a copy from the facility's website (www.whalemuseum.org).

Lighthouses

Orcas Island Eclipse Charters (360/376-6566 or 800/376-6566, www.orcasislandwhales.com) leads informative summertime tours to the four lighthouses within the San Juans: Turn Point Lighthouse on Stuart Island, Patos Lighthouse on Patos Island, and Lime Kiln Lighthouse and Cattle Point

Lighthouse on San Juan Island. **Outer Island Excursions** (360/376-3711, www.outerislandx.com) has guided boat-and-hike trips to the Turn Point Lighthouse on Stuart Island.

FISHING

Fishing for salmon (mainly king, silver, and sockeye) is best in August and September, with other fish—including blackmouth bass, bottom fish, halibut, and lingcod—available at other times of the year. Charter-fishing operators generally provide fishing gear and bait, but you'll need a current saltwater fishing license. Fishing trips on Haro Strait often provide the opportunity to see killer whales.

The **Washington Department of Fish and Wildlife** (360/902-2464, www.wdfw.wa.gov) oversees fishing, hunting, and clamming on the islands. Pick up the fat *Fishing in Washington* pamphlet at sporting goods or other stores that sell fishing licenses. Annual freshwater fishing licenses cost $30 for Washington residents or $85 for nonresidents. Combination licenses for both freshwater and saltwater fishing, plus shellfish (including clams), are $55 for Washington residents or $125 for nonresidents. A two-day combination license for nonresidents is $29. Be sure to get (and fill out) a catch record card for salmon, sturgeon, steelhead, halibut, and Dungeness crab from the vendor who sells your license.

Clams and other mollusks were a major part of the diet of the Coast Salish people who first lived on the San Juans, and they are still dug today along many island beaches. For information on clamming, including regulations and safety issues, contact the Washington Department of Fish and Wildlife (360/902-2464, http://fishhunt.dfw.wa.gov).

Some years, an overabundant growth of microorganisms causes clams to build up dangerous levels of toxins, including domoic acid, a chemical that can cause seizures, cardiac arrhythmia, coma, and even death. Before digging, it's always a good idea to check the Department of Health's **Shellfish Safety Hotline** (360/796-3215 or 800/562-5632, www.doh.wa.gov/ehp/sf) for the latest on the edibility of area clams.

DIVING

Locals say the San Juans offer the finest cold-water diving anywhere, with something for all levels of ability. Beneath the surface, the waters are chilly (48-52°F year-round), with currents that feed an abundance of marine plants and animals, from plankton to killer whales.

ESSENTIALS
RECREATION

fishing

Jacques Cousteau considered the San Juans one of his favorite places to dive.

The ocean floor around the archipelago is a garden of colors, with sponges, hydroids, corals, jellyfish, crabs, sea stars, sea cucumbers, kelp, and many species of fish, including sculpin, rockfish, scorpion fish, greenling, surfperch, prickleback, eel, ronquil, goby, clingfish, midshipman, and flounder. Many of the world's largest marine species are here, including the giant Pacific octopus, the two largest scallops, the world's tallest anemone (reaching three feet), and the largest sea slug, chiton, barnacle, and sea urchin. These waters are also home to dolphins, whales, seals, and other marine mammals.

All told, you'll find more than 500 dive sites here, covering a diversity that will please all levels, from those who learned at a beach resort to tech divers using rebreathers. In addition to wall dives, reefs, and pinnacles, there are dozens of wrecks to explore—including a 366-foot destroyer that was intentionally sunk off the southern Gulf Islands. Local currents are important in your dive planning, since they can reach seven knots when the tides are in full flux. There are, however, a number of beginning shore dives and some very good dives close to the islands. The best diving is often in the winter, when visibility increases due to less phytoplankton in the water.

For additional information, see Betty Pratt-Johnson's *99 Dives from the San Juan Islands in Washington to the Gulf Islands* or Edward Weber's *Diving and Snorkeling Guide to the Pacific Northwest.*

Anacortes Diving & Supply (2502 Commercial Ave., 360/293-2070, www.anacortesdiving.com) is a full-service shop that runs a variety of dive trips to the San Juans and surrounding areas. **Gone Diving** (1740 Iowa St., 360/738-2042, www.gonediving.org) is a Bellingham dive shop. There are no full-service dive shops in the San Juans.

Diving Safety

The diving around the San Juans is superb, but it can also be treacherous, with cold water, powerful currents, and a host of other hazards. Stay within your limits, and never take chances. If you lack experience in cold water and currents, get local training and go with a knowledgeable operator who can safely get you into these spectacular waters. At least five divers have died in the San Juans over the last decade or so.

Food and Drink

Food prices on the islands are somewhat higher than in Anacortes, Bellingham, or Victoria, so you may want to stock up on groceries before climbing on board the ferry. There are no 24-hour stores in the San Juans, and some dinner restaurants close as early as 9pm, so call ahead.

Given the location, it should come as no surprise that seafood gets center-stage treatment at many local restaurants. Fresh salmon and halibut are always favorites, along with fresh oysters from Westcott Bay on San Juan Island or Judd Cove on Orcas Island. Competition is stiff among island restaurants, and there are some real Northwest cuisine standouts.

Reservations are wise at the nicer restaurants, especially in peak season.

FARM FRESH

Farming was once a substantial business on the islands, and peas, fruit, hay, and dairy products were all important at one time or another. Many of the old apple, pear, and plum orchards dotted around the islands still produce fruit more than a century after they were planted.

Small-scale agriculture is increasingly popular, particularly on Lopez and San Juan Islands, where dozens of farms produce such specialty products as kiwifruit, goat milk and cheeses, organic wines, apple cider, and even oysters and clams. The **San Juan Islands Agricultural Network** (www.islandgrown. net) has details on local agriculture, including an interactive map of island farms.

Saturday **farmers markets** are a fun summertime event where you can buy local produce, flowers, crafts, clothing, and art. These take place not just on San Juan, Orcas, and Lopez Islands, but also in Bellingham, Anacortes, and Whidbey Island.

ALCOHOL

Local grocery stores all sell beer and wine, and you can buy the hard stuff from state liquor stores at Eastsound and Orcas Village on Orcas Island, Lopez Village on Lopez Island, and Friday Harbor on San Juan Island. Small wineries are located on Lopez, San Juan, and Whidbey Islands. Note that all Washington State bars and restaurants and most other public places are entirely **smoke-free.**

Accommodations

LODGING CHOICES

The lodging scene on the San Juan Islands comprises a mix of small hotels and inns, luxurious bed-and-breakfasts, resorts, and vacation rentals. Budget accommodations are scarce, and they are even more difficult to find when families start planning their summer vacations and school lets out. Most places on the islands have just a few rooms, so space is at a premium. It also costs a premium; only a handful of places have rooms for less than $125 d in the peak summer season. Hostel-type accommodations are available at Golden Tree Hostel and the Lodge on Orcas on Orcas Island and Wayfarers Rest on San Juan Island.

If you're in doubt about where to stay, visit **TripAdvisor** (www.tripadvisor.com) or **Yelp** (www.yelp.com) to see what other travelers say.

Throughout this book I list prices for lodgings as one person (single or s) or two people (double or d). Add 10.1 percent (8.1 percent sales tax plus 2 percent lodging tax) to all lodging rates quoted in this book, including bed-and-breakfasts.

The High-Season Shuffle

The San Juans are immensely popular in the summer, particularly during the peak season of July and August. If you plan a visit during these times, there may well be no room at the inn, and not a lot of mangers available either. Save yourself a headache by making reservations far in advance; at the older and more established bed-and-breakfasts and resorts, this means calling at least four months ahead for a midsummer weekend reservation. This is particularly true if you want a place for less than $160 a night in August. Do *not* arrive in Friday Harbor on a Saturday afternoon in July and expect to find a place—you won't. Anyone looking for space on Memorial Day, the Fourth of July, or Labor Day should make reservations up to a year in advance.

Many resorts, inns, and cottages also offer weekly rates and require a minimum summertime stay of at least two nights (sometimes up to a week). Also note that most island bed-and-breakfasts cater almost exclusively to couples and do not allow kids. Families are often better off with a vacation rental by the week or a campsite at one of the island parks.

In the winter you'll find fewer fellow travelers, lower lodging rates (sometimes less than half the summer prices), and less of a problem getting a room, but the weather won't be quite as inviting, the scenery won't be as green, and some businesses will be closed. The lowest rates are typically Sunday-Thursday October-April. Winter holidays (especially Christmas to New Year's) are likely to be booked well in advance.

Buying Paradise

Many San Juan visitors dream of moving to the islands and living out their fantasies of a simpler life, where they would sit on the deck along their private cove, sip champagne, and watch the sailboats, eagles, and killer whales play. OK, that works for Bill Gates and other billionaires but is a bit of a stretch for mere mortals. As with other resort areas, housing prices on the San Juans are high, and property values remain some of the highest in Washington. The severe recession of the last decade had a major impact on island home sales. At the market peak in 2008 the median home price was around $800,000, but by 2011 it had plummeted to under $300,000. Several real estate businesses closed over that time span, but the market has rebounded substantially. As of 2016, the median price was $577,000, but many places stay on the market for a long time, sometimes as much as three years. Feeling flush with cash? At the high end, you'll still see many waterfront mansions going for over $2 million. Want your own island? When I last looked, Trump Island, a 29-acre private island near Lopez with a 7,000-square-foot home was available for just $8.7 million.

Many of the homes are occupied only seasonally or belong to retirees. (Because of all these retired folks, the median age of islanders is 12 years over the statewide average.) Don't come to the islands with the expectation of getting rich, since half of the local jobs are in the services sector. The islands are, however, a great place if your money flows in from outside sources or a trust fund from your late Aunt Judy; dividends and investments make up more than half the income for the average islander.

Anyone considering a move to the islands should take into account not just the economics of the venture, but also the environmental problems associated with increased growth and development on the islands. Water is in short supply and will only become a greater problem as more people move to the San Juans. If you are planning a move to the islands, try to make it one that doesn't involve building a new place on undeveloped land.

If you're in the market, or just want to indulge your island dreams, local real estate companies will be happy to assist you. State ferry brochure racks are packed with glossy publications from island brokers, and you can cruise through property descriptions on their websites. Some of the larger companies include **Windermere Real Estate** (www.windermeresji.com), **Orcas Island Realty** (www.orcasislandrealty.com), **Coldwell Banker** (www.sanjuanislands.com), **Cherie L. Lindholm Real Estate** (360/376-2202, www.orcashomes.com), **Lopez Island Realty** (360/468-2291 or 866/632-1100, www.lopezislandrealty.com), **Lopez Village Properties** (360/468-5055, www.lopezisproperties.com), **Offshore Properties** (360/376-5166, www.offshoreproperties.net), **Orcas Island Realty** (360/376-2145, www.orcasislandrealty.com), and **T Williams Realty** (360/376-8374, www.twilliamsrealty.com).

Vacation Rentals and Home Swaps

Several real estate companies on the islands offer weekly and monthly home rentals starting around $800 per week. Another option is booking through one of the international online vacation rental brokers, such as **VRBO** (www.vrbo.com), **Airbnb** (www.airbnb.com), **Homeaway** (www.homeaway.com), and **Vacation Homes** (www.vacationhomes.com).

Visitors to the San Juans may also want to investigate a house exchange. Online companies list homeowners on the islands who are interested in a trade if you have an upscale home. If you live in Hawaii, Costa Rica, or Aspen, your home might be a hot property. If you live in North Dakota, good luck. Companies worth investigating include **Home Exchange** (www.homeexchange.com), **Home Link** (www.homelink.org), and **Intervac** (www.intervac-homeexchange.com).

CAMPING

Public campsites are most abundant at beautiful **Moran State Park** on Orcas Island, but even these fill up almost every day in July and August. San Juan Island has a handful of spots at **San Juan County Park,** and additional public camping can be found at **Odlin County Park** and **Spencer Spit State Park** on Lopez Island, along with **Shaw Island County Park.** County and state park campsites can be reserved ahead of time (strongly advised in the summer). Walk-in campsites (no reservations) are at **Obstruction Pass State Park** on Orcas Island, while **Griffin**

Bay Marine State Park on San Juan Island and **Point Doughty Marine State Park** on Orcas Island are accessible only by kayak. In addition to these, many of the more remote marine state parks have primitive campsites accessible by boat or kayak.

San Juan, Orcas, and Lopez Islands all have private campgrounds, offering a mix of standard tent sites and RV spaces with water and electrical hookups.

Travel Tips

CROSSING THE BORDER

Ferry and commercial aircraft passengers crossing between British Columbia and the San Juans will be checked by either the U.S. Customs Service or Canada Customs. **U.S. Customs and Border Protection** (800/562-5943, www.cbp.gov) has stations at Roche Harbor (360/378-2080, mid-May-Sept.) and Friday Harbor (360/378-2080, year-round) on San Juan Island. Travelers heading from the San Juans to Vancouver Island will need to clear customs in Sidney, where the facility is operated by the **Canada Border Services Agency** (204/983-3500, www.cbsa-asfc.gc.ca).

Crossing between the United States and Canada is not nearly as simple as it was in the days before bomb-sniffing dogs, surveillance cameras, and legitimate terrorism fears. Adult citizens of either country need a **valid passport** to cross the border in either direction. **Children under age 16** traveling with their parents will need either a passport or a certified copy of their birth certificate, and if only one parent is with the child, the parent will need to provide a signed and notarized permission note from the absent parent, including a phone number where they can be reached. Anyone 16 and older needs a passport, and it's wise to get a passport for all children to avoid any future hassles or travel delays at the border. All other foreign visitors must have a valid passport and may need

a visa or visitor permit depending on their country of residence.

Canadian law prohibits individuals from bringing guns, mace, pepper spray, and similar items into Canada, and a felony or DUI conviction will probably prevent you from crossing the border. Anyone **entering Canada by private plane or boat** must call the **Canada Border Services Agency** (888/226-7277) in advance for a list of official ports of entry and their hours of operation.

Driving in Canada

U.S. and international driver's licenses are valid in Canada. All highway signs give distances in kilometers and speeds in kilometers per hour. Unless otherwise posted, the maximum speed limit on the highways is 100 kph (62 mph).

Use of safety belts is mandatory, and motorcyclists must wear helmets. Infants and toddlers must be strapped into an appropriate child's car seat. Before venturing north of the 49th parallel, U.S. residents should ask their vehicle insurance company for a Canadian nonresident interprovincial motor vehicle liability insurance card. You may also be asked to prove vehicle ownership, so carry your vehicle registration form.

Returning to the United States

On reentering the United States, if you've been in Canada more than 48 hours, you can bring

Legal Marijuana

In 2012, Washington voters passed Initiative 502, making it the second state in the nation to legalize small amounts of marijuana-related products for use by anyone over age 21. It took another year or so before the law took effect, but the state now has a burgeoning *legal* cannabis market, with more than 150 recreational marijuana stores across the state and some 1,000 licensed producers. You'll see ads in the free Seattle papers for local pot shops, and a plethora of marijuana maps describing shops and their wares, including edibles, infused drinks, a "Bed Baked and Beyond" B&B, and restaurants that feature cannabis in their cooking. There are even tours of pot-growing operations and retail stores in the Seattle area from **Kush Tourism** (www.kushtourism.com) and **CannaBus** (www.theoriginalcannabus.com). Some shops provide free shuttles from downtown hotels so you don't need to imbibe and drive.

In addition to many shops around Seattle, there are 10 marijuana stores in Bellingham, two more on Whidbey Island, and one in Anacortes. **Token Herb** (360/376-8420) on Orcas Island is currently the only cannabis store on the San Juan Islands. Regional marijuana dealers can be found on websites such as **Leafly** (www.leafly.com) and **Weedmaps** (www.weedmaps.com).

Get details on the law by visiting the website of the **Washington State Liquor and Cannabis Board** (www.liq.wa.gov). Many travelers purchase marijuana at mainland Washington stores and carry it on board **state ferries** to the San Juan Islands, but this is a gray area. The **Coast Guard** could enforce federal laws prohibiting the transport of cannabis on the ferries, but that seems unlikely. Any prosecutions would lead to a firestorm of protests. It's wise to be discreet; keep in mind that smoking or vaping anything, even tobacco products, is prohibited on the ferries.

---

back up to $800 worth of household and personal items, excluding alcohol and tobacco, duty-free. If you've been in Canada fewer than 48 hours, you may bring in only up to $200 worth of such items duty-free.

If you're planning to make any large purchases in British Columbia, pick up a brochure describing what you can bring back without being charged extra duties.

TRAVELING WITH CHILDREN

The San Juans seem custom-made for families. They're a quick ferry ride from the mainland and provide all sorts of fun activities, from whale-watching and cycling to hiking and horseback rides. Children under age six travel free on **Washington State Ferries,** and older kids get reduced fares. Most attractions and activities have lower rates for children, and some also offer one-size-fits-all family rates.

Sea kayaking is a fun activity for older kids, and some companies provide special kayaks with middle seating for children as young as five. An impressive lavender farm on San Juan Island offers the chance to pick fragrant bouquets. Orcas is home to two great activity options: **The Funhouse,** where science and play meet, and **Orcas Island Skateboard Park**, one of the finest swaths of curving concrete in the Pacific Northwest.

Lopez Island is the most family-friendly island for **cycling,** with relatively level terrain, a diversity of scenery, good camping opportunities, and a paucity of traffic. Bikes, kid trailers, and strollers are available for rent on San Juan, Orcas, and Lopez Islands.

Several **summer camps** are scattered across the islands, including Camp Orkila, Four Winds-Westward Ho Camp, and Camp Indralaya on Orcas; Camp Nor'wester on Johns Island; and Canoe Island French Camp. In addition to traditional summer camps, the YMCA's Camp Orkila (360/376-2678 or 206/382-5009, www.camporkila.org) also offers reasonably priced day camps that are perfect if you're on Orcas for a week and need some time away from the kids. Drop-in **childcare centers** are available on San Juan, Orcas, and Lopez Islands.

SENIOR TRAVEL

The San Juans are an easy and popular summer destination for seniors traveling by car or RV. Island museums and some tour companies have discounted rates for those over 65. The ferry system has half-price rates for senior drivers and passengers over 65, but this only applies to the passenger portion of your ticket, not your vehicle.

TRAVELERS WITH DISABILITIES

Quite a few hotels, resorts, and bed-and-breakfasts in the San Juans provide ADA rooms with wheelchair-accessible facilities. A partial list includes Lakedale Resort, Roche Harbor Resort, Friday Harbor Inn, and Friday Harbor Suites on San Juan Island; Outlook Inn, Rosario Resort, and Turtleback Farm Inn on Orcas Island; and Lopez Farm Cottages and Edenwild Boutique Inn on Lopez Island.

Get wheelchair-friendly van rentals through **Wheelchair Getaways** (425/353-6563 or 800/854-4176, www.wheelchairgetaways.com) in Edmonds. Washington State Ferries have half-price fares for disabled passengers, but this is only for the passenger portion of your ticket, not your vehicle.

GAY AND LESBIAN TRAVEL

The San Juans are a fairly tolerant place, and most islanders don't care about one's sexual orientation. Several island B&Bs and restaurants have gay or lesbian owners and may promote themselves on such places as www.purpleroofs.com or www.gaytravel.about.com, while many other San Juan places are listed on these sites as gay friendly. A few conservative B&B owners may not be especially accepting of same-sex couples, but most lodgings welcome lesbians and gays.

PETS

The three main islands—San Juan, Orcas, and Lopez—all have veterinarians and kennels for dogs and cats. Anacortes has a veterinarian and pet boarding, along with a popular downtown dog park. Keep animals on a leash when traveling on ferries or around the islands, especially in natural areas. Some parks and preserves are closed to dogs.

HEALTH AND SAFETY

The closest full hospitals are in Anacortes or Victoria, but San Juan Island has a 10-bed hospital with limited services. Both Orcas Island and Lopez Island have medical clinics with at least one physician available 24 hours a day. All three islands also have dentists, massage therapists, and a range of alternative medical practitioners.

For medical emergencies and fires, call 911 from a landline or cell phone; EMTs and paramedics are available, and a helicopter or fixed-wing plane can transport patients to larger hospitals in Seattle or elsewhere.

Washington State has a comprehensive ban on smoking in all indoor public places and workplaces. **Smoking** is prohibited in all restaurants and bars and on Washington State Ferries, though it remains legal in some tribal casinos.

Safety in the Outdoors

There are no bears, mountain lions, or poisonous snakes on the San Juan Islands. Mosquitoes are not particularly bad, but yellow jackets can be a problem in the summer, particularly for those with allergies. They can also be a major nuisance for anyone dining outside, and you may end up fighting a losing battle keeping them off your burger. West Nile virus cases have occurred in Washington, so it's wise to use mosquito repellent. Visit www.doh.wa.gov for more on this potentially fatal disease.

Another potential threat is **hantavirus,** which is spread by deer mice. The disease it causes can be fatal, and at least one infection was reported from the San Juans. Prevention is the best strategy, and it simply means minimizing your contact with rodents. Never handle deer mice, stay away from their nests, and sleep inside a tent when camping—not on the open ground. For additional hantavirus information and safety precautions, see the Centers for Disease Control and Prevention website (www.cdc.gov).

Information and Services

TRAVEL INFORMATION

For maps and other information before you arrive, contact the **San Juan Islands Visitors Bureau** (360/378-6822 or 888/468-3701, www.visitsanjuans.com). You can also download their **San Juans Islands Insider** app from the Apple App Store or Google Play.

Chambers of Commerce

Each of the three main islands has its own local chamber of commerce visitors centers stocked with local brochures. Island chambers of commerce are **San Juan Island Chamber of Commerce** (360/378-5240, www.sanjuanisland.org), **Orcas Island Chamber of Commerce** (360/376-2273, www.orcasislandchamber.com), and **Lopez Island Chamber of Commerce** (360/468-4664, www.lopezisland.com).

For gateway cities, contact **Anacortes Visitor Information Center** (360/293-3832, www.anacortes.org), **Whidbey-Camano Tourism** (888/747-7777, www.whidbeycamanoislands.com), **Bellingham Whatcom County Tourism** (360/671-3990 or 800/487-2032, www.bellingham.org), **Seattle Convention and Visitors Bureau** (206/461-5800 or 866/732-2695, www.visitseattle.org), and **Tourism Victoria** (250/953-2033 or 800/663-3883, www.tourismvictoria.com).

Island Publications and Websites

Two free publications are found on board the ferries and in racks around Friday Harbor and Anacortes: *Springtide,* published by Sound Publishing (www.islandssounder.com), with helpful details on the islands, and *The Book of the San Juan Islands,* with relocation info and tons of factoids about the San Juans. It's published by the *Journal of the San Juans* (www.sanjuanjournal.com).

The **San Juan Islander** (www.sanjuanislander.com) is a web-only newspaper with community news, events, weather, classified ads, the local police blotter, and useful visitor information. Other private websites provide island information and links. Check out www.sanjuandirectory.com, www.sanjuanupdate.com, www.orcasisle.com, www.orcasisland.org, and www.orcasissues.com.

At **Island Cam** (www.islandcam.com), you'll find live webcam images from nine places around the San Juans, including Roche Harbor and the Friday Harbor ferry landing on San Juan Island, Rosario Resort and the ferry landing on Orcas Island, Fisherman Bay on Lopez Island, and the Anacortes ferry landing. It's a good way to check the ferry lines and weather.

MONEY

Canadian and other non-U.S. currency can be changed at banks on San Juan, Orcas, and Lopez Islands. The major **credit cards**—especially Visa and MasterCard—are accepted virtually everywhere. **Automated teller machines** (ATMs) are located at Friday Harbor on San Juan Island, Eastsound on Orcas Island, and Lopez Village on Lopez Island, but not on Shaw Island. These ATMs tack on a charge (typically $3) in addition to your own bank's fees, making this an expensive way to get cash, especially for small amounts.

COMMUNICATIONS AND MEDIA

Newspapers

Two surprisingly good weekly newspapers provide useful print and online info for the San Juans. In business since 1906, the *Journal of the San Juans* (www.sanjuanjournal.com) has its editorial staff in Friday Harbor on San Juan Island. The *Islands Sounder* (www.islandssounder.com) is headquartered at Eastsound on Orcas Island. Both papers come out on Wednesday. The *Islands' Weekly* (www.islandsweekly.com) is a free newspaper. Sound Publishing Company (360/376-4500, www.soundpublishing.com)—the state's largest newspaper publisher—owns all three of these papers.

Phone Calls

The area code for northern Puget Sound, including the San Juans, is 360. All phone calls among the various San Juan Islands are local calls. Cellular service is reasonably good on the main islands, but may be nonexistent in hilly areas or where other islands block the signal. Dial 911 for emergencies, even from your cell phone.

Internet Access and Wi-Fi

A number of places provide online access if you want to check email or surf the Internet while traveling in the islands. **Libraries** on San Juan, Orcas, and Lopez Islands all have computers you can use for free, as do those in Anacortes, Bellingham, and most other American cities. Computer rentals (with web access) are available in Friday Harbor on San Juan Island and Eastsound on Orcas Island.

Many hotels and B&Bs in the San Juans, along with quite a few cafés, coffee shops, and other businesses, provide free **Wi-Fi** access. These Wi-Fi hotspots can be found by popping open your laptop or tablet computer to see what's available.

Post Offices

Post offices are on Orcas Island at Eastsound, Deer Harbor, Olga, and Orcas. On San Juan, they are located at Friday Harbor and Roche Harbor. Lopez Island has its post office in Lopez Village, and the Shaw Island post office is right next to the ferry dock. Most of these are open 8am-5pm Monday-Friday, though some may also open for a few hours on Saturday. When closed, their outer doors usually remain open, so you can always go in to buy stamps from the machines. Many grocery store checkout counters also sell books of stamps with no markup.

WEDDINGS

Grand scenery, sunny weather, picturesque settings, luxurious bed-and-breakfasts, and excellent caterers combine to make the San Juans an idyllic place for weddings and honeymoons. The best source for details on island weddings—from venues and caterers to wedding planners and DJs—is the **San Juan Islands Visitors Bureau** (360/378-6822 or 888/468-3701, www.visitsanjuans.com/weddings). Request a printed wedding directory or pick one up in local visitors centers. **Orcas Island Weddings** (www.orcasislandweddings.info) has links to wedding service providers on Orcas.

Marriage licenses are issued by the **San Juan County Auditor** (360/378-2161, www.sanjuanco.com) and a three-day waiting period is required.

Resort Weddings

Anyone planning a wedding should start as early as possible: Some of the most popular island sites are booked a year in advance.

Roche Harbor Resort (360/378-2155 or 800/451-8910, www.rocheharborweddings.com) on San Juan Island is exceptionally popular with wedding parties, and the staff can help with all the arrangements. The location is particularly beautiful, with a gorgeous flower garden and a chapel that doubles as the only privately owned Catholic church in America. Wedding site fees range from $1,000 for a weekday in May to $9,500 for a Saturday afternoon in July. Only one wedding is allowed per day—and they have 100 or so annually—so book far ahead for the peak season.

At **Rosario Resort** (360/376-2222 or 800/562-8820, www.rosarioresort.com) on Orcas Island, the summertime wedding ceremony site fee is $4,000 for a service on a point of land affording a 360-degree bay view, but rates drop to half this in the off-season.

At both resorts, you'll need to add in the other associated costs (food and drinks, cake, entertainment, decorations, hair and makeup, musicians, and so on) for the reception. The average cost for a Roche Harbor or Rosario wedding including catering is around $20,000, and this doesn't include lodging, transportation, photography, flowers, cake, and other expenditures.

San Juan Weddings

In addition to Roche Harbor, several San Juan Island sites are popular for weddings, including the historic schoolhouse at **San Juan Vineyards** (360/378-9463, www.sanjuanvineyards.com), the lakeside lodge at **Lakedale Resort** (360/378-2350 or 800/617-2267, www.lakedale.com), and the eco-friendly **Juniper Lane Guest House** (360/378-7761, www.juniperlaneguesthouse.com). Groups looking for lodging together may want to consider the **Tucker House B&B** (360/378-2783 or 800/965-0123, www.tuckerhouse.com) and Harrison House Suites in Friday Harbor. These adjacent properties (aka San Juan Island Inn Collection) have the same owners and together provide space for 60 people.

Public places popular for weddings include **Lime Kiln Point Lighthouse, San Juan Island National Historical Park** (English

Camp, American Camp, and South Beach), and **San Juan County Park** on San Juan Island.

Orcas Weddings

Rosario Resort is especially popular for weddings, but equally picturesque is **Victorian Valley Chapel** (360/376-3289, www.victorianvalleychapel.com), a miniature New England-style church in a hidden valley. Also popular are **Outlook Inn** (360/376-2200 or 888/688-5665, www.outlookinn.com), **Deer Harbor Inn** (360/376-4110 or 877/377-4110, www.deerharborinn.com), and **Camp Orkila** (360/376-2678 or 206/382-5009, www.camporkila.org).

Orcas Hotel (360/376-4300 or 888/672-2792; www.orcashotel.com) is an extremely popular wedding destination. The lovely building has a big lawn and a restaurant for receptions, though noisy ferry traffic makes for a less-than-peaceful (or private) setting. One major advantage of Orcas Hotel is the ease of access for visitors. Guests won't need to take a car on the ferry since the hotel is right at Orcas Landing. Wedding packages are $1,200 plus the rental of all 12 hotel rooms (space for 32 guests overnight).

Also well worth a look are **The Inn at Ship Bay** (360/376-3933 or 877/276-7296, www.innatshipbay.com), near Eastsound, and **Doe Bay Resort & Retreat** (360/376-2291, www.doebay.com), with spacious grounds along a pretty bay.

For wedding planning on Orcas, contact **Orcas Events** (360/376-8376, www.orcasevents.com) or **Weddings on Orcas/Sandy Playa** (360/376-5531, www.springbayonorcas.com).

Resources

Suggested Reading

TRAVEL

Crockford, Ross. *Victoria: The Unknown City.* Vancouver, BC: Arsenal Pulp Press, 2006. Filled with little-known facts and interesting tales, this book describes how to get the best seats on BC Ferries, where to shop for the funkiest used clothing, the history of local churches, and more.

Harrison, Lorrie. *Kindred Spirits: Stories, Passions, and Portraits from the Heart of Community.* Anacortes, WA: Island Time Press, 2001. This book's sharp design and attractive black-and-white photos immediately grab your attention, and the stories of the eccentrics who populate the island keep your interest. Nowhere in the book is this mysterious place identified, but here's a hint: the island starts with "L" and ends with "Z."

Hempstead, Andrew. *Moon Victoria and Vancouver Island.* Berkeley, CA: Avalon Travel, 2014. A great source for coverage of Vancouver Island in nearby British Columbia.

Meyer, Barbara. *Sketching in the San Juans... and a Bit Beyond.* Eastsound, WA: Paper Jam Publishing, 1996. This attractive book is filled with hundreds of colorful and expressive watercolor sketches, created during Barbara Meyer's quarter century on the islands.

Mueller, Marge, and Ted Mueller. *The San Juan Islands: Afoot & Afloat.* Seattle: The Mountaineers, 2008. A relatively complete guide to natural areas within the San Juan archipelago, including the smaller islands.

Wilcox, Ken. *Hiking the San Juan Islands.* Bellingham, WA: Northwest Wild Books, 2001. A fine pocket-sized guide detailing dozens of hiking trails on the San Juans and surrounding areas, including Whidbey Island.

Wortman, Dave. *San Juan Islands: A Guide to Exploring the Great Outdoors.* Guilford, CT: FalconGuides, 2005. A helpful guide to hiking trails throughout the San Juans.

ON (AND IN) THE WATER

Bailey, Jo, and Carl Nyberg. *Gunkholing the San Juans.* Seattle: San Juan Enterprises, 2000. A chatty boater's bible with 300 fact-filled pages about cruising the islands. Worthwhile for sailors, motorboaters, and kayakers, and also of interest if you're just looking for details on hidden parts of the islands. Not only does it cover all the San Juans, but also surrounding areas, including Guemes, Cypress, and Lummi Islands, along with Deception Pass, Bellingham, Anacortes, and La Conner. Now out of print.

Canadian Hydrographic Service. *Canadian Tide and Current Tables Volume 5: Juan de Fuca Strait and the Strait of Georgia.* Canadian Hydrographic Service, www.charts. gc.ca. This detailed Canadian government publication is available at local marinas and bookstores. It provides vital information that is especially useful for those traveling in small boats and sea kayaks around the San Juans.

Douglass, Don, and Reanne Hemingway-Douglass. *Exploring the San Juan and Gulf Islands: Cruising Paradise of the Pacific Northwest.* Anacortes, WA: Fine Edge Productions, 2003. Part of a series of respected cruising guides by the authors, this one details anchorages and attractions in the islands, with suggested itineraries, GPS way stations, and distance tables.

Hale, Bob. *Waggoner Cruising Guide.* Bellevue, WA: Weatherly Press. An authoritative annual guide for boaters, this book covers the waters from Puget Sound to Prince Rupert, British Columbia, including the San Juans. It contains text on anchorages, piloting, and what to expect at each port, along with a bit of history.

Pratt-Johnson, Betty. *99 Dives from the San Juan Islands in Washington to the Gulf Islands.* Surrey, BC: Heritage House Publishing, 1997. The most up-to-date guide to island diving.

Scherer, Migael. *A Cruising Guide to Puget Sound and the San Juan Islands: Olympia to Port Angeles.* Camden, ME: International Marine/McGraw-Hill, 2004. A comprehensive spiral-bound guide for boaters.

Vassilopoulos, Peter. *Anchorages and Marine Parks.* Vancouver, BC: Seagraphic Publications, 2008. A useful guide for boaters along the British Columbia coast, this book also includes limited coverage of the San Juans.

Washburne, Randel. *Kayaking Puget Sound, the San Juans, and the Gulf Islands.* Seattle: The Mountaineers, 2002. Filled with details on destinations, routes, ratings, and launching information, this guide explores

the nooks and crannies of this fascinating waterway, including nine paddling trips in the San Juans.

Weber, Edward. *Diving and Snorkeling Guide to the Pacific Northwest: Includes Puget Sound, San Juan Islands, and Vancouver Island.* Houston: Gulf Publishing, 1993. A useful (but dated) guide for scuba divers heading to the San Juans.

FOOD

Bower, Holly, and Sarah Eppenbach. *With Love and Butter: An Island Cookbook and Memoir.* Lopez, WA: Hummel Lake Press, 2002. This is a beautiful blend of great recipes and Lopez Island history, with arty block prints. Author Holly Bower owns the respected Holly B's Bakery.

Veal, Janice, and Dawn Ashbach. *San Juan Classics Cookbook.* Anacortes: Northwest Island Associates, 1987. A delightful introduction to cooking, San Juan Islands style. Recipes are from local chefs and the authors' own collections.

Veal, Janice, and Dawn Ashbach. *San Juan Classics Cookbook II.* Anacortes: Northwest Island Associates, 1998. The second in a set of nicely illustrated books by local authors. The emphasis is on natural ingredients from the Northwest.

LITERATURE

Blanchet, M. Wylie. *The Curve of Time.* Sidney, BC: Gray's Publishing, 1968. This lovingly written book is the classic memoir of a newly widowed woman and her five children who explored the waters off Vancouver Island in the 1920s and 1930s. It's a wonderful book to read while boating in the San Juans and points northward.

Burn, June. *Living High.* Friday Harbor, WA: Griffin Bay Bookstore, 1969. A delightful autobiographical story about June and Farrar Burn, who homesteaded on tiny Sentinel

Island in 1919. The island is now managed as a natural area by the Nature Conservancy.

Burn, June; edited by Theresa Morrow and Nancy Prindle. *100 Days in the San Juans.* Friday Harbor, WA: Long House Printcrafters & Publishers, 1983. In 1946, June and Farrar Burn purchased an old sail-rigged rowboat from the Coast Guard and spent 100 days sailing through the San Juans. Their stories appeared that year in the *Seattle Post-Intelligencer* and were later collected to form this book. Out of print, but available in used bookstores in the area.

Glidden, Helene. *Light on the Island.* Woodinville, WA: San Juan Publishing, 2001. Originally published in 1951, when it was a regional best seller, this volume tells the adventures of a Patos Island lighthouse keeper and his family. A good read, but not necessarily the gospel truth.

Guterson, David. *Snow Falling on Cedars.* Vintage Books, 1995. This slow-paced but evocative novel is set in the San Juan Islands, and portions of the movie of the same name were filmed on the islands. The love story/murder trial tale is a fine read, bringing to the fore the nation's mixed emotions about Japanese Americans living in a white town after World War II. The movie is even sleepier than the book.

HISTORY

Morris, Gary J. *San Juan Island Indians.* A Xeroxed publication from 1980 available in island libraries, this work is filled with details about the lives of the islands' original settlers.

Orcas Island Historical Society and Museum. *Orcas Island.* San Francisco: Arcadia Publishing, 2006. Part of the Images of America series, this interesting history book is filled with historical photos from Orcas.

Peacock, Christopher M. *Rosario Yesterdays: A Pictorial History.* Eastsound, WA: Rosario Productions, 1985. Available from Rosario Resort and local bookstores, this book provides a fascinating history of Robert Moran and the mansion he built on Orcas Island.

Richardson, David. *Pig War Islands.* Eastsound, WA: Orcas Publishing, 1990. Written in a way that vividly brings the past to life, this book provides a detailed overview of island history with an emphasis on the Pig War and various scandalous events. His treatment of Native Americans is dated (the book was first published in 1971) and bordering on racist at times, but the book remains a fascinating read.

Stein, Julie K. *Exploring Coast Salish Prehistory: The Archaeology of San Juan Island.* Seattle: University of Washington Press, www.washington.edu/uwpress, 2003. Written by a curator of archaeology at UW's Burke Museum, this small book provides an introduction to Native Americans based on evidence from two important sites within San Juan Island National Historical Park.

Vouri, Michael. *The Pig War.* Friday Harbor, WA: Griffin Bay Bookstore, 1999. The definitive book on the Pig War by a longtime ranger from San Juan Island National Historical Park.

Vouri, Michael. *San Juan Island (Images of America).* Friday Harbor, WA: Journal of the San Juans, 2010. A fine collection of historical photos and commentary on San Juan Island.

Walker, Richard. *Roche Harbor (Images of America).* Friday Harbor, WA: Journal of the San Juans, 2010. A fine collection of historical photos and commentary on Roche Harbor.

NATURAL HISTORY

Adams, Evelyn. *San Juan Islands Wildlife: A Handbook for Exploring Nature*. Seattle: The Mountaineers, 1995. This isn't what you might expect. Although it does contain details about wild animals on the islands, it is primarily a series of Adams's nature essays. The writing is strong but a bit pompous.

Alt, David D., and Donald W. Hyndman. *Roadside Geology of Washington*. Missoula, MT: Mountain Press Publishing, 1984. A fine book for anyone with an interest in geology, with easy-to-understand descriptions of how volcanoes, glaciers, floods, and other processes shaped the state's topography over the eons.

Atkinson, Scott, Fred A. Sharpe, and David Macaree. *Wild Plants of the San Juan Islands*. Seattle: The Mountaineers, 1993. The definitive guide to island plants, with descriptions of more than 190 species, arranged by the habitat in which they are found.

Baron, Nancy, and John Acorn. *Birds of the Pacific Northwest Coast*. Renton, WA: Lone Pine Publishing, 1997. Nicely illustrated, this is the best all-around guide to identifying birds found on the San Juans.

Folkens, Peter. *Marine Mammals of British Columbia and the Pacific Northwest*. Vancouver, BC: Harbour Publishing, 2001. In a waterproof, foldaway format, this booklet provides vital identification tips and habitat maps for 50 marine mammals, including all species of whales present in local waters.

Ford, John K. B., Graeme M. Ellis, and Kenneth C. Balcomb. *Killer Whales*. Vancouver: University of British Columbia Press, 2000. Written by scientific experts, this is the finest book on the natural history and genealogy of orcas in Washington and British Columbia. It includes a photographic genealogy for field identification of individual whales and is nicely illustrated, too.

Lewis, Mark G., and Fred A. Sharpe. *Birding in the San Juan Islands*. Seattle: The Mountaineers, 1987. Detailed information on the islands' birds and where to find them. This is not, however, a field identification guide.

Yates, Steve. *Orcas, Eagles, and Kings*. Seattle: Sasquatch Books, 1994. This beautifully written and photographed book takes readers on a tour through the Salish Sea, the inland waterway that includes Washington's Puget Sound and British Columbia's Georgia Strait.

Internet Resources

San Juan Islands Visitors Bureau
www.visitsanjuans.com
This website has many links to local businesses and is an excellent starting point for Internet surfers.

San Juan Island Chamber of Commerce
www.sanjuanisland.org
Start here for specific San Juan Island information.

Orcas Island Chamber of Commerce
www.orcasislandchamber.com
The official Orcas Island business website.

Lopez Chamber of Commerce
www.lopezisland.com
A useful starting point for Lopez Island information.

Anacortes Chamber of Commerce
www.anacortes.org
A good source for info on the primary entry point to the San Juans.

Whidbey-Camano Tourism
www.whidbeycamanoislands.com
Whidbey Island details and links to local businesses.

Bellingham Whatcom County Tourism
www.bellingham.org
The official spot for information on visiting Bellingham.

Seattle Convention and Visitors Bureau
www.visitseattle.org
Everything you'll need for a visit to the Northwest's largest city.

Tourism Victoria
www.tourismvictoria.com
Tourism Victoria's website has all the details on British Columbia's beautiful capital city.

Travel to Canada
www.westerncanadatravel.com
Website of Andrew Hempstead, author of a comprehensive guide to Vancouver Island and the Gulf Islands (and the Victoria chapter in this book).

Washington State Parks
www.parks.wa.gov
This site has details on island state parks—including Moran State Park—along with many others across the state.

Washington Department of Fish and Wildlife
http://fishhunt.dfw.wa.gov
Head to this official website for details on fishing licenses and seasons. You can even buy your license online.

Washington State Ferries
www.wsdot.wa.gov/ferries
The state ferry system's very helpful website, with details on schedules, fares, system delays, and much more.

San Juan Island National Historical Park
www.nps.gov/sajh
This small national park offers a fine blend of history and scenery; check here for more information.

San Juan County Parks
www.co.san-juan.wa.us/parks
Check here to get details on county parks and to make campsite reservations.

San Juan Islands National Monument
www.sanjuanislandsnca.org
Created by President Obama in 2013, San Juan Islands National Monument covers many places, including Turn Point on Stuart Island and Cattle Point on San Juan Island.

San Juan Islands National Wildlife Refuge
http://pacific.fws.gov
The refuge is scattered across 83 islands, islets, and rocky reefs in the San Juans. Learn more at this website.

U.S. Customs & Border Protection
www.cbp.gov
Customs stations are located on San Juan Island at both Roche Harbor and Friday Harbor.

Canada Border Services Agency

www.cbsa-asfc.gc.ca

Travelers heading into Canada from the San Juans will need to clear customs at Sidney, British Columbia.

Tourism Vancouver Island

www.vancouverisland.travel

An excellent source for Vancouver Island details.

Don Pitcher

www.donpitcher.com

www.facebook.com/donpitcherphotography

Author Don Pitcher's website and Facebook page provide details on his guidebooks and photographic projects.

Index

List of Maps

Acknowledgments

For Rio Jalen
> *May you grow to love this earth's wild places*
> *May you never lose that delightful smile, inquisitiveness, and sharp wit*

I am indebted to many people who helped with this fourth edition of *Moon San Juan Islands*, particularly locals who took the time to offer tips on their home islands. Staff at the following chamber of commerce offices were particularly helpful: Mary Talosi of Anacortes Chamber of Commerce, Jacqueline Cartier and Cheryl Collins of Bellingham Whatcom County Tourism, Tom Kirschner of San Juan Island Chamber of Commerce, Sherry Jennings and Marc Esterly of Langley Chamber of Commerce, and Lia Noreen of Lopez Island Chamber of Commerce. Thanks also to Cindy Hansen at The Whale Museum for information on killer whales and Mike Vouri of the San Juan Island National Historical Park.

Three individuals deserve special thanks for above-and-beyond help and for their generous assistance with travel on the islands: Robin Jacobson of the San Juan Islands Visitors Bureau, and Lance Evans and Terri Gilleland of the Orcas Island Chamber of Commerce.

A number of individuals provided travel assistance and deserve my sincere appreciation, including William Diller of Islander Lopez Marina Resort, Shaun Andres of Trumpeter Inn B&B on San Juan Island, and the staff at Best Western Heritage Inn in Bellingham.

A huge tip of the hat goes to author Andrew Hempstead for providing text and photographs for the *Victoria* section of the *Gateways* chapter.

The many employees of Avalon Travel deserve thanks for extreme patience and for sending this book through the production process and onward to bookstores.

A very special thank you goes to Karen Shemet and our best-in-the-world children, Aziza and Rio, for sticking with me on yet another book project. This book update came at a time when I was recovering from a serious canoeing accident, and their help made a vital difference in my recovery—and sanity!

Also Available

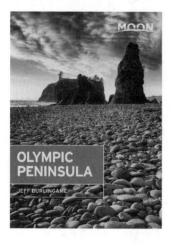

MAP SYMBOLS

▦ Expressway	★ Highlight	✕ Airfield	⚲ Golf Course
▦ Primary Road	○ City/Town	✈ Airport	ℙ Parking Area
▦ Secondary Road	◉ State Capital	▲ Mountain	⛩ Archaeological Site
▦ Unpaved Road	⊛ National Capital	✛ Unique Natural Feature	⛪ Church
------- Trail	★ Point of Interest		⛽ Gas Station
············· Ferry	• Accommodation	⚑ Waterfall	Glacier
⋯⋯ Railroad	▼ Restaurant/Bar	▲ Park	Mangrove
▦ Pedestrian Walkway	▪ Other Location	⬛ Trailhead	Reef
▦ Stairs	Λ Campground	⛷ Skiing Area	Swamp

CONVERSION TABLES

$°C = (°F - 32) / 1.8$
$°F = (°C × 1.8) + 32$
1 inch = 2.54 centimeters (cm)
1 foot = 0.304 meters (m)
1 yard = 0.914 meters
1 mile = 1.6093 kilometers (km)
1 km = 0.6214 miles
1 fathom = 1.8288 m
1 chain = 20.1168 m
1 furlong = 201.168 m
1 acre = 0.4047 hectares
1 sq km = 100 hectares
1 sq mile = 2.59 square km
1 ounce = 28.35 grams
1 pound = 0.4536 kilograms
1 short ton = 0.90718 metric ton
1 short ton = 2,000 pounds
1 long ton = 1.016 metric tons
1 long ton = 2,240 pounds
1 metric ton = 1,000 kilograms
1 quart = 0.94635 liters
1 US gallon = 3.7854 liters
1 Imperial gallon = 4.5459 liters
1 nautical mile = 1.852 km

°FAHRENHEIT °CELSIUS

WATER BOILS (100)
WATER FREEZES (0)

MOON SAN JUAN ISLANDS

Avalon Travel
An imprint of Perseus Books
A Hachette Book Group company
1700 Fourth Street
Berkeley, CA 94710, USA
www.moon.com

Editor: Kevin McLain
Series Manager: Kathryn Ettinger
Copy Editor: Brett A. Keener
Graphics and Production Coordinator: Rue Flaherty
Cover Design: Faceout Studios, Charles Brock
Interior Design: Domini Dragoone
Moon Logo: Tim McGrath
Map Editor: Mike Morgenfeld
Cartographers: Austin Ehrhardt, Brian Shotwell
Indexer: Rachel Kuhn

ISBN-13: 978-1-63121-425-7
ISSN: 1539-2295

Printing History
1st Edition — 2002
5th Edition — May 2017
5 4 3 2 1

Printed in Canada by Friesens